17.50
(2 vols)

PALESTINE

A STUDY OF JEWISH, ARAB, AND BRITISH POLICIES

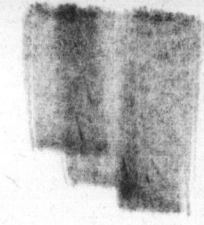

*Published for the
Esco Foundation for Palestine, Inc.*

VOLUME ONE

NEW HAVEN
YALE UNIVERSITY PRESS
LONDON · GEOFFREY CUMBERLEGE · OXFORD UNIVERSITY PRESS

COPYRIGHT, 1947, BY YALE UNIVERSITY PRESS

Printed in the United States of America

First published, March, 1947
Second printing, November, 1949

All rights reserved. This book may not be reproduced, in whole or in part, in any form (except by reviewers for the public press), without written permission from the publishers.

WE ARE privileged to dedicate this book to ROSE G. JACOBS through whose devotion and perseverance the Esco Foundation Palestine Study was consummated.

      THE FOUNDERS OF THE ESCO FUNDS.

FOREWORD

THE founders and sponsors of the Esco* Foundation for Palestine, Mr. and Mrs. Frank Cohen, realizing the importance of having objective, factual and comprehensive material on the subject of Palestine in readily available form, undertook to make this study possible. The trustees of the Esco funds sanctioned the project, and in 1942 the Esco Palestine Study was launched.

The Study was conducted by a staff of scholars and specialists. To assist and advise the Director a special committee known as the Esco Palestine Study Committee was selected, composed of members of the Board of the Esco Foundation for Palestine and Dr. Oscar Janowsky. On the basis of the resultant investigations and findings, the Director wrote the integrated text of this work.

As this book is divided into separate areas of discussion, there have inevitably been some repetitions of sources and ideas. These have been left unchanged so that each section would be self-sufficient.

Since the manuscript for the book was completed in the spring of 1945, a Chronicle has been added to summarize subsequent developments from the period of the San Francisco Conference, April, 1945, through the Report of the Anglo-American Committee of Inquiry, May, 1946.

New York, May, 1946

ROSE G. JACOBS, *President,*
Esco Foundation for Palestine.

* Esco is an acrostic of Ethel S. Cohen. The members of the Esco Boards are: Irwin M. Berliner, Dr. Israel S. Chipkin, Mr. and Mrs. Frank Cohen, Mark Eisner, Marian G. Greenberg, Harry Handler, Dr. Leo Honor, Rose G. Jacobs, Dr. Mordecai M. Kaplan, Leah Klepper and Dr. Israel S. Wechsler.

CONTRIBUTORS

THIS book is based on the work of a group of scholars and specialists who either contributed monographs on various phases of the Palestine problem or otherwise assisted in the preparation of the Study. Most of the material was correlated and rewritten by the Director of the Esco Palestine Study, with the exception of specific sections in the book accredited to contributors. The separate contributors assume no responsibility for statements made in the book. The contributing scholars and their contributions are listed below:

WILLIAM FOXWELL ALBRIGHT, Ph.D. Litt.; D.H.L., Th.D. (Utrecht); Dr. hon. caus. (Oslo); W. W. Spence Professor of Semitic Languages, Johns Hopkins University.

"The Christian Communities of Palestine"
"Some Observations on the Attitude of Christians to Moslems in the Near East"

ELIZABETH STRAUSS BING, Ph.D., Political Science, University of Geneva, Switzerland; Associate in Research, Research Department, Esco Palestine Study; Associate in Research, Research Department, American Zionist Emergency Council.

"Immigration into Palestine"

JOEL CARMICHAEL, B.A. (Oxon.).
"The Arab Movement"

EZRA CHAIKES, Ph.D., Marquette University, Wisconsin; Director, Verband Central High School, New York; Adviser, Economic Committee of *Histadruth*, New York.

"The Government of Palestine"
"Local Self-government in Palestine"
"K'Nesseth (Community) Israel"

AUGUSTA COHEN, Ph.B., University of Vermont; writer of *Chronicles: A Monthly Summary of Events of Jewish Interest*, published by the American Jewish Committee.

"Supplement: Chronicle—April, 1945–May, 1946"

WALTER J. FISCHEL, Ph.D., Heidelberg University, Doctor Rerum Politicum (Giessen); Fellow and Member, School of Oriental Studies, Hebrew University, Jerusalem; Fellow of the Royal Asiatic Society of Great Britain; Professor of Semitic Languages, University of California.

"The Jewish Communities in Islamic Countries"

EPHRAIM FISCHOFF, D.S.Sc., New School for Social Research; Master of Hebrew Literature, Jewish Institute of Religion, New York; Instructor, Department of Sociology and Anthropology, Hunter College; Lecturer in Sociology, New School for Social Research; Lecturer, Department of Sociology, College of the City of New York.

Editorial work on some sections of this book.

GUSTAVE E. VON GRÜNEBAUM, Ph.D., University of Vienna; Associate Professor of Arabic, University of Chicago.

"The Arab World"
"The Arab National Movement"
"Minorities under the Arabs"
Prepared abstracts and excerpts of sources

ROSE G. JACOBS, Former National President and now Honorary Vice-President of Hadassah, the Woman's Zionist Organization of America; Member of the Jewish Agency for Palestine.

"Jewish Social Service in Palestine"

*ISAAC J. KLIGLER, Ph.D., Columbia University; Research Fellow, Rockefeller Foundation; Director, Hadassah Anti-Malaria and Clinical Laboratory; Director, Palestine Government, Anti-Malaria and Clinical Laboratory; Director, Department of Hygiene and Bacteriology, Hebrew University, Jerusalem.

"Health in Palestine"

* Deceased.

ISAAC LEVITATS, Ph.D., Columbia University; Master of Hebrew Literature, Jewish Institute of Religion, New York; Executive Director, Bureau of Jewish Education, Akron, Ohio.

"External Zionist Policy"
"The Idea of National Restoration"
"The Period of the Balfour Declaration"
"The Period of the Mandate, 1918–1922"
"Zionist Policy—Formative Period, 1923–1928"
"The Working of the Mandate, 1920–1930"
"The Disturbances and Their Aftermath, 1929–1931"
"The Second Decade, 1931–1943"

JAMES G. MCDONALD, Assistant Professor of History, Indiana University, 1914–1916; Harvard University Traveling Fellow in Spain, 1915–1916; Professor of International Relations, University of Georgia, 1916–1917 (summers); Assistant Professor of History, Indiana University, 1916–1918; Chairman of the Foreign Policy Association, 1919–1933; League of Nations High Commissioner for Refugees Coming from Germany, 1933–1936; member of the editorial staff of the *New York Times,* specializing on international affairs, 1936–1938; President of the Brooklyn Institute of Arts and Sciences, 1938–1942; member of the Board of Education, New York City, 1940–1942; since 1933, Honorary Chairman of the Foreign Policy Association; since 1938, Chairman of the President's Advisory Committee on Political Refugees.

Supplement: Part Two.

NOAH NARDI, Ph.D., Teachers College, Columbia University; M.A., Hebrew Teachers College, Jerusalem; Principal, Progressive School, Tel-Aviv, Palestine, Consultant and Psychologist, Jewish Education Committee, New York.

"Twenty-Five Years of Education in Palestine"

MOSHE PERLMANN, Ph.D., University of London; M.A., Hebrew University, Jerusalem; Instructor, Brooklyn College, Department of Romance Languages; Instructor, New School for Social Research, Department of Political Science.

Consultant on Middle Eastern Affairs for The Esco Palestine Study

NATHAN REICH, Ph.D., Columbia University; Assistant Professor of Economics, Hunter College, New York; Lecturer, Columbia University (Extension Division); Lecturer, Teachers College, Columbia University (Summer Session); Director, Research Department, American Jewish Joint Distribution Committee.

"Industry and Commerce"

*ABRAHAM REVUSKY, B.S., Vienna; Minister of Jewish Affairs, Ukraine; editor of foreign news, *Jewish Morning Journal*, New York City.

"Land Relations in Palestine Agriculture"
"Population and Cultivable Area of Palestine since the Beginning of Jewish Settlement"
"Industry and Commerce"
"Absorptive Capacity"
"The Parallel Economics of Palestine and Their Probable Evolution"

AVRAHAM SCHENKER, B.S. in Education, College of the City of New York; Formerly, Executive Secretary, *Hashomer Hatzair;* Formerly, Executive Secretary, *Hechalutz;* Director, Youth Activities, Palestine *Histadruth* Campaign.

"The Bi-National Position of the *Hashomer Hatzair*"

MEIR SHERMAN, B.S., M.B.A., New York University.

"Arab Life in Palestine"
"The Arabs and the Jews"
"Arab Nationalism"

BENJAMIN SHWADRAN, Ph.D.; Research Fellow, Hebrew University, Jerusalem; Director of Research, American Zionist Emergency Council.

"Arab Relations, 1912–1937"
"The Plans for the Solution of the Palestine Problem"
"The Land, Its People, and Its Rulers"
"The Development of the Jewish National Home"

* Deceased.

"Palestine since the White Paper"
"Zionist Policy, 1920–1930"
Bibliography for this book

BERNARD D. WEINRYB, Ph.D., University of Breslau; Director, Jewish Teachers Seminary and Peoples University, New York; Editor, *The Jewish Review*.

"The Jewish Community in Palestine"
"The *Histadruth* and Other Professional Organizations"
"Social and Economic Forms of Jewish Life in Palestine"
"Arab-Jewish Relations in Palestine: Impressions"

ACKNOWLEDGMENT

ACKNOWLEDGMENT is gratefully made to those who in some measure, large or small, contributed to the book in its present form:

To the Director of the Esco Palestine Study, who performed his difficult task with painstaking care, applying his unique gifts and attainments of scholarship and knowledge to achieve a work which, it is anticipated, may for a long time be the definitive source book in the field of Palestinian affairs.

To the scholars and specialists whose monographs, prepared for the Study, have enriched the field of information on the subject of Palestine; to the research assistants, office staff and others whose patient and conscientious application helped make possible publication of this book.

To the scholars who were kind enough to read the preliminary draft of the manuscript either in part or whole, and to make many helpful suggestions. They are: Professor William F. Albright, Professor Salo Baron, Dr. Israel S. Chipkin, Harry Handler, Dr. Oscar Janowsky, to whom we owe special thanks for his devoted interest throughout, Professor Mordecai M. Kaplan, Dr. Paul Klapper, Dr. Emanuel Neumann, Dr. Koppel S. Pinson, Professor Louis Prashker, Dr. George N. Shuster, Dr. Abba Hillel Silver, and Dr. Israel S. Wechsler; as well as to the lay readers of the Board of Esco Foundation for Palestine, Marian G. Greenberg, Leah Klepper, and Rose G. Jacobs, and to Irwin M. Berliner, our attorney and Board member, who gave generously of his counsel.

We wish also to express our appreciation to Dr. Benjamin Shwadran, who compiled the exhaustive bibliography; to Ezekiel Schloss, cartographer, who adapted the maps for the book; to Effie Solis-Cohen, who read proof and prepared the index; and to the staff of the Yale University Press for their valued advice in the production of the book.

ETHEL AND FRANK COHEN

CONTENTS

FOREWORD v
ACKNOWLEDGMENT xii
TABLE OF CONTENTS xv
LIST OF MAPS AND FACSIMILES xxi

VOLUME I

PART I

I. THE DEVELOPMENT OF ZIONISM IN THE NINETEENTH CENTURY 1
II. THE FIRST WORLD WAR AND THE BALFOUR DECLARATION 55
III. THE PEACE CONFERENCE AND THE MANDATE FOR PALESTINE 119
IV. PROMISES, CLAIMS AND RIGHTS 178

PART II

V. EVENTS AND POLICIES: 1920–1929 256
VI. THE DEVELOPMENT OF THE JEWISH NATIONAL HOME 329
VII. THE ARAB WORLD AND ARAB POLITICS IN PALESTINE 428
VIII. COMMUNITIES, ATTITUDES AND ARAB-JEWISH RELATIONS 493

VOLUME II

PART III

IX. THE 1929 DISTURBANCES AND THEIR AFTERMATH 595
X. DEVELOPMENT DURING THE SECOND DECADE: 1930–1939 661
XI. POLITICAL EVENTS AND POLICIES: 1931–1936 739
XII. THE ROYAL COMMISSION AND THE PROPOSAL OF PARTITION 799

PART IV

XIII. THE 1939 WHITE PAPER 876
XIV. THE MIDDLE EAST AND PALESTINE DURING THE SECOND WORLD WAR 956
XV. THE SHAPING OF POLICIES AND SUMMARY OF PROPOSALS 1077
SUPPLEMENT: CHRONICLE OF EVENTS, 1945–1946 1187
BIBLIOGRAPHY 1238
INDEX 1281

TABLE OF CONTENTS
VOLUME I

PART I

I. THE DEVELOPMENT OF ZIONISM IN THE NINETEENTH CENTURY

Antecedents of Zionism, 1–12: British and general interest in the Restoration, 1; interest in the Near East and in Jewish restoration, 1; Jewish love for Eretz Israel, 7; precursors of Zionism: Hirsch Kalischer and Moses Hess, 8. *Currents of Zionist Thought in Eastern Europe,* 12–25: The Founders of Russian Zionism: 13; Leo Pinsker: father of Russian Zionism, 14; the cultural Zionism of Ahad Ha'am, 18; Labor Zionism, 22. *Theodor Herzl: Founder of Political Zionism,* 25–39: early interest in the Jewish question, 26, formulation of the Jewish state conception, 30; Zionist activities and conflicts of opinion, 36. *Formation of the Zionist Movement,* 39–54; the first Zionist Congress (Basle), 1897, 40; creation of the Zionist Organization, 42; Herzl's political negotiations, 42; criticisms of Herzl and the conflict over Uganda, 45; development of the Palestine Jewish community before the First World War, 51.

II. THE FIRST WORLD WAR AND THE BALFOUR DECLARATION

Treaties, Promises, and the British Conquest of Palestine, 57–74: secret treaties among the Allies, 57; the McMahon-Husain understanding, 63; the British conquest of Palestine, 70. *The British Alliance with Zionism,* 74–101: motivations for the Balfour Declaration, 75; first steps in the negotiations, 76; official conversations and proposals, 85. *The Balfour Declaration—Motivations and Meanings,* 101–118; drafts of the Declaration, 101; reactions and interpretations, 108; Great Britain's motivations, 114.

III. THE PEACE CONFERENCE AND THE MANDATE FOR PALESTINE

Events in the Near East, 120–134: temporary Allied administration, 120; Arab restiveness in the Levant, 121; the Military Administration in Palestine, 127. *Palestine and the Near East at the Peace Conference,* 134–151: Lloyd George and Clemenceau arrangements, 134; the Arab Delegation at the Peace Conference, 137; Allied disputes and the final settlement, 144. *The Drafting of the Mandate:* 151–177: programs for the Jewish homeland, 151; official Jewish proposals to the Peace Conference, 156; preparation of the final draft, 164.

IV. PROMISES, CLAIMS AND RIGHTS

British War Commitments and Arab Claims, 179–198; Palestine and the McMahon-Husain correspondence, 181; pronouncements after the

Balfour Declaration—the Hogarth Message, Bassett Letter, Declaration to the Seven, Anglo-French Declaration, 191. *Some other aspects of the Controversy*, 198–213: testimony of Lawrence, 198; Faisal's attitude toward Zionism, 202; Arab war services, 206. *Palestine and the Principle of Self-Determination*, 213–255: the King-Crane Report, 213; Article 22 of the League of Nations Covenant, 222; the Jewish claim of "historic connection", 230; the Mandate and its terms, 234. *American Interest in Zionism and in the Jewish National Home Policy*, 240; Woodrow Wilson's contribution and the American view at the Peace Conference, 242; the Congressional Resolution of 1922 and the Anglo-American Convention (1925), 251; American policy toward Palestine, 253.

PART II

V. EVENTS AND POLICIES: 1920–1929

The Shaping of British Policy, 256–296: changing lines of policy, 259; "As if there were no Balfour Declaration," 269; the Churchill White Paper, 281. *The Palestine Administration—Functions and Policies*, 296–328: the British Civil Administration, local self-government and religious communities, 297; government economic policies: aid to agriculture; concessions; taxation and tariffs, 306; regulation of immigration, 315; education and health, 319; appraisal of the British administration, 325.

VI. THE DEVELOPMENT OF THE JEWISH NATIONAL HOME

Instrumentalities of Development, 334–349: agencies of the Zionist Organization, 334; independent Zionist and non-Zionist public agencies, 343. *The Jewish Labor and Cooperative Movement*, 349–388: pioneering ideas and the labor philosophy of A. D. Gordon, 349; forms of cooperative living—*k'vutzah and moshav ovdim*, 354; the General Federation of Jewish Labor in Palestine, 359. *Economic Development*, 366–388: land purchase and reclamation, 366; growth of agricultural settlements and development of intensive farming, 375; industry and commerce, 381. *Health and Education*, 388–404: Jewish health services, 388; education, 393. *The Growth and Organization of the Jewish Community*, 404–414: population increase, 404; immigration, 405; Jewish community organization, 408. *Changing Zionist Policies and the Establishment of the Jewish Agency*, 414–427: postwar Zionist Congresses, 414; formation of the enlarged Jewish Agency, 422.

VII. THE ARAB WORLD AND ARAB POLITICS IN PALESTINE

The Character of the Arab World, 428–443: Arabism and Islam, 428; the political character of Islam and its attitude toward non-Moslem minorities, 432; the Arab lands—geographical diversities and social divisions, 437. *Arab Nationalism and Independence after the War*, 443–461: Arab nationalism before the First World War, 444; postwar development in Arab lands, 451. *Arab Affairs in Palestine*, 461–473: the general character of Arab Palestine, 461; personal factors in Palestine politics, 465; ideas and organization of early Arab political policy, 470. *The Course of Arab Politics in Palestine, 1918–1929*, 473–492: formulation of the Anti-Zionist position, 473; rejection of

Table of Contents

the 1922 White Paper, 476; internal Arab difficulties, 483; Arab intransigence and British optimism, 489.

VIII. COMMUNITIES, ATTITUDES AND ARAB-JEWISH RELATIONS

Social Class Differences among the Arabs, 500–516: the Bedouins or "unsettled" population, 501; the *fellahin* or peasants, 505; the urban population—the upper *effendi* class, the middle class, the lower class, 511. *The Moslem and Arab Attitudes toward the Jews*, 516–533: the traditional Moslem sense of superiority, 516; Arab-Jewish relations in Palestine before and after the First World War, 520; antagonism to Zionism in the first decade, 524. *The Christian Communities of Palestine*, 533–553: churches and missions—the Roman Catholic Church, the Greek Catholic Church, Protestant churches and missionary activities, 534; attitudes toward the restoration of Israel and toward Zionism, 541; the attitude of Eastern Christians to Moslems, 548. *The Jewish Community and Plans for Arab-Jewish Rapprochement*, 553–593: the social composition of the Jewish community, 555; attempts at political rapprochement, 562; the *Histadrut* and Arab-Jewish relations, 571; socialist views on Arab-Jewish relations, 573; the *Brith Shalom* point of view, 578; practical efforts aiding Arab-Jewish relations, 584.

VOLUME II

PART III

IX. THE 1929 DISTURBANCES AND THEIR AFTERMATH
(August, 1929—February, 1931)

The Wailing Wall Controversy and the Course of the Disturbances, 597–614: the incident of the Wailing Wall, 598; the outbreak of the disturbances, 603; after the disturbances, 609. *The Commission on the Palestine Disturbances of August, 1929*, 614–635: attitudes disclosed in the evidence, 615; the Shaw Commission Report, 621; reactions to the Report of the Shaw Commission, 629. *The Hope Simpson Report and the Passfield White Paper*, 635–660: the Hope Simpson Report, 636; the 1930 Statement of Policy, 644; the Jewish Agency analysis, 650; the MacDonald Letter, 656.

X. DEVELOPMENT DURING THE SECOND DECADE: 1930–1939

The Growth of the Population, 664–684: natural increase and immigration, 664; authorized immigration under the Ordinances, 671; the character of Jewish immigration after the rise of Nazism, 676; illegal immigration, 680. *Development in the Jewish National Home*, 685–704: growth of Jewish agricultural settlements, 686; urban and industrial development, 692; developments in education, 698. *Problems of the Arab Cultivator*, 704–722: *mushaa*, tithe and debt, 705; recommendations on credit facilities, 710; resettlement and development, 713; the question of Arab displacement, 717. *Government Policy and Economic Development*, 722–738: aid to agriculture, education and revenue policy, 722; foreign commerce, 729; comment on British administrative policy, 736.

XI. POLITICAL EVENTS AND POLICIES: 1931–1936

The Political Scene Among the British, Arabs and Jews, 739–768: British policy, 739; Zionist policy, 742; Arab policy in the Middle East, 750; Arab policy in Palestine, 761. *Political Developments from 1933 to 1936,* 768–798: Arab political parties, 773; the Legislative Council proposal, 782; disorders of 1936, 792.

XII. THE ROYAL COMMISSION AND THE PROPOSAL OF PARTITION

The Presentation of the Case, 799–818: the Jewish position, 799; views on immigration and land settlement, 804; Jewish land purchase and the Arab cultivator, 809; the Arab evidence, 813. *Conclusions and Recommendations of the Royal Commission,* 819–836: general analysis of the situation, 819; recommendations for restriction of land purchase and immigration, 825; supplementary recommendations on the Arab Agency, local self-government, public security, and education, 830. *The Repudiation of the Mandate and the Plan of Partition,* 836–875: the difficulties inherent in the Mandate, 837; the proposal of partition, 845; the reactions of the Jews and the Arabs, 852; the abandonment of the partition plan, 861.

PART IV

XIII. THE 1939 WHITE PAPER

Background of the MacDonald White Paper, 876–908: disorders during 1937–1938, 876; political discussions before the London Conference, 880; the London Conferences, 889; the White Paper of 1939 and its provisions, 901. *Reactions to the White Paper,* 908–931: Arab and Jewish rejection, 908; opposition in Parliament, 915; the Permanent Mandates Commission, 922; the Zionist Congress on the eve of the war, 928; implementation of the White Paper, 931; the Land Transfer Regulations of 1940, 933; immigration during the war period, 942.

XIV. THE MIDDLE EAST AND PALESTINE DURING THE SECOND WORLD WAR

The Arab Middle East and the United Nations, 960–1007: Saudi Arabia and Oil, 966; Egypt—non-committal and non-belligerent, 970; pro-Axis rising in Iraq, 975; independence in Syria and Lebanon, 981; Arab unity and federation, 988. *Affairs in Palestine,* 1007–1049: political attitudes among Jews and Arabs, 1008; Jewish military aid for the Middle East, 1020; the Jewish Army proposal, 1029; self-arming among Arabs and Jews, 1035; the outbreak of terror, 1039. *Economic Development during the War and Postwar Economy,* 1049–1076: developments in industry and agriculture during the war, 1050; the Government's conception of postwar reconstruction, 1061; the Jewish conception of postwar development, 1066; the Lowdermilk proposal, 1073.

XV. THE SHAPING OF POLICIES AND SUMMARY OF PROPOSALS

The Shaping of Policies in Recent Years, 1078–1120: formulation of Zionist positions, 1078; Jewish opinion for and against the Jewish

Table of Contents

Commonwealth, 1088; Palestinian opinions on the Jewish Commonwealth, 1098; British and American policies, 1106. *Current Proposals for the Future of Palestine*, 1120–1186: summary of Arab position, 1120; the official Zionist program: the Jewish Commonwealth, 1123; proposals using the term "Jewish State": the new Zionist Organization; the Jewish State Party; Vladimir Jabotinsky; other proposals for a Jewish State, 1134; cantonization and partition plans, 1146; cantonization; Federated State of Palestine; the partition proposal of the Palestine Royal Commission, 1150; the Jewish Criticisms of the Royal Commission proposal, 1154; criticism by the Woodhead Commission and recent partition proposals, 1156; bi-national plans based on parity, 1158; the League for Arab-Jewish Rapprochement; *Hashomer Hatzair* conception (bi-nationalism on the basis of an ultimate Jewish majority); Palestine Committee on Constitutional Development: bi-nationalism on the basis of a Jewish minority or of numerical parity, 1172; proposals for the international control of Palestine, 1178.

SUPPLEMENT

Part 1, A Digest of Events Pertaining to Palestine, April 1945, through April 1946, 1187; Part 2, Report of the Anglo-American Committee of Inquiry, 1217.

BIBLIOGRAPHY   1238

INDEX   1281

MAPS

SYKES-PICOT AGREEMENT, 1916   61
  Based on map in David Lloyd George, *Memoirs of the Peace Conference*, Yale University Press, New Haven, Conn., 1939, p. 664
  By permission of Yale University Press

PALESTINE AND SYRIA IN 1915   185
  Based on map in *Great Britain and Palestine* [reproduced by permission of the Controller of H. M. Stationery Office], Royal Institute of International Affairs, London, 1915–1945
  By permission of Royal Institute of International Affairs

ARAB TERRITORIES AND PALESTINE   211
  Based on map in *Documents Relating to the McMahon Letters*, Jewish Agency, London, 1939
  By permission of the Jewish Agency

FORECAST OF FUTURE POPULATION TRENDS   827
  Based on graph in *Palestine Partition Commission Report* [Peel Report] (Cmd. 5479), p. 281, London, 1937
  By permission of the Controller of H. M. Stationery Office

PROVISIONAL SCHEME OF PARTITION AS PROPOSED BY THE PALESTINE ROYAL COMMISSION, 1937   843
  Based on Map #8 in *Palestine Partition Commission Report* (Cmd. 5479), London, 1937
  By permission of the Controller of H. M. Stationery Office

PALESTINE PARTITION PLAN A, B AND C   865, 867, 869
  Based on maps in *Great Britain and Palestine* [reproduced from maps 8, 9, and 10 in *Palestine Partition Commission Report*, Cmd. 5854 by permission of the Controller of H. M. Stationery Office]
  By permission of Royal Institute of International Affairs

PALESTINE LAND TRANSFER REGULATIONS, FEBRUARY 28, 1940   935
  Based on map in *Documents and Correspondence Relating to Palestine, August 1939 to March 1940*, Jewish Agency, London, 1940
  By permission of the Jewish Agency

CANAL PROJECTS OF PALESTINE   1071
  Based on map of *Proposed Integrated Irrigation and Hydroelectric Development of Palestine*
  By permission of the Commission on Palestine Surveys, New York

FACSIMILES

AHAD HA'AM'S PROPOSALS FOR THE PEACE CONFERENCE IN VERSAILLES (1919); IN HIS OWN HANDWRITING   165

Reproduced from N. M. Gelber, *The Balfour Declaration and Its History*, Jerusalem, 1939, p. 232

OUTLINE OF TENTATIVE REPORT AND RECOMMENDATIONS PREPARED BY THE INTELLIGENCE SECTION, IN ACCORDANCE WITH INSTRUCTIONS FOR THE PRESIDENT AND THE PLENIPOTENTIARIES, JANUARY 21, 1919.   247, 249

Reproduced from David Hunt Miller, *My Diary at the Conference of Paris*, IV, 263–264; section on Palestine.

CHAPTER I

THE DEVELOPMENT OF ZIONISM IN THE NINETEENTH CENTURY

ANTECEDENTS OF ZIONISM

British and General Interest in the Restoration

THE Balfour Declaration which was issued by the British War Cabinet on November 2, 1917, and which stated that "His Majesty's Government view with favor the establishment in Palestine of a national home for the Jewish people," was no sudden decision. It resulted from the confluence of British and Jewish streams of interest centering around Palestine and came as the culmination of historical forces which had been gathering strength throughout the nineteenth century. In both the Jewish and the British interests there was an interplay of idealistic and practical motivations. Zionism among the Jews constituted a modern interpretation of the Jewish messianic idea taking on new form under the pressure of continued rightlessness in reactionary Eastern Europe and of the recrudescence of anti-Semitism in a supposedly liberal West. In a more positive sense Zionism arose in response to the desire to preserve Jewish life in the face of disintegrating forces in modern civilization. British interest in the Restoration had a background in the prophecies of the Old Testament. A sense of justice, the desire to rectify the wrongs committed by Christians against "God's chosen people," and a feeling of sympathy for the Jews and their aspirations, were also factors. With such religious and humanitarian impulses were mingled strategic and political considerations: the need for protecting Britain's life-line to India, and the urge to extend its influence over the Near East.

Interest in the Near East and in Jewish Restoration

Napoleon's campaign in Egypt and Palestine on the eve of the nineteenth century marked the entry of Europe into the affairs of the Near East and the beginning of a long rivalry between Great Britain and France for its control. Napoleon's object in organizing a French expedition in the Near East was to interrupt the communications between England and India. Although he succeeded in taking Gaza and Jaffa in Palestine, he was checked by the British, and the victory over his fleet at the mouth of the Nile by the brilliant Lord Nelson brought the campaign to an inglorious end. The outcome foreshadowed the ultimate triumph of Great Britain in the Near East which was to come after more than a century of struggle.

Napoleon's Near East campaign is directly relevant to our story of the development of Zionism. It was at this time that he issued his famous proclamation promising to restore the Jews to Jerusalem and to rebuild the Temple if they would aid him in his conquest of Palestine. The Jews paid no attention to his call, remaining loyal to the Turks, who were then the allies of Great Britain. Although of no practical importance at the time, Napoleon's proclamation, as Professor Baron has pointed out, was indicative of a prevalent mental attitude connecting the Jews with Palestine:[1]

The famous proclamation of Napoleon to the Jewish people during his Egyptian campaign in 1799, although of little immediate consequence, symbolized Europe's acknowledgment of Jewish rights to Palestine. Napoleon was no idealist, seeking to solve the Jewish question on an altruistic basis; his shrewd recognition of the intense interest of the Jews, whom he attempted to enlist in his expeditionary army, and of the support that Jewish hope had received from French and English writers, is a barometer of the extent to which the European atmosphere was charged with these messianic expectations.

There had been many suggestions for Jewish restoration to the Holy Land in previous periods, but the proposals multiplied as the nineteenth century advanced. Italians, Russians, even Americans—as well as the French and British—suggested plans, and among the proponents were Catholic Jansenists, Protestant Pietists and Puritans. Also, there were Jewish visionaries of all sorts, who identified themselves completely with the nations among whom they lived but who retained in their

1. S. W. Baron, *A Social and Religious History of the Jews*, Columbia University Press, 1937, Vol. II, p. 329.

hearts a love for the people and for the land of Israel. One of the most interesting of these plans was that of the Swiss, Henry Dunant, founder of the Red Cross, who tried to arouse among the Jews an interest in the resettlement of Palestine and who, in 1876, established an international Palestine Society for Jewish colonization in Syria and Palestine.[2] The motives of the many proposals were highly varied: millennial doctrines which held that the return of the Jews to the Holy Land was a prerequisite to the Second Coming and the establishment of the Kingdom of Christ, missionary hope to convert the Jews, love of the Holy Land and the desire to see it restored to its ancient beauty, genuine appreciation of the contribution that the Jews had made to Western civilization, and a belief that they could become creative again if restored to nationhood—such religious, philanthropic and humanitarian ideas were combined with the hard-headed *Realpolitik* of acquiring or strengthening spheres of influence in the Near East.

As the power of Turkey declined, a veritable scramble among the European Powers, particularly Great Britain and France, commenced after 1840 for influence over Palestine and Syria. In 1833 the Sultan had been forced to cede Palestine to Mohammed Ali, the ruler of Egypt, who was being backed by the French. The British—in alliance with Russia, Prussia and Austria—regained it for Turkey through the defeat, in 1840, of Mohammed Ali's son, Ibrahim Pasha, who had occupied Palestine. The gain was a costly one for Turkey: Syria and Palestine were opened up to European penetration and to "an unarmed crusade" by the clergy of all denominations and of all countries; churches, schools, hospitals and missions were established in great numbers. Even the Americans, who had no ostensible political interests, established missionary educational work, first in Palestine and then in Beirut, Syria. The Greek Orthodox Church, aided by Russia, became active, and the Czar acquired important properties in Jerusalem. The British strengthened their influence in 1838 by establishing a consulate in Jerusalem. In 1841, jointly with Prussia, England founded an Evangelical Episcopate at Jerusalem, exerting the predominating influence from the beginning and remaining in sole control after the Prussians withdrew in 1882. France did

2. Richard J. H. Gottheil, *Zionism*, Jewish Publication Society, 1914, pp. 42–43.

not lag behind: she also appointed a consul at Jerusalem, aided in the renewal of the Latin Patriarchate in 1847, and took over the protection of the Roman Catholic Church in Palestine.

British and French Jewry were drawn into Eastern affairs at the same time through the Damascus blood accusation in 1840,[3] an event which stirred the Jews in Europe and the United States, deepened the Jewish sense of mutual responsibility all over the world, and was an important factor in the growth of Zionism. It had implications also for the political struggle between the French and the British. The press of Europe was agitated with pro-Jewish and anti-Jewish articles. Austria tried to induce Mohammed Ali to give the Jews a fair trial, suggesting a court of four Consuls—besides her own, the representatives of England, Russia and Prussia. However, the French, undoubtedly regarding this as an attempt on the part of its rivals to strengthen their influence in the Near East, opposed the plan and it was never carried out. A great public meeting was held in London where prominent Christians expressed their sympathy for the Jewish cause. The English Jews decided to send a commission to the Orient and chose Sir Moses Montefiore and Adolph Crémieux, respectively the leading Jews of Great Britain and France. Montefiore went with the backing of the British Government; Crémieux, against the wish of the party in power in his government, which was collaborating with the clerical reaction. Mohammed Ali attempted to evade the issue but finally yielded to a petition of the European Consuls and liberated the prisoners. The Damascus Affair aroused the interest of Western Jews in the plight of the Oriental Jews and led to the establishment of philanthropic and educational work under Jewish auspices.[4]

Throughout this period, and a generation later, after the completion of the Suez Canal, there was noticeable an increase of interest in the Jewish restoration among the French and the

---

3. Father Tomaso, Capuchin monk living in Damascus, disappeared and the leading Jews of the city were arrested on the charge of murdering him for ritual purposes. The French Consul pressed the charges and ordered the prisoners tortured to elicit a confession.

4. The *Alliance Israélite Universelle*, which has done important educational work among the Jews in the Orient, was established under the leadership of Crémieux in 1860. Later, the Anglo-Jewish Association also established schools in Jerusalem and in Bagdad. The German society, *Ezra*, associated with the *Hilfsverein der deutschen Juden*, established an extensive system of schools in the first decade of the twentieth century.

British. In a book entitled *On the Oriental Question,* published in 1848, the Frenchman, Ernest Laharanne, pointed out the unique importance of Palestine in a settlement of the Near East problem, and suggested that the international diplomats take up the question of a revival of Judea and a restoration to her of the historic function that she had exercised in ancient times. The leading Jewish scholar in France, Joseph Salvador, proposed the establishment of a new Jewish state "on the coast of Galilee and in old Canaan." He urged this on the grounds of Christian sympathy for persecuted Jews and in the belief that Jewish restoration to Palestine would lead to the creation of a universal religion that would unite mankind. In his *Paris, Rome et Jérusalem,* he added a practical note:[5] "Certainly the political importance of Jerusalem and of the land of Israel cannot but be reborn through the same human genius that will cut the Isthmus of Suez and mingle the waters of the Red Sea with those of the Mediterranean."

The British proposals were more numerous and even more enthusiastic. In 1845, a former Governor of South Australia, Colonel George Gawler, published a pamphlet entitled *Tranquilization of Syria and the East,* in which he suggested the establishment of Jewish colonies in Palestine as "the most sober and sensible remedy for the miseries of Asiatic Turkey." On the romantic side, the movement for a restoration of Israel to Zion found expression in Disraeli's *Tancred* and in George Eliot's *Daniel Deronda.* A mixture of the religious, the humanitarian and the practical, is to be found in the writings of Edward Cazelet (1877–1883), Laurence Oliphant (1829–1888), and the Earl of Shaftesbury (1801–1885). Edward Cazelet, of Huguenot descent, was deeply moved by the tragedy of the long Jewish exile and felt that, though scattered and downtrodden, the Jews possessed within themselves the elements that go to form a united nation. Laurence Oliphant, a distinguished British official in India and a member of Parliament, imbued with the Christian millennial conception, formulated a scheme for colonizing Palestine with Jews and endeavored, in 1882, to induce the Turkish Government to grant him a concession for the purpose.[6]

5. Quoted in S. W. Baron, *op. cit.,* Vol. II, p. 330.
6. When he failed to get the concession he settled down near Haifa in a small village close to the Jewish colonies which were then beginning to be established.

The most ardent British promoter of the idea of restoration was the Earl of Shaftesbury (the former Lord Ashley), a broadminded Tory reformer, who induced Parliament to pass the Factory Act of 1833. He was of a religious disposition and throughout his whole life concerned himself with the problem of a Jewish restoration. In the summer of 1838, he laid his plan before Lord Palmerston, the Foreign Secretary, whom he apparently interested; the appointment of a British Consul to Jerusalem soon followed. In his diary, Shaftesbury expressed disappointment with Palmerston's hard-headedness: "I am forced to argue politically, financially, commercially; these considerations strike him home; he weeps not like his Master over Jerusalem, nor prays that now, at last, she may put on her beautiful garments . . ." But in 1876,[7] Shaftesbury wrote an article on Zionism which indicates that he had learned how to add practical and political arguments to his religious and humanitarian pleas. After explaining the future commercial importance of Palestine, and the part that the Jews could play in its revival as a center of world trade, he said:[8]

It would be a blow to England if either of her rivals (France and Russia) should get hold of Syria. Her Empire reaching from Canada in the West to Calcutta and Australia in the South-East would be cut in two. England does not covet any such territories, but she must see that they do not get in the hands of rival Powers. She must preserve Syria to herself. Does not policy then—if that were all—exhort England to foster the nationality of the Jews and aid them, as opportunity may offer, to return as a leavening power to their old country? England is the great trading and maritime power of the world. To England, then naturally belongs the role of favouring the settlement of the Jews in Palestine. The nationality of the Jews exists: the spirit is there and has been there for 3000 years, but the external form, the crowning bond of union is still wanting. A nation must have a country. The old land, the old people. This is not an artificial experiment: it is nature, it is history.

7. In the year before this, Prime Minister Disraeli out-generaled the French Government and acquired the controlling shares of the Suez Canal with the aid of a loan extended to him by his personal friend, Lionel Rothschild.

8. Nahum Sokolow, *History of Zionism*, Vol. I, pp. 206 ff.

Jewish Love for Eretz Israel

The Jewish sense of connection with *Eretz Israel*—as Palestine is always called by the Jews—has expressed itself not only in the well-known passages of the Hebrew Bible, but also in the Jewish prayer book, in Talmudic law and legend, and in the mediaeval literatures. It is remarkable as much for its character as for its persistence. Rabbinical regulation permits entering into a contract for the purchase of a house in Palestine on the day of rest when other business transactions would be regarded as the worst form of desecration. The Talmudic sayings are lavish in praise of residence in Palestine: "It is better to dwell in the deserts of Palestine than in palaces abroad" . . . "The merit of residence in Palestine equals that of the fulfillment of all the Commandments of Divine Law" . . . "If thou wouldst behold the Divine Presence in this life—go and study the Torah in Palestine." There is no religious service, whether at home or in the synagogue, which does not contain some allusion to the restoration of Israel and the rebuilding of Zion "quickly in our day." There are several ideas which recur constantly: the re-establishment of the House of David to kingship over Israel with the political implication; the religious motif of the restoration to Zion of the Divine Presence which has gone into exile with the people of Israel; and the simple human plea for freedom: "May the All-merciful break the yoke from off our neck, and lead us upright to our land." Throughout runs the concept of the messianic ideal, which in the Jewish tradition implies the social motive—the establishment of an era of justice and of peace when the people of Israel shall have returned to the land of Israel.

These ideas were not stored away in libraries; wherever the traditional form of Jewish life remained intact they were conned over each day in studies at school, repeated in prayers, and absorbed through the folklore. The character of modern Zionism is understandable only in the light of this all-pervading Zionist consciousness of the masses. This tradition accounts for the strong insistence on Palestine as the locus of the Jewish homeland and for the strong admixture of idealistic elements in the Jewish development of Palestine. To no lesser extent, however, Zionism must be regarded as incorporating modern trends which characterized the thought of the nineteenth century—particularly naturalism, nationalism and social liberalism. The idea of "back to the land" implied back to nature and back to the cultivation of the soil. The idea of "productivization" stressed by the Socialist Zionists, which demanded a return to the basic occupations requiring manual labor, was no doubt stimulated partly by economic need, but it was also prompted by the moral idea prevalent in certain circles of economic thought, that wealth was derived mainly from the cultivation of the soil and that business and professions were parasitic.

In another important phase, Zionism arose as an answer to anti-Semitism: it was a call to Jewish self-confidence and self-respect; it aimed to provide a haven of refuge from persecution, rightlessness and social discrimination; it offered an alternative to "assimilation"; it denied the idea that the Jewish problem could be solved by the complete merging of the Jews of each country with the majority of the population. Nineteenth century nationalism implied a national state for each national group. The prevailing belief did not envisage the possibility of Jewish restoration to statehood; the logical conclusion, therefore, was that the Jew must identify himself completely with the national state of which he was a part, that is, that the Jew must somehow disappear.[9] The Zionists took the radical step of asserting Jewish nationhood and the possibilities of Jewish statehood. Paradoxically, therefore, Zionism might be called assimilation par excellence: it hoped to solve the Jewish problem by assimilating the Jewish status to the current social form of nation-state, and with the Jews taking their rightful place on a basis of equality as one of the peoples of the earth.

Precursors of Zionism: Hirsch Kalischer and Moses Hess

The beginning of modern Zionism is sometimes placed in 1897 with the assembling of the First Zionist Congress at Basle under the leadership of Theodor Herzl. As a movement of resettling Palestine, it may properly be regarded as having been initiated in 1882, when the first agricultural colonies were established. From the point of view of the development of Zionist conceptions—and even from the point of view of organ-

---

9. S. W. Baron, *op. cit.*, Vol. II, p. 263.

izational activity—an earlier date must be chosen. Zionism in its modern form as a national revival and as a movement toward Palestine, probably began in the early 1880's, and was stimulated by the wave of liberal nationalism that spread throughout Europe in that year.[10] The stirring of nationalism among the Poles, Hungarians and Italians, appears to have been a decisive factor in influencing the first organizer of Zionist activity, Hirsch Kalischer, an orthodox but liberal-minded Rabbi of the town of Thorn in eastern Prussia on the Polish border. The first problem of Zionism was to overcome the belief that the restoration of the Jews to the land of Israel would be effected by supernatural means and must await the coming of the Messiah.

In 1832, Kalischer initiated a correspondence with a number of leading rabbis of the day, to try to convince them through Biblical and Talmudic citations that the redemption of Israel was destined to be accomplished in a natural way, and that the Messiah would come only after a great number of Jews were concentrated in Palestine. As early as 1836, we find him writing to Asher Meyer Rothschild of Frankfort and to other prominent Jewish leaders in Germany and France to induce them to supply funds and organize the work of settling Jews on the soil in Palestine. In 1861 and 1862, he published two tracts *(Emunah Yeshara* and *Derishat Zion)* in which, besides reiterating his major theses that the Redemption would come through self-help and that the way must be prepared for the Messiah by Jewish settlement in Palestine, he made the practical proposal that a society should be established for colonizing Jews in Palestine for the purpose of tilling the soil. He did, in fact, organize such a society in 1864 which was not very successful. However, he succeeded in influencing the *Alliance Israélite Universelle*—founded in 1860 for educational work among Jews in the Orient—to establish an agricultural school near Jaffa. The school, called *Mikveh Israel* (The Ingathering of Israel), was established in 1870 and is accounted the first Jewish agricultural settlement in Palestine.

The influence of Rabbi Hirsch Kalischer was largely in the field of practical activity. More significant from the point of

10. S. L. Citron, *Toledot Hibbat Zion* (History of the "Lovers of Zion" Movement), Odessa, 1914, p. 9.

view of the theory of Zionism, was Moses Hess,[11] who in 1862 published a small book entitled *Rome and Jerusalem. The Latest National Question.* Hess, sometimes humorously referred to by his colleagues as the "Communist Rabbi Moses," was the leader of a non-Marxist line of thought called "true socialism." [12] His interest in Jewish affairs was quiescent until he was aroused by the Damascus Affair in 1840. In Germany, the period was one of acute controversy with reference to the position of the Jews. The reactionary Frederick William IV, who succeeded to the throne in 1840, following the thesis of the German Christian state, wanted to apply to all of Prussia the principle that the Jews constituted a separate community, exempt from military service, and subject to certain political and civil disabilities. In protest, the Jewish leaders, carrying on the struggle for equal rights, became even more insistent on the idea that the Jews constituted a religious community only and in no sense a nationality; that is, they were Germans of Mosaic persuasion. In the cultural and social life there was a great effort to assimilate to accepted conventions. Even the religious practices and ideas were refashioned to fit in with liberal Protestant conceptions. Reform Judaism, which developed in this period, was assiduous in eliminating every mention of the return to Zion from the prayer book. The upper middle classes and the Jewish intellectuals tended to embrace the eighteenth century cosmopolitanism which was then fashionable in certain circles in Germany.

In Hess's philosophy there was an interaction between his Jewish and general conceptions. Though he earned the reputation of being the "Father of German Communism," his socialist ideas differed from those of Karl Marx, with whom he at times collaborated but more often quarreled. He conceived of Communism as a form of humanism, and humanism

---

11. Moses Hess was born in Bonn, Germany, on January 22, 1812, of a well-to-do family. His grandfather, who originally came from Poland, appears to have exerted a strong Jewish influence over him, and his father, though less learned in the Jewish tradition, was an orthodox Jew. In 1830, Hess entered Bonn University, but left without receiving a degree, to devote himself to the propagation of socialism both in Germany and France. After the Revolution of 1848, he was condemned to death and fled Germany. He spent much of his remaining life in France, where he died in 1875.

12. Sidney Hook, *From Hegel to Marx*, Reynal and Hitchcock, 1936, p. 188.

was for him love of mankind which, applied to society, meant social justice. He was particularly opposed to the idea of conflict which played such a large part in Marxism and to the emphasis on class stratification. He regarded the family and the nation, not the class, as the fundamental units of society. While believing that the real cause of social distress was economic, and that no ethics was significant which did not look to the tangible improvement of man, he regarded socialism not as a matter of bread primarily; its main purpose was the development of moral values, of truth and of human dignity, and it aspired to a social order marked by creative work in which effort and enjoyment would be fused. He rejected the cosmopolitan idea current at the time of humanity as an association of individuals, and conceived of world unity in terms of an association of nations.

His high evaluation of the family and the nation appears in—or, rather, was derived from—his philosophy of Judaism. A key thought in his writing is, "Judaism has never drawn any line of separation between the individual and the family, the family and the nation, the nation and humanity as a whole, humanity and the cosmos, nor between creation and the Creator. Judaism has no other dogma than the teaching of the unity." [13] The aim of Judaism, moreover, was not the salvation of the individual as in Christianity, but the perfection of social life: "With the Jews, solidarity and social responsibility were always the fundamental principles of life and conduct." [14] The Jews, like all other nationalities, have their unique contribution to make to the progress of humanity. Instead of self-obliteration, the Jews could serve the world best by a renascence of their national consciousness. In the new era emerging with the progress of liberalism and science, there would be a "regeneration of the historical civilized nations" and the small oppressed nationalities of Europe would be raised to the level of the mighty and dominant ones.[15] For the Jew, this regeneration could come only in his ancient homeland.

Hess realized the importance of legalizing Jewish efforts

---

13. Moses Hess, *Rome and Jerusalem. The Latest National Question* (translated by Meyer Waxman), Bloch, 1943, p. 84.
14. *Ibid.*, p. 52.
15. *Ibid.*, p. 75.

at resettlement in Palestine and laid emphasis on the idea of social justice. He summarized his conception as follows: "The acquisition of common ancestral soil, the organization of the work on a legal basis, the founding of Jewish societies of agriculture, industry and commerce on the Mosaic, i.e., social principles, these are the foundations on which Oriental Jewry will rise again and in its rise will kindle the glowing fire of the old Jewish patriotism and light the way to a new life for the Jewry of the entire world." He looked to France, which had given Jews individual freedom, to help them rebuild their nation. The projected Suez Canal, which would connect Europe and Asia, would bring in its train the restoration of the Jews to Palestine, the founding of colonies and the ultimate establishment of a Jewish state.

He regarded the attempt of the German Jews to estrange themselves from Judaism as far as possible and to become completely merged with the German people, as doomed to failure. No reform of the Jewish religion, however extreme, would be successful, for the Germans were not troubled about the religious distinctiveness of the Jews but by their racial difference.[16] Even conversion itself would not relieve the Jews from the enormous pressure of German anti-Semitism. He thought that the European nations generally considered the existence of the Jews in their midst as an anomaly. They might tolerate the Jews and even at times grant them emancipation, but they would never respect them as long as the Jews put material welfare and convenience above the great Jewish national memories. It was his belief that once progressive German Jews recognized this, they would work for the political regeneration of their people instead of expending their energy in fighting for so-called "emancipation."

CURRENTS OF ZIONIST THOUGHT IN EASTERN EUROPE

In Eastern Europe as well as in Germany, the intelligentsia for the most part embraced the doctrine of assimilation. But the social conditions in the Eastern European countries dif-

---

16. What Hess meant by race is not clear. He seems to have felt that each ethnic group is endowed with some unique characteristics which are not changeable and these "inborn instincts" and "typical inclinations" are the basis of the nation's social institutions.

fered greatly from those prevailing in Germany. The Jewish population was large and thickly concentrated. Jewish life was self-contained and the traditional educational institutions, the *Heder* and the *Yeshiva,* still occupied a central position in the cultural and religious life. The Russian Czars attempted in various ways to bring about the assimilation of the Jews, by introducing modern schools and prohibiting Jewish customs and dress, but these efforts were too superficial to bring about any fundamental change. Besides, these efforts were not accompanied by the introduction of democratic ideas or by the promise of equality for Jews. Another feature was that the doctrine of assimilation preached by the Jewish intellectuals was spread through the medium of Hebrew, which was the natural literary language of the Jewish scholars and of the educated Jewish classes. The *Haskalah,* as the enlightenment movement was called, thus led indirectly to a renascence of Hebrew and became the basis of a cultural revival. Moreover, within the *Haskalah* movement there had always been a more positive strain which emphasized the significance of Jewish history and the value of tradition, though criticizing superstition and religious bigotry.

The Founders of Russian Zionism

With Perez Smolenskin,[17] the *Haskalah* movement may be said to have been converted into the *Hatehiah,* or renascence. In the review *Hashahar* (The Dawn), which he began to publish in the late 1860's, he proposed to attack not only the bigots of the old school who hid themselves under the mantle of religious dogma, but in equal measure those "enlightened hypocrites who seek with honeyed words to alienate the sons of Israel from their ancestral heritage." [18] The work of shedding the light of knowledge was to go hand in hand with the regeneration of the beauty of the Hebrew language and the increase in the number of its devotees. In *Am Olam* (Eternal People), published in 1872, he taught that the Jews are the possessors of an historical and spiritual culture of enduring value, and propounded the idea that Jewish nationalism is

---

17. Born in 1842 in a little market town near Mogilev in the Russian Ukraine.
18. Quoted in Nahum Slouschz, *The Renascence of Hebrew Literature,* Jewish Publication Society, Philadelphia, 1909, p. 228.

compatible with the ultimate realization of the ideal of the universal brotherhood of men. In his philosophy there were three elements: an emphasis on the Jewish religious tradition in its fundamental aspects as accepted by the masses of the Jews; a revival of the Hebrew language as the medium of Jewish literature as well as of Jewish prayer; and an attachment to Palestine which the masses of the Jews had cherished throughout the ages.

Leo Pinsker: Father of Russian Zionism

The most important figure in the development of the Zionist movement before Theodor Herzl was Leo Pinsker.[19] For him disillusionment with the idea of emancipation was the starting point, in contrast to Smolenskin whose dominant motivation was a positive appreciation of the values of Hebrew literature and Jewish thought. Pinsker had been a firm believer in the idea of Russification; indeed, he was one of the founders of the "Society for Spreading Enlightenment among the Russian Jews." But the black reaction in Russia after 1881, the pogroms of that year, and the May Laws of 1882 restricting Jewish settlement to the Pale, led him to reconsider his position. He published a pamphlet under the name of *Auto-Emancipation: An Admonition to His Brethren by a Russian Jew*, which first appeared anonymously, written in German. Its central thought was that the Jews should no longer depend on others to emancipate them; they should emancipate themselves through reestablishing themselves again as a nation on a territory of their own. The pamphlet ended with the call: "Help yourself, and God will help you!"

The pamphlet contains the germ of a socio-psychological analysis of anti-Semitism. The tragic feature of the Jewish people in the Diaspora is that they can neither live nor die; they thus become a sort of strange, ghostlike phenomenon inspiring uneasiness and apprehension in the Gentile heart. Moreover, the Jews are always guests in the homes of other nations, and lacking a home themselves, can never reciprocate hospitality.

---

19. Leo (Judah Leib) Pinsker was born at Tomashov, Poland, in 1821. His father was a distinguished scholar and an authority on the history of the Karaites. Leo Pinsker studied medicine at Moscow University; after his graduation he went to Odessa where he soon distinguished himself in his profession.

Tolerance of the Jews by the host nation is never really a spontaneous expression of warm human feeling since the Jewish guest is in reality forced upon the host by circumstances. Emancipation thus takes on the character of "a rich gift, a splendid alms willingly or unwillingly flung to the poor, humble beggar whom no one, however, cares to shelter because a homeless, wandering beggar wins confidence or sympathy from none." [20] Under such circumstances, in the end the guest is bound to overstay his welcome. He summed up his idea in the pithy sentence: "They [the Jews] are everywhere in evidence and nowhere at home." The worst effect of this abnormal situation is the loss of self-respect and consciousness of human dignity on the part of the Jews:[21]

When an idle spectator on the road calls out to us: 'You poor Jewish devils are certainly to be pitied,' we are most deeply touched; and when a Jew is said to be an honor to his people, we are foolish enough to be proud of it. We have sunk so low that we become almost jubilant when, as in the West, a small fraction of our people is put on an equal footing with non-Jews. But he who must be *put* on a footing stands but weakly. If no notice is taken of our descent and we are treated like others born in the country we express our gratitude by actually turning renegades. For the sake of the comfortable position we are granted, for the flesh-pots which we may enjoy in peace, we persuade ourselves, and others, that we are no longer Jews, but full-blooded citizens. Idle delusion! Though you prove yourselves patriots a thousand times, you will still be reminded at every opportunity of your Semitic descent. This fateful *memento hori* will not prevent you, however, from accepting the extended hospitality, until some fine morning you find yourself crossing the border and you are reminded by the mob that you are, after all, nothing but vagrants and parasites, without the protection of the law.

As Pinsker saw it, the only solution is the re-creation of Jewish nationality and the acquisition of the normal attributes of a nation, i.e., "a common language, common customs, and a common land." The Jewish people must have a rallying point, a center of gravity and a government of their own. What the Jews needed was a land from which no foreign master could

---

20. Leo Pinsker, *Auto-Emancipation*, Maccabean Publishing Company, New York, 1906, p. 5.
21. *Ibid.*, p. 7.

expel them. As a first step Pinsker suggested that a national congress or "directory" of leaders be convened in which all Jewish forces would participate. The first task of the congress or the directory would be the discovery and purchase of territory adapted to Jewish needs, and large enough to permit the settlement of several million Jews. The land, as national property, was to be inalienable. In the days of Pinsker it was a major question in Russia whether Jewish immigration should be directed toward Palestine or America. He believed that Palestine was the more reasonable choice. But if Palestine[22] should be selected, it would have to be with the permission of Turkey and with international sanction. He suggested that it might be "a sovereign pashalic" in Asiatic Turkey, recognized by the Porte and the other Powers as neutral.

He concluded his memorable pamphlet with the following summary:[23]

The Jews are not a living nation; they are everywhere aliens; therefore they are despised. The civil and political emancipation of the Jews is not sufficient to raise them in the estimation of the peoples.

The proper, the only solution, is in the creation of a Jewish nationality, of a people living upon its own soil, the auto-emancipation of the Jews; their return to the ranks of the nations by the acquisition of a Jewish homeland.

We must not persuade ourselves that humanity and enlightenment alone can cure the malady of our people.

The lack of national self-respect and self-confidence of political initiative and of unity, are the enemies of our national renaissance.

That we may not be compelled to wander from one exile to another, we must have an extensive, productive land of refuge, a *center* which is our own.

The present moment is the most favorable for this plan.

The international Jewish question must have a national solution. Of course, our national regeneration can only proceed slowly. *We must take the first step.* Our descendants must follow us at a measured and not over-precipitant speed.

The national regeneration of the Jews must be initiated by a congress of Jewish notables.

22. Although later he accepted Palestine for the territorial basis of Jewish nationality, in *Auto-Emancipation* he expressed something of a prejudice against it on the ground that the Jews should not reattach themselves to ancient Judea where their political life was once violently destroyed.
23. *Ibid.*, pp. 15–16.

No sacrifice should be too great for this enterprise which will assure our people's future, everywhere endangered.

The financial execution of the undertaking does not present insurmountable difficulties.

Help yourselves, and God will help you!

Pinsker's brochure evoked a great deal of enthusiasm among Russian Jewish intellectuals and he was soon drawn into the leadership of the *Hovevei Zion* (Lovers of Zion) Movement which had been developing throughout Russia. Realizing the strong feeling for Palestine, he soon accepted the view that *Eretz Israel* was the only territory on which the Jews could re-establish themselves as a nation. At a conference held in Kattowitz in upper Silesia in 1884 to federate the *Hovevei Zion* societies and to stimulate fund-raising efforts for the aid of the Palestine colonies which had already begun to be founded, Pinsker was elected president. He was instrumental in the establishment of "The Society for the Support of Jewish Agriculture in Syria and Palestine," popularly known as the Odessa Committee, which was the principal organization for the development of Palestine work until the formation of the World Zionist Organization into which the Odessa Committee was later absorbed (1906).

The year 1882 marks the beginning of Zionist colonization in Palestine. After the pogroms, student national societies were organized with the idea of settlement on the land in Palestine. Of particular importance were groups organized by Israel Belkind in Kharkov in 1882 which were set up to raise funds for the purchase of land and the establishment of colonies in Palestine on cooperative principles. From these groups eventuated the *Bilu*,[24] a society of five hundred young people dedicated to the idea of pioneering in Palestine. Shortly after its organization in January, 1882, groups of the *Bilu* were already in Palestine—in Jaffa and the newly founded surrounding settlements. It was at this period, also, that Baron Edmond de Rothschild of the French section of the famous banking family,

---

24. The word "Bilu" is formed of the first letters of the passage in Isaiah, Chapter 2, Verse 5, of which the English version reads: "House of Jacob, come, let us go [in the light of the Lord]." The significance of the passage derives from the section immediately preceding with its central idea: "And they shall beat their swords into ploughshares, and their spears into pruning hooks; nation shall not lift up sword against nation, neither shall they learn war any more."

though not subscribing to Zionist principles, became interested in colonization in Palestine.

The Cultural Zionism of Ahad Ha'am

Pinsker's brochure was important not only for the practical work; it exerted a great influence on Asher Ginsberg,[25] who, under the pen name of Ahad Ha'am, became the proponent of a point of view which has since come to be known as "cultural" or "spiritual" Zionism.[26] His work extended over a lifetime and constituted an outline of a philosophy of Judaism. He has frequently been represented as an opponent of "political" Zionism. This is somewhat of a misapprehension; it is true that his views represent a different emphasis from that of "Herzlian Zionism," and in its totality represents quite a different outlook on Jewish life. But he was not entirely opposed to the political aspect of Zionism; indeed, he played an important part as an adviser in the course of negotiations which led to the Balfour Declaration, and his influence on those who were responsible for Zionist policy was considerable. He is credited with insisting that the concept of historic connection be included in the Mandate. In his proposal for a short formula to be presented to the Peace Conference he included the term "Jewish Commonwealth" as the ultimate aim of Zionism.[27]

Ahad Ha'am was greatly influenced by the English writers, Locke and Hume, the French philosopher, August Comte, and by the Russian, Pisarev, who was an interpreter of positivism. He treated the problems of cultural and practical life with a great directness and developed a crystal-clear style in Hebrew, something which was in itself a creative achievement at the

---

25. Asher Ginsberg (1856–1927) was born in the Province of Kiev. He came of a well-to-do Hassidic (pietist) family and spent his childhood and youth in the study of the Bible and Talmud, and later of Rabbinic Literature of which he became a recognized master. Later he studied literature and philosophy in Berlin, Breslau, Vienna and Odessa. His point of view is developed in many articles which were collected and published in 1913 in four volumes entitled *Al Pereshat Derachim* (At the Crossroads). His letters were published in six volumes (*Iggrot*, 1924–1925). He died in Palestine where he had settled in 1922.

26. The Hebrew term, though properly translated "spiritual" does not have the dualistic implications of the English word, and implies a union of moral and cultural conceptions. (See Leon Simon, "Introduction," *Selected Essays* by Ahad Ha'am, Jewish Publication Society, 1912, pp. 12–13.)

27. See below, Chap. III.

time. Like Hess and Smolenskin, he built his nationalism on a general universalistic philosophy of life and regarded Zionism as a modern conception of Judaism. He was a master of the Jewish sources and his Jewish outlook was well integrated with his modern conceptions. He was, however, quite uninfluenced by socialism and he ignored the problem of the interplay of social-economic factors with the moral life.

The basis of Ahad Ha'am's so-called "spiritual" Zionism is the concept that Israel is a nationality. Judaism is thus broader than the Jewish religion and includes all creations of the Jewish mind: ethics, law, prophecy, poetry and folklore. The Jewish mind or spirit has manifested itself throughout the ages in different forms, but the central element in Jewish national life is Jewish ethics. Jewish moral conceptions, he thought, were separable from the theological forms in which they were traditionally expressed. The foundation of Jewish ethics was the historical and national experience of the Jewish people, which had created its own ideas—religious, legal, and ethical. One might thus be "a good Jew" without being a religionist. It was an appreciation of the values of Jewish thought and of Jewish institutions that made one a Jew in the positive sense, not the performance of ritual or the maintenance of dogma.

In his view the nation was as real an organic unit as the individual. Just as the individual combines the memories of the past with hope for the future, so the nation represents a totality of memories and aspirations, a union of past and future. The fundamental characteristic of the Jewish people, its genius, was a tendency toward extremism or perfectionism in its striving for absolute truth; when applied to social life this meant the striving for absolute justice. This quest for truth and justice was the essence of Hebrew prophecy, the unique expression of Jewish experience and character. Since absolute justice is a messianic concept that never can be fully applied to life, the function of the Jewish people is eternal—the striving for ever greater justice in the life of society.

The motivation of Zionism was to be found in the inner urge to national survival and the fulfillment of Jewish character and spiritual destiny. Zionism was not in essence an answer to anti-Semitism which was a negative force and therefore could not be creative of cultural or spiritual values. Anti-Semitism would not be destroyed with the growth of Zionism. In the belief that anti-Semitism would soon be a matter of the past, the Zionists were no better than the "emancipated" Jews; for both were deluding themselves. The cure for anti-Semitism had to await the humanizing of Western civilization generally. Nor could Palestine offer a solution of the economic problem of the Jews; those who were concerned with improving the material lot of the Jews had better look toward America. Palestine was essential for the revival of the Jewish people: as the land of prophecy it was the site for such a revival. An early establishment of a Jewish state was not to be expected; it could come about only when internationalism was further advanced among other nations. This union of nationalism with internationalism was part of the teaching of Jewish history.

Zionism should aim to resolve not the problem of the Jews as individuals, but the problem of Judaism as an historical national culture. The value of Zionism lay in counteracting the petrification and the decline of religion, on the one hand, and assimilation and loss of Jewish values, on the other. Zionism had a moral object—the emancipation of the Jews from the inner slavery and the spiritual degradation which assimilation had produced, and the creation of a sense of national unity and a life of dignity and freedom. In the land of their original civilization, Jews would again become culturally and spiritually creative. Palestine was essential because it alone could arouse the Jewish people to the supreme effort needed; in no other country could the Jews establish a new form of life in harmony with their ancient and traditional culture. Zionism required "a revival of spirit" among the Jewish people at large. The means of this revival would be the renascence of Hebrew literature and thought. Only Hebrew could become the unifying language of the Jewish people and the schools in Palestine were even more important than the colonies, however essential the latter were for the development of Jewish life.

A unique element in Ahad Ha'am's thinking was that Palestine would form the center of cultural and spiritual influence for the Jews in the Diaspora. In marked contrast to other conceptions of Zionism, Ahad Ha'am thought that the establishment of the Jewish center in Palestine was not a substitute for Jewish life in other parts of the world, but a means of strengthening it. The Diaspora would not disappear: it would be the circumference receiving the spiritual influence of the center.[28] He offered no blueprint of the ideal society which he believed should be established in Palestine. His emphasis was on having the life Jewish in the ideal sense, but he did not otherwise describe the ideal. In explaining what he meant by the spiritual center, he frequently quoted a passage which he had first written in an essay on Dr. Pinsker in 1892:[29]

A national spiritual centre of Judaism, to which all Jews will turn with affection, and which will bind all Jews together; a centre of study and learning, of language and literature, of bodily work and spiritual purification; *a true miniature of the people of Israel as it ought to be* . . . so that every Jew in the Diaspora will think it a privilege to behold just once the centre of Judaism, and when he returns home will say to his friends: *'If you wish to see the genuine type of a Jew,* whether it be a Rabbi or a scholar or a writer, a farmer or an artist or a businessman—then go to Palestine and you will see it.'

Ahad Ha'am also devoted considerable attention to criticism of the practical work carried on by the *Hovevei Zion* Society in Palestine. In one of his earliest essays called "Truth from Palestine," written in 1891, he made a sharp criticism of the work in the new Jewish colonies and of the philanthropic administration of Baron de Rothschild who was then subsidizing the settlements. He was also one of the first to point out the potential gravity of the Arab question. He thought that it was a mistake to underestimate the Arabs: they were a shrewd people and were well aware of Jewish aspirations in Palestine. For the time being, they welcomed the Jewish activities; the peasants received high wages from the Jewish colonists and the large landowners were getting fantastically high prices for their rocky and sandy wastes. But if a time should come when they felt their position endangered, the Arabs would not view further Jewish settlement with equanimity. His purpose in

28. His conception of the spiritual center has sometimes been taken to mean that he did not regard the material basis of Jewish life in Palestine as important. He pointed out that this would be nonsense: in using the term spiritual, he meant to indicate that the influence of the center on the Diaspora could be only of a spiritual and cultural, but not of a material or political nature. (See "A Spiritual Centre," in Ahad Ha'am, *Ten Essays on Zionism and Judaism*, trans. by Leon Simon, Routledge, London, 1922, pp. 120 ff.)

29. *Ibid.*, pp. 154–155.

making these criticisms was not to discourage the Jewish development in Palestine, but, on the contrary, to impress upon the leaders the difficulties of the task and the necessity for careful thinking and planning. The difficulties could be overcome, not by underestimating them but by strengthening the Jewish will.

Labor Zionism

Before dealing with the political Zionism formulated by Theodor Herzl, a brief statement is in order on labor or socialist Zionism. Although later in development, it merits consideration at this point as one aspect of the East European trend in Zionism. The beginning of a "proletarian" conception of Zionism was in evidence during the last decade of the nineteenth century, and labor groups began to associate themselves with the Zionist movement in the first decade of the present century. Though a small minority, the Labor Zionists played on important part in Zionism, both in the practical work of developing Palestine and in the evolution of the Zionist conception.

With the growth of revolutionary thought in Russia, strong socialist-assimilationist tendencies developed among the intellectual Jewish youth, in the belief that the Jewish problem would be solved along with the general solution of Russia's economic and political problems. There were, however, Jewish socialist groups who wanted to maintain the sense of Jewish cultural or national distinctiveness, and a great variety of ideologies developed: some, along the lines of Jewish Diaspora cultural nationalism with Yiddish as the basis of Jewish nationality; others, which attempted to combine socialist ideas with Zionism.[30] To illustrate the socialist contributions to the development of Zionist thought, two writers who exercised an important influence on the character of the Labor Movement in Palestine may be chosen: Nachman Syrkin (1868–1924), who developed a non-Marxian line of Zionist socialist thinking, and Ber Borochov (1881–1917),[31] who attempted a synthesis of Marxism and Zionism which influenced the Russian *Poale Zion* (Workers of Zion) Movement.

30. See Oscar I. Janowsky, *The Jews and Minority Rights*, Chaps. 1 and 2.

31. A third writer was A. D. Gordon, who exercised a more direct and personal influence in Palestine. See below, Chapter VII.

Nachman Syrkin[32] began his work as a publicist in 1898 with a series of essays on socialist Zionism. He decried assimilationist tendencies: that of the socialists, who used internationalism as a cloak to cover the emptiness of their thought; and that of the bourgeoisie, to whom cosmopolitanism was an instrument of convenience. He deplored the elimination of the messianic idea from the synagogue service of the Reform Jews as a loss in idealism and in moral force. Zionism and socialism had a common basis, for both had their origin in a reaction against "suppression of human beings and the unequal distribution of power." Socialism might conceivably solve the Jewish problem in the distant future when human equality became firmly established in the world; it was already significant to all the oppressed for it aimed to increase the political power of the masses, to improve their economic lot, and to elevate their spiritual condition. But the abnormal economic structure of the Jewish people, its lack of political power, and its peculiar social conditions, made of the Jewish problem a special one which could not soon be resolved by socialism alone.

Anti-Semitism was a persistent force in European society. In the Middle Ages it appeared as religious prejudice; in modern times, as racial prejudice intensified by the tensions within capitalism. Anti-Semitism resulted from the unequal distribution of power and would therefore continue as long as there were weaker and stronger forces in the world. In a dormant form it was present in all classes of society, but it was particularly strong in the declining classes: among the lower middle class which was being undermined by the upper middle class, and the land-owning class which was being destroyed by the industrial capitalists, and in the peasant class which was being strangled by the landowners. Despite the moral degeneration of anti-Semitic leaders, and in spite of the real disgust which intelligent persons felt for anti-Semitism, the movement was steadily growing.

32. Nachman Syrkin was born in Mogilev, Russia. At the time of his graduation from the Minsk Gymnasium in 1884 he was already under the influence of the *Hovevei Zion*. He continued his university studies in Berlin and returned to Russia, participating in socialist and revolutionary movements. He studied medicine in Switzerland, but later devoted himself to the development of the Zionist Socialist Party in Europe. In 1907 he emigrated to America and became one of the outstanding leaders of the *Poale Zion* movement in the United States. *Essays on Socialist Zionism* is an English collection of some of his more important writings.

Zionism arose out of the inferior social position of the Jews, and in their lack of power. But it also contained the elements of moral protest rooted in traditional spiritual aspirations. The Jewish state would not be built on the basis of inequality; it could not be founded on a "social contract of servitude." Though idealistic, Zionism was not utopian, because it was founded on experience and need. The wheels of the Jewish state could not be turned without the powerful arms of the Jewish workers, and the Jewish masses willed a Jewish state built on social justice. Zionism, however, would be a solution for all Jews, not only for the working class: "Zionism must fuse with socialism in order to become the ideal of the entire Jewish people, of the proletariat, of the middle class, of the intelligentsia, as well as of the idealistic."

Syrkin's socialism was of a liberal popular type—non-Marxist in character. Ber Borochov,[33] although like Syrkin primarily a Zionist, attempted to apply the Marxist ideas of dialectical materialism to the Jewish problem. Differing from Marx, Borochov emphasized the significance of the principle of nationality in the organization of social life, but he combined this with a Marxist stress on the significance of class structure. Borochov believed that nationality arose out of common conditions of production as much as out of common tradition and common territory. In any given country, despite common elements, the nationalism of the various classes—of the landowners, of the middle class, of the petty bourgeoisie and of the proletariat—differed in important aspects. The landowners cherish their native land because it is the basis of rents; to the upper middle class, the country is the base of operations from which to capture the world market; to the petty bourgeoisie who serve the consumer, the native land represents the local market; and for the proletariat, their country is realisti-

---

33. Ber Borochov was born in the Ukraine, but after the pogroms in 1881 and 1882, the family moved to Poltava which was a center of the *Hovevei Zion* movement and also a place where the Czarist government sent exiled revolutionaries. Borochov thus came under both influences—Zionism and Socialism—early in his youth. He attended the *gymnasium* at Poltava, and in 1905 joined the *Poale Zion* party. In 1906 he was expelled from Russia for revolutionary activities and thereafter worked in various countries as a writer and editor of Yiddish papers. In 1914 he came to the United States and for a time was editor of *Der Yiddischer Kempfer*. He returned to Russia in 1917 after the March revolution and died there soon after.

cally enough the place of employment. Borochov emphasized the nationalist character of the proletariat which, in the interest of class consciousness, Marxists had obscured. In the attempt to understand anti-Semitism, he held, it was necessary to understand the nationalism of each class and how it cut across class consciousness.

The basic factor of the Jewish problem he found in the peculiar economic distribution of the Jews in the various occupations. On the basis of a statistical analysis of Jewish occupational distribution throughout the world, he concluded that "the concentration of Jewish labor in any occupation varies directly with the remoteness of that occupation from the soil." [34] The root of the Jewish problem lay in the fact that the Jews were absent from "the most important, most influential, and the most stable branches of production—far removed from the occupations which are at the hub of history." [35] The urgencies of modern capitalism were aggravating this evil and bringing the chronic ailment of the Jewish people to a severe crisis. Development in the direction of large-scale organization and monopoly was squeezing the Jewish petty bourgeoisie, creating an inner class war by setting Jewish capitalist against Jewish worker, and increasing the competition between the "native" worker and the "alien" Jewish worker. The Jewish problem thus rested essentially on the economic insecurity of the Jews, in their removal from the land and their absence from the basic industries of production. Because it would lead to a normalization of the Jewish economic status, "Zionism is the logical, the natural consequence of the economic revolution that has been going on within Jewish life for the last hundred years."

THEODOR HERZL: FOUNDER OF POLITICAL ZIONISM

The establishment of the World Zionist Organization and the conduct of negotiations looking toward the creation of the Jewish state in Palestine constituted the life work of Theodor Herzl, a Hungarian-born Viennese writer and journalist.[36] At

34. Ber Borochov, *Nationalism and the Class Struggle*, with an introduction by Abraham G. Duker, New York, 1937, p. 68.
35. *Ibid.*, p. 69.
36. He was born May 2, 1860, in the city of Pesth, which was united with Buda in 1872 to form the capital of Hungary.

the time that he wrote *Der Judenstaat* (The Jewish State), published in 1896, he was hardly aware of the writings of any of his predecessors, although he had heard of and rejected Zionism as a solution of the Jewish problem. His views had in one form or another been anticipated by others; even the political concept, the establishment of a Jewish state, had been adumbrated by Hess and Pinsker. But there was great originality in his insistence on the primary importance of the political factor, in his realization of the significance of a worldwide Jewish organization, and in his forceful, dynamic and dramatic envisagement of the Zionist idea. His remarkable personality added significance to his views: in his meticulous dress and manner, he was the perfect European; his dark coloring and deepset eyes gave a Semitic cast to his countenance, and his erect stature and full black beard were reminiscent of an ancient Assyrian prince. From youth he was marked for leadership.

Early Interest in the Jewish Question

Herzl has often been described as an assimilated Jew, suddenly aroused from his indifference to the Jewish question by the Dreyfus trial. This statement of the situation is far from correct.[37] He came from a well-to-do, conventional family which had adjusted itself to a Liberal-Reform type of Jewish practice comparable to the conservative synagogue in the United States. The language of the home was German, and Herzl's mother, a devotee of classical German literature, made a conscientious effort to imbue her children with a love for German culture. But there were also Jewish influences in his home life. At birth, he had, in the traditional manner, received a Hebrew name—Binyamin Ze'ev—and as a boy he regularly attended the synagogue with his father on the Sabbath and the Holy Days. He had the usual impressive *Bar Mitzvah*, accompanied by the confirmation party at home. He also received the conventional Jewish education of the middle-class culturally assimilated Jews, and though the instruction was neither inspiring nor profound, it appears to have exerted a certain sub-

---

37. An excellent biography of Theodor Herzl is available in English translation: Alex Bein, *Theodor Herzl, A Biography* (translated from the German by Maurice Samuel), Jewish Publication Society, Philadelphia, 1940.

conscious effect. The story of the Exodus, as he later related, appears to have been buried in his memory and he had a vivid recollection of the folk-tale of the Messiah King who the Jews believed would come riding on a donkey to lead them back to redemption.

Another significant element in his experience which has not been sufficiently emphasized, was his early interest in scientific progress and technology. When still a boy Herzl's imagination was first stirred by the rise of technical inventions, and his first hero was Ferdinand de Lesseps, who built the Suez, and projected the Panama Canal. His parents, taking his enthusiasm seriously, enrolled him in a technical high school, but it appears that he was less interested in the purely scientific aspects of the new discoveries than in the social aspects, i.e., what technology could do for the solution of human problems and the spread of international relations. He finally devoted himself to the study of law at the University of Vienna, but in this, too, he was concerned more in the human side of the law than in the legal technicalities. He had already determined to become a writer and he tried his hand at a novel and light drama soon after his admission to the University. Even at this period of his life he evinced a strong interest in the conflict between the European aristocracy and the rising upper middle class, a conflict in which the Jewish business and professional men were involved. He took an active part in the life of the student societies and was at the same time an omnivorous reader of German, French, English and American writers.

At the age of twenty-two, we find him very much concerned with the problem of the Jewish liberal middle class. The Jews in Hungary had received political and legal emancipation in 1867, but despite this they continued to be regarded as a separate group and moved largely in Jewish circles. Herzl seemed to be troubled by this "compulsion of the ring of the ghetto" which had persisted after the legal walls had been removed. What seemed to concern him most was that educated Christians still entertained the old prejudices. His solution for the problem of "the invisible ghetto" was the one usually put forward by the liberal intelligentsia of his day, that is, the complete merging of Jews and Gentiles through intermarriage which, as he said with the raillery that was characteristic of him, would improve both the "figurative and racial profile." In a more serious vein, he declared, "the crossing of the Western with the Oriental races on the basis of a common state religion—that is the great solution to be desired." [38]

The day after he wrote this sentence in his diary, he underwent a profoundly disturbing mental experience as a result of reading Eugen Dühring's *The Jewish Problem as a Problem of Race, Morals and Culture*. This book, published in 1881, was the first effort to find a "scientific" and "philosophic" basis for anti-Semitism. Dühring presented the Jewish question as a racial problem, maintaining that the Jews were, fundamentally and ineradicably, racially inferior. Emancipation, which aimed to permit the Jews to live among the Germans on an equal basis, had been an egregious error. Inasmuch as the Jews could not be settled in a state of their own, they should be driven "back to the ghetto": they should be subjected to special enactments, their influence over the press and the theater destroyed, their participation in public service restricted, and intermarriage with Jews, if not forbidden, should be subjected to social ostracism. The reading of the book was, for the sensitive and aristocratic Herzl, as Alex Bein says, "a blow between the eyes." He noted in his diary: "An infamous book . . . If Dühring who unites so much undeniable intelligence with so much universality of knowledge, can write like this, what are we to expect from the ignorant masses?" [39] After this he began to express himself more sharply in fraternity discussions on the question of intolerance and he soon resigned when his fraternity participated in a demonstration in honor of Richard Wagner at which an anti-Semitic address had been made and enthusiastically received.

In 1884, Herzl was admitted to the bar in Vienna and he practiced law for a short period. However, his main interest was in writing and after a few years he achieved considerable success in the field of light comedy, his plays being produced in New York, Berlin and Prague, as well as in Vienna. He became even more popular as a feuilletonist and was appointed on the staff of the liberal *Wiener Neue Freie Presse*, the most distinguished newspaper in the Austro-Hungarian Empire. His success as journalist was rapid and in 1891 he was ap-

---

38. Alex Bein, *op. cit.*, p. 35
39. *Ibid.*, p

pointed Paris representative and took up his residence in that city at the end of the year. France was in the throes of the conflict between the Royalist-Clerical reaction and the Republican-Middle Class progressive movement. The attempt of the Monarchists to establish a dictatorship supported by the army, had ended ingloriously in 1889 when their leader, General Boulanger, fled across the border to Brussels, where he committed suicide two years later. But the corrupt and meretricious forces of reaction persisted, using anti-Semitism as a chief weapon. Shortly after Herzl arrived in Paris, Edward Drumont, author of *La France Juive*,[40] had just founded his anti-Semitic paper, *La Libre Parole*.

During his early years in Paris, Herzl's diary indicates that he was troubled by the problem of anti-Semitism, and was groping for a solution. His first ideas were fantastic. He thought that Jews should challenge those who insulted them to duels; if the Jew were victorious he would have established his honor; if he were killed, the world would know that he had been a sacrifice to the "most unjust movement in the world." Another idea was to have the Jews of the older generation lead the children in a public procession to the doors of the Catholic Church and have them baptized en masse. At one moment he thought of socialism—of a liberal democratic variety—as the solution. A favorite idea was the establishment of a newspaper to combat anti-Semitism, emphasizing that no Jew, not even a baptized Jew, should work on the paper. Despite the peculiarity of these early suggestions, they have something in common with his mature Zionist proposals, namely, that the Jewish question must become a public matter; that both Jews and non-Jews must face the issue of anti-Semitism as a grave problem; that it must have a large-scale definitive solution.

In the fall of 1894, two months before the first Dreyfus trial which took place in December of that year, he was already completely obsessed with the Jewish problem. In the short period of seventeen days, while in a mood of great agitation, he wrote out a play which he entitled *The Ghetto*, later

---

40. This book, based upon the racial theories of Gobineau and on German anti-Semitic literature, appeared in 1885, and in the course of one year ran through one hundred editions. It was one of the greatest bookselling successes of the nineteenth century.

renamed *The New Ghetto*. Its theme is the social conflict between a German aristocratic mine owner and middle class businessmen, in which an idealistic Jewish lawyer becomes implicated. The last words of the hero of the play, the Jewish lawyer who is fatally shot in a duel, is the cry, "Out—of—the—ghetto." Herzl felt that this was the best play he had ever written and he wrote to his friend, Arthur Schnitzler, "This piece has to be produced! It has to speak from the stage!"

The Dreyfus trial had the final catalytic effect on him. In it he saw the failure of the emancipation theory in all its starkness. There on the military parade ground stood Alfred Dreyfus, the assimilated Jew who had broken all ties with Jewish life, who had chosen a military career, a vocation as far from the ghetto as possible, and who had become the one hundred percent French patriot. As the decorations were torn from his uniform, the hostile crowd cried hysterically, "*A mort! A mort les Juifs.*" Recollecting the scene, Herzl wrote four years later: "The Dreyfus case embodies more than a judicial error; it embodies the desire of a vast majority of the French to condemn a Jew and to condemn all Jews in this one Jew." And this had happened in France: "In republican, modern, civilized France, a hundred years after the Declaration of the Rights of Man. The French people, or rather the greater part of the French people, does not want to extend the rights of man to Jews. The edict of the great revolution has been revoked." [41]

Formulation of the Jewish State Conception

During the next year, until the publication of the *Judenstaat*, he was ceaselessly engaged in working out his final solution. He was still absorbed in the problem of how to get "out of the ghetto" and had now evidently come to the conclusion that the way out was by a large mass emigration to a new Promised Land. His idea was first incorporated in a sheaf of notes which he prepared for an interview with Baron de Hirsch, a leading Jewish philanthropist who was engaged in a large project for settling Jews in the Argentine. His effort to interest the Baron was unsuccessful, but it contributed to his development: he learned that the rich Jewish philanthropists did not have the imagination to grasp his plan. A central thought runs

41. Alex Bein, *op. cit.*, pp. 115–116.

throughout his new conception, namely, the significance of political leadership. He wrote in his notes: "Throughout the two thousand years of our dispersion we have lacked unified political leadership. I consider this our greatest misfortune. It has done us more harm than all the persecutions. It is this that is responsible for our inner decay." [42] The first task was the re-education of the people. There had to be a total repudiation of the principle of philanthropy. The Jews must be educated to understand their position and they had to be attracted by a great aim and a daring enterprise. He had already in his earlier thinking come to the conclusion that anti-Semitism was not only a religious but also a social problem. Now he had achieved the realization that it was a political problem and that its solution could be effected only by political means.

Throughout the summer of 1895, he wrote his ideas out under the stress of a great emotion—"walking, standing, lying down, in the street, at table, in the night"—as if under an unceasing compulsion. His outline assumed the form of an *Address to the Rothschilds*. He showed it to a number of friends; some thought him mentally unbalanced, others were impressed with his earnestness and powerful feeling. He had alternations of hope and despair. Finally he gained great encouragement from Max Nordau, another Hungarian-born Jew, a physician resident in Paris who had achieved international fame as a liberal writer and critic. Nordau introduced him to Israel Zangwill, the leading Anglo-Jewish writer, who used his good offices to obtain an invitation for Herzl to address the Maccabeans, the club of the leading Jews of England. In London a most favorable reception was accorded him, and here he received the first intimation that the Jews would insist on Palestine. The British Jews, both the businessmen and intellectuals, thought that Palestine alone could be considered as the place for national concentration of the Jews. Greatly encouraged by these conversations, Herzl hurried back to Vienna at the end of November 1895. At the suggestion of some friends, he had already deleted the title "Address to the Rothschilds" from his tract and crossed out every reference to the famous Jewish banking family. He revised his address with thoroughgoing changes of style and content, and it emerged as a new work

42. *Ibid.*, p. 127.

and was published in Vienna by a private printer under the title *Der Judenstaat*.[43]

The preface of *The Jewish State* sounds the theme with great simplicity and directness: "The idea which I have developed in this pamphlet is a very old one: it is the restoration of the Jewish State." The essence of the Jewish problem which Herzl proposes to solve is explained in ringing paragraphs:[44]

The Jewish question exists. It would be stupid to deny it. It is a hangover of the Middle Ages, of which the modern civilized nations, with the best will in the world, cannot rid themselves. They showed their magnanimity when they emancipated us. The Jewish question exists wheresoever Jews are to be found in larger numbers. Where it does not exist it is brought in by immigrating Jews. We move naturally toward those areas where we are not persecuted; our appearance in those areas is followed by persecution. This is true, and it must remain true, even in highly developed countries—France proves it—as long as the Jewish question is not solved politically. The poorer Jews are bringing anti-Semitism into England; they have already brought it into America.

I believe I understand anti-Semitism, which is an extremely complicated movement. I examine this movement as a Jew, without hate and without fear. I believe I recognize in it those elements which are merely brutal humor, mean belly-envy, inherited prejudice, religious intolerance; but I also recognize the element of unconscious self-protection. I consider the Jewish question to be neither social nor religious, even though it takes on these and other colorations. It is a national question, and in order to solve it we must, before everything else, transform it into a political world question, to be answered in the council of the civilized peoples.

We are a *people*, a people. Everywhere we have tried honestly to disappear in the surrounding community, and to retain only the faith of our fathers. We are not permitted to do it. In vain do we show our loyalty, and in some places an exaggerated patriotism; in vain do we bring the same sacrifices of blood and gold as our fellow-citizens; in vain do we exert ourselves to increase the glory of our fatherlands by achievements in art and science, the wealth of our fatherlands by our contributions to commerce. In our fatherlands, some of which we have lived in for many centuries, we are de-

---

43. A small English edition of five hundred copies appeared in London in 1896, translated by Sylvie d'Avigdor, under the title *The Jewish State: An Attempt at a Modern Solution of the Jewish Question*.

44. Quoted from Alex Bein, *op. cit.*, pp. 160–161. This version is a new translation by Maurice Samuel.

nounced as strangers: often by those whose forefathers were not yet in the land when ours were already sighing there. It is the majority which decides who is the stranger in the land: it is a question of power, as in all national relations . . .

Herzl believed that modern anti-Semitism was the result of a retarded emancipation of the Jews. While in the ghetto, the Jews had, by reason of discriminatory legislation, been forced to become a middle class people, and when they stepped out of the ghetto they were only too well prepared for competition with the rising non-Jewish bourgeoisie. In modern times, Jews are subjected to a double pressure: because they are Jews, and because they are members of the middle class. The remote cause of anti-Semitism is the separate existence of the Jews during the Middle Ages; the immediate cause is the overproduction of intellectuals who cannot find a wholesome outlet downwards or upwards. When they descend, the members of the Jewish intellectual middle class become a revolutionary proletariat filling the subordinate offices of the socialist parties; when the Jewish middle class rises, it is accused by the aristocracy of exercising its influence merely through the power of wealth.

Complete assimilation might theoretically be possible through inter-marriage, but this could not be realized on a large enough scale and could, in any case, be achieved with dignity only when the old social prejudices had disappeared. Those who wished to assimilate completely—and who could—should do so, but this offered no practical solution for the people as a whole: oppression and persecution could not exterminate the Jews, and anti-Semitism merely stripped off the weaklings. The Jewish people was indestructible: "The distinctive nationality of Jews neither can, will, nor must be destroyed. It cannot be destroyed, because external enemies consolidate it. It will not be destroyed; this is shown during two thousand years of appalling suffering. It must not be destroyed, and that, as successor to numberless Jews who refused to despair, I am trying once more to prove in this pamphlet. Whole branches of Judaism may wither and fall, but the trunk remains." [45]

45. Theodor Herzl, *The Jewish State* (translated by Sylvie d'Avigdor, revised edition, 1934), p. 18.

The plan, as Herzl saw it, was "in its essence perfectly simple":[46]

Let the sovereignty be granted us over a portion of the globe large enough to satisfy the rightful requirements of a nation; the rest we shall manage ourselves.

Two territories were to be considered: Argentina and Palestine. Argentina had the advantage of vast, fertile areas, a mild climate and a sparse population. Palestine was "our ever memorable historic home" and the magic of the name would attract the Jewish masses. The final choice was to be made by Jewish public opinion acting through a representative body. To implement the plan he proposed the establishment of two organizations: 1) The Society of Jews, which would have authority to speak in the name of the Jewish people and obtain recognition as "a state building power"; 2) The Jewish Company, which would be the financial instrument to settle the affairs of emigrating Jews and take charge of their settlement in the Jewish homeland. On one point he was particularly insistent, namely, that the infiltration of Jews without obtaining a political guarantee, as carried out in the past in Argentina and Palestine, was doomed to failure: "An infiltration is bound to end badly. It continues until the inevitable moment when the native population feels itself threatened, and forces the government to stop a further influx of Jews. Immigration is consequently futile unless based on an assured supremacy." [47]

There must be a mass immigration of Jews from Europe; this will, however, not happen in one day but will continue over many generations. The exodus of the Jews from Europe and the upbuilding of the new land should be arranged in accordance with a prearranged plan: first would go the labor force to construct roads, regulate rivers, cultivate the soil and build homes. These activities would stimulate trade and the trade would create markets; the markets would in turn attract new settlers. The upbuilding of the country would be based on modern principles, making use of all the instruments of science and technology. It would be a model state on the

46. *Ibid.*, p. 28.
47. *Ibid.*, p. 29.

social as well as on the technical side. Private initiative would be encouraged but it should be made to serve the public interest. The normal working day would be seven hours and, anticipating a contemporary idea, Herzl insisted that work should be a right as well as a duty.

The form of government, Herzl was inclined to think, should be an aristocratic republic; he would have preferred a constitutional monarchy but did not think it feasible because of the long interruption in the Jewish tradition of royalty.[48] Above all, he abjured theocracy and he thought that the "priesthood," though having a respected place in the state, ought to be confined strictly to its religious function. He conceived the Jewish state as neutral and as such it would require only a small professional army equipped with the weapons of modern warfare. He laid emphasis on the need of a flag and he suggested a white flag with seven golden stars: the white to symbolize the beginning of a new life; the stars were "the seven golden hours of our working day." His views on the question of language reveal how far removed he was from the roots of Jewish culture: he rejected Hebrew because he thought it could not be adapted to the needs of common life; he was even more opposed to Yiddish which he considered "the furtive language of prisoners of the ghetto." He believed that each group of immigrants should in the beginning keep the language of its native land, the memory of which it would always cherish; the language which proved itself of greatest utility would be adopted as the language of the Jewish state.

He ends the pamphlet on a note of exalted and determined conviction. The very initiation of the plan would immediately lead to a retreat from anti-Semitism and the emigration of the Jews would decrease the pressure and diminish the hatred toward them. In conclusion, he says: "Let the word be repeated here which was given at the beginning: The Jews who will it shall have their state. We shall at last live as free men on our own soil and die peacefully in our own homeland. The world will be liberated by our liberation, enriched with our wealth, made greater by our greatness. And that which we

---

48. Herzl believed that every state should contain a double principle—democratic and aristocratic. He thought "the aristocratic republic and the democratic monarchy are certainly the finest forms of the completed state." Alex Bein, *op. cit.*, p. 147.

seek, therefore, for our own use will stream out mightily and beneficently upon all mankind." [49]

Zionist Activities and Conflicts of Opinion

The *Judenstaat* aroused strong reactions—favorable and unfavorable. There was the usual crop of smart remarks: Herzl was dubbed a "crackpot adventurer who wanted to be King of the Jews"; the brochure was characterized as "poor in ideas and rich in imbecilities"; the plan was termed "a modern miniature of medieval Messianism." The *Allgemeine Zeitung des Judenthums* treated the pamphlet more seriously, but was not less opposed to Herzl's basic thesis. This leading German-Jewish newspaper, which had taken a prominent part in the struggle for Jewish equality, thought that the orthodox Jews should have nothing to do with the restoration of the Jews to Palestine until "the visible signs of God's direct intervention" were indicated; and that the Reform Jews should abstain from action because the re-establishment of Jewish nationality was opposed to the doctrine that the Jews had nothing in common but religion and to the belief that Israel was providentially dispersed throughout the world to be witness to "the prophetic promise of a time of all-human ennoblement." The leaders of the *Hovevei Zion* tended to be suspicious of this newcomer in Zionism who made no mention of the previous proposals for a Jewish state, and who was indifferent to Hebrew and diffident about Palestine. They were inclined to think that his ambitious political program would do nothing so much as alarm the Turkish Government and alienate the Jewish philanthropists who were now the chief supporters of colonization in Palestine.

There were, however, others who recognized that the *Judenstaat* opened up new perspectives and who felt that Herzl had the vision and the faith of a great leader. The response of the Zionists of Vienna was particularly encouraging. The students of the Zionist society, *Kadimah* (Eastward), formed in 1882 as a reaction to Dühring's book, called upon him to take the helm of the movement. David Wolffsohn, a Russian Jew established in business in Vienna and an important figure in *Hovevei Zion* activities, immediately became his devoted friend and remained his lifelong supporter. Outstanding writers, publicists, rabbis and communal leaders in the Jewish world, in

49. As translated in Alex Bein, *op. cit.*, p. 170.

Austria, Germany, France and England, rallied to his side. Thousands of letters were sent to him from the Jewish masses in the Austrian Empire and Eastern Europe, in which he was hailed as the new Moses, destined to lead the Jews out of their wretchedness to the Land of Promise. Among his followers were sober businessmen, but also visionaries, and no doubt some adventurers—Christians as well as Jews. There was the Reverend Hechler, chaplain to the English embassy in Vienna, who had written a tract prophesying that Palestine would be restored to the Jews about 1897–1898, and who became a devoted follower of Herzl's and later helped him in making contacts with the Grand Duke of Baden and the German official circles. The Ritter von Nevlinski, an imposing but impoverished descendant of a long line of Polish noblemen, who "belonged to the demi-monde of diplomacy," [50] was attracted by Herzl to the Zionist cause, partly because of the fantastic character of the idea itself, partly because of his knowledge and interest in the affairs of Russia, Turkey and the Balkans, and no less, it appears, because he still lived in the style of the *grand seigneur* and saw an opportunity for exploiting his political connections profitably.

Herzl had thought that the publication of his manuscript would end his work. However, the criticism of his plan as well as the enthusiasm which it had evoked led him on, and he became involved in activities designed to carry his idea into effect. Through Nevlinski, he tried to get an interview with the Sultan, and he proceeded to Constantinople for that purpose. His plan was again "simple": to pay the Turkish debt through a loan raised from the Jewish bankers, and by regularizing Turkish finances liberate the country from European tutelage; in exchange for this, the Sublime Porte would turn over Palestine to the Jews. Herzl did not obtain the desired audience with the Sultan, but Nevlinski, who was ostensibly in touch with highly placed Turkish statesmen, reported that though Turkey would never consent to renunciation of sovereignty over Palestine, she might recognize Palestine as a "vassal state" and permit large-scale Jewish immigration under Jewish management, if the Jewish financiers extended substantial help to Turkey.

Herzl thereupon hurried to London. There he got a rather cool reception from the Jewish leaders. They cautiously agreed

50. *Ibid., op. cit.,* p. 193.

to help him work for the vassal state under Turkish sovereignty provided that: a) the Powers agreed; b) the Baron de Hirsch Fund [51] (ICA) would place ten million pounds at the disposal of the plan; and c) that Baron Edmond de Rothschild entered the Executive Committee of the proposed "Society of Jews." Herzl attacked this dependence on philanthropy. He declared that he "wanted only the kind of colonization which would be protected by its own army." [52] If Rothschild would put himself at the disposal of the Jewish national effort, then the highest place would be accorded him, but he wanted none of his philanthropic endeavor, which he characterized "as a kind of rich man's sport." It is hardly surprising that the aristocratic Colonel Goldsmith, one of the British leaders, immediately wrote to Baron de Rothschild warning him against Herzl. Subsequently, Herzl went to Rothschild, but the Baron declined to support his political plan. Rothschild thought that a large mass immigration to Palestine would put the whole colonization enterprise into danger, and he saw no other possible method than that of gradual infiltration carried on in a fashion which could not attract hostile attention. Both Herzl and the Baron were adamant in maintaining their positions.

It has been pointed out that "the breaking up of negotiations with Rothschild may be designated as the beginning of the new Zionist movement." [53] While Herzl was in England a great meeting had been arranged for him in Whitechapel, the "East Side" of London.[54] Thousands of men and women had filled the streets cheering Herzl as he passed, and thronged the Working Men's Club where the meeting was held. Herzl now turned

51. The Baron had passed away in April, 1896. A day before his death, Herzl had tried to reach him again through Max Nordau. The following day Herzl wrote in his diary: "In any case, his death is a loss to the Jewish cause. Among the rich Jews he was the only one prepared to do something big for the poor ones. Perhaps I did not know how to handle him." (Alex Bein, *op. cit.*, p. 195.)

52. Alex Bein, *op. cit.*, p. 207.

53. *Ibid.*, p. 210.

54. Among those who took a leading part in the meeting were the Reverend Dr. Moses Gaster, Chief Rabbi of the Sephardic community, a scholar and orator, who had accepted the chairmanship when it had been turned down by other leaders of the community; young Jacob de Haas, English-born son of Dutch Jewish parents, already an impassioned follower of Herzl and later his secretary; Ephraim Ish-Kishor, a leading Hebrew teacher and enthusiastic devotee of the Hebrew renascence, who had a large part in staging and organizing the meeting.

to the Jewish public at large for support. He took up the idea of the Zionist Congress put forward by Nathan Birnbaum of Vienna, a philosophic-minded publicist, one of the founders of the *Kadimah* and the author of the term "Zionism." Herzl put his dynamic energy behind the Congress idea in the broadened form of a "World Congress of Zionists." Again there was much opposition, and history anticipated itself in the type of objections: some did not want the issue of Zionism to be publicly broached at all; some wanted to avoid the term "Zionist" and proposed that the meeting be called a "Conference of Pro-Palestine Societies" which would discuss the furthering of the practical work of colonization.

Dr. Hermann Adler, Chief Rabbi of the Ashkenazic community in Great Britain, led an attack, and Dr. Moritz Güdemann, Chief Rabbi of Vienna, followed with a pamphlet in which the irreconcilability of the national idea with the Jewish religion was expounded. Rabbi Güdemann had formerly supported Herzl, when the latter had confided his idea to him before the writing of the *Judenstaat*. Now Herzl employed his sharp pen, dipped in irony, to castigate Güdemann's conception of "the mission of Israel." The devotees of this idea among the Jews, Herzl pointed out, by no means resembled "the poor monks who set forth for the wild places of the world to carry the Christian gospel." "The Jewish 'mission'," he said, "is something sated, comfortable and well-to-do. For years now I have been observing the people who retort 'Israel's mission' whenever I come to talk to them about the wretchedness of the Jewish poor. These missionaries are all excellently situated." [55] On another occasion he said, referring to the anti-Zionist rabbis: "When they speak of Zion they mean, in God's name, anything but Zion." To describe the rabbis who opposed the Zionist cause, he coined the phrase, "Protest Rabbis," which has stuck to rabbinical opponents of Zionism ever since.

FORMATION OF THE ZIONIST MOVEMENT

Combating the philanthropic concept in Jewish life became one of Herzl's main purposes. In his announcement of the plans for the Congress, he said: "The Jewish question must be taken away from the control of the benevolent individual. There must be created a forum before which everyone acting

55. Alex Bein, *op. cit.*, p. 221.

for the Jewish people must appear, and to which he must be responsible." [56] He wanted to create a national congress which would meet at regular intervals and which would, in the period between the meetings, entrust the direction of Jewish affairs to an elected council. In this way the Jewish people would, through its representatives, formulate its needs, and Herzl established *Die Welt*, which became the official organ of the Zionist movement. The idea of a Congress gained general support of Zionists and others interested in the upbuilding of Palestine. When the Jews of Munich protested against holding the congress in that city, the place of the proposed meeting was transferred to Basle.

The First Zionist Congress (Basle), 1897

The First Zionist Congress convened in August, 1897, with 197 elected delegates. They came from all parts of Europe, from Palestine and from the United States. There were veteran leaders of the *Hovevei Zion*, recent converts to Herzl's ideas, orthodox religious Jews, and "secularists," well-to-do members of the upper middle class and representatives of the socialist groups. The greatest care was taken in making the arrangements and the sessions were conducted with great formality and dignity. The meeting was solemnly opened with the prayer of festive holidays: "Blessed art Thou, O Lord, our God, King of the Universe, who has kept us in life and preserved us and permitted us to reach this season."

Herzl presented the opening address and quickly proceeded to state the main object of the meeting: "We are here to lay the foundation stone of the house which is to shelter the Jewish nation." He summarized the main ideas of his program: The Jews must help themselves; there must be large-scale and well planned colonization in Palestine; the work must be conducted openly and with public approval. "The basis can be only that of recognized right and not of sufferance. We have had our fill of experience with toleration and with the protected Jew. Our movement can be logical and consistent only insofar as it aims at the acquisition of a publicly recognized legal guarantee." [57] At the end of his address he emphasized the need of creating a permanent organization to unite the Jews in their aim, one

56. *Ibid.*, p. 218.
57. *Ibid.*, p. 234.

that would be free from the domination or willfulness of individuals, which would "rise to the level of high impersonality." Max Nordau's address was the other highlight of the conference. He spoke on "The Condition of Jewry at the Close of the Nineteenth Century." An incomparable orator, Nordau's speech gave expression to the Jewish need in never to be forgotten words.

The task of formulating the program was entrusted to Nordau. The statement of Zionist purpose as adopted by the Congress, which was largely taken from his report, read:[58]

The aim of Zionism is to create for the Jewish people a home in Palestine secured by public law.
The Congress contemplates the following means to the attainment of this end:
1. The promotion, on suitable lines, of the colonization of Palestine by Jewish agricultural and industrial workers.
2. The organization and binding together of the whole of Jewry by means of appropriate institutions, local and international, in accordance with the laws of each country.
3. The strengthening and fostering of Jewish national sentiment and consciousness.
4. Preparatory steps towards obtaining government consent, where necessary, to the attainment of the aim of Zionism.

On the question of Palestine as the land where the Jewish home should be re-established, the Congress was fully agreed, Herzl having long recognized that he could get the support of the Jewish masses only by accepting Palestine. In the original German formulation, the term translated "home" was *"Heimstätte"* (homestead), which carried with it some implication of the autonomous self-sustaining manor and at the same time conveyed the overtones of the philosophy of practical and cultural Zionism. It was suggested by Nordau as a compromise which avoided the stronger word "state," to which the *Hovevei Zion* delegates objected and which, it was thought, would be repugnant to the Turkish Government. Herzl is reported to have said privately: "No need for worry [about the phraseology]. The people will read it as a 'Jewish State' anyhow." [59]

58. Nahum Sokolow, *op. cit.*, Vol. I, pp. 268 ff.
59. Jacob de Haas, *Theodor Herzl: A Biographical Study*, Chicago, 1927, Vol. I, pp. 194 ff.

The term chosen to indicate the public character of the guarantee which the Zionists wanted was *öffentlich-rechtlich*, sometimes translated as "publicly recognized, legally secured," but at other times more simply by the phrase "secured by public law." Some of the delegates had suggested "secured by international law," to indicate that they wanted to have the sanction of the European Powers and not of Turkey alone. In the debate Herzl defended the phrase *öffentlich-rechtlich*, which he had used in his address, and it was accepted as the best compromise.

Creation of the Zionist Organization

The second great task after the adoption of the program was the creation of the Zionist Organization. The Congress, originally designed to meet annually, was declared the "chief organ of the Zionist movement." An *Actions Committee* was to sit periodically to deal with important issues when Congress was not in session, and an *Inner Actions Committee*, consisting of five members, was to serve as a permanent executive. Theodor Herzl was elected President, and Max Nordau, Vice-President. A flag, designed by David Wolffsohn was accepted as the Jewish national flag. Wolffsohn, steeped in Jewish tradition, had chosen a white background and two broad blue stripes somewhat reminiscent of the *talith* (Jewish prayer shawl), and in the center, between the stripes, the intersecting triangle known as "The Shield of David." *Hatikvah* (The Hope) composed by the itinerant poet, Naphtali Herz Imber, and sung spontaneously throughout the period of the Congress, became the Jewish national hymn.[60] As soon as it was over, Herzl wrote confidently in his diary: "This day I have created the Jewish state." As President of the World Zionist Organization, he now felt he could speak as the representative of the Jewish people.

Herzl's Political Negotiations

Herzl's immediate aim was to obtain an audience with Abdul Hamid, the Sultan of Turkey, but several years were to pass before the meeting was arranged. He found it easier, with the

---

60. The melody is an adaptation of a Bohemian folksong which is recognizable in the second part of Smetana's symphonic suite, *The Moldau (Vladava)*.

Development of Zionism in the 19th Century 43

help of his millennial Christian Zionist friend, the Reverend Hechler, to reach the Kaiser. After preliminary conversations with Prince Eulenberg and Prince von Bülow, it was arranged that Herzl should meet Wilhelm II on the latter's trip to the Near East. The first audience took place in Constantinople during October 1898. Herzl, who by this time had learned to be cautious in his proposals, confined himself to suggesting a chartered Land Development Company which would operate in Palestine and Syria under a German protectorate, with the approval of the Sultan. Despite the fact that von Bülow, who was present at the meeting, attempted to restrain the Kaiser, the latter expressed himself enthusiastically about the proposal. However, it was evident that he was partly motivated by anti-Semitism: he thought it would be a good thing to remove some "usurious" Jews from Germany. But he seemed also to be impressed by the broadness of the conception and attracted by the idea of exhibiting his influence with the Sultan.

At the second audience in Palestine, which took place on November 2, 1898, the Kaiser appeared to have become colder to the idea. In Herzl's formal address, which had to be presented to the court official before the meeting, he was not permitted to make any reference to the aims of Zionism or to the Kaiser's protection of the projected Jewish land company. The interview, moreover, was less friendly, and the anti-Semitic remarks sharper. In the communiqué issued to the press, the interview was referred to only incidentally among a score of other unimportant notices: "Later the Kaiser received . . . also a Jewish deputation, which presented him with an album of pictures of the Jewish colonies in Palestine. In reply to an address by the leader of the deputation, His Majesty remarked that he viewed with benevolent interest the efforts directed toward the improvement of agriculture in Palestine as long as these accorded with the welfare of the Turkish Empire and as long as they were conducted in a spirit of respect for the Sultan." [61]

It is probable that the changed attitude was due primarily to a realization on the part of the Kaiser's advisers that the Sultan was opposed and that the idea would create difficulties with France, England and Russia, who would naturally view the Kaiser's protectorate of the Jewish development as an attempt

61. Alex Bein, *op. cit.*, p. 307.

to extend German influence over Turkish territory.[62] Everyone was discouraged by the failure of the negotiations with the Kaiser, but Herzl himself was determined not to lose heart. While recognizing the disappointment, he rationalized this defeat as an advantage from the long range point of view. He now thought that while a German protectorate would have been desirable at the time, it would have created great difficulties for the later development of the enterprise. He believed that England was the natural ally of the Jewish interest in Palestine.

The long-planned audience with the Sultan finally took place in May 1901. Even now Herzl was received, much to his disappointment, not as representative of the Zionist movement but because of his association with the *Neue Freie Presse*. He attempted to bring the question of Zionism up indirectly, indicating that the Jews could be of help in the reorganization of the Turkish finances and also that Jewish industrial initiative could play a part in the development of the unexploited natural resources of the Turkish Empire. Though the Sultan showed some interest in the latter idea, he was mainly concerned with the problem of the funding of the public debt. He indicated a friendly attitude toward the Jews and was ready on humanitarian grounds to allow a certain number of refugees to settle in Turkey. However, he evidently had been warned against the national aspects of Jewish colonization: he made it clear that there could be no mass immigration, only scattered settlements of a few families at a time in different sections of Turkey; the Jews would become Turkish citizens in the full sense of the term; and Palestine would not come into the picture at all as a place of Jewish settlement. Herzl made it clear that this would not be adequate.

Despite the wholly unsatisfactory character of the Sultan's proposals, Herzl seems nevertheless to have gone away with the impression that if the Jewish financiers would render very substantial aid to the Ottoman Empire, the Sublime Porte would be ready to consider the idea of a charter for a Jewish settlement in Palestine favorably. Herzl tried again to get the help of the Jewish bankers, of ICA, and of Rothschild, but they had no faith in his political plans. The financial support from the Zionist Organization was disappointing. In 1898, the Jew-

---

62. For an analysis of the reasons for the change of attitude on the part of the Kaiser, see Alex Bein, *op. cit.*, pp. 308–309.

ish Colonial Trust had been organized as the financial instrument of the Zionist movement, but despite considerable effort it had succeeded in raising only £250,000 in share capital. At the Fifth Zionist Congress, held in December 1901, Herzl was able to announce that the Jewish Colonial Trust was open for banking operations. However, the amount that had been collected was altogether inadequate for funding the Ottoman public debt, which Herzl calculated was a million and a half pounds. In the following year, in February 1902, Herzl was again called to Constantinople. Although he was invited to be the Sultan's guest during his stay, he did not see the Sultan himself, the negotiations being conducted by Izzet Bey. This time he was allowed to speak as a Zionist. He told Izzet Bey, the Secretary, that what he wanted was "a great, demonstrative declaration for the benefit of the Jews, such as would be represented by an offer of immigration rights without any restrictions." [63] The reply of the Sultan, received on the following day, stated that he could not admit the principle of unlimited immigration even if he wished to do so, because the opposition would be too great.

Criticism of Herzl and the Conflict over Uganda

In the course of Herzl's efforts, a certain amount of friction developed between him and his co-workers who were not always in agreement with his methods. Herzl was a somewhat imperious leader and headstrong in his ideas. In the winter of 1901, when the Fifth Zionist Congress was held, considerable internal opposition to Herzl was in evidence, particularly among the *Hovevei Zion* groups. The Russian Zionists had come to recognize Herzl's sincerity and his able leadership, but they had grown rather skeptical of the validity of the purely political approach as a result of Herzl's diplomatic failures. At this Congress an official opposition was formed which called itself the "Democratic-Zionist Fraction." It was a small but determined group whose leaders were destined to play important roles in the future development of the movement.[64] The group was deeply influenced by Ahad Ha'am: while not denying

---

63. Alex Bein, *op. cit.*, p. 379.
64. The leading spirits of the movement were Leon Motzkin, Chaim Weizmann, Victor Jacobson, Martin Buber, Berthold Feivel, Ephraim Lilien, Davis Trietsch.

the political character of the Zionist movement, it emphasized more the practical and cultural purposes of Zionism. It aimed for a Jewish nationalism more deeply rooted in Jewish culture, a greater degree of democracy in the leadership of the movement, and more attention to the program of *Gegenwartsarbeit*, i.e., of immediate, day-to-day activity throughout the Diaspora of a cultural nature designed to strengthen Jewish consciousness. It was at this Congress also that the Jewish National Fund was established to purchase land in Palestine as the inalienable possession of the Jewish people.

Herzl was further subjected to criticism after the publication of his *Altneuland,* which appeared in the fall of 1902. It was a utopian novel which painted a glorious picture of the future of Palestine under the Zionist development. Through the use of technology the face of the country would be transformed: its wastes would have been reclaimed; its arid areas irrigated; the fall of the Jordan to the Dead Sea and the difference of level between the Mediterranean and the Jordan Valley would be utilized for the generation of electric power; the chemical wealth of the Dead Sea would have been exploited. "The real creators of *Altneuland* were the irrigation engineers. Drainage of swamps, irrigation of the desert regions, and above all the system of power houses—there is the answer." [65] The social and economic life would also have been beautified and a "mutualistic" order, as Herzl called it, "the mediate form between individualism and collectivism" would have established life on the basis of justice and economic effectiveness. Health, social service and education would be provided for in accordance with the highest modern standards. Women would enjoy equal rights with men in all branches of life. There would be no race laws and the Arabs would live side by side with the Jews in friendship. This technological and social utopia did not produce the effect for which Herzl had hoped. One of its sharpest critics was Ahad Ha'am, who passed over the positive aspects of the book, its prophetic vision of technological development, its faith in Palestine, and the ethical impulse which informed the social conceptions, and derided its romanticism and sentimentality as the work of a dilettante. His most important criticism was that it lacked Jewish character: it was a colorless, utopian outline which might have been planned for any people

65. Alex Bein, *op. cit.*, p. 401.

and was suitable for none. It was not informed with Jewish feeling and it ignored the Hebrew language and literature.

A main issue between the Russian Zionists and Herzl centered around the question of Hebrew cultural activities. The Russian Zionists with their background in the tradition of *Hovevei Zion,* regarded the renascence of the Hebrew language and literature as an integral part of the Zionist movement, conceiving it as a means of spiritual revival as well as a great unifying influence. In his speech at the First Zionist Congress, Herzl had declared that "Zionism is the return of the Jews to Judaism even before their return to the Jewish land." By this he meant perhaps that the sense of attachment to the Jewish people had first to be deepened. He also appears to have been moved to an appreciation of the significance of the celebration of the traditional Jewish festivals in his own home. But he does not seem to have been aware of the close connection between the Hebrew renascence and the rise of Zionism as a national movement. In his own mind he tended to identify "culture" with Western liberal European thought. Most of all he feared an emphasis on Hebraic culture would introduce a divisive element into the organization. The Hebraists were opposed as secularists by the orthodox religious Zionists. While willing to unite with the Zionists in the practical and political work for Palestine, the orthodox elements were opposed to the promotion of educational work on the part of the Zionist Organization, fearing that there would be a departure from the religious emphasis. Herzl was much concerned with the problem of unity and wanted to eliminate the cultural question as well as social-economic problems from the discussions at the Congress.

Dr. Chaim Weizmann, destined to play the leading part in the promotion of the Zionist cause during the First World War and in the following generation, was already beginning at this time to develop a conception which has sometimes been referred to as "organic Zionism." He was a leading member of the so-called "democratic fraction," formed in 1901 at the Fifth Zionist Congress; in fact, he delivered the opening address at its first meeting. In it he emphasized two principles: first, the importance of a positive attitude on the part of the Zionist Organization toward the economic amelioration of the masses of the Jews; and, secondly, the importance of considering Hebrew cultural work an inseparable element of the Zionist program. He was one of the first expounders of the necessity for establishing a Hebrew University at Jerusalem. At the same time, he laid great emphasis on the work of colonization, both as a means of improving the material condition of the Jews and as a means of strengthening the historic claim of the Jewish people to Palestine. Although much influenced by Ahad Ha'am's conception, he was more appreciative of the personality and contribution of Herzl, and laid greater emphasis on the importance of political work designed to interest the statesmen of the Western Powers in Zionism. (At an early stage he looked particularly to England to further the Jewish cause.) In his conception of "organic Zionism," he aimed for a balanced synthesis of the practical, cultural and political trends.[66]

The growing difference of opinion came to a head at the Sixth Zionist Congress held in August 1903, when Herzl presented a British proposal for a Jewish settlement in Uganda, East Africa. The Jewish situation in Eastern Europe was becoming more desperate, culminating in 1903 in the massacres of Kishinev and Homel. Something over a year before this, in July 1902, Herzl had appeared as a witness before the British Royal Commission on Alien Immigration. He presented a plan for a chartered company somewhere in British dominated territory where the Jews would organize a large settlement and where they would be given the rights of autonomy and self-defense. In the fall of the same year, Herzl met Joseph Chamberlain, the Colonial Secretary, who proposed the investigation of the possibilities of El-Arish in the northwest part of Sinai Peninsula. The practicality of the project depended upon the possibility of diverting water from the Nile for irrigation, and it fell through because in the judgment of Lord Cromer, Governor of Egypt, a large enough water supply could not be spared. It was then that Chamberlain had suggested Uganda in East Africa.

Herzl proposed sending a Commission to investigate Uganda as the only possible place for an immediate settlement of a large number of Jews. However, he emphasized that this was to be only a temporary haven which would prepare the way for Palestine, a *Nachtasyl*, as Max Nordau termed it. The resolution to send the Commission passed, with the proviso that no

---

66. Joseph Klausner, "Dr. Weizmann in His First Period of Activity," *Hadoar* (Hebrew), February 16, 1945.

Zionist funds might be used for its expense, the vote being 295 for the resolution, 177 against it, and 132 abstentions. The opponents felt that the Zionist idea had been betrayed and marked the occasion as a day of mourning. Menahem Mendel Ussishkin, a leader of the Russian Zionists, who was in Palestine during the Congress session, convoked a conference of Zionist leaders at Kharkov on his return. A memorandum was prepared demanding that Herzl present no territorial projects before the Zionist Congress other than those connected with Palestine or Syria. The report of the Commission, which was delivered in May, 1905, indicated that the territory in question was unsuitable for any large number of Jewish agricultural settlers, and by a large majority the Congress rejected the project, either as a means toward settlement in Palestine or as an end in itself. Herzl was spared this final disappointment. He had died the previous summer (July, 1904), worn out by his exertions and by the internal conflicts.

The major difference of opinion in the Congress was now formulated in terms of an opposition between the "politicals" and the "practicals." The former group followed the line of Herzl in holding that the Zionist Organization should not engage in practical work in Palestine until adequate political guarantees were obtained. The practicals believed that the main effort of the Zionist movement should be devoted to colonization and to cultural work in Palestine, for the intrinsic value of such activity and also for strengthening the Jewish political position. An administrative committee was created, headed by David Wolffsohn, the lifelong friend of Herzl, which included three representatives each of the practical and the political orientations. Among those who supported the practical position was Otto Warburg, a German agronomist of the well-known banking family of that name. During the investigation of the Uganda project, he had headed a commission to study the possibilities of Palestine. Though critical of the unsystematic petty colonization conducted at the time, his impressive report indicated great possibilities for the promotion of agriculture and industry in Palestine if planned development were undertaken. At the Eighth Zionist Congress in 1907, the practicals had gained the upper hand, strongly supported by young pioneers in Palestine and the Zionist socialist groups in the Diaspora. A Palestine office was opened in 1908 in Jaffa, headed by

Dr. Arthur Ruppin,[67] which furnished information about Palestine, guided prospective settlers and immigrants, and aided in the purchase of land and in colonization. In 1911, the practicals, headed by Professor Otto Warburg, had won control of the Administration. For most Zionists, the difference between the practical and political aspects came to be of less significance.

The practical trend was also strengthened by political changes of far-reaching consequences which had in the meantime taken place in Turkey. The revolution against the absolutism of Abdul Hamid had been carried out by the Young Turks, and a constitution was granted in 1908, which was followed by the abdication of the Sultan in 1909. Official Zionist statements professed friendship for the new regime. The Young Turks, however, embarked on a strenuous policy of Turkification and were suspicious of any national movement designed to weaken the Ottoman Empire. In order to develop relations and understanding, the Zionist Organization decided to open a branch of the Jewish Colonial Trust in Constantinople. Dr. Victor Jacobson, one of its managers, a scholar as well as a banker, acted as the political liaison between the Zionist Organization and the Turkish capital.

In the decade before the outbreak of the First World War, the Zionist Organization continued to develop. The *Poale Zion*

---

67. Arthur Ruppin (1876–1943). After a brief period in business, Ruppin devoted himself to study of the social sciences and applied himself particularly to sociological investigations of Jewish life. In this connection he founded the Bureau for Jewish Statistics in Berlin, and later the *Zeitschrift für Demographie und Statistik der Juden*. The first edition of his work *Die Juden der Gegenwart* (1904) established his reputation and brought him into contact with leading Zionist personalities. At the behest of the Zionist Organization he came to Palestine in 1907 to direct colonization and continued to direct it as a member of the Jewish Agency until his death in 1943. A sympathetic and far-sighted administrator, he contributed greatly to the transformation of Jewish agriculture in Palestine from a system of independent farmers relying on philanthropic aid, to collective and cooperative farming based on mutual assistance.

Convinced that modern business methods should be employed in the reconstruction of Palestine, he established the Palestine Land Development Company and the Palestine Real Estate Company. After the Hebrew University was opened, he became a lecturer in sociology and ultimately a full professor. He also emphasized the necessity for Arab-Jewish cooperation and envisaged the creation of a bi-national state; to bring about the realization of this aim he helped found the society, *Brith Shalom*, which was established in 1925, with Ruppin serving as chairman until 1929.

Development of Zionism in the 19th Century

(Zionist Socialists) were now organized as a definite party and participated regularly in the work of the Zionist Congress. The *Mizrahi*—representing the religious point of view—was formed in 1902 in Vilna by the renowned Rabbi Isaac Jacob Reines. Its platform, adopted in 1904, read: "The Mizrahi is an organization of orthodox Jews who adhere to the Basle Program and who strive to perpetuate and develop the Jewish national life in the spirit of tradition." Emphasis was laid on the significance of Jewish ritual, the observance of the Jewish Sabbath and holidays in the traditional form, and the promotion of a religious form of education in which the study of the Talmud as well as the Bible would be included. With this emphasis on traditional and religious elements, the *Mizrahi* combined a strong adherence to the political purpose of the Zionist movement.

Development of the Palestine Jewish Community before the First World War

At the outbreak of the First World War, the *Yishuv* (settlement), as the Jewish community in Palestine was generally referred to, was already undergoing vigorous development. After the middle of the nineteenth century, with the strengthening of European Powers in the affairs of the East, there was an increase of immigration into Palestine by Jews from Eastern Europe who went there in response to the traditional religious motive. They were supported by the *halukah* (distribution or dole) maintained by contributions from the countries of their origin, and established educational institutions along traditional lines. The interest aroused among Western Jews led to the organization of philanthropic and educational activities for the native Jews. The *Alliance Israélite Universelle*, founded in 1860, established schools in which vocational training was combined with a modern course of study. The Anglo-Jewish Association followed suit some time later, and the *Hilfsverein der deutschen Juden* established an extensive system of schools, including a kindergarten and teachers' training school, in the beginning of the first decade of the twentieth century.

These endeavors were still largely in the nature of philanthropic activities extended to Jews already living in Palestine. The transition between the philanthropic effort and the more positive Zionist conception of resettlement is marked by the founding of the *Mikveh Israel* Agricultural School near Jaffa, in 1870, under the auspices of the *Alliance*. Its first director was Charles Netter, who had been influenced by Rabbi Hirsch Kalischer. A second landmark in Jewish agricultural colonization in Palestine is the year 1878, when Jews from Jerusalem acquired a stretch of land to the north of Jaffa and founded Petach Tikvah (The Door of Hope). Modern Zionist colonization in the full sense may be dated from 1882, when some Russian-Jewish settlers, who were members of the *Bilu*, established the colony of Rishon le-Zion (The First in Zion).

Colonization in Palestine before the War may be divided into three periods. In the first period, up to 1900, seven colonies were founded, devoted largely to the cultivation of grapes and oranges. They were mainly supported by the Rothschild administration. Between 1901 and 1907, a number of colonies were established in Lower Galilee, devoted to the cultivation of wheat. Though supported by the funds of the Baron Edmond de Rothschild, they were administered by the ICA Organization. The period from 1908 to the outbreak of the War marks the initial colonization on the part of the Zionist Organization. These colonies were intended for workers with small means and were established on small areas of land devoted to mixed farming, including dairy, vegetables and poultry.

At the time of the outbreak of the First World War, there were over forty Jewish agricultural settlements in Palestine, with a population of some 12,000. By that time, Jews had acquired some 400,000 Turkish dunams[68] of land, including the purchases made by private persons, the *Hovevei Zion* and the Baron de Rothschild organization. The Jewish National Fund which was established in 1901, had by this time acquired only a small area, something over 16,000 dunams.

A second important achievement of the new Palestine was the renascence of Hebrew as a spoken tongue and the establishment of a nucleus of a Hebrew school system in the Zionist spirit. Hebrew became the language of the Jews of Palestine, partly by necessity, partly as a result of the stimulus of the Hebraic renascence. The Jews of Palestine, gathered almost literally from the four corners of the earth, spoke a great variety of languages: Oriental Jews spoke Arabic, Persian or other

68. A dunam is about one-fourth of an acre.

languages of the countries from which they came; native Sephardic Jews, that is, Jews descended from the emigrés of the Spanish expulsion, used Ladino, or Español, based on a Castilian Spanish with an admixture of Hebrew; the Jews from Eastern Europe spoke Yiddish; the schools of the several foreign societies employed French, English or German, as the case might be, as the language of instruction. Hebrew was the only language which these various groups had in common.

Eliezer Ben Yehuda[69] who settled in Palestine in 1882, devoted his lifetime to the revival of Hebrew as the spoken tongue of the Jews, and to its renascence as the language of Jewish life and culture in all its aspects. He initiated the publication of the Modern Hebrew Thesaurus, and exercised an important influence in the introduction of Hebrew as the language of instruction in the Jewish schools in Palestine. His greatest opponents were the orthodox Jews who regarded Hebrew as a holy tongue which was not to be profaned by daily usage.

The use of Hebrew as the medium of instruction in the schools began in the elementary grades of the Zionist colonies. It gradually spread to the cities and to the secondary grades and to kindergartens. In 1913, the number of institutions using Hebrew as the sole medium of instruction had reached sixty, comprising 2,600 pupils. These included practically all the kindergarten and elementary schools in the colonies, a half dozen elementary schools in the cities, and two secondary schools in Jaffa and Jerusalem, a training school for woman teachers in Jaffa, the Bezalel Art School in Jerusalem,[70] and the agricultural school of *Mikveh Israel*. The *Alliance* schools and a number of orthodox schools had been affected by the movement. The schools using Hebrew were controlled by various authorities but were united by the idea of reviving Hebrew and the element of a common program of studies.

The population of the Jews also increased substantially with the Zionist development. In 1882, the Jewish inhabitants of Palestine numbered about 34,000 and were concentrated in Jerusalem, Hebron, Safed and Tiberias—the cities sacred to Jewish tradition. The population was about equally divided between the Ashkenazic or Yiddish-speaking Jews, and the Se-

---

69. His father's name was Jehuda Perlman, and Eliezer was born in 1858 in the Province of Vilna.

70. Founded by Boris Schaatz in 1906.

phardic, or Oriental Jews.[71] In 1897, at the time of the First Zionist Congress, the Jewish population was estimated at 50,000, of whom several thousand were then living in the agricultural settlements. Jewish settlement in Palestine was stimulated by the pogroms in Russia beginning in 1903 and by the abortive social-democratic revolution in 1905. In 1914, the population had increased to 85,000–90,000 and, as noted above, about 12,000 of these were in the Jewish agricultural settlements. By this time also there was the beginning of a Jewish communal organization and organized labor groups. Thus, before the First World War, the basis had already been laid for a Jewish national life in Palestine both in ideas and in practical work.

71. Arthur Ruppin, *The Jews in the Modern World*, Macmillan, 1934, p. 368.

CHAPTER II

THE FIRST WORLD WAR
AND
THE BALFOUR DECLARATION

AT THE outbreak of the First World War a beginning had been made toward the restoration of the Jews to Palestine. Colonization in Palestine had already made some progress, and Hebrew was striking root as the language of the new settlements. Zionism was a growing movement with a program of objectives, an organization comprising branches in many parts of the world, and a supporting body of thought. Serious political recognition of the Zionist purpose had been won through the negotiations conducted by Herzl with the heads of the German, Turkish and British Governments, even though these negotiations seemed abortive at the time. Despite these important achievements, the idea of the establishment of a home for the Jewish people in Palestine still lacked the sanction of public recognition and of law which the Basle Program had set down as a first principle. The necessary moral-legal basis for reconstituting the Jewish national home was obtained during the First World War and at the Peace Conference through two documents: 1) the Balfour Declaration issued by the British Government on November 2, 1917; and 2) the Mandate for Palestine, formally approved by the Council of the League of Nations on July 24, 1922.

The resolution to assign the Palestine Mandate to Great Britain was taken on April 25, 1920 at the San Remo Conference which decided on the terms to be imposed on the defeated Turks. On the previous day, the Supreme Council had agreed to include the Balfour Declaration in the proposed Turkish treaty. The partition of Turkey thus gave Zionism the opportunity to obtain the international political guarantee indispensable for the fulfilment of its program. It also opened up possibilities on a grand scale for realizing the aspirations of Arab nationalism. Besides allowing scope for the expression of the national strivings of the Jews and of the Arabs, the dismemberment of the Ottoman Empire held out the temptation of rich territorial prizes for the victorious nations and brought into play the rival imperialistic ambitions of the European powers. Three forces were involved in the Palestine problem: the aspiration of the Jewish people for a homeland; the struggle of the Arabs for political independence; the pressures of imperialism, particularly of French and British interests.

A decisive factor in the situation was Great Britain's need of protecting her life line to the East through the Suez Canal. For a century, Britain had followed the policy of bolstering up the Sick Man of Europe as a counterpoise to Russia's designs on the Dardanelles and as a means of keeping a friendly power on the Palestine side of the Suez. Germany's growing influence over Turkey in the generation before the war had weakened the validity of this time-honored British policy—particularly as a means of protecting the Suez—but the Foreign Office still hoped to keep Turkey neutral in the event of a war. However, Enver Pasha, the Prime Minister—ever hopping on the two branches of Turkish diplomacy, but partial to Germany at heart—decided the issue for the British when he signed a treaty of alliance with Germany on August 2, 1914, just one day after the outbreak of the war. At that time, it was still doubtful whether Britain would become a belligerent. When it became clear in the next few days that the British would certainly be involved, Enver Pasha began to make overtures to Russia, offering a military alliance in return for large concessions. The conditions were rejected, and Turkey, whether by design or by the force of circumstances, soon found herself on the side of the Central Powers.[1] The entrance of Turkey into the war netted Great Britain gains in the end, but at the beginning it was viewed with concern, for it brought to ruin the century-old policy of depending on Turkish neutrality for the protection of British interests in the East.

---

1. Herbert Sidebotham, *Great Britain and Palestine*, Macmillan, London, 1937, pp. 10 ff.; Arnold J. Toynbee and Kenneth P. Kirkwood, *Turkey*, Scribners, New York, 1927, pp. 54, 55.

TREATIES, PROMISES, AND THE BRITISH CONQUEST OF PALESTINE

Great Britain's need for a new Eastern policy after the collapse of her traditional alignment with the Turks was probably the main factor in her decision to support the Zionist policy during the First World War.[2] There were, of course, other factors: the purpose of this chapter is to describe the negotiations which led up to the Balfour Declaration and to make an analysis of what it signified at the time. Before we enter on this task, there are three subjects which require some consideration: 1) the secret treaties among the Allies concerning the disposition of the Ottoman Empire; 2) the promises made to the Arabs through Husain, the Sharif of Mecca; 3) the conquest of Palestine from the Turks.

Secret Treaties among the Allies

There were two secret treaties[3] among the Allies which concerned the disposition of portions of the Turkish Empire in case of an Allied victory: the Constantinople Agreement, and the Sykes-Picot Treaty, the latter being particularly important from the point of view of our discussion. The Constantinople Agreement consisted of a series of diplomatic exchanges between Russia, England, and France—and later of the three Allies with Italy—which were carried on during March-April, 1915.

Russia had pressed for a decision on the Dardanelles early in the course of the war. In March, 1915, the British agreed to Russia's annexation of Constantinople and to its control of the Straits, if the war ended successfully for the Allies and if the aspirations of England and France were adequately realized. The British made two specific conditions: that Russia should consent to British supervision of certain zones in Persia, hitherto considered neutral; and to the establishment of an independent Moslem power in Arabia with full control over the Moslem holy places. France was reluctant to act so far in advance of a successful outcome of the war, but she finally

---

2. Herbert Sidebotham, *op. cit.*, Chaps. II, III; H. W. V. Temperley, *A History of the Peace Conference of Paris*, Frowde, Hodder and Stoughton, London, 1924, Vol. VI, pp. 170 ff.

3. Royal Institute of International Affairs, *Great Britain and Palestine 1915–1939*, London, 1939, p. 7.

consented in principle to the Anglo-Russia arrangements stipulating that her agreement was contingent on a settlement of the whole problem of Asiatic Turkey which would safeguard her own interests in the Near East. The French indicated that they wanted to annex Syria, including the port of Alexandretta, and the province of Cilicia (Lesser Armenia) in Asia Minor. It was generally understood at the time that the term Syria included Palestine, but to make sure, Maurice Paléologue, the French Ambassador, made a special point of this in conversations with the Russian Foreign Office.[4] The Czar agreed to support the French demands, but no final settlement of the specific conditions was made at the time, and the question of the disposition of the Holy Land remained open.

British interests clashed with those of the French, especially in Syria and Palestine. The Foreign Office was on the verge of the negotiations with Husain to be presently recounted; they knew that the Arabs would be opposed to French rule of Syria. Palestine was a delicate problem. Prior to the war, the British generally considered it, along with Syria, as a sphere of French influence. There was always a party in England which believed that, as a foremost Protestant power, Britain should take a greater interest in the affairs of the Holy Land. But now there was a more urgent reason, as the strategic significance of Palestine began to be understood. Movement of Arab bands and Bedouin tribes over the southern borders of Palestine in the early months after the outbreak of the war, and a Turkish attack on the Canal in early February, 1915—although unsuccessful—confirmed the view that serious danger might come from a land attack through Palestine.

These considerations led the British government, in the spring of 1915, to appoint a committee under Sir Maurice de Bunsen to consider the question of the partition of Turkey with due regard to British interests. It was necessary for the British to prevent any strong foreign power from exercising domination in Palestine. Accordingly, the de Bunsen Committee, which reported in June, opposed yielding to the French in the matter of Palestine. They were, however, not prepared

---

4. E. Adamow, ed., *Die Europäischen Mächte und die Türkei während des Weltkrieges: Die Aufteilung der asiatischen Türkei nach den Geheimdokumenten des ehem. Ministeriums für Auswartige Angelegenheiten*, Dresden, 1932, pp. 26, 28.

to recommend British annexation. A new formula was devised: "Palestine must be recognized as a country whose destiny must be the subject of special negotiations, in which belligerents and neutrals are alike interested." [5] This principle became the pivot of British policy with reference to Palestine for the ensuing period. It was sufficient, at the time, for blocking the French claim to Palestine, and served also as a stepping stone for assuming greater control later. It may not have been planned, but it turned out that way.

In July, the negotiations with the Arabs had entered a formal stage through correspondence between Husain, the Sharif of Mecca, and Sir Henry McMahon, the chief British representative in Egypt. By the fall, the negotiations were coming to a head, and Sir Edward Grey thought it was time to inform Paul Cambon, the French Ambassador, of the situation in order to avoid further complication of British and French relations. The British proposed appointing a representative who would be empowered to confer with a French representative with regard to the questions at issue. After some preliminary discussions, Sir Mark Sykes, a distinguished Englishman who believed in the future of the East and in the part that the Arabs could play in its revival, was authorized to act on behalf of Great Britain. The French partner to the negotiations was M. Charles François Georges-Picot, formerly the French Consul at Beirut. By February, 1916, they had succeeded in working out a plan acceptable to the British and the French.

The main elements of this plan were as follows:

1) The British and French agreed not to acquire territorial possessions or to permit a third party to acquire territorial possessions in the Arabian Peninsula. Thus the basis was to be laid for a completely independent Arab state in Arabia.

2) Iraq and Syria—with the exception of Palestine—were to be divided into four zones—two alphabet zones, A and B, and two color zones, Blue and Red, as follows:

A Zone—The interior of Syria, from and including the cities of Damascus, Homs, Hama and Aleppo on the west, to and including the Mosul District on the east.

---

5. Great Britain, *Parliamentary Papers 1939*, Cmd. 5974: *Report of a Committee Set up to Consider Certain Correspondence between Sir Henry McMahon and the Sharif of Mecca in 1915 and 1916*, p. 51. Hereafter referred to as *Report*.

B Zone—The area lying south of A Zone, bounded on the west by a line running approximately from Gaza to Aqaba, and reaching across Trans-Jordan eastward to the Red Zone, with a north arm jutting into Persia and a south arm descending toward the Persian Gulf.

Blue Zone—The province of Cilicia in Asia Minor and all of coastal Syria west of A Zone with the cities of Damascus, Homs, Hama and Aleppo just outside the border.

Red Zone—The province of Basra and Bagdad in Persia.

3) Palestine, west of the Jordan and south of Galilee, was to constitute a fifth area designated as the Brown Zone.

In the alphabet areas, France and Britain were prepared to recognize semi-independent Arab states or a confederation of Arab states under an Arab chief, but they were to have—France in A Zone and Britain in B Zone—the right of supplying foreign advisers and officials and also were to be accorded economic privileges. In the colored zones, France—in the Blue Zone—and Britain—in the Red Zone—were to have such political control as they saw fit to establish after agreement with the Arab state or confederation.

Palestine, the Brown Zone, was to be placed under international control. The agreement[6] stated that: "With a view to securing the religious interests of the Entente Powers, Palestine with the Holy Places is separated from Turkish territory and subjected to a special regime to be determined by agreement between Russia, France, and Great Britain." In establishing the administration the other Allies and the Sharif of Mecca were to be consulted in accordance with the following paragraph: "In the Brown area there shall be established an international administration, the form of which is to be decided upon after consultation with Russia, and subsequently in consultation with the other Allies, and the representatives of the Shereef of Mecca."[7] Within the Brown Zone, Great Britain was to have the control of the ports of Haifa and Acre, which would thus form an enclave in the international zone. Haifa was to be a free port for the British. Great Britain was to be

---

6. According to Royal Institute of International Affairs, *Great Britain and Palestine, 1915–1939*, p. 8.

7. David Lloyd George, *The Truth about the Peace Treaties*, Gollancz, London, 1938, Vol. II, p. 1025. See also George Antonius, *The Arab Awakening*, Lippincott, 1939, p. 429.

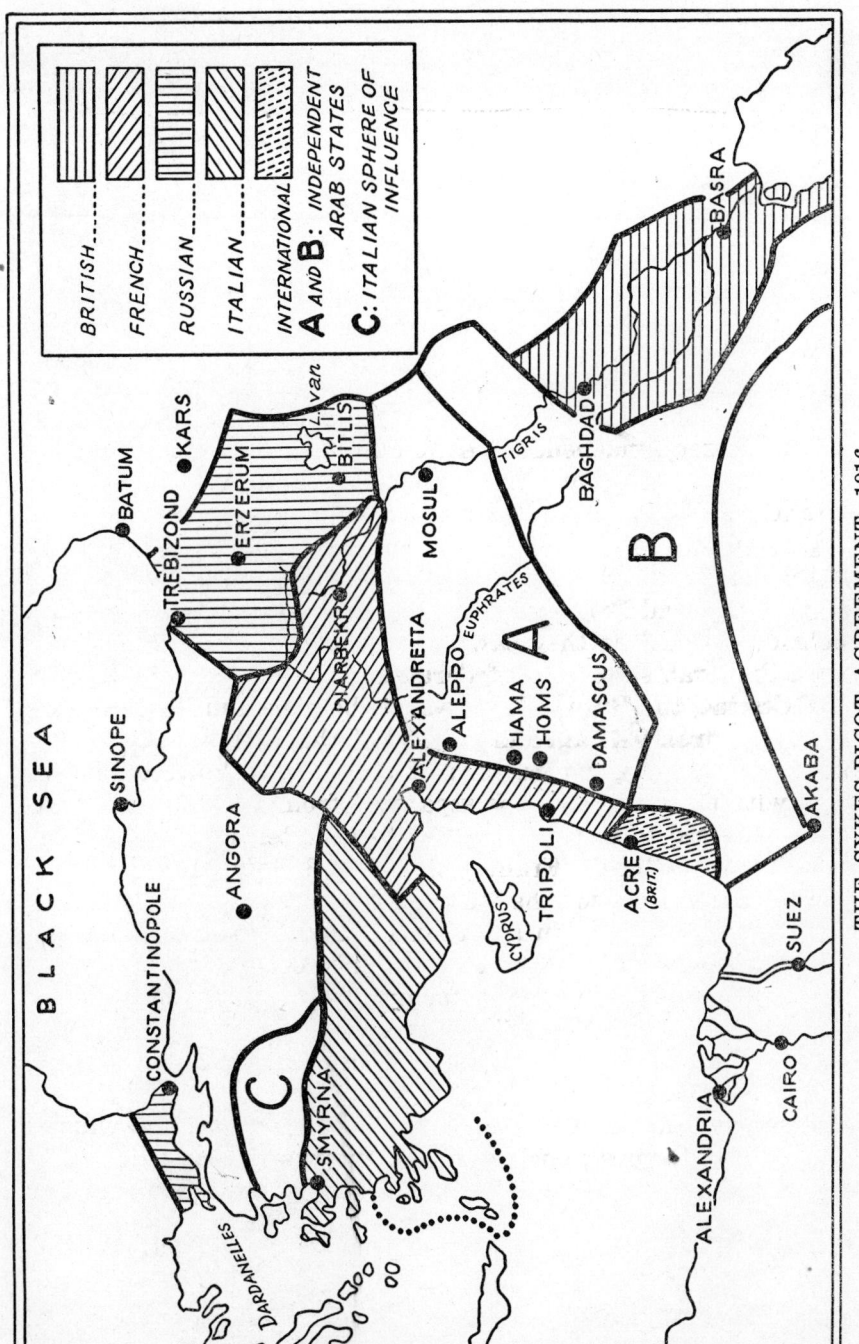

THE SYKES-PICOT AGREEMENT, 1916

assured also of the control of the projected Haifa-Persian Gulf railroad.

In March, the two emissaries, having gone to Russia for the purpose, presented the draft agreement to Sergei Sazonov, the Russian Foreign Minister. Russia accepted the draft in return for an agreement to allow the Russians to annex certain areas (Trebizond, Erzerum, Lake Van, Bitlis) in Asia Minor, south of the eastern end of the Black Sea. Paléologue, the French Ambassador, was still reluctant to lose Palestine and attempted to get Sazonov's consent to include it in coastal Syria, which had been assigned to the French. But Grey and Cambon, believing that Sykes and Picot had reached the most reasonable arrangement possible, pushed the agreement through. At this state of the negotiations, therefore, in the spring of 1916, the arrangement between England, France, and Russia was that Palestine should be under some form of condominium or international control. In the middle of May, the British government accepted the Sykes-Picot Agreement with a definite understanding that the cities of Homs, Hama, Damascus and Aleppo were to be assigned to the Arabs. This condition was in harmony with one of the main paragraphs of the McMahon-Husain correspondence.

The McMahon-Husain Understanding

In the period before the First World War, the British Foreign Office did not place much emphasis on relations with the Arabs. However, Lord Kitchener, the British Agent and Consul-General in Egypt, and others connected with the Arab Bureau in Cairo were developing the idea of creating an Arab state in the Levant, under British guidance, to offset the influence of Germany over Turkey. The Arab nationalists, whose center was in Syria, were ready to cooperate with the British as the less dangerous enemy, being most fearful of French ambitions. The figure in the Arab world who appeared to the Arab Bureau in Cairo as the most likely instrument of the British and Arab purpose was Husain ibn Ali, the Sharif of Mecca. He was reputedly a descendant[8] of the Prophet Mohammed, guardian of the Holy Places of the Hejaz, and an as-

---

8. He traced his descent through Fatima, and as Mohammed's family was of the Hashimi, the line of Fatima's progeny is sometimes referred to as Hashimite.

pirant for the Caliphate and for leadership in the Pan-Arab movement.[9] At the time, however, his position was precarious: the Turks were supporting his ancestral Arabian rival, Ibn Saud, against him, and he feared being deposed by the Committee of Union and Progress (C.U.P.), as the party of Young Turks was known.

In February, 1914, Abdullah, the second son of Husain,[10] passing through Cairo on his way to Constantinople, stopped to call on Kitchener, ostensibly on a courtesy visit. In the presence of Ronald Storrs, then Oriental Secretary to the British Agency, Abdullah told Kitchener of his father's difficulties, and tried to ascertain whether the British would support the Arabs of the Hejaz if they were to revolt against the Turks. Since the Foreign Office was then still committed to its pro-Turkish policy, Kitchener necessarily replied that Britain could not intervene. But Storrs was instructed to call on Abdullah the next day and to determine more precisely what Husain had in mind. After considerable talk, over chess and coffee, of the glories of the Arab past and the beauties of Arab

9. Although he enjoyed great prestige as a descendant of the Prophet and as the chief power in the Arabian peninsula, his reputation among the Moslems was none too good. John Van Ess (*Meet the Arab*, John Day, 1943, pp. 83–84) has given the following thumbnail description of him as he appeared at the outbreak of the war: "For a few years Hussein, in his position as sherif and controller of the pilgrimage, made hay vigorously—for himself, for he had his hand in pretty well everything that was lucrative. He sold the scant water supply to pilgrims at exorbitant prices, he controlled the sheep market where sacrifices were bought, he cornered the food supply and sold it again on his own terms, he forbore to punish looters, and gossip had it that he even shared the loot; in short he had his hand on everything save the air the people breathed and that, to be sure, was foul enough through the lack of the most primitive sanitation."

Some Britishers, particularly those associated with the India Office, were not enthusiastic about the choice of Husain, then sixty-six years old, and preferred his young rival, Ibn Saud, who was destined many years later to triumph over Husain. The preference for Ibn Saud was due in part to his younger years, and in part to the fact that he seemed more promising. The India Office evidently did not believe in the policy of an alliance with Arab nationalism, as sponsored by the Arab Bureau in Cairo. The interests of Ibn Saud were confined to Arabia and he was not regarded as a possible representative of the general Arab movement either in its nationalistic or religious phase.

10. Now the Emir of Transjordan. Ali, the eldest, was heir to the Sharifate and confined himself to affairs in the Hejaz. Faisal, the third son, was chosen by T. E. Lawrence to lead the Arab revolt. Zaid, a fourth son, is mentioned by Storrs as a youth.

poetry, Abdullah came to the point and "asked categorically whether Great Britain would present the Grand Sharif with a dozen, or even a half dozen, machine guns." [11] Storrs repeated Kitchener's refusal and said that Britain "could never entertain the idea of supplying arms to be used against a Friendly Power." Toward the end of April, when Abdullah was on the way back, he went to Storrs again, but still received no encouragement.

However, something had been started by these talks. Later in the year, when it looked as though Turkey were about to join the Central Powers, Storrs received authority from Kitchener, now in England as Secretary of State for War, to get in touch with Husain to find out whether he would support the British if the latter went to war with Turkey. Storrs' messenger, a trusted Arab, reached Mecca in October and had an interview with Husain. The Sharif in a roundabout way indicated that he was willing to work with the British. He said in the flowery Arabic typical of him: "Stretch forth to us a helping hand and we shall never at all help these oppressors. On the contrary we shall help those who do good." [12] In addition to this rather noncommittal response, Husain dispatched a letter, over Abdullah's signature, stating his readiness to reach an agreement with Great Britain but protesting his inability to take immediate action. Kitchener cabled to the British Agency in Cairo to send a reply to Abdullah which included the following: "If Arab nation assist England in this war England will guarantee that no intervention takes place in Arabia and will give Arabs every assistance against external foreign aggression." [13] Husain, pleased with this, which he took to be a warm support of Arab aspiration for national independence, and wishing to "give Kitchener just enough (but no more) encouragement to keep him in play," instructed Abdullah to inform Cairo that his father was definitely committed "to a policy of unavowed alliance with England." But Abdullah again stressed the inability of his father without further preparation to commit any overt act against the Turks. And he asked for time to find

11. Ronald Storrs, *Orientations*, Ivor Nicholson and Watson, London, 1937, p. 143.
12. *Ibid.*, p. 175, from Storrs' dictated rendition of the messenger's oral report to him.
13. *Ibid.*, p. 176.

his bearings, gather his forces and find a favorable opportunity for revolt.[14]

The British Foreign Office, now fully converted to Kitchener's plan of supporting Arab independence, tried to induce the Arabs to take some action against the Turks. On November 16th, the government made public through *The Times* that the British had no intention of undertaking operations in Arabia "except for the protection of Arab interests against Turkish or other aggression, or in support of attempts by Arabs to free themselves from Turkish rule." In April, 1915, the government let it be known through Sir Reginald Wingate, Governor-General of the Sudan, that Great Britain would make it a condition of peace with Turkey that the Arabian Peninsula and the Moslem Holy Cities in the Hejaz would remain in the hands of an independent Moslem state. In June, printed leaflets to this effect were distributed or dropped from airplanes in Egypt, Sudan and the Hejaz. Despite these efforts the Sharif of Mecca delayed taking any action. The only thing that he did which might be conceived as a gesture of aid to Britain was his refusal to allow the jehad to be preached in the mosques under his control.[15] However, he did not break with the Sultan as sovereign of Turkey.

In July, 1915, Husain took the first step toward active collaboration with the British. Under the Moslem date Ramadan 2, 1333 (July 14, 1915), he sent the first of a series of letters to Sir Henry McMahon in which he made definite proposals. Through his third son, Faisal, he had been in touch with the Syrian nationalists. They had agreed to accept the Sharif as spokesman of the Pan-Arab cause if he would present demands that included the very comprehensive ideal of a great Arab state as envisaged in the so-called Damascus Protocol.[16] If their terms were met they promised to raise a revolt in Syria in con-

---

14. George Antonius, *op. cit.*, pp. 132 ff.
15. The Turkish government attempted to mobilize the Islamic world against the Allies by having the war declared a jehad, i.e., a religious war against infidels. This presented difficulties from the viewpoint of Moslem law since Turkey was itself allied with infidels. But the jurisconsult of the Ottoman Empire managed to bring in a favorable opinion and the Sultan as Caliph declared the jehad on November 11, 1914. The British were worried about the possible effect of the jehad on the Moslems under their rule, but it proved a failure and the Moslems under the British took no action. (See Toynbee and Kirkwood, *Turkey*, pp. 55–56.)
16. Antonius, *op. cit.*, p. 157.

junction with the projected insurrection in the Hejaz. Accordingly, in this first letter to McMahon, Husain proposed that the British recognize Arab independence over a wide area which included the whole of the Arabian Peninsula (except Aden on the southeast corner which was already under British control) and all of what is now Syria, Palestine, Trans-Jordan and Iraq, running up to the borders of Persia on the east, and on the west to the Mediterranean up to Mersina and Adana, on the angle where the Syrian coastline joins Asia Minor. In addition to these territorial demands, he asked for the support of an Arab Caliphate and a treaty of mutual assistance between Britain and the projected Arab state. He indicated that the Arabs were ready to grant economic preference to Great Britain in the independent state proposed.

The British were not prepared for such comprehensive territorial demands.[17] In his answer (August 30), McMahon confirmed the promise made by Kitchener in 1914, that Britain would recognize an Arab Caliphate if a sufficient majority of Moslems chose to elect an Arab. But he evaded the question of boundaries on the ground that "it would appear to be premature to consume our time in discussing such details in the heat of war." McMahon pointed out that much of the territory mentioned by Husain was still in Turkish hands and that moreover some of the Arabs in such occupied portions were "lending their arms to the German and Turk, to the new despoiler and the old oppressor." As an evidence of good will, however, McMahon indicated that His Majesty's Government would be ready to ship quantities of grain and other charitable gifts due from Egypt to the Holy Cities in Arabia.

Things were not going so well with the British at this time and the Sharif in his reply, although retaining a courteous manner, did not yield any of his demands. His acknowledgment (September 9, 1915) began: "With great cheerfulness and delight I received your letter of the 19th Shawal, 1333 (the 30th August, 1915), and have given it great consideration and regard, in spite of the impression I received from it of ambiguity and its tone of coldness and hesitation with regard to our es-

---

17. Storrs (*op. cit.*, p. 177) writes: "As I struggled through his difficult writing and even more difficult Arabic, I found myself murmuring:
"In matters of commerce the fault of the Dutch
Is giving too little and asking too much."

sential point . . ." ¹⁸ He went on to say that the "coldness and hesitation" displayed by McMahon "might be taken to infer an estrangement or something of the sort." He made it plain that the boundaries demanded were not to be taken as the suggestions of one individual whose claims might await the conclusion of the war, but the demands of the Arab peoples who regarded the frontiers necessary for the establishment of the new regime for which they were striving.[19]

In the meantime, McMahon had been in touch with a certain Muhammad al-Faruqi, a young Arab officer who had deserted the Turks and gone over to the British lines at the Gallipoli Front. He was an ardent worker for Arab independence and a member of the secret nationalist society, al-Ahd.[20] Although he was not an accredited agent of the nationalists of Syria and Iraq, he stood in close relations with them and the British learned from him what the Syrian leaders were thinking and what their attitude was toward the Sharif.[21] Al-Faruqi appears to have given the British the impression that while the Arabs would have liked to obtain independence in all the Arab countries, they recognized the existence of British interests in Iraq and French interests in Syria. He indicated that the Arabs would insist on the independence of Aleppo, Hama, Homs and Damascus, but "they would accept a general reservation of the areas in which Great Britain was not free to act without detriment to the interests of the Allied Powers." [22]

With the background of this information, McMahon dispatched, under date of October 24, 1915, the so-called "key

---

18. Great Britain, *Parliamentary Papers, 1939*, Cmd. 5957: *Correspondence between Sir Henry McMahon, His Majesty's High Commissioner at Cairo, and the Sherif Hussein of Mecca*, July, 1915–March, 1916, p. 5. Hereafter referred to as *Correspondence*.

19. Following the version of Antonius, *op. cit.*, p. 417.

20. Al-Ahd [the covenant] was one of the secret societies of Arab patriots which continued to work underground in Turkey against the oppressive policy of the Young Turks after the Turkish Revolution of 1908. It was a brotherhood limited almost entirely to Arab officers in the Turkish Army, who swore to acquire the military knowledge of their masters, and turn it against them, in the service of the Arab people, when the moment of rebellion came. G. Antonius, *op. cit.*, pp. 11–12, 119, 155–7; T. E. Lawrence, *Seven Pillars of Wisdom*, Chap. 4, Doubleday Doran, 1935, p. 467.

21. Antonius, *op. cit.*, pp. 168–169.

22. *Ibid*. This account of al-Faruqi's views is based on *Report*, pp. 23–24.

letter." In this, Sir Henry accepted Husain's proposals as a basis but made significant reservations: 1) with reference to the territorial demands; 2) with reference to the degree of independence in the proposed Arab state. As to the territorial demands, the British excluded two areas: a) the Districts of Mersina and Adana in Asia Minor, and b) the coast of Syria lying to the west of the Districts of Damascus, Homs, Hama and Aleppo. The reasons given for the exclusion were: 1) that the territories excluded could not be considered purely Arab, and 2) that the interests of France were involved. With reference to limitations on complete sovereignty, Great Britain stipulated that the Arabs, in choosing outside assistance, will "seek the advice and guidance of Great Britain only, and that such European advisers and officials as may be required . . . will be British." Furthermore, that in the case of the vilayets of Bagdad and Basra, the Arabs should recognize that British interests demand special administrative arrangements.

In his reply (November 5, 1915), Husain agreed to the exclusion of Mersina and Adana on the border of Syria and Asia Minor, but did not consent to the exclusion of the vilayets of Aleppo and Beirut. Furthermore, he did not accept McMahon's proposals for special administrative arrangements in Iraq (Bagdad and Basra), but consented to temporary British postwar occupation on the understanding that there would be a subsidy by Great Britain to the future Arab state. But McMahon in the next letter (December 14, 1915) firmly refused to accede to Husain's request with reference to Aleppo and Beirut and repeated the argument that the interests of France were involved in both of these districts. Moreover, McMahon indicated that the British could make no changes from their limitations on complete Arab independence but he suggested that more detailed consideration would be given in the case of some of the areas.

On January 1, 1916, Husain replied that he would not at that time press the question of the Syrian coast in deference to the Anglo-French alliance, but that the Arabs would wish at the first opportunity after the war to take this matter up again. On this he was emphatic and said: "It is impossible to allow any derogation that gives France, or any other Power, a span of land in those regions." However, the British were equally emphatic in making it clear that the exclusion of coastal Syria was not temporary, and in the eighth letter, written on January 25th, McMahon warned Husain against expecting Britain to change its position. In the following letter, February 18, 1916, Husain accepted the British terms and detailed his monetary requirements.[23]

Palestine was not explicitly mentioned either by McMahon or by Husain in any part of the Correspondence, a circumstance usually explained by the fact that Palestine was not at that time either a political or an administrative entity, and the terms used throughout the Correspondence are those which were in vogue under Turkish rule. The omission of explicit reference to Palestine has made it possible for the Arabs to claim that it was not excluded from the area in which the British promised to help the Arabs obtain independence. The British Government and all of the officials connected with the negotiations have repeatedly declared that it was their intention to exclude Palestine from any commitments made to the Sharif. Sir Henry McMahon has put himself on record on two occasions—in 1922 and again in 1937—to the effect that he definitely intended to exclude Palestine and had reason to believe that Husain understood this at the time of the negotiations. The documents were re-examined by a committee set up by His Majesty's Government in 1939 and the letters have now been published in full. The publication of the documents and circumstantial evidence add further support to the British view of the matter. But the failure to make mention of Palestine by name has left the Arab contenders with a straw to which to cling, and the issue will be examined again in later chapters.[24]

The British Conquest of Palestine

Although Husain and McMahon reached a workable agreement by January 1916, the Arab revolt did not take place immediately. Husain was still waiting to make sure that he was "backing the right horse." [25] The indecisive attitude on the part of the Arabs was changed by the action of the Turks themselves. They had been suspicious of Arab loyalty and these

---

23. *Correspondence*, p. 15. Antonius, in *The Arab Awakening*, Appendix A, reproduced only eight of the letters, thus omitting reference to the Sharif's acceptance of McMahon's terms.
24. Chap. IV, p. 182 and Chap. XIII, p. 894.
25. J. de V. Loder, *The Truth about Mesopotamia, Palestine and Syria*, Allen and Unwin, London, 1923, p. 18.

suspicions were confirmed by the discovery of incriminating documents. A number of Arab nationalists who had relations with the Allies were executed. As a consequence, the uprising promised by the Syrian nationalists to coincide with the revolt in the Hejaz never came off. Husain was finally forced to act alone when the Turks, accompanied by a German Military Mission, ostensibly on its way to Yemen, approached the Hejaz.

On June 5th, Ali and Faisal, sons of the Sharif, rode out to the tomb of Hamza, where the recruits were encamped and proclaimed the independence of the Arabs from Turkish rule in the name of Sharif Husain, Lord of Mecca.[26] The Turkish garrison at Mecca was attacked on June 10th and later, after two British artillery companies from the Egyptian Expeditionary Force had come to the assistance of Husain's forces, was compelled to surrender. On November 2nd, Husain was proclaimed king of the Arab countries by an assembly of religious and secular notables gathered under his own inspiration. However, he was not recognized as such either by the other Arab princes or by the British. But he was recognized as King of the Hejaz and a formal notification of this was addressed to him on January 3, 1917 in identical British and French notes.[27] He did not, however, succeed in becoming master of the Hejaz until the end of the war, when Medina, which had held out, was finally taken.

The Arab revolt was helpful to Britain although its importance has been exaggerated by Lawrence's romantic descriptions. The main service rendered was provided by troops of the Sharif, trained and equipped by the British, and led by Faisal and Jafar Pasha under the guidance of Lawrence and other British officers. Moving north, the troops from the Hejaz captured Aqaba on July 5, 1917; they then joined Allenby's forces in Palestine and operated on the east side of the Jordan in company with Trans-Jordan tribesmen. In the final stages of Allenby's campaign in 1918 they cleared Trans-Jordan of Turkish troops and assisted in the conquest of Syria, capturing Homs and Hama.

The conquest of Palestine and Syria came late in the war, despite Lord Kitchener's advocacy of an aggressive campaign against the Turks from the very beginning. In the early stages

26. Antonius, *op. cit.*, pp. 194–195.
27. *Ibid.*, p. 213.

of the war the British Cabinet was averse to any active campaign in the Near East. Regarding the Western Front in France as the main issue, they were reluctant to spend their forces on what most of the military leaders called a "side show." The French leaders naturally joined with the British Cabinet in damping down the ardor for an aggressive strategy against the Turks. They were, of course, concerned about their own home front and had no arms to spare for the Near East campaign. But they were conscious also of the fact that if Britain carried on a campaign in the East without their help, French economic and political claims in the Levant would be weakened.

In defending Suez the British therefore followed a strategy of passive defense in the early stages of the war. During 1915, the military activity in the Near East centered around Gallipoli with its almost successful, but in the end altogether disastrous, result. A promising project for attacking Alexandretta in order to cut off the line of communications between Syria and Mesopotamia was abandoned after the failure at Gallipoli. However, in early 1916, Sir Archibald Murray assumed command of the Egyptian military forces and was permitted to advance into the Sinai Desert to create a new defense line for the Canal. In July, the Turks, urged by the Germans, who were anxious to keep as many of the British troops as possible occupied in Egypt, launched an attack. Their defeat at Romani on August 4, 1916, marked the turning point; the offensive now passed out of the hands of the Turks never to be regained.

A full change of strategy was indicated when David Lloyd George became Prime Minister in December, 1916. He favored the plan of attacking the Central Powers at their weakest point: to drive the Turks from Palestine as a means of forcing them out of the war. But the Near East strategy was still opposed by the General Staff and it was not until the summer of the following year that it began to be put into effect. Sir Edmund Allenby, who assumed command of the Egyptian Expeditionary Force in June, 1917, received instructions one month later to strike hard at the Turks. Things were not going so well with the Allies in the West and victory in Palestine was regarded as of great value in strengthening Allied morale. Allenby launched his attack in October, 1917. His forces captured Beer Sheba on October 31st, only a few days before the

World War I and the Balfour Declaration 73

Balfour Declaration was issued. By the middle of November, the Turks had been pushed back to Lydda, well within the borders of Palestine. The British then advanced against Jerusalem, which the Turks evacuated on the night of December 8th.

At noon on the 9th of December a Turkish representative conveyed the surrender of the city to Allenby who made his official entry two days afterwards. He entered Jerusalem on foot through the Jaffa Gate, followed by his staff and representatives of the French and Italian contingents. Standing at the top of the Citadel steps, he caused a proclamation to be read in English, French, Italian, Arabic and Hebrew. The proclamation was of a general character, emphasizing the international character of the city.[28]

> Furthermore, since your City is regarded with affection by the adherents of three of the great religions of mankind, and its soil has been consecrated by the prayers and pilgrimages of multitudes of devout people of these three religions for many centuries, therefore do I make known to you that every sacred building, monument, holy spot, shrine, traditional site, endowment, pious bequest, or customary place of prayer, of whatsoever form of the three religions, will be maintained and protected according to the existing customs and beliefs of those to whose faiths they are sacred.

After the capture of Jerusalem, Allenby proposed, if his troops were reinforced, to clear the Jordan Valley, cut the Hejaz railway in Trans-Jordan, and advance northward along the Syrian coast to dispose of the Turkish forces as quickly as possible. The great German offensive on the Western Front in the spring of 1918 interrupted this plan, although it had been approved by the British Government. However, in September he was ready to go forward. He caught the Turks off their guard and succeeded in scattering or destroying their forces. There was a swift advance north: Damascus surrendered October 1st; Beirut was occupied a week later by British troops, and Aleppo fell October 26th, after the capture of Homs and Hama by the Arab forces. On October 30, 1918, about a week before the general armistice in the west, Turkish repre-

28. Quoted in Harry Charles Luke and Edward Keith-Roach, *The Handbook of Palestine and Transjordan*, Macmillan, London, 1930, p. 28.

sentatives, met at Mudros on the island of Lemnos, agreed to what amounted to an unconditional surrender.

The conquest of Palestine and Syria was effected chiefly by the British. The Arabs from the Hejaz and Trans-Jordan who assisted Allenby were a relatively small force. The Syrian and Palestinian Arabs did not contribute to the victory; some of them deserted in miserable condition and were fed and clothed by the British armies, but most of them continued fighting with the Turks. In order to maintain the international character of the enterprise, the French sent some detachments, including a mixed brigade of Armenian and Syrian volunteers, and the Italians contributed a contingent of a few hundred infantry.[29] The operations of the Mesopotamian Expeditionary Force moving up the Tigris and Euphrates valleys from the Persian Gulf were another British contribution to the defeat of Turkey. The large part played by the British conquest of the Turks greatly strengthened British claims for extension of influence in the Middle East area. Their victory in Palestine gave a basis for extending their interest in Palestine which, under the Sykes-Picot Agreement, had been assigned to international auspices.

THE BRITISH ALLIANCE WITH ZIONISM

The Balfour Declaration marked a great historic triumph for Zionism. It was the first public recognition of the Jewish claim for a homeland in Palestine. Like the Sykes-Picot and the McMahon-Husain arrangements, the pledge to the Jewish people arose as a war commitment. But it differed radically from the other agreements in a number of essential ways. The Balfour Declaration was not a secret document of which the negotiators and Foreign Office alone were cognizant. The negotiations leading to the Balfour Declaration were carried on directly with the British Cabinet; its final formulation was made in close collaboration with the American Government; it was announced in a public letter from the Minister of Foreign Affairs to the leading British Jews; it was celebrated at a mass meeting in which leading British statesmen and representatives of many nationalities participated.

29. Loder, *op. cit.*, pp. 34, 35.

Motivations for the Balfour Declaration

It is generally held that the immediate causes that brought about the commitment of His Majesty's Government to the Jewish people were of two sorts. First was a long-term strategic reason: a few of the leading British statesmen had come to believe that the Jews, restored to statehood, would be the ideal people to guard the British bastion of defense on the Palestine land bridge between the Nile and the Near East. The other reason was in the line of propaganda: in the difficult days of 1916 and 1917, the British were anxious to get the moral support of the Jews, particularly of those in the United States, as a means of winning over America to the Allied cause. There was fear at the time that Germany would steal a march on the Allies by issuing, with the support of Turkey, a declaration in favor of Jewish restoration in Palestine. In a deeper sense of the term "propaganda," the Declaration was calculated to counteract the natural lack of sympathy that the Jews had for a war in which Czarist Russia was on the Allied side.

But there were also altruistic motivations in the British interest in Zionism. As Temperley says: "At a time when justice for oppressed races and small peoples had become an Allied slogan it was at least consistent to include the Jews among those whose wrongs might be righted as an outcome of the War." [30] Behind her sympathetic attitude, moreover, was an interest which Britain had shown in the restoration of the Jews to Palestine over a full century. The offer of the Uganda territory in British East Africa to Herzl in 1903 was an important first step in political recognition of Jewish claims to nationhood. While the offer could not be accepted by Zionists, it was in fact the first recognition by any government of the need of a land where the Jews might re-establish themselves as a people.

The continuity of British policy with reference to Zionism is exemplified in the person of Arthur James Balfour, whose name is forever attached to His Majesty's famous Declaration of November 2, 1917. He was Prime Minister when Joseph Chamberlain, as Colonial Secretary, offered the Uganda scheme to Herzl and he was a whole-hearted supporter of the pro-

30. H. W. V. Temperley, *op. cit.*, Vol. VI, p. 171.

posal. He was won over to Zionism in the stricter sense by Dr. Weizmann in a talk which they had together in Manchester when Balfour was campaigning in the General Election of 1906. He was at that time brought to the conviction "that if a home was to be found for the Jewish people, homeless now for nearly 1900 years, it was vain to seek it anywhere but in Palestine." [31] Balfour also reflected the mixture of strategic and idealistic motivations which has characterized the British interest in the restoration of the Jews to Palestine. In urging the Cabinet to accept the Balfour Declaration, he emphasized that it would be useful to the Allied cause in Russia and America; but the fact is that he had from youth a deep interest in Jewish history and civilization, and entertained a high appreciation of the Jewish contribution to Western culture and religion.[32]

First Steps in the Negotiations

At the outbreak of the war, various branches of the World Zionist Organization found themselves divided into opposing camps of the Allies and Central Powers. The major question among the leaders was whether the central office of the Zionist Organization should be continued at Berlin as heretofore or transferred to a neutral country. The six members of the Executive were dispersed. Professor Otto Warburg, the distinguished botanist, and Dr. Arthur Hantke, one of the pillars of German Zionism, remained in Berlin to direct the work in Central Europe. Dr. Victor Jacobson, one of the influential members of the Zionist Executive, established a bureau in the neutral city of Copenhagen. Nahum Sokolow,[33] the versatile journalist, left for England and was soon joined by the Russian Zionist leader, Dr. Yehiel Tschlenow, who was then technically

---

31. Nahum Sokolow, *History of Zionism*, Vol. I, pp. xxix, xxx.
32. Blanche E. C. Dugdale, *Arthur James Balfour*, Vol. II, Hutchinson, London, 1936, p. 216; also below, pp. 116 ff.
33. Nahum Sokolow (1859–1936) achieved early recognition as a linguist and litterateur. He is recognized as the founder of Hebrew journalism and as one of the pillars of the *Haskalah*. He published much in other languages besides Hebrew, e.g., English, German and Polish, and is regarded as the most prolific Jewish writer of his age. In 1908 he began to take an active role in the administration of Zionist affairs. Subsequently he became General Secretary of the Zionist Organization, was elected to the Inner Actions Committee, and became President of the Jewish Agency and the World Zionist Organization.

head of the World Zionist Organization. Shmarya Levin was already in America, where he remained for the duration of the war, helping to make the United States an important center of Zionist work.

American Jewry was to play a significant role in shaping the destinies of the Zionist movement. Louis Lipsky, President of the Zionist Federation of America, and Jacob de Haas, whom Herzl had sent from England to be its secretary, were the mainstays of the organization. Dr. Judah L. Magnes, later to become president of the Hebrew University, was one of the first Reform rabbis to espouse Zionism and maintain an official connection with the Zionist Organization. The entry of Louis D. Brandeis (later Justice Brandeis) into the organization in 1912, a visit to the United States by Nahum Sokolow in 1913, Shmarya Levin's activities during the war, were factors of inspiration and gave forceful leadership to the movement. At an Extraordinary Conference called on August 30, 1914 in New York City, a Provisional Executive Committee for General Zionist Affairs was formed and an emergency fund set up to support Palestinian institutions and to carry on Zionist propaganda. Brandeis was elected chairman and exercised his leadership in this capacity until he assumed his office as Justice of the Supreme Court in October 1916. After that, he exercised leadership through his personal contacts with the workers in the Zionist cause and by keeping in touch with the situation in Washington. The Zionist cause also had the backing of the Jewish Congress movement which was launched in 1915 to defend Jewish rights in Europe and Palestine.

The march of events soon gave to England the major role in formulating the political policy and in furthering the negotiations. The Zionist ideal had the warm encouragement of the majority of English Jews and the movement had exceptional leadership from among British as well as Continental Jews. The Zionist leaders in England hoped for an alliance with Great Britain, but in the early stages of the war they hesitated to tie the fate of the Jewish homeland too definitely with the Allied cause. The Executive in Berlin felt that the best policy would be to remain neutral and to formulate objectives in a way that would not make their success dependent on which side was victorious. Moreover, before America entered the war, American Zionists favored the policy of neutrality in line with the position of the United States Government. There was also a certain coolness to the Allied cause: the Jews from Eastern Europe could hardly be enthusiastic for the side with which the Russian Czar was associated; and the leaders of Jewish philanthropies, who were mainly of German-Jewish origin, undoubtedly harbored friendship for a Germany which, at that time, still had claims as a great center of culture and liberal thought.

The leading part in the negotiations with Great Britain was taken by Dr. Chaim Weizmann,[34] who came to England in 1904 when he was appointed to the staff of Victoria University, Manchester. The Zionist movement as a whole, and Weizmann particularly, had always looked to Great Britain for support; this position was held as well by Ahad Ha'am, who was also then resident in England. As early as September 9, 1914, Weizmann wished to begin making contacts with individuals influential in Government circles, but Ahad Ha'am, ever cautious, deterred him. However, when the war against Turkey was declared, Ahad Ha'am wrote to Weizmann (on November 15) that "the great historic hour for the Jews and for Palestine has struck." He wrote another letter the following week in which he indicated what he thought was the correct line of approach and, incidentally, forecast the sort of opposition that would be met:[35]

---

34. Chaim Weizmann was born on November 27, 1874, in a small town near the Pripet marshes in the Government of Pinsk. He received his early education in the village *heder* and then was sent to the technical school of Minsk, completing his studies in the Universities of Freiburg, Geneva and Berlin. He developed his scientific gifts at an early age, working in the field of biochemistry. Before going to England he was already known as the discoverer of a number of important chemical processes. As noted in the previous chapter, his participation in the work of the Zionist Congress began early. He was unable to be present at the First Zionist Congress because he was then taking his doctoral examinations, but has attended every one since. He participated in the Second Zionist Congress in 1898, and, as indicated above, became an important member in the "Democratic Fraction," an opposition group. After the death of Herzl, during the time when David Wolffsohn was President, he was the leader of a very sharp opposition. He was at that time also chairman of the Permanent Committee of the Congress, comparable to the committee on committees of American conventions, and thus exercised an important influence in the governing body of the Zionist movement.

35. Asher Ginsburg, *Iggrot Ahad Ha'am* (Letters of Ahad Ha'am), Jerusalem, 1924, Vol. V, p. 204.

As you know, I am of the opinion that we should be moderate in our demands and content ourselves with the right of colonization and cultural activity. At the same time, let us not conceal our hope that eventually, with the realization of these two objectives, we shall achieve in Palestine an autonomous life under England's banner. This moderate program will entail a struggle on the one hand, against our political rattleheads, who will undoubtedly find this historical moment most appropriate to wax pompous and, inflated with a windy phraseology, will concern themselves more with the splendor of their appearance than with the consequences. On the other hand, our notables will protest against any suggestion of the national character of the affair and against our hopes for the future and will endeavor to reduce it to a philanthropic enterprise to aid several thousand poor Jews. I am fully aware that everything depends on whether we shall have the strength to maintain a firm stand without faltering.

The first work of Weizmann was to make friends for Zionism. He had already established good relations with Lord Rothschild, recognized head of English Jewry, whose interest in the founding of a University at Jerusalem he had succeeded in winning shortly before the war. On December 14, 1914, he had a talk with Balfour who remembered clearly the meeting and conversation that he had had with Weizmann in Manchester eight years before. On this occasion the conversation turned about the position of the Jews in Germany as reflected in certain anti-Semitic remarks made by Frau Wagner to Balfour two years before while he was in Bayreuth. Weizmann commented on the paradox that while the German Jews were giving their best energies to Germany, and were trying to efface themselves as Jews and to identify themselves wholly with Germany, the Germans resented the large part that Jews played in German life. Here was the very crux of the Jewish tragedy—the assimilated German Jew was neither German nor Jew. Balfour asked whether there was anything he could do to help in a practical way. Weizmann answered: "Not while the guns are roaring." And added, "When the military situation becomes clearer, I will come again." In concluding the interview Balfour said: "Mind you come again. It is a great cause you are working for; I would like you to come again and again." [36]

36. Dugdale, *op. cit.*, Vol. II, p. 224.

One of the most important converts to Zionism that Weizmann made at this time was Cyril P. Scott, the distinguished editor of the *Manchester Guardian*. Through his good offices Weizmann became acquainted with Mr. Herbert Samuel, one of the outstanding liberals of England and the first unbaptized Jew to become a member of the British Cabinet. Weizmann found Samuel sympathetic—even enthusiastic—about the ideal of Jewish restoration. In personal talks that Samuel had with Sir Edward Grey and with Lloyd George as early as November 9, 1914, he gave expression to the idea that as soon as Turkey disintegrated "perhaps there might be an opportunity for the fulfillment of the ancient aspiration of the Jewish people and the restoration there of a Jewish State." [37] If such a state were established, he thought it might become the center of a new culture and a source of great literature, art and scientific development. The center would have an influence on the millions of Jews throughout the countries of the world who would for the most part necessarily remain dispersed. In early 1915, he presented his plans in a more formal way in a memorandum which he placed before the Cabinet. He urged that in the partition of the Turkish dominions the British should take Palestine, open it up to Jewish immigration, and reconstruct it as a Jewish center which in due course would achieve Home Rule.[38]

Toward the end of the year 1915, there is evidence of considerable favorable opinion toward the Zionist program in important British circles. The general conception of the restoration of the Jews to Palestine was beginning to be enforced by a more specific plan of the re-establishment of a Jewish State as a means of strengthening the British military position in the East. On November 22, 1915, a leading editorial article appeared in the *Manchester Guardian*,[39] in which, at consider-

---

37. Herbert Samuel, *Great Britain and Palestine*, The Second Lucien Wolf Memorial Lecture, The Jewish Historical Society of England, London, 1935, pp. 12 ff.

38. Leonard Stein, *Zionism*, Kegan Paul, London, 1925, p. 81. The memorandum was evidently permeated with warm feeling. Asquith (later Lord Oxford) who was "not attracted" by Samuel's proposal, mentions the memorandum in his diary (*Memories and Reflections*, Little, Brown, Boston, 1928, Vol. II, p. 78), describing it as a "dithyrambic memorandum."

39. An unsigned editorial written by Herbert Sidebotham; cf. his *Great Britain and Palestine*, pp. 24–27.

able length, a theory of the proper strategy for Great Britain in the Near East was outlined. The writer pointed out that with the loss of Turkey as an English ally, "the most vital spot in our communications with the East would be exposed to attack from the land, an attack from which the most powerful navy could not possibly secure us." He proposed that a buffer state be established in Palestine as a means of protecting the Suez Canal and Egypt and urged that the only people capable of forming such a state was the Jewish nation.

Mr. Harry Sacher, member of a notable group of young Manchester Zionists,[40] who was at that time a correspondent of the *Manchester Guardian,* brought the article to the attention of Weizmann. Sidebotham was asked to prepare a comprehensive memorandum elaborating on the idea. This was ready in February, 1916, and was submitted several months later to Sir Ronald Graham, head of the Near and Middle Eastern Section of the Foreign Office. Sidebotham notes: "At that time the official mind seemed to be leaning towards a policy that should substitute the Arab for the Turk as our friend." [41] Sidebotham urged as an alternative the reconstituting of the Jews as a large self-sufficing state extending over the whole of Palestine —"a modern state such as could ultimately, after a period of pupilage, form a self-sufficing State as a British Dominion, and not only become responsible for its own government and its own local defense but even, like other Dominions, tender voluntary help to the Empire in its trials." [42]

Throughout the lengthy memorandum the discussion concerned itself mainly with the arguments of political realism: with the basic thesis that the collapse of the Turkish policy made a new one necessary; that the defense of Egypt required advancing the line beyond the Suez Canal to form a bastion in front of the desert; that the only people capable of forming such a state were the Jews. In conclusion, however, having satisfied the claims of practicality, he urged the restoration of the Jews to Palestine as the necessary concomitant of the ideals for which the Allies were fighting:[43]

---

40. With him were associated his close friends, Simon Marks and Israel Sieff.
41. *Ibid.,* p. 33.
42. *Ibid.,* p. 38.
43. *Ibid.,* pp. 39–40.

We began this war on behalf of the conceptions of the international law and justice whose most conspicuous violation at that time was the invasion of neutral Belgium. Even if Belgium were all, there would still be among British people no regrets, no doubts. But great as the ideal of relieving Belgium from the invader may be, the ideal of restoring the Jewish State to Palestine is incomparably greater, as a new birth is a greater thing than a recovery from sickness . . . Before the magnitude of this war most ideals seem to shrink in size. But one ideal is the peer even of this war in magnitude and grandeur. It is the ideal of the restoration of the Jews to a country which, small and poor as it is, they made as famous as Greece and as great as Rome . . . Nor is there any achievement that would exhibit the contrast between English and German political ideals so favorably to us, and so eloquently vindicate our own, as the establishment of a Jewish State under the British Crown.

About the same time—winter of 1915 and spring of 1916—the War Cabinet appears to have come to a definite decision to support the idea of a restoration of the Jews to Palestine in some form. There is evidence that the government, wishing to have the backing of all ranks of Jewish public opinion, turned to a prominent British Jew of non-Zionist connections to ascertain what his attitude would be toward a declaration friendly to Zionism on the part of Great Britain.[44] His views, expressed in a memorandum written at the end of 1915, reflect the conceptions of the wealthy class of English Jewry who were generally opposed to Zionism. The author of the memorandum said that he was not a Zionist and regretted that a Jewish national movement had developed. But he recognized that Zionism had achieved great strength in consequence of the persecution of the Jews in Russia, and that the problem of Palestine would have to be dealt with, in any case, as part of the Turkish question. These facts could not be ignored and he admitted that "if one wishes to create a friendly attitude on the part of the Jews one must at the present time take full cognizance of the Zionist movement." In his recommendation of a policy, he suggested that the British Government, in making its declaration of sympathy with Zionist aspirations, should offer a promise that the Jews will be guaranteed the right of immigration and colonization, local self-government for the existing colonies,

---

44. D. Movshovich, "Behind the Scene with the Balfour Declaration" (in Yiddish), *Zukunft*, New York, Vol. XXII, 1937, pp. 391–397.

recognition of the Hebrew language as one of the languages of the country, and the right to establish a Jewish University. He declared further that although he recognized the difficulties in view of the existing agreement with France, according to which Palestine was to be part of Syria, "it would be imperative that the Zionists be made to understand that Palestine will be placed under the rule and protection of England."

It was evidently in line with such a conception that the Conjoint Foreign Committee (of the Board of Deputies of British Jews and the Anglo-Jewish Association), headed by Lucien Wolf, drew up a statement which they pressed on the Foreign Office.[45] In this statement, the "historic interest" of Palestine for the Jewish community is referred to, but the use of any terms which would give recognition to the national character of the Jewish people is studiously avoided. This formula, which was probably in the hands of the Foreign Office early in March, 1916, read as follows:[46]

In the event of Palestine coming within the spheres of influence of Great Britain and France at the close of the war, the Governments of those Powers will not fail to take account of the historic interest that country possesses for the Jewish community. The Jewish population will be secured in the enjoyment of civil and religious liberty, equal political rights with the rest of the population, reasonable facilities for immigration and colonization and such municipal privileges in the towns and colonies inhabited by them as may be shown to be necessary.

In the spring of 1916, the British Government began sounding out its Allies on the Zionist issue. On March 13th, Sir George Buchanan, the British Ambassador at Petrograd, sent an aide-memoire to Sazonov conveying to him the summary of a telegraphic communication received from Sir Edward Grey. The memorandum explains that while there are differences of opinion among the Jews on the question of Zionism, a numerous and influential section of Jewry in all countries would highly appreciate a proposal with reference to Palestine in the Jewish interest. Important political results might be achieved by utilizing this interest, and one of these results

45. Herbert Sidebotham, *op. cit.*, Vol. II, pp. 53–54.
46. Great Britain, Foreign Office, *Zionism Peace, Handbook*, No. 162, London, 1920, p. 39.

would be "the conversion to the side of the Allies of Jewish elements in the East, in the United States of America, and other places, whose present attitude toward the Allies is, to a considerable extent, hostile." As to the nature of the Jewish aspirations, the formula of the Conjoint Committee is quoted in the name of Lucien Wolf. The memorandum goes on to state that Sir Edward Grey has no objection to this or to any other formula and that:[47]

The only object of His Majesty's Government is to devise some agreement which will be sufficiently attractive to the majority of Jews to facilitate the conclusion of a transaction securing Jewish support. Having this consideration in view, it appears to His Majesty's Government that if the scheme provided for enabling the Jews, when their colonists in Palestine are sufficiently strong to be able to compete with the Arab population, to take in hand the administration of the internal affairs of this region (excluding Jerusalem and the Holy Places), then the agreement would be much more attractive for the majority of Jews. His Majesty's Government would not wish to express a preference for this or another solution of the question. However, it is informed that an international protectorate would meet with opposition on the part of influential Jewish circles.

The British proposal, indicating the possibility of the Jews taking a hand in the administration of the country, suggests more than is contained in the quoted Lucien Wolf formula, which confines itself to right of colonization, cultural and civic equality, and local self-government. Although Sir Edward Grey denied a preference for this or that solution, the reference to Jewish opposition against an international protectorate could be interpreted as a hint that Britain might herself wish to assume the protectorate. This construction is supported by the fact that while the Russians informed Great Britain that

---

47. Stein, *op. cit.*, p. 81. The source is in a collection of documents dealing with the partition of Asiatic Turkey, edited by E. A. Adamow. The original edition is in Russian and was published in Moscow in 1924. The document referred to will be found on pp. 161 ff. of the Russian edition. There is also a German edition, to which reference has already been made. Cf. above, p. 58, n. 4.

In summarizing the content of Grey's proposal, Hanna (*British Policy in Palestine*, p. 33) says "They [the Jews], in conjunction with the Arabs, might take over the administration . . ." This gives a rather different meaning from the present version which implies the ultimate predominance of the Jewish population. The translation quoted by Stein has been checked with the Russian original and found to be correct.

they would not object to a Jewish settlement of Palestine—so long as Russian religious interests in the Holy Land were safeguarded—it would appear that the French at this stage of the negotiations were dubious.[48] In any case, the Jewish claim to Palestine was a serious subject of negotiation among the Allies in the summer of 1916. "Zionism was now on the brink of being launched into the current. 'Before long politicians would be unable to brush it aside as the fantastic dream of a few idealists.' So wrote the first Lord Cromer in July 1916." [49]

Official Conversations and Proposals

In January 1916, a conference of Zionist leaders held in London appointed a Political Committee composed of the leading members of the World Zionist Organization,[50] and prominent British Zionists. The Committee outlined a course of action, independent of the Copenhagen bureau which was still, in a formal sense, the residuary legatee of the World Zionist Organization.[51] However, the English Committee worked in

48. Dugdale, op. cit., Vol. II, p. 227.
49. Ibid., pp. 227–228.
50. Joseph Cowen, outstanding English Zionist, was the chairman, and Paul Goodman, the historian and journalist, was the honorary secretary. Besides Weizmann and Sokolow, its leading members, it included Ahad Ha'am, Yehiel Tschlenow, Vladimir Jabotinsky, L. J. Greenberg, Herbert Bentwich and Boris Goldberg.
51. The Zionist leaders in the countries of the Entente naturally followed another line in the prosecution of their work. Thus Lichtheim and Jacobson, the members of the Executive who remained in Germany, continued their efforts to create a sympathetic attitude toward Zionism among the Central Powers. That they had a certain measure of success is evidenced by the fact that the governments of Germany and Austria expressed their sympathy with the objects of Zionism. Moreover, the intervention of the German Government contributed to the preservation of the *Yishuv*. That the Entente recognized the value of the Balfour Declaration as an important military move favoring the Allied cause appears from the fact that Germany entered into negotiations with Turkey in an effort to provide an alternative scheme that might win Zionist support. To this end, a German-Jewish society was formed, the Vereinigung Jüdischer Organizationen Deutschlands zur Wahrung der Rechte des Osten. At the instigation of the Germans the Grand Vizier Talaat in January 1918 made certain promises of legislation, "by means of which the justifiable wishes of the Jews in Palestine would be able to find their fulfillment." (Lloyd George, *The Truth about the Peace Treaties*, Vol. II, pp. 1140 ff.)
Lloyd George notes that the German General Staff "urged early in 1916 the advantages of promising restoration to Palestine under an arrangement to be made between Zionists and Turkey, backed by a German guarantee. The practical difficulties were considerable, the subject was

close cooperation with the American Provisional Committee, of which Louis D. Brandeis was the guiding spirit. British Zionism gained strength at this time also as a result of the formation of the British Palestine Committee, organized by Sidebotham in cooperation with Marks, Sieff and Sacher. This Committee published a weekly journal, *Palestine,* which reached liberal circles and had an important influence in developing sympathy for the Zionist cause in government circles.[52]

Weizmann was now connected with the Admiralty as a chemist. About this time, he placed at the disposal of the government an improved process for making cordite (a variety of smokeless powder). Lloyd George was Minister of Munitions and he greatly appreciated the service rendered. He suggested recommending Weizmann for some high honor, but the latter refused.[53] His good relations with the government strengthened his position among the Zionists and in 1917 he was elected

perhaps dangerous to German relations with Turkey; and the German Government acted cautiously." He observes that the Allies might have been forestalled in offering this supreme bid; and that in September 1917 the "German Government were making very serious efforts to capture the Zionist movement." (*Ibid.,* p. 1121.) Significantly, in the United States the pro-German sentiments cherished by Jews of German descent were buttressed by hints from official sources, e.g., Bernstorff, that a victory of the Central Powers, which included Turkey, would result in handing over Palestine to the Jews. (Stephen S. Wise, "The Balfour Declaration, Its Significance in the United States of America," in Paul Goodman, *The Jewish National Home,* John Dent and Sons, London, 1943, p. 41.)

52. Sidebotham, *op. cit.,* pp. 40–43.

53. The refusal to accept any reward for his discovery has given birth to the popular legend that the British granted the Balfour Declaration in return for his important chemical discovery. Lloyd George's account of the matter in *The Truth about the Peace Treaties* (Vol II, p. 1117) tends to confirm the story. J. M. N. Jeffries, the leading British protagonist for the Arabs, attempts to show in *Palestine: The Reality* (pp. 194 ff.) that Weizmann's discovery, while theoretically correct, was not extensively used in the army because of the scarcity of acetone and that, in any case, giving Palestine to the Jews for Weizmann's discovery was an outrageous price to pay. The line of argument is, of course, absurd. While Weizmann's discovery brought him closer to government officials, his chemical work did not play any part in winning the Balfour Declaration. Weizmann's leadership during this period was due to an unusual combination of qualities: his deep understanding of the Jewish problem, his knowledge of Western thought, his personal charm and quick, sensitive comprehension of ideas and situations. British interest in the Balfour Declaration, as indicated in this chapter, resulted from a carefully thought out policy with reference to the Middle East.

President of the English Zionist Federation. In January of that year, the political committee of the English Zionist Federation was dissolved and Weizmann and Sokolow were given full authority to speak in the name of British Zionism. In August, 1917, a London Bureau was set up as an organ of World Zionism, headed by Sokolow and Weizmann.

Returning to the story of the course of negotiations during the summer of 1916, we may note that, at first, the Zionists attempted to work together with the Conjoint Foreign Committee. But they soon learned that the attitude of the influential British Jews was less favorable to the Zionist idea than that of the British statesmen. On August 31, 1916, Lucien Wolf, writing to James de Rothschild, stated that the Committee could cooperate with the Zionists only on the assumption that the Jews constituted a religious community and only if the Zionists agreed not to place undue emphasis on Jewish nationalism or on political objectives. In a letter, dated October 11, 1916, Sokolow, on behalf of the Zionists, proposed that the Conjoint Committee should concentrate on obtaining equal rights for the Jews of Europe—a matter which was also of profound interest to Zionists—but to leave to the Zionists the negotiations with reference to Jewish resettlement of Palestine. Lucien Wolf refused to assume such an attitude of benevolent neutrality toward Zionism, arguing that a recognition of Jewish nationhood in Palestine would tend to weaken the Jewish position in the lands of the Diaspora. From this point on, the wealthy British Jews represented in the Conjoint Committee began to oppose the Zionists. But the leadership in the negotiations had now clearly passed into the hands of the Zionist Organization. This is evidenced by the fact that in October, 1916, Weizmann and Sokolow were given the privilege of sending an official Zionist cable, in code, through the Foreign Office channels.[54]

In the same month—October, 1916—the Zionists completed a carefully prepared draft of the Zionist proposals. This was entitled: "Outline of a Programme for a New Administration of Palestine and for a Jewish Resettlement of Palestine in accordance with the Aspirations of the Zionist Movement." [55]

---

54. Dugdale, *op. cit.*, Vol. II, p. 228.
55. *Reports of the Executive of the Zionist Organisation to the XIIth Zionist Congress*, I, *Political Report*, London, 1921, pp. 63 ff.

The program was submitted to the Foreign Office as the basis of negotiations. As the first official Zionist proposal and as the product of the thinking of the leaders of continental and British Zionism, the document is of particular significance.[56]

While there is no mention of a Jewish state in the proposal, quasi-governmental powers are to be granted to the Jewish chartered company for the purpose of developing the country. The program is based on the assumption that: "Palestine will come under the Suzerainty or the protection or within the sphere of influence of Great Britain or France or under the joint control of both governments." The "Suzerain," that is, the sovereign government, would have an exclusive control of foreign and international relations including military, naval and diplomatic affairs. With reference to the internal administration and development of the country the program is divided into two parts.

The first part which deals with *The Present Jewish Population of Palestine,* provides that the government should be based on the following principles:

1. Equality of civic rights for all inhabitants regardless of denomination, religion or nationality;
2. Equality of group rights, especially autonomy in educational and religious matters for every community;
3. Official recognition of the Jewish population of Palestine as a separate national unit, enjoying full equality in civic, political and community rights;
4. Proportionate representation for the Jewish population in legislative and executive bodies to be set up;
5. The recognition of Hebrew as a language equal and parallel to the Arabic language and any other language to be introduced by the sovereign government;
6. Protection of the smaller nationalities to prevent their being deprived by reason of their numerical inferiority of voice in the administration of government;
7. Autonomy in exclusively Jewish matters—educational, communal and religious, judicial, local self-government and local taxation, etc.

56. It was formulated largely by Sokolow and was the product of careful discussions. Participating in them, in addition to Weizmann, were Dr. Moses Gaster, Herbert Bentwich, as members of the Political Committee; also Ahad Ha'am and Boris Goldberg were frequently consulted. Herbert Samuel and the two Rothschilds (Lord Lionel Walter and James) agreed to the text.

The second part deals with *The Resettlement of Palestine by Jews from Other Lands*. The preamble states that "the Suzerain Government shall recognize the desirability of large scale immigration and resettlement of Jews in Palestine." It is urged that mass immigration is needed to alleviate the sufferings of Jews and as a means of the development of Palestine along modern lines. To make possible large immigration the program provides for the following:

1. A Charter for incorporation should be granted to a Jewish company for the colonization of Jewish Palestine.
2. This company would be recognized as representing the interests of the Jewish people in Palestine and should be authorized to act on their behalf.
3. The objects of the company should include: encouragement and aid for Jewish colonization in Palestine; promotion of undertakings of any kind, agricultural, commercial or industrial, for the development of Palestine; preservation of the Jewish settlements already in Palestine and furtherance of the establishment of new colonies.
4. The company should have *inter alia* the right of preemption of crown lands and of the acquisition of concessions; the right to improve, drain, irrigate and cultivate lands; the right to make and maintain harbors, roads and public utilities and systems of transportation of passengers and goods to Palestine.

The *Summary* recapitulates the program in six basic propositions:

1. The recognition of a separate Jewish nationality or national unit in Palestine.
2. The participation of the Jewish population of Palestine in local self-government insofar as it affects all the inhabitants without distinction.
3. The protection of the rights of minority nationalities.
4. Autonomy in exclusively Jewish matters, such as Jewish education, religious and communal organization.
5. The recognition and legalization of the existing Jewish institutions for the colonization of Palestine.
6. The establishment of a Jewish chartered company for the resettlement of Palestine by Jewish settlers.

When the Zionists submitted their program, they were not aware of the Sykes-Picot Agreement which had been completed about six months earlier, nor had the British Government informed Sykes of the negotiations with the Zionists at the time when he arranged an understanding with Picot. However, some time during the summer or fall of 1916, Sir Mark became aware of the British interest in the Zionist cause.[57] He quickly sensed the significance that a Jewish restoration to Palestine might have as a link between Europe and Asia and saw in the cooperation of the Arabs and the Jews the possibility of furthering the great renascence of the Middle East, in which he was deeply interested. When the Second Coalition Government was formed with Lloyd George as Prime Minister and Balfour as Foreign Secretary, at the end of 1916, Sykes was authorized to negotiate with the Zionist leaders, and after some preliminary talks between Weizmann and Sykes, a meeting was arranged at the home of Dr. Moses Gaster in London. This meeting, to which the leading British Zionists were invited, may be regarded as the first official discussion between the British Government and the Jews which led to His Majesty's Government undertaking the responsibility for Palestine. A record of this meeting, revealing the views of the Zionist leaders, has been preserved.[58]

Dr. Gaster opened the meeting with an exposition of the aims of Zionism; then proceeding to the question of administration, he expressed opposition to the idea of condominium or to international rule, insisting that the Zionist objectives could properly be realized only under British control. The Jewish community in Palestine should be organized under the status of a *millet*[59] in accordance with which it would be recognized as a national group with complete supervision over its religious and cultural affairs. The number of civil servants favorably inclined to Zionism should be large in order to insure the success of the enterprise. The Holy Places should be put under

---

57. S. Landman, "Balfour Declaration: Secret Facts Revealed," in *World Jewry*, London, February 20, 1935, pp. 6 ff., and March 1, 1935, pp. 6–9. N. M. Gelber, *Hazarat Balfour ve-Toledoteha* (The Balfour Declaration and Its History), Jerusalem, Zionist Organization, 1939, p. 57.

58. The summary given above is based upon Gelber (*op. cit.*, pp. 59–74) who had access to the Archives of the Zionist Organization in Jerusalem.

59. Non-Moslem communities in the Ottoman Empire could be organized in the form of the *millet*, a national-religious community, possessing delegated political power under its own ecclesiastical head. Cf. Werner J. Cahnman, "Religion and Nationality," *American Journal of Sociology*, Vol. XLIX, 1944, pp. 524–529.

British or Russian supervision. But he felt that Russia could not be granted any rule over the Jews of Palestine because of its record of persecution of the Jews.

Herbert Samuel agreed with the view expressed by Gaster and Rothschild that a condominium should be definitely avoided. Exception should be made, however, with reference to the Holy Places, which should be under international rule. He pointed out that since the creation of a Jewish nation in Palestine was being contemplated, it was necessary to define the concept "nation" to counteract the apprehensions of Western Jews who thought that the establishment of a Jewish regime in Palestine might lead to impugning their loyalty to the states in which they lived. The Jews of Palestine would receive the attributes of nationality in the full sense of the word, but this would not imply that the Jews living in England constituted a separate nationality. He also felt that the proposed charter company could not be granted an unlimited right to encourage Jewish immigration, without reference to the absorptive capacity of the country. For that reason it would be necessary to give the right of supervision over immigration to the sovereign power.

Sokolow emphasized that England had been regarded for generations as the nation most sympathetic to the Jews, and the Jews wanted England to be associated with the Jewish restoration to Palestine. He was sure that Russia would not be opposed to British rule. If Palestine were brought under the wing of England and a Jewish national entity created there, an eternal bond of friendship would be created between the Jews and England. Weizmann emphasized that the Jews were returning to Palestine for the purpose of recreating the Jewish nation and of remaining Jews in the complete sense and not to be turned into Arabs, Druzes or even Englishmen. The Power chosen to act as sovereign should not limit Jewish immigration in any manner. The Jews would be ready to agree to the supervision of immigration on the part of a Jewish authority but not on the part of the English or any other non-Jewish regime.

Harry Sacher made a clear distinction between the concept of statehood which involved the assumption of political obligations, and nationhood which signified a spiritual body, without political obligations. He expressed the view that the Jews of Palestine should constitute a Jewish state and be subject to its political responsibilities, while the Jews living in countries outside of Palestine should be considered members of the Jewish nationality, without political implication. He was opposed to condominium for he thought that such a regime might fragment Jewish unity and would make the creation of a Jewish nationality impossible. Palestine should be developed to the stage of self-governing dominion. He mentioned the fact that Brandeis as one of the advisers of Wilson supported the British protectorate and condominium.

James de Rothschild, like the others, opposed condominium, and strongly supported the idea of British control. The guardianship of the Holy Places, he thought, should remain under the French-Vatican control. This would silence the apprehensions of the French clericals. Mr. Joseph Cowen was certain that the British protectorate would be accepted not only by the English but also by the German Zionists. Mr. Herbert Bentwich expressed the opinion that the English Government had taken steps to overcome all difficulties and that the whole matter should be left in its hands. Toward the end of the presentation, Samuel spoke again, emphasizing the strategic argument and stressing the importance of British control over Palestine. At the same time he expressed appreciation of the English interest in the reconstitution of a Jewish Palestine because of the influence of the Bible.

Sir Mark Sykes, in reply, first assured his hearers that he was favorably disposed to the Zionist aspirations; that he understood the meaning of Jewish nationality and had no apprehensions on that side. But he wished to point out some of the major difficulties involved in the problem of a Jewish Palestine. He first referred to the position of Russia and conveyed the gist of conversations that he had had with Sazonov. The latter did not think that Palestine was large enough to absorb the Russian Jews, but agreed that the creation of a cultural center for the Jews would be valuable. In final analysis, Russia was not much concerned with Palestine from the political point of view, but wished to be reassured about the safety of the Holy Places; and she would insist on general guarantees for Russian pilgrims. More difficult, in his opinion, was the Arab problem. The Arab national movement, with its center in Syria, required delicate handling. The Arabs had already begun a struggle against Zionism, although he had succeeded in deterring them from action. The Arabs would possibly set up a claim for a united Syria and Palestine but "it would be possible to hold them in line if they would receive aid from the Jews in other matters." Italy would not constitute too serious an obstacle although she usually demanded everything that France demanded. The really serious obstacle would be encountered in the political program of the French. France was demanding all of Syria, including Palestine, and it was not difficult to see what national and clerical reasons drove her to this course. It would therefore be necessary to discuss the various questions with France openly and frankly. He strongly recommended that the Zionists get in touch with the French representative, Picot.

Then in the course of a presentation, which was frequently interrupted by questions, he proceeded to outline his conception of the program. The Jewish settlement should be organized under a chartered company, formed by the Zionists, under British protection. The chartered company would have the right of settlement in a part of Palestine, with certain enclaves under international control. The area under the control of the chartered company would be bounded on the north by a line running from Acco, eastward to the Jordan to the boundary of the Hauran. The southern boundary could be determined in agreement with the British government. International enclaves would include Jerusalem; the stretch of land west from Jerusalem to the Mediterranean Sea along the line of the Jaffa railroad; and the city of Jaffa, which was used by pilgrims from Russia.

The proposals aroused long discussions. The boundaries were considered inadequate since they left out large parts of Galilee already settled with Jewish colonies, and eliminated the Hauran, which would have lent itself to extensive Jewish immigration. Nor was the proposal of enclaves acceptable, since Jerusalem was considered a Jewish city and most of the Jewish colonies were situated along the Jaffa railroad. Samuel and Rothschild did not view with favor the suggestion that the Jews undertake the negotiations with France. They thought that Britain should establish its claim over Palestine directly. Dr. Gaster asked whether, failing to obtain British support for a Jewish Palestine, the Foreign Office would object to negotiations with the French on the part of the Zionists. Sykes assured him that there would be no objection. Sykes insisted that England had not given France any special privileges in Palestine and left the impression that the question of its disposition was still an open one. The trend of discussion gives the impression that the British were anxious to have the Zionists persuade the French of their opposition to a condominium and of their insistence on a British protectorate. Sykes reiterated his suggestion that the Zionists get in touch with the French. Despite the diffidence expressed by Herbert Samuel, the meeting followed Sykes' suggestion, and Sokolow was chosen for the purpose.[60]

At this meeting a summary of the Zionist proposals was made which include the following basic points:[61]

1. The right of the Jewish people over Palestine should receive international recognition.
2. The Jewish settlement in Palestine should be recognized as a nation in the juridical sense, with a large sphere of self-government, the right to use Hebrew, and the right to levy taxes.
3. A charter should be granted to a Jewish company with preferential right to acquire state and private lands, to obtain concessions on public works, to enjoy the right of free immigration and facilities for the naturalization of immigrants.
4. The whole area of historic Palestine should be united under one administration.
5. The Holy Places should enjoy the privileges of extra-territoriality.

Sokolow had a preliminary talk with Picot in Sykes' home on February 8th, the day after the meeting in Dr. Gaster's home. Sokolow emphasized the importance of a Jewish return to Palestine as a means of solving the Jewish problem, particularly of Eastern Europe. In answer to Picot's question as to the government which the Zionists favored as trustee, Sokolow

---

60. The view is advanced by Antonius that the major purpose of the meeting was to obtain a formal assurance from the Zionists that they were opposed to internationalization of the Holy Land even under an Anglo-French condominium, and that provided Great Britain would support them in their national aspirations, they would henceforth work for the establishment of a British protectorate in Palestine. (Antonius, *op. cit.*, p. 263.)

61. Gelber, *op. cit.*, p. 64.

answered candidly that with due recognition of France's great contributions to civilization, the Zionists would prefer to have Great Britain. Picot intimated that France would not easily give up its claim to Palestine, but, so far as he was concerned, he was ready to do everything in his power to have France recognize the Zionist purposes. The question of a charter to a Jewish company in Palestine to facilitate immigration and colonization was also raised. Picot expressed opposition to this also as an idea not familiar to the French. Picot raised the question of the relationship of the Jews to the Arabs and to the local Christian denominations and to the Holy Places. Sokolow expressed the view that no serious opposition would be encountered from the Arabs because they had never regarded Palestine as an important center, particularly in the light of the fact that an Arab dominion was to be set up for them elsewhere. As to the Holy Places, the Jews would not interfere in any degree whatsoever. A day or two later, Sokolow, Weizmann and Sykes met for a private talk and Sykes indicated that he was satisfied with the progress of the conversation with Picot.[62]

In March, Sokolow was sent to Paris to negotiate officially with the French government. He carried with him a six-point program generally referred to as the "Bases de l'accord." [63] The following is given as the official version used in the negotiations with France and later with Italy:[64]

62. Charles François Georges-Picot, "Les Origines de la Déclaration Balfour," in *Questions d'Israel*, Paris, 1939, p. 677; Gelber, *op. cit.*, pp. 71 ff.

63. An identical list of six points was included in an "Outline of Program for the Resettlement of Jews in Palestine" given to Ormsby-Gore as the Political Officer who accompanied the Zionist Mission to Palestine in February, 1918 (Medzini, *op. cit.*, p. 45); the "Bases de l'accord" also resembles in points 1 and 5 a "Scheme for a Jewish Resettlement of Palestine in Accordance with Jewish National Aspirations," which, it appears, was issued as propaganda material by the British War Office sometime during March or April, 1917. Jacob de Haas mentions such a document in several places: *Louis D. Brandeis*, pp. 89–90; *History of Palestine*, p. 484, and in his joint work with Stephen S. Wise, *The Great Betrayal*, pp. 32–33. Hanna, *op. cit.*, n. 82, pp. 174–175, states that he was unable to trace the document or the "War Aims Book" to which de Haas refers. Gelber, *op. cit.*, p. 65, refers to the same document and gives as reference a file in the Zionist Archives at Jerusalem.

64. Gelber, *op. cit.*, p. 65 and p. 276, n. 161.

1. *Recognition of Palestine as the Jewish National Home.*
2. *Regulations for Jewish Settlement in Palestine.* The Suzerain Government shall officially grant the Jewish population present and future in Palestine the status and right of a nationality. This population shall enjoy full national, political and civic rights.
3. *Immigration into Palestine.* The Suzerain Government shall grant full and free rights of immigration into Palestine to Jews of all countries.
4. *The Establishment of a Chartered Company.* The Suzerain Government shall grant a Charter to a Jewish Company for colonization and development of Palestine, the Company to have power to acquire and take over any concessions for works of a public nature which may have been or may hereafter be granted by the Suzerain Government and the rights of preemption of Crown Lands or other lands not held in private or religious ownership and such other powers and privileges as are usual in Charters or Statutes of similar colonizing bodies.
5. *Communal Autonomy.* The Jewish Community shall have the power to set up its own internal administration and prepare regulations for law and order. Full autonomy is to be enjoyed by the Jewish Community in all matters bearing upon their educational, religious or public life, as well as the right to levy a compulsory tax upon individuals of their nation for the purpose of the expenditures required for the above matters.
6. *Language.* The right to use the Hebrew language both in public and private affairs shall be recognized as the right of the Jewish Community that must not be infringed upon.

When he came to France in March, he first endeavored to make contact with French Jewry through the *Alliance Israélite Universelle*. Instead of giving him cooperation the *Alliance* launched a campaign of anti-Zionist propaganda. He was more successful in the negotiations with the French government. On March 22nd, he was received by the Ministry of Foreign Affairs, where he outlined the principles of the Zionist program in accordance with the "Bases de l'accord." Alexandre Ribot, the head of the Ministry, informed him that the French government was well disposed toward the Zionist plan and he was authorized to inform the Zionist Organization of Russia and America to this effect.[65] It is to be recalled that while the French government knew that the Zionists had expressed a preference for a British protectorate, formally speaking, the

---

65. Sokolow, *op. cit.*, Vol. II, p. 52; Gelber, *op. cit.*, p. 79.

question of the disposition of Palestine was regarded as open and a matter to be decided by the Allied Powers.

In April, Sokolow proceeded to Italy and despite a certain coolness on the part of some leading Italian Jews, he finally obtained an endorsement of the Zionist program from the Federation of Jewish Communities in Italy. In this he had the help of Angelo Sereni, President of the Jewish Community in Rome, and Luigi Luzzatti, the Minister of Finance, who was a Jew. On May 12th, Sokolow and Sereni were received by the Italian Prime Minister Boselli, who assured them of his full support.[66] While in Rome, Sokolow had conferences with the Cardinals, and especially with Gasparri, concerning the Holy Places. Through the good offices of G. H. Fitzmaurice, a British diplomat who was a devout Catholic, he was granted an interview with Pope Benedict XV. The Pope promised that the Vatican would not oppose Zionism so long as the Holy Places were fully safeguarded. From Italy he returned to Paris on May 28th, where he was received by Prime Minister Ribot and again he had a favorable interview. In a letter dated June 4, 1917, the French government gave written assurance of its favorable attitude, as follows:[67]

You were good enough to present the project to which you are devoting your efforts, which has for its object the development of Jewish colonization in Palestine. You consider that, circumstances permitting, and the independence of the Holy Places being safeguarded on the other hand, it would be a deed of justice and of reparation to assist, by the protection of the Allied Powers, in the renaissance of the Jewish nationality in that Land from which the people of *Israel* were exiled so many centuries ago.

The French Government, which entered this present war to defend a people wrongfully attacked, and which continues the struggle to assure the victory of right over might, can but feel sympathy for your cause, the triumph of which is bound up with that of the Allies.

While Sokolow was on the Continent, Weizmann was continuing negotiations with the British government. In March, he had an interview with Balfour who was the new Foreign Secretary. The British government's support of Weizmann was already assured and Balfour raised the problem of the

66. Gelber, *op. cit.*, p. 89.
67. Sokolow, *op. cit.*, Vol. II, p. 53.

difficulties arising out of the French and Italian claims. He suggested that "failing agreement with France, it might be best to aim for a joint Anglo-American Protectorate." [68] But Weizmann expressed his doubt of the validity of condominium on the ground that it would involve working under two masters having different conceptions of administration. He also expressed anxiety about the rumors of international administration of Palestine and of the division of Syria between Palestine and France, leaving the area of Galilee in the hands of the latter. The terms of the Sykes-Picot Agreement were evidently leaking out by this time and Balfour was still hesitant about Britain's sole control of Palestine. However, he seems to have been won over to the idea by Justice Brandeis whom he met when he proceeded the following month on a mission to the United States, after war had been declared against Germany. Brandeis assured Balfour that President Wilson was sympathetic both to the Zionist cause and to the idea of a British protectorate. He convinced Balfour that the United States would not participate since the prevalent opinion was opposed to entanglement in any foreign responsibilities. Some of the American Zionists favored the idea of American participation with Britain in the control of Palestine, but it is probable that the matter was settled in an interview held between Brandeis and Balfour on May 16, 1917.[69]

The British government must have made a definite decision to support the Zionist program before May 20th. On that day, Weizmann, at a special conference of the English Zionist Federation, announced: "I am entitled to state in this assembly that His Majesty's Government is ready to support our plans." However, he cautiously prepared those of his hearers who had been expecting the early establishment of a Jewish state against disappointment. He said:[70]

One reads constantly in the Press and one hears from our friends, both Jewish and non-Jewish, that it is the endeavor of the Zionist

68. Dugdale, *op. cit.*, Vol. II, p. 230.
69. Gelber, *op. cit.*, p. 135. Nevertheless, the idea of cooperation with the United States seems to have lingered in Balfour's mind for a short time longer. On June 13, he wrote in a Foreign Office Minute: "Personally I should prefer to associate the United States of America in the protectorate should we succeed in securing it." (Dugdale, *op. cit.*, Vol. II, p. 232.)
70. Sokolow, *op. cit.*, Vol. II, p. 56.

Movement immediately to create a Jewish State in Palestine. Our American friends went further than that, and they have even determined the form of this State, by advocating a Jewish Republic. While heartily welcoming all these demonstrations as a genuine manifestation of the Jewish national will, we cannot consider them as safe statesmanship. Strong as the Zionist Movement may be, full of enthusiasm as the Zionists may be, at the present time, it must be obvious to everybody who stands in the midst of the work of the Zionist Organization, and it must be admitted honestly and truly, that the conditions are not yet ripe for the setting up of a state *ad hoc*. States must be built up slowly, gradually, systematically and patiently. We, therefore, say that while a creation of a Jewish Commonwealth in Palestine is our final ideal—an ideal for which the whole of the Zionist Organization is working—the way to achieve it lies through a series of intermediary stages. And one of those intermediary stages which I hope is going to come about as a result of the war, is that the fair country of Palestine will be protected by such a mighty and a just Power as Great Britain. Under the wing of this Power, Jews will be able to develop, and to set up the administrative machinery which, while not interfering with the legitimate interests of the non-Jewish population, would enable us to carry out the Zionist scheme.

He proceeded to comment on the international aspects of the situation and brought to the attention of the meeting that Sokolow was absent because he was in France and Italy where he had received assurances and full sympathy of both governments. He pointed out that one of the important problems to be considered was the establishment of the Jewish national home and indicated that satisfactory relations had been established with the Vatican and the highest Catholic circles. In concluding, he turned the attention to the internal Jewish situation. He expressed disappointment at the lack of unity in the Jewish ranks. He said that it was "a matter of deep humiliation to every Jew that we cannot stand united in this great hour." He lamented the fact that "there still exists a small minority which disputes the very existence of the Jews as a nation." But he added that there need be no misgivings for "if it comes to a plebiscite and a test, there can be no doubt on which side the majority of Jews will be found." [71]

The test came soon enough, for only a few days later the Conjoint Foreign Committee published a statement on the Pales-

---
71. *Ibid.*, p. 57.

tine question in opposition to the Zionist program. It appeared in the form of a letter to *The Times* (written on May 17th and published on May 24th) signed by David L. Alexander as President of the Board of Deputies of British Jews and Claude G. Montefiore, President of the Anglo-Jewish Association. The Conjoint Foreign Committee stated that they had welcomed with deep satisfaction the prospect of a regeneration on Palestine soil worthy of the great memories of the Holy Land and promising to be a source of spiritual inspiration for the whole of Jewry. In the interest of a united effort, they had cooperated with the Zionists on the basis of this cultural policy, which had been adopted by previous Zionist Congresses. But now they found that they could no longer work together because the Zionists favored a much larger scheme of an essentially political character. Two points in the new Zionist policy seemed to the Committee to be open to grave objection, namely, first, that the Jewish settlement in Palestine should be recognized as having a national character in the political sense. In their view the Jews constituted a religious community only and could not therefore create in Palestine "a secular Jewish nationality recruited on some loose and obscure principle of race and ethnographic peculiarity." The second point in the Zionist program which aroused their misgivings, according to the authors of the letter, was the plan to invest a chartered company with certain exceptional political privileges and economic preferences. This, they felt, would be calamitous. It would contravene the principle of equal rights for all and endanger the position of the Jews in those countries where they were still struggling for equal rights, and make it more difficult to defend equality even in the countries where the Jews had already achieved it.[72]

A few days later, Dr. Weizmann published a brief reply. He denied the claim made by the Conjoint Committee that they had worked for Jewish regeneration of Palestine. He confined himself to making two points. First, the question of Jewish nationality was a question of fact not to be decided on by the convenience of individual Jews. "The fact that the Jews are a nationality is attested by the conviction of the overwhelming majority of Jews throughout all ages right to the present time, a conviction which has always been shared by non-Jews in all countries." In the second place, he stressed the fact that the Zionists were not demanding exclusive privileges in Palestine

---

72. Sokolow, *op. cit.*, Vol. II, pp. 58–61.

detrimental to the non-Jewish population. "It always was and remains a cardinal principle of Zionism as a democratic movement that all races and sects in Palestine should enjoy full justice and liberty, and Zionists are confident that the new Suzerain whom they hope Palestine will acquire as a result of the war will, in its administration of the country, be guided by the same principle."

Weizmann's stand was backed by public meetings all over the country. There were protests from some of the leading members of the Anglo-Jewish Association and the British Board of Deputies and from the institutions and synagogues which supported them. A vote of censure, proposed by Dr. Moses Gaster at a meeting of the Board of Deputies, passed by a small margin. A number of the officers of the Board of Deputies resigned. A new Conjoint Committee was formed and the question of Zionism was declared outside of its province. The response overwhelmingly demonstrated the Zionist sympathies of the great majority of British Jews. At the same time, however, anti-Zionist sentiment was crystallizing and some of the British leaders continued to work in opposition to the Zionist conception. As will be seen, the British government could hardly neglect the views of the wealthy anti-Zionist Jews, and their opinion ultimately led to a modification of the original formula of the Balfour Declaration.

THE BALFOUR DECLARATION—MOTIVATIONS AND MEANINGS

At the end of May, 1917, the British Government was definitely committed to the policy proposed by Weizmann— namely, a Jewish Palestine under British rule. After Balfour returned from the United States, negotiations between the Zionist leaders and the British Cabinet entered their final stage. Before the end of June, Weizmann and Lord Rothschild called at the Foreign Office and Balfour expressed his readiness to receive a draft of the Zionist proposals which might be put before the War Cabinet for its approval.

Drafts of the Declaration

The Political Committee of the Zionist Organization set to work to draft the formula. Many different texts were suggested by the members of the Committee and by British friends of Zionism.[73] Three main versions were thoroughly discussed at the meetings. The first proposal, considered on July 4th, was that of Dr. Ettinger. It laid emphasis on the National Home idea and was moderate in its formulation. It read as follows:[74]

His Majesty's Government, after considering that the Zionist aspirations are right and just, recognizes the right of the Jewish people to Palestine as its National Home, to be secured under the protection of the Sovereign Government that will rule Palestine in the future, following the victory of the Allied Powers.

The specific conditions for the realization of this plan shall be defined by negotiation with the representatives of the Zionist Organization. However, in any case, the constitution of Palestine as the Jewish National Home shall be based on the principles of internal autonomy; the recognition of Palestine as an independent country with boundaries that will be definitely fixed in advance; the granting of a charter to the Zionist Organization or to an institution duly created by this organization, for the development of Jewish colonization in Palestine.

A quite different version was discussed at the meeting of July 13. It was submitted in writing by Sidebotham. It made an unequivocal proposal for a Jewish state and contained the famous phrase that was to cause so much trouble later—that Palestine should ultimately become "as Jewish as England is English:" [75]

His Majesty's Government accepts as one of the chief aims of the war, the reconstitution of an integral Palestine as a Jewish State and as a National Home for the Jewish people. By a Jewish State is meant a state composed not only of Jews, but one whose dominant national character, after the realization of the hopes of its founders, shall be as Jewish as the dominant national character of England is English, of Canada, Canadian, and of Australia, Australian. Religious equality shall always be fundamental to the laws of this state.

His Majesty's Government also declares that it recognizes the Zionist Organization as the representative of the Jewish nation, and the Government agrees that as an instrument for the achievement of the aims mentioned in paragraph 1, a Charter Company shall be

73. Gelber, *op. cit.*, pp. 109–112, divides the proposals into six different types.
74. *Ibid.*, p. 294.
75. *Ibid.*, pp. 109–110. The version here given is not the original draft by Sidebotham, but a retranslation of Gelber's Hebrew rendition.

founded open to the Jews of the entire world. This Company shall facilitate immigration and assist in the economic development of the country. Except for matters relating to external defense and foreign relations, this Company shall appoint the Executive Government, but all its actions shall require the approval (right of veto) of the Suzerain Government or Governments of the country. After the work of this Company shall have been completed, it shall be liquidated and Palestine shall become an independent state.

It is necessary that the external defense and the foreign relations of Palestine shall be vested in a Suzerain Power or a group of Suzerain Powers either as Mandatory Administrations or as an International League having sovereign powers. The Administration shall assist the Charter Company in its stated aims and shall vest the Company with the required legal rights. After abolition of the Charter Company, the people of Palestine shall be heir to its political rights and functions.

The third formula, discussed at the meeting of July 17, was briefer and more general in character, as follows:[76]

The policy of His Majesty's Government with regard to the future of Palestine shall be guided by the principle that Palestine shall be set up as a National Home of the Jewish people.

His Majesty's Government shall consider with the Zionist Organization the methods and means for the reconstitution of Palestine as a National Home for the Jewish people as well as the grant of a charter with proper authority to the Zionist institutions.

The formula[77] chosen was a combination of the first and third drafts and did not mention the Jewish state. It was presented to the Foreign Office the next day, July 18, 1917, by Lord Rothschild as the official Zionist formula. It read as follows:[78]

H. M. Government, after considering the aims of the Zionist Organization, accepts the principle of recognizing Palestine as the National Home of the Jewish people, and the right of the Jewish people to build up its National Life in Palestine under a protection

---

76. Gelber gives two somewhat different versions, pp. 110 and 295.
77. The final formula was drafted after a thorough discussion in which Weizmann, Sokolow, Ahad Ha'am, Jacob E. Unger, Harry Sacher and James de Rothschild participated. The formula was shown to and approved by the following: Sir Mark Sykes, Baron Edmond de Rothschild and President Wilson. (Sidebotham, *op. cit.*, p. 59.)
78. *Reports of the Executive to the XIIth Zionist Congress*, I, p. 71 ff.

to be established at the conclusion of Peace, following upon the successful issue of the war.

H. M. Government regards as essential for the realization of this principle the grant of internal autonomy to the Jewish nationality in Palestine, freedom of immigration for Jews, and the establishment of a Jewish National Colonising Corporation for the re-settlement and economic development of the country.

The conditions and forms of the internal autonomy and a charter for the Jewish National Colonising Corporation should, in view of H. M. Government, be elaborated in detail and determined with the representatives of the Zionist Organization.

Of the members of the Cabinet besides Balfour, there were three others definitely in sympathy with the Zionist ideal: Lloyd George, Viscount Milner and Lord Robert Cecil. Lord Curzon's position was not so certain. He was ready to support cultural Zionism and some resettlement of Jews in Palestine, but he hesitated, he said, "to espouse a cause whose advocates had such different ideas of what they mean." He pointed out that whereas Sir Alfred Mond defined Zionism as the creation of "an autonomous Jewish State," Lord Rothschild postulated a much less definite political form: "a home where the Jews could speak their own language, have their own education, their own civilization, and religious institutions under the protection of Allied Governments." Lord Curzon, who appears to have been influenced by the outlook of the wealthy British Jews, was also dubious whether Jews would be willing to undergo the great physical hardships required for the upbuilding of Palestine. It appears, moreover, that he thought that Palestine did not have great possibilities for development. Under some European administration he was ready to secure to the Jews equal civil and religious rights and "arrange as far as possible for land purchase and settlement of returning Jews." [79]

The most strenuous objections in the Cabinet, however, were raised by Mr. Edwin Montagu, the Secretary of State for India. Montagu was one of the ablest Jews in England and a member of a distinguished family noted for its loyalty to Judaism. He recognized that the Jews were a religious community but he himself does not appear to have had a strong

---

79. For Lord Curzon's views, see David Lloyd George, *The Truth about the Peace Treaties*, Gollancz, London, 1938, Vol. II, pp. 1122–1132.

sense of attachment. He once wrote to Lord Morley: "I have been striving all my life to escape from the ghetto." He was apprehensive that if a Jewish national home were created in Palestine, the position of Jews elsewhere, in countries where equality of rights had already been attained, would be questioned. He urged this objection also against a modified draft prepared by Lord Milner, maintaining the point of view that the use of any phrase like "the home of the Jewish people" would be open to the same danger and might have a prejudicial effect on the status of Jewish Britons. Moreover, he thought that the creation of a national home would make it difficult, if not impossible, for a British Jew to exercise political authority on behalf of Great Britain. "How would he negotiate," he asked, "with the peoples of India on behalf of H. M. Government if the world had just been told that H. M. Government regarded his national home as being in Turkish territory?" [80]

As a result of the discussions in the Cabinet, the original draft was modified and a new draft was worked out by Lord Milner which was approved by the Foreign Office and the Prime Minister on September 19th. This formula was very brief and had two short clauses: "1) H. M. Government accepts the principle that Palestine should be reconstituted as the national home of the Jewish people; 2) H. M. Government will use its best endeavors to secure the achievement of the object and will discuss the necessary methods and means with the Zionist Organization." [81] The formula was submitted to President Wilson who approved the text, and the French and Italian Governments were informed.

However, in the meantime, the anti-Zionist forces among British Jewry exerted their influence and succeeded in getting the formula modified still further. The new version, forwarded to President Wilson on October 10th, read as follows:

The Cabinet after preliminary discussion suggest following amended formula: His Majesty's Government view with favor the establishment in Palestine of a National Home for the Jewish race and will use its best endeavors to facilitate the achievement of this object, it being clearly understood that nothing shall be done which may

80. Lloyd George, *op. cit.*, Vol. II, pp. 1132 ff.
81. Gelber, *op. cit.*, p. 295.

prejudice the civil and religious rights of existing non-Jewish communities in Palestine or the rights and political status enjoyed in any other country by such Jews who are fully contented with their existing nationality and citizenship.

The American Zionists, who were allowed to see the new formula, objected to the last clause—"the rights and political status enjoyed in any other country by such Jews who are fully contented with their existing nationality and citizenship." They pointed out that this based Zionism on a principle of discontent. They proposed that the final clause should read: "or the rights and political status enjoyed by Jews in any other country." They also asked that the word "people" be substituted for "race." On October 17th, President Wilson cabled his approval of the formula with the Zionist amendments.[82]

The amended draft was then sent by the Government to a number of leading Jews in England as well as to the Zionist Organization.[83] Sokolow and Weizmann accepted the draft on behalf of the Zionist Organization although they were much disappointed with the substitution of the clause, "establishment in Palestine of a national home for the Jewish people," for the original clause, "recognizing Palestine as the national home of the Jewish people." Moreover, they regarded the proviso: "not prejudicing the rights and political status enjoyed by Jews in any other country," as superfluous because self-evident. Dr. Hertz and Sir Stuart Samuel were in general agreement with the Zionist point of view. The other three persons who were consulted, Claude G. Montefiore, Sir Philip Magnus and Mr. Leonard H. Cohen, who represented the definitely non-Zionist view among British Jewry, raised objections particularly to the word "national." [84]

Lord Balfour presented the revised formula to the Cabinet

---

82. Jacob de Haas, *History of Palestine, The Last Two Thousand Years*, Macmillan, pp. 485 ff.; Gelber, *op. cit.*, pp. 136 ff., pp. 305 ff.

83. The following received copies: Sir Stuart M. Samuel, Chairman of the Jewish Board of Deputies; Mr. Leonard H. Cohen, Chairman of the Jewish Board of Guardians; Dr. Joseph H. Hertz, the Chief Rabbi of England; Mr. Claude G. Montefiore, and Sir Philip Magnus. The communication to the Zionist Organization was addressed to Mr. Nahum Sokolow, as chief representative in England of the International Zionist Organization, and Dr. Chaim Weizmann, as President of the English Zionist Federation.

84. *Reports of the Executive to the XIIth Zionist Congress*, I, p. 12 ff.

for a vote. He explained that the Zionist movement, though opposed by a number of wealthy Jews, had behind it the support of the majority, certainly in Russia and in America. He saw nothing inconsistent between the establishment of a Jewish national focus in Palestine and the complete assimilation and absorption of Jews into the nationality of other countries where they lived. Balfour read a sympathetic declaration from the French government which had been conveyed to the Zionists and he stated that President Wilson was extremely favorable to the movement. He pointed out that every member of the Cabinet now agreed that it was desirable that some declaration favorable to the aspirations of the Jewish people should be made. Such a declaration would be useful to the Allied cause both in Russia and America. "As to the meaning of the words 'national home,' to which the Zionists attach so much importance, he understood it to mean some form of British, American, or other protectorate, under which full facilities would be given to the Jews to work out their own salvation and to build up, by means of education, agriculture, and industry, a real centre of national culture and focus of national life. It did not necessarily involve the early establishment of an independent Jewish State, which was a matter for gradual development in accordance with the ordinary laws of political evolution." [85]

By this time, Lord Curzon had withdrawn his objections and the War Cabinet approved the formula which came to be known as the Balfour Declaration. On November 2nd, Balfour conveyed the decision of the Cabinet to Lord Rothschild in the form of a letter:

Foreign Office
November 2nd, 1917.

Dear Lord Rothschild,

I have much pleasure in conveying to you, on behalf of His Majesty's Government, the following declaration of sympathy with Jewish Zionist aspirations which has been submitted to, and approved by, the Cabinet.

"His Majesty's Government view with favour the establishment in Palestine of a national home for the Jewish people, and will use their best endeavours to facilitate the achievement of this object, it

---

85. This account of Balfour's presentation is taken from Lloyd George, *op. cit.*, pp. 1135 ff., the quoted matter being Lloyd George's understanding of Balfour's position.

being clearly understood that nothing shall be done which may prejudice the civil and religious rights of existing non-Jewish communities in Palestine, or the rights and political status enjoyed by Jews in any other country."

I should be grateful if you would bring this declaration to the knowledge of the Zionist Federation.

Yours sincerely,
ARTHUR JAMES BALFOUR.

Reactions and Interpretations

Among the great masses of the Jews of Eastern Europe or of Eastern European origin scattered throughout the world, that is, among Jews who had not broken with the historic, religious, national tradition of Israel, the Balfour Declaration was received as the announcement of the Redemption. In the synagogue services, in many public demonstrations, and in innumerable articles, one thought was dominant—that the era of Restoration for which Jews had hoped and prayed during two thousand years of dispersion was now at hand. Shortly after the Declaration, the Zionist Organization issued a Manifesto signed by Sokolow, Tschlenow and Weizmann, which declared that the aspirations which had found expression in the Basle program now found solid ground in the British Government's official Declaration of the 2nd of November, 1917.[86] "The period which then began was Expectation . . . the period which now begins is Fulfillment." The Manifesto called upon the Jewish people for unity in their own ranks; for cooperation with the British authorities; for ample means to support the endeavor on a large scale; for realism and discipline in every speech, thought and act. Its central thought was: "It all depends on you, the Jewish people, on you only."

In England, the Declaration was received with universal approval. Many articles appeared in the press heralding the Restoration of the Sons of Israel to the Promised Land. Some emphasized the moral and spiritual aspects of the Jewish return, conceiving it as an act of justice and as an exemplification of the idea of the rights of small nations for which the Allies were fighting the war. Others laid stress on the strategic importance of a Jewish State in close proximity to the Suez

---

86. Sokolow, *op. cit.*, Vol. II, pp. 124–127.

Canal and to Egypt, and drew attention to the part that the Jews might play in the economic development of Palestine and in the awakening of the Near East. At a great demonstration held in the London Opera House on December 2, 1917, leading British statesmen, Jewish leaders, and representatives of various governments and nationalities acclaimed the Declaration as a great historic event. The re-establishment of the Jews in their Homeland was regarded as one of the three great projects of liberation to which British policy was committed. As Lord Robert Cecil said in his speech at the demonstration: "Our wish is that Arabian countries shall be for the Arabs, Armenia for the Armenians, and Judea for the Jews." [87]

The group of wealthy British Jews who had fought so hard against the Declaration did not join in this general approval. Some weeks after the Declaration, a League of British Jews was formed in London with the object of counteracting the political implications of the Declaration. The major purpose of the League was to uphold the status of British subjects professing the Jewish religion. It proposed to facilitate settlement in Palestine of such Jews as might desire to make it their home, but at the same time, to resist any allegation that Jews constituted a separate political nationality. Some time later they took issue with the American Jewish Committee, which had published a favorable statement expressing its appreciation of Britain's promise to facilitate the establishment of a national home for the Jewish people in Palestine. Louis Marshall, the President and guiding spirit of the Committee, made it clear that while the American group did not support the idea of a Jewish State or Commonwealth, or that Palestine should be *the* Homeland of the Jewish people, they were ready to lend their aid to the establishment of *a* national home in Palestine.

In America, generally, as in England, favorable public interest was aroused by the Declaration. Here, too, many viewpoints were expressed with reference to its meaning. The usual interpretation was that the Declaration signified the ultimate establishment of a Jewish state, as is indicated by such expressions as: "Palestine to be set apart as a Jewish state under Allied protection"; "We shall see a Jewish republic founded in Palestine"; "The erection at no remote date of a

87. *Ibid.*, p. 101.

state, a Jewish state." [88] The following statement by Senator Charles L. McNary was typical of many others: [89]

The official pronouncements of our Allies in favor of the Zionist program mark a new epoch in the history of the Jews. These declarations give formal public recognition that Israel as a nation is still alive and will persist. This was necessary for the reason that some few people were skeptical as to the national entity of the Jews. All doubt as to this phase being totally dispelled now, it remains for those of the Jewish people who will settle in their old—but new—home, to make Palestine a veritable Jewish State as is looked for by their brethren all over.

Palestine is the connecting link between Europe and Asia. The Jews, originally hailing from Asia, but who have become Europeans in their Diaspora extending for two thousand years, may now also serve as a link between the people of these two great continents. It is, thus, a piece of good fortune that the Jews should become the governing people of Palestine. This, added to the fact that the Holy Land is their historic home, the land of their dreams and ambitions, makes the realization of Zionism at this time almost ideal. Europe may expect great results and much benefit from this promised State of Judea, and the Allied Governments will not be the losers in helping Israel in this accomplishment.

No objection to the Balfour Declaration was registered by the Arabs at the time of its announcement. There were two Arab speakers at the demonstration held at the London Opera House on December 2nd, and while the remarks were somewhat non-committal, sympathy with the Jewish cause was expressed along with the hope for Arab liberation. No comment was made by the Sharif of Mecca or his son, Faisal. The latter was in close touch with T. E. Lawrence in the campaign against the Turks in Trans-Jordan, and there can hardly be any question as to whether he knew about the Declaration. However, the Arab nationalists in Syria and Palestine may not have felt free at the time to express their views. That there was some apprehension of an unfavorable reaction from the Arab side

---

88. American Emergency Committee for Zionist Affairs, *The Balfour Declaration and American Interests in Palestine*, New York, 1941, pp. 8–10; for statements by members of the American War Congress on the Balfour Declaration and Zionism, see Zionist Organization of America, *The American War Congress and Zionism*, New York, 1919; American Zionist Emergency Council, *America and Palestine*, New York, 1944.

89. *The American War Congress and Zionism*, p. 60.

World War I and the Balfour Declaration

is evidenced in a speech made by Weizmann in Manchester, December 9, 1917, in the course of which he said:[90]

We all hope and believe that out of this welter of blood and destruction a better world will arise. If misunderstandings existed in the past between Arabs and Jews we have not created them; they have been created by those who were the masters of Palestine, by the deadening hand of the Turk, who can only rule over his Empire by playing off one part of the population against the other. All that, we hope, will disappear now. Is it not imperative, is it not logical, that we who have suffered so much from physical force should try and reconstitute in Palestine an age of justice and right for everybody? It is strange indeed to hear the fear expressed that the Jew in Palestine may become an aggressor, that the Jew who has always been the victim, the Jew who has always fought the battle of freedom for others, should suddenly become an aggressor because he touches Palestinian soil.

As to the meaning of the Balfour Declaration, the main point at issue has always been on the question whether it envisaged the foundation of a Jewish state in which the Jews would be the predominant element or merely contemplated setting up a home as a refuge for Jews oppressed in other lands and a cultural center for Judaism. Quotations might be culled from the press and the speeches at the time of the Declaration to illustrate the different meanings and shades of meaning. It is clear, however, that several of the members of the British War Cabinet had in mind the development of a Jewish state in due course, and that public opinion generally understood the Balfour Declaration in this sense.[91] Thus, Cyril P. Scott, the editor of the *Manchester Guardian,* wrote on November 10, 1917, when Lord Balfour's letter to Lord Rothschild was released: "What it means is that, assuming our military successes to be continued and the whole of Palestine brought securely

---

90. Jewish Agency for Palestine, *Memorandum Submitted to the Palestine Royal Commission*, London, 1936, pp. 89–90.
91. Vladimir Jabotinsky in evidence given before the Palestine Royal Commission in 1936 brought out the point that not enough attention had been paid to the introductory paragraph in the Balfour Declaration. In this preamble, the British Government declares its "sympathy with the Jewish Zionist aspirations." It was known at the time that "Jewish Zionist aspirations" were for the ultimate establishment of the Jewish State. (Palestine Royal Commission, *Minutes of Evidence*, 1936–1937, p. 371.)

under our control, then at the conclusion of peace our deliberate policy will be to encourage in every way in our power Jewish immigration, to give full security, and no doubt a large measure of local autonomy, to the Jewish immigrants, with a view to the ultimate establishment of a Jewish State." [92] Some characteristic utterances of leading British statesmen at the time are as follows:

In an address delivered at the Alexandra Theatre, Birmingham, on October 13, 1918, Mr. Neville Chamberlain remarked:

"If the new Jewish State which is to be established there is to be . . . associated with some great progressive people, such as those of the American Commonwealth or of the British Empire, then in such a case it seems to me that those fears which I have mentioned would be groundless, and that the existence of this new Jewish State would only add to the dignity and influence of Jews in other countries." (*Jewish Chronicle,* October 18, 1918.)

General Smuts, a member of the War Cabinet, told a meeting in Johannesburg on November 3, 1919:

"From those parts of the world where the Jews are oppressed and unhappy, where they are not welcomed by the rest of the Christian population, from those parts of the world you will yet see an ever-increasing stream of emigration towards Palestine; and in generations to come you will see a great Jewish State rising there once more." (*Zionist Bulletin,* December 10, 1919.)

Mr. Winston Churchill, then Secretary of State for War, wrote in the *Illustrated Sunday Herald,* February 8, 1920:

"If, as may well happen, there should be created in our own lifetime by the banks of the Jordan a Jewish State under the protection of the British Crown which might comprise three or four millions of Jews, an event will have occurred in the history of the world which would from every point of view be beneficial, and would be especially in harmony with the truest interests of the British Empire."

Lloyd George's summary of the situation is authoritative and in accord with the evidence:[93]

There has been a good deal of discussion as to the meaning of the words 'Jewish National Home' and whether it involved the setting

92. Quoted in a letter of James A. Malcolm to the editor of *The Spectator,* July 14, 1944, Vol. II, No. 455.
93. David Lloyd George, *op. cit.,* Vol. II, pp. 1138–1139. See also his statement to the Palestine Royal Commission, p. 24 of the *Report.*

up of a Jewish National State in Palestine. I have already quoted the words actually used by Mr. Balfour when he submitted the Declaration to the Cabinet for its approval. They were not challenged at the time by any member present, and there could be no doubt as to what the Cabinet then had in their minds. It was not their idea that a Jewish State should be set up immediately by the Peace Treaty without reference to the wishes of the majority of the inhabitants. On the other hand, it was contemplated that when the time arrived for according representative institutions to Palestine, if the Jews had meanwhile responded to the opportunity offered them by the idea of a National Home and had become a definite majority of the inhabitants, then Palestine would thus become a Jewish Commonwealth.

Paul L. Hanna, in his analysis of the wartime commitment to the Jews, expresses the following view:[94]

The Balfour Declaration was not precise in wording. Indeed, the conditions of compromise under which it was drafted rendered precision impossible. The Zionists themselves hesitated to ask for a Jewish state when they were in a minority and unable to protect themselves. Instead, they fell back upon the Basle program and spoke of a national home, a phrase which could mean much or little according to circumstances and the wish of the reader. Anti-Zionist opposition resulted in the declaration referring only to the *creation in* Palestine of *a* Jewish national home and not to the *reconstitution* of Palestine as *the* Jewish national home. Nevertheless, the Balfour Declaration, which was received with almost universal approval by the British press, was nearly everywhere accepted as a promise of a Jewish state to be created within some measurable future.[95]

94. Hanna, *op. cit.*, p. 37.
95. Professor Hanna's summary may be accepted as essentially correct. However, the sentence: "The Zionists themselves hesitated to ask for a Jewish state when they were in a minority and unable to protect themselves" suggests, perhaps, a somewhat wrong emphasis. The main issue was not the use of the term "Jewish National Home" vs. the term "Jewish State." It will be noted that Lloyd George used the terms "Jewish national home," "Jewish state" and "Jewish commonwealth" interchangeably. The real compromise made by the Zionists was the acceptance of the phrase "a national home in Palestine" instead of their original suggestion, "the reconstitution of Palestine as the Jewish national home." By the latter phrase the Zionists wished to indicate that the Jews had a "historical connection" with Palestine and that they were returning as of right; and furthermore, that this right applied to the whole of Palestine in its "historical boundaries." In their hesitancy to ask for "a Jewish state" the Zionists may have in part been motivated by expediency; but it should be remembered that Weizmann,

114   Palestine. Jewish, Arab, and British Policies

Summing up the matter, we may say that the Balfour Declaration was generally understood at the time it was issued as offering the Jews an opportunity of establishing a Jewish commonwealth in Palestine. Although its immediate establishment was not suggested, nor its ultimate development regarded as absolutely inevitable, the British statesmen and publicists who sponsored the idea desired and expected the development of a Jewish state in due course. If His Majesty's Government, as distinct from the individual statesmen who promoted the Balfour Declaration, made no absolute promise of a Jewish state, neither did they preclude it, as the Royal Commission has frankly conceded.[96] One eventuality to which the Zionists certainly did not look forward was remaining a minority in the country. Nor did anyone else. As Lloyd George has well said: "The notion that Jewish immigration would have to be artificially restricted in order to ensure that the Jews should be a permanent minority never entered into the heads of anyone engaged in framing the policy. That would have been regarded as unjust and as a fraud on the people to whom we were appealing." [97]

Great Britain's Motivations

Before concluding this chapter, a word may be said about the motives which impelled Great Britain to issue the Balfour Declaration. Here, too, there have been a great number of ex-

---

Sokolow and other leaders in the negotiations were strongly influenced by cultural and practical Zionism. While fully accepting the political aspect as an indispensable element of Zionism, they regarded the achievement of Jewish statehood as the culmination of a gradual process. Since this view was part of their own conception, they were not making any concession. Likewise, the term "national home" was, in any case, consonant with their general view. If anything, the idea of a Jewish state was more explicitly propounded by the non-Jewish British Zionists in whose plans the need of military strategy was an important element.

96. Great Britain, *Palestine Royal Commission Report*, London, 1937, p. 33. The Royal Commission, however, indicates that when Great Britain undertook to foster the development of a Jewish state, it was on the assumption that the Arabs would ultimately acquiesce to this. *Ibid.*, p. 42. This interpretation, however, is not tenable in the light of the facts. As M. Rappard, the vice-chairman of the Permanent Mandates Commission, pointed out in 1937: "When it was said that the success of the undertaking (i.e., the Jewish National Home) was based on the hypothesis of Arab consent, there was introduced an element that was entirely new and unforeseen and really absurd." (*Minutes of the Thirty-Second Session*, p. 32.)

97. David Lloyd George, *op. cit.*, Vol. II, p. 1139.

planations, most of which have been mentioned in the course of our discussion. The official explanations vary as widely as those given generally. Lord Curzon, who opposed the first formulation of the Declaration, stated in the House of Lords on June 29, 1920, that the chief reason was strategic.[98] Winston Churchill, in a statement to the House of Commons on July 4, 1922, declared that the motive for the Balfour Declaration was to obtain Jewish support both moral and financial all over the world, particularly in the United States and in Russia.[99] Ormsby-Gore (now Lord Harlech), connected with the Arab Bureau in Cairo and for a score of years concerned with the Jewish national home policy, declared in the House of Commons on July 21, 1937, that the outstanding motivation for the Declaration was the ideal of the restoration of the Jews to their ancient homeland.[100]

Lloyd George, who next to Balfour was the most consistent and determined exponent of the policy of the Declaration, has emphasized its propaganda value. As he wrote in his autobiography:[101] "The Zionist leaders gave us a definite promise that, if the Allies committed themselves to giving facilities for the establishment of a National Home for the Jews in Palestine, they would do their best to rally to the Allied cause Jewish sentiment and support throughout the world. They kept their word in the letter and the spirit . . ." Asquith has written, in connection with Herbert Samuel's proposal to the Cabinet in the early part of 1915:[102] "The only partisan of this proposal is Lloyd George, who I need not say does not care a damn for the Jews or their past or their future, but thinks it will be an outrage to let the Holy Places pass into the possession or under the protectorate of 'agnostic, atheistic France.'" A more kindly view is indicated by Mrs. Dugdale:[103] "Mr. Lloyd George's imagination was kindled, in the first place (Balfour always averred), because he knew his Bible." The truth is certainly near the second version. Lloyd George's interest

98. Great Britain, *Parliamentary Debates, Lords*, Vol. 40, col. 1028.
99. Great Britain, *Parliamentary Debates, Commons*, Vol. 156, col. 3289.
100. *Ibid.*, Vol. 326, col. 2237.
101. David Lloyd George, *op. cit.*, p. 1139.
102. Herbert Henry Asquith, *Memories and Reflections*, London, 1923, Vol. II, p. 78. Asquith's bitter memories of his defeat at the hands of Lloyd George may have colored his recollections.
103. Dugdale, *op. cit.*, Vol. II, p. 223.

in Zionism goes back, as does Balfour's, to the days of the Uganda project when, as a young man, he was asked to make a draft of the proposed Jewish settlement under Britain's protection.[104]

As for Balfour himself, he was without question profoundly moved by the ideal of a Jewish restoration. At times he frankly defended the Jewish national home policy on the grounds of its strategic and propaganda values to Great Britain. But practical motivations are not necessarily inconsistent with idealistic impulses. He had, as noted at the beginning of this chapter, a deep appreciation of the significance of Jewish history and thought. He was sensitive also to the "ancient stain upon our own civilization" [105] due to the persecution of Jews by Christendom, and as a recompense he wished to "give a chance, without injury to others, to this race of showing whether it can organize a culture in a Home where it will be secured from oppression." [106] As a Scotsman, moreover, he understood the possibility of "combining strong separate racial consciousness with a wider loyalty." [107] He was alive to the stabilizing forces in national traditions and saw in the Jewish heritage a conservative civilizing force. As his biographer says: "He had discerned a determination behind the Zionist ideology which appealed to him as a philosopher, and impressed him as a student of history. He became convinced that the revival of the sentiment of Jewish unity was no less worthy of respect than other national movements of the modern world, which were better understood because they sprang from geographically united peoples." [108]

In his defense of his policy in the House of Lords on the occasion of the debate as to whether Great Britain should

104. Emanuel Neumann, *The Birth of Jewish Statesmanship*, Scopus Publishing Co., New York, 1940, p. 44.
105. Great Britain, *Parliamentary Debates, Lords*, Vol. 50, No. 47, col. 1018, June 21, 1922.
106. *Ibid.* As a boy he was surrounded by Adventist influences. His mother, Lady Blanche Balfour, sister of Lord Salisbury, embodied in her person the tradition of Victorian piety. She chose for their county seat at Whittinghame a parish minister inspired by the evangelical doctrine. In his boyhood Balfour frequently heard such fervent Adventist messages as "The Jew must first return to Zion and then will come the final consummation." Cf. Norman MacLean, *His Terrible Swift Sword*, Victor Gollancz, London, 1942, pp. 30 ff.
107. Dugdale, *op. cit.*, Vol. II, p. 214.
108. *Ibid.*, p. 216.

accept the Mandate, he expressed his deep conviction of the significance of the re-establishment of the Jewish national home in the following memorable words:[109]

I do not deny that this is an adventure. Are we never to have adventures? Are we never to try new experiments? I hope your Lordships will never sink to that unimaginative depth, and that experiment and adventure will be justified if there is any case or cause for their justification. Surely, it is in order that we may send a message to every land where the Jewish race has been scattered, a message which will tell them that Christendom is not oblivious of their faith, is not unmindful of the service they have rendered to the great religions of the world, and most of all, to the religion that the majority of your Lordships' House profess, and that we desire to the best of our ability to give them that opportunity of developing, in peace and quietness under British rule, those great gifts which hitherto they have been compelled from the very nature of the case only to bring to fruition in countries which know not their language and belong not to their race? That is the ideal which I desire to see accomplished, that is the aim which lay at the root of the policy I am trying to defend; and, though it be defensible indeed on every ground, that is the ground which chiefly moves me.

All the reasons given and all the motivations mentioned in the various accounts undoubtedly entered into the British decision. But the reasons used at any particular time or the motivations of this or that individual do not give the key-explanation of what finally actuated Great Britain as a government to make the Declaration. The essential reason, accounts agree, was strategic and had to do with the need of strengthening Great Britain's lifeline to the East. More specifically, the Balfour Declaration helped Great Britain win the paramount position from the French.[110] Before the war, Palestine was recognized in the European Foreign Offices as a sphere of French influence. But the British soon came to the conclusion that it would be better from the point of view of defense of

---

109. Great Britain, *Parliamentary Debates, Lords,* Vol. 50, n. 47, cols. 1018–1019, June 21, 1922.
110. Hanna comes to a similar conclusion, although he may not give the same emphasis. He says: "It was evident . . . that an Allied declaration in support of Zionism would strengthen the British position when the time came to establish an administration for the Sykes-Picot Brown zone, and would make it easier to oppose French desires for a paramount position in Palestine" (*op. cit.,* p. 37).

the Nile not to have a rival imperialist state adjoining. To include Palestine in the scheme of Arab independence under British guidance was not practical at that time because of the French opposition. The first step, therefore, was to put it under the international control of the Allied Powers and this was done through the Sykes-Picot Treaty. But as time passed, some British statesmen saw the chance of establishing a British protectorate over Palestine. It seemed probable that a British army would conquer Palestine, and this would give a material basis for their claim. British backing of the Jewish aspiration for a national home in Palestine added moral weight to this claim. Through the Balfour Declaration Great Britain ultimately strengthened and extended her position in the whole Near East.

CHAPTER III

THE PEACE CONFERENCE AND THE MANDATE FOR PALESTINE

THE fate of Palestine was the subject of lengthy negotiations at the Peace Conference. It was linked with the problem of the partition of the Ottoman Empire and the final clauses of the Turkish Treaty were not decided until April 26, 1920, at the San Remo Conference. One day earlier the Supreme Council allocated the control of Palestine to Great Britain, under the newly devised system of Mandates, provided for in Article 22 of the Covenant of the League of Nations. The Mandate was assigned to Great Britain with the proviso that the Mandatory Power should be responsible for giving effect to the Balfour Declaration.

In the period of two and a half years between the Balfour Declaration and the San Remo decision much happened to complicate the Palestine problem. The Syrian Arab nationalists came out in unmitigated opposition to the Balfour Declaration, demanding inclusion of Palestine in a united, independent Syria. The Zionist question was not, however, the main one in complicating the issue. With the cessation of hostilities, the enforced harmony between France and Great Britain gave way to an intense rivalry for control of the Near East. Imperialistic motivations came into sharp conflict with the slogans of "self-determination" and "rights of small nations" which had been liberally employed during the war. The arrangements made in Syria and Iraq under Allied occupation did not satisfy the Arab demand for independence and the disappointment made Arab nationalism more intransigent; the bitterness engendered spread to Palestine with reference to which, it appears, the Arabs were at first prepared to compromise. Internal rivalries among the Christian Churches for the control of the Holy Places were aggravated with the removal of the common enemy of Moslem rule, and the religious dissensions were complicated by political considerations. The question of Palestine, which, in the early stages of the war had occupied a secondary place, became one of the major issues during the peace negotiations. Events in the Near East and in Palestine contributed to the difficulties.

EVENTS IN THE NEAR EAST

Temporary Allied Administration

The conquest of the Near East was achieved by two British Armies: the Mesopotamian Expeditionary Force operating from Iraq; and the Egyptian Expeditionary Force working its way across Sinai from Egypt. In the Egyptian Expeditionary Force—which conquered Palestine—there were some French and Italian troops taken along to demonstrate the joint character of the campaign. In April, 1917, also, an Anglo-French political mission under Sykes and Picot was attached to the military forces. The occupied territories, in accordance with international usage, were to be governed by Turkish law following the principle of administering such territories on the basis of the status quo. However, as the Turks retreated from Palestine and Syria they removed the governmental records and took along many of the local officials. It was therefore imperative to create some sort of civil administration, particularly since the campaign had left the land devastated. After the conquest of Palestine, the French indicated that they wished to have a condominium of Anglo-French control, but the British placed it under a purely British administration. Later, in August, 1918, after the conquest of Syria, the British made an effort to satisfy the claims of the French and at the same time to meet their obligations to the Arabs. In agreement with the French, the administration of Occupied Enemy Territory (O.E.T.) was divided into three zones: a South zone under English administration—Palestine north to Acre and east to the Jordan; a North zone under the Commander of the French detachment—the coastal area of Syria; an East zone under Faisal with Arab officers—Trans-Jordan and interior Syria. Iraq stood outside of these arrangements and remained under British control.

This arrangement was in general accord with the Sykes-Picot Agreement, if we consider the British in Palestine as acting temporarily for an international regime. Moreover, provided a fair and reasonable interpretation were given to the clauses concerning the degree of Arab independence in Syria and Iraq, the arrangement was not contradictory to the McMahon pledge. During the first period after the conquest, British troops supplied the main military forces for the whole area and General Headquarters in Egypt, under Allenby, exercised supervision over the French and Arab as well as over the British officials. In accordance with an Anglo-French Military Convention, signed September 15, 1919, O.E.T. West [1] was handed over to exclusive French control. The British took over the administration of O.E.T. South and withdrew to Palestine on a line approximating the Sykes-Picot division. In O.E.T. East (i.e., the Arab zone), the Arab administration at Damascus continued to function. This area included the A and B zones of the Sykes-Picot Agreement, in which the Arabs were to have independence under guidance. Accordingly, the arrangement was that the French should provide supervision in the A zone and the British in the B zone.

Arab Restiveness in the Levant

The Arab nationalists grew restive as they saw the British and French entrenching themselves. Even before the end of the war, feeling grew tense and in order to calm the Arab apprehensions and to make a show of a united front among the Allies, a joint Anglo-French declaration was made on November 7, 1918. It was couched in general terms and stated that the object aimed at by Great Britain and France in prosecuting the war in the East was "the complete and definite emancipation of the peoples so long oppressed by the Turks and the establishment of national Governments and Administrations deriving their authority from the initiative and free choice of the indigenous population." [2] This broadly worded declaration was distributed by the military authorities throughout the Levant, in Iraq, Syria and Palestine. Its publication made a difficult situation more difficult. Coming on the

---

1. O.E.T. North, the original French zone of administration, was renamed O.E.T. West, after the occupation of Cilicia in Asia Minor by the French in January, 1919.
2. The Royal Institute of International Affairs, *Great Britain and Palestine, 1915–1939*, p. 118. For the full text of the Declaration, see below, Chap. IV, pp. 197–198.

heels of the announcement of President Wilson's Fourteen Points[3] and taken together with the "Declaration to the Seven," [4] made earlier in June to a group of Arab leaders from Syria resident in Cairo, the Anglo-French Declaration was interpreted by the Arabs as a promise of independence throughout the whole Arab-speaking area in the Near East.

Even in Iraq, where the situation was regarded as satisfactory, the Anglo-French Declaration stirred things up and resulted in general uncertainty. Those desirous of Turkish rule saw in the announcement evidences of Allied weakness and were led to hope for a resumption of office under a re-established Turkish regime. Others went to the opposite extreme and took the Declaration as promising a completely independent government in Iraq without the benefit of any Allied "counsel." Speculation as to who would be the ruler of the Iraqi state became rife. The supporters of the aspirations of the Sharif of Mecca divided from those who wanted a local leader. The traditional animosities between the tribesmen and the settled population were aroused and the dissension between the Shiite and the Sunnite sects was sharpened. The Christians, comprising a small body of the population, became apprehensive at the growing truculence of the Moslems; and the Jewish community, comprising more than one-third of the population of Bagdad, expressed their desire to become British subjects if an Arab government was to be set up.[5]

To make matters worse, the type of British administration in Iraq, instituted in the early period, comported ill with the promise of a large measure of local autonomy to the Arabs. The Executive authority was placed in the hands of military governors and civil matters came under the direction of the government of India and the India Office. Indian currency was introduced and numerous officials provided from the Indian Service.[6] These measures were defended as necessary for practical reasons—the deficiency of local currency and the

---

3. Wilson had made his declaration in the Senate on January 8, 1918, but it was not known in Iraq until October, 1918, when notice of it appeared in Reuter's dispatches.

4. See below, Chap. IV, p. 198.

5. Gertrude Bell, *Review of the Civil Administration of Mesopotamia*, Cmd. 1069, 1920, pp. 126–127.

6. John de Vere Loder, *The Truth about Mesopotamia, Palestine and Syria*, p. 36.

lack of trained local personnel. But the Arabs, nevertheless, resented such measures as indicative of an attempt to introduce foreign domination. Propaganda was organized in Damascus, where Faisal evidently could not control the extreme nationalist element. It was particularly difficult to maintain peace in the border areas between interior Syria and Iraq. During 1919, while the Peace Conference was sitting, unrest assumed serious proportions in the Sanjak of Deir-ez-Zor, a frontier territory whose status was disputed. In December, Deir-ez-Zor was attacked by tribesmen and the life of the British political officer was threatened. An Arab agent arrived from Aleppo and demanded the withdrawal of all British influence, in the name of the local population.

The British attempted to satisfy the Arab feeling by giving greater recognition to local institutions and by introducing as many natives as possible into the work of administration. But this did not satisfy, and in March, 1920, when the Syrian Congress proclaimed an independent Arab state in Syria and crowned Faisal as king, a body in Mesopotamia, claiming to represent public opinion, pronounced itself in favor of a similar regime in Iraq and offered the crown to Faisal's brother, the Emir Abdullah. No effect could be given to this decision; for one thing Abdullah could not have accepted the crown without British consent. But the occasion gave concrete expression to the national sentiment. In July, 1920, an insurrection broke out which the British did not succeed in putting down until December, 1920. Peace was not restored until June, 1921, when a local government was established under the British Mandate with Faisal—who had in the meantime been ejected from Syria—as the king.[7]

7. The British decided on Faisal as king of Iraq at the Cairo Conference in March, 1921, and, by one of those miracles for which Egypt is famous, this decision happened to coincide with the majority will of the Iraqis. But miracles—the human variety at any rate—require very careful planning, as the authoritative work of Philip W. Ireland, *Iraq, A Study in Political Development*, shows (pp. 311 ff.). The "magic" used included a carefully arranged schedule of propaganda and political maneuvering: e.g., the suspension of the provisional Arab government, and the deportation of the Minister of the Interior, Said Talib Pasha, who was the strongest local candidate. Gertrude Bell, the very able Oriental Secretary to the Government, and a strong supporter of Emir Faisal, played the leading role in organizing public opinion in his behalf. The failure of the Iraqis to agree early enough on a local candidate gave Faisal and the British their opportunity. There was no election but only

In Syria the situation was much worse. The prospect of a French mandate provoked the Arabs to intransigence. There was mutual suspicion between the British and the French, both believing that each was arousing the Arabs against the other. Although in accordance with the McMahon-Husain understanding, coastal Syria was to have been excluded from the area of complete Arab independence, the extremists among the Arab nationalists never gave up their determination to create a state which would include all the territory originally demanded in the Damascus Protocol.[8] The French had difficulty in keeping order; the administrative staff was inadequate and there was no military force at hand. The garrisons were drawn to a large extent from Armenian battalions, which had been hastily recruited in Damascus after the armistice. These troops, only partially trained and poorly disciplined, could not resist the temptation to pay off old scores against the Moslems and their behavior did not add to the popularity of the French administration. On the borders between the French and Arab zones disorder was frequent, neither the French nor the Arabs being strong enough to control the situation. The Arab administration at Damascus, which was under the Emir Faisal, was headed by Ali Riza Pasha. He was president of the "Nadi el Arab," a nationalist society extreme in its demand for Arab independence and frank in its anti-French views. "In spite of orders prohibiting political activities, Arab propaganda was not checked. Inflammatory pamphlets circulated freely. Arms from depots surrendered by the Turks were openly sold to the civil population. Brigandage, in which irregular Arab levies participated, assumed large proportions. Raids, directed par-

---

a carefully organized referendum which, according to the High Commissioner's report, indicated that 96% of the Iraqis were in favor of the Emir Faisal. Concerning this referendum Ireland writes: "The referendum, as it was carried out, was hardly a gauge of spontaneous popular support for Emir Faisal, as official Reports would suggest, nor was it entirely the 'hasty pretence' assumed by some popular writers." Apart from the lip service to democracy, the choice was in itself a good one as Faisal's later career proved. Faisal was officially proclaimed king of Iraq on August 3, 1921. Great Britain recognized the kingdom by treaty on October 10, 1922, when it assumed the Mandate on behalf of the League of Nations. In 1930, the Mandate was abolished and Iraq was admitted to membership in the League of Nations as a sovereign state on October 3, 1932.

8. See Chap. II, p. 66.

ticularly against Christian villages on the Lebanon border, were frequent." [9]

The political restiveness was intensified when the King-Crane Commission came to Palestine and Syria in the summer of 1919 for the purpose of making a survey on the spot to determine whom the inhabitants wanted as Mandatory. A strong outburst of Arab national sentiment accompanied the presence of the Commission in Palestine and Syria during June and July. As Loder writes about the activities of the King-Crane Commission in the Middle East generally: "Attention was diverted for the moment from incitation to acts of mutual hostility to efforts to create a good impression, and the various sections of the community devoted themselves during the four months of the Commission's visit to a course of unlimited intrigue." [10] A Syrian Congress, claiming to speak for all the Arabs of Syria, Palestine and the Lebanon, assembled at Damascus on July 2nd. They adopted, for presentation to the American Commission, a program of "complete political independence" for a united Syria, including Palestine. The Congress protested against the mandatory status which the Peace Conference had prescribed for Syria but, failing absolute independence, a willingness was expressed to accept American or British guidance. On Palestine its statement was uncompromising: [11]

We oppose the pretentions of Zionists to create a Jewish commonwealth in the southern part of Syria, known as Palestine, and oppose Zionist migration to any part of our country; for we do not acknowledge their title but consider them a grave peril to our people from the national, economical, and political points of view. Our Jewish compatriots shall enjoy our common rights and assume the common responsibilities.

Emir Faisal was in Europe during most of the year 1919 in connection with the Peace Conference. When he returned to Syria in the middle of January, 1920, he found his personal authority weakened because of the moderate policy which he had been following. Faisal sympathized with the aspirations

9. Loder, *op. cit.*, p. 51.
10. *Ibid.*, pp. 64–65.
11. Hanna, *op. cit.*, p. 43.

of the nationalists, particularly since they were willing to recognize the leadership of the Sharif and his family. But he knew that he needed the help of the British for the proposed Arab State, and that the British would not support him to the extent of embarrassing Anglo-French relations. He was therefore willing to compromise on the range of his authority and the degree of independence. But this policy of moderation was unsatisfactory to his Syrian supporters. An assembly of notables, tribal chieftains, and leaders of religious communities was called together at Damascus in early March. This so-called "Syrian Congress" claimed to represent all of Syria, including Palestine and the Lebanon. On March 11th, they proclaimed Faisal the King of United Syria, and Faisal accepted. In April, the Peace Conference assigned the Mandate for Syria to France, but in May the newly formed Damascus government rejected the Mandate on the grounds that it was opposed by the great majority of the population.

Faisal's reign as King of Syria was short-lived. Some months before, in November, 1919, the French had sent out to Syria the able and resolute General Gouraud as High Commissioner and Commander-in-Chief. On July 14, 1920, Gouraud presented Faisal with an ultimatum which included: a) acceptance of the French Mandate; b) abolition of conscription which the Arabs had introduced; c) adoption of the Syrian currency in the eastern zone; d) French right of absolute disposal of the railway from Rayak to Aleppo which involved control of traffic in both the Syrian and Arab zones.[12]

The "Syrian Congress" was for opposing the French by force and the national die-hards began stirring the Arab population to rebellion. Faisal, realizing that resistance would be useless, played for time. He asked for an extension of twenty-four hours to reply, and then renewed the request for another twenty-four hours. He finally handed in his acceptance five hours before the expiration of the ultimatum but it appears that his message was delayed and the French forces began to advance on Damascus. Some resistance was offered by the Arab troops, but on July 25th the French entered Damascus and Faisal had to leave.[13]

12. Loder, *op. cit.*, pp. 77–78.
13. It has been claimed that the French were cognizant of Faisal's message but decided to expel him in any case.

The Military Administration in Palestine

The Arab restiveness in Iraq and Syria had its reflex in Palestine. Here, the dissatisfaction of the Arabs was deflected onto the Jews. The attitude of the Military Administrators was, on the whole, either hostile or unsympathetic to the Zionist aspirations. There were, it is true, conflicting pressures which made their task difficult: strictly according to the law, they were supposed to maintain the status quo, but this was impossible under the circumstances. The Jews expected the administration to live up to the Balfour Declaration; the Arabs could point to the Anglo-French Declaration of a year later which, while not mentioning Palestine, might be taken as implying general Arab independence. The personnel of the military administration had been hastily drawn from the army and from Egyptian civil service, and the officials were better acquainted with the Arab character, and as a whole more sympathetic to the Arab interests. To the military and to the colonial officials, the Jews often appeared as tactless, aggressive and demanding, and as lacking in consideration for the difficulties of administering the country under war conditions. The Jews often regarded the officials of the administration as reactionaries, and as anti-Semites, and refused to accord them that recognition of superiority which the colonial administrators expected from native populations.

There can be little doubt of the fact that many of the British administrators of the period of the occupation had no sympathy for the policy of the Jewish national home, and did as little to carry it out as was consistent with their instructions from the Foreign Office. General Allenby, while always correct in his utterances, is by some supposed to have been of the opinion that the British Government had made a mistake in issuing the Balfour Declaration and that it would have served the British interests better if the Arabs had been supported in their demand for a united Syria under British guidance.[14] A highly placed military officer has been frequently quoted to the effect that it would require a standing British army of no less

---

14. Charles Breasted, *Pioneer to the Past*, Scribners, 1943, pp. 247 ff.; p. 312.

than 50,000 men to carry through the Zionist program in the face of Arab opposition.[15]

The versatile Ronald Storrs, suave and brilliant, has always been an equivocal figure; dubious of the wisdom of Zionism and filled with the dislike of the conservative romanticist for the socialist ideas of the Jewish pioneers. Storrs, who later earned the reputation of being Sir Herbert Samuel's "evil genius," [16] brought to Palestine Mr. Ernest T. Richmond, who had been architect to the *Waqf* in Egypt. Richmond was an out-and-out opponent of Zionism and subsequently became associated with Haj Amin al-Husaini, the Mufti of Jerusalem, in his opposition to the Balfour policy and the Mandate.[17]

The Administration seems to have been dominated by men who believed that the British should not divide control of the Middle East with the French, that unified British rule could better be achieved through supporting the Arab movement, and that British power would ultimately be weakened by promoting Zionism. Hanna's summary is apropos: ". . . some officials cannot have failed to hope that events, if left to themselves, would present the world with a *fait accompli* in which both France and the Zionists would disappear from a Near East where British dominance would be assured." [18]

His Majesty's Government in London, however, did whatever they could to strengthen the Zionist position. Early in 1918, soon after the conquest of Palestine, the Zionists were permitted to send a Commission to Palestine. Its purpose was to assist in the rehabilitation of the *Yishuv*, to act as liaison officers between the government and the Jewish community, and to lay the foundation for the establishment of the Jewish National Home. At this time no decision had been made as to the Mandatory, and the Commission included representatives from the allied countries, Britain, France and Italy.[19] Ormsby-

15. J. M. N. Jeffries, *Palestine the Reality*, London, 1939, p. 293. The original statement is found in the report of the King-Crane Commission. Cf. "Report of American Section of Inter-Allied Commission on Mandates in Turkey," in *Editor and Publisher*, December 2, 1922, p. X, col. 2.
16. Marvin Lowenthal, *Henrietta Szold, Life and Letters*, Viking, 1942, p. 186.
17. Frederick H. Kisch, *Palestine Diary*, Gollancz, London, 1938, p. 34.
18. Hanna, *op. cit.*, p. 41.
19. The British Zionists were Joseph Cowen, Leon Simon, Israel M. Sieff and Dr. M. D. Eder; French Jewry was represented by Sylvain Lévi; Italian Jewry was represented by Dr. Artom and Commandante

Gore, assisted by Captain James de Rothschild, accompanied the party as political officer on behalf of the British Government. Weizmann, who headed the Commission, carried letters of introduction from Lloyd George and Balfour addressed to Allenby.

The Zionist Commission left for Palestine March 8, 1918 and arrived there via Egypt on April 20th. Weizmann was received courteously by the British officers in command. He found the British officials generally cold to the Zionist idea, although he appears to have made some impression on General Clayton and Colonel Deedes in his attempt to explain the cause of Zionism. He met a number of Arab notables in Egypt and a week after his arrival in Palestine, a reception was arranged for him by Storrs, now Military Officer at Jerusalem. In his address, Weizmann spoke frankly of the Zionist aim but at the same time endeavored to allay Arab apprehensions. He said that the Jews considered themselves as brother Semites; they were not strangers in Palestine, not "coming" to it but "returning." The Zionist aim was to create a moral and spiritual center which would bind the Jewish tradition of the past with the future. This was the inner meaning of the "Jewish national home." Such a center must rest on firm foundations and have deep roots in the soil of Palestine. It was therefore necessary to provide the conditions—material and moral—which would make it possible for Jews who wished, to return to Palestine. This, Weizmann emphasized, could be done in harmony with the interests of the existing communities—indeed, with benefit to them. He was convinced that Palestine had enough room to support a population many times as large as the number of its present inhabitants.[20] Storrs rendered the speech in Arabic and the Mayor of Jerusalem (Musa Kazem Pasha) replied courteously, thanking Dr. Weizmann for allaying any apprehensions which might have been aroused. He spoke of unity of aim which alone could bring prosperity to Palestine and he quoted a *Hadith,* or say-

---

Bianchini. The United States was unofficially represented by the officers of the Hadassah Medical Unit. Two delegates chosen by the Russian Zionists could not obtain passports in time because of the disturbed political situation. Menahem Ussishkin, one of them, joined the Zionist Commission in Palestine toward the end of 1919. (Medzini, *Eser Shanim shel Mediniut Artzi-Israelit* (Ten Years of Palestine Politics), Tel-Aviv, 1928, pp. 42–43.

20. Medzini, *op. cit.,* p. 59.

ing of the Prophet: "Our rights are your rights, and your duties are our duties." [21]

Weizmann had also planned to meet Sharif Husain but this did not come about. Instead he met Emir Faisal on June 4, 1918, at the latter's encampment at Gueira between Aqaba and Ma'an and there was a satisfactory interchange of views. At this time the relations with the Arabs seem to have been rather more favorable than with the officers of the British Administration. The attitude of the authorities in Palestine was discouraging and obstructive. They were annoyed at the extra trouble and expense involved in the use of Hebrew; they were outraged when the Zionist Commission undertook to pay subsidies to Jewish government officials of the junior service who, being classed as Palestinians, were receiving inadequate pay; they insisted that the poor economic situation did not permit any new immigration; they held that the disappearance of all Turkish registers rendered land transactions impossible. As Storrs says: "For one reason or another, every circumstance or step taken to implement the Balfour Declaration evoked a swelling chorus of protest against an admitted departure from the Laws and Usages of War." [22] Under these circumstances a general feeling of distrust and suspicion developed between the Zionists and the military administration.

Weizmann met the representatives of the Jewish community soon after his arrival. He had a double task: to dispel the feeling of disillusionment that had taken hold of the Jewish community as a result of the antagonistic attitude of the British Administration; on the other hand, he had to moderate the extreme expectations that had been aroused by the Balfour Declaration which the Jews in Palestine generally interpreted as a promise of a Jewish state. Ormsby-Gore made a long speech on this occasion which may be considered the first official interpretation of the Declaration. The gist of his definition was that the term "national home" meant, "That those Jews who come to Palestine of their own free will would live in the country as national Jews—that is, they would regard themselves only as Jews and would be free to establish a Hebrew educational system, to develop the country, to live there in freedom according to their own customs; but, together with

21. Storrs, *op. cit.*
22. *Ibid.*, p. 416.

this, they would be, along with the rest of the population, subject to the laws of the state." [23] Weizmann's statement was clearer and more direct. He said: "At present there is no point in talking about the foundation of a Jewish state in the full sense of the word for we do not have the power to conduct such a state. We must ask for some strong government, which we may trust to administer our "state" justly, to take matters under its direction, enable us to develop our abilities, our institutions and our colonies, until the time comes when we shall be fit to undertake the administration of the country ourselves." [24] The representatives of the *Yishuv*, however, were not conciliatory, as may be seen from the nature of the proposals which they prepared for presentation to the Peace Conference a year later.[25]

Weizmann left in September. Lord Allenby acknowledged that the Zionist leader had displayed wisdom and tact in handling the business of the Commission. But it does not appear that the attitude of the Administration improved or that any fundamental steps were taken to relieve the Jewish grievances. During the following summer, Justice Brandeis visited Palestine and had an interview with General Allenby and the Chief Administrator, General Sir Arthur Money. He urged the necessity of a more cooperative attitude on the part of the Palestine Administration toward the Zionist endeavor, particularly with reference to immigration. He received no encouragement: Allenby remarked that if the Zionists would bring in new immigrants before clearing the land of malaria, the number of deaths would equal the number of immigrants; General Money asked why the Zionists wanted to bring more Jews into Palestine when those already there were living on alms. On his way back to the United States Brandeis stopped in London and reported his impressions. His report helped the persistent efforts of the Zionist Commission and led the Government to dispatch a set of definite instructions to the Palestine Administration. It was made clear that the Administration should be guided by the policy of the Jewish national home; that this policy was not only that of Great Britain but also of the United States and France and was not subject to change; that the

---

23. Medzini, *op. cit.*, p. 57.
24. *Ibid.*, p. 24.
25. See below, p. 152.

Arab leaders should be informed of this and be impressed with the fact that propaganda against the Jewish national home policy was useless. General Money was removed and other changes in personnel favorable to the Zionist Organization were introduced.

However, the situation did not change essentially for the better. When the Syrian Congress met in March, 1920, and elected Faisal as King of United Syria, the fires of Arab nationalism flared up in Palestine. To the Arabs, the Jews now appeared as the chief obstacle to the achievement of a union of Palestine with Syria in the newly created independent Syrian State. The Arabs in Palestine, moreover, had reason to believe that "the Government was with them," that is, that the British Administration would not look with disfavor on action which would demonstrate Arab opposition to the French and to the Zionists.

The Moslem festival of Nebi Musa provided the occasion for setting off the explosive forces.[26] On this year the festival fell on April 4th. After several thousand pilgrims had arrived in

---

26. This festival, in honor of the Prophet Moses, takes place at the same time as the Christian Easter and the Jewish Passover. It probably has an ancient origin but in its present form is said to have been inaugurated by the Mameluke rulers of Palestine who feared the concentration of Christian pilgrims in the city during Easter and wanted to balance it with a similar concentration of Moslems. As distinct from the Christian and Jewish holidays falling at the same time, the Moslem festival retains a primitive, tribal and at times barbaric character. The celebration takes the form of a pilgrimage to the Tomb of Moses, situated in the hills about five miles from Jericho. The *fellahin* from the surrounding villages first gather in Jerusalem. The procession is picturesque and colorful, with the Hebronites carrying their many-hued flags embroidered with texts from the Koran; but at times the procession turns into ecstatic dancing, with swords flashing, drums beating, and spectators shrieking. Graves describes the procession in 1922 as follows: "As they entered the Old City the enthusiasm of the crowds reached its highest intensity. Men with the set blank stare of extreme excitement, danced round and round, bare-headed, their long locks flying wildly as they revolved. The singers strained their throats and now and again a fugleman would jump on the shoulders of a sturdy human horse who carried him up and down between the rows of dancers while he shouted, sang, or directed the dance with an amazing wealth of gesticulation." The first stop is on a high hill near the Mount of Olives where the Mufti of Jerusalem, sitting on horseback, prays briefly and blesses the people. Some of the marchers then return to the town while others continue to the Tomb of Nebi Musa several hours' march from Jerusalem. They stay at the grave for a whole week, which is spent in prayer, religious ceremonies, as well as in eating, drinking and making sacrifices.

Jerusalem, a political demonstration was staged in which a large picture of Faisal was displayed. Cries directed against the Jews were shouted by leaders in the procession, and agitators incited an attack. Marchers in the procession fell upon the Jews with sticks and knives; the Arab police remained passive or in some instances joined the rioting. The British troops finally succeeded in quelling the disorders and detained several hundred Arabs for the night in a mosque. Disturbances broke out again when they were released in the morning. The Government was finally forced to disarm the Arab police, proclaim martial law and hand over the control to the military. Order was not restored until two days after the outbreak.

The Jews accused the Military Administration, headed by Sir Louis J. Bols, of complicity. The Zionist authorities blamed the Government particularly for allowing the Moslem-Christian Associations to agitate against the Balfour Declaration. The actions of the military authorities after the riots confirmed the feeling that they were motivated by an anti-Jewish attitude. Severe penalties were inflicted on Jewish defense organizations which had armed the Jews for self-protection. Vladimir Jabotinsky who had been an officer in the British Army—one of the initiators of the Zion Mule Corps and the Jewish Legion, and the godfather of the *Haganah* (Jewish secret defense force)—and other members of the Jewish defense, were sentenced to fifteen years' imprisonment for the possession of firearms and ammunition.[27] The Jews were incensed at this, particularly because at the same time an exactly similar penalty was meted out to an Arab rioter convicted of rape. The Administration on its part made accusations against the Zionist Commission. Sir Louis Bols in a long memorandum charged the Commission with attempting to create a political *fait accompli* in the country before the Mandate had been determined. He implied that the Christians and Moslems were justified in feeling that the status quo was not being maintained, in view of the fact that Hebrew had been recognized as an official language, Jewish courts had been established, a quasi-governmental structure of the Zionist Commission had been introduced, etc. A local Committee of Inquiry was appointed to investigate the causes of the disturbances but the

27. These extreme sentences hastened the end of the Military Administration although Allenby reduced Jabotinsky's sentence to one year.

results of its inquiry were not revealed on the grounds that "their publication could serve no useful purpose."

The Foreign Office was not influenced either by the accusations of the Administration or the report of the local committee. General Allenby was instructed not to entertain the Moslem-Christian proposals which demanded the suppression of the Zionists and the disbanding of the Jewish Battalion. Plans were drawn up to change the existing regime. British public opinion joined the Zionists in urging a thoroughgoing reorganization of the Palestine Government. This first disturbance, which occurred before the Mandate was officially granted to Great Britain—unlike later disturbances—did not lead to a reaction unfavorable to the Zionist cause. On the contrary, it helped to expedite the decision of the Peace Conference to grant the Mandate to Great Britain, with the responsibility for the Balfour Declaration attached. A little over a month after the decision on the Mandate at San Remo (April 24, 1920), the Military Administration under Sir Louis Bols came to an end and the Civil Administration was initiated on July 1, 1920, under Sir Herbert Samuel as High Commissioner.

PALESTINE AND THE NEAR EAST AT THE PEACE CONFERENCE

Lloyd George and Clemenceau Arrangements

When the war ended, the Sykes-Picot Agreement, in accordance with which Palestine was to be placed under international auspices, was no longer considered binding by the French and the British. The validity of the agreement had come into question after it was repudiated by Russia who had been one of the original signatories. The British no longer were anxious to defend it, believing they could do better since their troops had conquered Palestine, Syria and Mesopotamia. France had never been enthusiastic about giving the Arabs as much independence as was provided in the Sykes-Picot Agreement. On November 30, 1918, Georges Clemenceau, the French Premier, paid a visit to London to determine where Lloyd George stood on the various questions involved in the partition of the Turkish Empire.

Lloyd George had evidently decided on two major changes from the previous arrangements. He wished to add the Mosul district with its rich oil fields to the sphere of influence which

The Peace Conference and Mandate for Palestine

had been allotted to Great Britain. In the second place, he wanted to substitute British control over Palestine for international supervision and to extend the boundaries from the narrow limits to which Sykes had agreed, to those of the Old Testament—"from Dan to Beersheba." Clemenceau was not loath to agree, if he could get a *quid pro quo* in each case. He demanded that French interests should get a proper share of the Mosul petroleum resources which were controlled by an English company. Furthermore, he wanted Lloyd George to agree that the French area of full control would include not only the "Blue Zone," i.e., coastal Syria as specified in the Sykes-Picot Agreement, but also the "A Zone," over which it had been given only advisory powers. This understanding was unofficial at the time, but it foreshadowed the arrangements finally adopted after the lengthy negotiations at the Peace Conference.

The deal between Lloyd George and Clemenceau was strictly in line with old style imperialistic politics and stood in striking contradiction to pronouncements that had been made against annexations by Great Britain and the United States. Lloyd George had declared in January, 1918, "Arabia, Armenia, Mesopotamia, Syria and Palestine are in our judgment entitled to a recognition of their separate national conditions." [28] In his "Fourteen Points" address on January 8, 1918, Wilson had said: "The Turkish portions of the present Ottoman Empire should be assured a secure sovereignty, but other nationalities which are now under Turkish rule should be assured an undoubted security of life and an absolutely unmolested opportunity of autonomous development." [29] These idealistic conceptions were not easily harmonized with the practical issues that faced the European statesmen who met in Paris. A complete withdrawal of European Powers from the East was not contemplated even by Wilson and would not have been welcomed by a large part of the native populations with their diverse religions and national minorities.

When the Peace Conference met in January, 1919, it was confronted with the knotty problem of reconciling the demands of *Realpolitik* with the many pronouncements about self-

28. Great Britain, *Parliamentary Papers 1918*, Cmd. 9005, London, 1918, pp. 230–235.
29. Woodrow Wilson, *State Papers and Addresses*, 1917, p. 470.

determination and the rights of small nations that had been made during the war. A way out was offered by a combination of two ideas: the League of Nations, urged by Wilson; and the mandate system suggested by Jan Christian Smuts, the South African statesman. In accordance with the mandatory system, the principal Allies would act as trustees for the new states to be created out of territories of the conquered Central Powers. These mandates would be subject to the supervision of the League of Nations. The new system offered a compromise between pure imperialism and gradual self-determination, and, accordingly, it was seized upon by the statesmen of Paris as a solution of the dilemma which confronted them. After discussion and modification of the original proposals, a Mandate System was provided for in Article 22 of the Covenant of the League of Nations. The first four provisions particularly relevant to our present discussion are:[30]

1. To those colonies and territories which as a consequence of the late war have ceased to be under the sovereignty of the States which formerly governed them and which are inhabited by peoples not yet able to stand by themselves under the strenuous conditions of the modern world, there should be applied the principle that the wellbeing and development of such peoples form a sacred trust of civilisation and that securities for the performance of this trust should be embodied in this Covenant.

2. The best method of giving practical effect to this principle is that the tutelage of such peoples should be entrusted to advanced nations who by reason of their resources, their experience or their geographical position can best undertake this responsibility, and who are willing to accept it, and that this tutelage should be exercised by them as Mandatories on behalf of the League.

3. The character of the Mandate must differ according to the stage of development of the people, the geographical situation of the territory, its economic conditions and other similar circumstances.

4. Certain communities formerly belonging to the Turkish Empire have reached a stage of development where their existence as independent nations can be provisionally recognized subject to the rendering of administrative advice and assistance by a Mandatory until such time as they are able to stand alone. The wishes of these communities must be a principal consideration in the selection of the Mandatory.

30. For full text see Quincy Wright, *Mandates under the League of Nations*, University of Chicago Press, 1930, pp. 591, 592.

In this way Palestine as well as all other countries of the Ottoman Empire fell under the mandatory system. At this time the mandatory power was still unnamed, the terms of the mandate unspecified, and the boundaries of Palestine undefined. Before the status of Palestine could be determined, the interests of the Arabs and of the French as well as of the British and the Jews had to be reconciled.

The Arab Delegation at the Peace Conference

Emir Faisal represented his father at the Peace Conference and was recognized as the spokesman of the Arab national movement. In a memorandum dated January 1, 1919,[31] he declared that he had come to Europe on behalf of his father, the King of Hejaz, and of the Arabs of Asia, to plead the cause of Arab unity. The aim of the Arab national movement (of which he claimed his father had become the leader) was eventually to unite the Arabs into one nation under one sovereign government. But he indicated that no attempt should be made immediately to force an artificial political unity on the whole Arab people. On the other hand, the development of Arab unity should not be hindered by dividing up the Arab lands as spoils of war among the great Powers. He made concrete suggestions for the disposition of each one of the main areas.

Syria, the most advanced area from an agricultural and industrial point of view, was sufficiently developed politically to manage her own affairs. Foreign technical advice would be appreciated and paid for. But the Arabs could not sacrifice any part of the freedom which "we have just won for ourselves by force of arms" for such help. In Mesopotamia (including Jezireh and Iraq), underdeveloped and thinly inhabited by semi-nomadic peoples, the Arabs realized that the system of government would "have to be buttressed by the men and material resources of a great foreign Power." They asked, however, that the government of these districts should be Arab in principle and spirit. In choosing officials "the selective rather than the elective principle" would necessarily be followed in the backward districts for some time to come. The main duty of the Arab government in these countries would be to supervise the

31. David Hunter Miller, *My Diary at the Conference of Paris*, Vol. IV, p. 297.

educational processes which would advance the nomadic tribes to the level of civilization in the cities.

The Hejaz was mainly a tribal area and the government should, as in the past, be suited to patriarchal conditions. For that reason the Arabs asked that complete independence should be retained. The Nejd and Yemen, the other areas in the Arabian Peninsula (which had remained neutral during the war) were not likely to submit their cases to the Peace Conference. They should be permitted to adjust their relations to the Hejaz and to the other tribes in Arabia. In Palestine, the Arabs wished for "the effective super-position of a great trustee." While the Jews and the Arabs were closely related and "in principles" were absolutely at one, "the Arabs could not assume the responsibility for maintaining peace among the various races and religions." They would be satisfied, therefore, if Palestine would come under a trusteeship, provided that the "representative local administration" actively promoted the material prosperity of the country.

Accompanied by Colonel Lawrence and several members of the Arab Delegation—Nuri Said, Rustum Haidar and Auni Abdul Hadi—Faisal appeared before the Supreme Council on February 6, 1919, to plead his cause. Here he presented his cause along the lines of the memorandum: he asked for the recognition of Arab independence in principle, and recommended leaving it to each area to decide which power was to act as the mandatory, and what degree of foreign control or assistance would be acceptable. When asked by President Wilson whether the Arabs would prefer a single mandatory or several, Faisal insisted that each people must make its own decision. To the question what his personal opinion was, he stated that he would prefer a single mandatory power over Syria (including Jezireh) and Iraq, the countries in question. There were two small areas which he specifically excluded: the Lebanon and Palestine. As to the Lebanon, he was satisfied to have an economic union between the surrounding countries; he did not insist on independence because the majority of the inhabitants were Christians. His position on Palestine was quite different. According to David Hunter Miller, "Palestine for its universal character, he left on one side for the mutual consideration of all parties interested." [32]

32. *Ibid.*, Vol. II, p. 226. These were obviously proposals reached in agreement with the British. For the American conception of the disposi-

The Peace Conference and Mandate for Palestine

Faisal's statement on Palestine was the result of conversations which had been held during the previous year, at the suggestion of the British, between the Zionist and Arab leaders. In Egypt, Weizmann and Ormsby-Gore had apparently succeeded in winning the confidence of Dr. Faris Nimr, one of the original members of the Syrian Arab nationalist movement and publisher of the influential daily, *al-Muqattam*.[33] The meeting between Faisal and Weizmann at Aqaba was, as noted above, attended with success, and in Weizmann's phrase, formed "the basis of a lifelong friendship." In November 1918 when Faisal entered Damascus, the Zionist Organization sent a congratulatory note and Faisal made a gracious acknowledgment.[34] At the end of 1918 Faisal met with the Jewish leaders in London, and at about that time he made a statement, marked by great cordiality, to Reuter's correspondent in London, which was published in *The Times* on December 12th:

"The two main branches of the Semitic family, Arabs and Jews [he stated], understand one another, and I hope that as a result of interchange of ideas at the Peace Conference, which will be guided by ideals of self-determination and nationality, each nation will make definite progress towards the realization of its aspirations. Arabs are not jealous of Zionist Jews, and intend to give them fair play; and the Zionist Jews have assured the Nationalist Arabs of their intention to see that they too have fair play in their respective areas. Turkish intrigue in Palestine has raised jealousy between the Jewish colonists and the local peasants, but the mutual understanding of the aims of Arabs and Jews will at once clear away the last trace of this former bitterness, which indeed had already practically disappeared even before the war by the work of the Arab Secret Revolutionary Committee . . ." [35]

The Emir expressed himself in a similar vein at a banquet given in his honor by Lord Rothschild at the end of 1918. Again in unmistakable terms he emphasized the kinship between the Jews and the Arabs, and the harmony between the Jewish nationalist and the Arab nationalist aspirations. Moreover, he pointed out that no state could be built up in the Near East

tion of these territories, see Document 246 in Miller, *op. cit.*, Vol. IV, pp. 263–264, a summary of which is given below, Chap. IV, pp. 245–246, n. 132.
33. Antonius, *op. cit.*, p. 270.
34. M. Perlmann, "Chapters of Arab-Jewish Diplomacy, 1918–22," *Jewish Social Studies*, New York, 1944, p. 132.
35. As quoted by M. Perlmann, *op. cit.*, p. 133.

without borrowing from the ideas, knowledge and experience of Europe, and that the Jews were the intermediaries who could best translate European experience to suit Arab life. When the Sykes-Picot Treaty was disclosed, he emphasized, in a discussion with Jewish leaders, that it was equally bad both for the Arabs and the Jews, and he again stated that he did not consider Arab and Zionist aims incompatible. On this occasion he gave his word of honor to support the Jewish demands at the Peace Conference.[36] It was in fulfillment of this pledge that he included the reference to Palestine in the January 1st memorandum. The paragraph, in its entirety, read:[37]

"In Palestine the enormous majority of the people are Arabs. The Jews are very close to the Arabs in blood, and there is no conflict of character between the two races. In principles we are absolutely at one. Nevertheless, the Arabs cannot assume the responsibility of holding level the scales in the clash of races and religions that have, in this one province, so often involved the world in difficulties. They would wish for the effective super-position of a great trustee, so long as a representative local administration commended itself by actively promoting the material prosperity of the country."

In conformity with this view, on January 3, 1919, a month prior to his appearance before the Supreme Council, he signed an agreement with Weizmann to act in the negotiations at the Peace Conference in accord with the Zionists. The agreement expressed friendship for the Jewish people on the grounds of racial kinship and ancient ties, gave recognition to the Balfour Declaration, provided that cordial relations should be maintained between "the Arab state and Palestine," guaranteed religious freedom and ensured Moslem control of the Moslem Holy Places, welcomed cooperation of the Jews in the development of the Arab state, provided that the Arabs and Jews should work in harmony at the Peace Conference; and, finally, stipulated that "any matters of dispute which may arise between the contracting parties shall be referred to the British Government for arbitration."

The main paragraphs of the agreement read:[38]

36. *Ibid.*, p. 360.
37. David Hunter Miller, *op. cit.*, Vol. IV, pp. 298 ff.
38. Jewish Agency for Palestine, *Memorandum to the Palestine Royal Commission*, London, 1936, p. 296.

Article I: The Arab State and Palestine in all their relations and undertakings shall be controlled by the most cordial goodwill and understanding, and to this end Arab and Jewish duly accredited agents shall be established and maintained in the respective territories.

Article III: In the establishment of the Constitution and Administration of Palestine all such measures shall be adopted as will afford the fullest guarantees for carrying into effect the British Government's Declaration of November 2nd, 1917.

Article IV: All necessary measures shall be taken to encourage and stimulate immigration of Jews into Palestine on a large scale, and as quickly as possible to settle Jewish immigrants upon the land through closer settlement and intensive cultivation of the soil. In taking such measures the Arab peasant and tenant farmers shall be protected in their rights, and shall be assisted in forwarding their economic development.

To the text of the Agreement, Faisal added a reservation in the form of a postscript. The reservation is written in Arabic, with a translation in Lawrence's handwriting, reading as follows: *"If the Arabs are established as I have asked in my manifesto of January 4th addressed to the British Secretary of State for Foreign Affairs, I will carry out what is written in this agreement. If changes are made, I cannot be answerable for failure to carry out this agreement."* This left a loophole for the denunciation of the agreement, if the Arabs failed to get independence in the other areas enumerated in the memorandum.

The French were opposed to Faisal as the prospective ruler of Syria and could produce Arabs who were ready to support their own plans and who were also ready to make concessions to the Jews. On February 13, a week after Faisal had appeared before the Supreme Council, Chekri Ganem, a Syrian resident in Paris, presented the views of *Le Comité Central Syrien*, a group sponsored by Clemenceau. Chekri Ganem denounced Faisal and his regime at Damascus and pleaded for the independence of Syria under French protection. Countering the British support of Zionism, he proposed French support of an autonomous Jewish settlement in a Palestine united with Syria:[39]

39. David Hunter Miller, *op. cit.*, Vol. XIV, pp. 399 ff. and pp. 414 ff.

Palestine is uncontestedly the southern portion of our country. The Zionists claim it. We have suffered too much from sufferings resembling theirs, not to throw wide open to them the doors of Palestine. All those among them who are oppressed in certain retrograde countries are welcome. Let them settle in Palestine, but in an autonomous Palestine, connected with Syria by the sole bond of federation. Will not a Palestine enjoying wide internal autonomy be for them a sufficient guarantee?

If they form the majority there, they will be the rulers. If they are in the minority, they will be represented in the government in proportion to their numbers.

Is it necessary, in order to establish them, to dismember Syria, to take from it its means of access and its historic safeguard against any invasion (which always took that route), and to constitute a State in the midst of a country which, as a consequence, would be hostile to them?

Toward the end of February, shortly after the Zionist delegates appeared before the Peace Conference,[40] Faisal, evidently pressed by Arab nationalist extremists, gave an interview to the representative of *Le Matin* in which he made remarks which appeared unfriendly to the idea of a Jewish state. He declared that the persecuted Jews were welcome to find a refuge in Palestine under a Moslem or Christian government responsible to the League of Nations, "but if the Jews desire to establish a state and claim sovereign rights in the country, I foresee and fear very serious dangers and conflicts between them and other races."[41] The Zionists were disturbed and called the matter to the attention of Faisal's secretary. He explained that all the Emir had said was that: "If the Zionists wished to found a Jewish state at the present moment, they would meet with difficulties from the local population." He also wrote a letter to *Le Matin* protesting against the published form of the interview.

To clear up the doubt which had been created, an interview was arranged between Faisal and (then) Professor Felix Frankfurter who represented the Zionists, with Lawrence present. Lawrence was delegated to summarize [in English] the substance of the position which Faisal had expressed. This was

40. See below, p. 159.
41. *Le Matin*, March 1, 1919; *Jewish Chronicle*, March 7.

done in the form of a letter to Professor Frankfurter, signed by the Emir. The letter was dated: Hejaz Delegation, Paris, March 3, 1919, and included the following statement:[42]

Our Deputation here in Paris is fully acquainted with the proposals submitted yesterday by the Zionist Organisation to the Peace Conference, and we regard them as moderate and proper. We will do our best, so far as we are concerned, to help them through; we will wish the Jews a hearty welcome home . . . We are working together for a reformed and revived Near East, and our two Movements complete one another. The Jewish Movement is national and not imperialist. Our Movement is national and not imperialist, and there is room in Syria for us both. Indeed, I think that neither can be a real success without the other.

There can be little doubt that at the time of the Peace Conference there was an entente among the British, the Arabs and the Jews with reference to the disposition of Palestine in accord with the Balfour Declaration. Each party to the entente may have had its own interpretation as to the ultimate meaning of the Balfour Declaration, but there cannot be any question on the main issue: that the Arab representatives at the time agreed that Palestine should be set apart from the Arab state, and that a regime safeguarded by Great Britain should be instituted, whose purpose would include the development of a Jewish national home. As the Royal Commission Report succinctly summarized the situation: "If King Hussein and the Emir Faisal secured their big Arab State, they would concede little Palestine to the Jews." [43] The Jews on their part were to support the Arab position at the Peace Conference and subsequently to lend whatever aid they could to the economic development of the neighboring Arab countries. The civil and religious rights of the Arabs in Palestine and the economic position of the peasantry were to be safeguarded by the British trustee.

42. The letter was reproduced in the *New York Times*, March 5, 1919. Its authenticity was questioned ten years later at the Shaw Commission which investigated the disturbances of 1929. Professor Frankfurter, however, reaffirmed its authenticity and gave a full account of how the letter was written, in *The Atlantic Monthly*, October, 1930, p. 49 of the Contributors' Column.
43. P. 27.

Allied Disputes and the Final Settlement

The French were absolutely determined to oppose any solution of the partition of Turkey which did not recognize clearly their claims to Syria. On February 15, Clemenceau brought in the Lebanese Delegation which asked for a French Mandate. On the same day, the French submitted to the British Government a written memorandum summarizing the understanding between Lloyd George and Clemenceau made several months before in London. The controversy between France and Britain was becoming acute. The French resented Britain's strong support of Faisal and suspected that Zionism was being used as a means of extending the Palestine boundaries northward. On March 20, the disagreement over the Syrian Mandate came to a head. Stephen Pichon, the French Foreign Minister, announced that his Government did not want to control Palestine but would insist on receiving a mandate for Syria, including the coastal and interior areas. Lloyd George said that he could not agree to this, in view of the Husain-McMahon correspondence, according to which Damascus, Homs, Hama and Aleppo and the area east of these cities were to be under Arab control. There was an impasse and President Wilson suggested that the peoples concerned in each case should be consulted on the question as to which Power should be named the mandatory.

In this suggestion he was espousing a proposal made a month before by Dr. Howard Bliss, an American born in Syria, President of the Syrian Protestant College (since 1920 the American University at Beirut), who had urged that an international commission be sent to the East to ascertain the wishes of the people concerning their political future. Lloyd George agreed at first and Clemenceau seemed prepared to acquiesce in principle. However, he made the condition that the inquiry should not be confined to Syria, but should include Palestine, Mesopotamia and Armenia, and the other parts of the Turkish Empire. Lloyd George said that he had no objection, but later in the discussion it seemed that he had some apprehensions about Mesopotamia. The suggestion to send an Inter-Allied Commission was accepted a few days later, but when the experts on Eastern questions were consulted, they expressed the view that the "presence of such a body in Syria would be a cause for intrigue and unrest." [44] The French soon placed difficulties in the way of the establishment of the Commission and indicated that they would not participate in an investigation intended to expose anti-French sentiment in Syria. In view of this attitude, the British, evidently not very enthusiastic about the proposition, now that it was to include Iraq, also withdrew their participation.

However, the American Section had already been appointed. President Wilson had chosen Dr. Henry C. King and Mr. Charles R. Crane as the members of the Commission responsible for the recommendations.[45] The question arose whether the American Commission should proceed without the others. After much discussion, they finally left toward the end of May. The Commission spent about six weeks in Syria and Palestine. The report recommended a single mandate for Syria under Faisal as Constitutional Monarch, the mandate to be assigned in accordance with the wishes of the people, to the United States or, as second choice, to Great Britain, but under no circumstances to France. Palestine was to be joined to Syria and become part of Faisal's dominion. The Commission took an unfavorable view of Zionism on the grounds that the majority in Palestine were Arabs and were opposed to a Jewish state. The report was delivered in Paris, after Wilson had left, and filed with the American Delegation. It was not made public at the time, and had no influence on the decisions at San Remo. But, as noted in the first part of this chapter, it had a disturbing effect on the general situation in Syria and Iraq as well as in Palestine.

Wilson left Paris on June 28, 1919, after the German Treaty was signed. After that, Lloyd George appeared in France only occasionally and the Peace Conference was permitted to expire gradually. The American Delegation remained without instruc-

44. Hanna, *op. cit.*, p. 53.
45. King was President of Oberlin College and had directed the religious work of the Y.M.C.A. in France during the war. Crane was a Chicago manufacturer who had gained some diplomatic experience on the Bullitt Commission to Russia in 1917. In addition to these two heads of the Commission there were three experts. (See below, Chap. IV, p. 213.) Captain Donald M. Brody was Secretary and Lawrence Moore, the business manager. (Harry N. Howard, "An American Experiment in Peace-Making: The King-Crane Commission," *The Moslem World*, April, 1942.)

tion during the summer and returned to the United States in December. There was a long period of delay marked by Anglo-French bickering and many abortive proposals. Professor William Yale, a member of the American Commission, who had an excellent knowledge of Syrian conditions, made a suggestion which won wide support, including that of T. E. Lawrence, Nuri Said and Rustum Haidar, members of the Arab Delegation.[46] It provided for:

Palestine: to be under the mandate of Great Britain and the Zionists permitted to carry out their plan.

Mount Lebanon: to be a separate political unit, under the mandate of France.

Syria: from Maan and Akaba to Aleppo with the ports of Tripoli and Latakia to be constituted as a "provisionally" independent state with an Arab Government representative of the inhabitants. This Arab state to be under the mandate of France.

Mesopotamia: to be divided into two areas, the northern one embracing the former Ottoman vilayets of Mosul and Bagdad; the southern one that of Bassorah and the Emirate of Mohammerah. The Northern area to be a "provisionally" independent state with an Arab Government representative of the inhabitants. This state to be under the mandate of Great Britain. A federal Council of representatives from each of the four Arab areas should meet at stated intervals.

In the absence of Wilson, the American Commission did not wish to take the responsibility for the plan and Yale could take no action. "It was a remarkable position. All the parties to a deadlock were prepared to agree to a solution which had been formulated—provided it were imposed upon them from the outside. But the Americans were not prepared to impose anything on any of them." [47]

The general outlines of a settlement of the Turkish question were finally determined in February, 1920, during a conference of the Supreme Council in London. Millerand, who had succeeded Clemenceau as Prime Minister, was, if anything, more intransigent than his predecessor with reference to France's claims in the East. Then came the unrest in Syria, with the

46. David Garnett, ed., *The Letters of T. E. Lawrence*, Doubleday Doran, 1939, p. 286.
47. Comment by David Garnett, *op. cit.*, p. 288.

election of Faisal as King, and the Nebi Musa riots in Palestine which followed. These events helped to impress the Allied statesmen with the imperative need for a final settlement of the Eastern problem. When the Supreme Council assembled at San Remo on April 19th, Lloyd George insisted on an immediate consideration of the Turkish question.

An agreement was finally reached on April 24, 1920. It followed the lines laid down in the Clemenceau-Lloyd George conversations in late November, 1918. Syria and Mesopotamia were to be recognized as provisionally independent states, subject to mandatory control. In Mesopotamia, Mosul was to be included, and French companies were to receive twenty-five percent interest in the Turkish petroleum in Mosul. France would, on its part, facilitate the building of oil pipe lines across Syrian territory to the Mediterranean. Palestine was to be excluded from Syria and, in accordance with the British proposal, the article on Palestine in the Turkish Treaty would recite the Balfour Declaration. To this the French at first objected. While agreeing that they had assented to Jewish settlement in Palestine, they preferred another formula which they thought would protect their rights more adequately as guardians of the Catholic interests in Palestine. But Francesco Nitti, the Italian Premier, and Lloyd George would not agree to this. As a compromise, Nitti proposed inserting in the Treaty a provision for the appointment of a special commission to define the status of the religious communities in Palestine. This satisfied Millerand and he withdrew his objections to the inclusion of the Balfour Declaration in the Turkish Treaty. The mandatory powers were not to be named in the treaty. On April 25th, the day after the agreement was made, a resolution naming the mandatories was adopted and recorded in the minutes, in the name of the principal Allied Powers. The San Remo Conference assigned to France the mandates for Syria and the Lebanon and to Britain those for Mesopotamia and Palestine.

On April 26th, after the completion of the final clauses of the Turkish Treaty, the San Remo Conference came to a close. The Ottoman Delegation finally signed the Treaty, under protest, on August 10, 1920, at Sèvres. The decision on Palestine is incorporated as Article 95 of the Treaty and reads as follows:[48]

48. J. Stoyanovsky, *The Mandate for Palestine*, Longmans, Green, 1928, pp. 24–25.

The High Contracting Parties agree to entrust by application of these provisions of Article 22 the administration of Palestine, within such boundaries as may be determined by the Principal Allied Powers, to a Mandatory to be selected by the said Powers. The Mandatory will be responsible for putting into effect the declaration originally made on the 2nd November, 1917, by the British Government and adopted by the other Allied Powers in favour of the establishment in Palestine of a national home for the Jewish people, it being clearly understood that nothing shall be done that may prejudice the civil and religious rights of existing non-Jewish communities in Palestine or the rights and political status enjoyed by Jews in any other country.

The Mandatory undertakes to appoint as soon as possible a special Commission to study and regulate all questions and claims relating to the different religious communities. In the composition of this Commission the religious interests concerned will be taken into account. The Chairman of the Commission will be appointed by the Council of the League of Nations.

Jewish popular opinion throughout the world acclaimed the San Remo decision with enthusiasm and demonstrations were organized in London and New York. Nordau, who only a few months earlier had declared that "anyone satisfied with less than a Jewish state is not a political Zionist," now averred that "we don't have to sing the *Hatikvah* any more because our hope has been fulfilled." [49] The Zionist leaders, Sokolow, Weizmann and Brandeis, however, took a more guarded view. They laid the emphasis on the need of unified endeavor and concerted practical effort for the upbuilding of the country. Sokolow said in June 1920:[50] "The chapter of politics is practically over and now begins the second chapter—the chapter of the realization of our aspirations. The first was written in the main not by us but by those in whose hands it lies to open the gates of the country; the second will be written only by us." Brandeis, speaking at the Zionist Conference in London in July, 1920, expressed the same trend of thought. "The work of the great Herzl was completed at San Remo. The effort to acquire the public recognition of the Jewish Homeland in Palestine for which he lived and died has been crowned with success. The nations of the world have done all that they could do. The rest lies with

---

49. Adolf Böhm, *Die Zionistische Bewegung*, Jerusalem, 1937, Vol. II, p. 65, n. 2.
50. Medzini, *op. cit.*, p. 128.

us."[51] Weizmann constantly spoke in the same vein during these years, appealing to America particularly to give the "golden key" that would open the doors of immigration in Palestine. He also endeavored to relieve the apprehensions of the Arabs in a speech delivered in Jerusalem toward the end of 1920. He said: "Our historical rights to the country can only be realized side by side with the Arab population. I trust that cooperation will convince them that we are not coming in the spirit of Prussian Junkers, but in the spirit of those serving a sacred national ideal, to whom right and justice are the supreme virtues."[52]

The British leaders who had helped to achieve the Balfour Declaration took a similar position. When the Zionists came to thank him for his efforts, Lloyd George said: "We gave you a start, now it is up to you."[53] In an address delivered in July, 1920, at Albert Hall, London, Balfour expressed the conviction that the Jewish renascence in Palestine would be crowned with triumph ultimately, but he emphasized the great difficulties that had to be overcome. One was the smallness of Palestine and its undeveloped condition; but he believed that skill, knowledge and perseverance combined with Jewish capital (by which he meant the contributions of the masses of the Jews who were imbued with the Zionist ideal) would conquer these difficulties. Another significant difficulty, in his opinion, was the danger of lack of unity among the Jews themselves, and the failure to trust their leaders sufficiently. But the greatest difficulty, he thought, concerned the Arab question:[54]

Among these difficulties I am not sure that I do not rate the highest, or at all events the first, the inevitable difficulty of dealing with the Arab question as it presents itself within the limits of Palestine. It will require tact; it will require judgment; above all, it will require sympathetic good-will on the part of both Jew and of Arab. So far as the Arabs are concerned—a great, and interesting, and an attractive race—so far as they are concerned, I hope they will remember that while we desire—this assembly and all the Jews whom it

51. *Brandeis on Zionism*, Zionist Organization of America, Washington, 1942, p. 113.
52. Jewish Agency for Palestine, *Memorandum to the Palestine Royal Commission*, p. 90.
53. Medzini, *op. cit.*, p. 126.
54. Stephen S. Wise and Jacob de Haas, *The Great Betrayal*, Brentano's, New York, 1930, pp. 166–67.

represents—under the aegis of Great Britain to establish this home for the Jewish people, the Great Powers, and among all the Great Powers most especially Great Britain, have forced them, the Arab race, from the tyranny of their brutal conqueror, who has kept them under his heel for many centuries. I hope they will remember it is we who have established the independent Arab sovereignty of the Hedjaz. I hope they will remember it, we who desire in Mesopotamia to prepare the way for the future of a self-governing, autonomous Arab State. And I hope that, remembering all that, they will not grudge that small niche, for it is not more geographically in the former Arab territories than a niche—being given to the people who for all these hundreds of years have been separated from it, but who surely have a title to develop on their own lines in the land of their forefathers.

Ahad Ha'am in the introduction to the third edition of his works, made a sharp analysis of what had been accomplished by the Balfour Declaration and the San Remo Conference. He warned against imagining more in these documents than actually was contained in them. The San Remo decision had, in his opinion, reaffirmed the Balfour Declaration and added to the British statement of policy an international recognition which was invaluable. It gave the Jews a chance to establish a national home, but it also gave the Arabs the right to develop their national home alongside the Jewish national home. Those who were interpreting the San Remo decision as a promise of a Jewish state which would dominate the country, were preparing the people for ultimate disillusionment. Besides, they were giving unnecessary support to the apprehensions of the Arabs, who were already fearful that the Jews would expropriate them and become masters in the land.

He also pointed out that, on the other hand, the vagueness of the document permitted whittling it down to almost nothing, and that, in the last analysis, all depended on the goodwill of the trustee on whom the San Remo Conference had laid the responsibility of carrying the "national home policy" into effect. He stated succinctly the difference between what the Jews demanded and what they got:[55]

It can scarcely be necessary to explain at length the difference between the two versions. Had the British Government accepted the

55. Ahad Ha'am, *Ten Essays on Zionism and Judaism*, trans. by Leon Simon, pp. 15–20.

version suggested to it—that Palestine should be reconstituted as the national home of the Jewish people—its promise might have been interpreted as meaning that Palestine, inhabited as it now is, was restored to the Jewish people on the ground of its historic right; that the Jewish people was to rebuild its waste places and was destined to rule over it and to manage all its affairs in its own way, without regard to the consent or non-consent of its present inhabitants. For this rebuilding (it might have been understood) is only a renewal of the ancient right of the Jews, which overrides the right of the present inhabitants, who have wrongly established their national home on a land not their own. But the British Government, as it stated expressly in the Declaration itself, was not willing to promise anything which would harm the present inhabitants of Palestine, and therefore it changed the Zionist formula, and gave it a more restricted form. The Government thinks, it would seem, that when a people has only the moral force of its claim to build its national home in a land at present inhabited by others, and has not behind it a powerful army or fleet to prove the justice of its claim, that people can have only what its right allows it in truth and justice, and not what conquering peoples take for themselves by armed force, under the cover of various "rights" invented for the occasion.

THE DRAFTING OF THE MANDATE

Throughout the year 1918, and during the beginning of 1919, numerous conferences, conventions and meetings were held to discuss the aims and programs of the Jewish Homeland in preparation for the Peace Conference. In many of these the term, Jewish Commonwealth, appeared and was frequently used interchangeably with Jewish Homeland. But there were different degrees of emphasis on the concept of Jewish statehood; and in most cases the Jewish state was conceived of as ultimate goal rather than as immediate objective. The Zionist plans emphasized religious freedom and civil rights for all inhabitants of Palestine. They give attention to the rights of the Arabs in cultural matters and in the safeguarding of the Moslem shrines.

Programs for the Jewish Homeland

One of the first of these proposals was incorporated in the Pittsburgh Program adopted by the Convention of American Zionists on June 25, 1918. The Zionist Organization was then under the influence of Brandeis and a group of young men imbued with the new democratic liberalism favorable to Labor and somewhat tinged with socialist notions. The Pittsburgh Program laid the emphasis on social justice and cooperative endeavor; it was a statement of social policy rather than a definite political program. It was in fact notably silent on political aspects. The following were its provisions:[56]

> We declare for political and civil equality irrespective of race, sex, or faith of all the inhabitants of the land.
> To insure in the Jewish National Home in Palestine equality of opportunity we favor a policy which, with due regard to existing rights, shall tend to establish the ownership and control by the whole people of the land, of all natural resources and of all public utilities.
> All land, owned or controlled by the whole people, should be leased on such conditions as will insure the fullest opportunity for development and continuity of possession.
> The cooperative principle should be applied so far as feasible in the organization of all agricultural, industrial, commercial, and financial undertakings.
> The system of free public instruction which is to be established should embrace all grades and departments of education.
> Hebrew, the national language of the Jewish people, shall be the medium of public instruction.[57]

Quite different in spirit was the program formulated in Palestine. At a conference held in Jaffa on December 18, 1918, an "Outline for the Provisional Government of Palestine" was drawn up and submitted to the Zionist authorities for their consideration in presenting the Jewish case before the Peace Conference. The resolutions may be summarized as follows:

> Palestine should be recognized as the National Homeland, in the affairs of which the Jewish people, as a whole, shall have a determining voice. England should be the trustee. A Jewish colonization society should be created with the sanction of the League of Nations.
> The colonization society should have broad powers: to organize Jewish immigration; to take over state lands and develop them; to obtain government concessions to construct railroads, harbors and irrigation works; to administer the agrarian bank of the former Ottoman government; to have the exclusive right to develop all sub-

---

56. "The Pittsburgh Program," *The Maccabaean*, XXXI, 1918, p. 237.
57. It is clear from the context that the reference is to Jewish schools and not to the language of instruction in non-Jewish schools, which are equally, with the Jewish schools, to be supported from public funds.

surface natural resources; to establish new agrarian institutions; and to grant concessions for these purposes.

The proposals aimed to bring about a large Jewish majority but, at the same time, to guarantee the rights of the various national and religious groups in all religious, cultural and philanthropic matters. Arabic as well as Hebrew were to be recognized as official languages. However, the purpose of creating a Jewish Homeland should receive recognition by adopting the name of *Eretz Israel* for the land and by recognizing the Jewish flag as the flag of the country.

The principal administrative agency of the land was to be an executive committee over whose action the Governor General should have veto power. The executive committee should have jurisdiction over all matters except military and foreign affairs, the protection of places holy to non-Jews and their religious, educational and communal affairs.[58]

About the same time, the American Jewish Congress meeting in Philadelphia (December 17, 1918) adopted a resolution, instructing their delegates to the Peace Conference to cooperate with the World Zionist Organization to the end that "the Peace Conference may recognize the aspirations and historic claims of the Jewish people in regard to Palestine . . . and there should be established such political, administrative and economic conditions in Palestine as will assure, under the trusteeship of Great Britain acting on behalf of such a League of Nations as may be formed, *the development of Palestine into a Jewish Commonwealth,* it being clearly understood that nothing shall be done which shall prejudice the existing rights of non-Jewish communities in Palestine or the rights and political status enjoyed by the Jews." [59] On March 2, 1919, the American Jewish Congress submitted to President Wilson a comprehensive memorial on "The Jewish Title to Palestine." Palestine is claimed as "the historic home of the Jews," the place where they achieved their greatest development and from which there emanated spiritual and moral influences of supreme value to all mankind. The Memorial recognized that the greater portion of the Jews throughout the world would remain in the lands of their abode and that the Peace Conference must be concerned with insuring for them, as for all others, equality of rights.

58. "Demands of Palestine Jews," *The Maccabaean*, Vol. XXXII, 1919, p. 197.
59. *Jewish Opinion*, No. 2, January 19, 1919, p. 2.

In Palestine, it would be the duty of the government to help the Jews to continue the development which they had already begun. Until such a period when the people of Palestine were prepared to establish a representative and responsible government, the following terms were deemed essential:[60]

1. In any instrument establishing the constitution of Palestine, the declaration of the Peace Conference shall be recited as forming an integral part of such constitution.
2. The Jewish people shall be entitled to fair representation in the executive and legislative bodies and in the selection of public and civil servants.
3. In encouraging the self-government of localities, the mandatory or trustee shall secure the maintenance by local communities of proper standards of administration in matters of education and communal or regional activities. In granting or enlarging autonomy, regard shall be had to the readiness and ability of the community to attain such standards. Local autonomous communities shall be empowered and encouraged to combine and cooperate for common purposes.
4. Assistance shall be rendered from the public funds for the education of the inhabitants without distinction of race or creed. Hebrew shall be one of the official languages and shall be employed in all documents, decrees and announcements issued by the Government.
5. The Jewish Sabbath and Holy Days shall be recognized as legal days of rest.
6. The established rights of the present population shall be equitably safeguarded.
7. All inhabitants of Palestine who, on a date to be specified, shall have their domicile therein, except those who, within a period to be stated, shall in writing elect to retain their citizenship in any other country, shall be citizens of Palestine, and they and all persons born in Palestine or naturalized under its laws after the day named shall be citizens thereof and entitled to the protection of the mandatory or trustee.

The view of the Zionist authorities in London was reflected in an interview which Weizmann had with Balfour on Decem-

---

60. "Jewish Title to Palestine," *The Maccabaean*, Vol. XXXII, March, 1919, Zionist Organization of America; quoted in Fannie Fern Andrews, *The Holy Land under Mandate*, Houghton Mifflin, Boston, 1931, Vol. I, p. 358.

ber 4, 1918, when he took up the thread of negotiations with the British Government. Weizmann's proposals were not official but they were made with the full knowledge and consent of the Zionist leaders and gave a preview of the Zionist policy. Weizmann presented as a basis for a proposal to be presented to the Peace Conference through the British Government the following three points: 1) recognition of the historical and national rights of Jews to Palestine, always with the proviso that the legitimate interests of the non-Jewish population would be fully safeguarded; 2) appointment of a Trustee for Palestine, it being understood that the Zionists would name Great Britain; 3) designation of an organization representing the Jewish people which would be empowered to make arrangements with the Trustee power necessary for the establishment in Palestine of a Jewish National Home. Balfour said that he was prepared to accept the purport of these recommendations and that the Zionists would probably have the opportunity of making their proposals directly to the Peace Conference. He said that Great Britain was definitely pledged to the policy of the national home and would support it at the Peace Conference.[61]

The view of the Zionist leaders, at this time, may be inferred also from the ideas expressed by Weizmann in the speech which he delivered before an assembly of Zionists in London toward the end of 1918.[62] Weizmann said that there were some who believed that the Jews ought to obtain "a Jewish State," like the Poles, the Yugoslavs and others, but in all these cases there was already a population and all that was necessary was the political structure. Before Palestine could become a Jewish state, it was necessary to have Jews living there. The essential political demands ought rather to be: 1) that the world should recognize that Palestine, the land of the Jews in the past, should again become so in the future; 2) that opportunities should be given for creating the conditions necessary for the restoration of the Jews to Palestine; 3) that the Mandate over Palestine should be given to a state which the Jews trusted implicitly, namely, to Great Britain. To those who claimed that such demands were not in harmony with the Basle Program,

---

61. *Reports of the Executive to the XIIth Zionist Congress*, 1921, I, p. 19.

62. Medzini, *op. cit.*, p. 89.

Weizmann replied that if the conditions he mentioned were granted, we would indeed have more than the Basle Program.

Official Jewish Proposals to the Peace Conference

It was still impossible to convene a regular session of the Congress or the Actions Committee, but a number of leading members of the Zionist Organization came together in London in January, 1919, to formulate an official policy.[63] Herbert Samuel was commissioned to draft a program in a form suitable for presentation to the Foreign Office. After some changes introduced by the members of the Zionist Political Committee, the draft was presented, unofficially, to the Ministry along with a large number of resolutions adopted at various conventions and meetings of Jews in England and other countries. At the end of January, the Zionist leaders were informed by the Foreign Office that it would be in order for the Zionist Organization to submit its proposals directly to the Secretariat of the Peace Conference. It was, however, intimated to them that the British Government would not accept the Mandate unless certain of the proposals considered excessive were eliminated. Among these were the demand that the head of the Palestine Government should be a Jew and that the majority of the Government officials should be Jewish.[64]

Another memorandum was then prepared under the title "Statement of the Zionist Organization regarding Palestine." This document, dated 3 February, 1919 (3 Adar, 5679), constituted the official Zionist proposal to the Peace Conference.[65] The memorandum begins with the following introductory remarks which convey the essence of the program:

---

63. Among these were: Dr. Shmarya Levin, who came from New York for the purpose, and Victor Jacobson from Copenhagen. There were two representatives of the Russian Zionists, I. L. Goldberg and Israel Rosoff, and the head of the Dutch Zionists, Mr. Jacobus Kahn.

64. Medzini, *op. cit.*, p. 91.

65. *Reports of the Executive to the XIIth Zionist Congress*, I, pp. 74–83. The statement was signed by the following: Lord Walter Rothschild; on behalf of the Zionist Organization, Nahum Sokolow and Chaim Weizmann; on behalf of the Zionist Organization of America, Julian W. Mack, Stephen S. Wise, Harry Friedenwald, Jacob de Haas, Mary Fels, Louis Robison and Bernard Flexner; on behalf of the Russian Zionist Organization, by Israel Rosoff; on behalf of the Jewish population in Palestine, in accordance with the Mandate received, Nahum Sokolow and Chaim Weizmann.

1. The High Contracting Parties recognize the historic title of the Jewish people to Palestine and the right of the Jews to reconstitute in Palestine their National Home.

2. The boundaries of Palestine shall be as declared in the Schedule annexed hereto.

3. The sovereign possession of Palestine shall be vested in the League of Nations and the Government entrusted to Great Britain as Mandatory of the League.

4. (Provision to be inserted relating to the application in Palestine of such of the general conditions attached to mandates as are suitable to the case.)

5. The mandate shall be subject also to the following special conditions:

(I) Palestine shall be placed under such political, administrative and economic conditions as will secure the establishment there of the Jewish National Home, and ultimately render possible the creation of an autonomous Commonwealth, it being clearly understood that nothing shall be done which may prejudice the civil and religious rights of existing non-Jewish communities in Palestine or the rights and political status enjoyed by Jews in any other country.

(II) To this end the Mandatory Power shall *inter alia:*

(a) Promote Jewish immigration and close settlement on the land, the established rights of the present non-Jewish population being equitably safeguarded.

(b) Accept the cooperation in such measures of a Council representative of the Jews in Palestine and of the world that may be established for the development of the Jewish National Home in Palestine and entrust the organization of Jewish education to such Council.

(c) On being satisfied that the constitution of such Council precludes the making of private profit, offer to the Council in priority any concession for public works or for the development of natural resources which it may be found desirable to grant.

(III) The Mandatory Power shall encourage the widest measure of self-government for localities practicable in the conditions of the country.

(IV) There shall be forever the fullest freedom of religious worship for all creeds in Palestine. There shall be no discrimination among the inhabitants with regard to citizenship and civil rights, on the grounds of religion, or of race.

(V) (Provision to be inserted relating to the control of the Holy Places.)

The proposals include detailed statements under the heads: The Historic Title of the Jews to Palestine; Great Britain as Mandatory of the League of Nations; the Boundaries of Palestine. Recommendations are made to the Mandatory Power which have as their purpose insuring the Jewish character of Palestine, e.g., Jewish representation on executive and legislative bodies, local government, control of education, facilities for naturalization, etc. The proposals emphasize the importance of the appointment of a Land Commission, on which the Jewish Council would have representation—with power to survey the land and to propose measures for development. Provisions are suggested for the election of a Jewish Council for Palestine to be elected by a Jewish congress representative of the Jews of Palestine and of the world. The Jewish Council should be recognized as a legal entity and have wide powers to cooperate and consult with the Government to act as the representative of the Jewish people in all matters affecting the government of Palestine. Finally, it is suggested that when, in the opinion of the Mandatory Power, Palestine will be ready for the establishment of a responsible government, such government shall be established on the basis of a democratic franchise without regard to race or faith, and that all inhabitants of Palestine shall continue to enjoy equal civil and political rights.

A meeting of the Actions Committee of the Zionist Organization was called and met in London a few weeks later on February 23, 1919. The statement prepared by the Committee for the Peace Conference was severely criticized. The delegates from Palestine, who had given their mandate to Weizmann and Sokolow, were incensed because certain demands made in their "Outline," such as giving voice to the whole Jewish people in the affairs of Palestine and recognition of the Zionist flag as the flag of Palestine, had not been included in the official proposals. There was criticism also outside of official sources. Israel Zangwill sharply attacked the official Zionist interpretation of the Balfour Declaration as being hardly serious. To him, it seemed that the Jewish national home, as proposed, was to be: "a British Crown Colony with predominantly Arab population . . . [The Jewish people] is to crawl into a corner of its own land like a leper colony, . . . representing on its own soil the humiliation and subservience of its two thousand years

The Peace Conference and Mandate for Palestine 159

of agony and ignominy. Such a Palestine has neither the glamour of poetry nor the practicality of prose. It is neither Jewish, nor National, nor a Home." In order to achieve a thoroughgoing settlement of the Jewish problem, he proposed that the Arabs of Palestine should gradually be resettled in the new and vast Arabian Kingdom to be set up in the conquered Turkish territories, to liberate which, Jews no less than Arabs had laid down their lives. With this new Arab state the Jewish Commonwealth would cultivate the closest friendship. "Only with a Jewish majority (not, of course, a Jewish totality), only with the land nationalized—and Jewish as well as Arab land must be expropriated with reasonable compensation—can Israel enter upon the task of building up that model state, the construction of which American Zionism in its trustful acceptance of the Declaration has already outlined." [66]

In the midst of the discussions of the Actions Committee, a call was received from the Government requesting the Zionists to appear before the Council of Ten at Paris.[67] The meeting took place in M. Pichon's room on the Quai d'Orsay on Thursday, February 27, 1919, at 3:00 P.M. Representing the Council of Ten were the following: for Great Britain, Balfour and Lord Milner; for France, Tardieu and Pichon; for America, Lansing and White; for Italy, Baron Sonnino; and a Japanese representative. Clemenceau was present when the meeting was opened, but left a few minutes later, yielding the chair to M. Pichon. On behalf of the Jews there were: Weizmann and Sokolow for the Zionist Organization; Ussishkin for the Russian Zionists; André Spire for the French Zionists, and Sylvain Lévi for French Jewry.

Nahum Sokolow opened the presentation, speaking in

---

66. Israel Zangwill, "Before the Peace Conference," *Asia*, February, 1919, pp. 105 ff.

67. Weizmann and Sokolow were invited on behalf of the Zionist Organization; Mr. Jacob de Haas for the Zionist Organization of America; André Spire for the French Zionists and Sylvain Lévi for French Jewry. De Haas could not arrange to come on time and the Zionists asked that Ussishkin be invited in his place as the representative of Russian Jewry. The Zionists asked whom M. Lévi was representing and they were told that he would speak on behalf of French Jewry. Accounts of the meeting will be found in the following: Miller, *My Diary at the Conference of Paris*, Vol. XV, pp. 104–5; *Reports of the Executive to the XIIth Zionist Congress*, I, pp. 21–23; Lloyd George, *op. cit.*, Vol. II, pp. 56–59.

French. He emphasized the need of a homeland for the masses of Jews living in Eastern Europe and elaborated on the first point in the Zionist proposals—namely, the historic right of the Jews to Palestine. He was followed by Weizmann, who noted that the war had left the Jews of Eastern Europe knocking around the world "seeking a refuge and unable to find one." Palestine possessed great possibilities for settlement and the solution proposed by the Zionist Organization was the only one which could, in the long run, solve the problem and, at the same time, transform Jewish energy into a constructive force. Basing his thesis on the density of the population in nearby Lebanon, he argued that there was room in Palestine "for an increase of at least four to five million people, without encroaching on the legitimate interests of the people already there." [68] He summarized the essence of the Zionist requirements under three heads: that the Mandatory Power should a) promote Jewish immigration and settlement on the land; b) cooperate with a Jewish council or agency—representative of Jewish Palestine and of world Jewry—in the development of the Jewish national home in Palestine and entrust the organization of Jewish education to such a council; c) offer to the Jewish council priority in obtaining concessions for development, on a non-profit basis, of natural resources which the Government might find it desirable to grant.

Mr. Ussishkin then spoke supporting the arguments of his colleagues. The speech was in Hebrew and according to Weizmann it made a great impression on the audience. André Spire, speaking in the name of the French Zionists, who, he admitted, were only a minority among the French Jews, associated himself completely with the ideas put forward by the representatives of the Zionist Organization. Then came the turn of M. Sylvain Lévi. He said that he greatly appreciated the honor of the invitation, particularly since he was not himself a Zionist: he was a Jew by origin and in sentiment, but French above all. He began by pointing out the splendid achievements of the colonies in Palestine under the auspices of Baron de Rothschild and emphasized the significance of the educational activities of the *Alliance Israélite Universelle*. After some complimentary remarks about the achievements of the Zionist movement, in which he, so to speak, damned them with faint

---

68. Miller, *op. cit.*, Vol. XV, p. 108.

The Peace Conference and Mandate for Palestine

praise, he proceeded to argue that Palestine was too small a country to absorb the millions of Jews who wanted to go there and also raised the question of the dual rights of citizenship, if a Jewish political center were to be established. In conclusion, he dwelt on the great part France had played in the development of the Jews in Palestine, and said that he trusted that France would be permitted to continue her beneficent educational work there.

The Zionist representatives were greatly disturbed by M. Lévi's remarks and then, as Dr. Weizmann put it: "There occurred a miracle." Mr. Lansing, the American representative, interpolated a question toward the end of Lévi's remarks and this gave Weizmann an opportunity for a rejoinder. Miller describes the incident as follows:[69]

Mr. Lansing asked Dr. Weizmann to clear up some confusion which existed in his mind as to the correct meaning of the words "Jewish National Home." Did that mean an autonomous Jewish Government?

Dr. Weizmann replied in the negative. The Zionist Organization did not want an autonomous Jewish Government, but merely to establish in Palestine, under a Mandatory Power, an administration, not necessarily Jewish, which would render it possible to send into Palestine 70,000 to 80,000 Jews annually. The Zionist Association would require to have permission at the same time to build Jewish schools, where Hebrew would be taught, and in that way to build up gradually a nationality which would be as Jewish as the French nation was French and the British nation British. Later on, when the Jews formed the large majority, they would be ripe to establish such a Government as would answer to the state of the development of the country and to their ideals.

There is also confirmation of the general position taken by the Zionists in a report of an interview given by Dr. Weizmann to Walter Duranty on February 28th, a day after the meeting with the Council of Ten. The main points of this interview, published in the *New York Times* on March 3rd, were:

1. Full recognition of the historic title of the Jewish people to Palestine, and of the Jews' right to reconstitute their national home there.

69. Miller, *op. cit.*, Vol. XV, pp. 104–117.

2. Choice of Great Britain as the trustee of Palestine because the British a) have been educated on the Bible and are sympathetic to the Jewish cause, b) have had great administrative experience. Another factor favoring the choice of Britain was the doubt as to whether the United States would accept obligations in the Near East.

3. Fixation of the boundaries of Palestine: "The whole of Palestine from the Lebanon Province to the Egyptian frontier and from the sea to the Hedjaz will be open to Jewish settlement, which will ultimately develop into an autonomous Jewish Commonwealth."

4. Request for creation by Great Britain of suitable political, administrative and economic conditions, promotion of Jewish immigration and land settlement, and cooperation with Jewish council representing the Jews of Palestine. "Concessions for the benefit of Palestine will be granted by Great Britain to the council with a proviso that the latter will be prohibited from using them for private profit."

Weizmann made it clear, however, that the establishment of the Jewish Commonwealth would not be immediate:

"We want it understood that the immediate formation of a Jewish State or Commonwealth is not contemplated. Today, and doubtless for some years to come, Jewish settlers in Palestine will actually be in a considerable minority as compared with the non-Jewish inhabitants of the country. There can be no question of that minority imposing its will on the majority. Our position will be the first experiment of the League of Nations' mandatory system by which people not yet ready for independent self-government will gradually rise thereto under the tutelage of great powers."

About a week later, in reporting the event to a Zionist conference held in London, Dr. Weizmann gave a very similar version of what had happened:[70]

Mr. Lansing, the American representative, who sat in a corner, and moved his chair further and further as Lévi was speaking, asked me what we meant by a "Jewish National Home." This gave me an opportunity. I declared that by a "Jewish National Home" we meant the creation in Palestine of such conditions as should enable us to establish between 50,000 and 60,000 Jews per annum there, and to settle them on the land. Further, that the conditions should be such

70. *Reports of the Executive to the XIIth Zionist Congress*, I, p. 22.

The Peace Conference and Mandate for Palestine

that we should be allowed to develop our institutions, our schools and the Hebrew language—that there should ultimately be such conditions that Palestine should be just as Jewish as America is American and England is English. Then I asked Lansing if I had made my point clear. He said: "Perfectly." Mr. Balfour was very pleased, so were the Italian representatives.[71]

Some insight into the view of Zionist leaders at this time is provided by the proposals to the Peace Conference formulated by Ahad Ha'am in 1919. He took an important though unobtrusive part in the formulation of the Mandate, as a trusted adviser in the negotiations with the British Government. His formulation is of considerable interest in the light of the fact that he has sometimes been regarded as having been opposed to the development of a Jewish Commonwealth:[72]

... That the historic right of the Jewish people to the re-establishment of its National Home in Palestine be recognized for all time as incontestable and that all possible assistance be given to facilitate the achievement of this object.

That with this ultimate purpose in view, the country of Palestine

---

71. The statement made by Weizmann to the effect that "Palestine should be just as Jewish as America is American and England is English" became in subsequent years the cause of much controversy. This expression has been exploited by pro-Arab writers to mean that the Jews expected to dominate Palestine, without giving consideration to the national character of the existing Arab population. It is interesting to note that in the first version, as reported by David Hunter Miller, Weizmann is reported to have employed the term "nationality," and in the context the emphasis is on the cultural and psychological aspects of this term. Weizmann expressed the desire for the completeness of the Jewish personality, and the consequent necessity of creating a Jewish milieu for the Jewish part of the population. The cultural and psychological emphasis of Weizmann's point is further strengthened by the fact that in the context, as reported in Miller's *Diary*, it comes in opposition to the emphasis on an autonomous Jewish government, which Weizmann had denied to be the immediate aim of the Jewish National Home. There is nothing in this much attacked phrase which indicates a deviation from the moderate position which Weizmann has held throughout the course of his leadership. It may be added also that the phrase "as Jewish as England is English" was anticipated in Sidebotham's formulation before the Balfour Declaration was issued. (See above, Chap. II, p. 102.)

The discrepancy in the figures quoted in the statement by Dr. Weizmann is due to a difference of sources. In *Reports of the Executive to the XIIth Zionist Congress*, 50,000–60,000 is mentioned, while according to Miller, *My Diary at the Peace Conference*, the number is 70,000–80,000.

72. Facsimile included in Gelber, *op. cit.*, facing p. 232.

within its historical boundaries to be defined by a Special Commission, shall at present be entrusted to the care of Great Britain, which in its capacity of Trustee, shall place the country under such conditions—political, administrative, economic, etc.—as will lead up to the steady enlargement and development of the Jewish settlement so that it may ultimately develop into a Jewish Commonwealth on national lines; it being clearly understood that nothing shall be done which may prejudice the civil and religious rights of the existing non-Jewish communities in Palestine or the rights and political status enjoyed by Jews in any other country.[73]

Preparation of the Final Draft

The British Delegation at the Peace Conference opened formal discussions with the representatives of the Zionist Organization on proposals for a draft of the Mandate for Palestine in the spring of 1919.[74] The course of negotiations may be discussed under seven stages.

First Stage.

The first stage is represented by a tentative draft mandate, of which there is a record in a letter sent by Felix Frankfurter to David Hunter Miller, dated Paris, March 28, 1919.[75] Summaries of selected main paragraphs follow:

---

73. It should be remembered that Ahad Ha'am had always insisted on the necessity of emphasizing the historically founded national claims of the Jewish people to Palestine. Thus, in a letter to Sokolow on November 7, 1917, he had suggested the addition of the clause: "the National Home of the Jewish people to be rebuilt by the same under a protection . . ." His reason was that without this addition it might appear that the term "National Home" was being applied to that tiny minority found in Palestine and that protection was being invoked primarily for it, "whereas in truth our eyes are directed above all to the future." (*Iggrot Ahad Ha'am*, V. 5, p. 304.) Cf. Gelber, *op. cit.*, pp. 297–298.

74. The drafting was carried out under the authority of Weizmann and Sokolow as heads of the Zionist Organization. Assistance was received from the American Delegation which included Felix Frankfurter and Benjamin V. Cohen, both of whom were in close touch with Justice Brandeis. In the first stages, a temporary political committee was in charge, consisting of Herbert Samuel, Dr. Victor Jacobson, Dr. M. Berthold Feiwel, Harry Sacher, S. Landman and Benjamin V. Cohen. In the later stages, Harry Sacher, Leonard Stein and Benjamin Cohen carried on. Drafts were prepared by Professor Frankfurter aided by an American lawyer, Mr. Gans.

75. Miller, *op. cit.*, Vol. VII, pp. 369 ff.

GLENSMORE ROAD
N.W.3

Proposals for
The Peace Conference.

The Peace Conference, having taken notice of the aspirations and claims of the Jewish People with regard to Palestine, hereby decides:

1) That the historic right of the Jewish people to the re-establishment of its National Home in Palestine be recognised for all times as incontestable, and that all possible assistance be given to facilitate the achievement of this object.

2) That, with this ultimate purpose in view, the country of Palestine, within its historical boundaries to be defined by a Special Commission, shall at present be entrusted to the care of Great Britain which in its capacity of Trustee shall

place the country under such conditions — political, administrative, economic etc. — as will lead up to the steady enlargement and development of the Jewish settlement so that it may ultimately develop into a Jewish Commonwealth on national lines; it being clearly understood that nothing shall be done which may prejudice the civil and religious rights of existing non-Jewish communities in Palestine or the rights and political status enjoyed by Jews in any other country.

General Suggestions

1. The Mandate should fit into the structure of the League of Nations.

2. The guiding principle for the Mandatory and the general objectives of the Mandate should be recited.

3. The authoritative utterances in regard to Palestine should be mentioned; i.e., the Balfour Declaration, concurrence by the Allies and the United States, and President Wilson's declaration in Washington on March 2nd.[76]

4. The means by which to carry out the defined aims within the framework of the guiding principles should be left to the Mandatory Power and the detailed structure of Government should be worked out in cooperation with the representatives of the peoples whose trustee they are.

5. The machinery of the League of Nations should be regarded as sufficient safeguard for the wise discharge of its functions and too many appeals to the League of Nations should be avoided.

6. However, certain specific limitations should be imposed: a) limitations applicable to all mandatory areas, such as non-discrimination and the development of natural resources for the benefit of the people; b) restrictions applicable to the specific mandatory area, having in mind the establishment of Palestine as the Jewish Homeland.

Clauses of the Preamble

1. Whereas the inhabitants of Palestine are unable at the present time effectively to constitute and to maintain an autonomous commonwealth, and

2. Whereas the League of Nations and the Signatory Powers recognize the historic title of the Jewish people to Palestine and the right of the Jews to reconstitute Palestine as their national home: and there to establish the foundations of a Jewish Commonwealth, and

3. Whereas it is the wish of the inhabitants of Palestine and of the Jews that governmental and administrative powers to be exercised over the territory and its inhabitants should be confined to Great Britain as the Mandatory of the League and as trustee of the Signatory Powers,

4. Now therefore the Signatory Powers hereby constitute Great Britain the Mandatory of the League of Nations for the Government and Administration of Palestine.

76. See Chap. IV, p. 242.

Constitutional Limitations on the Mandatory

1. All powers hereby conferred shall be exercised subject to the control which now is or hereafter may be vested in the League of Nations.

2. The establishment of Palestine as the Jewish National Home and its development into an autonomous commonwealth, dedicated to the advancement of Social Justice shall be the guiding purpose in the execution of the mandate. The Mandatory shall adopt measures appropriate for the creation of such political, administrative and economic conditions as will tend to the realization of these aims, insofar as such measures may be adopted without prejudicing the civil or religious rights and political status enjoyed by the Jews in other countries.

3. No law shall be made respecting the establishment of religion or prohibiting the free exercise thereof, and the free exercise and enjoyment of religious profession and worship without discrimination or preference shall forever be allowed. No political or religious test other than that of citizenship and an oath of affirmation to support the laws of the land and the Covenants and judgments of the League of Nations shall be required as a qualification to any office or public trust under the Government of Palestine or as a qualification for the exercise of any civil or political rights therein.

4. It shall adopt and enforce such measures as shall be adequate to protect both against physical impairment and against profanation the places within the land which are revered as holy by the adherents of the Jewish, Mohammedan and Christian faith, and to permit access thereto to the adherents of the faith or faiths by which they are held in reverence, and shall from time to time amend such measures to conform to such requirements, not inconsistent with the exercise of the general administrative and governmental functions hereinbefore conferred, as the League of Nations may impose.

5. All members of the League of Nations and the people thereof shall be assured the same opportunities for trade and commerce therein and with the inhabitants thereof as are assured to the Mandatory and its people.

6. Whenever in the opinion of the Mandatory or of the League of Nations the inhabitants of Palestine shall be fit to create and maintain an autonomous, representative and responsible government, the Mandatory shall take such steps as will permit them through the exercise of a democratic franchise, without regard to race, sex, or faith, to establish a representative and responsible Government in such form as the people of Palestine may devise.

Second Stage.

After consultation and revision the proposals were handed to the British Delegation under date of July 15, 1919. It was the first official draft and was intended to become part of the proposed Turkish Treaty. The following is a summary of the main points based on the account given in the *Reports of the Executive to the XIIth Zionist Congress:*[77]

1. Recognition should be given to the *"historical connection* of the Jews with Palestine and the claim which this gives them to found a *national home* in that country." [78]
2. The proposed mandatory should be made responsible for placing Palestine under such political, administrative and economic conditions as would secure the establishment there of the Jewish national home.
3. The ultimate aim of the mandate should be the creation in Palestine of a self-governing commonwealth.
4. A provisional—to be changed subsequently into a permanent—Jewish Council should be formed representing Jewish opinion in Palestine and in the world at large. This Council should constitute an agency to advise the government of Palestine on questions touching the welfare of the Jewish population, should be endowed with wide powers to carry out public works, and be granted preferential consideration in regard to concessions.
5. The Palestine administration should be under a Governor appointed by the Mandatory Power who would be assisted by an Executive Council. Not less than half of the members of the Executive Council should be representative of the Palestine population, Jewish and non-Jewish, and of the Jewish Council. Provision should also be made for a Representative Assembly of an advisory character, gradually to be given wider powers as the Palestinian nation progressed toward full self-government.
6. Jewish immigration and colonization should be facilitated by the British government.
7. Hebrew was to be recognized as an official language.

Third Stage.

The draft was a compromise and had been formulated in a manner which the Zionist leaders thought would possibly be

77. I, p. 28.
78. The phrase, "historical connection of the Jews with Palestine," is believed to have been suggested by Mr. Balfour.

acceptable to the British and the Peace Conference. At the meeting of the Actions Committee, held in July and August in London, where delegates from Palestine were also present, the draft was subjected to much criticism. As a result, representations were made in August 1919, in regard to a number of central points. The term, "historical connection," was regarded as inadequate. Only "historical title," as used in the Statement to the Peace Conference was regarded by the Zionists as adequate. A text was submitted which explicitly stated the recognition of the historic title of the Jews to Palestine and of the "right of Jews to reconstitute it as their National Home." It was also to be made clear that the Jewish National Home was not limited to a part of Palestine, but was to be co-extensive with the whole of Palestine. The Zionist memorandum requested that: "The Declaration should take cognizance of the fact that it is *the* National Home of the Jews which is to be re-established, and not merely *a* National Home in Palestine such as they may already be said to have in Poland and in Eastern Europe." Leading members of the Actions Committee urged that a reference to the eventual establishment of a Jewish Commonwealth should be included in the following form: "and there to establish the foundations of a Jewish Commonwealth." Among the alterations and additions suggested by the Actions Committee were the following:[79]

1. Insertion of words: "Establishment of the Land as the Jewish National Home and its development into an autonomous Commonwealth shall be the guiding purpose in the execution of the Mandate."
2. Insertion of a clause recognizing the Jewish Sabbath and holy days as official days of rest and legal holidays, without prejudice to the civil rights of non-Jews.
3. Provision to be made for public ownership or effective public control of the land and natural resources of Palestine and of public utilities with a view to prevention of exploitation for excessive profits.
4. Encouragement to be given to cooperative undertakings.
5. Instead of a Jewish Council an appropriate Jewish Agency to be recognized by the Mandatory and empowered to assist and cooperate in the establishment of the Jewish National Home with certain rights of preemption. The Zionist Organization to be recognized as

[79]. *Reports of the Executive to the XIIth Zionist Congress*, I, pp. 28–29.

such an Agency, and to have a right of preemption, carrying with it the right to be consulted in reference to concessions not undertaken by the Agency.

6. The Zionist Organization to cooperate with the Mandatory in regard to immigration and colonization.

7. Women to be entitled to vote and take office.

8. Change in the terms of the Mandate to be without prejudice to the principle of the Jewish National Home.

9. The Jewish Agency to have access to the Council of the League of Nations.

Fourth Stage.

The second official tentative draft was prepared by the Zionists and completed at the end of 1919. It apparently had the approval of the British Government. The new preamble still spoke of "historical connection" and not of "historical title," but it went on to add, "and the claim which this gives them to reconstitute Palestine as their National Home (*Eretz Israel*)." The draft also contains reference to the development of a self-governing Commonwealth as the ultimate outcome of the Jewish National Home. It included all the demands in regard to the recognition of the Jewish Agency and the acceptance of the Zionist Organization as this agency. It gave a preferential right to the Agency in public works, provided the rate of interest would be limited and excess profits utilized for the benefit of the country as a whole. The right of the Agency to cooperate in the facilitation of immigration and colonization was granted. The clause on naturalization provided that the acquisition of Palestinian nationality would be compulsory for all Jews who became permanent residents of Palestine. In connection with public works and the development of natural resources, the following important addition was made: "In the construction and operation of public works, services, and utilities, and in the development of the natural resources of the country, the establishment of the Jewish National Home shall be a guiding principle." The provision for public ownership and control of the land suggested by the Actions Committee was not conceded, but a land system was provided intended to counteract the evils of speculation. Close settlement and intensive cultivation of the land were to be stimulated and social legislation introduced to prevent the uneconomic use or non-use of land. In all of these clauses the Zionist Organization won points important for the development of the Jewish national home in Palestine. However, there was one fundamental point which the Zionists failed to obtain, namely, the reference to a Jewish Commonwealth. Weizmann received the definite intimation "that the British Government might not be prepared to accept the Mandate at all if this point were insisted upon." [80]

Fifth Stage.

In the spring of 1920, Lord Curzon succeeded Mr. Balfour as Foreign Secretary. It will be remembered also that the Arab situation in the East was growing more difficult and that Lord Curzon, never the most ardent of Zionist supporters, had very serious troubles in Iraq. The new situation was reflected in a less favorable attitude toward the Zionist demands. Fundamental changes make their appearance in a new draft of June 10, which may be considered the first official draft from the point of view of the British Government. The main changes made included the following:[81]

1. Omission in the preamble of the paragraph recognizing the historical connection of the Jewish people with Palestine.
2. Substitution of the term "self-governing Institutions" for "self-governing Commonwealth" in Article 3, with the inversion of the order of ideas in such a way as to relegate the Jewish aspect to a secondary place.
3. Withdrawal of the right conferred on the Jewish Agency to be consulted in regard to the granting of concessions.
4. Elimination of the statement making the establishment of the Jewish National Home the guiding principle in the execution of the Mandate.
5. Omission of the paragraph entrusting Jewish education to the Jewish Agency.
6. Omission of any express allusion to the Jewish Sabbath and holy days.

Sixth Stage.

In the light of the situation, the Zionists realized that if any improvement was to be secured, attention had to be concentrated on essential questions. While in their formal reply they

---

80. *Ibid.*, I, p. 30.
81. *Ibid.*

offered reasoned objections to all modifications in the draft, the main effort was centered on three cardinal points:[82]

1. In regard to the "historic connection" clause, the view was urged upon the British Government that as this clause set forth the fundamental basis of the policy which the Mandate embodies, it was fitting and expedient that it should be incorporated in the document which gives that policy its international sanction.

2. As to the "self-government" clause, it was pointed out that while Jewish opinion clearly recognized that a considerable time must elapse before Palestine would become fit for full self-government, a clause which expressly contemplated its gradual realization was essential, and consequently the change from "self-governing Commonwealth" to "self-governing Institutions" was unfortunate in its implications.

3. The Government of Palestine was, under the June draft, merely empowered to arrange with the Zionist Organization, upon fair and equitable terms, to construct or operate public works, etc. . . . insofar as these matters were not directly undertaken by the Government and subject to the limitation of profits . . . . These provisions were merely permissive, giving the Zionist Organization no assured right of first refusal, while on the other hand if the Zionist Organization obtained a concession, its profits, unlike those of other contractors, were expressly limited. It was pointed out that the right to be consulted in regard to concessions was of primary importance as a means of assisting the Zionist Organization to provide for Jewish labor.

Seventh Stage.

The Foreign Office first admitted the force of the Zionist arguments by reinstating the "historic connection" clause, refusing, however, to make any other modifications. Later the clause was again withdrawn, leaving the draft of the Mandate substantially in the same form as in June. Influential friends of Zionism in Government circles, including Balfour and Milner, exerted their influence in the direction of obtaining modifications consonant with the original intentions of the Declaration. Sir Herbert Samuel, already High Commissioner in Palestine, also supported the Zionist representations. Sir Alfred Mond and Major James de Rothschild, of the Jewish leaders, also aided. The Parliamentary Group for Palestinian

---

82. *Ibid.*, p. 31.

Affairs, of which Lord Robert Cecil was chairman, met on November 9, 1920, at the House of Commons and passed the following resolution: "That His Majesty's Government be urged to include in the terms of the Palestine Mandate definite recognition of the historic connection of the Jewish people with Palestine, and of the status of the Zionist Organization and of the policy of the development of Palestine into a Palestinian self-governing Commonwealth." [83]

Despite these great efforts on the part of the Zionists and British friends of the Jewish aspirations, only one change was secured, namely, the restoration of the phrase "historic connection" which had already appeared in the June draft. On December 6, 1920, Balfour submitted the approved draft of the Mandate to the League of Nations for ratification and it was published as an official document by the British Government.[84] The major points of difference between the original draft proposed by the Zionists and the final draft of the Mandate concern three points of paramount importance.

The Preamble. The Zionists had asked recognition of "the historic title of the Jewish People to Palestine and the right of the Jews to reconstitute Palestine as their National Home; and there to establish the foundations of a Jewish Commonwealth." [85] The Foreign Office at first attempted to omit any reference to the historic relation of the Jews to Palestine, but the Zionists finally won and the phrase "historical connection" was admitted as a compromise between "historical title" or "right" and the term "historic interest," which certain non-Zionists had suggested. The Zionists lost on two points: no mention of "Jewish Commonwealth" was granted; the phrase "to reconstitute Palestine as their National Home" was rejected and the much weaker, "establishment in Palestine of a national home for the Jewish people," was retained. The recital of the Balfour Declaration in the Mandate, however, was a distinct victory for the Zionists.

83. *Ibid.*, p. 32.
84. For a copy of his final draft which became the basis of negotiations between the United States and Great Britain, see United States Department of State, *Mandate for Palestine*, Washington, 1931, pp. 12–17.
85. This formulation and punctuation are taken from the tentative draft submitted by Felix Frankfurter to David Hunter Miller. See Miller, *op. cit.*

Self-Governing Institutions. In the Zionist draft the mention of self-governing institutions is always connected with the development of an autonomous Jewish Commonwealth. While the Zionists were willing to accept Great Britain as trustee for the time being, it was their hope that as Palestine grew stronger, self-governing institutions would be developed to represent Jewish interests, because by that time the Jews would be a majority. The final draft of Article II still begins with the clause: "The Mandatory shall be responsible for placing the country under such political, administrative and economic conditions as will secure the establishment of the Jewish national home," but the phrase "the development of self-governing institutions," which immediately follows is connected by the conjunction "and." This made it possible to regard the responsibility of developing self-governing institutions as a separate and independent clause, parallel, rather than instrumental, to the Jewish National Home. Later, the clause regarding responsibility for developing self-governing institutions was interpreted as designed to protect the Arab interests and as standing in a certain opposition to the Jewish national home.

Economic Development. In all Zionist proposals from the very beginning there is a recognition of the fact that Palestine could absorb large immigration only if the Jews were given the right to develop the natural resources of the country. Therefore, they always requested that the body representing the Jews, known in various drafts as the Charter Company, the Jewish Council, or the Jewish Agency, should have special powers with reference to obtaining concessions and executing public works. They never went so far as to demand a monopoly; what they wanted was the option on such undertakings when the Government itself was not able to carry out development projects. The final draft of the Mandate recognizes the Jewish Agency as a body with which the Government may cooperate in the development of the natural resources of the country and in the construction of public works. The arrangement, however, is merely permissive and does not give any special position to the Jewish Agency.

The draft of the Mandate submitted by the British Government was circulated for consideration of members of the Council of the League and as a result certain changes were made. A new draft of the Mandate, the so-called "final draft," was presented to the British Parliament in August, 1921. This version contained two changes of interest.[86] In the original Preamble the recital of the Balfour Declaration included only two clauses: 1) that a national home for the Jewish people should be established; 2) that nothing should be done which might prejudice the civil and religious rights and political status enjoyed by Jews in any other country. The clause safeguarding the civil and religious rights of all the inhabitants of Palestine irrespective of race and religion appeared in Article II of the 1920 draft, but not in the Preamble. In the 1921 draft, the clause "that nothing should be done which might prejudice the civil and religious rights of existing non-Jewish communities in Palestine," was included in the Preamble as well as in Article II. This was, however, essentially a change in form. The major substantial change comes in an entirely new Article numbered 25, which gives the Mandatory the right to withhold the application of the Balfour Declaration to the territories east of the Jordan. This was introduced to enable the British to have legal confirmation of the separation of Trans-Jordan, which had by this time been assigned to the Emir Abdullah.[87]

It took several years before all the legal formalities connected with the Palestine Mandate were completed. There were many factors that caused the delay. France did not wish to give its final consent until the arrangements for the Syrian Mandate had been completed and this was a difficult matter due to the necessity of composing national and religious differences, and meeting the demands of the Lebanese Christians, of the Druses and of the Turks in the Alexandretta district. The negotiations on the boundaries defining the limits between Mesopotamia, Syria and Palestine also consumed time. The Italians had their claims and the Vatican caused difficulties concerning the protection of the Holy Places.

86. A comparison of the two drafts is shown in parallel columns in United States Department of State, *Mandate for Palestine*, Washington, 1931, pp. 18–21.
87. This arrangement was regarded as an internal matter for the British in whose Mandate Trans-Jordan had originally been included. There had been lengthy negotiations on the questions of the boundaries of Palestine involving the interests of the French and the British as well as of the Jews. See *Reports of the Executive to the XIIth Zionist Congress*, I, pp. 33–39; also the summary and references in Hanna, *op. cit.*, pp. 63–64.

The Peace Conference and Mandate for Palestine 177

Particularly lengthy were the negotiations with the United States. The United States claimed that it should not be excluded from equality of rights in mandated territories because of its non-ratification of the Covenant of the League of Nations. The Americans wished, among other things, to protect American oil interests in the Mosul District. After long Anglo-American negotiations a treaty was signed on December 3, 1924, and the ratification proclaimed by the President of the United States one year later. The treaty recited the Palestine Mandate, making the United States a signatory to it, and provided for American participation in all rights and benefits extended to members of the League of Nations.[88]

The Mandate for Palestine was formally approved by the League of Nations July 24, 1922. Originally the mandates were connected with the Ottoman Treaty which the Turkish delegates were obliged to sign August 10, 1920, at Sèvres. The Treaty, however, was never ratified by the Turkish Government for, in the meantime, Mustapha Kemal had become master of the Turkish portions of the Ottoman Empire. Turkey made a general renunciation of its claims to the non-Turkish parts of the Ottoman Empire and this was regarded as sufficient. The legal formalities were not completed until more than a year later with the ratification of the Treaty of Lausanne on September 28, 1923. The Council declared the Palestine Mandate in effect as of September 29, 1923. Its main principles had actually guided the government of Palestine since the initiation of the Civil Administration under Sir Herbert Samuel, July 1, 1920.

88. The negotiations are reviewed in United States Department of State, *Mandate for Palestine*. For discussion see below, Chap. IV.

CHAPTER IV

PROMISES, CLAIMS AND RIGHTS

THE Arab representatives at the Peace Conference regarded the San Remo decisions as a betrayal of their cause. They denounced the division of Arab lands and the imposition of mandates without their consent. They were particularly incensed because Syria, the inland as well as the coastal regions, had been assigned to France. Although the mandates were in the "A" category which provided for the development of self-governing institutions, the Arabs had no confidence that France would administer the territories under her control in a liberal spirit. Nor were they satisfied with the degree of independence indicated for Iraq where the British had introduced a Colonial administration on the Indian model. Disillusioned about their major claims in Iraq and in Syria, the Arab nationalists were no longer willing to compromise on Palestine.

The grievance of the Arabs of Palestine against the Mandate is therefore part of the general disappointment with the decisions made at San Remo. As applied to Palestine the Arab case rests on two grounds,[1] and may be stated as follows: 1) The Balfour Declaration and the Mandate which incorporates its principle of the establishment of a Jewish national home constitute a violation of previous commitments given to the Arabs during the war period in return for the part they played in the overthrow of the Turks; 2) The Mandate violates the principle of self-determination, i.e., the right of any settled population to remain in possession of its land and to decide the political character of the country in accordance with the will of the majority of its inhabitants.[2]

The argument based on the principle of self-determination,

---

[1]. The Arabs of Palestine have also maintained that Jewish immigration and land settlement have been detrimental to the welfare of the native inhabitants. These complaints, which refer to the working of the Mandate, will be dealt with in Part II, below.

[2]. George Antonius, *The Arab Awakening*, Lippincott, 1939, pp. 390–392.

to be taken up in the latter part of this chapter, is by far the stronger of the two. It rests on the ancient right of possession and appeals also to the modern democratic consciousness. The question in this case will be whether this so-called "natural right" constitutes an "absolute right" so exclusive as to nullify the right granted to the Jews under the Mandate of establishing a national home in Palestine. The other claim revolving about the wartime commitments is at best a supplementary argument: even in the instances where no commitment can be claimed, the Arabs fall back on the major argument of self-determination, as is illustrated in the case of Syria. Moreover, the Arab claim to Palestine on the basis of specific commitments, in the light of evidence, is so weak as hardly to merit serious discussion. But the protagonists of the Arab cause have made much of the wartime pledges and these are constantly being put forward today as grounds for turning over Palestine to complete Arab control. It is therefore necessary to deal with them at some length.

BRITISH WAR COMMITMENTS AND ARAB CLAIMS

Before dealing with the specific documents and pronouncements which are alleged to give the Arabs a claim to the rule of Palestine, mention may be made of their complaint against the Sykes-Picot Agreement. This is attacked as a shocking document: "It is not only the product of greed at its worst, that is to say, of greed allied to suspicion and so leading to stupidity: it also stands out as a startling piece of double-dealing." [3] The Sykes-Picot Agreement is condemned on the ground that it placed artificial obstacles in the way of Arab unity and contemplated a topsy-turvy political structure in which the more advanced areas of Syria and Iraq would be placed under foreign control while the less developed portions in the Arabian peninsula were to be given independence. It is pointed out that the division into separate regimes with economic privileges for different governments was obstructive of the future economic development. But worse than these errors in judgment, it is maintained, was the breach of faith since the arrangement had been worked out by the Allies at the same time that Great

3. *Ibid.*, p. 248.

Britain was carrying on the negotiations with the Sharif of Mecca.

The Sykes-Picot Agreement was undeniably dictated by imperialistic motives and as such no less "shocking" than other arrangements of the same sort between Britain, France and Russia. But without attempting to whitewash Great Britain in the matter it must be said that it indicated something better than the pure power politics current at the time. It is also true that the agreement was secret and its contents were not revealed to Husain: but this too was playing the game according to the existing rules. Sykes did everything he could to include considerations beneficial to the Arabs: the British insisted on the inclusion of the important cities of Aleppo, Hama, Homs and Damascus in the territories under Arab control; and the Sharif of Mecca is specifically mentioned as one whose representatives would be consulted with reference to the international administration planned for the "Brown Zone" of Palestine. As pointed out by Lawrence, the terms of the Sykes-Picot Treaty were not inherently in conflict with the McMahon-Husain understanding. He says: "I see no inconsistencies or incompatibilities in these four documents, and I know nobody who does." [4] Lawrence held that the Sykes-Picot Treaty was not bad in itself but became unworkable because it no longer suited Lloyd George and Clemenceau.

When the British were confronted with the Agreement after the publication of the secret documents by the Bolsheviki, they tried, rather lamely, to explain it away as a record of provisional exchanges between Great Britain, France and Russia, not binding in character, and designed mainly to avoid difficulties between the powers in the prosecution of the war. They pointed out that Jemal Pasha, who was using the Agreement in his effort to win back the Arabs to the Turkish cause, had suppressed the stipulations which were designed to safeguard the Arab interest. They also pointed out that the Sykes-Picot arrangements had been completed before the Arabs had taken any steps to implement their promises of a revolt and that the subsequent success of the insurrection as well as the with-

---

4. David Garnett, ed. *The Letters of T. E. Lawrence*, Doubleday, Doran, 1939, pp. 281–282. The four documents referred to are (1) The British Promise to King Husain; (2) The Sykes-Picot Agreement; (3) The British Statement to the Seven Syrians of Cairo; (4) The Anglo-French Declaration of November 9, 1918.

drawal of Russia, created an altogether different situation.⁵ However, there is no denying the fact that the Sykes-Picot Agreement was not in harmony with the spirit of the McMahon-Husain understanding since the latter laid so much emphasis on mutual confidence between the British and the Arabs and on the theme of Arab independence.

The most that can be said is that the Agreement gave the Arabs more than they had before the war. They won full independence over the Arabian Peninsula and a large measure of freedom in the "A" and "B" zones. Even in coastal Syria and in Iraq, where the French and the British reserved control, the Arab position was improved in comparison with what it had been under the Turks. The following is a fair statement of the case:⁶

It is true that the division of the interior of Syria and Mesopotamia into Anglo-French spheres of influence could not be pleasing to Arab nationalists who wished to create a strong independent nation. Further, if the Sykes-Picot Agreement were to be merely a prelude to French annexation of the Blue and A zones, the English annexation of the Red and B zones, the frontiers laid down in the agreement were utterly out of reason on every ground of geography and economics. Yet if the agreement could have been carried out faithfully, and if both France and Great Britain had been sincerely interested in the welfare of the Arab state or confederation, the Sykes-Picot Agreement might have offered a workable compromise of English, French and Arab interests in the Levant.

Palestine and the McMahon-Husain Correspondence

The McMahon pledge was for a long time the trump card in the Arab deck of arguments. The British Government did not publish the complete texts of the correspondence until recently.⁷ It continued to maintain that the delay in publication had nothing to do with the Palestine situation but was in the interest of other aspects of British policy;⁸ however, the suppression of parts of the correspondence lent color to the Arab contentions. In 1939, in connection with the Round Table Con-

5. See the message conveyed to Husain in a telegram from Wingate. (Antonius, *op. cit.*, p. 257.)
6. Hanna, *op. cit.*, p. 30.
7. Great Britain, *Correspondence*, Cmd. 5957.
8. Great Britain, *Parliamentary Debates, Lords*, March 1, 1923, col. 232.

ferences held in London, a committee of British and Arab representatives was set up to examine the letters. Despite the fact that the original texts were made available in full, with accurate translations, the British and Arab representatives continued to disagree on the main issue—whether Palestine had been included in the area in which the Arabs were promised unconditional independence. The British representatives agreed that the language used to indicate the exclusion of Palestine from the areas reserved for Arab independence was "not so specific and unmistakable as it was thought to be at the time" but they maintained that "on a proper construction of the correspondence Palestine was in fact excluded." [9] In a special summary, the Lord High Chancellor (Lord Maugham), the spokesman of the British representatives, reiterated this view: "The Correspondence as a whole, and particularly the reservation in respect of French interests in Sir Henry McMahon's letter of the 24th October, 1915, not only did exclude Palestine but should have been understood to do so. . . ." [10]

Leading British statesmen of successive governments and officials connected with the Husain arrangements have testified to the same effect. The following represent a selection of such statements:

That letter [October 24, 1915, from McMahon to Husain] is quoted as conveying the promise to the Sherif of Mecca to recognize and support the independence of the Arabs within the territories proposed by him. But this promise was given subject to a reservation made in the same letter, which excluded from its scope, among other territories, the portions of Syria lying to the west of the district of Damascus. This reservation has always been regarded by His Majesty's Government as covering the vilayet of Beirut and the independent Sanjak of Jerusalem. The whole of Palestine west of the Jordan was thus excluded from Sir H. McMahon's pledge. (Statement of British policy in Palestine, June 3, 1922 [Churchill White Paper], Cmd. 1700, p. 20.)

Whether they [the promises] were expressed in the best terms or

---

9. Royal Institute of International Affairs, *Great Britain and Palestine, 1915–1939*, Oxford University Press, London, 1939, p. 6; Leonard Stein, *Promises and Afterthoughts*, Jewish Agency for Palestine, London, 1939, pp. 5–19.

10. Great Britain, *Report*, p. 46.

not, it is perhaps not for me to say, but undoubtedly there never was any intention, when the pledge was given, to recognize the independence of the Arabs so as to include Palestine. I think that is perfectly clear, and in my own mind I am certain of it. Although the terms may not have been expressed in the clearest possible language, I think it was the intention of both Sir H. McMahon and the Government at the time, when those pledges were given, that Palestine should not be included. (The Secretary of State for the Colonies [the Duke of Devonshire], *House of Lords Official Report,* March 1, 1923, col. 223.)

I was in daily touch with Sir Henry McMahon throughout the negotiations with King Hussein, and made the preliminary drafts of all the letters. I can bear out the statement that it was never the intention that Palestine should be included in the general pledge given to the Sherif. The introductory words of Sir Henry's letter were thought at the time, perhaps erroneously, clearly to cover the point. It was, I think, obvious that the peculiar interests involved in Palestine precluded any definite pledges in regard to its future at so early a stage. (Sir Gilbert Clayton [Chief Secretary of the Palestine Government, in a note to the High Commissioner, Sir Herbert Samuel, April 12, 1923], quoted by Lord Samuel, *House of Lords Official Report,* July 20, 1937, col. 629.)

I served in 1916 in the Arab Bureau in Cairo on Sir Henry McMahon's staff, and I wish myself to testify to the fact that it never was in the mind of anyone on that staff that Palestine west of the Jordan was in the area within which the British Government then undertook to further the cause of Arab independence . . . . I want it clearly and finally understood that His Majesty's Government, neither then nor now, can or will admit that Palestine west of the Jordan was included in the pledge given to the Sherif, and that they have always in mind that special considerations must obtain in regard to the future government of the Holy Land. The unique character of Palestine was recognized by the Arab Delegates to the Peace Conference. It is recognized all over the world. (Secretary of State for the Colonies [Mr. Ormsby-Gore], House of Commons, July 21, 1937, *House of Commons Official Report,* July 21, 1937, cols. 2249/50.)

Colonel C. E. Vickery, who was a master of Arabic, was sent from Cairo in 1920 on an official mission to inspect the original Arabic text of the letter as actually received by the Sharif. In a letter published in *The Times* on February 21, 1939, referring to this visit, he wrote:

I read the letter through very slowly .... It was quite evident that Palestine was not included in the proposals to the King .... I can say most definitely that the whole of the King's demands were centered around Syria, and only around Syria. Time after time he referred to that vineyard, to the exclusion of any other claim or interest. He stated most emphatically that he did not concern himself at all with Palestine and had no desire to have suzerainty over it for himself or his successors.

Finally we have testimony of Sir Henry McMahon himself. On March 12, 1922, Sir Henry wrote a letter to the Eastern Department of the Colonial Office in which he stated that he had intended to exclude Palestine from an independent Arabia. He had mentioned only the towns of Damascus, Homs, Hama and Aleppo because these were the places to which the Arabs attached vital importance. He could not at the time think of any other places in the area of Syria to which the Arabs attached such importance as deserved mentioning. He had explicitly excluded the coastal area of Syria west of the cities named and intended that this exclusion would apply to the southern as well as the northern part of the coast. He did not make use of the Jordan to define the limits of the boundaries because "he did not know whether at some later stage of the negotiations with the Grand Sharif a more suitable frontier might be found east of the river." In conclusion he wrote that he did not remember ever having heard anything from Husain which gave him the impression that the Sharif did not understand that Palestine was to be excluded from an independent Arabia.[11]

In a letter written to *The Times,* July 23, 1937, fifteen years later, McMahon reiterates his statement as follows:

Many references have been made in the Palestine Royal Commission Report and in the course of the recent debates in both Houses of Parliament to the "McMahon Pledge," especially to that portion of the pledge which concerns Palestine and of which one interpretation has been claimed by the Jews and another by the Arabs.

It has been suggested to me that continued silence on the part of the giver of that pledge may itself be misunderstood.

I feel, therefore, called upon to make some statement on the subject, but I will confine myself in doing so to the point now at issue— i.e., whether that portion of Syria now known as Palestine was or

---

11. Philip Graves, *op. cit.,* pp. 53–54.

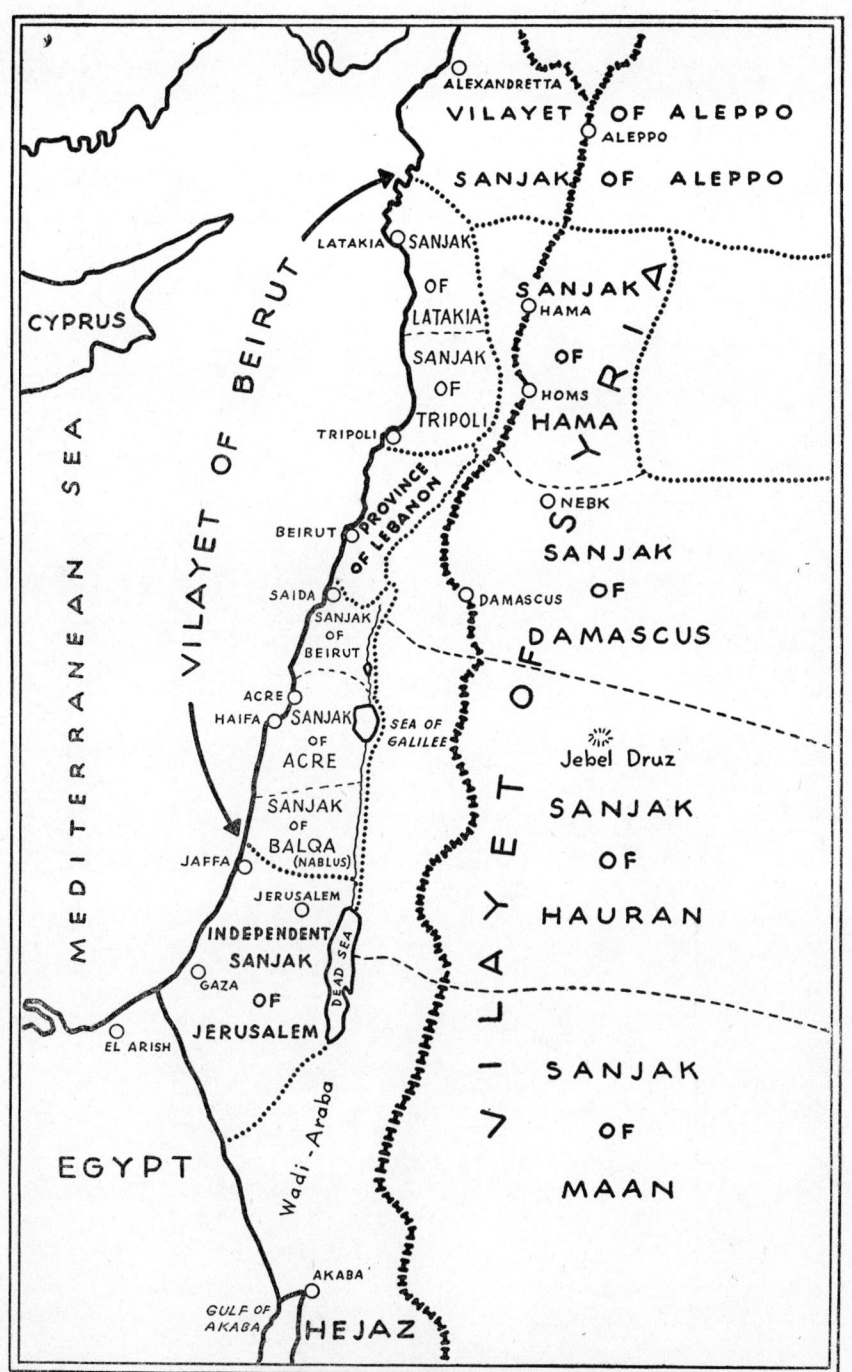

PALESTINE AND SYRIA IN 1915

was not intended to be included in the territories in which the independence of the Arabs was guaranteed in my pledge.

I feel it my duty to state, and I do so definitely and emphatically, that it was not intended by me in giving this pledge to King Hussein to include Palestine in the area in which Arab independence was promised.

I also had every reason to believe at the time that the fact that Palestine was not included in my pledge was well understood by King Hussein.

These definite statements made by British officials and statesmen of high standing received additional support—if this were needed—in the fact that Husain did not at the time claim that Palestine was included in the British promise, although he later made broad statements which led others to believe so. On July 29, 1920, he published a document in *al-Quibla* at Mecca which purported to give the definitive agreement between himself and the British, but the boundaries there mentioned are those which he asked for in his first letter, not those which the British in the course of the correspondence indicated they were ready to accept.[12] Emir Faisal raised the question with the Foreign Office in a conversation on January 20, 1921, more than five years after the conclusion of the correspondence. On that occasion, according to a statement by Winston Churchill, the Emir said that he was "prepared to accept the statement that it had been the intention of His Majesty's Government to exclude Palestine." [13]

Moreover, internal evidence in the correspondence confirms the British contention. The failure to mention Palestine specifically is in itself a point which strengthens the British case. The area under discussion was not usually called Palestine at the time. The Arabs have always insisted that Palestine does not constitute a special geographical entity and that it must be considered merely the southern part of Syria. This helps us to understand why McMahon thought that in excluding the reserved areas in Syria he was clearly excluding Palestine. The relevant clause in his letter of October 24th reads: ". . . por-

12. For the delineation of the boundaries in this letter, see William Ernest Hocking, *The Spirit of World Politics*, Macmillan, 1932, p. 247. Professor Hocking appears to have been unduly impressed by this document.

13. Great Britain, *Parliamentary Debates, Commons*, July 11, 1922, cols. 1032–1034.

tions of Syria lying to the west of the districts of Damascus, Homs, Hama and Aleppo cannot be said to be purely Arab and should be excluded from the limits demanded." [14] If a line were drawn running generally north and south through the cities mentioned and extended southward—roughly along the line of the Hejaz railroad—Palestine would clearly fall outside those areas. There is no doubt that McMahon intended in his description to exclude the southern as well as the northern part of the Syrian coast. The reason that McMahon gives for not including the northern part, namely, that the districts under discussion "cannot be said to be purely Arab," applies with greater force to southern Syria or Palestine. The other reason given, namely, that the interests of France were involved, applies also to Palestine.

There is confirmatory evidence in Husain's reply of November 5th. Husain, it will be remembered, agreed to the exclusion of the districts of Mersina and Adana in Asia Minor but took exception to the exclusion of Syria proper. Here he mentions the territories which he wishes to have included in the sphere of Arab independence in Syria by the names by which they were usually referred to in Turkish times, i.e., the *vilayet* of Aleppo and the *vilayet* of Beirut. The relevant passage in his letter is: "But the two *vilayets* of Aleppo and Beirut and their seacoasts are purely Arab *vilayets*, and there is no difference between a Moslem and a Christian Arab: they are both descendants of one forefather." [15] The district of Beirut includes northern and central Palestine. It will be recalled that McMahon very clearly refused to include the *vilayet* of Beirut in the Arab area of independence. Thus the larger part of Palestine was explicitly excluded by the British when they excluded the *vilayet* of Beirut, even though Palestine was not mentioned.

Of the southern part of Palestine, the *sanjaq* of Jerusalem, Husain makes no mention. In view of the fact that the Holy Land was the most questionable area, it is reasonable to assume that the Sharif did not think it worthwhile to enter a claim, it being generally understood that the Holy Land was of international interest and would not be made part of the independent Arab state. This view of the matter is confirmed

14. Great Britain, *Correspondence*, Cmd. 5957, 1939, p. 8.
15. *Ibid.*, p. 9.

by Faisal's statement at the Peace Conference that Palestine "for its universal character should be left on one side for the mutual consideration of all parties interested." [16] The area corresponding to the present Palestine was important from the point of view of the Syrian nationalists, but to Husain it was a poor country which, in any case, the Allied Powers would not yield to the Arabs. This conclusion is reconcilable with the view that some Syrian nationalists or the public at large may have believed that Palestine had been included in the McMahon promise since the exact nature of the correspondence was known only to a few. This, however, is quite a different thing from saying that a pledge was made by the British through McMahon. The weight of the evidence, factual and circumstantial, is wholly on the side of the British position that Palestine was definitely excluded from the territories of Arab statehood.[17]

Whatever may be the precise explanation—whether there was a genuine misunderstanding between McMahon and Husain, or whether the latter, though agreeing at the time, continued to harbor a mental reservation—the Arab argument on the basis of the Correspondence is at best auxiliary, designed to add weight to their primary claim, which rests on possession. Even had Palestine been unmistakably excluded, the Arab claim to it would not be withdrawn, as is illustrated in the case of those parts of Syria concerning the exclusion

---

16. See above, Chapter II, p. 138.
17. John S. Badeau (*East and West of Suez*, The Foreign Policy Association, New York, 1943, p. 45) says: "The McMahon-Hussein Agreements promised British support for Arab independence in an area understood by the Arab leaders to include Palestine. Although England has always denied that understanding, the fact is that nowhere in the correspondence was Palestine excluded *by name;* only by inference can the exclusion be maintained—and this seems to the Arabs distinctly artificial and forced. On the other hand, the Balfour Declaration of November 2, 1917, announced to the world that 'His Majesty's Government views with favor the establishment in Palestine of a national home for the Jewish people,' providing that 'nothing shall be done which may prejudice the civil and religious rights of existing non-Jewish communities in Palestine.' Both Arab and Jew thus entertained a justifiable claim to the country based on solemn promises, and in the Arab case, on national military participation in the war as an ally." In the light of the analysis submitted above, placing the promise to the Jews on the basis of the publicly announced Balfour Declaration on a par with the straw claim of the Arabs in the McMahon-Husain correspondence can hardly be deemed anything but a partisan formulation of the issue.

of which there can be no difference of opinion. The Emir Faisal made no reference to the Husain-McMahon Correspondence in presenting the Arab claims at the Peace Conference, but based his case on a number of other points, e.g., the military contribution of the Arabs to the cause of the Allies; the hoisting of the Arab flag at Damascus; the recognition of the Syrians as belligerents; etc., and on the general promises made at the end of the war to give the Arabs independence.[18]

From the point of view of international law, the claim on the basis of the Husain-McMahon arrangements has no validity, since the latter were not endorsed by the Allied powers or by the League of Nations. Great Britain was not sovereign over Palestine at the time and was not empowered to decide its future. At most, then, the disagreement with reference to the Husain-McMahon correspondence must be considered as an argument between the Arabs and the British, whether the latter helped the Arabs as much as they had promised. The British claim that they more than fulfilled their obligations, quite apart from paying very large sums to Husain and his followers for services rendered. British arms and money were mainly responsible for liberating the Arabs from Turkish rule, for laying the foundation for Arab independence in Arabia and Mesopotamia, and for preparing the way for independence in Syria.

Pronouncements after the Balfour Declaration

The messages and statements discussed in the following section were formulated and issued after the Balfour Declaration. They should be read in the light of the fact that the Declaration, having been publicly announced, was a matter of general knowledge among the Arabs as well as among the British. From the statements made by British leaders, it was evident that the Balfour Declaration envisaged the possibility of the ultimate development of a Jewish state.[19]

The first of the statements alleged to support the Arab case made after the Balfour Declaration was issued, was the "Hogarth Message" through which the British Government informed Husain of its intention relative to Palestine.

18. David Hunter Miller, *op. cit.*, Vol. XIV, p. 227.
19. See above, Chap. II, p. 104.

The Hogarth Message

According to Antonius, Commander Hogarth's[20] visit was in response to a request made by Husain, who asked for a definition of the meaning and scope of the Balfour Declaration.[21] Hogarth had two interviews with Husain during the first week of January 1918. After assuring the Sharif that the Entente Powers were determined to give the Arab race "full opportunity of once again forming a nation in the world," Hogarth proceeded to outline the policy with reference to Palestine as follows:[22] 1) the Allies were determined that "no people shall be subject to another;" 2) that in view of the fact that Palestine contains shrines and holy places sacred to the various religious groups "there must be a special regime to deal with these places approved of by the world;" 3) the Mosque of Omar would be considered as a holy Moslem concern not subject directly or indirectly to any non-Moslem authority.

After this introduction, he clearly stated that the British had resolved to support the return of the Jews to Palestine:

Since the Jewish opinion of the world is in favour of a return of Jews to Palestine, and inasmuch as this opinion must remain a constant factor, and, further, as His Majesty's Government view with favour the realization of this aspiration, His Majesty's Government are determined that in so far as is compatible with the freedom of the existing population, both economic and political, no obstacle should be put in the way of the realization of this ideal.

In this connection the friendship of world Jewry to the Arab cause is equivalent to support in all States where Jews have a political influence. The leaders of the movement are determined to bring about the success of Zionism by friendship and cooperation with the Arabs, and such an offer is not one to be lightly thrown aside.

After a satisfactory discussion on the question of the Holy Places, Hogarth took up the formula with reference to the Jewish settlement in Palestine. Hogarth's note is: "King seemed quite prepared for formula and agreed enthusiastically,

20. David George Hogarth, one of the leading members of the Arab Bureau in Cairo. He was an authority on Arab history and at one time Keeper of the Ashmolean Museum.
21. Antonius, *op. cit.*, p. 267.
22. Royal Institute of International Affairs, *Great Britain and Palestine, 1915–1939*, pp. 115–117.

saying he welcomed Jews to all Arab lands." In notes bearing on this conversation which Hogarth addressed to Sir Reginald Wingate, then High Commissioner in Egypt, Hogarth added that it was his impression that while the King was ready to assent to Jewish settlement in Palestine, he would not accept an independent Jewish state in Palestine. Hogarth notes: "Nor was I instructed to warn him that such a state was contemplated by Great Britain." Moreover, Hogarth attributed Husain's ready assent to Jewish immigration to Palestine to the fact that he did not know very much about the actual or possible economic development of Palestine; and he expressed the view that Husain's agreement was not "worth very much." On the other hand, Hogarth got the impression that Husain appreciated "the financial advantage of Arab cooperation with the Jews."

Whether Hogarth's impression of Husain's attitude is correct, it is clear beyond the shadow of any doubt that Husain understood that His Majesty's Government expected to facilitate the development of a Jewish national home in Palestine and that Palestine would not be made a part of the independent Arab state. Protagonists of the Arab case[22] have urged that Hogarth's statement to Husain implies a fundamental departure from the Balfour Declaration because the word "political" appears in the statement, viz., "freedom of the existing population, both economic and political," while the Balfour Declaration mentions only "civil and religious rights." However, in the context the term "political" can be taken to refer to local self-government; it certainly does not give the Arabs any claim of sovereignty in Palestine, nor does it reduce the Jewish settlement to a humanitarian enterprise as Antonius has tried to maintain.[23] The most that can be said is that the Hogarth Message gives assurance that there will be no domination of the Arabs by the Jews and that the Jewish development will take place under British auspices.[24]

22. Antonius, *op. cit.*, p. 268.
23. *Ibid.*, p. 298.
24. At the 36th Session of the Permanent Mandates Commission held in June, 1939, the Hogarth Message was injected into the discussion of the 1939 White Paper by Malcolm MacDonald. The Commission refused to consider it as a basis for the interpretation of the Mandate on the ground that it had not been brought to their notice prior to the issuance of the Mandate.

The Hogarth Message strengthens the view which maintains that the Balfour Declaration was generally understood by the British officials to imply the ultimate establishment of a Jewish state. While Hogarth did not himself believe the Jewish state policy to be wise, he nevertheless seems to have thought that this is what the British Government had in mind. In his Introduction to Philip Graves' *Palestine, The Land of Three Faiths*, Hogarth wrote "It was not realized by our Government of 1917 how far it (Palestine) was a settled land in occupation of a people Arab in tradition and hope, which had not been oppressed so greatly by the Turks as to welcome liberation at the price of new subjection. If the facts had been known, extremists like Jabotinsky and Ussishkin would never have been granted opportunity to raise the flag of coming domination among a people whose ancestors were on the land before the Normans landed in England. But it would be idle to blame the extremists. They were taking the Balfour Declaration at no more than its face value, putting upon it the most reasonable and natural interpretation." He called the Churchill White Paper of 1922 "depreciated currency" and praised Dr. Weizmann for his statesmanship in accepting this compromise as being necessary and in accord with the valid claims of the Arab position. He concluded: "The Balfour Declaration is as binding an engagement as Great Britain has ever been committed to." [25]

The Bassett Letter

During the winter of 1917, the British had to contend with an attempt on the part of Jemal Pasha, Governor of Syria, to win back the Arabs to the Turkish side. He sent a secret emissary to Aqaba with letters to Emir Faisal and Jaafar Pasha, one of the leaders of the Arab revolt. He appealed to them as one Moslem to another, inviting them to open negotiations for a return to the Ottoman fold. In a speech delivered in December, he made a public announcement of his overtures to Husain; he appealed to the Arabs on the ground of Moslem unity and referred to the Sykes-Picot Treaty, which the Russian Government had recently published, as proof that the Entente Powers intended to partition the Arab countries. He said that the revolt

---

25. Philip Graves, *Palestine, The Land of Three Faiths*, London, 1923, p. 6.

would destroy the religious unity of the Islamic world and in the end would fail in its object of securing Pan-Arab independence. Referring to the Sykes-Picot Agreement, he said: "In reality the Agreement was a device for bringing about an Arab revolt to suit the designs of the British who, needing tools and catspaws to serve their own ends, encouraged certain Arabs to rebel by giving them mendacious promises and hoodwinking them with false hopes . . ." [26]

The British Government found it necessary to try to dispel the doubts that had been raised by Jemal's intrigue. Wingate sent a telegram to Husain in which he said that the Turks had distorted the original purpose of the understanding between the powers and, furthermore, that the success of the Arab revolt and the withdrawal of Russia had long ago created a new situation. The telegram was followed by a formal note, dated February 8, 1918, signed by J. R. Bassett, acting British Agent at Jedda, in which His Majesty's Government reiterated in general terms their pledge in regard to the liberation of the Arab peoples, as follows:[27]

His Majesty's Government and their allies stand steadfastly by every cause aiming at the liberation of the oppressed nations, and they are determined to stand by the Arab peoples in their struggle for the establishment of an Arab world in which law shall replace Ottoman injustice, and in which unity shall prevail over the rivalries artificially provoked by the policy of Turkish officials. His Majesty's Government re-affirm their former pledge in regard to the liberation of the Arab peoples. His Majesty's Government have hitherto made it their policy to ensure that liberation, and it remains the policy they are determined unflinchingly to pursue by protecting such Arabs as are already liberated from all dangers and perils, and by assisting those who are still under the yoke of the tyrants to obtain their freedom.

Wingate's telegram and the Bassett note are couched in general terms and throw no light on the question of Palestine. In view of the fact that the Balfour Declaration had already been discussed by Hogarth with Husain, it cannot serve as a confirmation of the Arab claim with reference to Palestine.

26. G. Antonius, *op. cit.*, p. 255.
27. *Ibid.*, p. 432.

It is noteworthy that Jemal Pasha does not mention the Balfour Declaration as evidence of Britain's betrayal of the promises to the Arabs. He could not have done so because the Turks had also made overtures to the Zionists.

The Declaration to the Seven

This Declaration was made by the British in reply to a memorial submitted to the Foreign Office in the spring of 1918, through the Arab Bureau in Cairo, by seven Syrian leaders resident in Egypt. The memorialists were anonymous at the time,[28] and the contents of the memorial have never been published. From the reply it appears that questions were raised with reference to the disposal of the Arab territories in case of an Allied victory.

The British gave their answer on June 16, 1918. It was read out in English by an officer of the Arab Bureau at Army Headquarters in Cairo, and an Arabic translation was afterwards made for the benefit of those who did not understand English. The Declaration referred to four areas mentioned in the memorial: 1) territories which were free and independent before the outbreak of the War; 2) territories liberated from Turkish rule by action of the Arabs themselves; 3) areas liberated by the action of the Allied armies; 4) territories still under Turkish rule. In the case of the first two, that is of the territories previously free or liberated by the Arabs themselves, the British Government recognized complete Arab independence. With reference to the third category, i.e., territories liberated from the Turks by the Allied armies, the Declaration stated: "It is the wish and desire of His Majesty's Government that the future government of these regions should be based upon the principle of the consent of the governed, and this policy has and will continue to have the support of His Majesty's Government." [29] With regard to territories still under Turkish rule, the general statement was made that His Majesty's Government would continue to work for the freedom and independence of the oppressed peoples.

The Declaration to the Seven is alleged to be "by far the most important statement of policy publicly made by Great Britain

28. Antonius reveals their names in *The Arab Awakening*, p. 433.
29. Ibid., p. 434.

in connection with the Arab revolt." Its significance is supposed to lie in that "it confirms England's previous pledges to the Arabs in plainer language than in any former public utterance, and more valuable still, provides an authoritative enunciation of the principles on which these pledges rested." [30] A statement made to seven anonymous persons can hardly be regarded a public document, but whatever truth there may be in Antonius's interpretation, such a declaration cannot nullify the obligation undertaken by the War Cabinet in the Balfour Declaration. Moreover, T. E. Lawrence points out that the declaration to the seven Syrians in Cairo, to whom he refers in rather uncomplimentary fashion, as "an unauthorized committee of seven gothamites in Cairo," [31] is to be understood in terms of an arrangement agreed to between Allenby and Faisal.[32] In accordance with this arrangement, the Arab army operated almost entirely in the areas which the British had assigned to them under the Sykes-Picot arrangements. If Lawrence's interpretation is correct, then Palestine from the Jordan to the Mediterranean was excluded from any promises made in the Declaration.

In general, the purpose of the memorial is veiled in mystery. The anonymity of the memorialists is sometimes explained as being due to their fear of the Turkish authorities, but it is more likely that they wished to conceal their names from Husain. The memorial, it appears, was motivated largely by the fear that the British were going to establish the Sharif's family in the liberated territories without consulting the native inhabitants. In accordance with Antonius, "statements made by persons in King Hussein's entourage had given rise to a belief that he intended in the event of victory over the Turks, to set up his own administrations in those countries and make them answerable to himself in Mecca." [33] Thus, the Declaration to the Seven may have had as much to do with the internal difference between the Syrian nationalists and Husain as with the question of which territories were to be included in the sphere of Arab independence.

30. *Ibid.*, p. 271.
31. T. E. Lawrence, *The Seven Pillars of Wisdom*, Garden City, 1935, p. 555.
32. Garnett, *op. cit.*, 1939, p. 282.
33. *Ibid.*, pp. 270–271.

The Anglo-French Declaration

This Declaration, already referred to,[34] was issued on November 7, 1918. Its purpose was to assure the world of the solidarity of the Allied Powers in their attitude toward Arab independence. It forms the strongest basis for the Arab view that they were promised complete independence in all territories liberated by the Allies from the Turks. The Declaration, formulated ("authorized") by Lord Robert Cecil, a well known supporter of Zionism, read:[35]

The object aimed at by France and Great Britain in prosecuting in the East the War let loose by the ambition of Germany is the complete and definite emancipation of the peoples so long oppressed by the Turks and the establishment of national governments and administrations deriving their authority from the initiative and free choice of the indigenous populations.

In order to carry out these intentions France and Great Britain are at one in encouraging and assisting the establishment of indigenous Governments and administrations in Syria and Mesopotamia, now liberated by the Allies, and in the territories the liberation of which they are now engaged in securing, and recognizing these as soon as they are actually established.

Far from wishing to impose on the populations of these regions any particular institutions they are only concerned to ensure by their support and by adequate assistance the regular working of Governments and administrations freely chosen by the populations themselves. To secure impartial and equal justice for all, to facilitate the economic development of the country by inspiring and encouraging local initiative, to favor the diffusion of education, to put an end to dissensions that have too long been taken advantage of by Turkish policy, such is the policy which the two Allied Governments uphold in the liberated territories.

This document is more important than any of the previous ones in view of the fact that it was a public pronouncement which the Allies, after consultation, decided to issue jointly. It will be noted, however, that in so far as it is specific, it mentions Syria and Mesopotamia only, and the failure to mention

34. Chap. II, p. 121.
35. Great Britain, *Parliamentary Debates, Commons,* Fifth Series, Vol. 145, col. 36.

Palestine cannot be explained away as accidental.[36] No more than in the case of the Declaration to the Seven can its terms be regarded as voiding the specific undertaking entered into previously by the Balfour Declaration. This point was brought out clearly by Lord Halifax (formerly Mr. E. Wood), at that time Under-Secretary of State for the Colonies, in a speech he delivered in the House of Commons on July 25, 1921. He said: "I would remind my Hon. Friend that the Declaration of a National Home for the Jews in Palestine was made in November 1917, i.e., just a year before the Joint Declaration to which I have just referred [i.e., the Anglo-French Declaration]. It is obvious, therefore, that nothing contained in the latter can be regarded as abrogating in any way the earlier pledge." [37]

In fine, the various documents discussed: the Hogarth Message, the Bassett Letter, the Declaration to the Seven, and the Anglo-French Declaration of November 7, 1918, strengthen the Arab case in so far as these documents promise Allied or British support for Arab independence in Syria and Iraq. But there is no evidence in them of a change of the Allied or British attitude toward the Balfour Declaration or toward special treatment of Palestine. On the contrary, the failure to mention Palestine in any of these documents, even though it had become a controversial issue during this period, supports the view that the Balfour Declaration was accepted as determining the policy with reference to Palestine. What can be said is that these statements, which were worded so broadly, permit the Arabs of Palestine to hope that they might, through pressure, effect a change in the Jewish national home policy. And it appears that some of the highly placed British officials, particularly in the Military Administration, gave support to such a belief.

SOME OTHER ASPECTS OF THE CONTROVERSY

The Testimony of Lawrence

The opinion of Lawrence is of great importance in view of his close connection with the Arab revolt and his zealous support of the cause of Arab independence. He went to the Peace Conference with high hopes, believing that he could help to

36. Cf. David Garnett, *op. cit.*, p. 282.
37. Leonard Stein, *op. cit.*, p. 22.

win self-determination for the Arab peoples, but he was completely disillusioned by the decisions at San Remo. He felt "defeated and dishonored" by Britain's failure to live up to her promises to the Arabs. An echo of his disillusionment is reflected in the Introduction to the *Seven Pillars of Wisdom* as it appears in the Oxford text.[38]

This, therefore, is a faded dream of the time when I went down into the dust and noise of the Eastern market-places, and with my brain and muscles, with sweat and constant thinking, made others see my visions coming true. Those who dream by night in the dusty recesses of their minds wake in the day to find that all was vanity: but the dreamers of the day are dangerous men, for they may act their dream with open eyes, and make it possible. This I did. I meant to make a new nation, to restore to the world a lost influence, to give twenty millions of Semites the foundation on which to build an inspired dream-palace of their national thoughts. So high an aim called out the inherent nobility of their minds and made them play a generous part in events; but when we won it was charged against me that the British petrol royalties in Mesopotamia were become dubious, and French Colonial policy ruined in the Levant.

His belief that the Arabs had been let down, however, had nothing to do with Palestine or Zionism. Evidently he did not think that the Balfour Declaration was incompatible with the British pledge to the Arabs. He was the intermediary between Weizmann[39] and Faisal at the Peace Conference when the Agreement between them was signed. Moreover, he did not believe that the difficulty lay in any insurmountable conflict between the various agreements and promises, such as the Sykes-Picot Agreement, the McMahon understanding, the Declaration to the Seven or the Anglo-French Declaration.[40] The real trouble, he thought, was to be found in Lloyd George's and Clemenceau's disregard of all of these documents in the desire of the British to control the oil fields of Iraq and the determination of the French to keep a strong hand in the Levant. Lawrence

---

38. Garnett, *op. cit.*, pp. 262–263.
39. He held Weizmann in high esteem. In the draft of an unsent letter addressed to Dr. McInnes, the Anglican Bishop in Jerusalem who was accused of anti-Zionist propaganda, he referred to Weizmann as "a great man whose boots neither you nor I, my dear Bishop, are fit to black." (Garnett, *op. cit.*, p. 343.)
40. *Ibid.*, pp. 281–282.

was opposed to the suppressive colonial methods of administration adopted by the British in the early years after the war; he believed in ultimate Arab independence, but thought this should be achieved gradually under British guidance.

What his plan was for the solution of the conflicting problems is indicated by his readiness to accept the solution offered by Captain William Yale, a prominent member of the American Peace Delegation, in accordance with which Palestine was to be under the British mandate and "the Zionists permitted to carry out their plan." [41] In his note on the plan, Yale says: "Lawrence went over my projected solution and approved of it heartily saying that it gave the Arabs more than he had dared to hope to secure for them." [42] When all his efforts at the Peace Conference on behalf of the Arabs failed, Lawrence retired to Oxford in a state of nervous exhaustion and extreme depression.

He continued, however, to be interested in the problem of Arab independence, particularly in Iraq, and an opportunity came for him to help when Lord Curzon was replaced by Winston Churchill. There had been a strong newspaper campaign against the administration of Iraq under Lord Curzon, and the cry of "Evacuate Mesopotamia!" was started by a call for economy. This led Lloyd George to reverse the British policy in Mesopotamia, although he himself had initiated it. Lawrence joined the service, under the Middle East Department, at Churchill's persuasion in December 1920, and while still in London he cooperated in working out the lines along which the new Arab state was to be organized. Churchill accompanied by a staff went to the Middle East and the final decisions were made at the Cairo Conference held in March, 1921.[43]

At this conference it was decided to put forward the candidacy of Faisal for the throne of Iraq.[44] The Iraqis could not agree on any other candidate, and with the help of the British administration of Iraq and the persuasive influence of Gertrude

---

41. *Ibid.*, p. 286. See above, Chap. II, p. 146.
42. *Ibid.*, pp. 285–286.
43. Among those who participated in the conference were Sir Herbert Samuel, Sir Percy Cox, Miss Gertrude Bell, Jaafar Pasha, Sir Hugh Trenchard and General Geoffrey Salmond.
44. A careful schedule was worked out to assure Faisal's "election" in Iraq. See Philip W. Ireland, *Iraq, A Study of Political Development*, Macmillan, 1938, pp. 311–318.

Bell, Faisal was elected with "an overwhelming majority." At the same time, Churchill, Lawrence and Herbert Samuel, already the High Commissioner of Palestine, arranged that Abdullah should stay in Aman as Emir of Trans-Jordan.[45] The following year, after some eighteen months of service as political adviser on Middle East affairs, Lawrence felt that as much as was humanly possible had been done in redeeming the British pledge to the Arabs.[46] Complete independence had been established on the Arabian Peninsula under King Husain; Faisal was King of Iraq; and Abdullah had been made the Emir of Trans-Jordan.

Lawrence's opinion, however, was not accepted by the Arab nationalists in Palestine and in Syria. In later years some of them tried to find fault with his leadership in the Revolt, with his knowledge of Arabic, and his understanding of the Arab situation.[47] Lawrence's summary of the whole affair, of his relationship with the Arabs and his opinion of the critics of his policy is indicated in a draft preface that he wrote in November, 1922, to an abridgment of the Oxford text of the *Seven Pillars of Wisdom*, which was never published. He says:[48]

The book dates itself to 1919, when powerful elements in the British Government were seeking to evade their war-time obligations to the Arabs. That stage ended in March 1921, when Mr. Winston Churchill took charge of the Middle East. He set honesty before expediency in order to fulfill our promises in the letter and in the spirit. He executed the whole McMahon undertaking (called a treaty by some who have not seen it) for Palestine, for Trans-Jordania and for Arabia. In Mesopotamia he went far beyond its provisions, giving to the Arabs more, and reserving for us much less, than Sir Henry McMahon had thought fit.

In the affairs of French Syria he was not able to interfere, and the Sharif of Mecca can fairly complain that the settlement there is not yet in accordance with the Anglo-French Agreement of 1916, or with our word to him. I say "not yet" advisedly, since the McMahon proposals (being based on racial and economic reasons) were likely to have imposed themselves eventually, even if Mr. Churchill's progressive British military withdrawal from Mesopotamia had not come to prejudge the future of all the Arab areas.

45. *Ibid.*, pp. 328–329. See also below, Chap. V, p. 267.
46. T. E. Lawrence, *op. cit.*, p. 276 n.
47. Antonius, *op. cit.*, pp. 319–324.
48. Garnett, *op. cit.*, pp. 345–346.

I do not wish to publish secret documents, nor to make long explanations: but must put on record my conviction that England is out of the Arab affair with clean hands. Some Arab advocates (the most vociferous joined our ranks after the Armistice) have rejected my judgment on this point. Like a tedious Pensioner I showed them my wounds (over sixty I have, each scar evidence of a pain incurred in Arab service) as proof I had worked sincerely on their side. They found me out-of-date: and I was happy to withdraw from a political milieu which had never been congenial.

Faisal's Attitude toward Zionism

The protagonists of the Arab case have always found embarrassing Faisal's agreement during the Peace Conference to exclude Palestine from the area of Arab independence, as well as his cooperative attitude toward Zionism. Antonius omits all reference to Faisal's statement to the Council of Five recorded in Miller's *Diary*, when he explicitly agreed that Palestine should be "left on one side for the mutual consideration of all parties interested." [49] He also passes over in silence Faisal's memorandum of January 1, 1919—also included in Miller's authoritative record—in which he assumes that there would be a Jewish settlement in Palestine and asserts: "The Jews are very close to the Arabs in blood and there is no conflict of character between the two races. In principles we are absolutely at one."

However, Antonius does discuss the Weizmann-Faisal agreement and makes an effort to show that Faisal was subjected to undue pressure by T. E. Lawrence and the British Foreign Office. As Antonius describes the situation, Faisal, ignorant of English and unfamiliar with the methods of European diplomacy, found himself at a disadvantage. He knew that the French were opposed to him and to his plans, and he therefore had to rely on the British who indicated that his chances of obtaining the help of the Foreign Office would be greater if he came to some understanding with Weizmann. Antonius maintains that Faisal's views about the future Palestine, which did not differ from those held by "the great majority of politically minded Arabs," were as follows:[50]

49. See above, Chap. III, p. 137.
50. Antonius, *op. cit.*, p. 284.

In the Arab view, Palestine was an Arab territory forming an integral part of Syria and, as such, was bound to remain in the area of Arab independence. The fact that it was held in veneration by three of the world's religions, together with the existence of the holy sites and sanctuaries, gave it a special character which the Arabs were anxious to see respected and adequately safeguarded on a basis to be agreed upon by all the creeds concerned. Jewish settlement and colonisation would be welcomed on humanitarian grounds, subject to the limitations imposed by a proper regard for the welfare and the political and economic rights of the existing population.

Antonius' interpretation that Faisal's agreement with Weizmann envisaged Jewish settlement and colonization only on humanitarian grounds is forced and does not bear examination. It is true that the Emir vacillated, but those of his statements which give a certain support to Antonius' view came later and resulted from the change in the course of events and from pressure exerted by the Arab extremists. In May, 1919, Faisal was still friendly, and at a meeting held at Damascus he reiterated his view that Jewish and Arab aspirations were not incompatible.[51] However, it may be that he shifted his position in June, 1919, when the Arab Congress met at Damascus and declared its opposition to Zionism. In the fall of that year, while on a visit to London, he gave an interview to the *Jewish Chronicle* in which he expressed considerable resentment against a statement made by Israel Zangwill implying a transfer of Arabs from Palestine.[52] Faisal declared that he was still in agreement with Weizmann's conception of Jewish immigration and colonization in Palestine. But he did not believe that more than a thousand or fifteen hundred new settlers could be economically absorbed into Palestine annually, and he remarked: "So we needn't bother our heads about the time when the Jewish population will exceed that of the Arabs . . . ."[53] At most, the Jews might some day constitute a sub-province within the Arab kingdom.

The Emir was evidently under pressure from the Arab nationalists and his efforts to maintain the compromise were not

51. M. Perlmann, *op. cit.*, pp. 142–143.
52. See above, p. 139.
53. As quoted by M. Perlmann, *op. cit.*, p. 145, from the published interview in the *Jewish Chronicle*, October 3, 1919.

helped by the extreme expressions in some parts of the Jewish press. However, even at this time he was not prepared to break the entente with the Zionists and the British. In November, 1919, Herbert Samuel reported that he had a conversation with Faisal and what the Emir objected to was "the immediate establishment of a complete Jewish state in Palestine." He was opposed to this on the ground that it would mean placing a majority under the rule of a minority. But he was not opposed to what the authorized Zionist leaders wanted, namely, the promotion of Jewish immigration and land settlement. On December 10th Faisal wrote to Samuel, thanking him for clarifying the "misunderstanding" and reiterating that there was perfect agreement between himself and Dr. Weizmann.[54]

Faisal's attitude toward Zionism further deteriorated when the San Remo decisions failed to grant the Arabs their demands, and his reason for keeping the agreement ended altogether when he was ejected from Syria in 1921. As Temperley has remarked:[55] "Had . . . the Emir not been ejected from Syria by the French, much less might have been heard of his father's claim to Palestine." But whatever Faisal's later opinions were, the views he expressed at the Peace Conference, his statements to the press, the memorandum which he circulated, and the agreement with Weizmann, make it clear beyond any shadow of doubt that during that period he was prepared to accept a Zionist development of Palestine under British auspices.

There has been an attempt, also, to repudiate the letter which Faisal wrote to Frankfurter in which the Emir had said: "We are working together for a reformed and revived Near East and our two movements complete one another." [56] During the investigation by the Shaw Commission in 1929—ten years after the letter was written—Auni Abdul Hadi, now acting as one of the advocates for the Arab defense, sent a telegram to King Faisal in Iraq asking him whether, in his letter to Mr. Frankfurter, he had consented to the Zionist policy.[57] Faisal replied in a telegram signed by Rustum Haidar, who had also been one

54. *The Times*, January 12, 1922.
55. H. W. V. Temperley, *The History of the Peace Conference*, Hodder & Stoughton, London, 1920–1924, Vol. VI, p. 175.
56. Jewish Agency for Palestine, *Memorandum to the Palestine Royal Commission*, pp. 71–72. See above, Chap. III, pp. 143 ff.
57. *Ibid.*, p. 73.

of the members of the Arab delegation at Paris, and who was now Chief Political Secretary to His Majesty. The ambiguity of this reply might have done credit to the Delphic Oracle. It read: "His Majesty does not remember having written anything of that kind with his knowledge." Faisal's evasive answer is obviously the best that he could contrive without letting his former colleague down. His diplomatic forgetfulness can hardly be considered dishonest, and is pardonable perhaps in view of the fact that he himself did not draft the letter. This is what Faisal probably meant when he said that he did not remember having *written* anything of that kind; he only signed it.

In evidence which he gave before the Shaw Commission, moreover, Abdul Hadi tried to maintain the view that Faisal was representing only his father, the King of the Hejaz, at the Peace Conference, and thus had no authority to make commitments with reference to Palestine and Syria. He said that Rustum Haidar and himself had the sole authority to represent the Syrian demands which included Palestine. This, however, does not correspond with the fact as accepted by the Peace Conference, where it was understood that Faisal acted as the official representative of the Arab demands. Moreover, we have the testimony of Captain William Yale, that Nuri Said and Rustum Haidar, who were co-members with Auni Bey in the Arab Delegation at Paris, agreed to his proposals in accordance with which Palestine was to be under the mandate of Great Britain and "the Zionists permitted to carry out their plan." [58]

The evidence converges to confirm the view that the Arab Delegation at the Peace Conference was in agreement with Faisal and was ready to cooperate with the British in furthering the Zionist policy. The key to the understanding of the later change of heart lies in the reservation added as a postscript by Faisal to the Articles of Agreement with Weizmann. This reservation, it will be remembered, stipulated that if any changes were made in the projected Arab state as promised by the British, he would not be answerable for failing to carry out the agreement. The disappointment of the Arabs with reference to the decisions of the Peace Conference on Syria and Iraq was reflected in a change of policy toward Zionism. More-

58. Garnett, *op. cit.*, p. 286. See above, Chap. III, p. 138.

over, the failure of Faisal's moderate policy strengthened the hand of the extreme nationalists and these always had wanted a united Syria with Palestine included.

Arab War Services

As late as 1936, in evidence given before the Royal Commission, the Arabs brought up their war services in terms of fighting as another point in their claim for Palestine. The Arabs did give help to the British in their campaign against the Turks—how substantial, authorities differ. The main point is, however, that whatever the value of the services was, the natives of Palestine and Syria had nothing to do with the matter. During Allenby's campaign in Palestine and Syria, the native Arab either remained passive or aided the Turks. All the historians of the campaign agree on this.[60] Philip Graves writes:[61]

Most annoying, to anyone who has served with the British and the Sherifian Arab forces in the Palestine campaign and knows something of the history of that campaign, are the pretensions of the Arabs of Palestine to have rendered important military services to the Allies in the Great War.

Many of the Transjordanians and the Hejazis, whom, for all their talk of Arab union, the Palestine Arabs dislike and fear as rude and hardy men, played their part right well under the inspiring leadership of Emir Feisal and Colonel T. E. Lawrence; but the Palestinians confined themselves to deserting in large numbers to the British, who fed and clothed and paid for the maintenance of many thousand such prisoners of war, few indeed of whom could be induced to obtain their liberty by serving in the Sherifian Army.

As to the value of the services of the Arabs of the Hejaz, opinion differs. According to Antonius, these services were substantial: "The Arabs under Faisal covered the right flank of the British Army as it proceeded north into Palestine and Syria while Ali and Abdullah were harassing a large enemy force in the Hejaz." [62] Lawrence, on his part, makes a gallant acknowledgment of their contribution:[63]

60. A. Briscoe Moore, *The Mounted Riflemen in Syria and Palestine*, p. 64; W. T. Massey, *The Desert Campaigns*, p. 107; Guy Powles, *The New Zealanders in Sinai and Palestine*, p. 266; H. S. Gullet, *Official History of Australia in the War of 1914–1918*, Vol. VII, p. 100.
61. Philip Graves, *Palestine, The Land of Three Faiths*, pp. 112–113.
62. Antonius, *op. cit.*, pp. 232, 233.   63. Garnett, *op. cit.*, p. 312.

Faisal's courage and statesmanship made the Mecca revolt spread beyond the Holy cities, until it became a very active help to the Allies in Palestine. The Arab army, created in the field, grew from a mob of Bedouins into an organized and well-equipped body of troops. They captured thirty-five thousand Turks, disabled as many more, took a hundred and fifty guns, and a hundred thousand square miles of Ottoman territory. This was great service in our extreme need, and we felt we owed the Arabs a reward; and to Feisal, their leader, we owed double, for the loyal way in which he had arranged the main Arab activity when and where Allenby directed.

When Lawrence wrote this, he still felt that the British had not redeemed their pledge to the Arabs, and was inclined to estimate their contributions on the generous side. A careful reading of *The Seven Pillars of Wisdom* gives evidence of a somewhat different view and indicates that he agreed with the general view of British officers that the Arabs were not sufficiently disciplined for offensive operations, but that they could be used for defense.[64]

Blood feuds were nominally healed . . . All the same, the members of one tribe were shy of those of another, and within the tribe no man would quite trust his neighbour. Each might be, usually was, wholehearted against the Turk, but perhaps not quite to the point of failing to work off a family grudge upon a family enemy in the field. Consequently they could not attack. One company of Turks firmly entrenched in open country could have defied the entire army of them; and a pitched defeat, with its casualties, would have ended the war by sheer horror.
I concluded that the tribesmen were good for defence only. Their acquisitive recklessness made them keen on booty, and whetted them to tear up railways, plunder caravans, and steal camels; but they were too free-minded to endure command, or to fight in team.

An equally competent but less romantic authority, Major C. S. Jarvis, late Governor of Sinai, who spent eighteen years living and working with the Arabs, describes the situation in even more realistic terms:[65]

The truth of the matter is that the national desire for independence was confined solely to the few educated Arabs in the cause, such as

64. *Ibid.*, pp. 103–104.
65. C. S. Jarvis, *Three Deserts*, Dutton, 1937, pp. 299–303. See also Margret Boveri, *Minaret and Pipe-line*, pp. 178–179.

Feisal, and that among the fighting men and the sheikhs of the tribes who led them this feeling was conspicuous by its absence. . . . The only method of keeping these patriots in the field was by payment in gold, and when the Arab sees gold his natural avarice causes him to lose all control of himself so that squabbles as to the respective donations to various tribes were of daily occurrence.

In action they were entirely without discipline, and the first hint of loot meant that the greater part of the attacking force broke off the engagement before it was completed to rifle the enemy's captured baggage. After a successful raid when the Arabs were loaded with looted corn and rations nothing would keep them in the field, and they trickled back to their tents and womenfolk so that a striking force on which their commander was relying for another attack on the railway would scatter into the desert in a night.

Ronald Storrs, who played a principal role in making the early arrangements with Husain, does not conceal the less romantic aspects of the Arab Revolt. More elegant in his use of English than the tough-minded Jarvis, he says that he found the Arabs of the Hejaz "more esurient than the Greek himself." [66] The tribesmen's zeal to serve their kind and country had to be stimulated by very tangible rewards. One of the Arab attendants was overheard saying during the early negotiations: "Do the English not see that if the Sharif is not able to redeem his money promises to the Arabs, he will be a liar and lose his honour before them? Then where will be success?" [67] Nor was the understanding with the British lacking in monetary considerations for Husain himself. Storrs says: "Glancing hurriedly down the list of *talebs* (or requests) in the first document handed to me, I observed the mention of £50,000 with an additional £20,000 making a total of £70,000 . . ." [68] He estimates that the Arab Revolt cost the British taxpayers the sum of eleven million pounds, of which almost one million went to Husain in the way of a monthly subsidy of £125,000.[69]

The Zionists on their part do not lay emphasis on the Jewish war services as grounds for their claim to the re-establishment of the Jewish homeland. However, since the issue is raised, perhaps it is in order to point out that Jews fought in great numbers in the Allied armies whose victories made Arab free-

66. Storrs, *op. cit.*, p. 192.
67. *Ibid.*, p. 188.
68. *Ibid.*, p. 185.
69. *Ibid.*, n. p. 177.

dom possible; and, if an accounting is to be made, perhaps this ought not to be left out of the reckoning even though they fought as Americans, Britishers and Frenchmen and not as Jews. The Jews responded to whatever opportunities were offered to them to fight in special Jewish battalions for Palestine. In Palestine itself, their readiness to enter British forces stands in sharp contrast to the Arab reluctance. About twelve hundred Jews were recruited in Palestine during the war, as against 150 Arabs out of a population ten times the size of the Jews. A handbook prepared by the British Foreign Office in 1920[70] points out: "Practically the whole available Jewish youth of the colonies, and many of the townsmen of military age, came forward for voluntary enlistment in the Jewish battalions, took the oath to King George V, and were clad in British uniforms."

These facts about the Jewish service are added for the record as a reply to the Arab contentions. It should be understood that the Zionists on their part did not take the position that Arab rights in Palestine should in any way be diminished by the fact that their record of military service in Palestine is exceptionally poor. The Jewish Agency has taken the position that: "It goes without saying that the Palestine Arabs are entitled to the fullest safeguards for their legitimate rights and interests irrespective of whether they did or did not render services to the Allied cause." [71]

Moreover, as the Palestine Royal Commission has indicated, the Balfour Declaration and the Jewish support for the Allied cause it evoked the world over must not be omitted from any enumeration of the factors that contributed to the winning of the First World War:[72]

The fact that the Balfour Declaration was issued in 1917 in order to enlist Jewish support for the Allies and the fact that this support was forthcoming are not sufficiently appreciated in Palestine. The Arabs do not appear to realize in the first place that the present position of the Arab world as a whole is mainly due to the great sacrifices made by the Allied and Associated Powers in the War and, secondly, that, in so far as the Balfour Declaration helped to bring

70. Jewish Agency for Palestine, *Memorandum to the Palestine Royal Commission*, pp. 80–83.
71. *Ibid.*, p. 79.
72. Great Britain, *Palestine Royal Commission Report*, p. 24.

about the Allies' victory, it helped to bring about the emancipation of all the Arab countries from Turkish rule. If the Turks and their German allies had won the War, it is improbable that all the Arab countries, except Palestine, would now have become or be about to become independent States.

Summarizing the first part of this chapter which deals with the war pledges to the Arabs, we may say that whatever may have been the justification for Arab grievances with reference to other territories, the charge that the Balfour Declaration violated the British pledge to the Arabs is without foundation. There is no evidence that Britain included Palestine in the undertaking to the Sharif. On the other hand, there are explicit statements on the part of Faisal at the Peace Conference to the effect that Palestine should be excluded from the area of Arab independence; and more than this, there are definite statements on his part expressing friendship for the Zionist effort in Palestine. It is clear also that Husain knew that Palestine was to be opened up to Jewish settlement and that he expressed satisfaction with this eventuality. It should be added that both Husain and Faisal agreed to a Jewish Palestine on the assumption that the economic interests of the native population would be fully safeguarded and that the British trustee would see to it that no one people would exercise domination in Palestine.

For the disappointment of the Arabs with the San Remo decisions on Iraq and Syria, there is, on the other hand, much justification. The spirit of these decisions was not in harmony with the assurances that the Allies gave to support the Arabs in their aspiration for independence in the lands freed from the yoke of the Turks. These decisions moreover actually gave the Arabs not only less than what had been promised to them in the McMahon-Husain correspondence, but not even as much as what had been arranged in the less favorable secret Sykes-Picot treaty. Later, under Churchill, the British made whatever amends they could in increasing the degree of Arab independence and in rewarding Husain's sons, Faisal and Abdullah, for the services which they had rendered. All in all, the Arabs made important advances toward independence as a result of the First World War. If they got less than what was promised to them in the broad Allied propaganda, it should be remem-

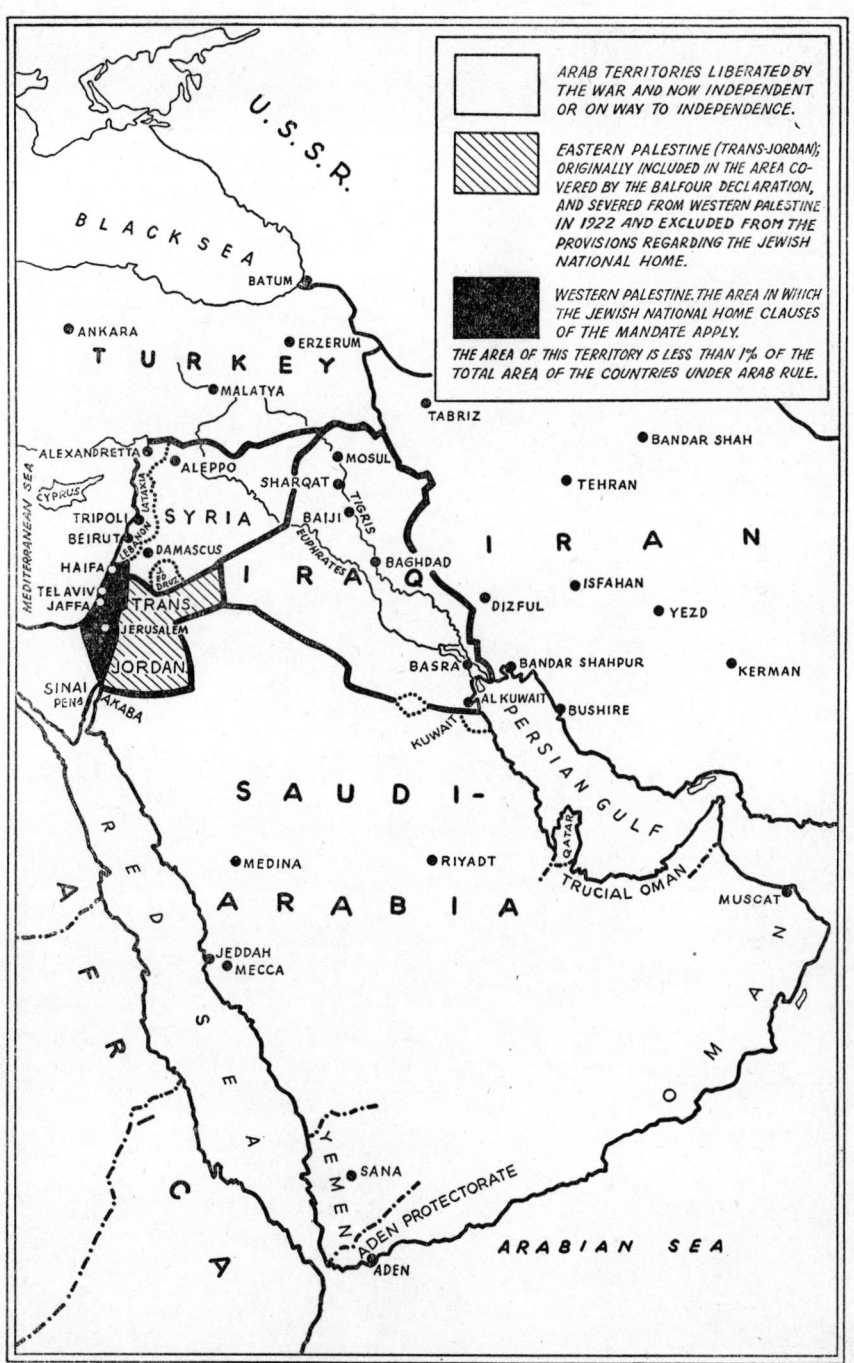

ARAB TERRITORIES AND PALESTINE

bered that this happened also in the case of other nations. If the issue is stated on the *quid pro quo* basis, as the Arabs are inclined to do, then it may be said that the Arabs received more in proportion to what they contributed than any other nation associated in the war effort.

PALESTINE AND THE PRINCIPLE OF SELF-DETERMINATION

The valid aspect of the Arab case lies not in the claims revolving around the war commitments, but in the second argument mentioned in the beginning of this chapter, namely, in their rights as inhabitants of the country. As indicated above, the real question concerns the nature of these rights. Does the fact that the Arabs constituted a majority of the inhabitants of Palestine at the time that the Mandate came into effect give them the right—contrary to the explicit terms of the Mandate—to prohibit Jewish immigration and to prevent the Jews becoming a majority, even if such a majority can be achieved without prejudicing the general welfare of the non-Jewish inhabitants? Involved in this is the question whether "self-determination" necessarily means absolute sovereignty—and whether it is tantamount to "domination" as the Arab position holds.[73]

The King-Crane Report

In connection with the argument of "self-determination" we may first take up the report of the King-Crane Commission which is cited as adding the weight of sound judgment and of scientific evidence to the claims of the Arabs in Palestine. A careful study of the work of the Commission is now available which makes it possible to evaluate more accurately the significance of its recommendations.[74]

---

73. In giving evidence before the Royal Commission in 1936 (p. 314), Auni Abdul Hadi, leader of the Pan-Arab movement in Palestine, made it clear that the Arabs "do not accept the formula laid down by the Jews, that there should not be any domination of the Arabs over the Jews or by the Jews over the Arabs."

74. Harry N. Howard, "An American Experiment in Peace Making: The King-Crane Commission," *The Moslem World*, Vol. XXXII, No. 2, April, 1942. The facts presented are taken from this study; the responsibility for the interpretation of the facts here given, however, rests with the Director of the Esco Foundation Palestine Study. See also I. B.

The Commission grew out of a letter sent by Dr. Howard Bliss, President of the American University in Beirut, to Wilson on February 7, 1919. Dr. Bliss told the President that the people of Syria were relying on his principle of self-determination and wanted "a fair opportunity to express their political aspirations." He expressed satisfaction with the report that an American Commission might possibly be sent to the Near East to study the situation there; he indicated that in his view an international commission would be preferable if it were backed up by the French and British authorities. He appeared quite sure of what such a commission would find.

I believe that the report of any Commission, made up of fair, wide-minded and resourceful men, would show that the Syrians desire the erection of an independent state or states under the care, for the present, of a Power, or of the "League of Nations." I believe the Power designated by the people would be America, for the Syrians believe in American disinterestedness; or England, for the people trust her sense of justice and believe in her capacity. I believe that French guardianship would be rejected for three reasons: serious-minded men in Syria fear that the people of Syria would imitate France's less desirable qualities; they do not consider the French to be good administrators; they believe that France would exploit the country for her own material and political advantage. They do not trust her. If America should be indicated as the Power desired I earnestly hope that she will not decline.

Bliss's conception fitted in perfectly with Wilson's thesis of self-determination. At the meeting of the Supreme Council on March 20th, when the question of the Syrian mandate had reached an impasse, Wilson as a way of breaking the deadlock threw out the suggestion that the wishes of the people concerned should be determined. He proposed sending an Inter-Allied Commission to Syria to report on the state of public opinion and to recommend such a division of territories and assignment of mandates as would be "most likely to promote the order, peace, and development of those peoples and countries." [75] Wilson wanted men of sound and liberal judgment

Berkson, "The Abortive King-Crane Recommendations—Science or Propaganda?" in *Hearings before the Committee on Foreign Affairs*, House of Representatives, Seventy-Eighth Congress, H. Res. 418 and 419, 1944, pp. 213–223.

75. *Ibid.*, p. 127.

rather than experts to head the Commission. He had said at the meeting on March 20th: "If we were to send a commission of men with no previous contact with Syria, it would, at any rate, convince the world that the conference had tried to do all it could to find the most scientific basis possible for a settlement." [76]

As noted above,[77] the French and the British who had originally appeared to agree, withdrew from participation. The American committee, however, was quickly appointed. Besides King and Crane, who as laymen were to be responsible for the recommendations, there were three technical advisers. Professor Albert H. Lybyer, a member of the Balkan section of the American Delegation whose work was about to terminate, applied for the position of Secretary, and was appointed the General Technical Adviser. The other two experts were: Dr. George R. Montgomery, for the northern regions of Turkey, and Captain William Yale, for the southern regions.

When the Commission was organized and ready to depart, many difficulties developed. Now that the French and British had withdrawn, Professor Westermann, Chief of the Western Asia (Turkish) Division of the American Commission to Negotiate Peace, was opposed to sending out the group. He thought that the Commission would do a great deal of harm, without achieving anything constructive or adding to the information already available in Paris.[78] Another difficulty developed from the Zionist side. Professor Felix Frankfurter, on behalf of the Zionist Organization, wrote to President Wilson on May 8, expressing his anxiety about the Commission. He pointed out that its report would not be delivered until after Wilson's stay in Paris, and this would further delay the disposition of the Zionist question. Wilson, after some time, finally replied that Frankfurter might rest assured of his adherence to the Balfour Declaration, but he made no promise with reference to detaining the King-Crane Commission. Responding to an urgent telegram from Syria, President Wilson and Colonel House decided to send the American group, regardless of the fact that with the non-participation of the French and English it would no longer be an Inter-Allied Commission.

76. *Ibid.*, p. 126.
77. Chap. III, p. 145.
78. *Ibid.*

216   *Palestine. Jewish, Arab, and British Policies*

The members of the Commission left toward the end of May. Traveling by way of Constantinople, the Commission arrived in Palestine on June 10, 1919. On June 12th, only two days after their arrival, the Commissioners sent an alarming telegram from Jaffa expressing their doubt that "any British or American official here believes that it is possible to carry out the Zionist program except through the support of a large army." [79] On July 11th, a week after the Syrian National Congress meeting in Damascus,[80] the committee, as if vibrating in complete sympathy with its resolutions, sent another telegram to Wilson from Beirut, in which they described the "unexpectedly strong expressions of national feeling" in Syria, the determined opposition to French supervision and the antagonism to the Zionist plans for Palestine.

The Commission remained in Palestine and Syria for a period of six weeks. In this time they interviewed a large number of delegations from some forty towns and rural centers, and received over 1,800 petitions. Dr. King, Mr. Crane and Professor Lybyer soon came to the conclusion that the correct solution of the problem would be a Syrian state under an American or British mandate with a constitutional monarchy under the Emir Faisal. In other words, their investigations confirmed the views of Dr. Bliss and the Syrian nationalists. Dr. Montgomery and Captain Yale disagreed with the methods of investigation and with the recommendations which were shaping themselves in the minds of the Commissioners and submitted their conclusions in separate memoranda. Dr. Montgomery recommended that Palestine be separated from Syria and placed under a British mandate, that Mt. Lebanon be autonomous under French mandate, and that Syria proper be placed under joint Anglo-French mandate with Faisal as King. Captain Yale suggested that Palestine be separated from Syria and constituted as a Jewish national home under British mandate.

The official report was formulated by Dr. King[81] and Pro-

---

79. *Ibid.*, p. 133.
80. See above, Chap. III, p. 125.
81. The plan itself, however, appears to have been the project of Mr. Crane who was the most forceful member of the Commission. Ronald Storrs remarks (*Orientations*, p. 417): "Few . . . will be disposed to doubt that, though the hands that signed their Report were the hands of King-Crane, the voice was the voice of Crane." An indication of his outlook and his general hostility to Jews is given in the diary of Am-

fessor Lybyer and completed on August 21st. They recommended a single mandate for Syria and Palestine, with autonomy for the Lebanon if the French insisted. This united Syria should be assigned, in accordance with the wishes of the majority of the people, to the United States,[82] and failing American acceptance, to Great Britain, but in no circumstances should the mandate be given to France. The form of government was to be a constitutional monarchy under the rule of Emir Faisal. The mandate should have a limited term, the time of expiration to be determined by the League. The Mandatory Power should make itself responsible for the development of economic undertakings and educational institutions, designed to promote the well-being and development of the Syrian people. One of the special functions of the Mandatory administration would be education for citizenship in a democratic State and the development of a sound national spirit—"This systematic cultivation of national spirit is particularly required in a country like Syria which has only recently come to self-consciousness." [83]

Although their major function was to determine which of the Powers should act as Mandatory, the Commission's report gave considerable attention to the question of Zionism. They

---

bassador Dodd, who remarked of him: "Jews are anathema to him and he hopes to see them put in their place. His advice to me was, of course: 'Let Hitler have his way.'" (William E. Dodd, Jr. and Martha Dodd, ed., *Ambassador Dodd's Diary,* Harcourt, Brace, 1941, p. 11.) At a subsequent meeting with Ambassador Dodd, later that year, Mr. Crane "talked of his coming interview with the Pope about a sort of a pact with the Islamic world whereby the followers of Mohammed may be protected against the Jews who are taking Palestine" (p. 42).

82. Storrs (*op. cit.*, p. 417) points out that the findings of the Commission were more favorable to the British than the report implies, since to the Eastern mind the nationality of the Commission would be taken into consideration in presenting the petition, and furthermore the known wealth and rumored liberalism of America had some influence. Moreover, from a conversation on March 29, 1919, at the Hotel de Crillon between Colonel House, Emir Faisal and Colonel Lawrence acting as interpreter (Garnett, *op. cit.*, p. 275), it would seem that the British were not opposed to having the Syrian Arabs vote an American mandate as the first choice, since they knew that the United States would not accept the mandate. Then if the British were the second choice it would fall to them without giving the impression that they had worked against the French. The major purpose of the Commission in the eyes of the British, it appears, was to show up the strong anti-French attitude in Syria.

83. Antonius, *op. cit.*, pp. 443–444.

re-echoed the current anti-Zionist allegations: that the Jews intended to dispossess the non-Jewish inhabitants of Palestine by buying up the land; that a military force of not less than 50,000 soldiers would be required to initiate the Zionist program; that to force Jewish immigration on the country where nine-tenths of its population were opposed would be a gross violation of the principle of self-determination. In addition to the objections voiced by Arabs and the British anti-Zionists in the Military Administration, the Commission added their own doubts. It seemed to them that the Jews could not possibly appear either to Christians or to Moslems as the proper guardians of the Holy Places or the custodians of the Holy Land as a whole. "The reason is this: the places which are most sacred to Christians—those having to do with Jesus—and which are also sacred to Moslems—are not only not sacred to Jews, but abhorrent to them." [84] They expressed extreme opposition not only to the idea of making Palestine a Jewish state, but also counseled a reduction of the Zionist program of establishing a Jewish homeland: "Jewish immigration should be definitely limited, and . . . the project for making Palestine distinctly a Jewish commonwealth should be given up." [85]

The opinions echoed by the Commissioners undoubtedly reflected the prevalent political attitude in Syria and Palestine. But this view of the situation, well known to those who are acquainted with Palestine and Syria, need not have been dressed up in the guise of a scientific survey. The investigation has all the earmarks of an organized piece of political propaganda of which the investigators may have been the witting or unwitting collaborators. The views were exactly those which had been expressed by Dr. Bliss in Paris; they coincided with the program of the extreme Syrian nationalists and were in accord with the propaganda of the Christian-Moslem societies in Palestine. They were, moreover, remarkably synchronized with the Syrian Congress at Damascus. The fact that the Committee was prepared to send an anti-Zionist telegram to Wilson only two days after their arrival in Palestine hardly testifies to patience in investigation. Their emphasis on petitions will hardly be persuasive to anyone who has lived in Palestine and

---

84. Antonius, *op. cit.*, Appendix H, Recommendations of the King-Crane Commission, p. 450.
85. *Ibid.*, p. 450.

knows that such petitions are easier to obtain there than in countries more literate and further along the road to democratic procedure than are the countries of the Near East.[86] A reliable Jewish authority reports that the investigation was replete with leading questions such as: "Do you want Jewish immigration? Would you like to have a Jewish State?" [87]

John de Vere Loder has described the situation as follows:[88]

It would have been difficult enough for the Commission to have achieved its object even had all concerned cooperated towards the discovery of a satisfactory solution. Under the conditions which existed it is not surprising that the Commission was somewhat baffled. The general conclusion of its report was that local opinion favoured independence without foreign control, but was prepared to accept a minimum of foreign assistance. Broadly speaking, the Christian communities in the Lebanon expressed themselves in favour of a French Mandate, but it is not improbable that considerations other than such as would have guided frank and free declarations influenced some of these decisions. The French and the Sherifians openly accused each other of putting unfair pressure on those who did not agree with their respective contentions. The Damascus administration was alleged to have used the censorship to suppress friendly references to France and to have picketed the offices of the Commission for the purpose of intimidating the delegations of the Christian communities. On the other hand, the French were supposed to be using equally unjustifiable if less crude means of obtaining the same end in Beirut and the neighborhood. On one point only does there appear to have been anything like unanimity, and that was in the demand for an integral Syria including Palestine, but not necessarily excluding special local administrations for certain areas.

The Commissioners, it should be stated, admitted the shortcomings of their investigation. In a special supplement[89] to

86. At Jerusalem eight of the twenty-three anti-Zionist petitions were practically identical in wording; in one case a printed form of the standard program for independence was handed in as a petition. The Commissioners remarked in their Report that "doubtless other printed copies had been models for many of the petitions."
87. Howard, quoted in *op. cit.*, p. 133.
88. John de Vere Loder, *The Truth about Mesopotamia, Palestine and Syria*, London, 1923, p. 36.
89. This supplement is omitted from the version of the King-Crane Commission's Report reprinted by Antonius in *The Arab Awakening*, pp. 443 ff.

their Report, pointedly entitled "For the Use of Americans Only," they gave instances of attempts at pressure on the part of the French, the British and the Arabs to influence the witnesses. In the body of the Report they said: "We were not blind to the fact that there was considerable propaganda; that often much pressure was put upon individuals and groups; that sometimes delegations were prevented from reaching the Commission; and that the representative authority of many petitions was questionable. But the Commission believes that these anomalous elements in the petitions tend to cancel one another when the whole country is taken into account, and that, as in the composite photograph, certain great, common emphases are unmistakable." [90] The Commission, however, does not indicate what "these anomalous elements" were; in a question as complex as this it is obviously important to know the nature of divergent opinions as well as of the single majority view. The fact that the two experts on the Commission who were best acquainted with Syria and Palestine offered other solutions would indicate that there were valid considerations which the Commissioners ignored.

It should also be noted that the recommendations made by the King-Crane Commission do not agree wholly with the facts presented in the full Report. According to the recommendations, the impression is given that the majority of the Arabs in Syria and Palestine voted for an American mandate, failing which they were ready to accept a British mandate. The truth is that on the question of a mandate, America received an insignificant number of votes.[91] The Americans were first choice only when a different question was asked: that is, whose "assistance" would be preferred. An analysis of the petitions would show that the petitioners wanted an independent Syria; they did not want to have any mandate. But if they had to take a mandate, a larger number wanted to have a French mandate than either a British or an American, although the total number voting for mandates (probably Christian Arabs) was so small as to be negligible. The preferred solution was an independent state, with "assistance" from one of the European Powers. In this, the feeling of the Arabs was almost equally

90. Quoted from Howard, p. 133.
91. I. B. Berkson, "The Abortive King-Crane Recommendations—Science or Propaganda?" *op. cit.*, p. 213.

divided between the British and the Americans, with the latter having somewhat the advantage.

The main fault of that part of the King-Crane Report which deals with Palestine does not lie in the procedures of the investigation, but in the whole approach to the problem. It is a "partial" report in the literal sense that it gave due consideration to only one part of the issue. Since the Commission was acting as an international agency, a truly "objective" approach would have required seeing the problem of Palestine in its international framework, giving equal consideration to the Jewish problem, together with the needs and views of the native inhabitants. Under the circumstances, it is questionable whether the wishes of the majority of the population could at that time be taken as the sole determining factor. In all of the discussions in Paris, the wishes of the peoples concerned were to be regarded as one factor, but not the only factor. In fact, this was also the view of President Wilson. The Commissioners responsible for the Report seemed to forget that the Allied nations, whom they were supposedly representing, had, after much discussion over a period of years, undertaken a definite commitment with reference to the establishment of the Jewish national home in Palestine which could not, in honor and justice, be evaded.

In the final analysis, the Report offered nothing in the way of a genuine workable recommendation; in reality, the proposals were self-contradictory. The preferred solution, according to the recommendations, was that the United States should assume the mandate over Syria and Palestine. This the United States was not prepared to do; but even if it had been so disposed, the problem of reconciling the Arab demand for complete self-determination with the policy of the Balfour Declaration would have stood, with all its difficulties. Wilson had given repeated allegiance to the Balfour Declaration in terms more extreme than the British declaration, and the American experts at the Peace Conference had explicitly conceived the future of Palestine in terms of a Jewish state. As for the British, who were the second choice, they certainly could not accept the mandate without the Balfour Declaration, since it was the issuance of the Balfour Declaration which had given them a claim to the mandate for Palestine.

The recommendations of the King-Crane Commission were

abortive for Syria as well as Palestine; recommendations were made that no one would, or could, carry out. The major effect was to weaken the French position and to strengthen the hand of Great Britain, but there was no constructive solution. This is well brought out in the comment made by Professor William E. Hocking:[92]

But in Syria, the effect was not nil. Such an enquiry has a logic which works in spite of itself. If men are offered a choice of supervisors, it becomes evident that they are to have supervisors. They may express their preference for independence; and do so in dominant numbers. But they are prepared for something less. But again, if they are offered a choice of supervisors, it is certainly implied that they have a choice, that the possibilities set before them are not mythical. If it is already determined that France is to govern here, and Britain there, it is misleading to ask people to choose between them, or between them and others. If it is not certain the United States will accept a mandate in those regions, it is misleading to present the United States as one of the possible advisers. Unless there is some possibility that those choices shall count, the work of such an enquiry as that of the King-Crane Commission can hardly be other than mischievous.

In the event, the work of the Commission, not discovering that France was the spontaneous choice of inner Syria, added materially to the difficulties of France in Syria. It was, so far, mischievous.

Whether the blame must rest on Wilson for sending the bootless Commission, or on France for insisting on the obtaining that which her professions had discountenanced, may remain open.

Article 22 of the League of Nations Covenant

Another line of attack in the self-determination argument relates to the incorporation of the Balfour Declaration into the Mandate for Palestine: it is alleged that this is a contradiction of the principles underlying the whole mandatory system. This contention was raised by the Palestine Arab delegation in its communications to the British Government in February and March, 1922, on the subject of the Jewish national home policy.[93] They submitted that the promise to the Zionists violated

92. William Ernest Hocking, *The Spirit of World Politics*, Macmillan, 1932, p. 255. Professor Hocking's comment is all the more interesting in view of his sympathy with the Arab point of view.
93. Great Britain, *Correspondence with the Palestine Arab Delegation and the Zionist Organization*, Cmd. 1700, 1922, pp. 1-4; pp. 11-15.

Article 20 of the Covenant in which the members of the League of Nations agreed to abrogate all understandings among themselves which were inconsistent with the terms of the Covenant, and that the Balfour Declaration was not in harmony with Article 22 of the Covenant, particularly with reference to paragraph 4, which provided that the wishes of the communities must be a principal consideration in the selection of the mandatory.[94]

On the legal side, the answer had already been given by the eminent British jurist, Sir William Finlay (now Mr. Justice Finlay) in response to an inquiry made by the Zionist Organization whether the terms of the Palestine Mandate, then being drafted, conflicted with Article 22. His opinion, written on April 8, 1921, reads:[95]

Article [Article 22] appears to me to have been, for perfectly intelligible reasons, drafted *in very general terms*. The first paragraph lays down the principle that the well-being and development of the *peoples* in question form a sacred trust of civilization. The second paragraph lays it down that the tutelage of such peoples should be entrusted to advanced nations as Mandatories. The third paragraph points out what is obvious and what really lies at the root of the inevitable vagueness of the whole Article, viz., that the character of the Mandate must differ according to the development of the people, the geographical situation, economic conditions, etc. My attention was called in conference to the last sentence of the fourth paragraph. But I do not think this sentence is relevant to the matter I have to consider (1) because I do not think this paragraph applicable to Palestine; (2) because it *is only in the selection of the Mandatory* that the wishes of the community must be a principal consideration; (3) because the words are *"a"* principal consideration and not *"the"* principal consideration.

Sir William Finlay also discusses the question whether Jewish immigration and settlement is inconsistent with the well-being and development of the inhabitants, which is, in

94. Quincy Wright, *Mandates under the League of Nations*, University of Chicago Press, Chicago, 1930, p. 591. The full text of Article 22 is given in this source. The first four paragraphs of this Article have been cited earlier, Chap. III, p. 136.

95. *Official Journal of the League of Nations*, August, 1921, pp. 443–444. See also Jewish Agency for Palestine, *Memorandum to the Palestine Royal Commission*, pp. 56 ff. and 293 ff.

accordance with Paragraph 1 of Article 22, a major object of the mandate system. His opinion is as follows:[96]

Article 22 of the Covenant does show that the general object is to secure the well-being and development of the mandated territories. Article 2 of the Mandate of course deals with a special scheme of immigration and settlement, viz.: that of the Jewish people. But I see absolutely no inconsistency between the two. It may well be that a judicious scheme of immigration is the best possible method of developing the resources of Palestine and securing the well-being of that country. It is in my view impossible upon any principle of construction to say that there is any inconsistency between this scheme and either the letter or the spirit of Article 22 merely because the scheme, which may benefit Palestine, may also benefit one particular people, viz.: the Jews. What is hoped is obviously that this scheme, while beneficial to the Jews will also prove in the best interests of Palestine. There is no inconsistency between these objects.

Article 22 came into force on January 10, 1920. When the San Remo Conference decided to assign the Mandate to Great Britain on April 24, 1920, and the League of Nations gave its approval on July 22, 1922, it was well understood that the establishment of the Jewish national home was an inseparable part of the responsibility of the mandatory power, and these international bodies saw no inconsistency between the Balfour Declaration and the League of Nations Covenant. Lord Balfour remarked on this in a speech in the House of Lords several months after the Arab delegation raised the question: "When my noble friend tries to maintain the paradox that the Powers who adopted the mandatory system . . . are so ignorant that they do not know their own child and are violating all their principles when they establish the policy of a Jewish Home in Palestine, I think my noble friend is not only somewhat belated in his criticism, but is asking us to accept a proposition which, as men of common sense, we should repudiate." [97]

Professor Rappard, the Vice-Chairman of the Mandates Commission, also argued: "The Mandate could only mean that the National Home was to be established and self-governing institutions be developed insofar as they did not prevent that

---

96. Jewish Agency for Palestine, *Memorandum to the Palestine Royal Commission*, p. 295.

97. Great Britain, *Parliamentary Debates, Lords*, June 21, 1922, cols. 1010–1011.

Home being established." [98] That there was no basic inconsistency may also be gathered from the fact that President Wilson and General Smuts, the foremost defenders of the idea of self-determination and the outstanding proponents of the mandatory system, were firm and enthusiastic supporters of the Balfour Declaration and of the right of the Jews to reconstitute themselves as a nationality in Palestine. While insisting on the significance of the principle of self-determination, Wilson never intended it to be a mechanical formula by which the situation in each country could be automatically determined. He seemed to have meant by it a broad principle which would secure for each people in the greatest measure possible the principle of life, liberty and the pursuit of happiness.[99]

The formal answer of the British Government to the Arab delegation was given in a letter dated March 1, 1922, written at the direction of Winston Churchill, who was then Secretary of State for the Colonies:

With regard to Article 22 of the Covenant of the League of Nations, I am to observe that this Article, in so far as it applies to territories severed from the Ottoman Empire, has been interpreted by the Principal Allied Powers in Articles 94 to 97 of the Treaty of Sèvres. Syria and Iraq are explicitly referred to in Article 94 of that Treaty as having been provisionally recognized as Independent States, in accordance with the fourth paragraph of Article 22 of the Covenant of the League of Nations. Article 95, on the other hand, makes no such reference to Palestine. The reason for this is that, as stated in that Article, the Mandatory is to be responsible for putting into effect the Declaration originally made on the 2nd No-

---

98. Permanent Mandates Commission, *Minutes of the Thirty-Second Session*, 1937, p. 190.
99. During the Peace Conference, Robert Lansing, the American Secretary of State, subjected the concept of determination to severe criticism. He conceded that the idea should exercise an influence on decisions, but opposed making it the controlling factor, pointing out that there were other factors—strategic and economic as well as ethnic—which should be taken into consideration in applying the principle. He noted that Wilson had himself been forced to abandon the principle in a number of important decisions and he prophesied that if used without qualification, the idea of self-determination would create difficulties in the solution of problems in many parts of the world, mentioning among others, Syria, Palestine, Morocco and Tripoli. He asked: "How can it be harmonized with Zionism, to which the President is practically committed?" (Robert Lansing, *The Peace Negotiations*, Houghton Mifflin, 1921, p. 97.) See also below, pp. 232–233.

vember, 1917, by the British Government, and adopted by the other Allied Powers, in favour of the establishment in Palestine of a National Home for the Jewish people, it being clearly understood that nothing should be done which might prejudice the civil and religious rights of existing non-Jewish communities in Palestine, and the rights and political status enjoyed by Jews in any other country. There is no question of treating the people of Palestine as less advanced than their neighbours in Iraq and Syria; the position is that His Majesty's Government are bound by a pledge which is antecedent to the Covenant of the League of Nations and they cannot allow a constitutional position to develop in a country for which they have accepted responsibility to the Principal Allied Powers, which may make it impracticable to carry into effect a solemn undertaking given by themselves and their Allies.

At the time when the mandatory system was being constructed, it was already recognized that Palestine along with Armenia would require special treatment.[100] In the case of Palestine the exceptional consideration required was the result of the special tie of the Jews to Palestine, which underlies the Jewish right to constitute their national home in that country. The constitutional position has been stated as follows:[101]

The present population of Palestine is, indeed, only a part of the much larger population whose connection with Palestine has been internationally recognized. The Jewish people as a whole may be considered, for this particular purpose, as forming virtually part of the population of Palestine. The mandates system has been applied to Palestine not merely on account of the inability of its present population to stand alone, as in the case with the other mandated territories, but also, and perhaps chiefly, on account of the fact that the people whose connection with Palestine has been recognized is still outside its boundaries. The mandatory power thus appears not only as a Mandatory, in the sense generally given to this term, but

100. J. C. Smuts, *The League of Nations—A Practical Suggestion*, Hodder and Stoughton, London, 1918, pp. 16–21.
101. J. Stoyanovsky, *The Mandate for Palestine*, Longmans, Green, 1928, pp. 41–42. A similar view has been expressed by Norman Bentwich, who holds that in the case of Palestine the Mandatory is acting as a trustee for the conscience of the civilized world in order to "administer that country not simply on behalf of the population which is there, but with a view to helping the people which desire to come there." ("Mandated Territories: Palestine and Mesopotamia (Iraq)," *The British Year Book of International Law*, 1921–1922, London, p. 51.)

as kind of a provisional administrator in the interest of an absent people. In this capacity the Mandatory has assumed an obligation not towards the actual but the virtual population of Palestine.

In accordance with the view outlined by Stoyanovsky, when the basic purpose of the mandatory system is borne in mind, it becomes clear that the pledge to the Jews contained in the Mandate is the exception that proves the rule. The main object of this mandates system may be stated as being "to guide towards independence and self-government those races, peoples or communities who for various reasons are not yet able to stand alone." [102] The League of Nations has recognized that the Jewish people is one of those peoples who cannot yet stand alone. In this case the primary reason is the lack of the territorial base requisite for self-determination; consequently the Mandate in its recognition of the Balfour Declaration provides this indispensable base. According to this view, the League of Nations has recognized two points: 1) The right of the Jews to nationhood and a national home as a logical consequence of the idea of self-determination for all peoples; 2) The right of the Jews, because of "historical connection," to establish the Jewish homeland in Palestine.[103]

The stock Arab reply to this claim is represented by the following passage written by Auni Bey Abdul Hadi.[104] "Stoyanovsky asks why the Jews are not entitled to self-determination. But supposing the Jews are able to organize a state which would be recognized by international law, would they have the right to organize such a state at the expense of another people's existence? What would the Irish people say, for instance, should the Jews choose Ireland for their national home? What would be the Spaniards' reply to an Arab demand for a national home in Spain?"

Clearly, however, the matter is not so simple. The fact that a people has lived in a certain land for a length of time, or lays a claim to it, is not sufficient to establish the principle of "historical connection." The following criteria are formulated by Stoyanovsky as essential:[105]

102. *Ibid.*, pp. 42–43.
103. Compare Quincy Wright, *op. cit.*, pp. 460–461.
104. "The Balfour Declaration," *Annals of the American Academy of Political and Social Science*, Philadelphia, 1932, p. 19.
105. *Ibid.*, pp. 64–68.

1. The nation which is recognized as having "historic connection" with given territory must have been at one time of its history in possession of that territory.

2. It is essential that the people claiming the benefit of "historical connection" with a given territory should not have previously renounced it, either explicitly or tacitly.

3. The people which claims the benefit of "historical connection" shall not have lost its distinct national character.

4. The people claiming the benefit of "historical connection" with a given territory shall not have acquired in the meantime any other national territory of its own.

5. Another essential condition is that such other rights and interests as may have been acquired in the meantime shall be safeguarded.

6. In order to be valid, "historical connection" is to be internationally recognized.

Ernst Frankenstein,[106] an authority on international law, has made a presentation of the legal claim of the Jews to Palestine. He points out that the Jews were the indubitable sovereigns of the land for more than a thousand years, until the destruction of the Jewish State by the Romans in the year 70. Palestine has never since constituted an independent political entity. The Romans perished without leaving a legal successor. The Arabs, who conquered it in 634, remained in possession for a relatively short time, when it passed successively to the rule of the Caliphs of Damascus, the Caliphs of Bagdad, the Tulinide Governors of Egypt, back to the Caliphs of Bagdad, then to the Egyptian Ikshidi princes, and finally to the Caliphs of Cairo. After 1071 Palestine was subjected to non-Arab conquerors, the Kurds, the Crusaders, the Mamelukes, and finally the Turks. In 1923, by the Peace Treaty of Lausanne, the Turks surrendered their rights to the Allied Powers. According to Frankenstein, "no one owns Palestine as a sovereign in his own right." Britain, as Mandatory Power, is acting only as trustee for the future sovereign. There are only two possible claims:

---

106. Ernst Frankenstein, *Justice for My People*, Dial Press, 1944, Chap. IX, "The Legal Position," pp. 82–115. Ernst Frankenstein, a German jurist, was formerly a member of the Berlin bar and legal adviser to the Italian Embassy, and served as lecturer at the Academy of International Law at The Hague. He is now a resident of London where he practices international law. He has published several volumes of a large work on private international law (*Privates Internationalrecht*).

that of the Jews and that of the present Arab-speaking inhabitants of Palestine.

According to the principles of international law, Frankenstein holds, the Jews have never lost their rights. Although the Romans conquered the country, international law admits the legality of conquest subject only to certain conditions. One of these conditions is that the conqueror must have been "in continuous and undisturbed possession" for a considerable time, but that "as long as other Powers kept up protests and claims, the actual exercise of sovereignty is not undisturbed." [107] Since the Jews were conquered after bitter resistance and have continuously, by word and act, asserted their claim, Frankenstein concludes that the Roman conquerors have never established a clear title to Palestine. The old Jewish claim, moreover, has received renewed vitality through the Balfour Declaration and the Palestine Mandate, in the Preamble which states: "Whereas recognition has thereby [the Balfour Declaration] been given to the historical connection of the Jewish people with Palestine and to the grounds for reconstituting their national home in that country."

The well-supported Jewish claim could be overcome only if the Arab claim proved to be a stronger one, which Frankenstein believes is not the case. He holds that the Arab claim by conquest is imperfect for a number of reasons. No Arab state can pretend to be the legal successor of those who conquered Palestine in 634. The Arabs ruled Palestine for a relatively short period (437 years). During the last 870 years, i.e., from the year 1071, there has been no Arab rule in Palestine. Moreover, unlike the Jews, the Palestine Arabs never struggled for their independence; they submitted to every conqueror and thus tacitly acquiesced in their domination. Even in 1917, when the Arabs of the desert revolted against Turkish rule, the Palestine Arabs took no action and the majority continued to fight for the Turks.

In addition, Frankenstein contests the argument based on possession from ancient days. He points out that the present-day inhabitants of Palestine are not in the main the descendants of the ancient inhabitants of the land, nor are they

---

107. Frankenstein, *op. cit.*, p. 86. Quoted "from the greatest English authority, Oppenheim, *International Law* (5th ed., London, 1937), Vol. I, p. 456."

predominantly the descendants of the Arab conquerors of Palestine. The Arab-speaking population of modern Palestine represents a highly mixed group. Palestine has been continuously replenished from the tribes of the Arabian desert; the Greeks, Romans and Crusaders have made their contribution to the racial make-up of the Holy Land; in modern times the Turkish governors and Egyptian conquerors introduced large contingents of foreign soldiers and settlers into the land. Authorities agree that the peasantry of Palestine who might be regarded as being most directly descended from the ancient inhabitants, had, by the nineteenth century, greatly dwindled in numbers. On the basis of an analysis of available statistics, Frankenstein estimates that, "in 1882 no more than about 106,000 settled Moslems had more than a half century's connection with the country." [108] Of the Arabs living in Palestine at the beginning of the First World War, no small proportion had immigrated from neighboring countries since 1882. His calculations led him to believe that only some 228,000 descendants of the 1882 Moslem settled population were living in Palestine at the outbreak of World War II. He thus comes to the conclusion: "In other words, *75 per cent of the Arab population of Palestine are either immigrants themselves or descendants of persons who immigrated into Palestine during the last hundred years, for the most part after 1882.*" [109]

The Jewish Claim of "Historic Connection"

Leaving aside this more formal type of argument, we may consider the commonsense of the situation. The Jews are not as a matter of fact choosing Ireland for their homeland, nor are the Arabs laying claim to Spain. It was not, obviously, an arbitrary act when the League of Nations with the concurrence of fifty-two of the leading nations of the world and with the formal approval of the United States recognized the Jewish claim to establish a national home in Palestine. It is not the single fact that the Jews once occupied Palestine, but a whole complex of facts that makes the Jewish claim acceptable to the international conscience.

The roots of Jewish civilization are in Palestine. The foundations of Jewish life, the writings of the Old Testament, were

108. *Ibid.*, p. 128.
109. *Ibid.*, p. 130.

there produced. The Jews were exiled from Palestine as the result of the conquest of the country despite stalwart resistance. Since the exile, the Jews have prayed for the restoration and Jewish ritual is replete with symbols of the hope for a return. The geography of Palestine to this day, the names of its hills and valleys and many of its towns and villages, are reminiscent of the connection of the Jews with the land in ancient times. The Jew who is rooted in the traditions of his people, who knows his Bible and prayer book, when he returns to Palestine, actually feels that he is returning to his ancient home. As the Royal Commission has recognized: "If Christians have become familiar through the Bible with the physiognomy of the country and its place-names and events that happened more than 2,000 years ago, the link which binds the Jews to Palestine and its past history is to them far closer and more intimate." [110]

The Jewish connection with Palestine, as seen by the Jews themselves, is only part of the story. Not less important is the fact that the Western world connects the Jews with Palestine. Whatever Palestine has meant to the Western world is due to what the Jews accomplished there. All those by whom the Bible is revered either as a religious book or as one of the great classics of the West tend by a certain mental compulsion to connect the Jews with Palestine. The recognition by Western nations of the right of the Jews to establish their home in Palestine never would have come about if the Jewish tie to Palestine were not deeply embedded in the Christian consciousness. "History" connotes not the record of the meaningless happenings of the dead past, but those events whose significance has impressed itself on the memory of civilized man. The term "historical connection" thus refers not only to the physical fact that Jews once occupied Palestine and that at least a remnant of the Jewish community has actually lived in Palestine up to modern times, but to the mental fact that all Western thought, Christian as well as Jewish, connects the Jews with Palestine.

Once having recognized the validity of the Jewish claim to, and need of, a homeland, the European mind cannot escape making Palestine the locus of the Jewish national home. Palestine is the only place where the Jews can hope to establish themselves as a people: the only place that can inspire the nec-

110. Great Britain, *Royal Commission Report*, p. 11.

essary idealism and sacrifice; the only place that the nations of the world can grant to the Jews as a homeland. The establishment of a national home for the Jews in Palestine would not be, as Abdul Hadi alleges, "at the expense of another people's existence." While Palestine has a certain importance for Arab culture and for Islam, the significance that it has for the Arabs is relatively less than it has either for Christians or for Jews. It is not an indispensable center of Arab culture; Arabia, Syria, Iraq and even Persia and North Africa are more important. Arab culture could develop in all its fullness even if Palestine were given over wholly to the Jews. But the only place that the Jews can develop their national home is in Palestine. It should be recalled also that the Jewish claim to develop their own culture in Palestine does not preclude the right of the Arabs to maintain and develop theirs. Even in a Jewish Palestine, the Arabs—in accordance with the Zionist view as well as in accordance with the Mandate—would have a greater degree of genuine self-determination than the Jews have in the Arabic countries.

It is not to be denied that there are difficulties inherent in the effort to harmonize the Arab right of self-determination on the basis of occupation and the Jewish right of self-determination based on "historic connection," which implies that they are in Palestine "as of right and not on sufferance." A just solution of this complicated problem would mean meeting the conflicting demands as fully as possible. No solution of the Arab claim versus the Jewish claim is possible if either be set up as an unconditioned absolute without reference to international judgment. It may be said that a "right," although always beginning as a desire, a need or a claim, does not achieve the status of a "right" unless it receives the sanction, intellectual, moral and legal, of an organized social body which stands above the contending parties. The essence of the Jewish argument is that at the time the Mandate was issued, such a judgment was rendered by the highest international authority that then existed, and that this judgment was made with the concurrence of all of the enlightened nations of the world.

The validity of the idea of absolute self-determination, when unqualified, is by no means beyond question. At the Peace Conference in 1919, Robert Lansing, the American Secretary of State, subjected it to a critical analysis, the force of which subsequent history has strengthened. He conceded that self-determination was a significant principle, meriting due consideration in the organization of states. But he thought it would be subversive of stable settlement to make the ethnic factor the all-controlling one, without giving consideration to other factors. As the affirmation of an unqualified right, self-determination was "one of those declarations of principle which sounds true, which in the abstract may be true, and which appeals strongly to man's innate sense of moral right and to his conception of natural justice, but which, when the attempt is made to apply it in every case, becomes a source of political instability and domestic disorder and not infrequently a cause of rebellion." [111]

Lansing thought that the principle as enunciated by Wilson was, to begin with, vague: "When the President talks of 'self-determination,' what unit has he in mind? Does he mean a race, a territorial area, or a community?" [112] Citing a usual example, he pointed out that if the individual state were the unit, the secession of the Southern states from the American Union in 1861 would have been wholly justifiable on the basis of the principle of self-determination. But, however carefully defined, the principle of self-determination was still bound to cause trouble in many lands. Wilson was forced to abandon the principle in important instances, and Lansing prophesied moreover that, if adhered to, the idea would sow the seeds of future trouble in many parts of the world and not least in Syria, Palestine, Morocco and Tripoli. He asked: "How can it be harmonized with Zionism to which the President is practically committed?" [113] Wilson agreed to eliminate mention of the principle of self-determination from the final draft of the Covenant of the League of Nations, but his failure to disavow it openly left an element of confusion in the arrangement of the peace treaties.

More recently, Walter Lippmann, in his criticism of Wilsonian principles, makes a similar and even more drastic statement. He declares: "To invoke the general principle of self-determination and to make it a supreme law of international

---

111. Robert Lansing, *The Peace Negotiations*, Houghton Mifflin, 1921, p. 102.
112. *Ibid.*, p. 97.
113. *Ibid.*

life, was to invite sheer anarchy." [114] He differentiates between self-government and self-determination, regarding the latter as a reactionary and barbarous conception. He says: "Despite its superficial 'democracy' the principle of self-determination is in an exact sense deeply un-American and uncivilizing. For it rejects the civilized ideal, which is the American ideal, that comes down to us from the Roman world and has persisted in the great tradition of the West. It is the ideal of a state within which diverse peoples find justice and liberty under equal laws and become a commonwealth." [115] Quincy Wright, an authority on the mandates under the League of Nations, who has proposed the internationalization of Palestine, has declared: "Palestine is perhaps the outstanding area of the world in which self-determination is inapplicable because of the greater weight of external, as compared to internal, political forces in shaping its destiny." [116]

The Mandate and Its Terms

The Royal Commission has succinctly stated the major objective of the Mandate as follows: "Unquestionably . . . the primary purpose of the Mandate, *as expressed in its preamble and its articles,* is to promote the establishment of the Jewish National Home." [117] Hanna also observes: "This document was framed in the Jewish interest, and the imperative obligations placed upon the Mandatory were in favor of the Zionists. It is significant that the word 'Arab' did not once appear, and that the native Palestinians were referred to throughout as non-Jews." [118] The Mandate, although designed to facilitate the establishment of a Jewish national home, makes full provision for the rights not only of the individual inhabitants of Palestine but of the non-Jewish communities.

The character of the Mandate may be discerned by dividing its major provisions into four categories: 1) obligations re-

114. Walter Lippmann, *United States War Aims*, Little, Brown, 1944, p. 173.
115. *Ibid.*, p. 174.
116. Quincy Wright, "The Future of the Near East," in Philip W. Ireland, ed., *The Near East, Problems and Prospects*, Lecture on the Harris Foundation, University of Chicago Press, 1942, p. 214.
117. Great Britain, *Royal Commission Report*, p. 39.
118. Hanna, *op. cit.*, p. 67.

sulting from the Jewish National Home policy; 2) obligations which relate equally to all inhabitants of the country as individuals or as grouped in communities; 3) obligations with reference to Holy Places and Antiquities; 4) international obligations.

The Jewish National Home Policy. The specific obligations arising from the responsibility of the Mandatory Power to facilitate the development of the Jewish National Home are indicated in the Preamble and Articles 2, 4, 6, 7 and in part of Article 11.

Historical Connection and Jewish National Home

Whereas the Principal Allied Powers have also agreed that the Mandatory should be responsible for putting into effect the declaration originally made on November 2nd, 1917, by the Government of His Britannic Majesty, and adopted by the said Powers, in favour of the establishment of a national home for the Jewish people, it being clearly understood that nothing should be done which might prejudice the civil and religious rights of existing non-Jewish communities in Palestine, or the rights and political status enjoyed by Jews in any other country; and

Whereas recognition has thereby been given to the historical connection of the Jewish people with Palestine and to the grounds for reconstituting their national home in that country; (From Preamble.)

The Mandatory shall be responsible for placing the country under such political, administrative and economic conditions as will secure the establishment of the Jewish national home, as laid down in the preamble, and the development of self-governing institutions, and also for safeguarding the civil and religious rights of all the inhabitants of Palestine, irrespective of race and religion. (Article 2.)

Recognition of the Jewish Agency

An appropriate Jewish Agency shall be recognized as a public body for the purpose of advising and cooperating with the Administration of Palestine in such economic, social and other matters as may affect the establishment of the Jewish national home and the interests of the Jewish population in Palestine, and, subject always to the control of the Administration, to assist and take part in the development of the country.

The Zionist organization so long as its organization and constitution are in the opinion of the Mandatory appropriate, shall be recognized as such agency. It shall take steps in consultation with His

Britannic Majesty's Government to secure the cooperation of all Jews who are willing to assist in the establishment of the Jewish national home. (Article 4.)

Facilitation of Immigration, Settlement and Development

The Administration of Palestine, while ensuring that the rights and position of other sections of the population are not prejudiced, shall facilitate Jewish immigration under suitable conditions and shall encourage, in cooperation with the Jewish agency referred to in Article 4, close settlement by Jews on the land, including State lands and waste lands not required for public purposes. (Article 6.)

The Administration may arrange with the Jewish agency mentioned in Article 4 to construct or operate, upon fair and equitable terms, any public works, services and utilities, and to develop any of the natural resources of the country, in so far as these matters are not directly undertaken by the Administration. Any such arrangements shall provide that no profits distributed by such agency, directly or indirectly, shall exceed a reasonable rate of interest on the capital, and any further profits shall be utilized by it for the benefit of the country in a manner approved by the Administration. (From Article 11.)

Nationality and Naturalization

The Administration of Palestine shall be responsible for enacting a nationality law. There shall be included in this law provisions framed so as to facilitate the acquisition of Palestinian citizenship by Jews who take up their permanent residence in Palestine. (Article 7.)

Obligations to Inhabitants—Individuals and Communities. Another group of articles have as their aim the promotion of the general welfare and development of the country as a whole. These are of course not opposed to but, rather indirectly, in the interest of the development of the Jewish national home.

Promotion of General Development and Land Settlement

The Administration of Palestine shall take all necessary measures to safeguard the interests of the community in connection with the development of the country, and, subject to any international obligations accepted by the Mandatory, shall have full power to provide for public ownership or control of any of the natural resources of the country or of the public works, services and utilities established or to be established therein. It shall introduce a land system appropriate to the needs of the country, having regard, among other things, to the desirability of promoting the close settlement and intensive cultivation of the land. (From Article 11.)

Individual Rights and Interests

The Mandatory shall be responsible for seeing that the judicial system established in Palestine shall ensure to foreigners, as well as to natives, a complete guarantee of their rights. (From Article 9.)

The Mandatory shall see that complete freedom of conscience and the free exercise of all forms of worship, subject only to the maintenance of public order and morals, are ensured to all. No discrimination of any kind shall be made between the inhabitants of Palestine on the ground of race, religion or language. No person shall be excluded from Palestine on the sole ground of his religious belief. (From Article 15.)

Group Rights and Educational Autonomy

Respect for the personal status of the various peoples and communities and for their religious interests shall be fully guaranteed. In particular, the control and administration of Wakfs shall be exercised in accordance with religious law and the disposition of the founders. (From Article 9.)

The right of each community to maintain its own schools for the education of its own members in its own language, while conforming to such educational requirements of a general nature as the Administration may impose, shall not be denied or impaired. (From Article 15.)

English, Arabic and Hebrew shall be the official languages of Palestine. Any statement or inscription in Arabic on stamps or money in Palestine shall be repeated in Hebrew, and any statement or inscription in Hebrew shall be repeated in Arabic. (Article 22.)

The Administration of Palestine shall recognize the holy days of the respective communities in Palestine as legal days of rest for the members of such communities. (Article 23.)

Self Government and Local Autonomy

The Mandatory shall be responsible for placing the country under such political, administrative and economic conditions as will secure the establishment of the Jewish national home, as laid down in the preamble, and the development of self-governing institutions, and also for safeguarding the civil and religious rights of all the inhabitants of Palestine, irrespective of race and religion.[119] (Article 2.)

119. This article is repeated from p. 235, where it was introduced in connection with the Jewish national home.

The Mandatory shall, so far as circumstances permit, encourage local autonomy. (Article 3.)

Religious Sites, Holy Places and Antiquities. In accordance with the Mandate, the British Government undertook full responsibility for preserving existing rights and securing free access to the Holy Places, subject to the League of Nations. Special precaution was taken to ensure complete authority to the Moslems with reference to the sacred shrines of Islam. In addition to the general article mentioned below with reference to Antiquities, the Mandate contains under Article 21 carefully worked out rules for excavations and archaeological research.

Holy Places and Religious Shrines

All responsibility in connection with the Holy Places and religious buildings or sites in Palestine, including that of preserving existing rights and of securing free access to the Holy Places, religious buildings and sites and the free exercise of worship, while ensuring the requirements of public order and decorum, is assumed by the Mandatory, who shall be responsible solely to the League of Nations in all matters connected herewith, provided that nothing in this article shall prevent the Mandatory from entering into such arrangements as he may deem reasonable with the Administration for the purpose of carrying the provisions of this article into effect; and provided also that nothing in this mandate shall be construed as conferring upon the Mandatory authority to interfere with the fabric or the management of purely Moslem sacred shrines, the immunities of which are guaranteed. (Article 13.)

Commission on the Holy Places

A special Commission shall be appointed by the Mandatory to study, define and determine the rights and claims in connection with the Holy Places and the rights and claims relating to the different religious communities in Palestine. The method of nomination, the composition and the functions of this Commission shall be submitted to the Council of the League for its approval, and the Commission shall not be appointed or enter upon its functions without the approval of the Council. (Article 14.)

Law of Antiquities

The Mandatory shall secure the enactment within twelve months from this date, and shall ensure the execution of a Law of Antiquities based on the following rules. This law shall ensure equality of treatment in the matter of excavations and archaeological research to the nations of all State Members of the League of Nations.

International Obligations. The international undertakings are designed to prevent discrimination by the Mandatory against other States Members of the League of Nations to facilitate adoption of international conventions with reference to traffic in drugs, combating disease, freedom of travel, cultural communication and international arbitration. However, apart from reporting to the Council of the League, the Mandate does not provide for effective international control.

Non-Discrimination

The Mandatory shall see that there is no discrimination in Palestine against the nationals of any State Members of the League of Nations (including companies incorporated under its laws) as compared with those of the Mandatory or of any foreign State in matters concerning taxation, commerce or navigation, the exercise of industries or professions, or in the treatment of merchant vessels or civil aircraft. Similarly, there shall be no discrimination in Palestine against goods originating in or destined for any of the said States, and there shall be freedom of transit under equitable conditions across the mandated area. (Article 18.)

Adherence to International Conventions

The Mandatory shall adhere on behalf of the Administration of Palestine to any international conventions already existing or which may be concluded hereafter with the approval of the League of Nations, respecting the slave traffic, the traffic in arms and ammunition, or the traffic in drugs, or relating to commercial equality, freedom of transit and navigation, aerial navigation and postal, telegraphic and wireless communication or literary, artistic or industrial property. (Article 19.)

The Mandatory shall cooperate on behalf of the Administration of Palestine, so far as religious, social and other conditions may permit, in the execution of any common policy adopted by the League of Nations for preventing and combating disease, including diseases of plants and animals. (Article 20.)

Report to the League of Nations

The Mandatory shall make to the Council of the League of Nations an annual report to the satisfaction of the Council as to the measures taken during the year to carry out the provisions of the mandate.

Copies of all laws and regulations promulgated or issued during the year shall be communicated with the report. (Article 24.)

Acceptance of International Arbitration

The Mandatory agrees that, if any dispute whatever should arise between the Mandatory and another Member of the League of Nations relating to the interpretation or the application of the provisions of the mandate, such dispute, if it cannot be settled by negotiation, shall be submitted to the Permanent Court of International Justice provided for by Article 14 of the Covenant of the League of Nations. (Article 26.)

The Mandate gives all inhabitants of Palestine equal rights as individuals and thus includes the principle underlying Western democratic constitutions. But it goes beyond this and makes equality the basis of the rights of the various communities, cultural as well as religious, allowing to each full scope for development. To the Christian world outside of Palestine are guaranteed special rights arising out of the religious connection, and this principle applies also—with special safeguards for autonomy—in the case of Moslems. The Jews have, besides the implied right of access to their holy places, the unique right that grows out of their historical connection with the land, which in essence means the right of Jews to come to Palestine as persons returning to their home. It may truly be said that there is no constitution in the world in which the rights of divergent peoples and religions and the interests of the international outlook are so fully safeguarded as in the Mandate for Palestine.

AMERICAN INTEREST IN ZIONISM AND IN THE JEWISH NATIONAL HOME POLICY

Underlying the American attitude toward Zionism, there is a sympathetic interest in the advancement of Jewish equality and in the restoration of the Jews to Palestine which goes back to the early days of the republic. In 1818, in a letter to Major Mordecai M. Noah,[120] John Adams, second President

---

[120] The brilliant and erratic Mordecai Manuel Noah, playwright and politician, was a pioneer American Zionist. In 1825, he bought Grand Island near Buffalo and issued an invitation to all suffering Jews to come

Promises, Claims and Rights 241

of the United States, manifested a strong concern for extending to the Jews "all the privileges of citizens in every part of the world," and also expressed a warm interest in the Jewish restoration to Palestine. He wrote: "I really wish the Jews again in Judea, an independent Nation." [121] An indication of the religious interest in Jewish restoration is afforded by a remarkable enterprise undertaken in 1858 by "The Church of the Messiah" in New York City. In order to stimulate the return of the Jews to Palestine in accordance with prophecy, they dispatched thirty of their own families to settle in the Holy Land to be an example to the Jews and to encourage agriculture among them. They bought land near Jaffa and devoted themselves completely to their mission, but the experiment was finally abandoned after the group was decimated by hunger and disease.

In 1891, the Reverend William E. Blackstone, a prominent Protestant clergyman, moved by the outrages against the Jews in Russia, presented a memorial to President Benjamin Harrison and Secretary of State James G. Blaine, urging them to exert the influence of the United States for the purpose of holding an international conference to consider the plight of the Jews and promote their claim to Palestine as their ancient homeland. The petition was signed by outstanding Americans and read in part:[122]

Why not give Palestine back to them [the Jews]? According to God's distribution of nations, it is their home—an inalienable possession from which they were expelled by force—under their cultivation it was a remarkably fruitful land, sustaining millions of Israelites, who industriously tilled its hillsides and valleys. They were agriculturists and producers as well as a nation of great commercial importance—the center of civilization and religion.

If they could have autonomy in government, the Jews of the world would rally to transport and establish their suffering brethren in their time-honored habitation. For over 17 centuries they have patiently waited for such a privileged opportunity . . . A million exiles, by their terrible sufferings, are piteously appealing to our

and settle there in an autonomous state. After the failure of this project, he became an advocate of the return of the Jews to Palestine under the protection of the United States.
121. Reuben Fink, ed., *America and Palestine*, American Zionist Emergency Council, 1944, p. 20.
122. Reuben Fink, *op. cit.*, p. 21.

sympathy, justice and humanity. Let us now restore to them the land of which they were so cruelly despoiled by our Roman ancestors.

Woodrow Wilson's Contribution and the American View at the Peace Conference

Woodrow Wilson's interest in the restoration of the Jews to Palestine, no doubt greatly strengthened by his contact with Louis D. Brandeis, appears to have been originally stimulated by the influences in his Presbyterian home.[123] His response to the Zionist idea was quick and wholehearted. Early in the spring of 1916, at the beginning of the negotiations which led to the British declaration, Wilson seems to have assured the American Zionists of support for their plans. It was not, however, until shortly before the Balfour Declaration was issued that Wilson gave a definite indication of his approval. In early September, 1917, Lord Robert Cecil cabled Colonel Edward House, Wilson's close friend and adviser, asking him to ascertain unofficially if the President favored the proposed declaration of sympathy with the Zionist movement. Colonel House followed this up with a memorandum to Wilson on September 7th, in which he asked him what answer to make to Lord Cecil. At the same time he warned: "There are many dangers lurking in it, and if I were the British I would be chary about going too definitely into that question." [124] Wilson's answer came six weeks later—he had been carrying House's memorandum in his pocket. He explained that he had "concurred in the formula suggested by the other side," and would be obliged if Colonel House would so inform them. Wilson evidently had reference to his approval of the text of the Declaration which had been shown to him in October.

It would seem that Wilson's warm attitude was not shared by Colonel House or by Robert Lansing, the Secretary of State, although it is not clear whether their hesitancy was due to coolness to the Zionist idea or to an unwillingness to involve the United States in the complex Palestine issue. On December 13, 1917, Lansing wrote to the President indicating that pressure was being brought by the Zionists to get the Government to

---

123. Norman Maclean, *His Terrible Swift Sword*, Gollancz, London, 1942, p. 31.

124. Ray Stannard Baker, *Woodrow Wilson, Life and Letters*, Doubleday, Doran, Vol. 7, 1939, p. 256.

express its attitude. He advised that the United States proceed cautiously, giving three reasons: the United States was not at war with Turkey; the Jews were not unanimous in their desire for independent nationhood; and there would be resentment if the Holy Land were turned over "to the absolute control of the race credited with the death of Christ." He indicated that only the first reason, that is, that the United States was not at war with Turkey, should be publicly stated. The President returned the letter to Lansing at a Cabinet meeting the following day, stating, according to Lansing, that "he was forced to agree with me, but said that he had an impression that we had assented to the British Declaration regarding returning Palestine to the Jews." [125]

The State Department's caution or reluctance was further illustrated in the letter written to Wilson by Lansing on February 28, 1918, regarding the authorization of the proposed Zionist Medical Unit and the granting of passports to the representatives of the Zionist Organization who wished to proceed to Palestine as part of the Zionist Commission. Lansing advised against fulfilling these requests, arguing that the United States Government had not "accepted Mr. Balfour's pronouncement with reference to the future of Palestine, and has expressly refrained from accrediting consular agents to the territory, in which action the British Government had entirely acquiesced." He felt that the presence in Palestine of individuals sponsored by an organization having a distinct political aim would be embarrassing. Again, the President was not deterred, for Lansing's letter carried the notation signed by F.L.P.:[126] "March 13–18 President authorized the Unit."

The Balfour Declaration was received in the United States with wide approval and it was generally regarded as the promise of a Jewish state. In June, 1918, the Zionist Organization of America addressed a letter to the members of Congress, requesting them to express their opinion on the Zionist question.[127] Most of the Senators and Representatives declared their support of the Balfour Declaration, giving the following reasons: the Jews were entitled to the same national rights en-

---

125. *The Lansing Papers*, Vol. II, pp. 107–8.
126. Frank L. Polk, Under-Secretary of State.
127. The statements were collated in *The American War Congress and Zionism*, edited by Reuben Fink, 1919.

joyed by other peoples; the establishment of the Jewish homeland would enable the Jews to contribute further to world progress and civilization; it would render justice to a persecuted race and was the fulfillment of a duty that had long been withheld. A number of the statements specifically referred to the formation of a Jewish state.[128]

Official support was slow in coming, although there were a number of indications that the United States had accepted the British position. On August 31, 1918, Wilson wrote to Dr. Stephen S. Wise expressing satisfaction "in the progress of the Zionist movement in the United States and in the Allied countries since the Declaration by Mr. Balfour on behalf of the British Government." [129] In the autumn, Lansing prepared a memorandum to serve as guide to the American Peace Commissioners in which he stated that "Palestine should be an autonomous state under a general international protectorate or under the protectorate of a Power designated to act as the Mandatory of the Powers." [130] Lansing did not refer to Jewish settlement of Palestine but seemed to imply this in separating Palestine from other areas in Turkey and in intimating that it was to have a mandatory. That the American point of view implied a Jewish state, is clearly indicated through the Recommendations[131] made at the Peace Conference in January 1919

---

128. See statement by Representative William E. Cox of Indiana in Reuben Fink, *op. cit.*, pp. 38–39; also the statement by Senator Charles M. McNary given above, Chap. III, p. 110.

129. Baker, *op. cit.*, p. 373.

130. Lansing, *op. cit.*, p. 196.

131. The document is given in David Hunter Miller, *My Diary at the Conference at Paris*, Vol. IV, pp. 263–4, entitled "Outline of Tentative Report and Recommendations Prepared by the Intelligence Section, in Accordance with Instructions, for the President and the Plenipotentiaries." A facsimile of the recommendation on Palestine is shown herewith on pages 247 and 249.

The Intelligence Section appears to have been the outgrowth of a group referred to as The Inquiry, which consisted of a body of experts appointed by Colonel House in the fall of 1917 at the suggestion of President Wilson. Dr. Sidney F. Mezes of the College of the City of New York was the Director, and Walter Lippmann, the Secretary; David Hunter Miller of the New York Bar was Treasurer. Among the staff members were: Dr. Isaiah Bowman, then of the American Geographical Society, who was Chief Territorial Specialist; James T. Shotwell, then of Columbia University, who acted as Librarian and Specialist in History; and W. L. Westermann, then of the University of Wisconsin, who was Regional Specialist for Western Asia. The Inquiry had the function of collating material which would be of use at the Peace Conference. This

by the Intelligence Section for the use of the President and the American Delegation.

The report recommends that Palestine be established as a separate state under Great Britain as a mandatory of the League of Nations, and that the Jews be invited to return to Palestine to settle there, being given the assurance that it would be the policy of the League of Nations "to recognize Palestine as a Jewish state as soon as it is a Jewish state in fact." The Peace Conference should render all possible assistance in the development of a Jewish Palestine consistent with the protection of the personal, religious and property rights of the non-Jewish population. The Holy Places and religious rights of all creeds would be placed under the protection of the League of Nations and its Mandatory. In discussing the boundaries of Palestine, emphasis is laid on the problem of irrigation, with the recommendation that the new state should control the resources of water power on Mt. Hermon to the east of Jordan. In discussing the recommendation of a Jewish state, the memorandum declares unequivocally:

It is right that Palestine should become a Jewish state, if the Jews being given the full opportunity make it such. It was the cradle and home of their vital race, which has made large spiritual contributions to mankind, and is the only land in which they can hope to find a home of their own; they being in this last respect unique among significant peoples.

The recommendations made by the Intelligence Section are of particular significance for understanding the American view at the time of the Peace Conference because they are part of a comprehensive report on various questions—territorial, economic and labor—designed to guide the Peace Conference in making postwar arrangements. The proposals on Palestine are in turn part of a complete plan devised for the Arab areas, including Syria, Mesopotamia and Arabia, in the light of the economic and social conditions in each area.[132] But the solu-

group appears to have been incorporated later into the "Section of Territorial, Economic and Political Intelligence of the American Commission to Negotiate Peace."

132. Under the section entitled "Arabia" the Report recommends that the desert portion of the Arabian Peninsula (exclusive of Syria and Mesopotamia) be treated as a separate block, with reference to which no action should be taken by the League of Nations. The policing of the

tion for Palestine is markedly different from the proposals for the other countries because it is definitely set apart from the Arab countries and Great Britain is named as the Mandatory of the League of Nations.

The view of the Inquiry Commission appears to have been generally accepted at the Conference. During February, when Weizmann returned to London from Paris, where he had seen Wilson, House and Westermann, he stated that the President had promised unqualified support for "a Jewish Palestine, full and unhampered." [133] This was confirmed by the President himself somewhat later on March 2, 1919, at the White House, when he met a delegation of the American Jewish Congress, consisting of Dr. Stephen S. Wise, Judge Julian W. Mack, Mr. Louis Marshall, and Bernard G. Richards, Secretary of the Congress. The statement read:[134]

As for your representations touching Palestine, I have before this expressed my personal approval of the declaration of the British Government regarding the aspirations and historic claims of the Jewish people in regard to Palestine. I am, moreover, persuaded that the Allied nations, with the fullest concurrence of our Government and people, are agreed that in Palestine shall be laid the foundations of a Jewish Commonwealth.

By this time, support of the Balfour Declaration had become the *de facto* policy of the American Government. In 1921, writ-

---

coasts of Arabia on the Red Sea, the Indian Ocean and the Persian Gulf, was to be left to the British Empire. The Report is not favorable to the domination of Husain. It declares: "In spite of the political prominence of the King of the Hedjaz [Husain] he be not aided to establish an artificial and unwelcomed dominion over tribes unwilling to accept his rule." The discussions following the recommendations explain that the chieftains of the inner desert tribes, especially Ibn Saud, and the sheikhs of Asir and Yemen, would look with hostility on the consolidation of the power of the King of the Hejaz or of his sons. The movement toward Arab unity in the Arabian Peninsula should receive encouragement only if it could be shown that such unity might be developed without the use of force. Syria and Mesopotamia are treated in separate sections but their recommendations are similar. In each case it is recommended that a separate state be established and that the mandatory principle be applied, but no recommendation is made as to the Power to be selected to carry out this principle. Furthermore, it is proposed that no solution be adopted which would preclude the incorporation of Syria or Mesopotamia in an Arab confederation if a tendency toward such a solution would develop in either of the two countries.

133. *The Maccabaean*, February, 1919, p. 30.
134. *The New York Times*, March 3, 1919.

*26. PALESTINE.

It is recommended:

1) That there be established a separate state of Palestine.

2) That this state be placed under Great Britain as a mandatory of the League of Nations.

3) That the Jews be invited to return to Palestine and settle there, being assured by the Conference of all proper assistance in so doing that may be consistent with the protection of the personal (especially the religious) and the property rights of the non-Jewish population, and being further assured that it will be the policy of the League of Nations to recognize Palestine as a Jewish state as soon as it is a Jewish state in fact.

4) That the holy places and religious rights of all creeds in Palestine be placed under the protection of the League of Nations and its mandatory.

DISCUSSION.

1) It is recommended that there be established a separate state of Palestine.

> *The separation of the Palestinian area from Syria finds justification in the religious experience of mankind. The Jewish and Christian churches were born in Palestine, and Jerusalem was for long years, at different periods, the capital of each. And while the relation of the Mohammedans to Palestine is not so intimate, from the beginning they have regarded Jerusalem as a holy place. Only by establishing Palestine as a separate state can justice be done to these great facts.
>
> As drawn upon the map, the new state would control its own source of water power and irrigation, on Mount Hermon in the east to the Jordan; a feature of great importance since the success of the new state would depend upon the possibilities of agricultural development.

2) It is recommended that this state be placed under Great Britain as a mandatory of the League of Nations.

*79
OUTLINE OF TENTATIVE REPORT AND RECOMMENDATIONS ON PALESTINE FOR THE PEACE CONFERENCE IN VERSAILLES, 1919

Palestine would obviously need wise and firm guidance. Its population is without political experience, is racially composite, and could easily become distracted by fanaticism and bitter religious differences.

The success of Great Britain in dealing with similar situations, her relation to Egypt, and her administrative achievements since General Allenby freed Palestine from the Turk, all indicate her as the logical mandatory.

3) It is recommended that the Jews be invited to return to Palestine and settle there, being assured by the Conference of all proper assistance in so doing that may be consistent with the protection *of the personal (especially the religious) and the property rights of the non-Jewish population, and being further assured that it will be the policy of the League of Nations to recognize Palestine as a Jewish state as soon as it is a Jewish state in fact.

It is right that Palestine should become a Jewish state, if the Jews, being given the full opportunity, make it such. It was the cradle and home of their vital race, which has made large spiritual contributions to mankind, and is the only land in which they can hope to find a home of their own; they being in this last respect unique among significant peoples.

At present, however, the Jews form barely a sixth of the total population of 700,000 in Palestine, and whether they are to form a majority, or even a plurality, of the population in the future state remains uncertain. Palestine, in short, is far from being a Jewish country now. England, as mandatory, can be relied on to give the Jews the privileged position they should have without sacrificing the rights of non-Jews.

4) It is recommended that the holy places and religious rights of all creeds in Palestine be placed under the protection of the League of Nations and its mandatory.

The basis for this recommendation is self-evident.

*80

OUTLINE OF TENTATIVE REPORT AND RECOMMENDATIONS ON PALESTINE FOR THE PEACE CONFERENCE IN VERSAILLES, 1919

ing of the Turkish dismemberment, W. L. Westermann said: "Palestine has been set aside as a homeland for the Jews of the world, under the mandate of Great Britain." [135] In discussing the secret agreements reached by the Powers during the war period, he noted: "A change was made in regard to Palestine when the British Government published the Balfour Declaration of November, 1917, granting to the insistent Zionists the privilege that Palestine should be set aside as the homeland of the Jews. This was an open covenant published to the world and fought for in the open. It received official and public recognition from the French and Italian Governments. President Wilson declared his adherence to it, and many of our State legislatures passed resolutions urging the national government to support it." [136]

The Congressional Resolution of 1922 and the Anglo-American Convention of 1925

The American Government finally gave its formal stamp of approval through the Congressional resolutions in the spring of 1922, several months before the British Mandate was sanctioned by the League of Nations. The British Government was meeting some difficulty in having the Mandate approved in Parliament, the House of Lords actually rejecting it. The activity of the Zionists in getting American approval was welcomed. A joint resolution favoring the establishment of a national home for the Jewish people in Palestine was adopted in the Senate on May 3, and in the House of Representatives on June 30. It was passed unanimously despite the fact that it was opposed by a group of Jewish anti-Zionists and a number of Palestine Arabs resident in New York. The Resolution was signed by President Harding[137] on September 21st and read as follows:

---

135. W. L. Westermann, "The Armenian Problem and the Disruption of Turkey," in *What Really Happened at Paris*, Edward M. House and Charles Seymour (eds.), Scribners, 1921, p. 176.

136. *Ibid.*

137. President Harding had already made a number of statements favorable to the rehabilitation of Palestine as the homeland of the Jewish people. Similar statements were made subsequently by President Calvin Coolidge, on June 13, 1924; President Herbert Hoover, on September 21, 1928; and President Franklin Delano Roosevelt, on July 2, 1938. (Reuben Fink, ed., *op. cit.*, p. 88.)

Resolved by the Senate and House of Representatives of the United States of America in Congress assembled, that the United States of America favors the establishment in Palestine of a national home for the Jewish people, it being clearly understood that nothing shall be done which may prejudice the civil and religious rights of Christian and all other non-Jewish communities in Palestine, and that the holy places and religious buildings and sites in Palestine shall be adequately protected.

The Anglo-American Convention of 1925[138] is regarded by some as a further indication of American support of the Balfour Declaration, but by others it is viewed rather as a step in the direction of indifference. The Convention resulted from the American claim that despite the fact that the United States was not a constituent of the League of Nations, it was entitled to the rights and privileges enjoyed by League members in areas which had passed to the control of the Allies as a result of the war. The basis for this claim was that the United States had participated in the defeat of Germany and her allies. The British for a time resisted the claim, but finally agreed. During the course of the negotiations it was indicated that His Majesty's Government were anxious that the Convention with regard to Palestine should "contain a specific allusion to the policy of establishing a national home for the Jewish people in Palestine." [139] As a result, it was decided to incorporate the whole Mandate in the Convention, thus making the United States a signatory to the Mandate. After the recital of the Mandate in full, Article I of the Convention states: "Subject to the provisions of the present Convention, the United States consents to the administration of Palestine by His Britannic Majesty, pursuant to the Mandate recited above." [140]

138. It was consummated December 3, 1924 and proclaimed by President Calvin Coolidge after ratification on December 5, 1925.
139. Department of State, *Mandate for Palestine*, U. S. Government Printing Office, 1931, p. 82. See also, *Great Britain Parliamentary Papers 1921*, Cmd. 1226, and *Parliamentary Papers 1924–25*, Cmd. 2559, pp. 107–115. The following Zionist publications give a summary of the American interest in the Palestine Mandate: *A Survey of the Diplomatic Negotiations and Relevant Circumstances Bearing on the Right of the United States to Participate in Any Disposition of Palestine; Memorandum Submitted to the Palestine Royal Commission on American Interest in the Administration of the Palestine Mandate*, 1936.
140. Department of State, *Mandate for Palestine*, p. 91.

American Policy Toward Palestine

The Articles of the Convention provided that: the United States and its nationals should enjoy all the rights and benefits secured under the terms of the Mandate to the members of the League of Nations and their nationals; vested American property rights in the mandated territory should be fully respected; the nationals of the United States should be permitted to maintain educational, philanthropic and religious institutions in Palestine; extradition treaties and similar conventions in force between the United States and Great Britain should be applied to the mandated territory; and a duplicate of the annual report to be made by the Mandatory to the League of Nations should be furnished to the United States. Article 7 states: "Nothing contained in the present convention shall be affected by any modification which may be made in the terms of the mandate, as recited above, unless such modification shall have been assented to by the United States." [141]

Article 7, taken in conjunction with Article 1, has been interpreted in Zionist literature to mean that no part of the Mandate could be changed without the consent of the United States. Moreover, Article 27 of the Palestine Mandate provides that no change can be made in the Mandate without obtaining the consent of the Council of the League of Nations. Since the United States claimed all privileges of members of the League with reference to the Mandate for Palestine, it has been held that the United States has a voice in determining changes in the Mandate. The State Department, however, has taken the view that the rights of the United States are much more limited, that the Convention does not, in fact, empower the Government of the United States to prevent modification of the Mandate. Under its provisions, however, "this Government can decline to recognize the validity of the application to American interests of any modification of the Mandate unless such modification has been assented to by the Government of the United States." [142]

---

141. *Ibid.*, p. 92.
142. Carl J. Friedrich, *American Policy toward Palestine*, American Council on Public Affairs, Washington, 1944, p. 23, n. 1. The statement was made on October 14, 1938, in a press release. President Roosevelt indicated the same view in a letter written a few days later, on October 19th. (See Reuben Fink, ed., *op. cit.*, p. 56.)

Carl J. Friedrich, in his little book, *American Policy toward Palestine,* interprets Article 7 in this light: namely, that the consent of the United States is required only if the proposed changes in the Mandate affect the rights (mainly economic) of American citizens as individuals in the matters specifically provided for in the Articles of the Treaty, but is not called for if the changes apply to Articles in the Mandate which do not affect the rights of Americans as such. Moreover, he thinks that there is no intimation in the Convention that the consent of the United States would be denied if the alterations proposed affected provisions of the Mandate other than such as would affect the rights of American citizens.

He therefore comes to the conclusion that by 1924, "the United States had actually abandoned Palestine and the Jewish National Home to Britain and her good offices." [143] This passive acquiescence of the United States Government in the British policies, which departed more and more from the Balfour Declaration, was not due necessarily to a lessened interest in Palestine on the part of the American people, but was part of the general policy of indifference and isolationism in foreign affairs which set in with the Harding administration in reaction against the Wilsonian idealism.

Quincy Wright [144] has taken the position that in general the claim of the United States to be consulted with reference to the administration of the mandated areas rests on moral and political rather than on strictly legal grounds. He questions the soundness of the argument that the United States has a claim because she contributed to the defeat of Germany and her allies. He points out that in the first place the United States was not at war with Turkey; and secondly, that a claim based on the right of conquest is not in consonance with the position taken by the United States on other occasions. He agrees, however, that the United States could claim a share in the decisions with regard to the mandated territories on moral and political grounds. If this is the case, then obviously the influence of the United States need not be limited to the specific matters indicated in the Convention.

The sum of the matter seems to be that the United States Government could have exercised a significant influence on the

143. Carl J. Friedrich, *op. cit.,* p. 23.
144. Quincy Wright, *Mandates under the League of Nations,* pp. 483 ff.

Palestine policy if it had so desired. There was apparently considerable difference between the attitude of the State Department on the one hand, and of the Executive and Legislative branches of the Government on the other. The State Department was more narrowly concerned with American business interests and, to a degree, with the educational and philanthropic work of Christian missionary bodies in the Near East. The Executive and Legislative branches, representing a wider public opinion, reflected the traditionally sympathetic attitude of the American people toward the restoration of the Jews to Palestine as a nation.

CHAPTER V

EVENTS AND POLICIES
1920-1929

THE SHAPING OF BRITISH POLICY

THE period to be treated in this chapter begins with the Civil Administration which came into force on July 1st, 1920, when Sir Herbert Samuel assumed office as the High Commissioner of Palestine. The outbreak of the grave disturbances in the late summer of 1929 has been taken as marking the end of the period. There had been one other serious case of disorders—in May, 1921—but taking the period from the Occupation in 1918 to the end of World War II, the years from early May, 1921, to late August, 1929, represent the longest period free from disturbances in the history of the British administration of Palestine. Sir Herbert was succeeded as High Commissioner by Lord Plumer in 1925, and the latter was followed by Sir John Chancellor in 1928. The official policy which guided the administration during the seven years between 1922 and 1929 was worked out in the first two years of Samuel's administration and incorporated in the 1922 Statement of Policy, usually referred to as the "Churchill White Paper."

As interpreted in the 1922 Statement and as implemented through government ordinances and administrative practices in Palestine during this period, the Balfour Declaration—to employ the usual phrase—was "whittled down." Under the Mandate, Britain had accepted the responsibility of *facilitating* the establishment of the Jewish national home; the actual policy adopted by the administration in Palestine was rather that of *permitting* the homeland development, if the Jews made an obstinate effort and supplied the means. From the positive function of encouragement, Great Britain changed in practice to acting as the arbiter between the contending interests of Jews and Arabs. In some respects, the policy was to counterbalance the theoretical primacy given to the Jewish interest in the Mandate by practical measures which were designed especially to advance the welfare and development of the Arab part of the population.

There is a tendency to attribute the course of British policy to the influence of the administrative officers in Palestine. Some go so far as to ascribe the ambiguous policy of the British Administration to the impress made upon it by Samuel: to his softness of character, his well-intentioned but misdirected liberalism, and to his leaning backward in the attempt to show that as a Jew he could be fair to the Arab. Factors in the local administration and the influence exerted by personalities should not be neglected; but in the light of analysis, such explanations are over-simplifications essentially erroneous. The development of British policy in Palestine will be better understood if it is viewed in the framework of the international situation, with full reference to the rise of Arab nationalism and British interests in the Near East, and in relation to attitudes and happenings in the Jewish world itself.

The weakness of the League of Nations and the inadequacy of its control in the administration of the mandates was one great factor of crucial importance. The opinions of the Permanent Mandates Commission were not altogether without their influence with reference to this or that point, but on the whole they constituted little more than comments on the British policy which His Majesty's Government could disregard if they ran contrary to their interests. Moreover, the Commission being without responsibility for action, often appeared confused and contradictory in its recommendations. In Britain itself there were many factors which contributed to lack of clarity in the formulation of policies, and lack of firmness in carrying them out: the disillusionment with the idealistic aims of the war, the trend toward pacifism and anti-imperialism, and the general let-down of spirit to which Gilbert Murray's phrase "the loss of nerve" has sometimes been applied. The Russian Revolution with its widely ramifying effects played a part. It made the British Tories grow suspicious of the Russian-Jewish labor immigration to Palestine. It deprived Zionism of the support of an important branch of Jewry particularly well-adapted to understand the significance of the upbuilding of Palestine. To a part of the younger Jewish generation, Communism for a time held out the hope of a total solution of the Jewish problem, along with all other social problems, and this made the effort in Palestine appear petty and "reactionary" in its emphasis on the Jewish national and spiritual tradition.

Not to be neglected in the accounting of factors which led to the depreciation of the Jewish national home policy is the division of opinion among the Jews themselves which continued to persist. The well-to-do Jews in the United States and Great Britain who contributed the larger share of funds to organized Jewish communal endeavor never, as a group, became genuinely convinced of the practicability or the desirability of the Jewish national home. While many of them lent aid, their best efforts went to other projects, philanthropic in nature. They supported Jewish colonization with greater enthusiasm when it was not in Palestine, ever fearing the bogey of the ultimate establishment of a Jewish state.

The middle class of American Jews were generally sympathetic to the Zionist aspiration; in terms of contribution to the Zionist funds they probably gave a larger share than any other Jewish community in the world. But they were more numerous and better off on the whole than other comparable groups, and the Zionist leaders have often complained that they did less than might have been expected, and certainly less than the task of upbuilding required. It was a favorite expression among Zionist leaders that "the New York Jews alone could build Palestine twice over." [1] It should be recalled, however, that the tasks facing American Jews were many: families and communities in Eastern Europe had to be assisted; Jewish religious, educational and communal institutions had to be built for the growing body of American Jews; the Jews were expected to do their share in general charities and public endeavors. The essence of the matter is that the re-establishment of the national home in a poor and neglected Palestine required unprecedented energies, careful planning and gradual development. Ten years was a short time for such an immense and complicated task to get under way. But these ten years were crucial from the point of view of political developments in the Near East and in Palestine. This gap between the objective requirements of economic development and the political urgencies was not the least important of the factors

1. Schmarya Levin in *New Palestine*, October 17, 1923, p. 157.

which played their part in the depreciation of the British policy in Palestine with reference to the Jewish national home.

The central document of this period was the 1922 Statement of Policy. It carries the name of Churchill, who was Secretary of State for the Colonies at the time, and was probably influenced by him in the first place, as well as approved by him in the last instance; but there is evidence that Samuel had a great part in formulating it even if he did not work out its main lines.

Changing Lines of Policy

The position of High Commissioner of Palestine was offered to Herbert Samuel at San Remo by Lloyd George. The recommendation of a Jew to be head of the Palestine Government was undoubtedly an expression of Lloyd George's belief that a Jewish Commonwealth was in the making in Palestine. There was some criticism of his failure to appoint a Christian, but on the whole British opinion was favorable. The attacks against the appointment were generally from political enemies of the Lloyd George government and were not taken too seriously. Samuel had a high reputation for liberality of view and for his sense of justice; his loyalty to British interest was unquestioned.

The Jews accepted the appointment as an earnest of the intention of Great Britain to fulfill her promise in the Balfour Declaration. The *Yishuv* was overjoyed and hailed Samuel as a second Nehemiah, come to establish the Third Jewish Commonwealth. An outstanding exception was Israel Zangwill who had, since San Remo, parted from the Zionist leaders in their conception of policy. In a letter to *The Spectator* published on July 3, 1920, he wrote: "The appointment of Sir Herbert Samuel is a mere cover for the practical repudiation of the Balfour Declaration." Zangwill's criticism must be understood in the light of his belief that mass immigration, Jewish predominance in Palestine, and the ultimate establishment of a Jewish state ought to have been the clearly stated aims of British and Zionist policy. Of Samuel as an administrator he had a high opinion, but he thought him "too timid and weak-hearted" for the hard task of establishing a Jewish national home in a country predominantly Arab. "England is to be congratulated on so able and high-minded a servant, though his appointment is to Zionism proper a shorter way of spelling disappointment."

The Zionist leaders recognized negative as well as positive elements in the appointment. On the negative side they realized that the presence of a Jewish High Commissioner on the Mount of Olives would serve to feed the fires of Arab and anti-Semitic propaganda—the cry would be raised that the Holy Land was being turned over to Jews. The Conservatives in England would be angered by the appointment of a Liberal to such an important post. Samuel would undoubtedly be accused of favoring the Jewish side, no matter how fair he would be. But in the last analysis they heartily welcomed the appointment, as did the masses of the Jews. Nordau said that Samuel was "the right man in the right place." Jabotinsky, who vehemently attacked Samuel's later policy, said at the time of his appointment: "Sir Herbert Samuel is truly the most fitting man for this great task. He is unexcelled in tolerance, consistency and courtesy. We may place great hopes in him." [2]

The Arabs, on their part, also regarded the appointment of Samuel as a victory for the Zionists. They were generally in a mood of dejection at this period; they felt the English had let them down by permitting the expulsion of Faisal from Damascus and that nothing was left to them except to reiterate their old protests. The tone of the newspapers was somewhat subdued. *Al-Kuds* wrote: "The appointment of Herbert Samuel will not break the national spirit in the heart of the Arab people. We regard the rejection of our demands on the part of the Powers as an affront to our rights. Our demand has been for self-rule, for unity of territory, for a rejection of Zionist immigration—from these demands we shall not move. And we shall not permit our land to become a national home for the Jews." Nevertheless, the writer adds: "Some say that Samuel will treat the Arabs more favorably than the Jews in order to demonstrate justice and equality to all peoples. Who knows, perhaps Samuel may change his mind when the justice of the Arab cause and their love for their fatherland become clear to him." [3]

From the very beginning, Samuel followed a "good will" policy. He retained a number of officials from the Military Ad-

2. Medzini, *op. cit.*, p. 139.
3. *Ibid.*, p. 143.

ministration whose position on Zionism was doubtful or even negative—with the hope evidently of winning them over by his own fairmindedness and tolerance. Colonel Storrs,[4] whose behavior in the riots of the spring had aroused Jewish suspicions, became one of his closest advisers. Mr. Ernest T. Richmond, known to be definitely pro-Arab and anti-Zionist, became his official expert on Arab affairs.[5] He followed the same trusting method when he granted a general amnesty soon after his arrival to those who had been involved in the disturbances in Jerusalem in 1920, and a month later, at the request of Arab notables, he agreed to pardon two of the chief participants in the Nebi Musa riots, whom he had formerly excluded from the pardon because they had failed to appear in court.[6] By some, Samuel's method has been ascribed to weakness of character, by others to an undue faith in the practical effectiveness of the twice-blessed quality of mercy.

Before coming to Palestine, Samuel shared the views of the other British statesmen who believed that the Balfour Declaration implied the ultimate establishment of a Jewish state or commonwealth with a large majority of Jews. In a speech which he delivered on November 2, 1919, on the occasion of the second anniversary of the Balfour Declaration, he expressed himself in no uncertain terms as follows:[7]

The immediate establishment of a complete and purely Jewish State in Palestine would mean placing a majority under the rule of a minority; it would therefore be contrary to the first principles of democracy, and would undoubtedly be disapproved by the public opinion of the whole world. The policy propounded before the Peace Conference, to which the Zionist leaders unshakeably adhere, is the promotion to the fullest degree that the conditions of the country allow, of Jewish immigration and of Jewish land settlement, the concession to Jewish authorities of many of the great public works of which the country stands so greatly in need, the active promotion of Jewish

4. For a characterization of Storrs as seen by Henrietta Szold at the time, see Marvin Lowenthal, *op. cit.*, pp. 186–187.
5. Frederick H. Kisch, *Palestine Diary*, Gollancz, 1938, p. 34.
6. One of these was Haj Muhammed Amin al-Husaini who had been the chief fomenter of the Arab excesses in 1920 (Storrs, *op. cit.*, p. 388) and who after years of political intrigue and intransigent opposition to the Jews was the instigator of the Axis-aided revolt against the British in Palestine in the period preceding the outbreak of the war.
7. From a speech at the London Opera House on November 2, 1919, reprinted in *Zionist Bulletin*, November 5, 1919.

cultural development and the fullest measure of local self-government, in order that with the minimum of delay the country may become a purely self-governing Commonwealth under the auspices of an established Jewish majority.

During the first week of July, 1920, some days after his arrival in Palestine as High Commissioner, Sir Herbert Samuel made a statement of policy before a gathering of representatives of the different communities. He read the Message of King George V, addressed to the inhabitants of Palestine, in which the main paragraphs were:[8]

I desire to assure you of the absolute impartiality with which the duties of the Mandatory Power will be carried out, and of the determination of my Government to respect the rights of every race and every creed represented among you, both for the period which has still to elapse before the terms of the Mandate can be finally approved by the League of Nations, and in the future when the Mandate has become an accomplished fact.

You are well aware that the Allied and Associated Powers have decided that measures shall be adopted to secure the gradual establishment in Palestine of a National Home for the Jewish People. These measures will not in any way affect the civil or religious rights or diminish the prosperity of the general population of Palestine.

After reading the general declaration, Samuel proceeded to outline in considerable detail his own program for the future development of the country.[9] He first spoke of the beneficent character of British rule throughout the world: complete freedom for all faiths, the same justice for all men, the maintenance of security with a firm hand, the interest of the government in economic development and its concern with the happiness of the inhabitants. He then touched upon the steps leading to gradual development of self-government, beginning with the establishment of an Advisory Council and the enlistment of cooperation of the people in various ways. He laid particular emphasis on the importance of economic development and went into detail in his analysis of projects to be undertaken: a Land Commission to determine what lands were

8. Jewish Agency, *Documents Relating to the Balfour Declaration and the Palestine Mandate*, London, 1939, p. 8.
9. Medzini, *op. cit.*, pp. 145–146.

fit for intensive cultivation; a cadastral survey to ascertain boundaries and titles; banks for agricultural credit; development of railroad, telegraph, telephone and electricity; the building of a harbor at Haifa; the draining of marshes; improvement in health conditions; the elimination of malaria.

The question of the Jewish national home he approached cautiously, linking its development with the program for the general improvement of conditions in the country. The Jews, he indicated, would supply the large amounts of capital needed and Jewish immigration would provide the additional manpower needed for development. He was careful to add immediately that the number of immigrants would be kept strictly within the bounds of the economic potentialities of the country and the possibilities of employment. In closing, as if to give concrete illustration of the spirit of good will which pervaded his address, he announced the pardon of those who had taken part in the riots during the Nebi Musa festival. He gave a warning, however, that such pardoning should not be regarded as a sign of weakness, and that if disturbances should recur, they would be suppressed with all possible firmness and that the act of clemency would not be repeated.

If there is a change of policy indicated in this cautious statement from that which was indicated in the address some six months earlier, it must be borne in mind that now he spoke not as an individual but as the High Commissioner whose pronouncement carried with it Government responsibility. It should be recalled also that British policy in Middle Eastern affairs was undergoing a change at the time. The Arab nationalists were also becoming more active. Having given up hope of a union with Syria following Faisal's expulsion in the summer of 1920, they began to agitate for the recognition of an independent Arab Palestine under a British mandate. Meeting in the middle of December, 1920, the Third Palestine Arab Congress made a formulation of the Arab demands. This included the right of self-determination and the establishment of a national government responsible to a council elected by the Arabic-speaking people who were living in Palestine at the outbreak of the Great War.[10] The Congress also appointed an

10. Hanna, *op. cit.*, p. 153; Matiel E. T. Mogannam, *The Arab Woman and the Palestine Problem,* Herbert Joseph, Ltd., London, 1937, pp. 125–127. See also below, p. 475.

Executive Committee to present the demands of the Arabs of Palestine to the British Government.

In the meantime, as a result of the difficulties that the British were experiencing in Mesopotamia, Lloyd George placed the Near Eastern affairs in the hands of Winston Churchill, then associated with the War Office. Churchill organized a new Middle Eastern Department, inviting T. E. Lawrence, among others, to join. Responsibility for mandated territories, formerly divided among the Foreign, India and War Offices, was now united under the Colonial Office which took over the administration of Mesopotamia and Palestine early in 1921. Winston Churchill, now Secretary of State for the Colonies, aided by a group of experts in Near Eastern affairs, went out to the Near East in March 1921 with the idea of improving relations with the Arabs, which had been disturbed by the San Remo decisions. Their immediate and major task was to work out a quasi-independent government for Iraq, permitting the gradual evolution of an elective element. A similar type of development, it appears, was to be applied to Palestine, with the expectation that the Arabs and Jews could be induced to cooperate jointly in the government of the country.

The Palestine Arab Executive Committee tried to see Churchill in Cairo, where the conference of the experts was being held, but they failed to do so. However, they succeeded in presenting their views in a memorandum submitted to him when he visited Palestine in March, 1921. In this memorandum the Balfour Declaration was denounced as contrary to McMahon's pledges and a protest was expressed against the text of the draft mandate. The following demands were made: 1) repudiation of the Jewish national home policy; 2) creation of a national government in Palestine to be elected by the inhabitants of the country in their pre-war proportions; 3) cessation of Jewish immigration; 4) reconstitution of the pre-war system of laws until the establishment of a national government; 5) no distinction between Palestine and other Arab countries.[11]

Churchill had been greeted at his arrival by a minor anti-Jewish demonstration at Haifa which was suppressed after two of the rioters were killed. Undisturbed by these events, he characteristically maintained a firm position in his reply

11. Medzini, *op. cit.*, p. 170.

to the Arab Executive Committee. In unmistakable terms he made it clear that he neither wished, nor was able, to repudiate the Balfour Declaration or to halt immigration. He said that Great Britain had, through Mr. Balfour, promised to facilitate the development of the Jewish national home in Palestine and this necessarily involved Jewish immigration. The promise had been approved by various governments and it should, therefore, be looked upon as one of the facts which had been determined with finality with the achievement of a victorious end to the war. It was on the basis of the Balfour Declaration that Great Britain had received the Mandate; and that on this basis the Mandate would be implemented.

He went on to say that it was right that the Jews scattered throughout the world should have a national center and a national home to which many would return. This was a good thing for the world, good for the Jews, good for the British Government, and good for the Arab inhabitants of the land. On the other hand, he attempted to reassure the Arabs and said that there was no intention on the part of Great Britain to create a Jewish government that would dominate them. However, he made it clear that there was no ground for hoping that His Majesty's Government would yield to the demands for an Arab state. The creation of self-government, he indicated, was a long way off: "Step by step we shall develop representative institutions leading to full self-government, but our children's children will have passed away before that is completed." [12]

Immediately thereafter he received the representatives of the National Council of the Jews of Palestine (*Vaad Leumi*) to whom he outlined the same series of ideas that he expressed to the Arab delegation. He reassured the Jewish representatives that Great Britain was determined to fulfill the terms of the Balfour Declaration. At the same time he impressed on them the need for moderation and the importance of developing friendly relations with the Arabs. He concluded by saying: "I believe faithfully that your endeavor will succeed . . . The Jewish people throughout the world must provide me with the means of answering the criticism of opponents. My wish is to be able to say that a great event is coming into being in this place." [13] The Jews accepted Churchill's statement with mixed

12. Quoted by Hanna from *The Times*, April 2, 1921 (*op. cit.*, p. 80).
13. Medzini, *op. cit.*, p. 173.

feelings. On the one hand, they were comforted by his firm reiteration of the Balfour pledge; on the other hand, they were not happy to hear again the pointed distinction between "*a national home for the Jews in Palestine*" and "the establishment of *Palestine as the Jewish homeland*." However, in the light of the circumstances and general atmosphere of the time, Churchill's stand was regarded as a victory for the Zionists.

Churchill's statement did not preclude the development of the Jewish state in the future. In a statement made about a year earlier he had said: "If, as may well happen, there should be created in our own lifetime by the banks of the Jordan a Jewish State under the protection of the British Crown which might comprise three or four millions of Jews, an event will have occurred in the history of the world which would from every point of view be beneficial, and would be especially in harmony with the truest interests of the British Empire." [14] However, while he evidently favored a Jewish state, he did not envisage the deprivation of the social or political rights of the Arabs, expecting them to exercise their due influence on the government. This is brought out in the answers which he gave to questions raised in a meeting of the Cabinet on June 22, 1921, soon after his return to England. Lloyd George quotes from the minutes of the meeting as follows:[15]

Mr. Meighen: How do you define our responsibilities in relation to Palestine under Mr. Balfour's pledge?

Mr. Churchill: To do our best to make an honest effort to give the Jews a chance to make a National Home for themselves.

Mr. Meighen: And to give them control of the Government?

Mr. Churchill: If, in the course of many years, they become a majority in the country, they naturally would take it over.

Mr. Meighen: *Pro rata* with the Arab?

Mr. Churchill: *Pro rata* with the Arab. We made an equal pledge that we would not turn the Arab off his land or invade his political or social rights.

Despite Churchill's fair and friendly attitude, his visit to the East resulted in a major defeat for the Zionists. It was at this time that Trans-Jordan was definitely separated from

14. *Illustrated Sunday Herald*, February 8, 1920.
15. David Lloyd George, *The Truth about the Peace Treaties*, Vol. II, p. 1193.

Palestine as part of the plan to pay Britain's debt to Husain. Trans-Jordan was part of the area included in the British Mandate for Palestine and until February 1921, it appears, the plan was still "to include Trans-Jordan in Palestine, to make it indistinguishable from Palestine, and to open it to Jewish immigration." [16] In November 1920, however, Emir Abdullah, the son of Husain, had occupied Ma'an. He had come up with a force of 1200 troops from the Hejaz to attack the French in reprisal for his brother's expulsion in July of the previous year. The British did not wish to have a French occupation of Trans-Jordan in the attempt to crush Abdullah, nor were they anxious to engage in the suppression of Abdullah themselves. Meanwhile Abdullah had gotten to Amman, capital of Trans-Jordan. The British decided to come to some understanding with him. When Churchill was in Palestine, Lawrence "fetched Abdullah to Jerusalem," [17] and there, in a half hour's talk in which Samuel, Churchill and Lawrence participated, the arrangement was made with Abdullah to turn Trans-Jordan over to him to be administered under the control of the High Commissioner of Palestine. In April, Samuel paid a formal visit to Amman and explained the arrangement to the tribal leaders, and in July, Parliament voted 180,000 pounds as a grant-in-aid for the new government.[18]

The separation of Trans-Jordan from Palestine came as an indirect result of the failure of Great Britain and France at the Peace Conference to honor their pledges to the Arabs. If the full McMahon pledge had been carried out by the British, Faisal would have been the head of an extensive Arab state

---

16. Quoted by Hanna (*op. cit.*, p. 75) from L. B. Namier, "Lawrence of Arabia," *The Manchester Guardian Weekly*, May 24, 1935, p. 416.
17. David Garnett, ed., *The Letters of T. E. Lawrence*, p. 333.
18. Royal Institute of International Affairs, *Great Britain and Palestine, 1915–1939*, pp. 14 ff. The arrangement was originally made for a six-months period, but the British found it convenient and it was made permanent. On September 16, 1922, the Council of the League of Nations gave its assent to the separation of Trans-Jordan from Palestine, and in April, 1923, the British Government made a formal announcement to this effect. In 1925 Aqaba and Ma'an were definitely attached to Trans-Jordan. The semi-independence of Trans-Jordan was finally embodied in a treaty between His Majesty's Government and the Emir Abdullah on February 20, 1928, and ratified October 31, 1929. The agreement provided for British supervision over foreign affairs, finances and the maintenance of military forces and for the administration of Trans-Jordan under the British mandate for Palestine under the High Commissioner.

with its capital at Damascus, and Abdullah could have been made King of Iraq. Husain was King of the Hejaz domain which would in the natural course of events have been inherited by his eldest son, Ali. This was the original plan, the so-called "Sherifian solution," by which a large united Arab state would have been created under the leadership of the Hashimite family. When Faisal was expelled from Damascus, the British gave him Iraq as consolation prize, and a third prize had to be found for Abdullah at the expense of a divided Palestine.

The first "whittling down" of the Mandate, therefore, was accomplished by limiting the area in which the national home policy could be implemented. As a consequence of the arrangement with Abdullah, Jews were denied the right to enter and settle in Trans-Jordan or to engage in commerce and industry there. The separation had serious effects on the Jewish development in Palestine. Trans-Jordan had a relatively large area with a sparsely settled population, and its elimination as a place of Jewish settlement greatly cut down possibilities of Jewish colonization. It had also an indirect political effect on the discussion of land settlement in Palestine: by considering Palestine as a separate unit, the area available for Arab agricultural development was also reduced and a case could be made out to the effect that Palestine, already overcrowded, could not accommodate much new Jewish colonization. If Trans-Jordan had been included in the Palestine area available for land settlement, it would have been obvious that the main problem lay not in the lack of land but in lack of development of the sparsely settled areas. In the third place, the higher standard of living in Palestine as a result of the economic development set in motion by Jewish immigration made Palestine a magnet to attract illicit immigration from Trans-Jordan.

The Jewish Agency felt forced at the time to accept the Government's decision to exclude Trans-Jordan from the area of the Jewish national home. The Government justified their action on the grounds that Trans-Jordan had been included in the McMahon understanding as an area of Arab independence.[19] But the Agency protested the policy of excluding Jews

19. According to McMahon's own testimony, however (see Graves, *Palestine, The Land of Three Faiths*, pp. 53–54), the eastern boundary of Palestine was not fixed at the time: "He did not make use of the Jordan to define the limits of the southern area because he did not know whether at some later stage of the negotiations with the Grand Sharif a more suitable frontier might be found east of that river."

from entering Trans-Jordan altogether as a violation of the articles of the Mandate which provided for equality of rights in mandated areas irrespective of faith or race. The exclusion of Jews from Trans-Jordan was held to be a particularly bad case of discrimination in view of the fact that the Arabs of Trans-Jordan retained their customary right to cross into Palestine without passports. The Jewish Agency maintained that even though His Majesty's Government might not be obligated to *facilitate* immigration into Trans-Jordan, it was violating the Mandate when it *prevented* such immigration. It also pointed out that setting up official barriers between these two parts of Palestine was harmful to both countries from the economic point of view. The Permanent Mandates Commission tended to agree with the position of the Jewish Agency. In July, 1929, at the XVth Session of the Permanent Mandates Commission, M. Rappard declared: "If it was a question of general exclusion [of Jews from Trans-Jordan], the terms of the mandate had been broken." [20]

"As If There Were No Balfour Declaration"

The severance of Trans-Jordan from Palestine reduced the Balfour promise in the quantitative sense, so to speak; the Churchill White Paper of 1922 diminished it qualitatively by weakening the Mandate's emphasis on the primacy of the Jewish national home. Violent disturbances which occurred in early May, 1921, appear to have contributed to the growing tendency on the part of the Government to conciliate the Arab opposition. The Nebi Musa festivals had passed off without any untoward event; the Government was fully prepared and the Arabs were aware of this. An occasion for violence, however, presented itself on Labor Day. An illegal parade of Jewish Communists clashed with the regular Labor Day procession of the Jewish Labor organizations which had been authorized by the Government. The excitement offered an opportunity for Arab bands to attack both. A bloody riot ensued, followed by a horrible massacre in the Immigration House at Jaffa and thirteen Jews were killed. On the outskirts of Jaffa, Joseph Chaim Brenner, a leading Hebrew writer, was murdered together with

---

20. Jewish Agency for Palestine, *Memorandum Submitted to His Majesty's Government*, May, 1930, p. 66. For a discussion of the Trans-Jordan problem, see also Jewish Agency for Palestine, *Memorandum to the Palestine Royal Commission*, pp. 210–213.

the whole family whom he had visited at the time. There were reprisals on the part of the Jews in and around Jaffa; a number were killed and many on both sides wounded.

The general excitement spread throughout the country; armed bands of Arabs attacked and looted several Jewish colonies. Petach Tikvah, the oldest Jewish agricultural settlement, which employed many Arab agricultural workers and which was reputed to have good relations with the Arabs, was subjected to a serious attack in which Bedouins of the neighboring Abu Kishk tribe participated. The attackers were about 2,000 strong and some of them had rifles, but the colony managed to defend itself for several hours until it was saved by a squadron of Indian cavalry which happened to be on the march from Jenin to Jaffa. Another attack was held up by a squadron of planes and then dispersed by an Indian regiment. About fifty Arabs were killed in the encounter and there were four deaths among the Jewish colonists. An attack against Rehovoth was repelled by the inhabitants.

The Civil Administration proved powerless to maintain order; the police, mostly Arab, proved unreliable. The troops had to be called in before order was restored. In all, 88 persons were killed and 238 wounded. The disorders were followed by a period of unrest; a boycott, commenced by the Arabs, soon became mutual. When the outbreak began, the military authorities in Jaffa halted the landing of Jews, and on May 14th Samuel announced a complete suspension of immigration pending the revision of existing legislation. Special courts, civil and military, tried a number of persons, but the sentences were lenient and the Jaffa police, who had torn off their shields and participated in the attack, were let off scot-free on the grounds of insufficient evidence. The Jews believed that the attacks had been planned. The late Henrietta Szold recorded: "Early in the morning of May Day, a number of Jews were warned by Arab friends that something was brewing, and they had better take measures of protection." [21] Around Petach Tikvah, gauze bandages and other material for binding wounds were found on the bodies of the Arabs killed in the encounter.

A local Commission of Inquiry under the chairmanship of

21. Lowenthal, *op. cit.*, p. 177.

Chief Justice of Palestine, Sir Thomas W. Haycraft, was appointed to investigate the disturbances.[22] In its report[23] the Commission said that while the immediate occasion of the Jaffa riots was the clash between the Jewish Communists and Labor processions, the underlying cause was rooted in the Arab opposition to the Zionist program, in the Arab belief that Great Britain was favoring the Jews over the Arabs, that there was a disproportionate number of Jews in the public service, that the Zionist Commission had too much authority. The Arabs, it was alleged, were pervaded by the fear that the country was being inundated by aliens who were displacing Arab workers, and that with their superior commercial ability and greater amount of capital the Jews would undermine Arab enterprise. Though careful to say that "the general body of Jews was anti-Bolshevist," the Commission placed considerable emphasis on the socialistic ideas of the immigrants and implied that an aggressive group of Russian-Jewish immigrants were planting the seeds of communism in Palestine. They summarized their conclusions as follows:[24]

The Commission found that the racial strife was begun by Arabs who were generally the aggressors; that the outbreak was unpremeditated and unexpected; that the general body of Jews was anti-Bolshevist; that the fundamental cause of the riots was a feeling among the Arabs of discontent with, and hostility to, the Jews, due to political and economic causes, and connected with Jewish immigration, and with their conception of Zionist policy as derived from Jewish exponents.

While the Commission agreed that the outbreak had been started by the Arabs, and that the police had been inefficient and in some cases had participated in violence, the general

22. The other members were: H. C. Luke, Assistant Governor of Jerusalem; J. N. Stubbs, Assistant Controller of Land Registries. The Commissioners were assisted by three "assessors"—Aref Pasha Dajani, Elias Effendi Mushabbek, and Dr. M. Eliash, representing respectively the Moslems, the Christians and the Jews. (Fannie Fern Andrews, *The Holy Land under Mandate*, Vol. II, pp. 78–79.)

23. *Parliamentary Papers 1921*, Cmd. 1540. The Haycraft Commission's report constitutes the official version of the disturbances. A Jewish point of view is represented by Horace Samuel, *Unholy Memories of the Holy Land*, pp. 70–75.

24. Philip Graves, *op. cit.*, p. 65.

tendency of the findings was to place the blame on the Jews for creating the conditions that made the attack possible. The Zionist Organization came in for particularly drastic criticism. The Commission deplored the pressure exercised to employ only Jewish labor, and they regarded the policy of subsidizing Jews in public services, in order to enable them to accept positions, as undesirable. Above all, they took issue with the position of the Political Department of the Zionist Organization. According to the Commission, the views held by the Zionist Organization with reference to the British policy in Palestine were at variance with the view of the national home as presented by the Secretary of State and the High Commissioner. They described at some length an interview with Dr. Eder, then the head of the Political Department, and summarized his position as follows:[25]

As Acting Chairman of the Zionist Commission, Dr. Eder presumably expresses in all points the official Zionist view, if such there be, and his statements are, therefore, most important. There is no sophistry about Dr. Eder; he was quite clear that the Jews should, and the Arabs should not, have the right to bear arms, and he stated his belief that this discrimination would tend to improve Arab-Jewish relations. . . . We do not comment upon his opinions because the discussion of the questions raised is not our concern, but it is relevant to our report to show that the acting Chairman of the Zionist Commission asserts on behalf of the Jews those claims which are at the root of the present unrest, and differ materially from the declared policy of the Secretary of State and the High Commissioner for Palestine. It is perhaps worth noting as an instance of the diversity of manner in which Jews and Arabs look upon the same questions, that, whereas Arab witnesses denounce the Government of Palestine as a Zionist Government, Dr. Eder stigmatizes it as an Arab administration.

The attitude of responsible Zionists as revealed above is not negligible, as it is one of the irritant causes of the present discontent. It arises, perhaps, from a habit of regarding Palestine as "a deserted, derelict land," sparsely inhabited by a population without traditions of nationality, where political experiments may be launched without arousing local opposition. Such a conception is considerably at variance with the spirit of the authorized Zionist policy as defined in the declared intentions of the Secretary of State and the Local Government.

25. *Ibid.*, pp. 171–172.

The Zionists rejected the Haycraft Commission's analysis of the situation and protested that its presentation of the Zionist attitude was unfair. They maintained that whatever Dr. Eder's views were, these could not be regarded as nullifying the frequently expressed official statements of the Zionist Organization in which they denied intention to dominate. Moreover, the views of Dr. Eder carried a different connotation if other parts of his statement were taken into consideration, as follows:[26]

The Balfour Declaration provides for a National Home for the Jewish people in Palestine. The interpretation we have put upon this is that Jews should be free to enter Palestine to build up their own civilization and culture, and eventually when the Palestinians are fit for it by their experience and political judgment, representative Government shall be conferred upon Palestine by His Majesty's Government. We look eventually to Palestine being in the position of one of the free dominions, inhabited by Arabs and Jews, and that both will play their part, the only difference being that the League of Nations has a certain control over the Government. . . .

This country has to be built up by the Jews and the Arabs. Jews do not come here for domination. I claim predominance. My own view is this: in the remote future there could be a Federate State of the Near East. Syria, Mesopotamia, Hedjaz, Palestine, Transjordania, could all be independent. Palestine would be predominantly Jewish. . . . I do not say that they [the Arabs] are foreigners. Every respect would be paid to their civil and religious rights in this country. We do not think there is room for an Arab National Home in Palestine. Their National Home is in Syria, Transjordania, Mesopotamia and Hedjaz. . . . There is no room for an Arab National Home [in Palestine]. We can have them both united in one home.

They also rejected the Commission's analysis of the fundamental causes of the riots. The Zionists maintained that the anti-Jewish sentiment was neither natural nor widespread among the people, that it had been artificially stimulated by the *effendi* class who were fearful of losing the political preferment which they had enjoyed under the Turkish regime. The *effendis* knew that the establishment of an efficient government with modern methods of taxation would deprive them of their traditional position as publicans and tax gatherers, and,

26. Loder, *op. cit.*, p. 127, n.

more fundamentally, they feared that their exploitation of the peasant would become impossible in the atmosphere of social ideas which were being introduced by the labor movement in Palestine.

In the Government's reaction to the May riots, the Zionists saw the beginning of a policy of making concessions to Arab violence. They were particularly outraged by Herbert Samuel's decision to halt immigration. Even moderates like Miss Henrietta Szold were indignant. She wrote at this time: "The whole policy—stopping immigration, promising a representative assembly at this moment, apprehending the Bolsheviki, arresting the Jews who bore 'concealed' arms and defended themselves, while the Arab assailants go scot free because no convincing evidence can be found against them—it is all a policy of cowardice. There isn't one of us who would not rather fall in a general massacre than be saved by such methods. Of course, I admit that Sir Herbert cannot say for me that I should prefer to be killed to being saved—by him. But he could have resigned." [27]

As a result of Samuel's decision on May 14th to suspend immigration, the major bodies representing the Jews—the Zionist Commission and the Executive of the *Vaad Leumi*—tendered their resignations and did not resume their offices until they received assurance from Churchill that immigration would be resumed. Samuel on his part also threatened to resign if the Zionist leaders did not show a greater understanding of the realities of the situation and of his problems. In the ensuing months, he formulated, in agreement with the Colonial Office, a revised statement of policy with reference to the Jewish national home which he incorporated in an address delivered in Jerusalem on June 3, 1921 on the occasion of the King's birthday. He sought to assure the assembled Arab notables that their interests would not be sacrificed in favor of the Jews; that Great Britain as the Mandatory Power would never consent to setting up a Jewish government to rule a non-Jewish majority. He announced that the Government was considering the setting up of a legislative council on a partially elected basis. Furthermore, he laid emphasis on the necessity of limiting immigration by the economic absorptive capacity of the country. He interpreted the Balfour Declaration to mean that:

27. Lowenthal, *op. cit.*, p. 182.

"Jews, a people who were scattered throughout the world, but whose hearts are always turned to Palestine, should be enabled to found here their home, and that some among them, within the limits that are fixed by the numbers and interests of the present population, should come to Palestine in order to help by their resources and efforts to develop the country to the advantage of all the inhabitants." [28]

The new policy which had been taking form in Samuel's mind is expressed in the High Commissioner's Interim Report submitted in the summer of 1921.[29] The central idea is epitomized in the following striking phrase: "The measures to foster the well-being of the Arabs should be precisely those which we should adopt in Palestine if there were no Zionist question and if there had been no Balfour Declaration." In context the phrase does not have the sharp effect that it does when so stated in isolation; it evidently refers to the internal development of the country and not to the right of the Jews to establish a home in Palestine. Nevertheless, the general tone and spirit of Samuel's formulation at this time clearly differs from previous formulations of the British policy with reference to the Jewish national home. The following are the main paragraphs of this statement:[30]

The policy of His Majesty's Government contemplates the satisfaction of the legitimate aspirations of the Jewish race throughout the world in relation to Palestine, combined with a full protection of the rights of the existing population. For my own part, I am convinced that the means can be found to effect this combination. The Zionism that is practicable is the Zionism that fulfills this essential condition.

It is the clear duty of the Mandatory Power to promote the well-being of the Arab population, in the same way as a British Administration would regard it as its duty to promote the welfare of the local population in any part of our Empire. The measures to foster the well-being of the Arabs should be precisely those which we should adopt in Palestine if there were no Zionist question and if there had been no Balfour Declaration. There is in this policy nothing incompatible with reasonable Zionist aspirations. On the contrary, if the growth of Jewish influence were accompanied by Arab degradation,

28. Graves, *op. cit.*, p. 66.
29. *An Interim Report on the Civil Administration of Palestine During the Period 1st July, 1920–30th June, 1921*, London, 1921, Cmd. 1499.
30. *Ibid.*, pp. 7–8.

or even by a neglect to promote Arab advancement, it would fail in one of its essential purposes. . . .

Simultaneously, there must be satisfaction of that sentiment regarding Palestine—a worthy and ennobling sentiment—which, in increasing degree, animates the Jewries of the world. The aspirations of these fourteen millions of people also have a right to be considered. They ask for the opportunity to establish a "home" in the land which was the political, and has always been the religious, centre of their race. They ask that this home should possess national characteristics—in language and customs, in intellectual interests, in religious and political institutions.

This is not to say that Jewish immigration is to involve Arab emigration, that the greater prosperity of the country, through the development of Jewish enterprises, is to be at the expense, and not to the benefit of the Arabs, that the use of Hebrew is to imply the disappearance of Arabic, that the establishment of elected Councils in the Jewish Community for the control of its affairs is to be followed by the subjection of the Arabs to the rule of those Councils. In a word, the degree to which Jewish national aspirations can be fulfilled in Palestine is conditioned by the rights of the present inhabitants.

The Zionists recognized that despite the fine words about the Jewish national home, the essence of the pronouncement lay in the limitations placed on its development as indicated in the last sentence quoted: "the degree to which Jewish national aspirations can be fulfilled in Palestine is conditioned by the rights of the present inhabitants." Nevertheless, the Zionists felt that they could not repudiate Samuel; such action might be misinterpreted as a rejection of the policy of moderation for which he stood and would play into the hands of those who had been representing the Zionists as unreasonable in their demands. As a matter of fact, the Zionists were doing their utmost to conciliate the Arabs. At the Twelfth Zionist Congress which met in the late summer, the following resolution was passed:[31]

It was with sorrow and indignation that the Jewish people have lived through the recent events in Palestine. The hostile attitude of the Arab population in Palestine incited by unscrupulous elements to commit deeds of violence, can neither weaken our resolve for the

31. *Reports of the Executive to the XIIth Zionist Congress*, London, 1922, I, p. 150.

establishment of the Jewish National Home nor our desire to live with the Arab people on terms of harmony and mutual respect, and together with them to make the common home (*Wohnstaette*) into a flourishing commonwealth (*Gemeinwesen*), the upbuilding of which may secure to each of its peoples an undisturbed national development. The two great Semitic peoples, united of yore by the bonds of common creative civilization, will not fail in the hour of their national regeneration to comprehend the need of combining their vital interests in a common endeavor. The Congress calls upon the Executive to redouble its efforts to secure an honorable entente with the Arab people on the basis of this Declaration and in strict accordance with the Balfour Declaration. The Congress emphatically declares that the progress of Jewish colonization will not affect the rights and needs of the working Arab nation.

Despite the concessions made by the British Government and the conciliatory attitude of the Zionist Organization, the Arabs remained obdurate. Late in May, the Fourth Palestine Arab Congress met in Jerusalem to reaffirm its unalterable opposition to Britain's Jewish national home policy. They decided to send a delegation to Europe to campaign against including the Balfour Declaration in the Mandate. The delegation was headed by Musa Kazem al-Husaini and included two other Moslems and two Christians. One of the latter, Shibly Jamal Effendi, acted as Secretary, and Miss Frances Newton, a British resident in Palestine, strongly opposed to the Balfour Declaration, accompanied them as adviser. Samuel tried to dissuade them from going, assuring them that the Government stood ready to meet their lawful demands in harmony with the Balfour Declaration, and warning them that they would not obtain any more in London than he was empowered to propose to them in Jerusalem. To all his appeals their only response was the question: "Would they obtain the passports for their journey?" [32] Samuel permitted them to go after making it clear that they went as individuals and not as official representatives of the Palestinians.

After a short visit to Cairo where they consulted the Egyptian Nationalists who were then agitating for the end of the British Protectorate, they went on to Rome where they had a favorable interview with the Pope. The delegation then proceeded to London, but finding many of the parliamentarians

32. Medzini, *op. cit.*, p. 192.

away for the summer, they repaired to Geneva to submit their protest against the "Zionist clauses" in the draft mandate. Their main contention was that the Mandate as proposed did not conform to Article 22 of the Covenant and that no plebiscite had been held to determine the people's choice of the Mandatory Power. On their return to England they issued a pamphlet entitled *The Holy Land: The Moslem-Christian Case Against Zionist Aggression*. They initiated a campaign of propaganda which received the support of a mixed group—of conservatives opposed to the Lloyd George coalition government, of hard-bitten English anti-Semites, and of genuine sympathizers with the Arab cause.[33]

Pressure was organized to force the Colonial Office to change from its pro-Zionist orientation. Churchill and the Colonial Office officials whom the Arab delegation had attempted to influence on many occasions urged the Arab leaders to try to arrive at a direct understanding with the Zionists and suggested a meeting with Dr. Weizmann. At first the Arabs categorically refused, but then evidently feeling that it would not be wise to antagonize the Government, they consented to meet on "neutral ground." The meeting took place in the Middle East Department of the Colonial Office. Graves records: ". . . in spite of the efforts made by the Head of that Department [Churchill] to further an understanding, and the distinctly conciliatory attitude of Dr. Weizmann, no agreement was reached." [34] The Arabs wanted the draft mandate to be amended to include a provision for a Legislative Council in Palestine with powers which would enable the existing majority to prevent the Mandatory Power from carrying into effect the policy of the Jewish national home. The British Government was ready to introduce reasonable modifications in the direction of self-government, but they were adamant in their refusal to nullify the Balfour Declaration.

In their effort to satisfy the Arabs, the Government proposed the establishment of a legislative council, and a draft proposal was prepared by the legal advisers to His Majesty's Government in August, 1921. The draft provided for an administration composed of a British High Commissioner, an official Executive Council and a partially elective Legislative Coun-

33. Hanna, *op. cit.*, p. 80.
34. Graves, *op. cit.*, p. 68.

cil. Under this Constitution, no ordinances which were repugnant to the Mandate could be enacted and the High Commissioner retained veto power. The Legislature, of which ten members would form a quorum, was to consist of the High Commissioner, ten officials and twelve elected members, one person nominated by the Associated Chambers of Commerce and two persons nominated by the High Commissioner.

The Arab delegation was permitted to study the proposed constitution. They gave a flat refusal and declared it was futile to consider the terms of a constitution unless the Government denounced the Balfour Declaration, stopped all non-Arab immigration and granted full self-government to Palestine. They pointed out, moreover, that under the proposed constitution the High Commissioner would control fourteen out of the possible twenty-seven votes of the full meeting and that he could, if he desired, transact business with a quorum of ten official members. The mention of these details led the Government to believe that the Arabs were ready to negotiate despite their first bald rejection of the proposal. In its reply the Government made clear that it would not consider any constitution or parliamentary regime that would lead to the abrogation of the British pledge to the Jews, but that it would be ready to consider modifications in the composition of the Legislative Council and arrange to give the Arabs a voice in the control of immigration. But these concessions did not move the Arabs. In concluding a letter written on March 16th, the delegation reiterated their original stand and said: ". . . the Delegation has not entered into the details of the Constitution since no object could be gained in discussing details when the foundation on which these details are built is a subject of disagreement."[35]

Negotiations had dragged on for the better part of a year without any progress having been made. On April 11, 1922, a letter[36] signed by Shuckburgh expressed Churchill's regret that the delegation had not adopted a more responsive attitude toward his proposals. The letter summarizes the Government's policy as follows: There would be "no question of rescinding

35. Great Britain, *Correspondence with the Palestine Arab Commission and the Zionist Organization*, Cmd. 1700, June 1922, p. 15. (Henceforth in this chapter referred to as the *Correspondence.)*
36. *Ibid.*, pp. 15–17.

the Balfour Declaration"; the Declaration provided first for the establishment of a national home for the Jews in Palestine, and secondly, for the preservation of the rights and interests of the non-Jewish population of the country. The point to which the Colonial Secretary had addressed his efforts in the negotiations with the Arab delegation was to provide adequate safeguards for the fulfillment of the second part. He expressed his disappointment that the delegation declined to cooperate with him in seeking a practical solution to the problem and he failed to see what advantage they or their advisers could expect from the purely negative attitude which they had assumed.

Sir Herbert Samuel, however, did not give up his search for a formula which he thought could enable moderates among the Arabs to accept the Mandate. The Mandate had not as yet been approved and he feared that the national home would be jeopardized. Parliamentary opinion had changed for the worse, as became evident in the debate on the Rutenberg concession for harnessing the waters of the Jordan to produce electric power. The British press was becoming more and more anti-Zionist. Lord Northcliffe, a powerful newspaper magnate, had lost his Zionist sympathies on a visit to Palestine, partly, it appears, on account of the tactless behavior of the socialist-minded *halutzim* who had not accorded him a friendly welcome, and in part because of his realization of the strength of the Arab opposition. Philip Graves, who was a prominent journalist sympathetic to a moderate implementation of the Balfour Declaration, and who had accompanied Northcliffe to Palestine, published letters in *The Times* defending the British officials against the attacks by Zionists and condemned the Zionist Commission for exacerbating the situation through excessive demands. *The Daily Mail* and *The Post* were even more extreme in their opposition to Zionism. The Conservative opposition to Lloyd George was growing.

In May, 1922, Sir Herbert Samuel came to England in an endeavor to work out a policy in cooperation with the Colonial Office. In addition to the central purpose of conciliating the Arab position there were other factors that he had to reckon with: British public opinion was against expending large sums in the Near East on military forces; the Palestine issue was being used in the attack against the Lloyd George coalition; the Mandate for Palestine had not yet been approved by the

League of Nations. From these various considerations there emerged the new statement of policy which was incorporated in the famous Churchill White Paper of 1922.

The Churchill White Paper

The 1922 Statement, usually referred to as the Churchill White Paper, was first drawn up in the form of a Memorandum entitled "British Policy in Palestine." An advance draft was communicated to the Arab delegation on May 30th, and its terms were discussed in detail with the members of the delegation on June 1st by Sir Herbert Samuel and a representative of the Colonial Office. The comments which were offered by the Arab representatives indicated no change in their attitude and presaged a rejection of the statement.[37] On June 3rd the draft was communicated formally to the Zionist Organization. The statement included a paragraph which entered the British Government's official denial of the Arab delegation's contention that Palestine west of the Jordan was included in Sir Henry McMahon's pledge to King Husain. The main principles of the new statement of policy, in accordance with the Government's official summary, were as follows:[38]

1. His Majesty's Government reaffirm Declaration of November, 1917 which is not susceptible of change.
2. A Jewish National Home will be founded in Palestine. The Jewish people will be in Palestine as of right and not on sufferance. But His Majesty's Government have no such aim in view as that Palestine should become as Jewish as England is English.
3. Nor do His Majesty's Government contemplate disappearance or subordination of Arab population, language or culture.
4. Status of all citizens of Palestine will be Palestinian. No section of population will have any other status in the eyes of the law.
5. His Majesty's Government intend to foster establishment of full measure of self-government in Palestine, and as the next step a Legislative Council with a majority of elected members will be set up immediately.

---

37. These comments were later summarized in a letter dated June 17th to the Secretary of State for the Colonies from the Arab delegation; see *Correspondence*, pp. 21–28.
38. As telegraphically transmitted on June 29th by the Secretary of State for the Colonies to the officer administering the Government of Palestine. (See *Correspondence*, Cmd. 1700, pp. 30–31.)

6. Special position of Zionist Executive does not entitle it to share in any degree in government of country.

7. Immigration will not exceed economic capacity of the country at the time to absorb new arrivals.

8. Committee of elected members of Legislative Council will confer with Administration upon matters relating to regulation of immigration.

9. Any religious community or considerable section of population claiming that terms of Mandate are not being fulfilled will have right of appeal to League of Nations.

The following are the main paragraphs of the Churchill White Paper:[39]

Unauthorised statements have been made to the effect that the purpose in view is to create a wholly Jewish Palestine. Phrases have been used such as that Palestine is to become "as Jewish as England is English." His Majesty's Government regard any such expectation as impracticable and have no such aim in view. Nor have they at any time contemplated, as appears to be feared by the Arab Delegation, the disappearance or the subordination of the Arabic population, language or culture in Palestine. They would draw attention to the fact that the terms of the Declaration referred to do not contemplate that Palestine as a whole should be converted into a Jewish National Home, but that such a Home should be founded *in Palestine.*

It is also necessary to point out that the Zionist Commission in Palestine, now termed the Palestine Zionist Executive, has not desired to possess, and does not possess, any share in the general administration of the country. Nor does the special position assigned to the Zionist Organisation in Article IV of the Draft Mandate for Palestine imply any such functions. That special position relates to the measures to be taken in Palestine affecting the Jewish population, and contemplates that the Organisation may exist in the general development of the country, but does not entitle it to share in any degree in its Government.

So far as the Jewish population of Palestine are concerned, it appears that some among them are apprehensive that His Majesty's Government may depart from the policy embodied in the Declaration of 1917. It is necessary, therefore, once more to affirm that these fears are unfounded, and that the Declaration, re-affirmed by the Conference of the Principal Allied Powers at San Remo and again in the Treaty of Sèvres, is not susceptible of change.

During the last two or three generations the Jews have recreated

39. *Ibid.,* pp. 18–21.

in Palestine a community, now numbering 80,000, of whom about one-fourth are farmers or workers upon the land. This community has its own political organs; an elected assembly for the direction of its domestic concerns; elected councils in the towns; and an organisation for the control of its schools. It has elected Chief Rabbinate and Rabbinical Council for the direction of its religious affairs. Its business is conducted in Hebrew as a vernacular language, and a Hebrew press serves its needs. It has its distinctive intellectual life and displays considerable economic activity. This community, then, with its town and country population, its political, religious and social organisations, its own language, its own customs, its own life, has in fact "national" characteristics. When it is asked what is meant by the development of the Jewish National Home in Palestine, it may be answered that it is not the imposition of a Jewish nationality upon the inhabitants of Palestine as a whole, but the further development of the existing Jewish community; with the assistance of Jews in other parts of the world, in order that it may become a centre in which the Jewish people as a whole may take, on grounds of religion and race, an interest and a pride. But in order that this community should have the best prospect of free development and provide a full opportunity for the Jewish people to display its capacities, it is essential that it should know that it is in Palestine as of right and not on sufferance. That is the reason why it is necessary that the existence of a Jewish National Home in Palestine should be internationally guaranteed, and that it should be formally recognised to rest upon ancient historic connection.

For the fulfillment of this policy it is necessary that the Jewish community in Palestine should be able to increase its numbers by immigration. This immigration cannot be so great in volume as to exceed whatever may be the economic capacity of the country at the time to absorb new arrivals. It is essential to ensure that the immigrants should not be a burden upon the people of Palestine as a whole, and that they should not deprive any section of the present population of their employment. Hitherto the immigration has fulfilled these conditions.

It is the intention of His Majesty's Government to foster the establishment of a full measure of self-government in Palestine. But they are of opinion that, in the special circumstances of that country, this should be accomplished by gradual stages and not suddenly. The first step was taken when, on the institution of a civil Administration, the nominated Advisory Council, which now exists, was established. It was stated at the time by the High Commissioner that this was the first step in the development of self-governing institutions, and it is now proposed to take a second step by the establishment of a Legislative Council containing a large proportion of members elected on a wide franchise. . . . After a few years the situation will be again reviewed, and if the experience of the working of the constitution now to be established so warranted, a larger share of authority would then be extended to the elected representatives of the people.

The 1922 statement of policy, it is generally agreed, redeemed the Balfour promise in "depreciated currency," to use Hogarth's expression.[40] Often the view is expressed that the Churchill White Paper denied the possibility of a Jewish state. One view is that: "In the Churchill Statement the purely Jewish state is substituted by a 'bi-national' state. . . ."[41] Hanna says more cautiously: "It foreshadowed the creation of Samuel's ideal of a duo-cultural state in the Holy Land."[42] Mr. Leonard Stein, well acquainted with the course of negotiations from the beginning of the Balfour Declaration, made the following statement before the Royal Commission:[43]

. . . There is a good deal of evidence that what was contemplated at that time when the Balfour Declaration was issued was a Jewish State or a Jewish Commonwealth in Palestine. . . . Between 1917 and 1922 when the Mandate was issued, just as many other things and conceptions changed in the flux of public affairs, so there was a change . . . a change in the conception and reading of the Balfour Declaration. It was to some extent cut down. It may be a good thing that it was, but it was cut down by the time we reached 1922. The British Government made it clear in their White Paper in that year they did not contemplate a Jewish State in the sense in which that word would commonly be used.

Read literally, however, the Statement does not explicitly deny a Jewish state, and as the Royal Commission has declared, Churchill himself did not intend such a denial. Referring to the White Paper, the Commission has stated: "This definition of the National Home has sometimes been taken to preclude the establishment of a Jewish State. But, though the phraseology was clearly intended to conciliate, as far as might be, Arab antagonism to the National Home, there is nothing in it

40. Graves, *op. cit.*, Introduction, p. 6.
41. Josef Cohn, *England und Palastina*, Kurt Vowinckel, Berlin, 1931, p. 175.
42. Hanna, *op. cit.*, p. 82.
43. Palestine Royal Commission, *Evidence*, p. 281.

to prohibit the ultimate establishment of a Jewish State, and Mr. Churchill himself has told us in evidence that no such prohibition was intended.[44] Apart from the change in spirit— from warm encouragement of the national home to a somewhat apologetic defense of it—there are several modifications of emphasis which reduce the primacy of the Jewish, and increase the consideration of the Arab, interest. Although the historical connection of the Jews with Palestine is mentioned, the Jewish national home is seen as developing out of the existing Jewish community in Palestine rather than as resulting from a large and rapid immigration facilitated by the Government. The condemnation of the phrase, "as Jewish as England is English," coupled with the emphasis on the persistence of Arab language and culture, is tantamount to the denial of Jewish cultural predominance and assertion that Palestine is to be built on a dual-cultural foundation. In the Mandate, it is implied that self-governing institutions would be developed only when such political, administrative and economic conditions were established as would secure the Jewish national home; in the Churchill White Paper, a promise is made to initiate steps immediately toward the establishment of representative institutions and that the situation will again be reviewed "after a few years," with a view of giving a larger share of government authority to the existing population.

The Zionist Organization felt itself constrained to accept the White Paper, though fully realizing its limitations. Jabotinsky as well as other members of the Executive signed it, although he later regretted doing so.[45] There was one sentence in the Statement that made it possible for the Zionists to regard it as a continuation of Britain's friendly policy to the Jewish National Home: "It is essential that it [the Jewish people] should know that it is in Palestine as of right and not on sufferance." [46] Under date of June 18, 1922, Weizmann wrote: "The Executive of the Zionist Organization, having taken note of the statement relative to British policy in Pales-

---

44. *Palestine Royal Commission Report*, Cmd. 5479, p. 33.
45. He claimed that he had done so under pressure from Weizmann and out of a sense of loyalty to his colleagues.
46. This is a transcription of a statement made by Theodor Herzl at the First Zionist Congress: "Die Basis kann nur ein Zustand des Rechtes und nicht der Duldung sein." (Protokoll des I. Zionisten Kongress, Prag, 1911, p. 17.)

tine, transmitted to them by the Colonial Office under date of June 3, 1922, assure His Majesty's Government that the activities of the Zionist Organization will be conducted in conformity with the policy therein set forth."

Dr. Weizmann went on to say that the Executive observed with satisfaction the re-affirmation of the Balfour Declaration and the acknowledgment that it was necessary for the Jews to increase their numbers in Palestine. He attempted to strengthen the immigration clause by giving a positive interpretation to the "economic capacity" phrase. The White Paper says: "This immigration cannot be so great in volume as to exceed whatever may be the economic capacity at the time to absorb new arrivals." The Executive states that it understands this policy to mean "that the volume of such immigration is to be determined by the economic capacity of the country from time to time to absorb new arrivals." The Executive reiterated its desire to work in harmonious cooperation with all sections of the population and said that "it has repeatedly made it clear both in word and deed that nothing is further from its purpose than to prejudice in the smallest degree the civil or religious rights or the material interests of the non-Jewish population."

The Arabs communicated their rejection of the Churchill White Paper in a letter dated June 17, 1922, in which they summarized all their previous arguments and reiterated all their objections to the Jewish national home. In commenting on the Government's view that the White Paper policy would "serve to establish a spirit of association on which depends the development and prosperity of the country in the future," they observed:[47]

Whereas we see division and tension between Arabs and Zionists increasing day by day and resulting in general retrogression. Because the immigrants dumped upon the country from different parts of the world are ignorant of the language, customs, and character of the Arabs, and enter Palestine by the might of England against the will of the people who are convinced that these have come to strangle them. Nature does not allow the creation of a spirit of cooperation between two peoples so different, and it is not to be ex-

---

47. *Palestine Correspondence with the Palestine Arab Delegation and the Zionist Organization*, Cmd. 1700, 1922, p. 28.

pected that the Arabs would bow to such a great injustice, or that the Zionists would so easily succeed in realising their dreams."

The 1922 Statement of Policy thus failed to effect the major purpose that Sir Herbert Samuel had hoped to attain, namely, reconciling the Arabs to Jewish immigration and to a moderate development of the Jewish national home if they were convinced that this would not lead to Jewish domination. But the White Paper did succeed in defeating the opposition which had developed in the British Parliament to accepting the Mandate with the inclusion of the Balfour Declaration. On June 21st, Lord Islington had raised the question of Palestine in the House of Lords and succeeded in obtaining the passage of a resolution which declared the Palestine Mandate unacceptable on the grounds that it violated the McMahon promise. However, after the White Paper was laid before Parliament during the first week of July, Sir William Joynson-Hicks, leader of the Conservative opposition in the House of Commons, failed in an attempt to bring the Mandate before the House of Commons for parliamentary examination.

When the Mandate was approved the next month, the Government made it clear that it accepted the responsibility of implementing it with the understanding that it would be carried out in the light of the 1922 Statement of Policy.[48] After the approval of the Mandate by the League of Nations, Samuel pushed the matter of the Legislative Council. To meet some of the objections which had been raised by the Arab delegation, the number of non-official appointed members was reduced and provision was made for an advisory committee on immigration. However, the Fifth Palestine Arab Congress which met in Nablus on August 22, 1922, rejected the Legislative Council and proclaimed a boycott against the elections. Samuel, nevertheless, promulgated an Order-in-Council on September 1, 1922, providing for the elections and issued instructions for holding them early in the following year.

When the Lloyd George coalition fell in October, 1922, the Arabs again made a desperate attempt to have the Palestine policy changed. Their strongest supporters had been among the Conservatives who, with Bonar Law as Prime Minister,

48. As communicated by the British Government to the Council of the League of Nations under date of July 1, 1922, Cmd. 1708, p. 2.

now replaced the Lloyd George coalition. However, in January, 1923, the Duke of Devonshire, the new Colonial Secretary, informed the Arab delegation that the Conservatives did not propose to repudiate the Balfour Declaration and that there would be no change in Government policy from that indicated in the White Paper. His view of the matter is indicated in a speech which he made in the House of Lords on June 27, 1923, when he said: "The Mandate is not merely a national obligation, it is an international obligation, and the Balfour Declaration was the basis on which we accepted from the principal Allied Powers the position of Mandatory Power in Palestine. . . . It is not possible for us to say that we wish to reserve certain portions of the Mandate and dispense with others." [49]

The Government proceeded with the primary elections to the Legislative Council designed to nominate the electors during the month of February. Only 68 out of 663 Moslems and 14 out of the 59 Christians were chosen. The time for elections was extended to March 7, and 39 additional Moslems and 4 Christians were elected. The Moslems thus elected one-sixth of their nominees, and the Christians, one-third. The Jews elected their full complement of 79, and 8 electors were chosen by the Druzes. Clearly, the Arab Executive Committee had secured a clear victory over the Government, and the attempt to secure cooperation on the basis of a legislative assembly had failed. The apathy of the peasantry may have been a large factor in the poor election turn-out, but the Arab Executive had undoubtedly been the major influence. It is significant that propaganda based on religious grounds conducted by Sheikh Muzafar, an adherent of the Husainis, occupied an important place in the anti-election campaign.

Sir Herbert, still persistent in his endeavor to gain the co-operation of the Arab section of the population, announced the suspension of the Legislative Council clauses of the Constitution and revived the plan of an Advisory Council. This was to include an unofficial membership of eight Moslems, two Christians and two Jews. The Arabs, however, having succeeded in their boycott of the Legislative Council, were encouraged to believe that their policy of non-cooperation would again yield concessions. Pressure was exerted on the persons

---

49. Jewish Agency, *Documents Relating to the Balfour Declaration and the Palestine Mandate*, London, 1939, p. 27.

chosen for the Advisory Council to refuse to serve, and the Moslem and Christian members refused their appointments. Later, in August, six of the ten Arab nominees were induced to give a promise to serve, providing their acceptance would not be taken as an approval of the Palestine Constitution. But again pressure was brought to bear by the Arab Executive Committee; there were new difficulties, and the Government gave up the plan to compose an Advisory Council with participation of the local population.

A third attempt to appease the Arab Executive was made by the new British Cabinet, now under the leadership of Stanley Baldwin. The new proposal was to establish an Arab Agency to occupy a position analogous to that accorded to the Jewish Agency. In a dispatch of October 4, 1923, the Secretary of State (the Duke of Devonshire) wrote to the High Commissioner as follows:[50]

His Majesty's Government are accordingly prepared to favour the establishment of an Arab Agency in Palestine, which will occupy a position exactly analogous to that accorded to the Jewish Agency under Article 4 of the Mandate, i.e., it will be recognised as a public body for the purpose of advising and co-operating with the administration in such economic, social and other matters as may affect the interests of the non-Jewish population, and, subject to the control of the administration, of assisting and taking part in the development of the country. As regards immigration [Article 6 of the Mandate] the Arab Agency will have the right to be consulted as to the means of 'ensuring that the rights and position of other [i.e., non-Jewish] sections of the population are not prejudiced.'

There were certain differences between the proposed Arab Agency and the Jewish Agency: the Arab Agency was to represent the Palestine Arabs, while the Jewish Agency represented the Jews of the world as well as those in Palestine in matters relating to the establishment of a Jewish national home. Moreover, the members of the Arab Agency were to be elected by the High Commissioner and not by the Arabs themselves, as was the case with the Jewish Agency. But quite apart from these differences, the Arabs were not ready to accept the Arab Agency within the framework of the Mandate. Sir Herbert Samuel put the offer to a representative meeting of Arab no-

50. *Palestine Royal Commission Report*, p. 181.

tables on October 11, 1923. The Arab leaders immediately indicated that the proposal did not meet the demands of the Arab population, and this attitude was confirmed in the letter from the President of the Arab Executive to the High Commissioner, in which he said: "The object of the Arab inhabitants of Palestine is not an Arab Agency analogous to the Zionist Agency. Their sole object is independence. The Arab owners of the country cannot see their way to accept a proposal which tends to place them on an equal footing with the alien Jews." [51] As Hanna points out, the Arab Executive Committee had gained concessions through their method of non-cooperation, and there was no reason for them to change their tactics. "They had induced the government to accelerate its plans for the establishment of representative institutions, had secured in the Churchill paper an official denouncement of efforts to create a Jewish state, and had obtained an offer of an Arab Agency, all through non-cooperation. Adhering to this apparently successful policy they therefore unanimously rejected the government's proposal." [52] Finally convinced that no cooperation could be obtained from the Arab leaders short of renunciation of the Balfour Declaration, the British Colonial Office instructed the High Commissioner to terminate the negotiations with them and to administer the country with the help of an advisory council composed entirely of British officials. This form of government was initiated in December 1923.

In the seven year period from the Churchill White Paper to the outbreak in 1929, there were no unsurmountable political impediments to the Jewish development of the country. The limitations imposed on Jewish immigration by the economic absorptive capacity principle were not so stringent as to prevent a large Jewish immigration. In 1925, 33,801 Jews immigrated into the country and 2,151 emigrated; in 1926, 13,081 entered and 7,365 left. In 1927, emigration was larger than immigration, 2,713 having come in, and 5,071 having departed, leaving a minus quantity of 2,358. The decline in immigration and the increase in emigration during these years was due to economic factors which had their origin mainly out-

51. Royal Institute of International Affairs, *Great Britain and Palestine, 1915–1939*, p. 37.
52. Hanna, *op. cit.*, p. 85.

side of Palestine. The fall of the value of Polish currency left the middle class immigration of the Fourth *Aliyah* without sufficient capital to complete projects initiated, and this had catastrophic results on the employment situation. In 1927 the beginnings of a world-wide depression began to have their effect on Palestine, and occurrences in Palestine added to the unfavorable economic trend: there was a drought in 1926, an earthquake in 1927, and an invasion of locusts in 1928. The growth of unemployment caused the Zionist Executive of its own accord to cease their request for labor certificates.

The year 1925 with its record immigration of almost 34,000 and its crowning cultural event, the opening of the Hebrew University, was the high point of Jewish development in the first decade. It is not surprising therefore that many who had opposed Samuel's policy began to believe that he had after all followed the right course. Whatever the doubts were, the Jewish population gave Sir Herbert a friendly farewell when he left. At a gala performance of the Opera in Tel-Aviv on June 30, 1925, the day on which Samuel's term of office came to an end, there was an enthusiastic demonstration from the audience when Samuel rose to leave.[53] In the *Report of the Executive to the XIVth Zionist Congress,* the Zionist Organization paid Samuel a glowing tribute:[54]

Sir Herbert has, by common consent, acquitted himself of his historic task with dignity and distinction, and he carried with him in his retirement the enduring gratitude of the Zionist Organization and of the Jewish world at large. The contrast between the Palestine of 1920 and the Palestine of 1925 speaks for itself. Political unrest has subsided; a stable and efficient Administration has been built up; and there has been a marked and general quickening of economic life. Not only have the past five years brought Palestine peace, order and good government, but they have witnessed the successful completion of the first and most difficult stage in the establishment of the Jewish National Home.

Sir Herbert Samuel's summary of the situation is contained in his *Report of the High Commissioner on the Administration of Palestine, 1920–1925.* After tracing the great economic

53. Frederick H. Kisch, *Palestine Diary,* Gollancz, London, 1938, p. 190.
54. P. 16.

and social improvement in Palestine after the inauguration of the British administration, he says:

> Some of the Arab political leaders are accustomed to assert that the Government of Palestine devotes its chief efforts to promoting the establishment of the Jewish National Home, favouring the Jews unduly in the allocation of land, in matters of education, in the appointment of officials, and in other ways. From the Jewish side, on the other hand, the complaint is often made that the Government is inactive in all these matters; that it does less than is required by the articles of the Mandate; that the up-building of the National Home has been left to the efforts, almost unaided, of the Jewish people themselves. So far as there is any truth in these criticisms, it is the latter that has most substance. For the reasons that I have given the Government has found it possible to do little in the provision of land for Jewish settlement. The school system as it stands, although a reform is already under preparation, leaves almost the whole burden of the education of the Jewish child population upon the shoulders of the Jews themselves, in addition to the contribution which they make through their taxes to the Government system of Arab schools; of the many competent Jews who have offered themselves for Government positions, it has not been possible, without injustice to others, to employ more than a small number. But the consequence has been that the Jewish movement has been self-dependent. If it has had the moral encouragement of the Balfour Declaration and of the official recognition of the Hebrew language, if it has been able to rely on the Government of Palestine to maintain order and to impose no unnecessary obstacles, for all the rest it has had to rely on its own internal resources, on its own enthusiasm, its own sacrifices, its own men. What the future will bring it would be foolish to try to forecast. There are too many factors involved to enable anyone to foretell with assurance how successful will be the Jewish agricultural colonies and industries, how much support will be forthcoming from other countries, how efficient will be the direction of the community's affairs, and how fast, in consequence, its numbers will increase. But this one factor at least is propitious; that the building of the National Home has not been the work of any Government; it is not an artificial construction of laws and official fostering. It is the outcome of the energy and enterprise of the Jewish people themselves.

His general opinion of the situation had not changed ten years later. In an address delivered before the Jewish Historical Society of England on November 25, 1935, he said as follows:[55]

55. Herbert Samuel, *Great Britain and Palestine*, the Second Lucien Wolf Memorial Lecture, London, 1935, pp. 19–21.

From the outset it was obvious to the Government at home and to the administration in Palestine, that the Arab question was the predominant issue. There were over 600,000 Arabs in the country. Rooted there for a thousand years, regarding themselves as trustees of Moslem interests and Moslem Holy Places on behalf of the Mohammedan world, they were apprehensive as to the ownership of their lands, and anxious as to the possibility of being supplanted by the incursion into Palestine of millions of Jews, drawn from the reservoirs of Jewish population and backed by the resources of Jewish wealth all over the world. It was necessary to show that these anxieties were unjustified and to allay these fears. It was plain that the establishment of the Jewish National Home must be conditioned, not only by safeguards for the existing rights of the Arab population, but also by a constant and active care, on the part of the Mandatory Power, for their economic and cultural progress. No other policy was consistent with the principles that prevailed throughout the British Empire in the administration of backward territories. No other policy would be approved by the House of Commons and British public opinion. None other could be endorsed by the League of Nations, whose Permanent Mandates Commission held a close and impartial watch over all the mandated territories.

By common consent Lord Plumer, the High Commissioner who followed Samuel, gave the country an exemplary form of government. At first the Jewish community was suspicious of the appointment of a military man who had passed the prime of life, but he proved to be a perfect, non-political governor, interested in the economic development of the country and bent on single-minded execution of the policy of His Majesty's Government. As Kisch notes in his *Diary*, after his first official interview with Lord Plumer: ". . . I conclude that Plumer's attitude to our submissions will be 'Is the request justified under the policy of H. M. Government?—If so, I must grant it, and carry it through.' The last High Commissioner's first reaction was: 'What will the Arabs say to this?' " [56]

The Arab leaders lost no time in presenting Plumer with a long list of demands condemning the regime of his predecessor in no uncertain terms. Plumer bluntly answered that he expected to follow in the footsteps of Samuel, and that it was his intention to lay the emphasis during his administration on economic improvement and agricultural development of the country. He made it clear beyond any shadow of a doubt that

---

56. Kisch, *op. cit.*, p. 201

he would not be intimidated by threats of trouble. A deputation of Arab notables once requested permission for a demonstration of sympathy with the Syrian Arabs, warning him that if their request was not granted they could not be responsible for the tranquility of the country. Plumer coolly replied that he never expected them to take such responsibility, that he himself would see to it that the security of the country was assured. The old Field Marshal hated political intrigue. Some officials in the Government had been in the habit of supplying Samuel with reports on the political situation. Plumer wanted no such reports, saying: "There is no political situation; create none."

The situation appeared so secure under his administration that the Government gradually removed the major part of the defense forces. This process had already begun in Samuel's time. After the disturbances of May, 1921, the Administration issued rifles and ammunition to the outlying Jewish colonies. These were kept in sealed armories and could be opened only by the head of the colony who was held responsible for the proper use of the weapons. In June, 1924, the Government thought the situation so well improved that the number of arms in the Jewish colonies could be reduced. Withdrawal of the sealed armories was completed under Plumer's administration. A Trans-Jordan frontier force established in 1926, numbering 772, was reduced to 687 by 1928, most of the withdrawals being in the British section.

After the disturbance of 1929, the Shaw Commission severely criticized the Palestine Administration for the reduction of the defense forces to a point which had endangered the security of the land. As early as 1926, at its Ninth Session, the Permanent Mandates Commission drew the attention of the British Government to the "danger of not maintaining adequate local forces," [57] and repeated its warning at the Sixteenth Session held in July, 1929. It may appear paradoxical that Lord Plumer, an experienced and competent soldier, agreed to this reduction. It should be remembered, however, that the depletion of the forces was primarily for the purposes of economy and was inspired from London. The Colonial Office was anxious to demonstrate that Palestine was largely self-

---

57. Permanent Mandates Commission, *Minutes of the Ninth Session*, p. 184.

supporting. As a matter of fact, Lord Plumer wanted a larger force left in Palestine and he consented to the Government's plan only when he was promised that reinforcements could be obtained from Egypt in case of emergency.

Undoubtedly Lord Plumer's soldierly qualities were a factor in maintaining peace despite the reduction of forces. Bentwich notes: "Lord Plumer's personality in the country . . . was worth a battalion; and it was not sufficiently appreciated that, when he left the country, a battalion might be necessary to make up for him." [58] Granting this, it should be borne in mind also that the conditions in the immediate neighborhood of Palestine helped Plumer to begin successfully, and that there were a number of factors during his short period of tenure that contributed to the absence of trouble. Furthermore, when he took office, the British in Egypt and the French in Syria were dealing successfully with the revolts which had broken out there. In Palestine itself the leadership of the politically dominant Husaini family was under internal attack, and opposition parties were springing up. The reduction of Jewish immigration on account of the economic crisis may have been a factor in temporarily diminishing the Arab antagonism.

Plumer devoted himself to the practical aspects of the Palestine situation. He gave attention to improving the lot of the Arab peasant, he helped the Jews to cope with the problem of employment, and earned their gratitude by extending a government loan to Tel-Aviv when that newly built city was threatened by the economic crisis. In politics, he "let sleeping dogs lie," quite satisfied to rule the country with the aid of the Advisory Council made up of official members. In the 1928 report on the administration of the country he laconically stated: "No steps have been taken to set up a representative legislature." [59] However, some progress was made in legislation for local self-government and autonomy of the religious communities through ordinances passed in 1926 and 1927. By all accounts his administration was efficient and non-partisan and he won the respect of both the Jewish and Arab sections of the population. But seen in retrospect he did little, as Hanna says, "to-

---

58. Norman Bentwich, *England and Palestine*, London, 1932, p. 149.
59. *Report on the Administration of Palestine and Trans-Jordan for the Year 1928*, Colonial No. 40, p. 4.

ward solving the basic problems arising from Arab-Jewish habitation of a single homeland." [60]

Having had a certain success with one military man the Government decided to appoint another as Plumer's successor. Sir John Chancellor had also had considerable colonial experience as Governor of Mauretius, Trinidad and Rhodesia. In view of the favorable experience with Lord Plumer, the Jews welcomed his coming. There was also a turn for the better in the economic situation and his administration opened with high hopes. The first year of Sir Chancellor's administration was uneventful. The country slowly recovered from the economic depression and the number of Jewish immigrants began to exceed the number of emigrants. From the first, however, Sir John Chancellor showed himself more ready than his predecessor to lend an ear to the complaints of the Arabs with reference to the failure to establish a parliamentary government. At the Seventh Arab Congress which met in June, 1928, a united front of the Nashashibi and Husaini factions, the chief Arab Palestinian parties, had finally been achieved. The chief place in the new program was given to a demand for self-governing status of an "A" Mandate. In a meeting of the Arab Delegation with Sir John Chancellor in January, 1929, soon after his arrival, the latter promised to consider revival of the representative Legislative Assembly. Shortly before he went on his leave in June, 1929, he made public his intention of consulting the Colonial Office with reference to the suspended Legislative Council, and confirmed this when he appeared at the Permanent Mandates Commission in July. While in England, he initiated discussions with the Secretary of State on the subject of constitutional changes in Palestine. In the midst of these discussions the course of events was marred by the outbreak of the disturbances which occurred in late August, 1929.

THE PALESTINE ADMINISTRATION—FUNCTIONS AND POLICIES

For an understanding of British policy, it is necessary to supplement the statements made in public pronouncements and documents with an account of the form of administration established, the ordinances enacted, and the practices followed by

60. Hanna, *op. cit.*, p. 88.

the Government of Palestine. Many charges have been leveled from time to time: e.g., that the Arabs had enjoyed a greater measure of self-government under the Turks than they did under the British Mandate; that the Arabs' cause was favored as against that of the Jews—or vice versa; that the Administration in Palestine rather than the Colonial Office in London was responsible for the weakening of the Jewish national home policy; that Government was not active enough in promoting the welfare and the development of the country as a whole, and that this was due to a lack of social consciousness on the part of the colonial officials, if not to a deliberate British policy of preventing the industrialization of Palestine and the Near East. In the brief account which is to be given of the functions and policies of the Administration in Palestine, no attempt will be made to give an exact appraisal of these charges, but the account may throw some light on the problems involved and serve as background for a further discussion of the problems in later chapters.

The British Civil Administration, Local Government and Religious Communities

Under the Turkish regime, Palestine was not a separate country, nor even a simple administrative unit. In the area now included in Palestine west of the Jordan there were three sanjaks or districts; two of these were in the Vilayet (province) of Beirut: the Sanjak of Acre, which included the sub-districts of Acre, Haifa, Safad, Nazareth and Tiberias; the Sanjak of Nablus, which included Nablus, Jenin and Tulkarm. Jerusalem and the southern part of Palestine constituted an autonomous district, i.e., it was not part of the vilayet, and was directly responsible to Constantinople. This third area was called the Independent Sanjak of Jerusalem, and included Jerusalem, Jaffa, Hebron, Gaza and Beer Sheba.[61] In 1913, the Turkish Government had taken steps to put into effect the provisions of the new constitution of 1908 which related to promoting self-governing institutions in the provinces. Provincial, district and sub-district councils were organized with functions relative to the development of public works, agriculture and education. Each province, moreover, sent a number

---

[61]. H. C. Luke and Edward Keith-Roach, *The Handbook of Palestine and Transjordan*, Macmillan, London, 1930, p. 208.

of delegates to the National Parliament in Constantinople. On the basis of these reforms, apparently, in their petitions to the Permanent Mandates Commission, the Arabs claimed that the Turkish regime prior to the war gave them a greater degree of self-government than they later enjoyed under the British.[62] The British Government described the Arab statement as inaccurate: while the councils contained elective elements, the majority of the members were officials; the powers granted were limited and confined to administrative matters; the governors who had the final decision were mostly Turks and not Arabs; the members elected from Palestine to the Turkish Parliament, like other delegates from Arab countries, exercised little effective influence.[63]

The evacuation of the Turks left Palestine without governmental machinery, and the first task of the Military Administration established by the British was to restore the essential functions of government. Palestine was divided into districts—at first into thirteen, and then in 1919 into ten—each under a military governor; and departments of Finance, Justice, Health, Agriculture, Education and Public Works were organized. Under the Ottoman regime, the important offices in government service were filled by Turks, frequently sent from Constantinople. The Military Administration reserved the senior positions for the British, but introduced native Palestinians, Arabs and Jews, in the junior services. Turkish had been the official language in government service, but now Arabic became dominant. The Military Administration obstructed the introduction of Hebrew, on the grounds that its use was time consuming and expensive. Even after the Civil Administration was introduced, the pattern of administration established by the Military Government of the period of the Occupation persisted. To it may be traced the germ of the conception later enunciated by Sir Herbert Samuel, that Palestine was being administered "as if there were no Balfour Declaration."[64]

The Civil Administration, established July 1, 1920, continued to function as a prolongation of the Military Govern-

62. Permanent Mandates Commission, *Minutes of the Seventh Session,* 1925, p. 161.
63. *Ibid.,* p. 174.
64. He repeated this view when he appeared before the Permanent Mandates Commission in 1924, in the following form: "The underlying idea pursued by the Government was that it should deal with the Arabs

ment, in view of the fact that the Mandate was not finally ratified by the Council of the League of Nations until July, 1922. Immediately thereafter, a constitution was promulgated for Palestine in the form of an Order-in-Council.[65] The government established was of the "Crown Colony" type. According to this, the High Commissioner is the representative of the King in whose name he discharges his functions. He is the commander-in-chief of the armed forces and has very broad executive, legislative and administrative powers, limited only by the terms of the Mandate, the Order-in-Council, and instructions received from time to time from the Colonial Office. He is assisted by an Executive Council consisting of the Chief Secretary, the Attorney General and the Treasurer, as *ex officio* members, and of other persons holding office in the public service that the High Commissioner may appoint. The High Commissioner is to consult with his Executive Council, but he is not bound by their decisions. His broad powers include trusteeship over the property of the State: all rights in the public lands are vested in him; he may grant pardons to any offender convicted of any crime; and he is the supreme authority in removal of prisoners or deportation of political offenders from Palestine.

In October, 1920, Sir Herbert Samuel had set up a nominated Advisory Council to function side by side with the Executive Council. This consisted of ten British officials who were departmental heads and ten nominated non-official persons representative of the communities of Palestine. Of these non-official

in regard to their possession of their land, their religion, their development generally, exactly as if no Balfour Declaration has been made at all. The policy of the Palestine Government was therefore precisely the same as would be the policy of the British Government towards the local inhabitants in India, Ceylon or in any British colony. As he had already stated publicly, the object of the Government was to stimulate and aid both an Arab and a Jewish revival." (*Minutes of the Fifth Session*, 1924, p. 56.) The Arab Executive took the second sentence out of context and accused Samuel of attempting to govern Palestine as if it were a colony like India or Ceylon instead of a mandated territory. In their observations on the Arab petition presented to the Seventh Session of the Permanent Mandates Commission, the British Government took occasion to point out that Samuel's statement referred to the internal administration of the country and not to its constitutional status, and that it was aimed to give assurance that the Government was equally interested in Arab and Jewish development. (*Minutes*, pp. 173–174.)

65. This form of legislation was regularly used by the British Government for the establishment of its jurisdiction in foreign countries over which it exercised power. The Order is issued by His Majesty in private Council, i.e. does not require the approval of Parliament. (Norman Bentwich, *The Mandates System*, Longmans, Green, 1930, p. 28.)

members, four were Moslem Arabs, three Christian Arabs, and three Jews—a distribution which indicated that the country was conceived as being composed of three major religious communities. The 1922 Palestine Order-in-Council provided for a Legislative Council along the same lines: it was to consist of twenty-two members (in addition to the High Commissioner), of whom ten were to be official members and twelve unofficial members (who were to be elected). The twelve elected members were to include eight Moslems, two Jews and two Christians. As a result of the refusal of the Arabs to participate in the elections for the Legislative Council, an amendment to the Palestine Order-in-Council was passed in 1923 which declared that until a Legislative Council should have been duly constituted, all the powers of the Legislature formerly conferred on the proposed Legislative Council were to be reassigned to the High Commissioner. The amendment provided for an Advisory Council of the nominated type, but the Arab opposition made it impossible to obtain the participation of Arabs in such an Advisory Council and after 1923 the Advisory Council was composed entirely of departmental members.

A well-organized system of courts was established, including Magistrates' courts, District courts, Land courts and a Supreme Court. In the Magistrates' courts, the judges are Palestinians, either Jews or Arabs. In the other courts, in addition to Palestinian members, there are British judges who preside. Large scope is given to religious courts: there are Moslem religious courts, courts of the Christian community and Rabbinical courts for the Jewish community. The religious courts have jurisdiction in cases of religious law and personal status, i.e., marriage, divorce and inheritance. The Moslem courts also have jurisdiction over *Waqfs*, that is, properties belonging to the Moslem Church. A special feature of the judiciary system of Palestine are the tribal courts for the Bedouin where minor cases are disposed of in accordance with custom by the courts of the Sheikhs. The Order-in-Council also confirmed the establishment of the Supreme Council for Moslem Religious Affairs which had been authorized December 20, 1921.

The Palestine Order-in-Council amplified Article 22 of the Mandate which prescribed recognition of Arabic and Hebrew, in addition to English, as official languages. It provided that all ordinances and official notices both of the Government and of local authorities in areas of mixed population should be published in the three languages, and that any of these languages might be used in the Government offices and in the law courts. Owing to the delay in completing the Turkish treaty, citizenship was not regulated until 1925 by a later Order-in-Council. All previous Turkish subjects residing in Palestine were automatically to be considered Palestinians; any person born in Palestine who does not at birth register as a national of another state automatically becomes a Palestinian; the children of Palestinian citizens born abroad may inherit citizenship for one generation. The requirements of naturalization were simple: the applicant must have resided in Palestine for a period of not less than two years out of the three years preceding the date of application; possess good character and an adequate knowledge of one of the three official languages; intend to reside permanently in Palestine. Britishers who become citizens of Palestine do not thereby lose their British citizenship.

Under the Civil Administration, Palestine was divided for administrative purposes into three major districts: the Northern District (Haifa, Beisan, Tiberias, Galilee); Southern District (Jaffa, Gaza, Beer Sheba); and the Jerusalem District (Jerusalem, Ramallah, Bethlehem and Jericho). The District Commissioners, as well as the departmental heads of the Central Administration at Jerusalem, were Britishers, a number of whom had been taken over from the Military Administration. Among the chief officers during Samuel's regime—and for a considerable time thereafter—were two prominent British Jews: Norman Bentwich, who occupied the post of Attorney General, and Albert A. Hyamson, head of the Department of Immigration.[66] In the junior services, Palestinians—Christians, Moslems and Jews—were the predominant element. The major part

---

66. Both of these men were Zionists of the Ahad Ha'am school. They have written extensively on Zionism and Palestine affairs and have advocated a "cultural-center" conception of Zionism. Despite Bentwich's well-known moderation, the Arabs objected to him on the ground that a Zionist should not have been permitted to occupy the important post of Attorney General. After the riots of 1929, he was shot by an Arab youth and sustained a slight wound from which he recovered. He retired soon after. Hyamson observed the immigration regulations in more than a meticulous manner and was constantly subject to Jewish criticism. He retired in 1934 in the period when there was a great outcry by the Arabs against the increased Jewish immigration.

302   *Palestine. Jewish, Arab, and British Policies*

of the police force consisted of Arabs, but the officers were British. After the riots of 1921, when the Arab police proved utterly undependable, a British constabulary—originally numbering 762—made up largely of enlistments from Ireland, was organized.

The policy of the Government was gradually to reduce the numbers of Britishers in the lower ranks of the service, partly for reasons of economy and partly in response to the pressure to allot Palestinians a greater share in the administration. The number of Christians in Government services was much larger than their ratio in the population. The Jews, though underrepresented in some departments, appear on the whole to have had a share in the main branches of government services not less than their ratio in the population. The Moslems were least well represented, except in the railroads where there were a large number of manual workers. The large proportion of Christian Arabs is partly explained by their better education. But if education and fitness were the only factors, the proportion of Jews should have been larger. No doubt the preferences of the British heads of the departments entered into the situation, at least to some degree.

In 1924, taking all services, the Christians, who were about 10 percent of the population, held over 30 percent of the posts; the Jews, who were roughly 15 percent of the population, occupied close to 20 percent of the posts. The Moslems, who constituted 75 percent of the population, held something less than 15 percent of the posts. Taking all services outside of the railroads, the discrepancy between the Christians and others is even more striking: the proportion of Christians was 45 percent, of Moslems 25 percent, while the Jews were 30 percent.[67]

67. Permanent Mandates Commission, *Minutes of the Fifth Session*, 1924, p. 59, p. 76. The following chart illustrates the situation:

	Senior Service Officers			Junior Service Officers		
	Total	Railway	Other	Total	Railway	Other
Christians	231	24	207	1,212	526	686
Moslems	76	—	76	1,943	1,583	360
Jews	47	1	46	764	316	448
Others	2	—	2	6	2	4
Total	356	25	331	3,925	2,427	1,498

Local Self-Government and Religious Communities

The Ottoman constitution had provided for municipal councils in the cities and for rural self-government under *mukhtars* (head men of the villages) assisted by a council of elders. These authorities were elected by male suffrage limited to owners of immovable property. As in the case of the provincial and district councils, practice and theory did not go together: the municipalities, the village councils and the *mukhtars* were subject to complete control by Turkish governors and district officers. Article 3 of the Mandate enjoined on the Mandatory Power encouragement of local autonomy and some steps were taken in this direction during the first decade. In 1921, a local ordinance was enacted which enabled the High Commissioner, on the recommendation of the District Commissioner, to declare that any large village should be administered by a local council. Under this article the larger Jewish colonies obtained the right to form councils and to regulate their affairs under the supervision of the Government. This Local Council Ordinance also permitted a group of villages to unite for common purposes such as building of roads and the supply of water. A provision that the local council might be "constituted in a quarter of a town which is distinguished by its needs and character from the rest of the municipal area," made it possible for Tel-Aviv to obtain its independence from the Jaffa Municipality.

During Samuel's administration, the effort to promote self-government was largely exhausted in the abortive Legislative Council project, although he fully recognized the significance of local autonomy. At the Fifth Session of the Permanent Mandates Commission when the Mandate for Palestine first came up for review, Sir Frederick Lugard, the British member of the Commission, raised the question whether the plan for a legislative council on the Western model was appropriate for the conditions in the Orient. It seemed to him that it would be better to develop the indigenous forms of self-government, particularly those which centered in village councils, and in this connection suggested: "Would it not be possible that Arab village councils and Jewish village councils, gradually expanding into district councils composed of both races, later into central councils, might gradually recognize the value of cooperation if it were introduced in this way and not all of a sudden in a full-blown legislative council based on a foreign model?" [68] In his reply, Sir Herbert Samuel said that Lord Lugard had touched on the very heart of the problem and that the real line of advance for the future should be the development of local government from the bottom up. He indicated that the Arab villages were particularly interested in local self-government from the point of view of the promoting of local schools. However, he made it clear that the Arab political leaders on their part would not accept the development of local autonomy as a substitute for their ambition to dominate the country through a form of representative government on the basis of rule by the majority.

Lord Plumer, never an enthusiast for the Legislative Council idea, emphasized local self-government from the beginning of his administration. At the end of 1926, a Municipal Franchise Ordinance was promulgated. The statute was based on the municipal laws derived from the Ottoman sources. It provided that if there were in any municipality members of all three communities—Moslem, Jewish and Christian—separate registers should be prepared for the members of each community. The number of members elected on the municipal council from each community was to be proportionate to the number of names contained in the register. The new ordinance went a step beyond the Ottoman law in the democratic direction: under the Turks the right to vote was restricted to the owners of immovable property who paid a certain tax; the statute of 1926 granted the right also to tenants who paid municipal rates of a certain amount. The Municipal Ordinance was not received with great enthusiasm either by the Jews or by the Arabs, although for different reasons. The Jews considered the property and the age (25 years) qualifications too high and severely criticized the administration for not granting suffrage to women. The Arab leaders were satisfied with the restrictive voting qualifications, but demanded greater power and independence for the municipal councils.

Local autonomy was also promoted along religious-national lines. Under the Ottoman code, religious communities enjoyed wide powers of jurisdiction in matters affecting the personal status of their members, including inheritance and religious

---

68. *Minutes of the Fifth Session*, 1924, pp. 66–67.

endowments. However, the regulations governing the powers of the local *waqfs* were loose, resting mostly on custom, and depending to some extent on the character of the local administration. In the case of the Moslems, moreover, the affairs of the community were, in final analysis, subject to the jurisdiction of the central Ottoman legislative authority, since the Empire was a Moslem State and the Government considered itself supreme in all matters concerning Moslems, civil as well as religious. With the establishment of the British Civil Administration, it became necessary to create an authoritative body for the direction of specifically Moslem affairs. In the first draft of the ordinance, the British Government tried to retain some supervision over the administrative and financial side, allowing full control to the heads of the Moslem community in matters of law and internal affairs. This conception met with opposition from the Moslem notables and *ulema,* and in December, 1921, a new order was issued along the lines suggested by the Moslem authorities. In accordance with this, a Supreme Moslem Council was established with complete authority over the *Waqfs* (Moslem Religious Endowments) and the *Sharia* (Moslem Religious Courts in Palestine). As a result of the establishment of the Supreme Moslem Council, the Moslem authorities in Palestine gained a far greater degree of control over Moslem affairs than they had possessed under the Turkish regime, when their decisions had been subject to the authorities at Constantinople.

The Jewish community was organized under powers conferred by the Religious Community Ordinance of 1926. The regulation provided for both religious and lay authorities. The religious authority was vested in a Rabbinical Council composed of two Chief Rabbis, one belonging to the Sephardic and the other to the Ashkenazic sections of the Jewish communities, and six associate rabbis, three from each section. The powers of the Rabbinical Courts were an inheritance of the Ottoman regime and extended, as in the case of the Moslems, to matters of personal status and to Jewish religious endowments. However, there was one fundamental difference: the courts exercised jurisdiction only over those Jews who were registered as members of the Jewish community, and any Jew could by declaration exclude himself from the jurisdiction of the Rabbinical

Courts.[69] The Religious Community Ordinance of 1926 also permitted the Jews to place on a statutory basis the *Vaad Leumi* (National Committee) organization which had grown up on a voluntary basis among the Jews in Palestine to represent the *Yishuv*. The regulation permitted the *Vaad Leumi* to impose taxes on its members for communal purposes, support of the Rabbinical Courts, and education and charitable undertakings. As in the case of the Religious Courts, a Jew may avoid the responsibilities involved in membership in the Jewish community by requesting that his name be stricken off the register.

Government Economic Policies: Aid to Agriculture; Concessions; Taxation and Tariffs

Traditionally, the major occupation of Palestine has been agriculture. Industry on a modern scale was almost unknown before the First World War. Such industrial production as existed was carried on in small workshops employing members of the family, and was confined to traditional industries such as carpentry, smithing, stone cutting, pressing of olive oil, milling of flour. There were a number of native handicrafts, e.g., weaving of mats, plaiting of belts, pottery and glass making and tanning of skins. Industry in its larger sense was limited to the wine cellars at Rishon le-Zion and Zikhron Jacob, established by Baron Edmund de Rothschild, and to native soap industry conducted in fair-sized but primitive factories at Nablus and Jaffa. There were bazaars and shops for domestic trade and tourist traffic. Although well situated, the harbor facilities at Jaffa and Haifa were inadequate for modern shipping.

Under the Turks, agriculture, although the basis of the Palestine economy, was very poorly developed. There were several well conducted German colonies and the Jewish agricultural settlements, although hardly self-supporting, employed modern methods. Arab cultivation—by far the larger part—was carried on by the most primitive methods: land was rarely manured, the crops were hand-sown and harvested with sickle, the grain trodden by cattle on the village threshing floors. Forests

---

69. This development took place largely as a result of the opposition of the ultra-orthodox Agudists to the organization of the Jews on a community basis. See below, Chap. VI.

had been cut down and the terraces on the hillsides had deteriorated, and the drainage and irrigation works built in ancient times had been neglected. Much of the land in the plains was marsh and swamp; throughout the country large areas were left untilled; the sources of water supply and of water power were undeveloped. During the war the country was devastated, olive trees were felled for fuel, the remainder of the forests almost altogether cut down, and many ploughing animals lost.

Social factors prevented the *fellah* from improving his poor methods of cultivation, even when he wished to. A large part of the land was in the hands of great landowners, some of whom lived abroad on the income derived from the exploitation of the tenants. No cadastral survey had ever been made, and whatever land registers there were, were mostly removed by the Turks when they evacuated. More than half of the country was held in *mushaa,* an antiquated system of common undivided shares in the village lands, which made it impossible for any individual to point to a piece of land which he could call his own. This system robbed the *fellah* of the initiative to improve his land. Taxation based on the tithe rested inequitably on the cultivator. Most of the *fellahin* were subject to a heavy burden of debt accumulated as a result of payments at usurious rates of interest.

Through the Agricultural Department, established in 1920, the Government introduced a number of activities designed to improve the general condition of agriculture. Measures were enacted to limit losses due to droughts, locust invasion, depredations of field mice, insect pests, and plant diseases. Experimental farms at Acre and Beisan, horticultural stations at Jerusalem and Jericho and stud farms at Acre, and a number of forest nurseries and model plantations were established. Veterinary and quarantine services were instituted to control contagious animal diseases and to improve the sanitary conditions of stables, and to advise with neighboring countries concerning the outbreak of infectious cattle disease. While the major work of reafforestation in Palestine was initiated by Jewish bodies, particularly the *Keren Kayemeth,* the Department of Agriculture recognized the importance of this work in the organization of a special Forestry Service.

The measures taken by Government to improve the agricultural situation in the country as a whole included initiating a cadastral survey, legislation to protect tenants against eviction, financial help in the form of loans, conservation of forests and water supply, and agricultural instruction. In the early years after the war the Government issued small loans, mostly to Arab cultivators. These helped to tide the peasant over to the next season, but did not put him on a sound financial basis. In September, 1920, a Transfer of Land Ordinance was enacted, designed to protect the tenant from dispossession. It empowered the District Commissioner to withhold his consent to a transfer of land until he was satisfied that the tenant had obtained adequate money compensation or was allowed to retain sufficient land for the maintenance of himself and his family. In 1921 the Ordinance was amended in two ways: the decision was placed in the hands of the central administration, through the Registrar of Land; secondly, money compensation was no longer regarded as adequate, and the Registrar had to be satisfied that the tenant had found adequate land elsewhere. Some improvements were also made in the registration of land.

The Land Transfer Ordinance, designed to protect the tenant cultivator from eviction, was not welcomed by the Arab political leaders who were themselves landowners. In their evidence before the Haycraft Commission which reported on the riots of 1921[70] and in their petitions to the Permanent Mandates Commission,[71] they maintained that the Government's purpose in introducing land legislation was to make farming unprofitable, and to depress the price of land so that it might be the more easily bought up by the Jews. The Land Transfer Ordinance did not, in fact, lead to a decrease in prices —quite the contrary—nor did it prevent land sales. The quantity of land offered for sale continued in excess of the purchases, and yet the prices paid were about two or three times the pre-war figures.[72] Moreover, this early ordinance was not in general effective since, as the Government of Palestine later pointed out, the "purchaser paid the tenant to decamp and

70. See above, p. 271.
71. Permanent Mandates Commission, *Minutes of the Fifth Session*, 1924, p. 168.
72. Government of Palestine, *Report of the High Commissioner on the Administration of Palestine and Transjordan, 1920–1925*, Colonial No. 15, London, 1925, p. 16.

the latter usually left the land before the land was brought before the Land Registry." [73]

The well-meaning—although not necessarily beneficial—attitude of the Government toward the Arab cultivator is illustrated in the famous case of the Beisan lands. This was a large tract of marshy and poorly cultivated land owned by the Crown. The inhabitants lived in mud hovels and were poverty-stricken, infected with malaria, constantly at feud with their neighbors on both sides of the Jordan. In the light of Article 6 of the Mandate, under which the Government was enjoined to "encourage in cooperation with the Jewish Agency close settlement of Jews on the land including state lands and waste lands not required for public purposes," the Zionists had hoped that the Beisan area or a part of it would be devoted to a large development project, conducive to the growth of the Jewish national home. However, in a visit to the area, Samuel was confronted by a sullen and hostile attitude on the part of squatters who claimed the land as their own. Samuel evidently was much disturbed, both by their plight and their rebellious attitude. After investigation, he found that the Arabs had no legal right under the Turkish law which the Administration had inherited. But he believed that they had moral rights which the Government was in duty bound to recognize. Accordingly, the land was made available to the existing population for very small sums payable over a period of fifteen years.

While not opposed to settling the native Arabs who had been working the land, the Zionists attacked the transaction on a number of grounds: that it had been made as a result of intimidation, that land was sold to persons of doubtful title, that the plots assigned to each family were too large to permit adequate cultivation, that some of the Arabs offered the land for resale to the Jews at greatly increased prices, that the Jews had not been given any opportunity to acquire land on the same basis as the Arabs. Their main complaint was that while the allotments were too large for individual families, dividing up the area made irrigation difficult and a large unified plan of development impossible. At the Ninth Session of the Permanent Mandates Commission, where the matter was taken up,

73. Great Britain, *Memoranda Prepared by the Government of Palestine*, London, 1937, Colonial No. 133, p. 56.

Colonel Symes, the British representative, in his defense of the agreement, admitted that it had been made under political pressure, and that "from an economic point of view the agreement might be criticized unfavorably." [74]

In marked contrast with the method of disposing of the Beisan lands was the procedure followed in the Kabbara concession granted to PICA. The former was speedily dealt with, the Arabs made no investment for development, and no part of the lands was assigned to the Jews; in the case of the latter, the negotiations dragged on for many years, PICA invested large sums for reclamation and the Arabs received substantial benefits. The Kabbara concession evoked considerable protest from Arab circles, despite the fact that the PICA organization was generally regarded as treating the Arabs with consideration.

The Kabbara concession had originally been arranged for in 1914 with the Turkish Government, and was confirmed by the British in November, 1921. The concession was part of a tract of land near the seashore halfway between Jaffa and Haifa. It consisted of 25,510 dunams of marshland and sand dunes. After the concession was confirmed by the British Administration, PICA invested about £92,000[75] in reclamation, provided the Bedouins who had been deprived of their grazing grounds 2,500 dunams of freehold land elsewhere, and paid them, in addition, £2,000 compensation in cash in order to enable them

---

74. Permanent Mandates Commission, *Minutes of the Ninth Session*, 1926, p. 161. The question of the disposition of the Beisan lands has been subject to much controversy; both John Hope Simpson and Lewis French who investigated agricultural development in Palestine agreed that the Government had not dealt with the Beisan matter efficiently. For various aspects see: Government of Palestine, *Report of the High Commissioner on the Administration of Palestine, 1920–1925*, pp. 41–42; Jewish Agency for Palestine, *Memorandum Submitted to His Majesty's Government*, May, 1930, pp. 22 ff.; Lewis French, *Reports on Agricultural Development and Land Settlement in Palestine*, Jerusalem, 1931–1932, p. 25; *Report of the Palestine Royal Commission*, pp. 259 ff. The last named report concludes: "This case has been explained at some length, as it shows, in our opinion, an error of judgment on the part of the Administration. The original agreement in 1921 was hastily made without sufficient examination. There was a disregard of possible development and unduly generous terms were given to Arabs, who are not in a position to take advantage of them without sufficient safeguards against abuse."

75. Great Britain, John Hope Simpson, *Palestine, Report on Immigration, Land Settlement and Development*, Cmd. 3686, London, 1930, p. 40.

to move to their new lands.[76] It appears, however, that Arabs in the vicinity made other claims and PICA was unable to obtain possession of the Kabbara land. In 1928, the Government laid claim to the area as waste, or unassigned, land (*mewat*) so as to permit the case to be brought before the Land Court. The judges were divided in their opinions and the case dragged on, being still unsettled in 1936 when the Royal Commission conducted its investigation. In the light of the judicial opinions rendered, the Royal Commission recommended that the Arabs should be offered in exchange a consolidated plot of 2,655 dunams in some other part of the country, so that PICA could be permitted to continue its work of reclamation. The Royal Commission offered the opinion that in this case the Jews had a valid claim because of delay in the land settlement proceedings.[77]

In accordance with Article 11 of the Mandate, the Administration at its discretion might make arrangements with the Jewish Agency for the construction or operation of public works designed to develop the natural resources of the country. Strictly speaking, no such arrangements were made during the first decade,[78] but the Rutenberg concession for the development of electricity, which was organized through Zionist initiative, may be regarded as such. This concession also elicited a great deal of protest, not only from Arabs but also from British anti-Zionist circles.

The so-called Rutenberg concession was granted to the Palestine Electric Corporation and included the right to generate electricity through harnessing the waters of the Auja River near Jaffa, and of the Jordan River below the southern point of Lake Tiberias at the junction with the River Yarmuk. The concession to develop the resources of the Auja was granted by the High Commissioner in February, 1921. A contract for developing the hydroelectric resources of the Jordan River, which was by far the more important project, was signed in September of the same year. The contract was made after a statement on the concession had been published in the press

76. Jewish Agency for Palestine, *Memorandum Submitted to His Majesty's Government*, May, 1930, p. 38.
77. *Palestine Royal Commission Report*, pp. 262–263.
78. In the second decade, arrangements were made with the Jewish Agency for the development of the Lake Huleh area. See Chap. X, p. 1070.

and was signed by the Crown Agents, who acted on behalf of the High Commissioner. Rutenberg, who represented the Palestine Electric Corporation, was given the concession on the condition that he form a company with a capital of not less than a million pounds, of which £200,000 were to be subscribed during the first two years. The contract included a clause limiting the profits of the company, and provided that a share of the profits above ten percent would go to the Government. The Government also stipulated that Arab as well as Jewish labor should be employed.

The concession was attacked in the House of Commons and a full length debate took place on July 4, 1922. It was brought out that the concession was a matter of common knowledge among engineering firms for several years before. One of the members declared: "I myself and my firm had the very concession offered twice. It was hawked all over London and refused by house after house . . . I would not give a bob for it now." [79] Winston Churchill, who was the Colonial Secretary at the time, vigorously defended the concession. Nevertheless, it was again attacked by the Arabs as a "secret" concession, and they brought the matter before the Permanent Mandates Commission—at its Fifth Session held in Geneva, October-November, 1924—in a memorandum submitted by the Palestine Arab Executive. After a full explanation on the part of the British Government at a later session (the Ninth), the Permanent Mandates Commission justified the British Administration in granting the concession.[80]

The Rutenberg concession was originally designed to apply to the whole of the country. However, in the pre-war period, the Ottoman Government had granted a concession to a Mr. Euripides Mavrommatis, a Greek subject, for supplying electricity in the Jerusalem area. There were long negotiations between the owner of this concession and the Palestine Government, and the case was finally brought before the International Court of Justice at The Hague. The International Court decided that the Mavrommatis concession was valid with some modifications.

79. Great Britain, *Parliamentary Debates, Commons*, Vol. 156, No. 90, cols. 313, 337.
80. Permanent Mandates Commission, *Minutes of the Ninth Session*, June, 1926, p. 224.

Another concession was that granted by the Palestine Government on January 1, 1930, to the Palestine Potash Ltd. for extracting salts and minerals from the Dead Sea. Like the Palestine Electric Corporation, this group was established largely as the result of the efforts of an individual, Mr. Moses Novomeysky, formerly a mining engineer in Siberia. He worked for many years investigating the Dead Sea's resources. Though the company was formed through Jewish initiative, it had strong British representation on the Board of Directors, which included both non-Jews as well as Jews. The company was obligated to pay the Government a royalty of five percent of the value of the products, and in addition, was to allot the Government a certain share of the profits. It was stipulated further that the company should procure its labor from Palestine and Transjordan, and employ workers from other sources only with the permission of the Government. Both Arabs and Jews have been employed, and in accordance with the Government report, "the two races in the workingmen's camp remained all the time friendly and no incidents occurred." [81]

In its Customs policy, the Government followed a free trade, "tariff for revenue only," principle. The Government was reluctant to introduce protective tariffs to aid new industries, alleging that such import duties would increase the cost of living, an argument frequently put forward by the Arab leaders. Some protection for established local industries was given in 1927 through exempting certain raw materials from duty, e.g., yarns for the textile industry, hides and skins for tanneries, olive oil for soap manufacture and for refining as a food. In the same year also some import duties were introduced for protecting industries based on local raw materials, e.g., olive oil and soap, wines and spirits, confectionery and pastry, leather products and furniture, salt and cement. In the following years, more items were gradually added to the list of exempted raw materials and rates of duty on imported commodities were raised.[82] A Customs Agreement, along free trade lines, was signed with Syria in 1921, and revised in 1929. In 1928, a Com-

[81]. Great Britain, *Report to the Council of the League of Nations for the Year 1929*, Colonial No. 47, pp. 182 ff.; *Report for the Year 1932*, Colonial No. 82, p. 264.

[82]. Great Britain, *Report on Palestine for 1926*, p. 14; *for 1927*, p. 15; *for 1928*, p. 10. Cf. also *Reports of the Experts Submitted to the Joint Palestine Survey Commission*, Boston, 1928, p. 60.

mercial Agreement was concluded with Egypt, granting each country "most favoured nation" treatment for agricultural and industrial produce.

Other taxes were: an immigration tax amounting to £P 1 per person, revenue stamps which were affixed to bank checks and commercial transactions, and tobacco excise duties. The two basic taxes of Palestine, both continued from Turkish times and resting heavily on agriculture, were: the tithe (*osher*) on agricultural produce; the *werko,* or tax on immovable property; there was also an animal tax. The *werko,* instituted by an Ottoman law of 1886, was assessed on the capital value of improved or unimproved property. The Palestine Government divided the land into different categories with different rates for each category, taxing less heavily such lands as were subject to the tithe. In 1928, an urban property tax, replacing the *werko,* was promulgated, and amended in 1929. The new tax was payable by the reputed owner of the property, the rate not to exceed ten percent of the value prescribed annually by the High Commissioner. The tithe, in Turkish times, was estimated at one-eighth of the crop. In 1927, it was experimentally replaced by a commuted tithe based on the aggregate amount paid during the number of preceding years. In 1929, the system was applied generally to all districts of Palestine with the exception of certain Bedouin areas in Beer Sheba. Dating from Turkish times was also an animal tax levied on sheep, goats and cattle, designed to collect revenue from graziers, who owned no land, as well as from those who did.

As a measure of assistance in the general development of the country, the Palestine Government undertook the organization of postal, telephone and telegraph services under one department, following the model of the British Post Office. The Government improved the railway, built good motor highways, and gave technical assistance in the development of village roads. However, little attention was paid to land routes between Palestine and neighboring countries during the first decade, despite the obvious advantages of such a development.[83] Seaborne trade continued to pass through the old ports of Jaffa and Haifa; toward the end of the decade, the Government

---

83. *Reports of the Experts Submitted to the Joint Palestine Survey Commission,* p. 31.

undertook the construction of a new harbor at Haifa, a project which was completed in 1933.

An idea of the amounts derived from the various sources of revenue during the first decade may be obtained from the following tables:[84]

	1926–1927 £E	1929 £P
Customs	783,573	917,050
Port and Marine	7,045	8,677
Licences, Taxes, etc.	704,481	761,823
Fees of Courts and Office, etc.	239,997	230,844
Posts and Telegraphs	151,679	207,288
Railways	369,680	
Revenue from Government Property	19,286	16,541
Interest	2,659	104,207
Miscellaneous	19,902	16,650
Land Sales	7,466	6,774
	2,305,768	2,269,854
Grant-in-Aid	84,314	24,523
Colonial Development Fund	......	29,195
	2,390,082	2,323,572

Regulation of Immigration

Under the British military occupation, immigration into Palestine was prohibited, except for returning residents. Some amelioration of the rule was obtained by Dr. Weizmann in February, 1920, when the Government gave an assurance that there was no objection to the immigration of 700 to 1,000 skilled workers. It may be estimated that between January, 1919, and September, 1920, a total of 6,843 immigrants were admitted into Palestine.[85] The first Immigration Ordinance was enacted under date of August 26, 1920. This was a general enabling ordinance: it laid down usual requirements, such as possession of passport, conditions of health, and ability to sup-

---

84. *Statistical Abstract of Palestine 1937–1938*, Jerusalem, 1938, p. 111.

85. There are no official statistics for this period. The estimate has been made in the following way: according to the *Memorandum* submitted by the Jewish Agency to the Permanent Mandates Commission for the year 1929 (p. 6) a total of 21,506 Jews entered Palestine between January, 1919, and the end of December, 1921. According to the Government records, the Jewish immigration from September, 1920, to December, 1921, amounted to 14,663.

port himself and dependents, and provided that the entry into Palestine for permanent or temporary residence should be regulated by the High Commissioner from time to time. On the basis of this, the High Commissioner issued Regulations authorizing the following classes of immigration: 1) persons whose maintenance was guaranteed by the Zionist Organization for one year; 2) persons of independent means or who could produce evidence that they would become self-supporting; 3) persons of religious occupation who had means of maintenance in Palestine; 4) members of familes of present residents. The number of immigrants which the Zionist Organization could bring in on its guarantee was limited to 16,500 heads of families for the year.

A new ordinance was promulgated after the report of the Haycraft Commission which was appointed to investigate the May Day riots of 1921. The Commission, it will be remembered, had emphasized that Jewish immigration was one of the prime causes for discontent among the Arabs because of the alleged fear of causing unemployment. As a result, the Government eliminated the provision of the previous ordinance in accordance with which the Zionist Organization had a right to bring in a specified number of immigrants on its own responsibility. Instead, a new category was introduced which provided for "persons with definite prospects of employment with specified employers." In accordance with this "labor certificates were assigned first to employers, then to private applicants with assured prospects of work, and finally the unexpended certificates were given to the Zionist Organization which was permitted to request the entry of persons for whom it estimated that work might be found and for whom it stood ready to promise a year's maintenance." [86]

The labor certificates were estimated on a quarterly basis and the final decision was in the hands of the Government. According to the Pronouncement of the High Commissioner of June 3, 1921, the ordinance was revised to include the following categories of immigrants: a) travelers who did not intend to remain in Palestine for more than three months; b) persons of independent means who intended to reside permanently in Palestine; c) members of professions who intended to

---

86. Great Britain, *Parliamentary Papers 1921*, Cmd. 1499, pp. 18–19.

follow their calling; d) wives, children and other dependents of persons resident in Palestine; e) persons with definite prospects of employment with specified employers; f) persons of religious occupation who could show that they had means of maintenance in Palestine; g) returning residents.[87]

The 1922 White Paper (Churchill) which established absorptive capacity as the limiting principle on Jewish immigration, therefore, did not in reality introduce any new regulation or administrative practice. It merely transformed an administrative system that had already been established by the High Commissioner in the Ordinance of 1921 into a definitive political policy. In April, 1924, certain administrative changes were made to insure better control. In September, 1925, as a result of the large middle class (so-called "capitalist") immigration, a new immigration ordinance was issued, designed primarily to define more carefully the category of persons of independent means, the determination of which had previously been left to administrative regulation. The Immigration Ordinance of 1925 remained in effect for the rest of the period under review.[88] Its main provisions were as follows:[89]

A. Persons of independent means, which term shall be deemed to include:

(i) any person who is in bona fide possession, and freely disposes of a capital of not less than £P500, and is qualified in a profession or intends to engage in commerce or agriculture; and

(ii) any person who is in bona fide possession, and freely disposes of a capital of not less than £P250, and is skilled in a trade or craft; and

(iii) any person who has a secure income of not less than £P60 per annum, exclusive of earned income; and

(iv) any orphan of less than sixteen years of age whose maintenance is assured until such time as he is able to support himself; and

(v) any person of religious occupation whose maintenance is assured; and

87. John Hope Simpson, *Report on Immigration, Land Settlement and Development*, London, 1930, Cmd. 3686, p. 119.
88. In 1927, after the economic crisis, the capital requirement for immigrants in Category B (independent means) was in practice raised from £P500 to £P1,000. This practice was incorporated in a regulation in April, 1930, and made part of the revised Ordinance of 1933.
89. Luke and Keith-Roach, *op. cit.*, p. 235.

(vi) any student whose maintenance is assured until such time as he is able to support himself.

B. Persons who are not in bona fide possession, or do not freely dispose, of a capital of the full amount of £P500, but would otherwise have belonged to Category A (i).

C. Persons who have a definite prospect of employment in Palestine.

D. Dependents of permanent residents or immigrants belonging to Categories A, B, and C, other than Categories A (iv) and (vi).

The original Immigration Ordinance enacted in 1920—which provided that the Zionist Organization could bring in a specified number of persons on their guarantee for the period of one year—had evolved into Category C—persons who have a definite prospect of employment. Category C became known as the Labor Schedule and entrance under it was regulated by the following procedure:[90] twice each year the Palestine Zionist Executive was authorized to present an estimate of the number of workers who could be absorbed into the country in the following period of six calendar months, ending alternately on the 30th of September and the 31st of March. The Department of Immigration of the Executive of the Jewish Agency prepared a schedule showing in what trade and callings the immigrants could be employed. The memorandum of the Zionist Executive was considered by the Chief Immigration Officer, and in the light of his recommendations the High Commissioner made a decision as to the number of Labor Schedule certificates which could be granted for the period in question. A small number of the certificates were retained by the Chief Immigration Officer to be placed at the disposal of employers—Jews and non-Jews—who wished to bring a specified number of workers to Palestine. The remainder of the certificates were then issued in blank to the Palestine Zionist Executive which took the responsibility for the distribution.

Under the Immigration Ordinances from September 1, 1920, through December 31, 1929, a total of 106,525 immigrants entered Palestine, of whom 99,806 were Jews and 6,719 non-Jews, including Moslems and Christians. There was, however, a considerable amount of emigration: Jews, 23,977; Moslems, 5,339; Christians, 6,145. The number of emigrants was 38.7

---

90. Great Britain, *Report of the Commission on the Palestine Disturbances of August 1929*, Cmd. 3530, 1930, p. 103.

percent of the number of immigrants.[91] Among the Moslems and Christians the amount of emigration exceeded the recorded immigration. These figures, though official, must be considered as accurate in a general way only. There was a considerable amount of unrecorded Jewish and non-Jewish immigration of persons who came in on travelers' passports or of those who came across the borders. The figures on emigration are also only roughly accurate, since many persons left the country without notification. On the basis of the census of 1931, it was estimated that 15,000 persons must have left the country between the years 1926 and 1931 over and above the number recorded officially.[92]

It may be noted that the Immigration Ordinances do not contain any definite provision for Jewish immigration, except in so far as the special arrangements made with the Jewish Agency in connection with the Labor Schedule may so be regarded. Non-Jews as well as Jews may enter under the same regulations. Beginning with the pronouncement of the High Commissioner on June 3, 1921, the Ordinance and regulations were designed to restrict and control Jewish immigration rather than to facilitate it. The motivation for the control of immigration was political rather than economic. At the same time, it should be realized that it would have been possible to bring in a larger number of Jewish immigrants than actually entered under the existing Ordinances if economic conditions had warranted. In other words, there may have been some political ceiling in the minds of the Administration even during this period. If so, it was not brought into play, for the economic ceiling was even lower than the political ceiling.

The development of population (including the nomadic population but excluding His Majesty's forces) during the first decade is indicated in the table on pages 320 and 321 :[93]

Education and Health

The new Turkish constitution of 1908 provided for a system of compulsory and free education. However, little progress was

91. Some of the emigrants were previous residents and not immigrants who came in after the British occupation.
92. Government of Palestine, *Report on the Administration of Palestine and Trans-Jordan for 1931*, p. 22.
93. *Statistical Abstract of Palestine 1937–1938*, p. 19; *Statistical Abstract of Palestine 1943*, p. 2.

RECORDED IMMIGRATION AND EMIGRATION*

	1922	1923	1924	1925	1926	1927	1928	1929	Total
Immigration									
Jews	7,844	7,421	12,856	33,801	13,081	2,713	2,178	5,249	85,143
Moslems	60	168	187	99	218	124	198	200	1,254
Christians	224	402	510	741	611	758	710	1,117	5,073
Total	8,128	7,991	13,553	34,641	13,910	3,595	3,086	6,566	91,470
Emigration									
Jews	1,503	3,466	**507	2,151	7,365	5,071	2,168	1,746	23,977
Moslems	720	768	**251	748	559	1,094	407	792	5,339
Christians	716	713	**353	1,201	1,505	813	547	297	6,145
Total	2,939	4,947	**1,111	4,100	9,429	6,978	3,122	2,835	35,461
Net Immigration									
Jews	6,341	3,955	12,349	31,650	5,716	−2,358	10	3,503	61,166
Moslems	−660	−600	−64	−649	−341	−970	−209	−592	−4,085
Christians	−492	−311	157	−460	−894	−55	163	820	−1,072
Total	5,189	3,044	12,442	30,541	4,481	−3,383	−36	3,731	56,009

* From September 21, 1920, to January 1, 1922, the official statistics do not differentiate between Moslem and Christian immigration nor are any figures indicated for emigration. Immigration for the fifteen months may be estimated at 15,055: Jews, 14,663; non-Jews, 392.

** Figures for July-December only.

Year	Total	Moslems	Jews	Christians	Others
1920	673,000	521,000	67,000	78,000	7,000
1922 (Census)	752,048	589,177	83,780	71,464	7,617
1923	778,989	609,331	89,660	72,030	7,908
1924[94]	804,962	627,660	94,945	74,094	8,263
1925	847,238	641,494	121,725	75,512	8,507
1926	898,362	663,613	149,500	76,467	8,782
1927	917,315	680,725	149,789	77,880	8,921
1928	935,951	695,280	151,656	79,812	9,203
1929	960,043	712,343	156,481	81,776	9,443
1930	992,559	733,149	164,796	84,986	9,628
1931	1,023,734	753,812	172,028	87,870	10,024

made in putting the law into effect in the outlying parts of the Ottoman Empire, and Moslem elementary education never became a reality on any considerable scale. The northern districts of Palestine in the Vilayet of Beirut were better provided than the Sanjak of Jerusalem, where the education law of 1913 remained practically a dead letter. In and around Jerusalem, education was largely in the hands of Christian missionaries from various countries, each school teaching in the language of the foreign organization which sponsored it. In none of the schools for Arabs—except in the old Koran schools—was Arabic the language of instruction. In public school classes, Turkish was used in place of the Arab vernacular, and in missionary schools, the language of instruction was that of the missionary body.

Schools for Jews were also conducted by foreign Jewish bodies: the *Hilfsverein der deutschen Juden;* the *Alliance Israélite;* and the Anglo-Jewish Association. All these schools taught some Hebrew, but their chief medium of instruction was the language of the country of the respective organizations. However, in the generation before the First World War, modern schools in which Hebrew was the language of instruction had developed in all of the Jewish agricultural settlements and in some of the cities as well. Shortly before the War, as a result of a conflict with the *Hilfsverein* concerning the language of instruction in the newly built Technion in Haifa, a Board of Education (*Vaad Hahinukh*) was formed, which undertook the direction of a number of the modern He-

---

94. Figures for 1924 and following years are official estimates as of June 30th of each year.

brew schools. During the War, when former sources of support were cut off, a special drive was initiated by the Zionist Organization of America for the support of the schools of Palestine. The number of schools under the *Vaad Hahinukh* greatly increased, and in 1920 the Zionist Commission established a Department of Education to which it gave a substantial subsidy. In addition to elementary, secondary and teachers' training schools, the Jewish system included a large number of kindergartens, a type of work which had been initiated by the *Hilfsverein*.

The basis of an Arabic Public School System was laid by the Military Government during the years 1918–1920. Schools that had existed before the War were reopened in the larger towns, and training colleges for men and women were instituted in Jerusalem. Arabic was made the medium of instruction. In 1919, the Administration voted £P53,000 for the educational budget. The grant was increased to £P78,000 in 1920–1921, the first year of the Civil Administration. The schools subsidized by the Military Administration remained "Government Schools," and were developed into the Arab Public School System. The Government Department of Education regarded the Arab need as more urgent than that of the Jews, since the latter were in large measure provided for by the Zionist Organization and other Jewish bodies.[95] Although differently motivated, the Jewish attitude in the matter played in with the Government's decision to confine itself to the development of Arab education. While Jews believed that Hebrew as well as Arab education ought to be supported by Government, there was a widespread apprehension that the Government might interfere with the autonomy of the schools or the spirit of the teaching, and they were willing to sacrifice a possible subsidy for complete independence. As a result, the Jewish schools remained in the status of private schools. At the end of 1921, when it was decided to give small per capita grants to private schools, the Jewish schools received a sum of about £2,500. The total budget of the Government Educational Department during the early years averaged upwards of £P100,000. The Zionist grant to the schools of the *Vaad Hahinukh* averaged over £P80,000.

As the enrollment in Jewish schools grew, and the pressure

95. Humphrey Bowman, *Middle East Window*, Longmans, Green, London, 1942, pp. 252–254.

of colonization needs increased, the Zionist Organization found it difficult to meet the educational obligation which they had undertaken. Moreover, *Keren Hayesod* collections, being derived from voluntary contributions, fluctuated and were generally less than estimated. The Jewish authorities became less and less satisfied with foregoing their share of the Government expenditure on schools. In their Memorandum to the League of Nations in 1926, the *Vaad Leumi* submitted that the Jewish schools under Zionist control should receive a proportion of the educational grant equal to the ratio of Jews to the population. The Permanent Mandates Commission regarded this request as justified, and in 1927 Lord Plumer agreed to a Jewish school grant calculated on the basis proposed. It amounted to £P20,000 and was given in the form of a fixed bloc grant-in-aid to the Zionist Executive to be applied by them through the *Vaad Hahinukh* to the Hebrew schools under its control. This amount was added to the former Government educational budget, so it did not lead to any deduction from the amount previously given to the Arab schools. At the same time, the Government recognized the Zionist school system as the Hebrew Public School System and introduced a Jewish inspectorate in its Department.

There thus developed a dual system of public education in Palestine, one Arab and one Hebrew. The Arab Public School System was conducted by Government which employed and paid the teachers directly. The Hebrew Public School System was conducted by the *Vaad Hahinukh*—under the auspices of the Zionist Organization during the period under discussion. Its main support was derived from the Zionist Organization, supplemented by the Government subsidy, tuition fees and contributions from local communities. The Government laid down certain minimum requirements and exercised rights of inspection, which, however, did not interfere with the educational autonomy of the Hebrew school system. The major expense of the schools, it will be understood, was borne by the Jewish bodies. The Government grant represented only one-eighth of the sum spent by the schools affiliated with the Zionist system. In addition, Jews spent considerable sums on schools maintained by other public bodies or privately.

The Government spent roughly £1 on every Jewish child attending the Zionist school system, as against £5 for Arab children attending the Government Public School System. On the other hand, it should be realized that a far larger proportion of the Jewish school-age population attended school. The funds provided by Government sufficed to give some education to only one out of every five Arab children of school age. The Jews are able to give schooling to most—although not to all—of the children by supplementing the Government grant from the various sources noted above.[96] Government did not enact a compulsory education law even for the elementary grades; this would have involved a greatly increased educational expenditure. The Arab leaders have constantly complained about the inadequacy of the funds provided for education; however, apart from the provision of school buildings by a number of Arab villages, the Arab section of the population has done little on its part to promote education. The Arabs have also objected to direct control of education by the British Government heads. They would wish to have Government supply the educational funds, but demand a degree of autonomy comparable to that enjoyed by the Hebrew school system.

The Jerusalem District was relatively well endowed with hospitals, largely due to missionary effort and to Jewish endeavor dating from before the War. For the period under review, as far as the Jews were concerned, the major health effort was conducted by the Hadassah system established by American Zionist women under the inspiration of the late Henrietta Szold. This large-scale effort was supplemented by the activities of the Labor Federation through its *Kupat Holim* (Sick Benefit Fund). The Government established a competent Health Department which compared favorably with those organized in Syria or Iraq. In view of the fact that other sections were better provided for, its main effort was on behalf of the Moslem section of the population.

The Palestine Department of Health was established as a centralized service, responsible for the public health of the country as a whole. The Department includes the usual functions, i.e., registration of medical practitioners, registration of death and birth, quarantine, inspection of sanitary conditions, control of infectious diseases. Hospitalization is largely provided, as indicated above, by voluntary bodies, but the Govern-

---

96. However, a considerable proportion of the Jewish children—particularly among the Oriental families—receive only a few years of schooling.

ment conducts a number of hospitals and aids municipal hospitals in several of the cities. Some Jews as well as Christians take advantage of the Government services, but they are patronized mostly by Moslem Arabs. The Government also established a number of epidemic and casualty posts in Arab towns and villages and organized a number of infant welfare centers and pre-natal and post-natal clinics in cities with a large Arab population.

Nurses' training centers were established in connection with Government hospitals in the cities, and a school for midwives was conducted at the Maternity Hospital in Jerusalem. A special school medical service was organized to train school teachers in hygiene, to treat children affected with eye diseases and malaria and vermin, and to control infectious diseases. Owing to the considerable incidence of rabies among dogs and jackals throughout Palestine, anti-rabic measures, both therapeutic and preventive, were instituted at Government expense. The Department also maintained a Laboratory Section whose work included the preparation of vaccines for the anti-rabic campaign and for the control of cattle diseases. The Department of Health also engaged in anti-malarial work including the destruction of mosquitoes, medical treatment of infected persons, and drainage operations under the Sanitary Engineering Section. These activities together with the anti-malarial work done by the Jewish colonization agencies, by Hadassah, and the Hebrew University, served to reduce greatly the incidence of malaria in Palestine.

Appraisal of the British Administration

The High Commissioners of Palestine—each in accordance with his ability and insight—undoubtedly tried to carry out the policy of His Majesty's Government, and the administration of Palestine was not less well conducted than other parts of the British Colonial system. This means that the administration was efficient, honest, and, within the confines of its limited conceptions, directed to the promotion of the welfare of the inhabitants of the country. Nevertheless, the active development of the Jewish national home was prejudiced from the beginning by a number of factors. Sir Herbert Samuel, the first High Commissioner, leaned backward in his desire to be fair to the Arabs and to conciliate the opposition to the Jewish national home. Among the British officials there were a number friendly to "reasonable Zionist aspirations," but the main body of officials were by training and outlook better prepared "to understand the Arab" than to appreciate the significance of the Zionist purpose. The difficulties encountered in administrating the Mandate no doubt irritated some of the officials. There were also persons in government who believed that the Balfour Declaration was a mistake and that British interests would be served better if an out-and-out pro-Arab policy were followed in Palestine as well as in other parts of the Near East.

However, it was not primarily the attitude of the personnel, but rather the effect of the principle enunciated—"as if there were no Balfour Declaration"—which worked against a rapid development of the Jewish national home. While the Mandate clearly involved an obligation to facilitate the development of the Jewish national home, the most that the British administration in Palestine ever assumed was the principle of a parallel development of both peoples. This easily came to mean that Government should help the Arab section of the population more than the Jewish, because the latter was better provided with education, health and other services. It was a constant uphill fight for the Jewish authorities to obtain a due share of assistance in health and education, and in employment in public works, despite the fact that it was admitted that the Jews contributed a far larger share of Government revenue.

Preferential treatment of the Arab section of the population designed to raise their standard of living and their educational opportunities to that of the Jews would have been justified if Government policy had been genuinely directed toward a full development of the natural resources of the country for the interests of both peoples. This would have required a system of taxation which would have stimulated—and in certain cases compelled—the Arab landlords to contribute their due share to the improvement of the life for all classes. Moreover, it would have involved far-reaching agrarian reforms which would have benefited the *fellahin*. However, as Sir Herbert Samuel indicated, "the policy of the Palestine Government was the same as that which the British Government followed toward the local inhabitants in India, Ceylon, or in any British colony." This implied gearing the development of Palestine to the standards of life accepted in the Near East for native populations. The Government, however, was satisfied to conceive of improvement in the life of Palestine in terms of eliminating the grosser evils resulting from the neglect and corruption of the Ottoman regime; it did not project any program of development in terms of modern conceptions. There was no interest in studying the fundamental social and economic causes of the backwardness of the life in Palestine; there was no aggressive attempt to attack such problems as raising the living standard of the peasantry, or eliminating illiteracy among the Arab masses.

The colonial attitude of the British Administration in Palestine had as great a part in the retardation of the Jewish development as its political attitude. The Jewish national home demanded imaginative, dynamic, broad vision and courageous development. The general mood of the British Government was conservative; it urged "slow and sound" development, tending to regard new enterprise as impractical. At bottom there was the reflex of the attitude of colonial officials who were born and bred to the idea that the needs of the British Empire required that British dependencies should be suppliers of agricultural products and raw materials. Accordingly, many excuses were found for failing to promote modern industry. Palestine was regarded as an agricultural country; improvement in the lot of the *fellah* was not to be so great as to change his status; indeed, the expense involved in improvement was at times urged mainly on the ground that "a contented tenantry and peasantry will in the end be much cheaper to govern." [97] The general colonial attitude led to a tendency on the part of the Administration to look upon the landowning class as representing the Arabs.

The Government did not undertake—rather it did not think that it was within its province to undertake—any large-scale developments which would have been necessary equally for an adequate increase of the economic absorptive capacity of Palestine and for raising the general level of life among the non-Jewish inhabitants. It conceived its function mainly in terms of acting as a judge between the contending parties for an equal division of the little there was, instead of devoting itself with the help of Jewish energy to the development of the potentialities of Palestine. Quite apart from the political moti-

97. *Palestine Royal Commission Report*, p. 232.

vations that were consciously or unconsciously responsible for this policy, British colonial administrative practice—in its experience, habits and outlook—was not prepared for the dynamic task that the establishment of a Jewish national home on a modern basis implied. Perhaps this is no more than saying that the British administration was British—that it was guided by *laissez faire* conceptions of government, characteristic of the British tradition generally and particularly in evidence in colonial administration.

CHAPTER VI

THE DEVELOPMENT OF THE JEWISH NATIONAL HOME[1]

THE progress made in developing the Jewish national home during the first decade was disappointing to those who had expected a mass immigration of Jews to Palestine and the early establishment of a Jewish majority. In retrospect—considering the tremendous practical difficulties—the achievement appears to have been far greater than could have been anticipated on a realistic view of the situation. By the end of 1929, the Jewish population had grown to about 160,000—twice the pre-war number.[2] Large development projects had been undertaken: drainage of swamp areas, afforestation of bare hills, harnessing of the waters of the Jordan for electric power, and exploitation of the mineral resources of the Dead Sea. The number of Jewish agricultural settlements had multiplied and their methods of cultivation had been improved. Industry and urban life likewise underwent a marked development; modern suburbs had spread around Jerusalem and Haifa, and the all-Jewish city of Tel-Aviv had sprung up on the sands of the Mediterranean near the ancient port of Jaffa. A high standard of medical care had been provided for all classes of the Jewish population and a scientific attack made on malaria, to the benefit of the country as a whole. Schools established by various organizations in the pre-war period were reorganized under the supervision of a united Board of Education (*Vaad Hahinukh*) and they were later recognized by the British Administration as the Hebrew Public School System. The inner life of the Jewish community began

    1. Main attention will be given to the development during the first decade when the Jewish national home took shape. However, the statistics available are not always divided to suit our purpose, and the developments between the first and second decade cannot always be strictly separated.
    2. Almost three times the number in 1919. During World War I the Jewish population in Palestine was depleted by emigration, deportation by Turkish authorities, and rise in the death rate.

to undergo a profound change as the Zionist spirit of rebuilding and the Labor ideal of "self-work" spread through the country.

The instrumentalities in the upbuilding of the Jewish national home included administrative agencies, financial institutions, labor organizations, and training centers for the pioneers. Organization interfused with ideas which, to echo a phrase of Walt Whitman's, "breathed into the material tissues the breath of life": the all-pervading Zionist aim of *binyan haaretz* (building the land), youth ideals of *shomer* and *halutz* (watchman and pioneer), and the labor slogan of *kibbush avodah* (conquest of labor). The Zionist Labor movement played a particularly significant part in the shaping of the character of the new Palestine in the decade following the First World War. But it should be understood that the growth of the Jewish national home was the product of the thought and work of Jews with diverse religious and social outlooks, with varying conceptions of the ultimate aims of Zionism—or with no explicit views regarding its ultimate aim. Some of the settlers came for the romance and adventure of the new life; others were inspired by the idea of a Jewish cultural and social renascence; still others were following the old religious tradition of living in the Holy Land. Most were no doubt impelled by the need of making a living and by the desire to find a life free from oppression or restriction. Every country in the world contributed its share of immigrants and pioneers; among them were rich and poor, capitalists, middle class and workers. Likewise, the agencies which contributed to the development were many and varied, and included activities of private individuals, of local committees and of public organizations, some of which had been initiated in the generation before the First World War. It was the Zionist Organization, however, which carried the major responsibility for facilitating immigration, promoting colonization, and generally stimulating and aiding the development of the Jewish national home.

With the successful conclusion of the negotiations which led to the recognition of the Balfour Declaration as part of British and international policy, the main emphasis of the Zionist Organization shifted from political to practical work. Between 1918 and 1920 the Zionist leaders differed radically on the principles and methods of upbuilding the national home. Max

Nordau, one of the ardent followers of Theodor Herzl, sponsored the idea of a mass immigration into Palestine. In his speeches before the Congress he had always emphasized the part that Zionism could play in solving the problem of the persecution of the Jews in Eastern Europe; now he also pointed out the importance of quickly establishing a large settlement in Palestine as a means of counterbalancing the numerical superiority of the Arabs. He felt that all other questions should be subordinated to the major problem of how to bring the maximum number of Jews into Palestine in the shortest possible time. At the other extreme was Justice Brandeis, who placed all the emphasis on assuring sound foundations for subsequent developments; careful planning, business methods, scientific knowledge, and in general the separation of the practical tasks of economic development from "politics." Nordau, whose views were vague and who offered no concrete program, constituted no serious threat to Weizmann's leadership. The Brandeis objections to the policies hitherto followed by the Zionist Executive in its Palestine work, however, led to a conflict within the organization and to the eventual withdrawal, for a period at least, of the Brandeis forces from the Zionist leadership.

Behind the views of the two leading personalities in the Zionist movement of the period, Weizmann and Brandeis, were two different orientations which at the time were characterized as a struggle between Western and East European conceptions.[3] The Brandeis view was shared by some of the European Zionist leaders, particularly those from Western countries. Only a small—though important—group of American Zionists followed it,[4] but it clearly reflected an American approach. It emphasized the importance of material factors and efficiency of operation: no place should be settled until malaria had been eliminated and sanitary conditions assured; adequate funds should be available before projects were initiated; funds collected for one purpose should not be used for another; investments should be differentiated from non-returnable expendi-

---

3. Cf. Jacob de Haas, *Louis Dembitz Brandeis*, Bloch, New York, 1929.
4. Stephen S. Wise and Jacob de Haas aligned themselves with Brandeis in the anti-Weizmann opposition. Strong support came from Judge Julian W. Mack, whose name is frequently coupled with that of Brandeis in describing the group. The Hadassah organization tended to follow the Brandeis point of view during this period.

tures; outlays for economic development should have priority over the use of national funds for cultural activities. Brandeis conceived the national task in terms of specific lines of endeavor—in agriculture, industry, education and health—to be developed under the leadership of experts, and he was ready to accept the services of any person of competence for a particular task without inquiring into his Zionist affiliation. Indeed, he tended to oppose giving the Zionist Organization any control over the economic activities and wished to divest it of any pretensions of behaving as if it were the precursor of a Jewish government. In fine, he conceived the upbuilding of Palestine as essentially a practical and economic undertaking in which political or ideological views should play no part. Although his view was permeated with an ideal of social justice, and although he was more than sympathetic to the cooperative movement in Palestine, he placed the emphasis on self-reliance and individual responsibility. His idealism had a definite American tang about it, and differed from the collectivist inspiration which animated the European socialist idealists in the Zionist movement.

The opposing view entertained by the rank and file of the Zionists was that the rebuilding of Palestine was a movement of national renascence in which the economic, cultural and political elements were interfused at every turn. The task of upbuilding was a task for the whole Jewish people, not for a few leaders aided by experts. The Zionist Organization which expressed and organized the will of the Jewish people for this upbuilding had to be kept strong and maintained intact as the directing agency of the historic endeavor. As a democratic movement maintained by the voluntary allegiance of its members, the leadership must be responsive to the needs and ideals of the masses, and different trends and views must be given full opportunity for expression. Obviously, political factions and a party organization were indispensable for maintaining this kind of organized expression of opinion. Moreover, the method of building the national home could never be completely divorced from its purposes, and expert advice would be of little significance if it lacked sensitiveness to the objectives of the Zionist movement. Devotion to the Zionist cause, willingness to make sacrifices and, above all, perseverance were even more important than expert knowledge and efficient administration. The Jewish need for Palestine was urgent and the immigrants could not always wait for careful planning; activity and endeavor were creative of resources; in a national undertaking it was not always possible to separate profitable from non-profitable investments. The main thing was to go forward, to purchase land wherever possible, to settle people on the land as quickly as possible, and to enable them to live in consonance with their ideals.

The difference in points of view came to a head at the London Conference in 1920, the first Zionist Assembly convened after the close of the war. The method of financing the Zionist enterprises was under discussion. Weizmann and Sokolow, representing the General Zionist group, proposed the creation of a fund to be called *Keren Hayesod* (Foundation Fund) which could be used for all purposes: facilitation of immigration, colonization, education and health services, etc. It was to be launched as a mass offering and the Jews were to be called upon to give one-tenth of their fortunes and incomes in the manner of the old Biblical tithe. The Brandeis group wished to separate non-returnable expenditures, such as were required for the elimination of malaria, afforestation, preparation of the land, etc., from capital investments which could normally be expected to draw interest and ultimately be repaid. Education, they believed, should be met largely from local sources in Palestine, aided by special collections organized for the purpose. The London Conference, nevertheless, resolved to establish the *Keren Hayesod* as an overall fund, part of which would go to the Jewish National Fund for land purchase, part to be invested in economic undertakings, and part to be devoted to education, social welfare, and the promotion of immigration.

In the desire to reach an understanding with the Mack-Brandeis group, the Zionist Executive sent a reorganization committee to Palestine in the fall of 1920 to observe the administrative methods of the Zionist Commission which was at this time acting as the representative of the Zionist Organization in Palestine work. The Commission consisted of Julius Simon, Nehemiah de Lieme and Robert Szold, who were in agreement with the Brandeis point of view.[5] The Reorganiza-

5. Julius Simon was born in the United States of German Jewish parents, and was brought back to Germany as a child. He returned to the

tion Commission recommended the concentration of Zionist funds on the developmental activities of immigration and colonization, and suggested the reduction or elimination of the educational budget which at that time constituted a considerable proportion of the whole. The recommendations were rejected by the Zionist Executive, whereupon Simon and deLieme resigned from the Executive. After the Cleveland Convention in 1921, the Brandeis group as a body left the Zionist Organization of America, although in specific projects they continued to cooperate both individually and collectively. In 1926, members of the Brandeis group were instrumental in creating the Palestine Economic Corporation,[6] and in later years some of the members returned to active participation in the Zionist Organization. On the other hand, it may be noted that the Zionist Organization adopted some of the methods and principles of work advocated by the Mack-Brandeis group.

INSTRUMENTALITIES OF DEVELOPMENT

Agencies of the Zionist Organization

The responsibility for the practical as well as the political aspects of the Jewish national home was thus concentrated in the Zionist Organization. The Mandate provided for the recognition of an appropriate Jewish agency "as a public body for the purpose of advising and cooperating with the Administration of Palestine in such economic, social and other methods as may affect the establishment of the Jewish national home and the interests of the Jewish population in Palestine, and subject always to the control of the Administration, to assist and take part in the development of the country." It also provided that the Zionist Organization should be recognized as such an agency as long as its organization and constitution were considered appropriate by the Mandatory Power. Although these provisions did not grant the Zionist Organization any governmental powers, as has sometimes been suggested,

---

United States about the time of the outbreak of the First World War and was a member of the Zionist Executive at the time of his appointment to the Reorganization Commission. Nehemiah de Lieme, also a member of the Executive, was a Dutch Zionist; Robert Szold was a New York lawyer closely affiliated with the Brandeis group of Zionists.

6. See below, p. 345.

this recognition further enhanced the central position of the Zionist body in the work of upbuilding Palestine.

The World Zionist Organization. The Zionist Organization, which carried the responsibility for representing the Jewish people in the development of the Jewish national home, is a democratic body, international in scope. It is composed of two types of membership: 1) Federations organized according to countries whose core consists of "General Zionists"; 2) Unions or parties—international in character—based on a conception or ideology. During the early period, the main unions or parties were the *Mizrahi* and Labor.[7] The *Mizrahi* stand for a fusion of orthodox religious principles with Zionist aims. The Labor group looks forward to the creation of a synthesis of Zionism and socialism. Among the Labor group there were a number of fractions, or internal parties, the most important of which at the time were the *Poale Zion*[8] (Workers of Zion), which espoused a so-called Marxist ideology; and the *Zeire Zion* (Young Zionists), whose views were of a more general labor or socialist character. The *Mizrahi* and Laborites were minority parties, the majority strength during the first decade lying with the General Zionists.

The highest authority of the Zionist Organization is the Zionist Congress, which meets bi-annually in some centrally located European city—in the past, most often in Switzerland. The delegates to the Congress are chosen by the national federations and party units and elected by all who pay the *shekel*— a sum amounting to about twenty-five cents. The number of delegates sent by each federation or group depends on the number of *shekel* payers. The Zionist Congress decides major lines of policy in political and practical work, approves an estimated budget of expenditure for each department of activity, and elects a president and an executive body charged with the responsibility of carrying out the resolutions of the Congress

---

7. The Revisionist Union, a minority group organized to frame maximalist Zionist demands and to further the Jewish state idea, was formed in 1925.

8. The theoretical foundations of the *Poale Zion* party were laid by Ber Borochov who endeavored to synthesize Marxism and Zionism. It should be observed in regard to this somewhat artificial amalgam that the purpose of Borochov's work was apparently not so much to give Zionism a Marxist tinge as to win Marxists over to Zionism.

and supervising the work between sessions of the Congress. The executive power is vested in a Greater Actions Committee, consisting of between twenty-five to fifty members, and a Smaller Actions Committee, comprising five to seven members. The former, also known as the General Council, meets periodically in the years between sessions of the Congress, to make decisions on matters of principle. The Smaller Actions Committee, later called the Executive, is the superior executive body. It has the task of carrying on the daily work of the Zionist Organization and managing Zionist activities throughout the world. Some of the members of the Executive are assigned to London, the center of political activity, and others to Jerusalem, to conduct the practical affairs.

The Palestine Zionist Executive. In 1907 the Zionist Organization established a Palestine Office under the direction of the late Dr. Arthur Ruppin for the purpose of supervising the practical work initiated at that time. The Palestine Office devoted itself mainly to assisting the Zionist agricultural settlements. After the Balfour Declaration, the Zionist Commission, which was charged with the task of representing the interests of Zionism and the Jewish community in Palestine, took over the work of the Palestine Office. The XIIth Zionist Congress (Carlsbad, 1921), the first to meet after the First World War, assigned a number of the members to the Executive to service in Palestine, and these came to be known as the Palestine Zionist Executive. The Palestine Zionist Executive had a double function: on the one hand, it took over the duties formerly belonging to the Palestine Office and the Zionist Commission; on the other hand, it was the official Jewish agency with which the Palestine Administration consulted in matters relating to the building of the Jewish national home.

Each member of the Executive was responsible for one or more departments of work. These included: Political, Immigration and Labor, Colonization (including Trade and Industry), Education and Health. The various departments had different degrees of authority. Broadly speaking, the functions were administrative and advisory rather than directive. The Political Department represented the Executive in its contacts with the British Administration in Palestine. It was not responsible for the formation of Zionist political policy, which was in the hands of the President and the London Office, and its relations with the British Administration were of course purely consultative.⁹ The Immigration Department maintained emigration offices and supported training camps in various countries, made arrangements with the Labor Federation and other local organizations for the placement of immigrants and advised on absorptive capacity and labor schedules. The Colonization Department cooperated in the establishment of new settlements, worked out agricultural and financial schemes for settlement, and carried on experimental work for the improvement of agriculture. Both the Immigration and Colonization Departments cooperated with local committees and institutions, and the General Federation of Jewish Labor exercised an important influence on decisions. Educational work was conducted under the supervision of the *Vaad Hahinukh* (Board of Education), the function of the Palestine Zionist Executive being limited mainly to the financial aspect and the appointment of the chief executive officers. Health work was largely financed and administered by the Hadassah Medical Organization of America and by *Kupat Holim,* The Sick Benefit Fund of the Labor Federation. The Health Department of the Palestine Zionist Executive was principally an advisory body and liaison agency for the various health institutions working in the Jewish community.

The appropriations made for the departments included allotments for maintenance, grants in aid, and investments. The expenditures of the Palestine Zionist Executive, therefore, do not represent the total cost of the services reported, although some rough idea of the extent of the activities may be gathered from the departmental budgets. During the first decade, from 1920 to September, 1929, the Zionist Commission and the Pal-

9. The Arab opposition has frequently charged that the Zionist Executive had a "privileged position" with quasi-governmental powers. In accordance with the provisions of the Mandate it had, of course, special functions related to the policy of the Jewish national home. But as the Government pointed out officially in the 1922 White Paper (and on many other occasions): "It is also necessary to point out that the Zionist Commission in Palestine now termed the Palestine Zionist Executive has not the desire to possess, and does not possess, any share in the general administration of the country. Nor does the special position assigned to the Zionist Executive in Article 4 of the draft Mandate of Palestine imply any such functions." In order to offset the Arab apprehension, Great Britain offered to establish an Arab Agency analogous to the Jewish Agency, but this was turned down by the Arab representatives. See above, Chap. V, p. 289.

estine Zionist Executive expended about £5,000,000, of which a little less than nine-tenths was derived from the *Keren Hayesod* and one-tenth from local sources, tuition fees, etc. About 60 percent of this sum was spent by the Departments of Immigration, Colonization, Labor, and Public Works; 30 percent on cultural activities and health; something over 10 percent on political work, security, administration and miscellaneous expenditures. For the second decade (1929–1930 to 1938–1939) the figures are not exactly comparable because of changes in the system of bookkeeping and methods of administration. A total expenditure of about £4,500,000 is recorded, of which as much as £1,100,000 came from local sources. A somewhat larger proportion of the funds—about 65 percent—was expended on economic activities—immigration, colonization, industry, etc.; a considerably smaller amount, only about 15 percent, on health and education.[10]

The Palestine Foundation Fund (Keren Hayesod). Before the First World War there was no general Zionist fund for the practical work in Palestine. The main Zionist institutions were: the Jewish Colonial Trust which operated through the Anglo-Palestine Bank in Jerusalem and Jaffa and granted credits for commercial and industrial purposes; Jewish National Fund (*Keren Kayemeth*) whose main purpose was the purchase of land and which in some measure participated in the improvement of the land and afforestation. The amounts at the disposal of these organizations before the First World War were relatively small. Between 1918 and 1920 the Zionist Organization, under the leadership of Weizmann and Sokolow, launched the Palestine Restoration Fund which raised almost £100,000 for the work of rehabilitation, settlement, education, etc.

Keren Hayesod was created by the Zionist Conference in London in 1920 to serve as the major financial instrument of Zionist work in Palestine. It was established with its own

10. This was largely due to a drastic reduction in the educational appropriation of the Executive of the Jewish Agency. The reduction was partly real and partly apparent: the grant-in-aid to education was considerably reduced; besides, after 1932, the major responsibility for the educational work was transferred to the *Vaad Leumi*, and income derived from tuition fees and local contributions were no longer recorded on the books of the Executive.

Board of Directors who were independent of the Zionist Congress. However, it was provided that half of the members of the directorate of the *Keren Hayesod* should be appointed by the Executive of the Zionist Organization and the fund is thus *de facto* under its control. The statement of the purposes of the *Keren Hayesod* included the facilitation of immigration, afforestation, colonization, road building, the development of arts and crafts; in short, all measures designed "to bring about the settlement of Palestine by Jews as a well ordered plan and in steadily increasing numbers." [11] Side by side with these undertakings, adequate provision was to be made for the social welfare of the population, for public health and for education. The *Keren Hayesod* was officially registered as an English company in March, 1921; its main office remained in London until 1927, when it was moved to Jerusalem.

The net income of the *Keren Hayesod* for the period April 1, 1921 to September 30, 1929, for all countries, was £3,965,200. For the period October 1929 to October 1939, it was £3,390,474. As indicated in the following table, the main sources of collections were from Jews in English speaking countries.[12]

	Apr. 1, 1921 to Sept. 30, 1929 (£P)	Oct. 1, 1929 to Sept. 30, 1939 (£P)	Total (£P)
United States	2,190,340	1,235,074	3,425,414
Europe (except England)	928,518	972,589	1,901,107
South Africa	293,246	528,162	821,408
England	173,380	277,369	450,749
Canada	147,328	92,762	240,090
South and Central America	108,757	84,099	192,856
Palestine	39,176	127,035	166,211
Other Countries	84,455	73,384	157,839
	3,965,200	3,390,474	7,355,674

The Jewish National Fund (Keren Kayemeth Le-Israel). The establishment of this fund was first suggested by Dr. Hermann Schapira, professor of mathematics at Heidelberg University,

11. *Keren Hayesod Book*, Leonard Parsons, London, 1921, pp. 5 ff.
12. A. Ulitzur, *Two Decades of Keren Hayesod 1921–1940*, Jerusalem, 1940, pp. 14–15.

and a leader of the pre-Zionist *Lovers of Zion* movement, at the Basle Congress in 1897.[13] The plan provided that two-thirds of the fund should be earmarked for the acquisition of land and one-third for conservation and cultivation. The land acquired by the fund should be allotted on lease for a period not exceeding forty-nine years and should never be alienated. While expressing its approval of the fund, the Congress refrained from carrying the suggestion into effect so as not to interfere with the Jewish Colonial Trust which Herzl had suggested as the main financial instrument of the Zionist Organization. However, in 1901, when the Jewish Colonial Trust had become firmly established, the Zionist Congress adopted a resolution establishing the fund for the purpose of purchasing land in Palestine and Syria as "an inviolate possession of the Jewish people." The fund was incorporated as an English company in 1907. Its constitution provided that only members of the Actions Committee elected by the Zionist Congress were eligible for membership on the Board of Directors, and gave the Zionist Executive two members on the Board with the right of vetoing resolutions.

While the fund has always been popularly known as the *Keren Kayemeth* (Perpetual Fund), the registered name of the corporation was *Juedischer National Fond Ltd.*, which in 1922 was officially changed to the Hebrew, *Keren Kayemeth Le-Israel*. When the *Keren Hayesod* was established by the London Conference in 1920, the functions of the *Keren Kayemeth* were re-defined as follows:[14]

1. The fundamental principle of Zionist land policy is that all land on which Jewish colonization takes place should eventually become the common property of the Jewish people.

2. The organ for carrying out the Jewish land policy in town and country is the Jewish National Fund. The objects of this body are: To use the voluntary contributions received from the Jewish people in making the land of Palestine the common property of the Jewish people; to give out the land exclusively on hereditary leasehold and on hereditary building right; to assist the settlement on their own

---

13. Dr. Schapira was also the earliest recorded proponent of the idea of the Hebrew University at Jerusalem.
14. *Keren Hayesod Book*, pp. 47–48.

farms of Jewish agricultural workers; to see that the ground is worked, and to combat speculation; to safeguard Jewish labour.

3. The credit resources of the Zionist Organization are to be placed, in the first instance, at the service of such settlers as undertake to comply with the principles of the Jewish National Fund.

To make sure that the land leased by the *Keren Kayemeth* should be worked by Jewish hands, the leasehold agreement provided that in case the lessee required additional labor for cultivation or the erection of buildings, only Jewish workers should be employed. This provision was further surrounded with safeguards which prevented any member of the household of the lessee or any persons living with him or any sublessee, to employ non-Jewish labor in connection with any activities directly or indirectly connected with the use of the Jewish National Fund land. These strict clauses in the *Keren Kayemeth* leasehold agreement have been subject to considerable criticism as indicating an exclusive spirit. They were introduced in the first instance to ensure fulfillment of the main purpose of the Jewish National Fund and to prevent conversion of the leasehold to the uses of private property through the exploitation of cheap Arab labor. At the time of the organization of the Jewish National Fund, the Jewish colonies generally resorted to the employment of Arab labor for cultivation, thus turning the settlements into plantations with the Jews as the owners and the Arabs as the workers.

The amount of land acquired by the Jewish National Fund up to 1917 was small—totaling 16,379 metric dunams.[15] In the following decade, to the end of 1927, over 180,279 metric dunams were bought, and in the third recorded period, from 1928 to 1937, the area acquired was 188,390 metric dunams. The total net income of the Jewish National Fund from 1902 to 1917 was about £260,000. After this, collections increased greatly: the total income from 1918–1929 was close to £1,750,000, and by 1937 the amount almost doubled, equalling over £3,400,000. The expenditures for the same period are indicated in the following table:[16]

15. The Turkish, or old dunam, was 919.3 square metres; the standard, or metric dunam, is 1,000 square metres, or about a quarter of an acre.
16. A. Ulitzur, *Hahon Haleumi Uvinyan Ha'aretz* (National Capital and the Building of the Land), Jerusalem, 1939, pp. 132 ff.

	1902–1917 (£S)	1918–1929 (£S)	1930–1937 (£S)
Rural Areas			
Land Purchase & Improvement	30,478	475,619	1,729,880
Water Supply, Buildings, etc.	67,222	141,421	69,527
Planting & Afforestation	41,491	93,323	49,363
Total	139,191	1,710,363	1,848,770
Urban and General			
Purchase of Land	912	142,259	173,125
Investments and Loans	44,571	32,022	42,941
Miscellaneous	—	22,942	40,454
Total	45,483	197,223	256,520
Grand Total	184,674	1,907,586	2,105,290

Palestine Land Development Company (Hachsharat Hayishuv). After the establishment of the Palestine Office in 1907, a plan was adopted by the Actions Committee meeting the following year, designed to centralize the acquisition of land in Palestine, both for the Jewish National Fund and for private colonization companies and individuals. Dr. Ruppin, as head of the Palestine Office, was placed in charge of this work, and he organized the Palestine Land Development Company in 1908. The company was registered in England in 1909; the major shareholders being the *Keren Kayemeth,* Jewish Colonial Trust and Anglo-Palestine Bank; the *Keren Hayesod* acquired shares later when it was formed. In October, 1920, the Palestine Land Development Company was registered by the Palestine government as the first "company of public utility."

Between 1910 and 1914, the Palestine Land Development Company acquired about 62,000 Turkish dunams of mainly agricultural land at a value of over £P90,000, in various parts of Palestine. From 1921 to 1928, it bought some 330,000 Turkish dunams at a value of £P1,302,300. In the decade 1929–1938, it acquired about 560,000 metric dunams at a value of £P2,375,785. It has also bought urban property in a total amount of 20,516,764 square metres (some 20,516 metric dunams) in Jerusalem, Haifa, Tel-Aviv and in the environs of these cities.[17]

17. Palestine Land Development Company, *Report and Balance Sheet for 1938*, p. 10.

The Palestine Land Development Company purchased for private individuals and groups as well as for the Jewish national bodies. About seventy percent of the land acquired by the Jews was bought through it.

Independent Zionist and Non-Zionist Public Agencies

In addition to the above agencies which are controlled by the Zionist Organization, there are a number of public bodies which serve the Zionist purpose but which are autonomous or altogether separate. Among these the most important are: the Palestine Jewish Colonization Association (PICA); the Palestine Economic Corporation; and the two women's Zionist organizations—Hadassah, which is the American Women's Zionist Organization; and the Women's International Zionist Organization (WIZO), with a central office in London. Both of these organizations cooperate closely with the Zionist Organization and the Jewish Agency, but they have independent status and raise their own funds.

Hadassah (Women's Zionist Organization of America). Hadassah was established in 1912 by Miss Henrietta Szold for the purpose of teaching Zionism to the women of America and encouraging their active participation in Palestine work in the fields of medical care and public health. The need of raising the standard of health and sanitation in Palestine was impressed on Miss Szold during a visit the previous year. Hadassah's first activity was to send, with the help of Nathan Straus, two registered nurses to Palestine in 1913 to organize infant and prenatal care, and to combat the scourge of trachoma. In 1918, shortly before the termination of the War, Hadassah, at the request of the Temporary Committee for General Zionist Affairs in the United States, organized a unit to be dispatched to Palestine, consisting of a staff of doctors, dentists and nurses, furnished with medical supplies and equipment. The unit had an estimated budget of £90,000 to cover the first year's operations, of which the Joint Distribution Committee contributed £40,000, the Zionist Organization the same amount, and the American public the balance.

The unit functioned for three years and performed a wide range of services: sanitation work in the cities and in the rural communities, physical examination and treatment of immigrants; conduct of hospitals, dispensaries and polyclinics; hygiene instruction and treatment of trachoma, ringworm and tuberculosis through the schools; and a nurses' training school. At the end of 1921, the medical unit was reorganized as the Hadassah Medical Organization and placed on a permanent basis. It expanded its program in a number of directions, including school luncheons and children's playgrounds. A particularly important part of its program was the work done in malaria control, under the direction of the late Dr. Israel J. Kligler. In 1929, Hadassah incorporated collections for the Jewish National Fund into its program of work in the United States, thereby assisting in reclamation and afforestation. In the early years of the second decade it contributed to the development of a social work program. In 1935, it adopted the Youth *Aliyah* project, serving as the American agency for maintaining and educating Jewish refugee children brought into Palestine. In the decade to 1929, the Hadassah Medical Organization spent £1,064,838 on health and other activities in Palestine. By 1942, the amount had risen to £2,754,874, exclusive of expenditures on social work; and, in addition, £415,410 were spent on educational and cultural activities. Close to £1,000,000 ($4,000,000) has been spent on the Youth *Aliyah* program.[18]

The Women's International Zionist Organization (WIZO). The Women's International Zionist Organization was organized in London in 1920 by a group of women prominently connected with the Zionist work.[19] The organization selected as its special tasks the provision of vocational and agricultural training for pioneer women in Palestine, promotion of child welfare in Palestine, and enlisting the support of women in the *Keren Hayesod* and *Keren Kayemeth*. In fulfillment of its practical program, during the first decade WIZO helped to support a number of women's agricultural training schools and farms, conducted infant welfare and mothercraft training centers, and opened a number of baby homes and day crèches. It has also promoted tree nurseries and garden work in the cities, in gardens attached to private houses, schools and public buildings. Evening classes in cooking, sewing and homemaking,

---

18. For accounts of Hadassah work, see the *Memorandum Submitted by Hadassah Medical Organization to the Palestine Royal Commission*, New York, 1936; *Twenty Years of Medical Service to Palestine, 1918–1938*, Jerusalem, 1939; and *Facts about Hadassah Medical Organization in Palestine*, issued by Hadassah, New York, January, 1944.

19. Mrs. Edith Eder, Mrs. Rebecca Sieff, and Dr. Vera Weizmann.

Hebrew and Jewish history, were conducted at Tel-Aviv. WIZO has also trained personnel in connection with its baby homes and other activities. During the last decade, it has also participated in the training of the girls of the Youth Aliyah.

By 1941, WIZO had organized federations and clubs in forty-five countries throughout the world. In accordance with an agreement between Hadassah in America and WIZO, the latter does not function within the United States. Through 1941 WIZO had spent about one-half million pounds in Palestine on its program of activities. In addition, it had stimulated its individual members to contribute to the various Zionist funds.

The Palestine Economic Corporation. The development of the Palestine Economic Corporation can be traced to the ideas enunciated by the Mack-Brandeis group and the Zionist Organization of America. In line with the views of this group, a Palestine Cooperative Company was organized in September, 1921, with a capital of $1,000,000,[20] of which $400,000 was subscribed during the first year. The organization undertook two enterprises, both incorporated in London: 1) the organization of the Central Bank of Cooperative Industries in Palestine;[21] 2) the Palestine Mortgage and Credit Bank. As an outgrowth of these activities the Palestine Economic Corporation was formed in 1926. A substantial amount of new money was subscribed by American investors, who included some of the outstanding non-Zionist members of American Jewry.

In the formulation of its program, it was stated that the object of the corporation was to afford an instrument through which aid might be given to Palestine "on a strictly business basis," with the end in view that through sound economic activities an increasing number of Jewish immigrants could be established in Palestine as self-reliant and self-supporting citizens. It was explained that the term "business methods" referred to the mode of operation and not to the making of large profits. At the end of 1929 the paid-up capital and surplus of the Palestine Economic Corporation was over $2,000,000, and

20. Robert Szold was the president and Israel Brodie one of the chief founders.
21. In cooperation with the American Joint Distribution Committee, the Economic Board for Palestine of London, and the Jewish Colonization Association (ICA).

at the end of 1939 it had capital reserves and surplus in excess of $3,500,000. In the first eight years of its operation it showed a small net profit averaging about one percent per year, but no dividend was declared until 1933, when payments at the rate of two percent per annum were initiated and continued.

The following activities were initiated during the first decade:

The Central Bank of Cooperative Institutions in Palestine. The Central Bank, organized in 1922, devotes itself to the development of a sound cooperative movement in Palestine. It grants loans to many kinds of cooperative groups in the agricultural and industrial fields. It also carries on an educational program to further the adoption of the best cooperative practice.

The Palestine Mortgage and Credit Bank Ltd. This subsidiary engages in the financing and construction of housing for workers both rural and urban. Prior to 1926 the Bank financed the construction of houses for teachers, officials and small merchants in the suburbs of Jerusalem and around Haifa. Since 1926 it has been engaged in erecting low cost housing in the cities for urban workers and in rural communities for farmers and farm laborers.

The Bayside Land Corporation Ltd. This corporation was formed in 1928 in conjunction with the Jewish National Fund and acquired a large area of waste and marsh land in the Haifa Bay district. A comprehensive development scheme was outlined, dividing the area into well defined industrial, residential and agricultural zones. In this way speculation in real estate was eliminated, haphazard building avoided, and sanitary conditions ensured.

During the second decade the activities have been expanded. A loan bank was acquired from the Joint Distribution Committee in 1932. This bank, originally created for relief purposes, later developed as an agency for granting small loans to artisans and shopkeepers. A new type of activity was the Palestine Water Company, created to supply water for irrigation to a group of agricultural colonies around the Haifa Bay and industrial area. In addition to these activities which the Palestine Economic Corporation administrates or controls, it has participated in the initiation and development of a number of the important industries of Palestine: the Palestine Potash Company in which it is the largest single investor with the sum of $456,000; the Palestine Electric Corporation (popularly known as the Rutenberg concession) in which it has invested $134,000; the modern King David Hotel in which it has invested $92,000. Together with the Palestine Government and other financial institutions, it has established the Agricultural Mortgage Company in which it has invested $122,000.

The Palestine Jewish Colonization Association. Among the important public agencies working for the development of the Jewish national home is the Palestine Jewish Colonization Association (PICA) which, in 1924, took over the management of the Baron de Rothschild enterprises in Palestine. The interest of the Baron Edmond de Rothschild in promoting colonization in Palestine dates back to 1883, when he stepped in to save the early Jewish settlements. In addition to extending financial aid for the work of colonization, he supplied subsidies for education and health and sent out a staff of experts and supervisors to manage the work of the colonies. However, paternalistic supervision and philanthropic methods, as well as the concentration on viticulture, led to a new crisis. In 1889, in the interest of a better administration, the Baron entrusted the management of his enterprises to the ICA (Jewish Colonization Association) which had been established by Baron de Hirsch for agricultural settlement of Jews in various parts of the world. Rothschild continued his interest and contributed additional funds for the work. Under the new administration the plan was gradually to turn the colonies over to the colonists themselves, and in 1906 the management of the great wine cellars of Rishon le-Zion became their property. There was also a change in the type of cultivation, and the new colonies founded under ICA's management turned back to grain cultivation and dry farming.

When the Baron turned over his interests to the PICA in 1924, he again supplied the organization with additional funds for the development of existing colonies and for new efforts. The PICA is managed by a council of seven, the original members of which were appointed by the Baron before his death in 1925. In the postwar period several new settlements were established but the main emphasis was on the consolidation and improvement of the existing colonies. During the second decade, PICA gave special attention to the improvement of the water supply and irrigation. It cooperated with the Emergency

Fund [22] in re-establishing Beer Tuvia, one of the early colonies, on a new basis, after it had been destroyed in the 1929 riots; it also participated in the development of two Jewish Agency settlements established through *Keren Hayesod* funds. There are today twenty-two PICA settlements in Palestine. There is no public record of the exact amount spent by the Baron de Rothschild funds in Palestine. An authoritative estimate indicates that a sum of £5,600,000 was expended during the various administrations from 1883 to 1937. Of this sum, £3,000,000 were expended in the postwar period (1918–1937), of which £2,300,000 was spent on agricultural and colonization work, and £700,000 for education, health and social services in the colonies.

The following table indicates the investment and expenditures made by the major Jewish national funds in the quarter of a century between 1917 and 1942: [23]

	£P
Restoration Fund, 1917–1921	850,860
Keren Hayesod, 1921–1942	11,016,855
Keren Kayemeth, 1918–1942	7,016,054
Hadassah, 1918–1942	2,843,627
WIZO, 1921–1942	520,037
Hebrew University, 1923–1942	1,490,394
Emergency Fund for Palestine, 1929–1939	731,698
Funds for German Jews, 1933–1942 (including Youth Immigration)	1,469,681
	£25,939,206

In addition, it is estimated that the Joint Distribution Committee spent for relief between 1914 and 1937 approximately £2,000,000 ($9,613,718). It is further estimated that individuals and private companies brought something like a hundred million pounds into Palestine in the last quarter of a century.[24] Including both public and private sources, it is probable that

22. A fund gathered for relief after the riots of 1929, the surplus of which was later used for constructive colonizing activities.

23. *Bulletin of the Economic Research Institute of the Jewish Agency*, Jerusalem, 1943, Vol. VII, Second Issue. (The total shown here differs somewhat from the original in which an error in addition was discovered.)

24. Joshua Ziman, *After Sixty Years of Palestine Reconstruction*, Jerusalem, 1943, p. 83.

the Jews brought into Palestine a sum of over £125,000,000 during the last generation. Money was also sent to Palestine through the post office, of which there is no estimate.

THE JEWISH LABOR AND COOPERATIVE MOVEMENT

During the 1920's, the Jewish Labor movement in Palestine grew into a powerful instrument for the development of the Jewish national home. It became the characteristic expression of the Zionist aspiration and achieved a position of moral leadership in the *Yishuv*. The Jewish Labor movement evolved as an interweaving of economic needs and idealistic impulses. Its idealism was drawn from the old reservoir of Biblical thought, from the streams of the modern Hebrew renascence and from the currents of the socialism prevalent in Eastern Europe and in Russia. The Labor movement developed gradually in the course of the three decades before the First World War; though different in social-economic outlook, it contained an element of continuity with the ideals of the *Bilu* who came to Palestine with the first wave of immigration in the 1880's to found a society based on justice, equality and self-labor in the land of Israel. Form was given to the Labor movement through the organization of the *Histadrut* (the General Federation of Jewish Labor in Palestine); its élan was the product of the impelling forces of ideas—of *halutziut* (pioneering)—of *kibbush avodah* (conquest of labor)—and the concepts of cooperation and comradeship embodied in the organization of the *moshav ovdim* (workers' settlement) and *kvutzah* (collective). tive).

Pioneering Ideas and the Labor Philosophy of A. D. Gordon

The Hebrew word for immigration into Palestine—*aliyah*—means "ascent," a term derived from the Old Testament where the verb meaning "going up" is always used for entry into Palestine.[25] As a result of its frequent connection with the Exodus from Egypt to the Land of Israel, the word *aliyah* has acquired the connotation of a delivery from slavery to freedom.

---

25. Probably because of the geographical fact that for the Hebrews, coming into the hill country of Palestine from Egypt or from the desert was actually an ascent.

It also carries an overtone of the joyous pilgrimage to Jerusalem in the times of the festivals, and in later Hebrew suggests the sense of an exaltation of the spirit. Throughout Jewish history, departure from the lands of exile to the land of Israel bore the high sense of a pilgrimage and sacred duty, and this feeling pervaded the Zionist pioneers who went up to Palestine in the hope of rebuilding the land and establishing a reign of peace and justice there. To this theme of spiritual and social dedication, the note of heroism was added by the *Hehalutz* organization, founded by Joseph Trumpeldor in Eastern Europe during the First World War. *"Halutz"* is a Biblical term which connotes a vanguard; in the Old Testament, it has the meaning of an armed force going before the main body of the people to conquer the land.[26] But the military meaning of the word has been submerged and it is associated with the idea of conquest of the soil through labor.

The emphasis on manual labor was in part an answer to the accusation leveled against the Jews that they were "economic parasites" because they lived on commerce and trade. Occupational restratification, in which the Jews would become workers in all vocations—from the lowest to the highest, in agriculture as well as in industry—was the favorite idea in the *Haskalah* movement both in Central and Eastern Europe, and this theme of the "normalization" of Jewish life entered into the Zionist ideal. Redemption through engaging in manual work became one of the main concepts in the Zionist movement toward the end of the nineteenth century. For the Russian Zionist youth, the cry "back to the land" had a threefold meaning: back to the land of Israel, back to contact with nature, and back to cultivation of the soil. The idea of salvation through labor had already found some expression among the early settlers in the first immigration of the 1880's; but the devotees were few in number and they were inspired by abstract idealism rather than by their own concrete needs. Instead of conquering the land through work, most of them were vanquished by the hard

---

26. As in the King James' translation of Numbers XXXII:32: "We will pass over armed before the Lord into the Land of Canaan, that the possession of inheritance on this side of the Jordan may be ours." The translation of the word *halutzim* as "armed" persists in all the versions; however, its root meaning has the sense of becoming released from confinement or to become free. Whatever may be the connection between the concept "armed" and the concept of "release" in modern Hebrew, the word has come to imply a vanguard or pioneer.

conditions of agricultural labor in Palestine; they were defeated by the competition of the poorly paid Arab workers, and by the hostility of the Jewish colonists who had themselves succumbed to the paternalistic philanthropy of Baron de Rothschild.

The small groups who remained true to the labor idea were later strengthened by the new wave of immigrants who came to Palestine after the abortive Russian Revolution in 1905. The third wave of immigration in the early 1920's, after the Bolshevik Revolution, also brought renewed strength for the workers' movement. The number of immigrants was larger, and now there was also an economic drive since, in the postwar world, immigration to other countries was limited and the opportunities for a professional career greatly curtailed. Moreover, a larger number held the socialist idea more consciously: although the youth who came to Palestine were of middle-class parents, they wished to identify themselves with the working class of the world in the march to an era of justice and peace which many at this time believed would come in the wake of the Russian Revolution.

The ideal of self-labor as a means of personal and national redemption found a particularly significant expression in the life and thought of Aaron David Gordon. Until he was almost fifty, he lived the obscure life of a bookkeeper on the estate of Baron Guinzberg in Podolia, for whom he had worked for twenty-seven years. He left his wife and children and went to Palestine in 1904 to become an agricultural laborer and to preach the doctrine of the salvation of work. Gordon raised the concept of work to a philosophic idea and to the height of a religious emotion. The Hebrew word *avodah* means both work and service, and the term is used—as always in the case of Temple worship—to signify service of God. In Gordon's writings, the word *avodah* signifies an intermingling of the concepts of work, creative effort and religious exaltation. To permit others to work for oneself and to do the hard work which one should do for oneself, is to commit the cardinal sin of *avodah zarah*, which, reminiscent of the Bible worship of strange gods, is the later Hebrew term for idolatry. In his conception of the significance of work there enters the spirit of pantheistic naturalism:[27]

27. Shalom Spiegel, *Hebrew Reborn*, Macmillan, New York, 1930, p. 412.

One works, simply works, at rough, hard tasks. Yet, at times, one feels that which cannot be better expressed than by saying that one works oneself organically into the work of nature herself, that one grows into her life and creation. Something seizes one, a something large as the world, wide as the heavens, deep as the lowest abyss; and it seems to a man suddenly that he too has taken root in the soil in which he digs, that he too is nourished by the rays of the sun, that he too, like the grasses and bushes and trees, is merged more deeply into nature, more greatly into the great world.

In Gordon's view, only devoted labor applied to the soil of Palestine could give the Jews a rightful claim to the land; military force gave no claim, the contribution of money was not enough, and the historic right of the Jews to Palestine had to be renewed by a creative union of the people with the land which could come only through manual labor. He taught that the division of labor which frees the more capable from manual work was not suited to the character of the Jewish people, which, Gordon asserted, rejected the idea of class divisions. The separation of the Jews from the soil and from the crafts during the long period of the Diaspora was the cause of their failure to create living literature and new values; the Jews had become middlemen for other people's creations—at best, the Jews completed what others had begun. "We have no ground under our feet. And we are parasites, not merely in the economic sense, but also in spirit, in thought, in song, in literature, in the finer traits of character, in idealism, in high human strivings." Gordon's strong ethical impulse led him to demand that the philosophy of labor must be embodied in a way of life for the individual. "He believed that no social movement had meaning if it did not change the life of the individual while it sought to change the life of the social organism." [28]

Gordon stated the relation of work and culture to each other in the following terms: [29]

A living culture embraces the whole of life. Everything that life creates for life's necessities, *that* is culture—digging the earth, building houses and roads; such work, such labour, such activity is culture, or, rather, the basis and substance of culture. The order and manner and way according to which these things are done pro-

28. Maurice Samuel, *Harvest in the Desert*, 1944, p. 113.
29. Ludwig Lewisohn, ed., *Rebirth*, Harpers, 1935, pp. 75–77.

duce the *form* of a national culture. All that the workers feel and do and experience working or resting, and the relations which arise the while with that nature which is alive in each—this it is that creates civilization. From this the highest culture—science, art, philosophy, poetry, ethics, religion, draws its nourishment. . . . What we need today in our great poverty is not an academic culture, but a culture of life itself, in the cells and atoms of which that academic culture is embedded . . . All that we desire in Palestine comes to this, that we create with our own hands all that constitutes life; that with our own hands we perform all the work and labour that is needed from the highest and most complicated and easiest down to the coarsest and hardest and most contemptible, and that way thus come to feel and think and experience all that labouring human beings in the performance of all these varied tasks can come to think and feel and experience.

His strong Jewish national motivation led him to emphasize the significance of historical continuity. He said: "Nor must we forget to build a bridge of life, a living bridge between our present and our past." His socialism—if, indeed, it may be so called—was anti-Marxist. He was strongly opposed to the idea of class consciousness and espoused the doctrine of the unity of the nation. For him, the true basis of the collective life was nationality. The principle of nationality had been debauched in modern times by chauvinism, by individualism and by cosmopolitanism. It was for the Jews to restore the genuine character of the meaning of nationality as a basis for the cooperative life and the life of culture and of the spirit. The Jews had been the first to assert the idea of individual man created in the image of God; in this day of catastrophe for the world, the Jews had the task of creating a national life which would typify universal man (*am-adam*) created in the image of God.[30]

Through the doctrine of the redemption of the land, the people and the self through labor, the arduous physical tasks which might have been unbearable for the town-bred youth of Eastern Europe became suffused with national, ethical and religious emotion. It was merit to choose the hardest forms of labor, the *avodah schehorah*, of building wasteland and draining malarial swamps. *Zehut kibbush* (the privilege of conquest

30. Translated from *The Writings of A. D. Gordon* (Hebrew), Tel-Aviv, 1925, Vol. 2, p. 267.

of the land by labor) was demanded as a right even when it meant danger to health and risk of life—as in the case of the Kabbara Concession, which the PICA administrators wanted to clear with Arab labor. The Baron—it was said—did not want the lives of Jews sacrificed; and anyway there was plenty of other employment at the time. But, as one worker wrote: "Ours is the privilege of dying for Kabbara because we claim for ourselves the privilege of living on it." The burden of toil was eased also by the sense of comradeship and equality which pervaded the life of the groups.

Forms of Cooperative Living—Kvutzah and Moshav Ovdim

The *kvutzah* was one form of organization which embodied these ideas. Although no doubt influenced by socialist concepts, it grew up—as in the case of the idea of "the conquest of labor"—as the result of national and individual needs. The young people who came to settle, in most instances, had no funds with which to purchase lands and establish private homesteads, and the Jewish National Fund offered them an opportunity. For the Jewish National Fund there were advantages in leasing to a group instead of to an individual. By working in groups all could benefit by the knowledge of those who had already had training and experience; when one worker dropped out he could be replaced by another without destroying the continuity of the work; savings could be effected in housing and equipment. These considerations led the Ninth Zionist Congress to inaugurate an experiment in cooperative colonization at Merhavia along the lines proposed by Professor Franz Oppenheimer, the noted German economist and sociologist. Another line of development which led to this group form of organization was the contract system, by which a group undertook to run a farm or carry out a development project on a cooperative basis. One of the earliest experiments of this kind was that instituted under the leadership of Manya Schochet at Sedjerah, one of the PICA colonies in lower Galilee. Another example is that of the Zionist settlement of Dagania, which undertook work for the Palestine Land Development Company.

Contracting for work on a group basis made it possible for the Jewish workers to compete with Arab labor: economies in the purchase and preparation of food could be made through the communal kitchen; there could be division of labor giving each the work for which he was best fitted; large tracts could be cultivated and better machinery employed. The morale of the group could be kept up: the assignment of the work was not from above as in the case of the PICA colonies, but was decided on at a meeting of the workers themselves; when there was not enough for all, the available work could be divided. The young people who came to Palestine as pioneers were of the middle class; they wanted to be workers but not employees; and the collective form of organization offered them a relationship of dignity and equality. Here, they could work for themselves and their people at the same time and not exploit any man. Hard work and the simple life were transformed; they were no longer privations but the necessary sacrifices which, as members of a fellowship, the pioneers were called on to make for their people and for the creation of a new society. Originating in practical need as much as in idealism, the collective settlement came to be envisaged as the basis of a Utopia where private property and its attendant evils of inequality and strife would be eliminated. One of the early organizers of the *kvutzah* summarized its purposes as follows:[31]

To create a settlement form which obliged us to work by ourselves; to obtain work where there will be no owners and no overseers; to give an example of work done by employing modern technological methods; to enable the newcomer to become accustomed to work; and finally the highest purpose of the *kevutzah,* "to create the possibility of becoming masters of our own life and establish a form of life based on economic and social equality between the members."

The term *"kvutzah"* applies to many kinds of cooperatives, in the cities as well as in the rural communities. There are cooperatives that go by this name in the fields of building, transportation, planting and irrigation of citrus groves, in reclamation and afforestation work. However, the term has come to be used particularly to define a certain type of agricultural settlement, sometimes referred to as a "communal" or "collective" settlement. The *kvutzah* is an idea rather than a fixed form; it has undergone considerable change in the course of development, and there are several types, large and small. In the broad sense, the *kvutzah* has been defined as "a group having similar

31. Joseph Bussel, in *Pirke Hapoel Hatzair*, Tel-Aviv, 1936, Vol. VIII, 2, p. 140.

religious, political, economic or social background" who "pool their resources and substitute collective for individual property." [32] The typical *kvutzah* is situated on land of the Jewish National Fund, the lease being held in common ownership. The Jewish cooperative settlements in Palestine differ from the Soviet collectives in essential points: in the Zionist collectives association is voluntary and the members may leave on their own volition; each member of the collective is part owner of the leasehold and shares the profits of the farm; no wages are paid, all earnings being pooled, and all needs—food, clothing, medical attention, spending money, cash assistance to relatives, etc.—are met within the limitations of the funds available.

In many respects the *kvutzah* has the character of a large family: there is a common dining hall; the infants are housed in a crèche under the care of nurses and a physician; the young children most frequently live in a central building under the care of teachers; the older children who are able to take care of themselves live at the parents' quarters. Men and women have the same rights. In the early days there was a tendency to make no differentiation in distributing tasks, but today, generally speaking, the women are assigned to the lighter branches of farming—poultry, dairying, nurseries—as well as to household duties and care of children. All work is done by the members of the collective, but physicians, teachers and other specialists may be engaged from the outside. These receive wages in accordance with the scale of the Federation of Labor, but do not share in the benefits or losses of the *kvutzah*. The final authority is the General Assembly of the members which convenes at least once a year, receives reports of committees, plans activities, resolves on the budget, etc. There are generally two main standing committees: an executive committee, consisting of a treasurer and coordinator of work and other officers; and a members' committee which makes recommendations for new admissions and concerns itself with social relations.

In the course of their development the Zionist collectives have shown an increasing regard for individual differences. In the beginning, when the emphasis was wholly on the significance of manual labor and equality, the members were as-

32. Harry Viteles, "The Cooperative Movement," *The Annals of the American Academy of Political and Social Science*, November, 1932, p. 131. (Issue, *Palestine: A Decade of Development*.)

signed by rotation to every kind of unskilled work. In some cases, however, even at the outset, the nature of the work, e.g., administration, excluded some members. Later, it was realized that to use skilled workers for unskilled work was wasteful; division of labor and assignment to permanent tasks became the practice. Another instance is the attitude toward personal ownership of wearing apparel. In the early days, clothing was regarded as common property and all articles of apparel were obtained from the general storeroom. Later, in most of the collective settlements each member retained his own garments and only working clothes were taken from the general store. Although there is equality of living standards within each collective settlement, differences have developed in standards of living as between one settlement and another. It may be borne in mind also that, while the inner organization of the *kvutzah* is on a socialist basis, the settlements are part of a society which is basically capitalistic and must adjust themselves to the conditions of the general economic life.

Another form of the cooperative settlement is the *moshav ovdim* (workers' settlement) which is only partly collective. This type of settlement reflects the views of the *Hapoel Hatzair*, a Labor grouping much influenced by Gordon's non-Marxist conceptions. Like the *kvutzah*, it is an instrument of colonization and absorption of Jewish workers, and includes many cooperative features. However, *moshav ovdim* gives greater range to private initiative and private property. The settlement as a unit leases the land from the Jewish National Fund but then subdivides it among a definite number of families. The leaseholder cannot sell the land or the equipment; if he wishes to leave the colony the land and equipment revert to the community. He may, however, turn it over to another family with the consent of the community. Purchasing and selling are cooperative; also there is some joint cultivation, e.g., in grain farming and afforestation. Chickens and cows belong to the individual settlers. In the main, each family cultivates its own leasehold and enjoys the profits of its own labor. In the course of time one family may accumulate more than another, either because of luck or greater ability, or a combination of both. On the other hand, taxation is graduated, so a part of the differences in earning is neutralized. In fine, in the *kvutzot,* both ownership and profits from cultivation are collective; in the *moshav,* ownership is collective but earnings are not pooled.

An essential element of the *moshav ovdim* philosophy is the non-employment of hired labor. Thus, although the family keeps profits earned, these profits must be made by the work of the members of the family themselves. The aim is to avoid the exploitation of labor. For this reason, as in the case of the collective settlements, no Arab labor is utilized. Eliezer Yaffe, a leader of the *moshav ovdim* movement, has expressed its purpose as follows: "What we are striving for are Jewish colonies in which there will be place for families of small farmers who work by themselves and not with the help of hired labor; and that in these colonies the workers' families will extract from their farms their bread and all their needs; they will extract it in an entirely economic manner, in use of land and in the application of labor. The colonies shall be built on national land which cannot be bought or sold and which belongs only to the worker as long as he works it." [33] The internal government of the workers' settlement is similar to that of the collective: the highest authority is the General Assembly which meets at least once a year. At that meeting the General Committee and the Council are elected. The former carries out the program of work decided upon by the Assembly and manages the business of the settlement; problems and complaints are brought before the Council and the final decision rests with the General Assembly.

At the end of the first decade there were 34 workers' agricultural settlements of both types. There were 17 workers' smallholders settlements with a population of 2,994, and 17 collectives with a population of 1,885. They were organized around three nationwide associations, each with its philosophy and political orientation: *Moshavim Ve-irgunim* (Settlements and Organizations). This represented the workers' smallholders settlements and cooperatives with a similar philosophy. In 1940, it included 46 settlements with 8,753 members. *Hakibutz Hameuhad* (The United Collective). This represented the main group of collectives of the *kvutzah* type. In 1940, it had 38 settlements and 8,957 members; *Hakibutz Haarzi Hashomer Hatzair* (The National Collective of the *Hashomer Hatzair*).

33. Eliezer Yaffe, "Hoshavei Ovdim," *Pirke Hapoel Hatzair*, Vol. VIII, 2, p. 187.

This organization represented the collectives with the *Hashomer Hatzair* philosophy, described later.[34] Although associated with the Labor Federation it constitutes a separate party which generally stands in opposition to the Palestine Workers' Party (*Miphleget Eretz Israel,* usually abbreviated as Mapai), which is the majority Labor party. In 1940, there were in this group 42 settlements with 4,902 members. In addition to these three organizations which were established in the first decade, there is a fourth grouping known as the *Hever Hakvutzot, Igud Gordonya* (Association of Collectives, Gordon Grouping). It represents the point of view of the "small *kvutzah*" as against the "large *kvutzah*." In 1940, there were 34 settlements with 2,819 members in this grouping.

The General Federation of Jewish Labor in Palestine

The General Federation of Jewish Labor in Palestine—generally referred to as the *Histadrut*[35]—is the organized expression of the Labor movement and of its national-social conceptions. It was formed in 1920 as an amalgamation of labor organizations that had developed in Palestine prior to the war. The *Report of the Experts of the Joint Palestine Survey* declared that the *Histadrut* had become "an arm of the Jewish Agency in Palestine." [36] With equal justice it might be said that the Zionist Organization became the instrument of the *Histadrut* in the fields of labor, immigration and colonization. The Jewish Labor Federation in Palestine is unique among labor organizations of the world, both in the comprehensiveness of its influence—it has organized the white collar, industrial and agricultural workers—and even more distinctively, in its combination of trade union purposes with Zionist ideals of rebuilding the country and with the socialist aim of establishing Palestine as a society of workers.

As expressed in its statutes: "The General Federation of Jewish Workers in Palestine unites and binds all the workers—

34. See below, p. 349.
35. The word *Histadrut* means "organization" and is the first word of the lengthy title *Histadrut Hakelalit shel Ha-ovdim Haivrim be-Eretz Israel,* which may be translated General Organization of the Jewish Workers of Palestine.
36. Leo Wolman, "The Labor Movement and Its Activities," *Reports of the Experts Submitted to the Joint Palestine Survey Commission,* Boston, 1928, p. 517.

who live by their own work and do not exploit the labor of others—for the purpose of conducting the economic, colonizing, and cultural activities of the working class in Palestine, with the aim of establishing a Jewish Workers' Society (*Hevrat Haovdim*) in Palestine. All the members of the Federation are at the same time members of their respective trade union." The further paragraphs of the statutes enumerate the following activities: trade union organization, including sick funds and mutual aid; industrial, agricultural and consumer cooperatives; development of cooperative farms; stimulation of workers' immigration; maintenance of relations with the Pioneer Movement (*halutz*) abroad; reception of immigrants and provision of employment after arrival; promotion of the Hebrew language and general cultural activity among the workers; publication of periodicals, trade papers and newspapers; maintenance of friendly relations with Arab workers in Palestine; the cultivation of bonds between the Jewish international and labor movements throughout the world.

The attempted combination of these varied purposes has presented peculiar problems and has led to paradoxical situations. In other countries, the purpose of the trade union was to protect the existing class of wage earners against the established employers. In Palestine, the *Histadrut* often had to help create the working class whose interests it would then protect, and for this reason had often to assume the function of entrepreneurs. It had to fix wage standards as well as to fight for them; and it was under the urgency of setting the standards at an economically feasible level. Trade unions in other countries are generally opposed to immigration; in Palestine, because of its function as an instrument of national upbuilding, the *Histadrut* was always the strongest supporter of a large Jewish immigration. In their relations with the Arabs, both because of their socialist ideology and their desire to avoid the competition of cheap labor, their aim was to raise the standard of wages and living. They carried out organizing activities among Arab workers; at the same time, in order to secure more places for Jewish immigrants, the *Histadrut* promoted a policy of employing Jewish labor only in Jewish enterprises.

There were beginnings of workers' organizations in the colonies in the 1880's and 1890's. These did not last long but are interesting because they foreshadowed the character of the subsequent labor movement: they combined self-help activities with elements of political organization. Beginning in the late 1890's and during the following decade there were attempts at trade union organization in Jerusalem in an effort to organize the printers for better conditions. At that time the printing industry worked mainly on production of Jewish religious books, and the employers did not hesitate to make use of the weapon of excommunication in their struggle against the workers. With the second wave of immigration which was associated with the abortive social-democratic revolution in Russia, the organization of the workers became more clearly political in character. In 1906, two party organizations, the *Hapoel Hatzair* and the *Poale Zion,* were formed; the former was social-democratic in its tendencies, and the latter, Marxist in its orientation. These party organizations fulfilled the purposes of trade unions and also supplied medical care. Several other organizations were formed about this time which contained a labor element. The *Hashofar* (The Trumpet) was founded in 1907 to defend the Jewish colonies from Arab marauders; the *Hahoresh* (The Plowman), founded in 1908, was an agricultural workers' association; and the *Ha'avodah* (Work) founded in 1909, emphasized the idea of cooperative settlement.

In 1911, an agricultural organization was formed under the name *Histadrut Haklait,* in Judea, later also in Galilee, which may be regarded as the precursor of the *Histadrut* of today. It embarked on a wide program embracing trade union activities, projects in colonization and cultural development. It showed continuity and growth, and in 1913 a sick fund, or *kupat holim,* was formed under its auspices. During the war, food shortages and the high prices of food led to the formation of the consumers' cooperative (*Hamashbir*), which was later incorporated as the purchasing agent for the cooperatives of the *Histadrut*. The connections between the various groups of agricultural workers' organizations in Judea, Samaria and Galilee were strengthened and some collective settlements and producers' cooperatives were formed. After the cessation of hostilities, a union was effected (in 1919) between the *Poale Zion* and the *Histadrut Haklait* under the title of *Ahdut Ha'avodah* (Union of Work). Finally, after the establishment of the Civil Administration and the beginning of the large immigration of workers, a conference to discuss the problem of unification was called in Haifa for *Hanukah* (December, 1920). It was at this conference that the *Histadrut,* or General Federation of Jewish Labor in Palestine, was formed as a nonpartisan workers' association.

Within the *Histadrut* there were several political groupings during the first decade. The *Ahdut Ha'avodah,* or Jewish Socialist Party, was the largest and comprised more than half of the membership; the *Hapoel Hatzair* (The Young Worker) was next in size and represented almost one quarter of the membership. A group in the original socialist party which had refused to merge with the *Ahdut Ha'avodah* constituted a more extreme socialist party and came to be known as *Poale Zion Smol* (Left Poale Zion). In the very early years there was a small communist group in the membership of the *Histadrut,* but when, under Russian influence, the party engaged in anti-British demonstrations and sought to provoke uprisings among the Arabs, it was expelled from the *Histadrut.*

Later, also, two new groupings, one more radical and the other religious, developed. The former, the *Hashomer Hatzair* (The Young Watchman) grew out of a Jewish youth movement founded in Austria, in which elements of the British Scouting Organization, the German *Wandervogel* movement, and Marxist socialism, were fused. Later, as the Jewish position in Eastern Europe deteriorated and the outlook in Palestine became more promising, *Halutz* Zionism was introduced as part of the synthesis and later became the dominant element. Groups of the *Hashomer Hatzair* began to arrive in Palestine in the early twenties, and in 1924 the first *Hashomer Hatzair* colony was established in Beth Alpha. A religious organization known as *Hapoel Hamizrahi* (*Mizrahi* Worker) was founded in 1922. At first it joined the *Histadrut,* but later left. The organization continued as an autonomous body working closely with the *Histadrut* and uniting in some of the activities.

There are also a number of labor organizations outside of the *Histadrut* and, in some cases, opposed to it. Of these, the most important are the Revisionists, whose extreme nationalist policy has led them to oppose any union organization which sets the worker against the employer. In the early 1920's many Revisionists were members of the *Histadrut;* in the 1930's, however, with the growing divergence in political ideas, they formed their own organization known as "Organization of the Nationalist Workers," in which, besides Revisionists, some General Zionists, Oriental Jews and other dissidents joined. The Revisionist workers' organization has its own unions, sick benefit funds, and labor exchanges. Oriental Jews have also attempted from time to time to organize separate unions, partly because of different standards of living and difference in social-religious attitudes; ambitions of local leaders also play a part. The extreme orthodox non-Zionist group, *Agudath Israel,* has established its own workers' organization which has conducted some union activities as well as colonization work.

At the time of its organization, the *Histadrut* took over the existing workers' institutions and infused new content into them. It also established new endeavors: training groups and labor exchanges for immigrants; a bureau of public works (*Misrad Kablani*) to carry out projects in afforestation, drainage, road construction and building; and a workers' bank for the development of cooperative enterprises. In 1923, the *Histadrut* organized itself as the *Hebrat Haovdim* (Society of Workers) which became a holding company directing and controlling the various economic activities.

At the end of the first decade the major economic institutions of the *Histadrut* were as follows:[37]

Kupat Holim (Sick Fund). The Sick Fund furnishes to its members and their families hospital and medical services, medicines, and pays sick benefits. It is maintained by fees collected from both employers and employees, and from the Zionist Organization. As noted, it was started in 1911; at that time it had a small membership of 150; by 1930 it had grown to 15,000 with a budget of about £50,000 per year. It is also concerned with the improvement of the sanitary and hygienic conditions of the workers' settlements. It maintains sanitaria, X-ray institutes, dental clinics and infant welfare stations.

Solel Boneh (Leveling and Building). This is a cooperative contracting agency which originated in road building and public works projects. The *Solel Boneh* was organized in March 1925 and in that year and the next its contracts aggregated nearly £600,000. Including the work done by the preceding building cooperatives, the total

37. Leo Wolman, "The Labor Movement and Its Activities," *op. cit.,* pp. 528 ff; Walter Preuss, *Die Juedische Arbeiterbewegung in Palestina,* Wien, Fiba Verlag, 1936, p. 296; I. Kanievsky, *Social Policy and Social Insurance in Palestine,* Tel-Aviv, 1942, p. 26.

amount of contracts handled was close to £1,400,000. However, it was forced into bankruptcy, partly because of poor management and over-anxiety to make work for immigrants. Some of its activities were taken over by the *Yakhin,* founded in 1927, which conducts the planting, irrigating and other work connected with citrus groves, and by the *Misrad Kablani,* a general contracting agency in Tel-Aviv. The *Solel Boneh* was re-established in 1934.

Hamashbir and Tnuvah (Consumers' and Marketing organizations). In the decade of the twenties, the *Hamashbir* operated retail stores throughout the country, purchased the products of the agricultural colonies, and sold them foodstuffs, clothing and machinery, etc. It thus performed the double function of a retail and wholesale cooperative and a cooperative marketing agency. It became involved in the difficulties of the *Solel Boneh,* and later reorganized, concentrating on the wholesale aspects. *Tnuvah* began to form as a separate division of the *Hamashbir.* Its primary purpose was to sell the products of the cooperative agricultural settlements, particularly milk and other dairy products.

Workers' Bank (Bank Hapoelim). The Workers' Bank was organized in May 1921 and is the financial institution of the labor cooperatives. Part of its support has come from the Zionist Organization which subscribed a good portion of its shares. During the first ten years of its existence the bank made loans of £P1,603,377, as follows: 1) for agricultural effort, £512,122; 2) for building and public works, £308,350; 3) to producing associations, £359,368; 4) to credit associations, £39,161; 5) to workmen's institutions *(Kupat Holim,* etc.), £329,770; 6) for miscellaneous purposes, £54,606.

The Labor Federation also conducted educational and cultural activities under a special committee which was during this period known as the *Vaadat Hatarbut* (Cultural Committee), organized in 1922. A system of kindergarten and elementary schools was established, which grew from one institution of 19 pupils in 1921 to some 55 schools with 1,500 pupils in 1929. While the Labor schools have representation on the Board of Education (*Vaad Hahinukh*) and receive a grant-in-aid, they are not fully maintained as are the General and *Mizrahi* schools. They fulfill the minimum essentials of the school program laid down by the Board of Education, but enjoy complete autonomy and are practically free from control or supervision.

The Cultural Committee of the Labor Federation has given particular attention to educational activities for adults. These include instruction in Hebrew for new immigrants, lectures in literature, fine arts, music and drama, and seminars for education in social and political questions. Reading rooms supplied with newspapers and books have been opened up, particularly in rural communities. Excursions to historic places in Palestine form an important part of the educational program. In 1925, a dramatic company, *Ohel* (The Tent), was organized and soon became the leading theatrical group in Palestine. In the same year the Labor daily *Davar* began publication. The *Histadrut* has also published many books on a variety of subjects of professional and general interest.

In 1925, the membership of the *Histadrut* was 9,000 and including wives numbered 10,085. In 1930, the number had grown to 20,200, or 25,400 with the wives included, constituting about three-fourths of the working population of Palestine. From the above description of its activities, the *Histadrut*, it will be seen, has something of the character of an autonomous society within the community of the Jewish national home: it has its settlements and other economic institutions; its hospitals, schools and cultural activities; its newspapers and political parties; its interests, loyalties, and its philosophy of life.

While the main cooperative endeavor in Palestine has been associated with the Labor Federation, the cooperative idea is widespread among other parts of the population. To a certain extent cooperative enterprises existed in Palestine even before the Zionist immigration. The new Jewish quarters in Jerusalem outside of the old city, established in the later decades of the 19th century, were initiated on a cooperative basis. Among the older, middle-class cooperatives are the wine cellars of Rishon le-Zion and Zikhron Jacob (1896) and the Pardess Cooperative Society of orange growers (1900). Both of these are marketing associations. There are numerous cooperative credit unions for every type of population—small trades, artisans, farmers and workers; the outstanding being the *Halvaah Vehisakhon* (loan and savings) with its main office in Jerusalem and branches in the towns and larger colonies. Although the basic structure of the Palestine economy is capitalistic and depends on private initiative, the influence of the Labor Federation and of the many cooperatives have greatly affected the spirit of the Jewish community in Palestine: mutual aid and group benefits involved in the cooperative form of organization have reduced inequalities, minimized competitive elements, and generally tended to mitigate the harsher aspects of the unrestrained competitive type of society characteristic of Western capitalism.

ECONOMIC DEVELOPMENT

The main effort of the Zionist Organization in developing the Jewish national home during the first decade was concentrated on land settlement and agriculture. It regarded the settlement on the land as a rooting of the people in the soil, as a means of normalizing Jewish life, and as the basis of a just as well as stable Jewish community life. Some attention was given to the development of trade and industry by the Palestine Zionist Executive, but the major development was left to private initiative. From the point of view of the transformation of the character of Jewish life and occupational distribution, the accomplishments in agriculture are the most striking. But from the point of view of the total economy of Palestine, the most significant changes have been in the fields of industry and commerce. In the last quarter of a century Palestine has definitely moved from a land nearly wholly devoted to agriculture to a semi-industrial country, and its position at the crossroads of three continents has inherent in it the potentialities of a great commercial development. This transformation of Palestine did not become apparent until after 1933, when the rise of Nazism led to a large capitalist immigration into Palestine; but the beginnings of the change were already in progress in the decade of the 20's. The concern of the Zionist agencies, however, was largely with land purchase and settlement.

Land Purchase and Reclamation

Article 6 of the Mandate charged the Palestine Administration with encouraging close settlement by the Jews on the land in cooperation with the Jewish Agency. Article 11, which deals with the general development of the country, directed the Administration to introduce an appropriate land system suitable to the promotion of intensive cultivation. The Mandate thus assumed that there was a connection between the encouragement of close settlement of Jews on the land and the general improvement and intensification of agriculture. The Jewish Agency on its part fully recognized the interrelations between the possibilities for large Jewish settlement on the land and the development of the land resources of Palestine generally for the benefit of the population as a whole and, more particularly, of the rural population. It took the view that "apart from more general considerations of a moral order it is essential in the interests of the Jewish National Home that the fellaheen should be raised to a higher standard of life. On a long view, the Jewish village cannot prosper unless the Arab village prospers with it." [38]

As noted in the preceding chapter, the Government's Department of Agriculture and Fisheries engaged in activities designed to improve agriculture: afforestation, stock and poultry breeding, veterinary and entomological services, regulation of water supply, etc. However, these measures hardly sufficed to improve the existing situation and contributed little to the intensive development required for encouraging new settlers in the spirit of the provisions of the Mandate. The main tasks in land reclamation, drainage, and agricultural experimentation were left to the Jewish organizations. Referring to the Arab sector, Mr. Ramsay MacDonald, speaking in the House of Commons in 1930, said: "If during the last few years the Administration had done its duty, closer Arab settlement would have been established by now and further development of the land would have been possible." [39] As for the Jews, Professor Rappard of the Permanent Mandates Commission observed "the Government had practically done nothing concrete . . . to encourage close settlement by Jews on the land. Government had not prevented it but he did not see that they had taken any positive action to encourage it." [40] In its report on the work of the Seventeenth Session, the Permanent Mandates Commission intimated that "the obligation to encourage close settlement by the Jews on the land implied the adoption of a more active policy which would develop the country's capacity to receive and absorb immigrants in larger numbers with no ill results. . . . It is quite clear, however, that the Jewish National Home, so far as it has been estab-

38. Jewish Agency, *Memorandum to the Palestine Royal Commission*, p. 128.
39. Great Britain, *Parliamentary Debates, Commons*, November 17, 1930, col. 117.
40. Permanent Mandates Commission, *Minutes of the Seventeenth Session*, 1930, p. 81.

lished, has in practice been the work of the Jewish Organisation . . . the Mandate seemed to offer other prospects to the Jews." [41]

The Mandate specifically mentions State lands and waste lands in connection with the encouragement of close settlement by Jews on the land. Despite this practically no lands were made available to the Zionist Organization for Jewish settlement during the first decade.[42] The list of lands claimed as State Domain, as estimated at this time, comprise an area of some 960,000 dunams.[43] Of this total, over 397,000 dunams were granted to Arab cultivators under the Beisan Land Agreement of 1921, while only 83,000 dunams were leased or promised to various Jewish organizations. Of the relatively small area granted to the Jews, some 65,000 dunams consisted of sand dunes of no agricultural value near Acco, Caesarea and Jaffa. Moreover, two of the concessions involving over 60,000 dunams—the Kabbara-Caesarea Concession to the Palestine Jewish Colonization Association and that of the Jaffa dunes to the colony of Rishon le-Zion—had already been granted before the war by the Turkish Government and were only confirmed by the British Administration.[44] In all, the Zionist bodies were granted 3,385 dunams—the Rushmia area in the Haifa subdistrict—which was leased to the Jewish National Fund.

The Jews had to purchase land for colonization purposes at high prices and then invest large sums in the work of reclamation to make the lands fit for settlement. The total Jewish hold-

---

41. *Ibid.*, p. 142.

42. In 1934, the Jewish Agency acquired the concession to the Lake Huleh area under conditions which required that the Jewish bodies would be responsible for reclaiming a certain part of the area reserved for Arab settlement. (See below, p. 691.)

43. According to a list provided by the Colonial Office to the Jewish Agency in 1930. (See Jewish Agency for Palestine, *Memorandum Submitted to His Majesty's Government*, May, 1930, p. 22.) A later estimate prepared by the Government of Palestine for the Palestine Royal Commission gives the State Domain as totaling 1,263,497 dunams. (See Great Britain, *Memoranda Prepared by the Government of Palestine*, London, 1937, Colonial No. 133, p. 192.)

44. Jewish Agency for Palestine, *Memorandum Submitted to His Majesty's Government*, May, 1930, p. 23. Beside the areas mentioned, it should be stated that the Government leased some 75,000 dunams to the Palestine Potash Company in connection with the exploitation of the minerals of the Dead Sea. The Palestine Potash Company, although established through Jewish initiative, is a public company in which there is a large non-Jewish as well as Jewish capital.

ings of land at the end of 1920, when the Land Register was reopened, were 650,000 metric dunams. During the next ten years, an additional 536,800 metric dunams were acquired. Thus, at the end of 1930, Jewish organizations and individuals owned close to 1,200,000 metric dunams. More detailed figures are available as of June 30, 1936.[45] At that time there were in Jewish hands outside of State lands, an area of 1,340,782 metric dunams, or roughly about five percent of the cultivable area of Palestine which is estimated to be about 26,300,000 metric dunams. The cultivable land in Jewish hands on June 30, 1936, in this case including the cultivable area of State lands, was estimated to be 1,040,070 metric dunams, or about one-ninth of the total area of cultivable land estimated by Government to be 8,760,000 dunams.[46]

The greater part of the land acquired by the Jews was purchased from large proprietors. Evidence of this is afforded by the figures of the Palestine Land Development Company through which the greater part of all land acquired by the Jews was purchased. According to their records, about 92 percent of the land was bought from large proprietors, of whom more than three-quarters were absentee landowners.[47] Moreover, in accordance with the Land Transfer Ordinance of 1921, all land transactions had to receive the consent of the Government; in the case of agricultural land leased to tenants, such consent was given only when the Register of Land was satisfied that "any tenants in occupation will retain sufficient land in the District or elsewhere for the maintenance of himself and his family." Once the transfer had been completed no obligation rested on the purchasers; nevertheless in certain cases the Jewish bodies added *ex gratia* payments to tenants when they felt this was justified. Despite these precautions,

---

45. Jewish Agency for Palestine, *Memorandum to the Palestine Royal Commission*, pp. 130 ff.

46. The Government—following Sir John Hope Simpson's *Report on Immigration, Land Settlement and Development*, pp. 21 and 22—defines cultivable land as "land which is actually under cultivation or which can be brought under cultivation by the application of the labour and financial resources of the average Palestinian cultivator." The Jewish Agency's estimate of the cultivable area of Palestine is larger than that of the Government. Accordingly, it holds that the Jews own a smaller proportion of the cultivable land than indicated in these figures.

47. Jewish Agency for Palestine, *Memorandum to the Palestine Royal Commission*, London, 1936, p. 139.

much was made before the hearings of the Shaw Commission of displacement of Arabs by Jewish purchasers. Later investigations indicated that there were some Arabs who had been displaced but their proportion was very small.[48]

The main point, however, is that while some families might have discontinued cultivation of the soil, the total number of Arabs living off the land in Palestine increased during the period of Jewish settlement. This is indicated by the fact that the number of non-Jews living in the rural communities increased considerably between the years 1922 and 1931. In 1922 the total number of non-Jews living in the rural districts amounted to 477,693; in 1931 the total was 602,387, an increase of 124,694. Furthermore, there is no substantial difference in the ratio of the rural to the urban population: in 1922 the rural non-Jewish population constituted 70.9 percent of the total non-Jewish population; in 1931 the ratio was 69.9. In other words, the increase in the rural population was practically all absorbed in the rural districts. Moreover, in the 1922 census, the figure for the rural population includes 103,000 Bedouins; in the 1931 census it includes only 66,553 Bedouins. The rural population of 1931 thus includes a larger number of settled families than the 1922 figures. It is not improbable that a substantial number of Bedouins became settled cultivators between 1922 and 1931; and of these some at least drifted from Beer Sheba and Trans-Jordan into the settled portions of Palestine.

Moreover, the 1931 census indicated that the increase in the Arab population has tended to be most marked precisely in those areas in which Jewish settlement was concentrated, as the following table shows.[49]

Sub-district	Non-Jewish Population 1922	1931	Increase
	Affected by Jewish Development		
Haifa	13,933	34,802	194%
Jaffa	13,619	30,519	124%
	Not Affected by Jewish Development		
Tulkarm	31,622	40,853	29%
Nablus	40,747	51,513	26%

48. See below, Chap. IX, p. 812.
49. Jewish Agency Memorandum, p. 251.

Although the major part of the land purchased by the Jews is counted as cultivable at the present time, a considerable part of it became so only as the result of the reclamation work done by the JNF, PICA, and private Jewish investors. Moreover, the work done in reclaiming Jewish land—such as draining of swamps, elimination of malaria, providing water supply, etc.—opened up surrounding districts occupied by Arabs which were previously uninhabitable. Rehovoth, one of the most prosperous of the Jewish colonies, was established on land which could never have been brought under cultivation "by the application of the labour and financial resources of the average Palestinian cultivator." Testifying before the Shaw Commission in 1929, Moshe Smilansky, one of the founders of Rehovoth, pointed out that thirty-eight years previously the colony which now supported some 2,500 Jewish settlers was a waste occupied by a dozen Arabs.[50] In "Jewish Colonization and the Fellah," Smilansky has also given us a graphic picture of the development of Hedera which was founded in 1890, a year before Rehovoth.[51]

The colony of Hedera has been established on lands which, like those of Mulebbis, seemed to be permanently unfit for human habitation. No Arab village could remain for any length of time on these fever-ridden lands, where all efforts at settlement ended in disaster. Not a single Arab village was to be found in the neighborhood, and the settlement of Circassians from Transjordan was in terrible condition and on the verge of extinction. The 30,000 dunams of Hedera lands were all a gigantic breeding-ground for malaria infection, and a source of danger to the whole district. When Jewish settlers acquired these lands, for which they paid 600,000 gold francs, they became the laughing-stock of the local wiseacres, and when they actually went out to settle there with their families amidst the fever-infested marshes, they were regarded as little short of mad. True, of the 540 original settlers, 214 perished in the first few years, but they have worked that miracle—they have made the desert blossom as the rose.

The green fields of Hedera now extend over an area of 50,000 dunams. There are 4,000 dunams of irrigated and 4,400 of non-irrigated plantations, and the largest eucalyptus forest in Palestine,

50. *Report of the Commission on the Palestine Disturbances of August 1929*, pp. 121–122.
51. M. Smilansky, *Jewish Colonisation and the Fellah*, Tel-Aviv, 1930, pp. 33–34.

having over half a million trees. On the border of the colony's lands, on the spot which was once one of the most poisonous of marshes, there now stands the railway station, through which Hedera sends and receives yearly not less than 1,500 wagon-loads of goods. The Railway brings to the colony building materials, fuel, fertilisers and various manufactured articles, and takes from the colony grain, water-melons, fodder-crops, almonds and oranges. The population numbers 1,200, consisting of farmers, workers, artisans, traders and professional men, in addition to hundreds of Arab workers who find permanent employment in the colony.

Some of the most fertile lands were covered with swamps at the time when the Jews purchased them. Striking examples of the drainage and reclamation work are the clearing of the Kabbara swamps in Samaria and the development of the Valley of Esdraelon. The former was carried out by PICA, which reclaimed some 4,000 metric dunams, making them suitable for intensive cultivation. The work of the Valley of Esdraelon was carried out by the Jewish National Fund, which reclaimed for settlement about 100,000 dunams in several blocs. Sir Herbert Samuel's description of this accomplishment has now become classic:[52]

The most striking result in this sphere that has been achieved during the last few years has been in the Valley of Esdraelon. This is a belt of rich deep soil which stretches for forty miles from the sea at the Bay of Acre eastwards down into the Jordan Valley; it is some nine miles abroad, between the range of Mount Carmel and the hills of Samaria in the South and the hills of Galilee about Nazareth and Mount Tabor in the North. When I first saw it in 1920 it was a desolation. Four or five small and squalid Arab villages, long distances apart from one another, could be seen on the summits of low hills here and there. For the rest the country was uninhabited. There was not a house, not a tree. Along a branch of the Hejaz railway, an occasional train stopped at deserted stations. A great part of the soil was in the ownership of absentee Syrian landlords. The River Kishon, which flows through the valley, and the many springs which feed it from the hillsides, had been allowed to form a series of swamps and marshes, and, as a consequence, the country was infested with malaria. Besides, public security had been so bad under

52. *Report of the High Commissioner on the Administration of Palestine, 1920–1925*, Colonial No. 15, London, 1925, pp. 34–35.

the former regime that any settled agriculture was in any case almost impossible.

By an expenditure of nearly £900,000 about 51 square miles of the valley have now been purchased by the Jewish National Fund and other organisations; twenty villages have been founded, with a population numbering at present about 2,600; nearly 3,000 dunams (about 700 acres) have been afforested. Twenty schools have been opened. There is an Agricultural Training College for Women in one village and a hospital in another. All the swamps and marshes within the area that has been colonised have been drained, and cases of malaria are proportionately rare. An active trade in dairy produce has sprung up, mostly finding a market, by means of the railway, in Haifa. The whole aspect of the valley has been changed. The wooden huts of the villages, gradually giving place to red-roofed cottages, are dotted along the slopes; the plantations of rapidly growing eucalyptus trees already begin to give a new character to the landscape; in the spring the fields of vegetables or of cereals cover many miles of the land, and what five years ago was little better than a wilderness is being transformed before our eyes into a smiling countryside.

Another type of problem presented itself in the hills, which were formerly terraced for vineyards and olive trees, but which are now almost bare. Despite the recognition of the difficulty of restoring the fertility of the hills, the Zionist Organization engaged in experimental colonization near Jerusalem: at Kiryat-Anavim on the road to Jaffa to the south, and Atarot on the road to Nablus toward the north. The hills were terraced and fruit trees planted; dairies supplied with pure-bred cattle were established, and poultry raising developed. A successful attempt at development of hill country was made by a private settler at Motza near Jerusalem which evoked commendation on the part of John Hope Simpson, despite the fact that the latter believed that colonization of the hills was, generally speaking, impractical from the economic point of view. Discussing the colonist's achievement "on what seemed to be sterile and barren rock," he says: "The trees and vines have flourished, and what was a wilderness without vegetation of any kind is now a fine orchard producing a large income for its proprietor. The result is the more praiseworthy in that the planter received no assistance from any Jewish or other sources, but created the property by his own exertions." [53]

53. John Hope Simpson, *op. cit.*, p. 78.

JEWISH AGRICULTURAL SETTLEMENTS IN 1920 AND 1929

(These tables are based on data given in *Palestine Land Settlement, Urban Development and Immigration,* Jewish Agency, London, July, 1930, pp. 48–51. The information given indicates 117 settlements; in the tables shown below some of these were omitted either because they are mentioned later as agricultural schools or because they do not fall strictly under the categories of agricultural settlements.)

	1920	1929		
	No. of Settlements	No.	Area	Population
Settlements According to Land Ownership				
PICA	26	32	381,881	20,248
JNF	13	47	155,628	6,230
Private	11	32	163,411	10,394
Total	50	111	700,920	36,872
Settlements According to Geographic Location				
Coastal Plain	26	51	372,642	29,129
Hill Country	4	7	17,998	240
Valley of Jezreel	2	27	137,245	4,305
Lower Galilee	11	17	109,503	2,004
Upper Galilee	7	9	63,532	1,194
Total	50	111	700,920	36,872
Settlements According to Type				
Moshavot[1]	28	47	466,163	29,087
Moshav Ovdim[2]	7	24	83,899	4,245
Kvutzot[3]	11	28	103,718	2,690
Miscellaneous	4	12	44,140	850
Total	50	111	700,920	36,872

1. *Moshavot*—villages in which both land and equipment are private property.
2. *Moshav ovdim*—workers' settlements.
3. *Kvutzot*—communal settlements.

Growth of Agricultural Settlements and Development of Intensive Farming

Through large investments of capital and by dint of hard labor, the colonies were greatly enlarged, in number, in area of cultivation, and in population. At the end of 1919, there were some fifty agricultural settlements with an area of 425,000 dunams and some 13,000 inhabitants. By the end of 1929 these had increased to 110 colonies with an approximate area of 700,000 dunams and about 37,000 inhabitants. The tables on page 374 indicate the distribution in accordance with sponsorship and type of settlement. The largest group consisted of *moshavot,* that is, villages in which both the land and equipment were privately owned. In this group there were 47 settlements with a population of over 29,000; the *moshav ovim* type (workers' settlements) numbered 24 with 4,250 inhabitants; there were 28 *kvutzot* or communal villages with a total population of 2,700.

Besides these settlements there were a number of agricultural schools and farms. The most important of these was the Mikveh Israel Agricultural School, founded in 1870 under the auspices of the *Alliance Israélite Universelle.* This institution owned an area of 650 acres and engaged in every type of agriculture. During the decade after the establishment of the British Administration the work was expanded along several lines including: extension of the area under fodder cultivation and citrus plantation; improvement of cattle by crossing with Dutch breeds; introduction of high breeds of poultry and the improvement of apiculture. A Zionist Agricultural School for women in Nahalal was founded in 1924 and is now supported by the WIZO. The school occupies an area of 125 acres and embraces the principal branches of agriculture—cereal cultivation, plantation, vegetable growing, flower gardening, and apiculture. Two "children's villages" were established, one at Ben-Shemen maintained by a German organization, and the other at Meir Shfeya supported by Junior Hadassah of America.[54] The children's villages combine general education with agricultural training in which practical work and self-labor occupy a prominent part. Six women's agricultural training

54. A third children's village was maintained for a few years at Ain Harod in the Emek Israel, but was later closed.

farms were also established; the principal phases of agriculture on which they specialized were dairy, poultry, vegetable raising and nursery gardening.

For the purpose of research in agriculture, the Zionist Organization established in 1921 the Institute of Agriculture and Natural Science (generally called the "Experimental Station"). The offices, laboratories, the citrus and several other divisions are at Rehovoth where about 1,300 dunams are devoted to plantation, field crops and vegetables; the major agricultural division is at Gevat in the Emek (Valley of Esdraelon) where about 1,360 dunams are devoted primarily to experiments in grain culture; in addition, about 2,000 dunams in various parts of the country are maintained for experimental purposes. The research covers a very wide field of study: insect pests and noxious plants; disease-causing fungi and bacteria; types of soil in different parts of the country; soil improvement, crop rotation, fertilizers, systems of irrigation; seed varieties, selection of citrus plants; poultry husbandry, etc. In addition to the research and scientific work, an Extension Department is maintained for the purpose of increasing productivity and profitability of agriculture through demonstration films, publications, lectures, courses and tours of farms.

The purpose of the experimental work is to find suitable types of cultivation and the most economical farm units for each area, to improve the yield of grains and better the breeds of poultry and cattle. The Jewish experts are working toward mixed farming units; however, their plans provide for three different cores adapted to different agricultural conditions: the *falha* (grain) zone, mainly in the valleys; a plantation zone, in the coastal plain; orchards and vines, in the hill country. For the *falha* zone, a three crop rotation plan is recommended instead of the two crop rotation traditionally practiced by the Arab *fellah*. Moreover, the endeavor is to diversify the farm production by including dairying, cattle raising, poultry, plantation, and vegetable growing. This plan would make the farmer less dependent on a single product and the rotation of crops would lead to conservation of the soil. The effort to diversify agriculture involves more economic use of water resources. As a result of the changed methods of cultivation, the Jewish farmers produced considerable quantities of milk, eggs, chickens, table grapes and vegetables. In 1920, the Jewish farmers frequently did not raise a sufficient quantity of these commodities for their own use.[55]

The center of the diversified farming, with grain culture as the core, was in the settlements in the Valley of Esdraelon supported by the Zionist Organization. The plantation area on the coastal plain was to a large extent under private ownership, although some of the settlements were assisted by PICA and other public organizations. The plantation colonies established before the First World War generally contained two types: non-irrigated plantations, such as grape vines, almond trees and olives; and irrigated plantations of citrus fruits, mainly oranges. Before 1920 about four-fifths of the area of plantation was devoted to the non-irrigated plantations. In the decade after the establishment of the British Administration the citrus area was greatly increased, from about 15,000 dunams to 58,000 dunams,[56] many plantations being now devoted exclusively to the citrus industry. Traditional methods of cultivation were replaced by systems used in advanced countries, particularly those in the United States, with the use of machines in preparing the land for planting and in the cultivation of the groves. On the completion of the Rutenberg Power Development, electric motors, cheaper and easier to run, replaced the gasoline motors formerly used for irrigation. More careful selection of saplings was introduced and plant diseases brought under better control. Mechanized cleaning, sizing and packing gradually replaced hand grading. New markets in Europe were developed, and cooperation among exporters—in which Arab growers participated—reduced competition and decreased freight costs.[57]

Farming in the hills is still in the experimental stage, and

55. J. Elazari-Volcani, "Jewish Colonization in Palestine," *op. cit.*, p. 89.

56. Jewish Agency, *Palestine Land Settlement, Urban Development and Immigration*, Memorandum submitted to Sir John Hope Simpson, London, July, 1930.

57. Under normal conditions a family in Palestine can be maintained by a grove of 10 to 20 dunams of citrus. However, prices are subject to large fluctuations since the major part of the crop is exported. In the second decade the citrus industry was over-expanded. While under normal conditions the larger crop might have been absorbed in the European markets, the onset of the Ethiopian War brought about a crisis in the citrus industry and the Second World War led to its virtual bankruptcy.

there has been severe criticism on economic grounds of the two settlements established by the Zionist Organization in the hill country. Nevertheless, the local Jewish experts insist that the hills will ultimately be proved to be cultivable on an economic basis. History supports this contention, for in ancient times—in fact, until the seventh century when the Arabs conquered Palestine—the hill country was thickly populated. Due to neglect of the terraces and the destruction of the forests, the hills have suffered from severe erosion as the heavy winter rains each year sweep away the remaining layers of the soil. While admittedly a great deal of patient labor is involved in building up the soil again through terracing and afforestation, experts are agreed that this can be done. Dr. W. C. Lowdermilk, of the Soil Conservation Service of the United States, has recently written: "In spite of their desolation, the high lands of Palestine can still play an important part in the rebuilding of the country. Even where remaining soil, after centuries of erosion, is too thin for grain or vegetable crops, this extensive area is suited for grazing and forestry management and for certain tree crops which may improve the food balance of the country directly or indirectly." [58]

The Jewish experts believe that the farms in the hills should be based largely on fruit plantations supplemented by poultry raising and dairying. In addition to grapes, the most suitable trees for cultivation in the hills are the olive, fig, nut (almond, walnut and pistachio), and last, but by no means least, the carob tree. This humble fruit, more popularly known as "St. John's bread," is a large pod rich in honey, and has a high food value as a forage plant for livestock. Once the problem of feed —the transportation of which into the hills is now costly—is solved, the hilly country can become suitable for high yielding dairy and poultry farms, for which the climate is ideal.[59]

Preliminary to the formation of the enlarged Jewish Agency,

---

58. W. C. Lowdermilk, *Palestine, Land of Promise*, Harpers, 1944, p. 45.

59. For cultivation of the hill country, see Joseph Weitz, "Settlement in the Hill Country," in *Palestine Land Settlement, Urban Development and Immigration*, Jewish Agency, London, 1930, pp. 55–56; also a recent article with a more carefully elaborated plan in *Palestine and Middle East*, April, 1944; and J. Elazari-Volcani, "Planned Agricultural Settlement in the Hill Region" (mimeographed), Jewish Agency, September, 1938.

the non-Zionist leaders dispatched a commission of agricultural experts to Palestine under the chairmanship of Dr. Elwood Mead, United States Commissioner of Reclamation.[60] In their conclusions they expressed the view that Jewish colonization in the hills was not satisfactory from an economic point of view and recommended that no additional settlements in the hills should be attempted. They also objected to some of the administrative arrangements of the Zionist Organization with the settlements as "unbusinesslike" and expressed doubt as to the economic soundness of colonies "organized on the communistic basis," as the *kvutzot* were described. However, the major conclusion of the Joint Palestine Survey Commission was favorable: while Jewish agriculture in Palestine was not as yet paying its own way, in every case sufficient progress had been made to give assurance that under right methods success was possible. As their main judgment they stated: "That the success of Jewish agriculture has been demonstrated along the Coastal Plain, in the *Emek,* and in the Valley of the Jordan where water for irrigation has been made available . . . The accomplishments of the Jewish people toward establishing agriculture on a modern basis in Palestine deserve the heartiest commendation of all. In the face of unusual difficulties they have laid the foundations of a Jewish life on the soil that will be the controlling factor in the successful upbuilding of the Jewish national home." [61]

Some of their criticisms on methods of administration were undoubtedly well taken. In their strictures of the cooperative settlements considerable prejudice on social grounds seems to have entered into their judgment. Sir E. J. Russell, outstanding British economist, whose "Report on A Visit to Palestine" is included in the *Reports,* appears to have had a better appreciation of the human elements that entered into the success of Jewish colonization. Among the factors which he mentions as giving promise of good prospects for Palestine's agriculture,

---

60. Other experts were Dr. J. G. Lipman, Director of the Agricultural Experiment Station at the New Jersey College of Agriculture; A. T. Strahorn, Soil Technologist, U. S. Department of Agriculture; Prof. Frank Adams, in charge of Irrigation Investigations and Practice, University of California; K. A. Ryerson, Horticulturist, Agricultural Experiment Station, Service Technique, Haiti; and C. Q. Henriques, Irrigation Engineer of the Zionist Organization in Palestine.

61. *Reports of the Experts, op. cit.,* pp. 40–41.

he emphasizes "the deep attachment of the people and especially of many of the younger ones, to the land which would enable them to do much more than ordinary pioneer farmers." Moreover, while insisting, as do the other experts, that the agricultural work should be done as economically as possible, he nevertheless points out that in a total evaluation of the Zionist accomplishment its concern for human factors must be taken into consideration. The following are paragraphs from his report:[62]

This distinguishes the Jewish colonization of Palestine from any other with which I am acquainted; the nearest approach, which however, is a long way off, being the Mormon colonization of Utah. In any part of Canada or of the United States (apart from Utah) a farmer will loudly sing the praises of his farm, describing it as undoubtedly the best spot on earth and will then immediately offer to sell it so that he can go elsewhere. Farmers are perpetually moving from East to West, from South to North and vice versa. In Palestine, so far as I could see this is not happening . . .

Every settlement of a new country is bound to be costly especially when, as in Palestine, there had previously been such mismanagement and misgovernment. The price may be paid in money or in human suffering. In older settlements the first colonists, especially the women and children, have often suffered greatly; the story of the first years of the Red River settlement, now one of the richest parts of Canada, while a stirring record of human achievement is a pathetic tale of human suffering; the Mormon settlement endured some tragic episodes in the beginning as also have others. In Palestine, the price of colonization has been paid in large part in money; the Palestine Zionist Executive and other agencies that have provided the funds have the satisfaction of knowing that the human suffering has been minimized. I have rarely seen healthier looking children.

It may be said that three propositions which had been the subject of much question in 1920 appeared to have been demonstrated in the course of the first decade of the intensive development of the Jewish national home under the auspices of the Zionist Organization: 1) that the Jews, despite their long separation from the soil, could become good farmers again; 2) that Palestine, despite the long period of neglect and misgovernment under Arab and Turkish rule, could be restored to its original fertility; 3) that the social concepts of the young Jew-

62. Sir E. J. Russell in *ibid.*, pp. 488, 490.

ish pioneers imbued with labor ideals was an important factor in the success of the agricultural colonies—and not, as some of the experts believed, an economic handicap from the practical point of view.

Industry and Commerce

Before the First World War, there were some 1,235 establishments but these were mainly small, employing only a few workers each. The enterprises were chiefly concentrated in four groups: olive and sesame oil presses and soap manufactories; food, drink and tobacco; textiles and apparel; and metal work. The primitive character of the operations is illustrated in the olive and sesame oil industry, where the presses were operated by the circumambulation of a blinkered donkey or camel. It is probable that no more than five percent of the Palestine community were engaged in some form of industrial production before the First World War. According to the 1931 census, the population dependent on industry represented about 14 percent of the total population. A government census of industries was taken in 1927 which showed that the number of industrial establishments had grown to 3,505. Of these, 2,395 were Arab enterprises, of which more than half (1,373) had been founded after the war. The growth in Jewish industrial establishments is even more vigorous, these having developed from 213 enterprises in the pre-war period to 1,110 in 1928. These figures do not take into account the size of the industry; taking capital investment as the index, the Arab industries grew from 100 to 312; while the Jewish industries grew from 100 to 459.[63] The average size of the industrial enterprise increased and there was a tendency to substitute motor power for hand and animal power.

A survey of Jewish industry was made in March 1939 by the Statistical Department of the Jewish Agency. This showed that there were 2,475 establishments in which 10,968 employers and workers were engaged. The capital invested in these industries was £2,235,000 and the value of the annual production was estimated at £2,510,000. The industries were concentrated in the urban localities in which there were 2,276 enterprises giving work to 9,362 persons. The industries are divided into

---

63. D. Horowitz, "Industry in Palestine, Achievement and Possibilities," (mimeographed) Economic Research Institute, Jewish Agency for Palestine, Tel-Aviv, 1941.

three groups: Group A—enterprises selling their products direct to private consumers, employing less than five persons; Group B—industries employing from five to nine workmen and selling only part of their products direct to private consumers; Group C—industries that employ more than ten men and work for the wholesale market. From the following table it will be seen that Group C, although forming only six percent of the total number of enterprises, represents the most important part of the industry, accounting as it does for 38 percent of the total number of persons employed, 40 percent of the wages paid, 45 percent of the production, and 59 percent of capital invested.[64]

	Number of Enterprises	Persons Employed	Invested Capital £P	Annual Wage Bill £	Value of Finished Articles £
Group A	1,725	3,200	134,563	180,039	371,409
Group B	418	2,626	274,915	110,435	526,125
Group C	133	3,536	589,426	185,978	737,933

The table below indicates the distribution among the various industries:[65]

JEWISH INDUSTRIAL ENTERPRISES IN ALL TOWNS IN 1929

Industries	Number of Enterprises	Number of Employees	Value of Production	Capital
Food	177	1,336	394,701	202,057
Textiles	40	533	85,561	30,929
Clothing	486	1,359	163,030	72,935
Metallurgical	454	1,413	229,392	115,975
Wood	298	1,032	162,025	57,739
Leather	380	1,010	207,769	95,178
Printing & Stationery	121	1,030	126,328	141,747
Chemical Industry	24	235	70,755	31,254
Stone and Cement	55	605	105,601	199,493
Electricity	13	66	12,356	5,986
Miscellaneous	228	603	77,938	45,611
Total	2,276	9,362	1,655,462	998,904

64. Jewish Agency, *Palestine Land Settlement, Urban Development and Immigration*, pp. 59 ff.
65. *Ibid.*

The Palestine industries are partly based on native resources, partly established to meet the consumer needs of the European immigrants, and partly the creation of skills brought in by the Jews. In the first category are the industries based on agricultural products. The following are several large industries based on agriculture:

1. *Wine cellars of Rishon le-Zion and Zikhron-Jacob.* About £200,000 was invested in these wine cellars originally established by PICA and then transferred to the colonists. The annual turnover is about £65,000. The number of workmen employed was 70. The cellars produced approximately 40,000 hectolitres of wine a year. In addition to the manufacture of wine, the cellars have started the production of concentrated grape juice and are engaged in the distillation of alcohol from grapes.

2. *Grands Moulins and Matzoth Bakeries.* These flour mills at Haifa were also established by PICA with an investment of some £200,000 and the annual turnover about £240,000. The daily capacity of the mills is 50 tons of flour and 70 workers are employed during eight months of the year and an extra 20 workers during the four other months.

3. *The Shemen Oil Press.*[66] This establishment is engaged in the manufacture of refined olive and sesame oil, toilet soap and oil cakes for cattle fodder. It has a nominal capital of about £100,000 and in all £150,000 have been invested in buildings and machinery. The annual turnover is about £170,000 and its annual output is 3,000 tons of oil, 3,500 tons of cakes, and 900 tons of several varieties of soap. The establishment at the end of the first decade employed about 160 workers.

In another category may be placed the enterprises developed in Palestine for the creation of electric power, the exploitation of the mineral resources of the Dead Sea and the use of limestone for the making of cement. Although established by Jews, these industries also employ Arabs as workers.

The Palestine Electric Corporation, Ltd. This company, formed by Pinhas Rutenberg, first began operations in 1923. It obtained the concession for development of the hydroelectric resources of Palestine. Through a subsidiary company it also holds the concession for

66. This large oil press situated in Haifa was established by Jews but later passed into the hands of an international group with strong British participation. The management and labor, however, have remained Jewish. *Ibid.,* p. 59.

the utilization of the waters of the Yarkon River north of Tel-Aviv for irrigation purposes. The company began supplying electricity to Tel-Aviv, Jaffa, Haifa and Tiberias from power plants run by Diesel engines. However, its main project was to develop the hydroelectric plant at the juncture of the Yarmuk and Jordan below the Sea of Galilee. In 1926 the company sold 2,344,000 kilowatt hours of electricity. In 1930, 5,352,630 kilowatt hours were sold throughout Palestine, exclusive of Jerusalem.[67]

Palestine Potash Syndicate. This was organized as a British corporation in 1929 with exclusive rights to extract the minerals from the Dead Sea, which contained large quantities of potassium salts, bromine and magnesium. A concession was granted by the Governments of Palestine and Trans-Jordan to Mr. Moses Novomeysky, a Russian-Jewish mining engineer, and to Major T. G. Tulloch, who represented British interests, which have invested considerable amounts in the syndicate. The Palestine Economic Corporation was one of the founders and the largest single stockholder. The Palestine Potash Company began operations in 1930; in 1931 the syndicate started its first factory for the refining of bromides.

Portland Cement Company, 'Nesher' Ltd. This company owes its existence to Mr. Michel Pollak, a Russian-Jewish capitalist. The factory, located near Haifa, is one of the largest and most important factories in Palestine. About £P350,000 was invested in Nesher in the middle 1930's. The capacity of this factory at the end of the first decade was 120,000 tons a year. It not only supplied most of Palestine's cement requirements, but began to export to other countries as well. It employed over 700 workers, Arab and Jewish.

As A. P. S. Clark, manager of the Palestine branch of Barclay's Bank, notes: "The third category is the most interesting from the point of view of the postwar development of Palestine —the category of industries that have been made possible primarily by the knowledge and skill of the new immigrants—and it includes a host of articles never before made (many never before seen) in Palestine." [68] He gives a variegated list of manufactures in Palestine introduced by the Jewish immigrants, among which are: Iron bedsteads, biscuits, preserved fruits and fruit juices, cigarettes, refrigerators, aerated waters,

---

67. The concession to supply electricity to Jerusalem was allotted to Euripides Mavrommatis, a Greek subject, to whom the Turkish Government had granted a concession in 1914.

68. A. P. S. Clark, "Commerce, Industry and Banking," *The Annals of the American Academy of Political and Social Science,* November, 1932, pp. 98–99 (Issue, *Palestine: A Decade of Development*).

knitted goods, concrete pipes, stoves, bathing costumes, praying shawls, neckties, umbrellas, candles, scouring powder, fertilizers, poultry feed, perfumes, matches, lithographic stones, automobile bodies, mirrors, envelopes, toothpaste, insect powder.

The following may be selected to indicate the degree of growth:

Hosiery. Before the First World War there was only one establishment making hosiery in Palestine, operated by the owner with a capital of £15. In 1931 there were six hosiery factories, with a combined capital of nearly £56,000, employing over two hundred people. In 1925 the value of the imports of hosiery amounted to £52,700, while the exports were only £400. In 1928 the imports had decreased to £42,400, while the exports had increased to £17,500.

Cardboard Boxes. Seven establishments for making cardboard boxes, particularly for cigarettes, were established. This led to a decrease in the import of cigarette and tobacco boxes from £22,200 in 1927 to only £200 in 1931. At the same time exports rose from nothing in 1926 to £600 in 1927 and £2,234 in 1931.

Handbags and Wearing Apparel. A factory for making leather handbags was established in 1927. Exports began in 1928 with £900 of goods, increasing to £3,900 in 1929; to over £16,000 in 1931. Similarly, the export of wearing apparel went up from £2,200 in 1925 to almost £16,000 in 1931.

Artificial Teeth. A factory for artificial teeth was established in 1926 by a Mr. Blum of Philadelphia. It represents an example of a successful industry which depends on labor and skill and in which the main element is not the cost of material or transportation. The factory, which is in Tel-Aviv, exports to many cities in the Near East and to Europe. In 1927 the value of its exports was £1,000, increasing year by year until it exceeded £16,000 in 1931.

Building activity formed an important industry in this period of immigration. During the period 1924–1928, in accordance with Government reports, a total of £4,873,700 was invested in building in the cities: in Tel-Aviv, £2,224,000; in Jerusalem, £1,558,000; in Haifa, £498,700; in Jaffa, £458,000; and in Tiberias and Safed, over £135,000. In Tel-Aviv the building was done entirely by Jewish labor, although the materials were to no small extent purchased from Arabs. In the cities of mixed population it is probable that the building operations by the Jewish section were larger than their proportion in the population. Around the old cities, new Jewish suburbs grew up, built largely by Jewish labor and capital. A great deal of new building also went on in the Jewish rural sections; over half a million pounds in accordance with the estimate made by the *Vaad Leumi*. In a report submitted to the Permanent Mandates Commission in 1930, the *Vaad Leumi* estimated that the Jewish community had invested over £5,000,000 in building houses for new settlers in the decade ending with the year 1929.[69]

Along with the development of industry went an expansion in commerce. In 1913 the imports amounted to £1,616,000, and the exports to some £1,093,000. In 1920 the imports had increased to approximately £5,550,000, and the exports were reduced to £771,700. In 1930 imports had further increased to almost £7,000,000, while the exports amounted to nearly £2,000,000. The large increase in imports was due in part to the demand for consumers' goods for the larger Jewish population, but in major degree to the importing of industrial machinery, electrical plants, wood for orange cases, fertilizers, etc., i.e., goods which improved the internal productive capacity of the country. It is noteworthy that the imports during this period include raw materials used in manufacture, not only consumers' goods, which was universally the case formerly. Chemical fertilizers required for the expanding citrus plantations are a case in point: in 1921, the import of chemical fertilizers amounted to £12,462; in 1929, it had risen to over £59,396. An indication of the expanding industry is given by the imports of motor cars: in 1914, there was only one automobile in the whole country; from 1922 through 1931, over 6,400 automobiles were imported, mostly from the United States.

The so-called "adverse" balance of trade, i.e., excess of imports over exports, during the first decade was considerable. This adverse balance was covered in a number of ways: by capital brought in by the settlers; incomes derived by some of the immigrants from investments in their countries of origin; money spent by pilgrims and tourists; remittances received by religious organizations, orphan homes and hospitals; income of the various Zionist bodies. It has been conservatively estimated that in the ten years between 1919 and 1929 "the

---

69. The National Council (*Vaad Leumi*) of the Jews of Palestine, *Memorandum Submitted to the Permanent Mandates Commission of the League of Nations*, London, June, 1930, p. 8.

amount of capital brought into Palestine *by Jews alone* amounted to no less than £40,000,000." [70] Thus, the heavy balance of trade against Palestine was partly righted through these forms of income usually referred to as "invisible exports." An unfavorable balance of trade of the dimensions indicated would generally be regarded as symptomatic of an unsound economy. However, the special conditions surrounding the development of Palestine make it a not abnormal situation.[71]

The Jewish bodies have complained that the Government tariff policy was not conducive to a development of export trade. Palestine's customs tariff remained one of the lowest in the world. Moreover, in accordance with Article 18 of the Mandate, Palestine had to admit without discrimination the products of all members of the League of Nations. It thus, in its initial stage, had a largely unprotected and unsupported industry which had, in the period under discussion, to meet high tariffs, quotas, bilateral agreements and other obstacles of international trade which developed in the postwar period. The Joint Palestine Survey Commission pointed out that it was essential in Palestine, as in other countries, that infant industries should enjoy some measure of protection in their initial stages. Without suggesting that protective duties should be levied indiscriminately they concluded that: "The judicious use of tariffs for the encouragement of industries having a reasonable prospect of establishing themselves on a self-supporting basis, will have a beneficial effect on the condition of life in Palestine, and will be to the advantage of the population as a whole." [72]

In summing up significant points about the development of Jewish industry in Palestine, the *Memorandum* submitted by the Jewish Agency to Sir John Hope Simpson in July 1930 makes the following points:[73]

1) Jewish industry in Palestine, in the main, a postwar growth, was fairly well established, as evidenced by the fact that there was no unemployment and that there had been no failures of any im-

70. A. P. S. Clark, *op. cit.*, pp. 101–102.
71. For discussion of this point, see below, p. 729.
72. *Reports of the Experts, op. cit.*, p. 108.
73. Adapted from Jewish Agency, *Palestine Land Settlement, Urban Development and Immigration*, pp. 83–84.

portance. In 1930 it directly employed some 14,700 people who, with their dependents, constituted a population of 33,000. It had absorbed about one-third of the postwar immigration.

2) Jewish industry had filled an economic vacuum and was not dependent on taking away any occupation from Arabs. On the contrary, the development of the Jewish town population had provided a good market for the *fellahs'* agricultural products and further growth of Jewish industry indirectly gave additional occupation to Arabs.

3) "Absorptive capacity" with reference to industry could only be thought of in dynamic terms. The industrial capacity of the country depended "on the willingness and ability of Jewish capitalists to start industries which they understood and the products of which they could market, and of Jewish labor to come in and work in these industries." There were great prospects for the future provided Government would encourage the immigration of men of experience and skill and offer protection for the nation's industries. In order to further the development of industry "the immigration policy of the Government of Palestine must be *creative*, not *contemplative*; *active*, not *passive*; *bold*, not *timid*."

HEALTH AND EDUCATION

Jewish Health Services

Jewish health activities were conducted by two bodies—the *Kupat Holim* of the Labor Federation, and Hadassah, the latter organization carrying the main responsibility for supplying the health services for the Jewish section of the population. Toward the end of the decade the Jewish health work was coordinated by a Health Council (*Vaad Ha-Briut*) constituted by the Palestine Zionist Executive. Its function was to advise on medical policy and coordination of the work and to maintain contact with the Government Department of Health.

The membership of the *Kupat Holim* grew from 2,000 in 1920 to 18,000 a decade later. Counting the families, it provided health services to about 30,000 persons. At the end of the first decade the budget of the *Kupat Holim* was about £60,000, of which almost half was contributed by the members and workers' cooperatives; a third by the *Keren Hayesod* and Hadassah, the remainder being from employers' contributions, patients' fees, and miscellaneous. After 1930 the *Keren Haye-*

sod contribution was reduced and in 1932 ceased entirely. In the latter years of the decade of the 1930's the workers provided over four-fifths of the entire income, with one-fifth coming from employers' contributions and miscellaneous. Contrary to practice in other countries with regard to similar organizations, no support was given by Government. Five out-patient departments were maintained in the principal cities, and physicians and nurses were provided for over fifty rural districts. A central hospital was maintained in the *Emek* (Valley of Esdraelon) and two convalescent homes were established. In 1930, 73 physicians, 49 nurses, and 9 pharmacists were employed.

The Hadassah Medical Organization, after its reorganization in 1921, expanded its activities continuously throughout the decade. The following is a brief summary of the main branches of its work.

Hospital Service. Five hospitals were maintained in the cities (Jerusalem, Tel-Aviv, Haifa, Tiberias and Safed) with clinics, laboratories and pharmacies attached. It also maintained a rural service in more than fifty colonies. In 1930 it had a staff of 44 physicians, 127 nurses, 41 public health nurses and over 200 lay and technical staff.

The Nurses' Training School. The Nurses' Training School was established by Henrietta Szold in 1918. At the outset it admitted students with an elementary school education, but later changed this requirement to the completion of a high school course. In 1930 the school had graduated 135 nurses and had earned the reputation of being one of the two nursing schools of high standards in the Near East.[74] In 1936, in honor of the founder's seventy-fifth birthday, it was re-named the *Henrietta Szold Hadassah School of Nursing*.

The Straus Health Center. In 1929 the Nathan Straus and Lina Straus Health Center for All Races and Creeds was opened in Jerusalem. The buildings were provided through a gift of £50,000 presented by Mr. Nathan Straus of New York. The Center has as its object the coordination of preventive health services in Palestine and the dissemination of health information. It operates a prenatal and health welfare service, serves as headquarters for the Jerusalem school hygiene work and for the Clara Wachtel Dental Clinic. Its program of work includes orthopedics, education in nutrition, sex

---

74. In the opinion of the Executive Secretary of the International Association of Graduate Nurses. (See Hadassah Medical Organization, *Twenty Years of Medical Service to Palestine, 1918–1938*.)

hygiene and mental hygiene clinics. A pasteurization plant opened in 1931 is also housed in the Center.[75]

Infant Welfare Stations. The first Infant Welfare Station was established in Jerusalem in 1921. The Station, directed by an American nurse trained in public health, covered the field of prenatal, postnatal, maternity and pre-school care. By 1927 Hadassah Medical Organization was maintaining 17 Infant Welfare Stations in Palestine.

School Hygiene and School Luncheons. Practical courses in hygiene were organized in the schools, the work being done by specially trained nurses. A school luncheon project was instituted in 1923 with the object of providing at least one adequate meal a day for undernourished children, and educating the child in the selection of proper foods and in proper eating habits. This program was later coordinated with cooking classes and domestic science courses.

Playgrounds. In 1925, through funds contributed by Mrs. Bertha Guggenheimer of New York, a playground was opened in the old city of Jerusalem, designed to provide facilities for play for both Jewish and Arab children. In 1928 Hadassah took over the administration of the Guggenheimer playground funds and later further developed this work in other cities. Hadassah also supervised a number of playgrounds maintained by local communities.

Hadassah played a leading part in the reduction of the incidence of trachoma and malaria, the two major endemic diseases. Trachoma, not infrequently causing blindness, was widespread both among the Arabs and the Jews, though the incidence was smaller among the latter. In the Government schools attended by Arabs, 68 percent of the children in the towns and 75 percent of those in the villages suffered from this disease in 1922. The incidence was somewhat reduced by Government activity, but in 1928 at least half of the children in the towns and almost three-quarters in the villages were still afflicted. Although there was some improvement in the following years, the situation was still bad a decade later: in 1937, the incidence in the town schools was 59 percent, and in the villages 73 percent. Hadassah attacked the problem of trachoma more successfully, its work being done through the schools. The following tables indicate great improvement in

---

[75]. In 1928, Mr. Straus also presented £15,000 to Tel-Aviv for a health center in that city, which was at first conducted by Hadassah and later transferred to the local municipality.

the course of the decade of work and even more remarkable improvement in the second decade.

	1919	1928	1938
Jewish Urban Schools			
Jerusalem	21.6	13.0	4.8
Tel-Aviv	64.8	6.6	3.9
Haifa	49.0	11.8	3.5
Tiberias	78.3	34.9	9.6
Safed	55.0	24.4	2.3 (1937)
Jewish Rural Schools			
Judea	49.0	11.7	3.8
Samaria	45.0	14.0	4.9
Lower Galilee	46.0	17.3	0.9
Upper Galilee	64.5	15.8	0.5

Malaria is still the worst scourge of the Middle East and in Palestine it had for centuries decimated the population and operated as an effective bar to the settlement of large tracts of fertile land. At times it assumed an epidemic character, wiping out entire villages in the space of a few months. Nearly all of the new Jewish colonies before the First World War were placed in malarial districts, since these lands were the best watered. The disease carried off a large part of the first generation of pioneers in Petach Tikvah, Hedera, and the colonies in the Jordan Valley. During the period of the war a large part of the British forces suffered from the disease. In 1921, malaria was epidemic in all the rural malarious districts and close to 30,000 patients attended the dispensaries for treatment.

In 1921, Hadassah began a control demonstration in three selected areas of Palestine under the direction of the late Dr. I. J. Kligler of New York, who had been trained at the Rockefeller Institute. The results were encouraging and in 1922 the Joint Distribution Committee of America contributed funds for the organization of a Malaria Research Unit in the Palestine Department of Health. The Unit instituted countrywide control in the rural areas and freed the Government to devote its efforts to controlling urban malaria. In 1930, the Malaria Research Unit had expended, under the supervision of the Government Department, some £40,000 in reducing malaria in areas of Jewish agricultural settlements. As a result of the combined work of the Government Department of Health in the cities, the drainage and reclamation work done by the various Jewish organizations and the efforts of the Malaria Research Unit, the incidence of malaria was radically reduced. As against the 30,000 cases in 1921 out of a total population of about 650,000, the malaria cases were reduced to an average of something over 7,000 in 1928 when the population was close to 800,000.[76] In the regions of Jewish settlement the disease was largely brought under control. In non-Jewish areas—Acre, the Huleh Plain, and the region east of Beisan—malaria was still highly prevalent. The efforts of the first decade, however, had indicated that malaria could, for all practical purposes, be eliminated with proper control, the drainage of swamps, and the extension of settlements.

Despite the necessity of adapting themselves to new climatic conditions and to a new type of life, the vital statistics indicate that the Jews made a satisfactory adjustment. The death rate during the early decade was fairly low: 13.62 per thousand during the years 1922–1925, and 11.66 per thousand from 1926 to 1930.[77] This compares favorably with the death rate in advanced countries; in the United States, for instance, the death rate for the comparable periods was 11.9 and 11.8 per thousand. The low death rate among the Jews is in part due to the fact that the Jewish population represents a selection of the younger age groups; the main factors, however, are social: the excellent provision for health and child care, and general social and cultural environment. A major factor is the low incidence of mortality among infants and children up to the age of five.[78]

The Jewish death rate stands in marked contrast to the Moslem death rate which, during the period 1922–1925, was 26.83 per thousand, and during 1926–1930, 28.31 per thousand. This strongly resembles the death rate of Egypt which, during the years 1929–1933, fluctuated from 24.9 to 28.8, with an average of 26.5.[79] The death rate among the Christian Arabs in

76. In 1929, the year of the Wailing Wall disturbances, and the following year, the malaria cases increased again to about 11,500. However, the number receded to a low of about 3,000 in 1932, and then ranged between that number and about 6,000 in 1939.

77. During the second decade the death rate was reduced even further: 9.32 per thousand during 1931–1935, and as low as 7.78 in 1937.

78. See I. J. Kligler, *op. cit.*, p. 172.

79. Great Britain, *Palestine Partition Commission Report*, Cmd. 5854, London, 1938, p. 25.

Palestine, who are largely urban and who represent a relatively high economic, cultural and social stratum of the population, is more in line with the Jewish death rate, although still appreciably higher: during the years 1922–1925 it was 16.13, and for 1926–1930, 17.91. However, in rates of infant mortality the figures for the Christians, though closer to the Jewish rate for 1922–1925, is closer to the Moslem death rate in subsequent years. This is due to the fact that the Jewish infant mortality was very greatly decreased after 1925. On the other hand, the *crude* birth rate among the Moslem Arabs of Palestine is exceedingly high, averaging over fifty per thousand for the period under discussion. The natural increase of Moslems, as compared with that of Jews, is not very great but still of appreciable significance. The comparisons are indicated in the following table.[80]

	Birth Rate per M	Death Rate per M	Natural Increase per M	Infant Mortality per M
Jews				
1922–1925	34.81	13.62	21.19	122.90
1926–1930	34.29	11.66	22.63	95.83
Christians				
1922–1925	36.37	16.13	20.24	144.35
1926–1930	38.55	17.91	20.64	158.56
Moslems				
1922–1925	50.09	26.83	23.26	190.39
1926–1930	53.45	28.31	25.14	193.46

Education

The *Vaad Hahinukh* (Board of Education), which was organized in 1914 as the result of the conflict with the *Hilfsverein* concerning the language of instruction in the newly built technical school in Haifa, continued to function during the First World War under the auspices of the Palestine Office of the Zionist Organization. Twelve schools had been taken over by the Zionist Board of Education at that time, the entire budget being underwritten by the Zionist Organization. By 1918 the number of schools had grown to forty. After the British occupation, a Department of Education was formed as part of the

80. *Ibid.*, p. 24.

Palestine Commission with the *Vaad Hahinukh* continuing to direct educational policy. In 1919, the Zionist school system included ninety-four institutions of all grades, including kindergartens, elementary schools, secondary schools, and two teachers' training schools. The enrolment in the schools was over 10,000 pupils.

During the first few years, the educational work was literally supported by the Zionist Organization; its contribution to the budget averaged about £100,000 and constituted about 90 percent of the total expenditure of the schools. At this time the Board of Education was supporting a number of Jewish schools in Syria with Hebrew as the language of instruction. There was considerable criticism against the large expenditure on cultural work, and the Zionist Reorganization Commission, mentioned at the beginning of this chapter, at the end of 1921, proposed transferring the responsibility for education from the Zionist Organization to the *Yishuv*. This proposal was rejected, but the budget of the Education Department was reduced and during the next few years ran between £70,000 and £75,000. At the same time the number of school children was increasing and economies had to be made. The schools in Syria were given up, and in Palestine the emphasis was laid on elementary education.

In 1927, as a result of negotiations that had been carried on for several years, and in accord with the recommendations made by the Permanent Mandates Commission, the Palestine Administration consented to contribute a fixed grant-in-aid to the Zionist educational system. This was calculated on the basis of the proportion of the Jews in the population and was set at £20,000, less an amount to be deducted for a Government inspector of the Jewish schools. At the same time the Government recognized the Hebrew schools under the direction of the Zionist Board of Education as the Hebrew Public School System. It laid down certain conditions for giving the grant which included strengthening the authority of the Government Department over the Jewish schools and establishing a Budget Commission, participation of two representatives of the Government in the meeting of the *Vaad Hahinukh*, and the establishment of a permanent Finance Committee in which the Government would be represented, to examine into any new financial commitments to be made.

The Fourteenth Zionist Congress in 1927 decided on a further curtailment of their education grant in a general plan to reorganize the finances of the Palestine Zionist Executive. The number of pupils in the schools had meanwhile increased and the Government grant was not sufficient to offset the Zionist reduction. A period of difficulty followed and the schools were closed for several months. With the aid of some special contributions made by Baron de Rothschild and Junior Hadassah, the schools were reopened and their finances reorganized and put on a sounder foundation. Wherever possible, the main responsibility of the kindergartens was transferred to local committees, and the grants to secondary schools were drastically reduced. A great deal of effort was put into an endeavor to raise tuition fees and contributions from local sources so as to free the schools from dependence on the fluctuating income of the *Keren Hayesod* collections. After 1929, the Zionist budget was again increased to £75,000, but in 1931, reduced to £40,000, and in 1932, the financial responsibility for the schools was transferred to the *Vaad Leumi*, the Jewish Agency now making its contribution in the form of a fixed grant-in-aid.

During the first decade the schools continued to expand from year to year, particularly in the elementary branch. In the academic year 1929–1930, the enrolment in the schools maintained or assisted by the Department of Education of the Jewish Agency reached the figure of over 21,000 pupils. Of these, 4,650 were in the kindergarten grades, 13,700 in the elementary grades, about 1,500 children in the secondary classes, over 500 in the training colleges, and the remainder in vocational or other schools. From the financial point of view, the schools were divided into a number of categories; some were wholly maintained by the Zionist Organization and some were merely assisted with financial subsidies. In 1929–1930, the total expenditure of the Jewish Agency Education Department was £127,350. Of this, the Jewish Agency contributed £76,200, the Government Department about £19,195, the Palestine Jewish Colonization Association in respect of its schools, £5,645, the local communities, including Tel-Aviv, £26,000, and the remainder, £310, from other sources. In view of the fact that some of the schools were only assisted, the total amount spent by the schools affiliated with the *Vaad Hahinukh* system was larger. The table on this page shows the total expenditure of the Jewish Agency schools in the year 1929–1930, where the distribution was not far different.

The Jewish school system in Palestine includes kindergartens, elementary, secondary and teachers' training schools.

ESTIMATED INCOME AND EXPENDITURE OF SCHOOLS MAINTAINED BY OR AFFILIATED WITH THE DEPARTMENT OF EDUCATION (1929–1930)

Expenditure	Categories A and C £P	Category B £P	Category D £P	Total £P
1. Kindergartens	12,368	4,813	8,486	25,667
2. Elementary Schools	82,069	8,559	2,050	92,678
3. Secondary and Teachers' Training Schools	11,722	23,206	7,735	42,663
4. Vocational Schools	—	680	3,850	4,530
5. Administration and General Expenses	13,669	459	—	14,128
Totals	119,828	37,717	22,121	179,666
Income				
1. Jewish Agency	68,685	7,522	—	76,207
2. Government	19,195	—	172	19,367
3. PICA	5,645	—	—	5,645
4. The Yishuv (Tuition Fees and Local Participation)	26,079	26,642	14,871	67,592
5. Miscellaneous	224	3,553	7,078	10,855
Totals	119,828	37,717	22,121	179,666

Source: *Report of the Executive to the XVIIth Zionist Congress at Basle*, London, 1931, p. 292.

A—schools provided and maintained by the Jewish Agency; C—schools provided by PICA but maintained by the Jewish Agency; B—assisted schools, including Labor schools; and D—schools which receive no financial assistance but which are under supervision.

The term "kindergarten" covers the pre-school and nursery ages. The work of these groups is of particular importance in the Palestine scene: the kindergartens serve as centers for health care and instruction in hygiene; relieve working mothers; introduce the children to Hebrew speech, an important function in view of the fact that in many of the homes some European language is spoken. The elementary schools are attended from the ages of six to fourteen, and follow an eight-year course of study similar to that of the German *Volkschulen* or the American public elementary school. There are a number of significant differences, however, arising out of the Jewish tradition or the fact that Palestine is a bilingual country. The Hebrew Bible and Jewish history occupy an important place in all elementary schools; and in the *Mizrahi* school for boys, the Talmud is taught in the upper classes. Moreover, in accordance with Government requirement, an additional language besides Hebrew, either English or Arabic, must be taught in the four upper grades of the elementary school; most of the schools have chosen English.

The secondary schools in Palestine are organized on the continental pattern; their course of study is intensive and is a separate system in itself, not based on the ordinary elementary school. After a preparatory period of four years, from the age of six to ten, the child may enter the secondary school at that age and continue for an eight-year period until he is eighteen, when he is ready to enter the university. Thus, the four lower grades of the secondary school are parallel to the four upper grades of the elementary school. As in the European system, the poorer children go to the elementary schools and the middle classes attend the secondary schools. As is indicated by the tables, only a small proportion of the children attend secondary schools. There are two types: one following the humanistic *Gymnasium;* the other, of the *Realschule* type, in which the sciences are emphasized. In the humanistic type, no Latin or Greek is taught, the emphasis being on the Hebrew classics. All the Jewish secondary schools teach Arabic, essentially of the classic style. The teachers' training schools were also originally modeled on the German system: five years' training after the elementary schools, in which a general high school course and special training in pedagogy are combined. More recently, the lower two classes have been eliminated in the teachers' training school, making it more of a professional school with a three-year course after what in our case would be the junior high school.

In respect to point of view and curriculum, the schools are divided into three types: General, *Mizrahi*, and Labor. Each of these types has a special committee which has the power to appoint teachers and to make the final decisions as to curriculum. The "General" schools include over 60 percent of the children in the Zionist school system. These vary among themselves in accordance with locale and views of teachers and parents. These schools are generally considered "secular": however, the Bible—that is, the Old Testament—regarded as the basis of Jewish literature, history and thought, occupies a central place in the course of study. In some of these schools the more important prayers and blessings are taught in the lower grades as part of the Jewish tradition. In deference to Jewish customs, when the "religious" subjects are taught, e.g., prayers, Bible or *Mishnah,* caps are worn by the boys, which, in accordance with tradition, indicates that the study is regarded as sacred. Despite the fact that the course of study in the General schools contains many elements which would be called "religious," there is no explicit inculcation of religious ideas or practice, this being regarded as the function of the home. The *Mizrahi* schools, representing an enrolment of about one-third of the population in the Zionist groups, are explicitly religious schools in the orthodox manner (although their orthodoxy does not satisfy some of the more extreme groups). They aim for a synthesis between the traditional religious curriculum and the essentials of a European course of study. They give first place to religious studies, and in the boys' schools the teachings of the Talmud are emphasized. The Labor schools are to a large extent situated in cooperative settlements, although one important school is maintained in Tel-Aviv. The Labor schools emphasize the connection of education with life and lay particular stress on work as an element in the educational program. In the schools in the agricultural settlements the program consists of four hours of study and four hours of work, in the shops or in the fields. With the schools are associated agricultural plots which afford opportunity for practical training and also for experimental work and application of scientific principles. The number of Labor schools and their enrolment increased with the growth of the Jewish settlements, but during the first decade they were still in the minority; as indicated in the table on page 399, they represented less than 10 percent of the total enrolment. Moreover, they were self-supporting to a larger extent than the other schools, being in the assisted class and receiving a fixed grant-in-aid from the Department of Education.

There has been a good deal of difference of opinion among Zionists concerning the validity of this system of separate schools with different points of view and doctrines. The General Zionists have for the most part held that there should be only one common public school system, non-religious in char-

ENROLMENT, ETC., IN SCHOOLS MAINTAINED BY OR AFFILIATED WITH THE JEWISH AGENCY FOR PALESTINE (1929-1930)

Table I

(In accordance with grades of instruction)

	No. of Schools	No. of Pupils
Kindergarten	126	4,650
Elementary	90	13,705
Secondary	4	1,465
Teachers' Training	4	526
Vocational and Others	6	685
Totals	230	21,031

Table II

(In accordance with social and religious viewpoint)

	No. of Schools	No. of Pupils
General	125	13,133
Mizrahi	54	6,392
Labor	51	1,506
Totals	230	21,031

Table III

(In accordance with financial categories)

	No. of Schools	No. of Pupils
Category A (Maintained)	81	14,169
Category B (Assisted)	71	3,546
Category C (PICA)	20	807
Category D (No financial assistance)	58	2,509
Totals	230	21,031

acter, as in the Western countries. It should be understood that there is a basic curriculum for all the three schools laid down by the Board of Education. A fundamental unity is achieved through the fact that the instruction is in Hebrew, that the teaching of the Bible occupies a central place, and that all of the schools are imbued with the idea of the Jewish revival and the building of the Jewish national home. The *Vaad Hahinukh* includes representatives of the three groupings and provides a forum for the discussion of common problems. It may be said that despite certain difficulties of administration and a certain amount of duplication, the tripartite system is warranted by the situation in Palestine. There is a great deal of diversity within each type and the first task is to reduce the differences of outlook to three main points of view. The present system provides a basic unity of program and allows at the same time adjustment to the main differences of outlook which exist in the *Yishuv*. A more completely homogeneous system must await the time when the Jewish community in Palestine will grow to be more homogeneous in fact.

As indicated above, the schools are under the supervision of the Government Department of Education, which maintains a special staff of inspectors for the Jewish schools. The Government educational code provides for a minimum course of study in all schools recognized as such by Government. This minimum curriculum includes the basic subjects usually taught in elementary schools and, as noted above, requires that either English or Arabic should be taught in the four upper grades of the elementary schools. The Government inspectors charged with the supervision of the Jewish schools are Jews who have been selected for their high qualifications. These inspectors visit the schools regularly and confer with the teachers, making suggestions and recommendations. However, their function is advisory only and they cannot compel changes in the curriculum other than those required for fulfilling the minimum essentials of the public school program. There was in the beginning some apprehension on the part of the Jews that the Government might attempt to influence unduly the character of the Jewish schools through its inspectors, but these fears proved to be groundless. The main complaint against the Government in the matter of education is its failure to provide sufficient funds. The grant-in-aid did not suffice to maintain a universal system of education even of several years' schooling for all children. The Jews have supplemented this through the Jewish Agency grant, local self-taxation, and tuition fees. While most of the Jewish children of elementary school age receive some education, a certain proportion do not go to school. It should be understood also that there is no compulsory education law, and not all the children finish an elementary school course. In fact, the majority have only six years' elementary schooling, and a fairly large proportion of the children, particularly the girls in Oriental families, drop out after a few years of instruction. In the case of the Arabs, the Government grant provided only for one out of five or six children of school age.[81]

In the better organized Jewish communities, such as Tel-Aviv and the well established colonies, the Jews have been able to increase self-supporting schools through local taxation. However, in the cities of mixed population it has been particularly difficult for the Jews to support educational work, as, for example, in Haifa and Jerusalem, especially the latter. The Arab members in the municipalities who are always of the upper class, do not wish to tax themselves for general education. In Jerusalem, the situation is complicated by the fact that the Christian Arab population enjoys relatively good educational facilities provided by the mission bodies and are averse to paying a rate which will mainly benefit the Moslems and Jews.[82] An education ordinance published in 1927 provided that if a local education authority failed to collect a rate adequate to maintain schools within its area, the High Commissioner would have the power to impose and force the payment of the necessary rate as if it were a Government tax. This ordinance did not come into effect until January, 1933, and even at that time Government took no steps to enforce the ordinance.

In addition to the children enrolled in the schools of the Jewish Agency, over 10,000 Jewish children attend non-public schools. About one-third of these attend private schools in which the language of instruction is Hebrew and in which the national outlook does not differ significantly from that of the general public schools. The most important single group of

---

81. The failure of Government to provide more adequately for education evoked drastic criticism from the Palestine Royal Commission. See below, Chap. XII.

82. *Government Educational Report*, 1936–1937, pp. 7–8.

Jewish schools outside of the Zionist system is that of the *Alliance Israélite Universelle*, which conducts eight schools with an enrolment of 3,000 pupils. Hebrew and French are the languages of instruction, and English is now taught in the upper grades of the elementary schools. In recent years the schools of the *Alliance* have been markedly influenced by the Hebraic and Zionist movement in Palestine. The Evelina de Rothschild School in Jerusalem, established by the Anglo-Jewish Association, had an enrolment at this time of about 500 pupils. In this school Hebrew and English are the languages of instruction. The spirit of the school has not been sympathetic to Zionism, but this too has yielded in recent years to the pressure of events.

Altogether unaffected by modern forces are the *Talmud Torahs* and *Yeshivas* of the orthodox religious type, in which Yiddish is still the language of instruction. Hebrew is regarded as the holy tongue, not to be profaned by use as a medium of discourse. Practically no secular instruction is imposed in these schools outside of arithmetic in some schools. About 3,000 children and youth attend these schools. Vocational education is largely in the agricultural field although there has been a growing interest in trade and technical education. Besides the special institutions devoted to agricultural training mentioned above, school gardens are conducted in both town and rural schools. Something is done in the way of manual training in most of the elementary schools and sewing is part of the regular course in girls' classes. There are several special trade schools, one for boys and two for girls. For many years the *Alliance* conducted a trade school in Jerusalem but it was eventually closed. There are a number of private secondary schools which give commercial training. The Max Pine Vocational School for Youth and Adults, associated with the *Histadrut*, was opened in Tel-Aviv toward the end of the decade.

The outstanding institution for technical training is the Hebrew Technical Institute at Haifa (usually called the *Technion*). The school was established by the *Hilfsverein der Deutschen Juden* of Berlin through special donations for the purpose, and the foundation stone for the building was laid in April, 1912. Reference has already been made above to the conflict with regard to the language of instruction at the *Technion* shortly before the outbreak of the First World War. After the war the buildings were registered in the name of the *Keren*

Hayesod which supplied the funds for repairing the damage caused during the war and for equipping the Institute. The Hebrew Technical Institute was officially opened on February 9, 1925. The first branch opened was that in civil engineering, this being followed by a course in architecture. Evening classes were inaugurated for vocational education for adult workers. In 1929, the Technical Institute also opened a trade school. There were at the time 125 students in the Technical Institute and 55 in the trade school.

The establishment of a Hebrew University in Jerusalem was one of the dreams of the early Zionists. It was a genuine expression of the deeply cultural motif in the Hebraic renascence. Professor Hermann Schapira, the founder of the Jewish National Fund, proposed the idea in a series of articles a number of years before the Zionist Congress in 1897, and submitted it as a definite project at that time. The cornerstone of the Hebrew University was laid by Dr. Weizmann soon after the British occupation in 1918. The site chosen was Mount Scopus which commands a magnificent view of the hills of Jerusalem, of the Valley of the Dead Sea, and of the mountains of Moab. A number of institutes for research were organized, including Jewish study, chemistry and microbiology. Dr. Judah L. Magnes, one of the first Zionists of the Reform wing of Judaism and a leader of the Jewish community of New York before the First World War, came to Palestine in the early twenties and devoted himself to the upbuilding of the Hebrew University. It was formally opened by Lord Balfour in 1925 amid festivities and in the presence of representatives from universities throughout the world. It continued to expand in departments and in number of students. During 1925–1926 the School of Oriental Studies, the Institute of Palestine Natural History and the Department of Bacteriology and Hygiene were opened, and in the following year the Institute of Mathematics was added. At the end of 1928 a Faculty of Humanities was established, consisting of three divisions, i.e., Jewish Studies, Oriental Studies and General Humanities. In 1925 there were 64 regular students and about 100 non-matriculated; in 1930, the total was 177 students, of which as many as 130 were matriculated. The first class completed its studies in 1932, the students receiving the degree of Master of Arts. Associated with the University is the Library, which is an outgrowth of the Jewish National Library founded in 1892 by Dr.

Joseph Chasanowitz, a physician who used to accept rare books as fees from his patients. In 1930 the Library contained a quarter of a million volumes, among which were invaluable manuscripts and incunabula. A reading room with periodicals and newspapers is conducted for the general public and a quarterly bibliographical review is published. In 1927 work on the construction of the buildings for the University Library was begun and it was completed in 1929.

The cultural activities of the *Yishuv* are abundant and diversified. Several dramatic groups were established, the most important being the *Habima,* organized by former members of the Moscow Jewish Theatre of that name. There were amateur and semi-professional attempts to develop chamber music and symphony orchestras, and a number of operatic performances were given. It was not, however, until the second decade that a competent orchestra was developed. There are many publications: periodicals, books and newspapers, and Palestine has become the most important market for Hebrew books published abroad. Several daily newspapers were established during the first decade; the most important was *Haaretz* (The Land). This was the newspaper of the intellectual and literary leaders of Palestine and, though reflecting the viewpoint of the General Zionists, was sympathetic toward Labor. Contrasted with it was the *Doar Hayom* (The Daily Mail), promoted by native-born Palestinian Jews, which was highly nationalistic, opposed the leadership of the Russian Jews in the *Yishuv,* and was antagonistic to the *Histadrut.* It was later acquired by the Revisionists as their organ. In 1925 the *Histadrut* began to issue its own paper, *Davar* (The Word). Its standard of journalism and literary level were high, comparing favorably with *Haaretz*. It continued to grow with the development of the Labor movement and subsequently became the leading newspaper in Palestine.

THE GROWTH AND ORGANIZATION OF THE JEWISH COMMUNITY

Population Increase

In 1914, it is conservatively estimated that the Jews in Palestine numbered about 85,000 persons. In 1919, after the war, the number had been reduced to about 55,000, due to the increase of the death rate during the war, deportations by Turkish authorities, and emigration of settlers. At that time the Jews were 9 percent of a total estimated population of 590,000. These are rough estimates; the first set of reliable figures are derived from the census of 1922, according to which the Jews numbered 83,790 persons, constituting 12.9 percent of the settled population of 649,048. The total population—including Bedouin nomads estimated at 103,000—was 752,048.[83] At this time there were 486,177 Moslems (74.9%), 71,464 Christians (11.0%) and 7,617 others (1.2%), mostly Druses. In the midyear of 1929, the Government estimated Jewish population at 156,481, which would constitute 17.7 percent of the total estimated population of 882,511. The Moslems now numbered 634,811 (71.9%), Christians 81,776 (9.3%), and others 9,443 (1.1%). These figures are based on the settled population. If we should take the figures for the total population including the Bedouins, then in 1922 the Jews constituted 11 percent, and in mid-year of 1929, 16.3 percent of the total of 960,043.

The growth of the population from year to year is shown in the accompanying table:[84]

Year	Total	Moslems	Jews	Christians	Others
1922 (Census)	752,048	589,177	83,790	71,464	7,617
1923	778,989	609,331	89,660	72,090	7,908
1924	804,962	627,660	94,945	74,094	8,263
1925	847,238	641,494	121,725	75,512	8,507
1926	898,362	663,613	149,500	76,467	8,782
1927	917,315	680,725	149,789	77,880	8,921
1928	935,951	695,280	151,656	79,812	9,203
1929	960,043	712,343	156,481	81,776	9,443
1930	992,559	733,149	164,796	84,986	9,628

Immigration

The increase in the Jewish population was largely due to immigration. Under the Military Administration it is estimated that 6,843 Jews entered Palestine and 2,246 left, leaving a total

83. Palestine Government, *Statistical Abstract of Palestine 1941*, p. 21. These figures differ slightly from the original census report which showed 83,794 Jews out of a total population of 757,182, a figure which includes H. M. Forces.

84. *Statistical Abstract of Palestine 1937–1938*, Jerusalem, 1938, p. 19. For the years 1923 onward the figures are as of June 30th of each year (exclusive of British forces).

net immigration of 4,597. A proportion of the immigrants were returning residents of Palestine. The doors of Palestine were officially opened to Jewish immigration in September, 1920. From then until the end of December, 1929, a total of 99,806 Jewish immigrants are recorded as having entered Palestine; during the same period 23,977 Jews left the country, leaving a net Jewish immigration of 75,829 in the first decade. The average number of immigrants per month was 891, or 10,692 for the average twelve month period. The annual net immigration was 8,124. There were large fluctuations: the highest point was reached in 1925, with a gross immigration of 33,801 and a net of 31,650; the year of lowest immigration was 1928, with 2,178 immigrants and 2,168 emigrants, leaving a net increment of 10. The worst year was 1927: there were 2,713 immigrants—a larger number than the following year—but 5,071 Jews left the country, leaving a minus figure of 2,358.

There were two large waves of Jewish immigration during this period, generally referred to as the third (1920–1923) and the fourth (1924–1926) *aliyah*.[85] In both of these waves of immigration there were Jews from various parts of the world, but the third *aliyah* is sometimes referred to as the "Russian *aliyah*" because there was a large immigration from that country. This immigration consisted of workers and small capitalists and was largely supported by the Zionist funds. During the three-year period between 1921 and 1923, about 25,000 Jews came in; 5,000 emigrated, leaving a total immigration of about 20,000. The fourth *aliyah* is frequently referred to as the "Polish *aliyah*"; it was stimulated by the increasing pressure of the boycott on Jewish industry and commerce during the regime of Premier Grabsky. During the three years 1924–1926 inclusive, a total of approximately 60,000 Jews came into Palestine, while 10,000 emigrated, leaving a total net immigration of 50,000. Inflation in Poland and an economic depression in Europe generally, which began in 1927, stopped the flow of capital and an economic crisis followed in Palestine. As noted, immigration was greatly curtailed, and 1927 enjoyed the dubi-

---

85. *Aliyah* means ascent or immigration. The first *aliyah* began in 1880–1881 under the impact of the Russian pogroms; the second *aliyah*, after 1903, was stimulated by the Kishenev massacres and by the abortive Russian Revolution of 1905.

ous distinction of being the only year of Palestine under the Mandate in which emigration exceeded immigration.[86]

During the first decade, roughly speaking, about 82 percent of the immigrants came from Russia and East European countries. The next largest contingent—about 9 percent of the immigrants—came from Asia and Africa and consisted of Sephardic and Oriental Jews. About 6 percent came from Germany, Austria and the United States, and about 3 percent from all other countries. Looked at from the point of view of the populations of the various countries, the Orient shows the highest figure. From Yemen and Aden about four Jews out of a hundred left for Palestine; and Turkey, Syria, Lebanon, Iran and Iraq similarly sent relatively large numbers. Despite the fact that the largest contingent of Jews came from Poland, only about one out of every hundred Polish Jews emigrated to Palestine; the proportion for Russia being even smaller. From Germany and Austria, only four out of every thousand Jews went to Palestine, and from the United States, only five out of every ten thousand. The relatively great immigration of Oriental Jews to Palestine is explained partly by the geographical proximity of these countries to Palestine, partly because emigration to Palestine did not mean a complete change in the mode of life, partly because in most instances it meant an improvement in the standard of living.

As a result of the waves of new immigration, of the agricultural and industrial development in Palestine, and of the ascendancy of the Zionist idea, the *Yishuv* underwent a profound change in its general character and appearance: the ratio of native, Oriental and Sephardic Jews, on the one hand, to the growing settlement of European Jews (Ashkenazic); in proportion of the "old" *Yishuv*, which consisted of the pious Jews who lived in the towns and were dependent on the religious dole called *halukah*, to the "new" *Yishuv*, who lived by the labor of their hands in agriculture and industry; and in the general relation of the rural population to the town population. Despite the great variety of Jews of all types from

---

86. It was in general not a good year: during July, 1927, there was a severe earthquake which killed 272 and wounded 833 persons in Palestine and Trans-Jordan and caused much damage to property. In the spring of 1928 there was a particularly heavy invasion of locusts.

all countries with exceedingly diverse social and religious outlooks, the *Yishuv* maintained a certain unity and developed an authoritative and responsible community organization (*Knesset Israel*), of which the *Vaad Leumi* was the executive body.

Jewish Community Organization

As early as 1903, attempts were made on the part of Zionists in Palestine to create an organized Jewish community. In that year, Menahem Ussishkin, leader of the Russian Zionists, came to Palestine and, with the assistance of local forces, organized a *Knessiah* (Assembly) of the Jews of Palestine. It disintegrated, however, in the following year. Another attempt made by another Russian leader, Israel Belkind, in 1913, fell through with the outbreak of the First World War. The first steps toward a continuous development of a national organization were taken at the end of 1917, immediately following the occupation of Palestine by the British. It consisted of representatives of organizations, agricultural settlements and Zionist agencies, and elected a Provisional Council whose main task was to arrange for a constituent assembly elected by direct, equal, secret ballot and universal suffrage, including women. The preparations for the constituent assembly lasted several years, the delay in calling it being due to disagreements among various parties and organizations. The major opposition came from the leaders of the old *Yishuv* who looked askance at the growing influence of the Zionists in the life of the Jewish community and who were opposed to uniting with non-religious Jews for communal purposes, no doubt also fearing the break-up of the *kolelim* which were then the major form of Jewish communal organization. The most extreme opposition was centered in the *Agudath Israel*, made up of some of the leaders of the old Yiddish-speaking and ultra-orthodox elements of the *Yishuv*.

The more liberal elements in the Orthodox wing under the leadership of the *Mizrahi* and some sections of the Sephardic Jews were prepared to cooperate in the formation of a united communal organization but were opposed to giving women the vote, believing that if woman suffrage were eliminated, a union might be effected with the *Agudath Israel*. However, the attempted compromise proved fruitless, and finally a constituent assembly was called and met on April 19, 1920. There was an excellent response of the 28,765 registered voters, almost 80 percent going to the polls. The Assembly opened on October 7th. The twenty groups that composed the 314 members merged into three wings: a Right wing composed of Sephardic *Mizrahi* and other orthodox Jews; a Left wing consisting of the two strong Labor parties—the *Ahdut Avodah* and the *Poale Zion* —and a Center which included the General Zionists and Farmers' Federation.

The Assembly proclaimed itself to be "the supreme organ in conducting the communal and national affairs of the Jewish people in Palestine and its sole representative internally and externally." [87] It elected a National Council (*Vaad Leumi*) of 36 members, which was directed to prepare a draft of the constitution for the inner self-government of the Jewish community and to negotiate with the Palestine Administration for formal recognition. The preparation of the draft lasted five years, and was finally adopted by the third session of the Elected Assembly which was held on June 15, 1925. Difficulties were encountered in the negotiations with the Government. The *Vaad Leumi* wished that the organization be based on obligatory membership: every person born a Jew was to be considered subject to the responsibility of the Jewish community unless he declared himself outside the ranks of Israel. It also proposed that the national organization should be granted the right to levy compulsory taxes to meet the internal requirements of the *Yishuv*. The *Vaad Leumi* was following conceptions recognized under the Turkish regime which gave the non-Moslem communities or *millets* extensive privileges of self-government.[88] Under this law, the Turks had given wide power to the Greek, Armenian and Jewish communities. The British, on the other hand, were accustomed to conceive of national self-government on a territorial—not a communal—basis. They tended to conceive of Jewish communal organization along the lines of a voluntary religious community. Nevertheless, the Government was ready to give consideration to precedent; moreover, the Mandate implied that the communities of Palestine were to be given a degree of self-government.

87. Vaad Leumi, *Sekiroth al Peulot* (Survey of Activities), Jerusalem, 1922, pp. 50–56.
88. *Millet* was "the term given to distinct religious communities having in most cases also some national characteristics of their own." Stoyanovsky, *The Mandate for Palestine*, 1928, p. 244.

An important factor in the discussions was the attitude of the *Agudath Israel,* which opposed the organization of a united community on all but a strictly orthodox religious line. This ultra-orthodox group organized as a separate community—under the name *Vaad Ha-eer Ashkenazi*—and applied to the Government of Palestine for official recognition—claiming to represent 600 families of the city of Jerusalem. On the rejection of its claim, the *Agudath Israel* forwarded an appeal to the Permanent Mandates Commission in which it declared its opposition to uniting in the organization of a community based on secular and national principles. The petition asserted that the organization of the Jewish community along lines contemplated would deprive the strictly orthodox members of the possibility of shaping their lives in accordance with their religious views and with the genuine Torah tradition of Israel. The appeal failed to prevent the organization of the Jewish Community. However, the opposition of the *Agudath Israel* had the effect of strengthening the hand of the Government in declining to make it compulsory for any individual or congregation to come under the control of the *Vaad Leumi.*

The promulgation of the Religious Communities Organization Ordinance in 1926 gave the framework for the organization of the Jewish Community the following year. A compromise was effected. Under the provisions of the new Ordinance, the Jewish community obtained juridical personality and powers of taxation. However, the purposes for which the community could tax were limited to charity and education. Furthermore, while membership in the community was automatic for all Jews after a residence of three months, any person who desired to have his name struck from the Register might do so within one month after notification. This was intended to give satisfaction to the *Agudath Israel,* who could thus vote themselves outside of the authority of the *Vaad Leumi,* but it also made it possible for anyone who wished to avoid being taxed for communal purposes to do so. However, all but a few thousand Jews in Palestine remained members of the Jewish Community, and the regulations were regarded as an important step forward in the organization of Jewish life in Palestine. Nevertheless, its function as an organ of public opinion was more significant than its effectiveness as an administrative agent.

The regulations of the Jewish Community provide for religious as well as lay authorities. The highest religious authority is vested in a Rabbinical Council in which the Ashkenazic and the Sephardic sections of the community have equal representation. As in the case of the other religious authorities of the Moslem and Christian communities, the Rabbinical Courts established under the Rabbinical Council have wide jurisdiction in matters of personal status and inheritances. The powers of the Rabbinical Courts are as follows:[89]

(i) exclusive jurisdiction in matters of marriage and divorce, alimony, executive and confirmation of wills of Jewish Palestinian subjects;

(ii) jurisdiction in any other matter of personal status of Jewish persons, where all the parties to the action consent to their jurisdiction;

(iii) exclusive jurisdiction over any case as to the constitution or internal administration of a *waqf* constituted before the Rabbinical Court according to Jewish Law.

The lay bodies include: the *Kehillah* (Community), *Asefat Hanivharim* (the Elected Assembly), and the *Vaad Leumi* (National or General Council). The *Kehillah* is the local representative body; in purely Jewish communities there is a certain overlapping between the *Kehillah*, as the local representative body organized under the Religious Communities Ordinance, and the municipality or local committee, organized under the Local Government Ordinance. In the mixed Arab-Jewish cities, functions connected with schools, orphanages and hospitals are in the hands of the *Kehillah*, while the municipality in which both Jews and Arabs are represented, deals with economic or neutral matters not affected by religious or cultural differences.

The Elected Assembly is the supreme organ of the Jewish Community. It is composed of 71 members and is chosen by a general franchise open to all classes and to both sexes. The principle of proportional representation safeguards the rights of minority groups. The Elected Assembly holds a session once a year at which the General Council of the Jewish Community of Palestine (*Vaad Leumi*) is elected. The constitution provides that the General Assembly may pass resolutions for

---

89. H. C. Luke and Edward Keith-Roach, *The Handbook of Palestine and Transjordan*, Macmillan, London, 1930, p. 219.

the guidance of the *Vaad Leumi;* it has the authority to vote a budget for both *Vaad Leumi* and Rabbinical Council. The first election under the new constitution was held on January 5, 1931. The *Agudath Israel* refrained from participation and carried on propaganda to induce Jews to have their names removed from the Register. According to figures published by the *Vaad Leumi,* 89,656 Jews had joined the organized Jewish Community by the end of 1927.

The political policy of the *Vaad Leumi* generally follows that of the Palestine Executive of the Jewish Agency. It is more concerned with those aspects which affect the internal life of the Jewish community of Palestine. In a memorandum submitted to the Permanent Mandates Commission in June, 1930, the *Vaad Leumi* presented a number of major grievances which it had against the Palestine Administration. It held that the Administration failed to make adequate provisions for Jewish security. It pointed out that the number of Jewish policemen on the force, particularly in cities with a mixed population, was altogether disproportionate to the Jewish element, and that experience had shown that a police force composed for the most part of Arabs could not be relied upon in the event of an Arab attack on the Jewish community. It complained also of the removal of sealed armories from the villages despite the fact that the Bedouins were permitted by law to carry arms. A third source of dissatisfaction was the exclusion of Jews from the Trans-Jordan Frontier Force.

Another type of infringement related to the use of the Hebrew language. Despite the provision of the Mandate which made Hebrew one of the official languages, it held an inferior position in the Department of Police and in other Government departments. Moreover, the religious rights of Jewish Government officials—policemen and railway employees—were infringed upon by not permitting Jews to observe the Sabbath and Jewish holidays. In the mixed municipalities, the Jews were generally under-represented, and the Government had a tendency to favor the Arab notables in appointing the mayors and deputy mayors. In Jerusalem the situation had so deteriorated that the Jewish councillors had been forced to resign from the municipality.

A standing complaint of the Jewish community was that despite the large Jewish contribution to the public revenues—

Development of the Jewish National Home

estimated at this time as being 45 percent of the total—Jews benefited little from the major Government services. The proportion of Jews employed in the public works was very small— from 3 to 6 percent. In the years 1927–1928, which were critical years for the city populations, and when Lord Plumer made a special effort to assist, the share of Jewish labor in public works was not more than some 15 percent despite the fact that during those years the proportion of Jewish unemployed rose to 50–75 percent of the total unemployed. The Department of Agriculture concerned itself mainly with the interests of Arabs and spent less than 10 percent of its total budget on Jewish agricultural interests. The Government schools were in Arabic and the subsidy granted to the Jewish schools at this time constituted only 10 percent of the total cost of the Jewish schools. The most serious grievance was against the Department of Health, whose attitude toward Jewish physicians and the Jewish population generally was described as "notorious." The Department of Health employed 30 out of the 100 non-Jewish doctors in the country and only 6 out of the 500 Jewish doctors. The Government hospitals made inadequate provision for Jewish patients; on the other hand, the clinics supported by the Jewish organizations gave medical treatment to a very great number of non-Jewish patients. In some districts the Hadassah Organization had gone so far as to establish clinics in neighborhoods which were predominantly Arab, and where the number of Arabs treated was far in excess of the number of Jews. As the *Vaad Leumi* analyzed the situation, the Jews were not only carrying the main burden for their own education and health services, but the surplus of revenue derived from Jews paid for the major part of the services rendered to the Arabs through Government.

In fine, the plea of the *Vaad Leumi* was for equality of treatment with the non-Jewish sections of the population in the matter of Government assistance; its view was summed up in the following paragraph:[90]

A country the population of which is as mixed as that of Palestine does not belong to one race only, and each of the two or three races which form its population must be granted full equality of rights

---

90. *Vaad Leumi, Memorandum Submitted to the Permanent Mandates Commission of the League of Nations*, June, 1930, p. 39.

and national development, even if the Palestine Mandate be ignored, together with the express obligation undertaken by His Majesty's Government with regard to the establishment in Palestine of a Jewish National Home—an obligation which has been confirmed by the League of Nations itself. At present, despite all this, not only are obstacles placed in the way of the establishment of the Jewish National Home at each and every stage, but even the elementary principle of equality of rights for Jews has not hitherto been applied in Palestine.

CHANGING ZIONIST POLICIES AND THE ESTABLISHMENT OF THE JEWISH AGENCY

Postwar Zionist Congresses

The first Congress to meet after the war was the Twelfth Zionist Congress which convened in Carlsbad in the summer of 1921. There were 445 delegates from forty different countries, representing 778,407 *shekel* payers. In accordance with the continental fashion, the Congress divided itself into three main divisions: a right wing, representing the *Mizrahi*, or religious party, which consisted of 97 delegates; a left wing, representing socialist and labor groupings—the *Poale Zion* (Workers of Zion) and the *Zeire Zion* (Young Zionists) being the most important—consisting of 38 delegates; while the large majority was made up of General Zionists who formed the center. Poland led with a delegation of 65; followed by the United States with 42; Galicia was third with 24; and Palestine, despite its small Jewish population, sent 21 delegates. No Zionist election took place in Russia on account of the hostile attitude of the Soviet Government, but a Russian delegation of 64 was admitted in a consultative capacity. Many problems faced the Congress in organizing immigration and promoting the economic development of Palestine. The political problems were no less grave. The Mandate had as yet not been approved by the League of Nations although it was already in draft form. Sir Herbert Samuel had been in office for over a year and had given an indication of the nature of British policy in practice. The May riots of 1921 had brought the question of the relations with the Arabs to the forefront of attention.[91]

---

91. The Congress had to deal also with a conflict which had broken out between the main body of Zionists, headed by Weizmann, and the so-called Mack-Brandeis group in the United States. See above, p. 331 n.

As the leader who had played the central part in the negotiations which led to the Balfour Declaration and the Mandate, Weizmann had the confidence of the great body of Zionists. However, even at this early date, there were voices of disapproval. Berl Katznelson of the Labor Party criticized the leadership adversely for too easy acquiescence in the policy of Sir Herbert Samuel, whom he attacked as attempting to gain for the Government "the sympathies of the Arabs at the price of our blood." Solomon Kaplansky, also of the Labor group, blamed the Executive for not proposing any definite program for the development of Arab-Jewish understanding. Nehemiah de Lieme, a Dutch Zionist and former member of the Executive associated with the American Mack-Brandeis group, was of the opinion that the best approach to the Arab problem was through leaving politics alone and concentrating on "economic persuasion," i.e., by developing the country so that the Arabs would recognize the benefits of Jewish settlement.

In his reply on behalf of the Executive, Weizmann attributed the slowness of progress in the practical work and the defeats sustained on the political front mainly to the inadequacy of funds. Larger funds would have permitted the Executive to initiate projects to stimulate immigration, encourage a firmer policy on the part of Great Britain and to provide the means of promoting better relations with the Palestine Arabs and with the neighboring Arab countries. He declared that he had protested against every serious mistake made by Sir Herbert Samuel, but he counseled a policy of cooperation with the Administration nevertheless. Throughout he emphasized that political gains could be obtained only by progress in the development of the country, by acquisition of land, and by more intensive agricultural and industrial development.

On the question of Arab-Jewish relations, Weizmann declared in his opening address:[92]

Our policy in regard to the Arabs, as in regard to all our other problems, is clear and straightforward. We intend to abate no jot of the rights guaranteed to us by the Balfour Declaration, and recognition of that fact by the Arabs is an essential preliminary to the establishment of satisfactory relations between Jew and Arab. Their temporary refusal to recognize that fact compels us to give thought to

92. *Reports of the Executive to the XIIth Zionist Congress*, London, 1922, p. 44.

the means by which we can best safeguard our Yishuv against aggression. Self-protection is an elementary duty. But we proclaim most solemnly and unequivocally that we have in our own hearts no thought of aggression, no intention of trespassing on the legitimate rights of our neighbors. We look forward to a future in which Jew and Arab will live side by side in Palestine, and work conjointly for the prosperity of the country. Nothing will stand in the way of such a future, when once our neighbors realize that our rights are as sacred to us as their rights are to them.

The Congress expressed its confidence in Weizmann and in the Executive by a large majority of 348 votes, being supported by the General Zionists and the *Mizrahi*. The Labor group submitted resolutions incorporating their criticisms of the Executive. The Congress was united in protesting emphatically against the temporary stoppage of immigration after the May 1921 riots, and against the restrictions introduced subsequently in the immigration regulations. It resolved: "The Congress declares before the entire world that large immigration to Eretz Israel is an uncontestable right of the Jewish people of which under no circumstances it may be deprived. The internal regulation of immigration into Eretz Israel, according to the economic capacity of the country, is a matter for the Jewish people, represented by the Zionist Organization, in agreement with the Administration of Palestine." [93]

While protesting in strong terms against the May riots, the Congress was in full accord with Weizmann's position on the Arab-Jewish question. The following resolution, adopted at the Twelfth Zionist Congress, became the guiding line of Zionist policy:

With sorrow and indignation the Jewish people have lived through the recent events in Palestine. The hostile attitude of the Arab population in Palestine incited by unscrupulous elements to commit deeds of violence, can neither weaken our resolve for the establishment of the Jewish National Home, nor our determination to live with the Arab people on terms of concord and mutual respect, and together with them to make the common home into a flourishing commonwealth, the upbuilding of which may assure to each of its peoples an undisturbed national development. The two great Semitic peoples united of yore by the bonds of common creative civilization will not

---

93. *Ibid.*, pp. 149–150.

fail in the hour of their national regeneration to comprehend the need of combining their vital interests in a common endeavor.

The Congress calls upon the Executive to redouble its efforts to secure an honourable entente with the Arab people on the basis of this Declaration and in strict accordance with the Balfour Declaration. The Congress emphatically declares that the progress of Jewish colonisation will not affect the rights and needs of the working Arab nation.

Before the Thirteenth Congress convened in Carlsbad in 1923 a number of political events of importance had occurred. In May and June, 1922, the United States Congress had passed a joint resolution favoring the establishment of the Jewish national home in Palestine, and in July, the Council of the League of Nations had confirmed the Mandate for Palestine. However, along with these favorable political developments there were major disappointments: Trans-Jordan had been separated from the area in which the Jewish national home clauses in the Mandate were to apply, and the Churchill White Paper had been issued and accepted by the League of Nations as the official interpretation of British policy. It was generally felt that the 1922 White Paper was a serious limitation on the original purposes of the Balfour Declaration. As part of the 1922 White Paper policy, Government was promoting the idea of the Legislative Council which the *Vaad Leumi* in Palestine thought dangerous to the development of the Jewish national home. There were also disturbing rumors of negotiations between the British Government and the representatives of Husain, King of Hejaz, concerning the formation of an Arab federation which would include Palestine.

The Executive of the Zionist Organization, however, continued its policy of complete cooperation with the British Government, and in line with this persuaded the *Vaad Leumi* to participate in the elections of the Legislative Council. As evidence of the desire for close cooperation with the Palestine Administration, the Executive in 1922 appointed Colonel Frederick H. Kisch—a former officer of the Indian Civil Service, who had served in the First World War with distinction—as head of the Political Department.[94] As a Britisher with experi-

---

94. Colonel Kisch acted as the Political Head of the Executive until 1933. At the outbreak of the Second World War he enlisted and served as

ence in the Civil Service, it was thought that Colonel Kisch would get along better with the Government personnel in Palestine than his predecessor, the East European M. M. Ussishkin, who was blunt in his manner and urgent in his demands. The Report of the Zionist Executive to the Congress discussed the proposed treaty between Great Britain and King Husain and stated that there was nothing in it to warrant serious anxiety:[95]

> ... It has already been officially intimated that no change in the political status of Palestine is implied by the Treaty, and it may be safely assumed that none is contemplated. In a word, there is not the smallest reason to suppose that Great Britain has any intention whatever either of whittling down her obligations under the Mandate or of putting herself in a position in which she would be unable to fulfill them. At the moment of writing the Treaty still remains to be finally settled, but whatever the form in which it may eventually emerge, it may be confidently anticipated that when the full text is published, it will prove to contain nothing inconsistent with the faithful execution of the Mandate in the spirit as well as in the letter.

The Congress was composed of 292 elected delegates and 42 members of the Actions Committee who had the right to vote. The General Zionists still predominated, with 171 representatives, but the wings were gaining strength: there were 70 representatives of the *Mizrahi* and 51 Labor delegates. The two main issues before the Thirteenth Congress were the attitude of the Executive vis-à-vis the Mandatory Power, and the question of the enlargement of the Jewish Agency by the inclusion of non-Zionists. There were sharp attacks against the Executive from different quarters. Vladimir Jabotinsky had resigned from the Executive in January, 1923, principally because of his disagreement with the policy of the 1922 White Paper.[96] Isaac Gruenbaum, the leader of a General Zionist group from Poland which called itself Radical Zionists, accused

---

chief engineer of the Eighth Army. He was killed before the capture of Tunis when the car in which he was riding struck a mine.

95. *Report of the Executive to the XIIIth Zionist Congress*, London, 1923, p. 15.

96. He had, as a member of the Executive, originally agreed to accept the 1922 White Paper, but he later explained that he had yielded to Dr. Weizmann's urging against his better judgment and that he had not been given time to consider the matter fully.

Dr. Weizmann of "defeatism and capitulation"—defeatism in his attitude toward the British Government, and capitulation to the non-Zionists. Ussishkin objected to the extension of the Jewish Agency because the non-Zionist forces, which Weizmann proposed to bring in, were opposed to the political aims of the Zionist movement. Israel Mereminski, of the *Zeire Zion* from Poland, was sharp in his criticism, particularly in the matter of the immigration restrictions. He epitomized his view in the phrase: "Samuelism is supplanting Zionism." He also opposed extending the Jewish Agency on the ground that it would give power to a handful of philanthropists who did not understand the aims of Zionism. A bitter attack came also from the side of the *Mizrahi*. Hershel Farbstein, one of its leaders from Poland, demanded the resignation of the Executive for accepting the 1922 White Paper.

The most comprehensive criticism was made by Kaplansky of the Labor Zionists, who had at the previous Congress already attacked the Executive for its failure to work out a concrete plan of Arab-Jewish collaboration. In his indictment, Kaplansky pointed out that immigration was being hampered, that the *Vaad Leumi* had failed to obtain autonomy, that the Palestine Administration included anti-Zionists, that the Executive had done nothing to prevent the separation of Trans-Jordan from Palestine. He attacked the British Tory elements as attempting to dominate the Arab East through an alliance with the Arab ruling classes against the interests of the Arab *fellahin*. He warned the Zionists not to trust England as an intermediary between Jews and Arabs, and that an understanding with Arabs could be achieved only by direct relations with them. He asked that Congress take steps to consider the agrarian problem in Palestine as a means of fostering good relations with the peasants.

In his reply, Dr. Weizmann answered all the criticisms with great patience, along the now customary lines. Political gains in Palestine could only be made through constructive work in Palestine, and for that reason the cooperation of all Jews—non-Zionists as well as Zionists—should be sought, providing they were willing to accept the Mandate and the Balfour Declaration. He did not deny the seriousness of the political situation, but insisted that the cornerstone of the Zionist policy must be sincere cooperation with the British Government.

Summing up his position, he said: "The irrevocability of the Mandate, the good faith of the Mandatory, and the sympathy of the enlightened people throughout the world, are the foundations upon which we must rebuild our policy." [97] To the Arabs he repeated his offer of neighborly relations based on mutual respect and trust.

The resolution for a vote of confidence omitted reference to political questions and limited itself to an expression of thanks on the part of the Congress for the efforts of the Executive in the confirmation of the Mandate, the colonization in Palestine, and the successful results of the *Keren Hayesod*. Despite this effort to conciliate Weizmann's opponents, several of the groups refrained from voting, including the *Mizrahi,* Labor groups and the Radical Democrats. One group, which called itself the Zionist Socialists, went so far as to vote against the Executive. The resolution of confidence was supported mainly by the General Zionists and passed by a vote of 147 to 72. The Congress also yielded to Weizmann in approving the plan for extending the Jewish Agency to include non-Zionists. It went on record—somewhat vaguely—as expecting "that the future Trans-Jordania will be shaped in conformity with the legitimate demands of the Jewish people." It also passed a lengthy resolution reiterating the Jewish desire to live in complete harmony with the Arabs in Palestine, and emphasized the benefits which would accrue to the Near East and to the world at large through cooperation between the Arab and the Jewish peoples.

The Fourteenth Zionist Congress met in Vienna, August 18–31, 1925, amid favorable circumstances. Immigration had reached an unexpectedly high figure and the Hebrew University at Jerusalem had been opened, with Balfour delivering the main address. Improved relations with the Arabs were indicated in a visit by a Jewish delegation from Palestine to King Husain at Amman in January, 1924. The Executive had indicated its satisfaction with the Administration in its report to the Congress, in which it stated: "Sir Herbert Samuel has, by common consent, acquitted himself of his historic task with dignity and distinction, and he carries with him in his retirement the enduring gratitude of the Zionist Organization and

---

97. *Report of the Executive to the XIIIth Zionist Congress*, pp. 355–356.

of the Jewish world at large." In his opening speech, Weizmann said that Zionism had now been established as a reality through the practical developments in Palestine, and expressed the view that the relations between the Arab and Jewish peoples had become less tense. He reported progress in the negotiations with the non-Zionists and explained that the representation in the governing bodies would be organized on a fifty-fifty basis, i.e., it would consist of half Zionists, half non-Zionists. The program of the enlarged Jewish Agency would be based on the Mandate and "on the cardinal principles of our work in Palestine, namely, national land, national labor, national language and culture."

In the face of the favorable situation, criticism of the Executive was less strong, but dissatisfaction was still expressed by the *Mizrahi* and Labor wings. The *Mizrahi* accused the Executive of being opposed to middle-class immigration, and attacked the colonization policy which favored cooperative and collective forms of agricultural settlement. Hershel Farbstein, its spokesman, also thought that the Executive should have insisted on being consulted in the matter of the appointment of the new High Commissioner, Lord Plumer. The criticism of the Labor representatives was milder in tone and more general in character. Although they complained of the Executive's lack of determination in promoting the Zionist policy, there was in evidence a tendency to follow the line of cooperation with the Government.

The most important criticism now came from Vladimir Jabotinsky, who outlined an approach which foreshadowed the development of "Revisionism." His presentation re-echoed the political emphasis of Herzlian Zionism. He restated the ultimate aim as the achievement of a majority of Jews in Palestine, urging that all activity should be concentrated on attaining this objective in the shortest possible time. He proposed a planned immigration of 40,000 Jews a year for twenty-five years, stating his belief that such an immigration would be realizable with no great difficulty if active measures were taken, with the encouragement of the Government, to increase the absorptive capacity of the country. All waste and uncultivated land should be nationalized and leased to Jews for colonization purposes on the payment of small sums. Agriculture, moreover, should be supplemented by a rapid development in industry and trade, and an appropriate tariff policy should be instituted by Government. Immigration should be controlled by the Zionist Executive and the Jews should be consulted in the appointment of officials. He also declared that in view of the insecurity in Palestine, it was necessary to form Jewish defense units.

Dr. Weizmann admitted that there were shortcomings in achievement and that the Arab-Jewish situation was far from settled. Nevertheless, he defended his policy as the only constructive one. He pointed out that the Executive had to depend on factors beyond its control and could only utilize such forces as were provided by the Zionist movement. He maintained that the Arab problem could be solved only in the measure that the Arabs became convinced that the Jews were in earnest about upbuilding a Jewish national home, and, at the same time, that the "spirit in which we build our home is based on the considerations of liberty, of tolerance and of fraternity."

The debate on the vote of confidence showed that opposition was growing, particularly in the middle-class groups and among the *Mizrahi*. The resolution of confidence was passed, but Dr. Gruenbaum, one of Weizmann's opponents, pointedly remarked that half of the delegates had abstained. Thereupon, Dr. Weizmann declared that the members of the Executive would not accept re-election. This confounded the opposition, for they had no united slate to offer. The Congress then adopted a resolution instructing the Executive to carry on until the next meeting of the Actions Committee, which was to convene within three months. In pursuance of this recommendation, the Actions Committee met in Berlin the following October and extended the power of the Executive to the next Congress.

Formation of the Enlarged Jewish Agency

The Fifteenth Congress met in Basle during August-September 1927. This Congress indicated a further weakening of the General Zionists, some accession of strength to the Laborites, and the development of two new groups—the Radicals, led by Isaac Gruenbaum, and Revisionists, led by Vladimir Jabotinsky. The main question before the Congress was the formation of the enlarged Jewish Agency. The negotiations in America between the non-Zionist group, headed by Louis Marshall and Felix Warburg, on the one hand, and the Zionist Organization, led by Stephen S. Wise, had been retarded because of a controversy which had arisen with reference to fund raising. The Joint Distribution Committee, in which the non-Zionists were prominent, had launched a large campaign for Jewish colonization in Russia, and in response, Dr. Wise had organized a United Palestine Appeal. However, after the arrival of Dr. Weizmann in the United States, an agreement was reached and officially signed in January, 1927. The agreement expressed "the unanimous accord in principle of both parties as to the desirability and feasibility of organizing the Jewish Agency in accordance with the terms of the Palestine Mandate, as confirmed by the Council of the League of Nations on July 24, 1922, and along the general lines of the resolutions adopted by the Zionist Congress at Vienna in August 1925." [98]

The economic crisis in Palestine had now assumed serious proportions: emigration was exceeding immigration, and there were many unemployed. Economic difficulties in Europe, which preceded the depression in the United States by a year or two, had led to a reduction in the collections of the *Keren Hayesod* and the Zionist budget was unbalanced. In the light of this situation and the prospective inclusion in the enlarged Jewish Agency of non-Zionist members, who were critical of the economic ideas and methods of the Zionists, the Executive wished to put its financial house in order. For this purpose they suggested a small, "homogeneous" Executive consisting of General Zionists without the party wings, which would concentrate on problems of organization and economics. This aggravated an internal political situation which was already difficult. The Radical and Revisionist groups, representing the middle class in Eastern Europe, were dissatisfied with the economic policy of the Executive which favored agriculture and labor. The *Mizrahi,* also largely made up of middle-class groups, tended to follow the anti-Labor opposition. The Labor groups, on their part, looked with suspicion on the proposal of a "homogeneous" Executive in which they would not be represented, fearing it might be hostile to the new Zionist coopera-

---

98. *Report of the Executive to the XVth Zionist Congress,* London, 1927, p. 9. The agreement also provided for a Survey Commission to study at first-hand in Palestine the resources for agricultural, industrial and commercial development. The commission of experts was to be formed under a committee composed of Sir Alfred Mond, Great Britain, Director; Oscar Wassermann, Germany; Mr. Felix Warburg and Dr. Lee K. Frankel of the United States.

tive colonies on the ground that these were not self-supporting. However, in view of the fact that none of the groups had a constructive policy to offer, Labor decided not to oppose the formation of the new Executive. Weizmann's proposal won out by a relatively small margin: he was re-elected President of the World Zionist Organization by 113 votes against 84, with many abstaining. The other members of the Executive were elected by even narrower margins, of 83 against 62.[99]

The Sixteenth Zionist Congress met in Zurich from July 28 to August 11, 1929. It again showed a weakening of the General Zionist representation, with a considerable growth in the strength of the Labor forces. The greatest relative increase came in the ranks of the Revisionists and Radicals. The economic situation in Palestine was improving; the new Executive had made considerable progress in balancing the budget and the stream of immigration into Palestine was renewed. However, a tragedy was in the making: agitation arising from the Wailing Wall incident, which had occurred on the Day of Atonement in October, 1928, was in full swing and gave cause for concern. Although some of the delegates to the Congress sensed the seriousness of the situation, none of them expected the violent outbreaks that were to occur shortly after the closing sessions of the Congress.

Weizmann was optimistic: though he made reference to the Wailing Wall issue, he expressed hope that it would be settled in amity. He was grateful to Lord Plumer for what the latter had done to aid the unemployed and to help Palestine weather the economic crisis. While expressing some dissatisfaction with the Government's immigration and land policies and with the failure of the Administration to employ a proportionate number of Jews in Government and municipal institutions, Weizmann pointed out that the Government had adopted a number of constructive measures, e.g., easing of agricultural taxation and of customs duties, and recognition of the Zionist school system as the Hebrew public school system with the allotment of a grant. He announced that the plan for uniting all the Jews interested in the upbuilding of Palestine—whether Zionists or

99. The officers elected were: Weizmann, President of the Zionist Organization; Sokolow, President of the Zionist Executive; Dr. M. D. Eder, Col. F. H. Kisch, Louis Lipsky, Felix Rosenblueth, Harry Sacher and Henrietta Szold. Sacher, Kisch, and Henrietta Szold formed a "triumvirate" to direct affairs in Palestine.

non-Zionists—was about to be consummated through a meeting of the newly constituted Council of the Jewish Agency, immediately after the meetings of the Zionist Congress.

At this Congress the Labor movement definitely shifted to the support of Weizmann's policies. Dr. Chaim Arlosoroff, who had risen to a position of leadership, praised the method of *suaviter in modo, fortiter in re,* which Weizmann had followed, though he urged constant watchfulness in the coordination of economic and political work. He turned attention to the need of inner Zionist discipline, and without mentioning the Revisionists by name, pointed out that under the slogan of "Herzlian Zionism," this group was planning to secede from the Zionist Organization. He also urged that Great Britain use her good offices to save the Zionists in Russia who were languishing in concentration camps. Solomon Kaplansky, one of the older leaders of the Labor group, hailed the advent of the Labor Party to power in England and thought that this presaged a friendly attitude toward the Zionist endeavor in Palestine.

Outside of the Labor group, however, there was still sharp criticism of Weizmann. Jabotinsky again demanded the repudiation of the 1922 White Paper and defined the Jewish national home as a "national state with a preponderant Jewish majority." He expressed the fear that the Wailing Wall incident would be followed by grave consequences. Ussishkin also considered the Wailing Wall affair as disquieting and accused the British Administration of dilatory tactics. He also decried the efforts made by Dr. Judah L. Magnes and the *Brith Shalom* Organization in the direction of Arab-Jewish rapprochement, expressing the view that as long as the Jews had no power in Palestine, such declarations of friendship were meaningless. Rabbi Meyer Berlin, one of the leaders of the *Mizrahi,* joined in deprecating the activities of the *Brith Shalom;* though praising their aspiration for peace as in harmony with the religious spirit in Jewish nationalism, he opposed the *Brith Shalom's* conception that Palestine belonged to the two peoples equally. In accordance with the Bible, Palestine was the Land of Israel. Dr. Stephen S. Wise was critical both of the Mandatory Power and of the Weizmann-led Executive. He thought that the Mandatory Power had adopted an attitude of non-cooperation toward the Jews and that the Executive had failed to make sufficiently strong representations to the Government in the matter of the Wailing Wall incident. But Weizmann was reelected President of the Zionist Organization, the Executive was enlarged and again included representatives from both Labor and *Mizrahi* groups.

The first meeting of the Council of the enlarged Jewish Agency including Zionists and non-Zionists took place in Zurich on August 11, 1929. The final agreement between the Zionist Organization and the non-Zionists was signed on the 14th. The basic objectives of the Jewish Agency were stated to be: 1) Jewish immigration to Palestine; 2) fostering of the Hebrew language and culture; 3) acquisition of land under title of the Jewish National Fund as the inalienable property of the Jewish people; 4) promotion of agriculture and colonization based on the principle of Jewish labor; 5) provision for religious needs without infringing on individual freedom of conscience. An important provision was that the President of the Zionist Organization would be the President of the Jewish Agency unless three-fourths of the membership of the Council voted otherwise. The *Keren Hayesod* remained the main financial instrument in the enlarged Agency.[100]

The material presented in this chapter shows that the main effort in Palestine was devoted to the upbuilding of the land in its economic, social and cultural aspects. The analysis of Zionist policy indicates the same interest: the amounts expended on what might be called political and propaganda activities, including Arab-Jewish relations, were very small. Likewise, the political demands of the Zionist majority were minimal; indeed, as modest as they could possibly have been without wholly repudiating the Balfour Declaration. In ad-

---

100. Dr. Chaim Weizmann was elected President of the Jewish Agency, Mr. Louis Marshall, Chairman of the Council, and Lord Melchett, Associate Chairman. Mr. Felix Warburg was elected Chairman of the Administrative Committee. The Council elected Baron Edmond de Rothschild as Honorary President. The members of the first Executive of the enlarged Jewish Agency were: on the Zionist side, Rabbi M. Berlin, Professor Brodetsky, Colonel Frederick H. Kisch and Dr. Arthur Ruppin; on the non-Zionist side, Dr. Maurice Hexter, Dr. Bernard Kahn, Dr. Werner Senator and Mr. Julius Simon. Mr. Nahum Sokolow, Honorary Vice-President of the Agency, acted as Chairman of the Executive. Louis Marshall, the moving spirit of the non-Zionists in the Jewish Agency and the first Chairman of the enlarged Jewish Agency Council, died in Zurich shortly after the close of the sessions, following a few days' illness.

mitting the non-Zionists to an equal share in determining the policies of the Jewish Agency, the Zionist Organization went far in compromising the objective of creating a Jewish state in Palestine. Indeed, the leaders of the Zionist movement in effect accepted the policy laid down by His Majesty's Government. There were minority groups which demanded a more aggressive program, but even these had in mind mainly the facilitation of immigration and land settlement. Those who insisted that the Jewish state was the major goal of Zionism had been reduced to a secondary position with no part in the leadership; "practical" and cultural Zionism had become dominant.

The political restrictions imposed by the depreciated British policy were, during the first decade, not the only—perhaps not the main—factor in limiting the development of the Jewish national home. Even under the 1922 White Paper policy it would have been possible to introduce a larger number of Jewish settlers if funds had been available. Far greater progress could have been made if the non-Zionist Jewish bodies concerned with the amelioration of the condition of the Jews in Europe had joined with the Zionists a decade earlier in aiding the Jewish development in Palestine under the British Mandate. At the time when the non-Zionists decided to enter, the economic depression had set in in the United States and American aid proved less than expected. Failure of Jews throughout the world to grasp the significance of Zionism and to recognize the possibilities of Palestine must be accounted an important cause in limiting the success of the Jewish national home. In the light of the grave obstacles—the weakness of British policy and the coolness of the Jewish philanthropists—the achievement of the Zionist Organization in successfully laying the foundations of the Jewish national home in the first decade after the establishment of British rule, must appear the more remarkable. This is not to minimize the difficulties of the political problem. Subsequent events indicated that the Zionist Organization was over-optimistic about the possibility of reducing the political friction through improvements in economic conditions. The warnings of Vladimir Jabotinsky were not without foundation. But whether stronger political policy would have been possible is still open to question, in the light of the inadequate support given to the Zionist Organization.

CHAPTER VII

THE ARAB WORLD AND ARAB POLITICS IN PALESTINE

THE CHARACTER OF THE ARAB WORLD

LIKE the Jews and the Christians, the Arabs of Palestine are part of a larger community. Although, as Lawrence says in *Seven Pillars of Wisdom*, the Arabic-speaking peoples are "as varied as a field full of poppies," they have "an equal and essential likeness."[1] Students of Arab life are somewhat troubled in attempting to define what constitutes this "essential likeness." They are agreed that the Arabs do not comprise a distinct race or homogeneous stock. While most Arabs are dark, as are other peoples living in the Mediterranean area and in the Middle East, they range in color from blonde to coal black. Some Arabs are obviously of Negro race. The Hejaz in the Arabian Peninsula, the home of the "original Arabs," is today one of the most racially mixed communities on earth, and Mecca is a city of mulattoes and quadroons of all racial blends. One of the reasons for Islam's rapid spread is undoubtedly its complete disregard of the color line. In the term "Arab" there is a sense of consanguinity, but it is symbolic rather than actual. The amount of "pure Arab blood" among the people commonly classed as Arab today is insignificant, and it is probable that even at their emergence into history the Bedouins were to some degree at least a racially mixed group.[2]

Arabism and Islam

Lawrence wrote: "A first difficulty of the Arab movement was to say who the Arabs were. Being a manufactured peo-

1. T. E. Lawrence, *Seven Pillars of Wisdom*, Doubleday, Doran, New York, 1933, p. 33.
2. Although all members of the same clan consider themselves as being of one blood, kinship may be acquired by the simple process of sucking a few drops of a member's blood (Philip K. Hitti, *The Arabs, a Short History*, Princeton, 1943, p. 14).

ple, their name had been changing in a sense slowly year by year. Once it meant an Arabian. There was a country called Arabia, but this was nothing to the point. There was a language called Arabic; and in it lay the test." [3] On this prerequisite, all writers agree; it should be added that the common language referred to is not primarily the vernacular—which differs considerably in the various countries—but rather the classic tongue which is the language of the literature studied in the schools throughout the Arab and Islamic world. The community of the language and literature, moreover, implies a heritage of attitudes, beliefs and aspirations enshrined in the Arabic literature. Part of this heritage is a memory of the political domination of the Arabs under the Caliphate over the major part of the then civilized world. Still the heart of Arabic unity is missing without the Islamic factor, for it was Islam that transformed the crude pagan Bedouin into the standard bearer of a universal idea, and converted the bond based on ethnic kinship into a community based on a way of life and a mode of belief. H. A. R. Gibb has included these several elements in the following brief definition: "To the question 'Who are the Arabs?' there is—whatever enthnographers may say—only one answer which approaches historic truth: All those are Arabs for whom the central fact of history is the mission of Mohammed and the memory of the Arab Empire, and who in addition, cherish the Arabic tongue and its cultural heritage as their common possession." [4]

Arabism—as the synthesis of Arab literature, of the recollection of, and aspiration for, an Arab state, and of the religion of Islam—is the product of the life and work of Mohammed who preached the monotheistic doctrine, "There is no God but Allah," to the people of Western Arabia in the beginning of the seventh century. The new religion, which made "submission to the will of Allah" its pervading principle, had a disciplinary effect on the loose-living and ever-quarreling Arabian tribes. Wine—along with gambling—was strictly forbidden, song was frowned upon, and women—the indulgence "dearest to the Arabian heart,"—were limited to four at a time, in the moderated polygamy which the Koran permitted. These virtues made not only for cleaner living but also for

3. T. E. Lawrence, *op. cit.*, p. 33.
4. H. A. R. Gibb, *The Arabs*, Oxford, 1941, p. 3.

better fighting. Moreover, all Moslems were declared brothers and the internecine raiding and looting hallowed by Arabian tradition were forbidden against members of the Islamic fraternity, though these activities were still deemed pleasing in the sight of Allah when exercised against non-Moslems. Energy saved through abstention from drink and cessation of tribal warfare was put to use in a great campaign of conquest. The Prophet had established a tiny state at Medina in 622 A.D. soon after his migration from Mecca to that city, and the early victories of the new Islamic community were not those of the Islamic religion but of the Islamic state. "It was Arabism and not Muhammadanism that triumphed first." [5] Within a century the arms of the Arabians, strengthened by religious fevor, had conquered the whole of Western Asia up to the mountains of Afghanistan, and across North Africa to the Atlantic seaboard.

The general view that Islam was spread by the sword—that the Arabian Moslems offered death with one hand and the Koran with the other—is only partly true. There was a third alternative—that of paying tribute—and this, it appears, was the preferred method with Jews and Christians, who as "People of the Book" were deemed less sinful than the pagans; besides they were also generally of the wealthier part of the population. The Koran enjoined: "Make war . . . upon such of those to whom the Book has been given until they pay tribute offered on the back of their hands, in a state of humiliation." [6] The economic element was probably a larger factor in the spread of Islam than imposition at the point of the sword. Converts to Islam, as members of the privileged Arab aristocracy, were exempted from a large part of the taxes, and were given a share in the benefits accruing from exploitation of infidels. Islam admitted peoples of all races, colors and nationalities, and "the economic benefits proved so great that the Arabs were eventually shouldered aside by peoples their own religion had made it impossible to exclude." [7] The remarkable spread of the Arab language and the Islamic religion "were not the results of a brutal military policy but the final

5. Hitti, *op. cit.*, p. 50.
6. As quoted in *ibid.*, p. 48.
7. Joel Carmichael, "The Arab National Movement" (manuscript prepared for the Esco Foundation Palestine Study).

consequences of an economic process the Arabs had neither foreseen nor desired." [8]

At first, to keep up the appearance of ethnic affiliation, the new converts were provided with Arab genealogies on the tribal pattern, but in the end the Islamic principle of equality and fraternity was victorious over the Arabian idea of tribal solidarity. All peoples who accepted the religion of Mohammed were absorbed into the unity of the brotherhood of Islam, and became part of the community which possessed the Arabic language and literature in common. As a result of the inclusion of many nationalities in the Islamic fraternity, the Arabs lost their power as a ruling class, and the Bedouin heritage became a minor element in the new Moslem Arab civilization. The conquered peoples, the Arameans, Persians and Greeks who accepted Islam, brought along with them a rich and diversified heritage of the ancient cultures of which they were the custodians. Arabia brought the spirit of vitality and renascence, together with the gift of brilliant poetry. But the scientific and philosophic content of the glorious mediaeval civilization attributed to the Arabs was largely the work of peoples who were Arabs not by descent but through their adoption of the religion of Islam and the language of the Koran. Arab predominance in the new Islamic state lasted no more than a century and a quarter, the decline of Arab power being signalized by the removal of the capital from Damascus to Bagdad. Islam became the designation of a universal civilization which inherited and synthesized the cultural heritage of the Iranian East and the Hellenic West.

And yet it is true that Islam and Arabism are largely identical, and that the central part played by the Arabs in creating and propagating the Islamic faith has had a permanent influence. It remains the fact that Islam was founded by an Arab prophet, that it is codified in an Arab sacred book, that it was developed by an Arab state.[9] Today, the believer still

---

8. P. K. Hitti, *History of the Arabs*, Macmillan, 1940, p. 218; *Cambridge Medieval History*, 1926, Vol. II, pp. 362 ff.; C. H. Becker, *Islam Studien*, Vol. I, 1924, pp. 10–12, 152–155, Vol. II, 1932, pp. 5–10; R. Levy, *An Introduction to the Sociology of Islam*, Williams and Norgate, London, 1931–1933, Vol. I, pp. 82–92; J. Wellhausen, *The Arab Kingdom and Its Fall*, University of Calcutta, 1927, pp. 277–282, 304–310.

9. Gustave E. von Grunebaum, "The Arab World" (manuscript prepared for the Esco Foundation Palestine Study).

turns in prayer to Mecca as the foremost sanctuary of Islam, and every Moslem is in duty bound to perform, once in his life, the pilgrimage to this hallowed place and to participate in ceremonies which Mohammed had adopted from age-old Arabian rituals. Like Judaism, Islam has remained, in a certain sense, a national religion, despite its international expansion and its claim to universality.[10] This is particularly true of the Arabic-speaking part of the Islamic world. The interplay of national and religious elements is more clearly realized when we remember that Islam is not, as Western religions are today, in the main, a matter of belief or ritual, but a complete way of life. Islam "not only creates personal beliefs about God, but gives form and substance to the communal life. The legal code of the State, the basis for marriage and divorce, the rights of property and inheritance, the detailed rules for personal conduct—all are in large measure a creation of the religious system. Islam is not so much a state religion as a religion which is a state, embracing every part of life." [11]

The Political Character of Islam and Its Attitude toward Non-Moslem Minorities

In defining what is Arab, therefore, it is of the very essence to bear in mind the interplay of the several factors—of literature, of political connection, of religious unity—which have given Arabs a sense of group solidarity. At its core is the consciousness of belonging to a people with a significant cultural heritage. It is this which makes the Arabs "an entity of political relevance," rather than the common geographical, ethnic, historical and religious factors, which, of course, also have entered into the making of this unity of group feeling.[12]

The substratum of common ways of belief, common attitudes and common modes of behavior is more important than the explicit avowal of Islamic religion. The social and political base of the Moslem-Arab consciousness is well expressed in the following paragraphs by Professor Jeffery:[13]

10. *Ibid.*
11. John S. Badeau, *East and West of Suez*, Foreign Policy Association, 1943, pp. 22, 23.
12. G. E. von Grunebaum, *op. cit.*
13. Arthur Jeffery, "The Political Importance of Islam," *Journal of Near Eastern Studies*, University of Chicago Press, October, 1942, pp. 383–386.

.... There are men in the Near East today who never perform a single cult practice of Islam, who never pray, never fast, never attend the Friday mosque services; who think it naive to believe in a personal god, in the survival of the soul apart from the body, in a revelation supernaturally given to a man or men; but who, nevertheless, consider themselves Muslims, and who would fiercely resent any suggestion that, because of their lack of belief or laxity in practice, they did not belong to the community of Islam. To be sure, such men are at present exceptional, but they well illustrate the fact that, quite apart from its religious importance among the world-religions, Islam is something else of importance—a social and political body in which men can feel that they are at home even when Islam as a religion has ceased to have any appeal to them ....

.... If, therefore, the Qur'an, as the final revelation from Allah never to be superseded, and the Sunna, or custom of the Prophet, as the perfect ideal for men to follow, are to remain as the two primary sources from which Islam derives its pattern for life, then Islam will always have a sociopolitical aspect, as well as a more narrowly religious aspect, and it will always be possible for this sociopolitical Islam to function as a culture pattern for community life, even where the religious teaching of Islam may cease to have binding force on men's lives. To some extent this is true, of course, of other religions; but it is more significant in the case of Islam, where those who still ardently believe in the religion, feel that this political aspect is something not to be divorced from religion.

The political character of Islam has found expression in a number of important tenets which play their part in the present struggle of the Arabs for independence and unity, even though this struggle is carried on today under the banner of Arab nationalism. First may be mentioned the *jehad,* which is defined in classic works on Moslem jurisprudence as "the religious duty of spreading Islam by force of arms." [14] Any Moslem who dies fighting in the *jehad* or holy war is a martyr (*shahid*) and as such is assured of special privileges in Paradise. Although a large-scale *jehad,* such as the Sultan-Caliph attempted during the First World War, is for a number of reasons not likely to succeed, the idea still has some power to move the Moslems. Another idea is the interest in the restoration of the Caliphate. This hope, too, is unlikely of realiza-

14. *Ibid.,* p. 387. The duty of the *jehad* just missed being included among the five absolute obligations of Moslems. It was raised to the dignity of a sixth pillar of Moslem faith by a formerly powerful but now minor sect, the *Kharijites.*

tion: efforts to restore the Caliphate permanently after its abolition by Kemal Ataturk in 1924 have so far proved abortive. Nevertheless, as a means of strengthening the solidarity of Arabs and Moslems the conception still has power, as was exemplified by the Islamic Conference in Jerusalem in 1931.[15] A third factor is the concept of divine right of occupation. To Moslems, all lands conquered by them—as they believe with the help of Allah—in former times are the inalienable possession of the Arab people. Professor Jeffery is of the opinion that: "Deeper than either of these [the fear of economic competition and the resentment against newcomers] as a source of Arab resistance to Zionism is the feeling that Palestine is a Muslim land by divine right." [16]

Another factor which should not be excluded in estimating the political force of the Arab tradition is the tenet of the superiority of the Moslem over non-Moslems. In Judaism and Christianity, the sense of being chosen has long been sublimated into a cultural and religious conception. It is not only that Moslem belief is "Islam is the final religion, the right way, the ultimate truth;" [17] other religions share this attitude with reference to their own creed. The point is that this world, as well as the next, belongs to the true believer, and that the elect of Allah are convinced that they have a divine right to rule over others. A fundamental fact to be borne in mind is that legally there cannot be political equality of Moslem and non-Moslem.[18] Jews and Christians, even though considered "People of the Book," nevertheless are "marked by the sign of the anger and the malediction of the Almighty." [19] They are to be tolerated but at a price: they have the status of *dhimmi*, that is, of persons in possession of a protective treaty by which they renounce certain rights and in return enjoy the practice of their religion and their customs. The famous covenant of Umar,[20] frequently regarded as evidence of Moslem toleration

15. See below, Chap. XI.
16. Jeffery, *op. cit.*, pp. 388, 389.
17. Jeffery, *op. cit.*, p. 392.
18. G. E. von Grunebaum, *op. cit.*
19. A *fetwa* (judicial opinion) of the fourteenth century (*Journal Asiatique*, Vol. 18, Paris, 1851, p. 408), as quoted by G. E. von Grunebaum, *op. cit.*
20. Probably an abstract from many individual covenants, or better still, an approximate description of actual affairs in the ninth century

and liberalism, is a good illustration of the Moslem point of view. It isolates the non-Moslems within their own religious groups and guarantees the safety of person and property at the price of permanent inequality and social inferiority. The general trend of the covenant is indicated in the following:[21]

When you came to us we asked of you safety for our lives, our families, our property, and the people of our religion on these conditions: to pay tribute out of hand and be humiliated; not to hinder any Muslim from stopping in our churches by night or day, to entertain him there three days and give him food there and open to him their doors; to beat the naqus—the wooden board which serves as "bell" amongst the Eastern Christians—only gently in them and not to raise our voices in them in chanting; . . . not to build a church, convent, hermitage, or cell, nor repair those that are dilapidated; nor assemble in any that is in a Muslim quarter, nor in their presence; not to display idolatry, not invite to it, nor show a cross on our churches, nor in any of the roads or markets of the Muslims; not to learn the Koran nor teach it to our children; not to prevent any of our relatives from turning Muslim if he wish it; . . . not to resemble the Muslims in dress, appearance, saddles, . . . ; to honor and respect them, to stand up for them when we meet together; not to make our houses higher (than theirs); not to keep weapons or swords, nor wear them in a town or on a journey in Muslim lands; . . . not to strike a Muslim; not to keep slaves who have been the property of Muslims. We impose these terms on ourselves and on our co-religionists; he who rejects them has no protection.

In practice, under the Moslems, minorities were sometimes treated worse and sometimes better than the legal arrangements provided. On the whole, the Moslems seem to have felt greater kinship with the Jews than with Christians, possibly because of the common Semitic background of the two peoples or because of the emphasis in Islam on the unity of God. Moreover, the political power of Christians created a degree of tension, as the Moslems were conscious of the fact that Christians might receive support from the West. The Crusades had led to a deterioration of the attitude toward Eastern as well as

rather than the work of the Caliph of Umar (ob. 644 A.D.), to whom it is attributed. (Quoted by G. E. von Grunebaum, *op. cit.*)

21. A. S. Tritton, *The Caliphs and Their Non-Moslem Subjects*, Oxford University Press, London, 1930, pp. 4–5. (Quoted by G. E. von Grunebaum, *op. cit.*) R. Levy, *op. cit.*, Vol. I, p. 95, Vol. II, pp. 161–162.

Western Christians. The greatest resentment was reserved for Christians of Arab descent; these were felt to be renegades from a natural loyalty to Islam. Although Jews and Christians attained high positions among the Moslems, they held their positions on sufferance, and strictly speaking, illegally. Pious circles always fought against the laxness which permitted non-Moslems to have a share in government. "The decisive point is not that in certain periods Jews and Christians trespassed without punishment the several restrictions imposed on them, but that both communities, the Muslim as well as the non-Muslim, were constantly aware of the fact that there were irrevocable restrictions incorporated in the Sacred Law and that there obtained in every-day life conditions of *laissez faire* not compatible with the sterner ordinance of this Law." [22]

The conception of a specially tolerated status for non-Moslem groups led to the development under the Ottoman Turks of the "millet" system which persisted until the Young Turkish revolution in 1908. The personal status before the law of an Ottoman subject depended on the privileges enjoyed by the religious community or *millet* to which he belonged.[23] The *millet* was self-governing in its internal affairs; its head, elected by the community with the confirmation of the Sultan, had just enough executive power to enable him to collect the taxes imposed on his community by the State.[24] The gradual westernization of the Ottoman regime after 1839 resulted in a diminution of the local autonomy of the minorities—some matters being withdrawn from the jurisdiction of the religious communities and settled uniformly for all Ottoman subjects. A certain contempt for the non-Moslem groups, for the "raya" (the Turkish pronunciation of the Arabic *ra'aya*, meaning herd animals) lingered on, along with their exclusion from the policy-making bodies of the old Turkish Empire. The *millet* system had its advantages and represented a satisfactory adjustment in the light of prevailing conditions.[25] While the

22. G. E. von Grunebaum, *op. cit.*
23. F. van den Steen de Jehay, *De la situation légale des sujets ottomans non-muselmans*, Société Belge de Librairie, Oscar Schepens and Co., Bruxelles, 1906, p. 7 (quoted by G. E. von Grunebaum, *op. cit.*).
24. *Ibid.*, pp. 347 ff.
25. G. E. von Grunebaum, *ibid.*

minority groups were inferior in point of their legal status, they enjoyed a great deal of freedom in internal affairs and a high degree of security. The change to the democratic constitution of 1908, in accordance with which all individuals were made equal before the law, abolished these special securities and rights of the minorities, but it could not readily do away with the traditional habit of mind that non-Moslems were inferiors.

The Arab Lands—Geographical Diversities and Social Divisions

As defined and characterized in the preceding pages, the Arabs are the predominant element in the area stretching from the Valley of the Euphrates to the western coast of North Africa. There are four regional units: (1) the Levant which consists of Iraq, Syria (including Lebanon), and Palestine (including Trans-Jordan); (2) the Arabian Peninsula including Saudi Arabia (now comprising the Hejaz and the Nejd), Yemen, Oman and Kuwait; (3) Egypt and the Anglo-Egyptian Sudan; (4) North Africa, including Libya, Tunisia, Algeria and Morocco.

To the religious and cultural factors that have given these countries a common character must be added a natural feature which has left indelible traces on Arab life, and which must be included in the definition of Arabism, namely, the background of desert. Despite great variation of climate and topography in all of the lands named, the proportion of cultivated to arid land is relatively small. With the exception of the oases in the interior and the coastal areas, the Arabian Peninsula is all desert. In Egypt, the fertile valley of the Nile supports a very dense population, but the country as a whole is ninety-seven percent arid. Trans-Jordan is four-fifths arid, while Syria and Palestine are, at the present time, half fertile and half uncultivated. The cause of infertility is not poor soil but the lack of water supply, and for that reason the so-called "uncultivable" area is a variable depending on factors of knowledge, skill, effort and organization. There is a never-ceasing struggle to extend the area of "the sown" and to prevent the desert from encroaching on it. The physical struggle between "the desert and the sown" is paralleled by a cultural struggle between the "tent and the town," between the tribal life—its vitalities and barbarisms—and civilized life, with its own peculiar virtues and vices.

Arab life is characterized by a dialectic social division into two opposites—the settled townsmen and the nomad herdsmen. There is a third group, sometimes the major social class, which consists of a fluctuating body of cultivators, half settled but still remembering their nomadic origin. The Bedouin, although exalting the free life of the desert and looking with contempt at the sedentary cultivator, always is tending toward settling down on the fringes of the desert. The Bedouin knows that settling down is the only means of escaping the insecurity and poverty which constantly haunt him. "The Bedouin is no gypsy roaming aimlessly for the sake of roaming." [26] His wandering is due to following the seasonal growth of grass or to the constant search for better pasture. The Bedouins' life represents an adaptation to desert conditions on the edge of civilization. They are shepherds, breeders of horses, and, particularly herdsmen of camels. The tribes in Southern Arabia especially like to call themselves "the people of the camel." The camel, the "gift of Allah," is the basis of their economic life; it not only provides transportation, but its flesh provides food and its milk drink; its skin and hair are made into clothes and habitation; its dung is fuel and its urine is used as a hair tonic and medicine. The camel may be regarded as the Bedouins' means of production, and the horse as their instrument of exploitation since its chief use is to provide the speed necessary for the success of Bedouin raids. The raid on the village to rob the *fellahin* of their harvest and animals is an indispensable part of Bedouin economy.[27] That the raid is essentially economic in its object, is indicated by the well-established mores

---

26. Hitti, *op. cit.*, p. 7.
27. The raid or *ghazw* (corrupted into "razzia"), otherwise considered a form of brigandage, is raised by the economic and social conditions of desert life to the rank of a national institution. It lies at the base of the economic structure of Bedouin pastoral society. In desert land, where the fighting mood is a chronic mental condition, raiding is one of the few manly occupations. Christian tribes, too, practised it. An early poet gave expression to the guiding principle of such life in two verses: "Our business is to make raids on the enemy, on our neighbor and on our own brother, in case we find none to raid but a brother!" (Hitti, *op. cit.*, p. 12.)

that no blood should be shed except in cases of extreme necessity.

The basis of Bedouin life is the clan organization: each tent represents a family; each encampment a clan; a number of kindred clans together make up the tribe. All members of the same clan consider each other of one blood, submit to the authority of one chief, and use one battle cry. "The spirit of the clan demands boundless and unconditional loyalty to fellow clansmen, a passionate chauvinism. His allegiance, which is the individualism of the member magnified, assumes that his tribe is a unit by itself, self-sufficient and absolute, and regards every other tribe as its legitimate victim and object of plunder and murder." [28] There are elements of primitive democracy in Bedouin life, as there are in all tribal civilizations; the Bedouin meets his fellow clansmen on an equal footing. But he looks down on those outside the group, regarding himself as "the consummate pattern of creation." He takes infinite pride in the purity of his blood and the nobility of his ancestry. The universal aspect of the religion of Mohammed, who was after all a townsman, rests lightly on him, and no element of humanitarianism characterizes his relationship to other men. The shedding of blood, whether with intent or without, according to the primitive law of the desert, calls for blood, or its compensating tribute; and vengeance is a responsibility which the next of kin must assume until the debt is paid. A feud between clans may last for a generation or more. The family is, of course, polygamous, and the man is master, but the woman is at liberty to choose a husband and leave him if ill-treated; the Bedouin woman has a greater measure of freedom than Moslem women in the towns. A high Bedouin virtue is that of hospitality; this mitigates the general harshness of his outlook and way of life. As long as the guest is in the area of his abode, the Bedouin is "loyal and generous within his laws of friendship." [29]

The Bedouin background sometimes shows through in the character of the villager and even of the townsman. Traits that are understandable as an adjustment to the desert environment often become distorted in the milieu of rural and urban

28. Hitti, *op. cit.*, pp. 14, 15.
29. *Ibid.*, p. 13.

life. In the political instability of the Arab may be seen traces of the individualism and impulsiveness of the Bedouin; vestiges of the clan feud are discernible in the lifelong opposition of rival families and in the political murders that are sometimes their accompaniment. The Bedouin devotion to his chieftain may reappear as the blind following of the leader of the party; the tribal loyalty may turn into national chauvinism; the absence of "half-tones in their register of vision"—to use Lawrence's phrase—may lead to intransigence and to inability to compromise. The tradition of raiding remains as a tendency toward looting; the conscious concern with blood revenge may break out from time to time in a veritable blood lust. As Professor Albright has graphically written: "Those who have seen the 'teetotal' peasants become intoxicated with blood lust at Nebi Musa and on other occasions, know how little is required to start an orgy of brutal murder almost anywhere in Syria or Palestine." [30]

The towns and the cities have always been the centers of Islamic and Arabic civilization. Despite their modernization, they are still picturesque, with remnants of beautiful old architecture, winding streets, and colorful bazaars. The cities are the centers of trade; they serve as residences for the wealthy landowners; they are the places of pleasure and the seats of government. The townsman has been the guide of the political destiny of the Arab as well as the standard bearer of Arab culture. However, the glory of the Oriental city as a seat of science and philosophy has long departed; today its mixed population and polyglot civilization too often produce the superficial Levantine, who speaks many languages but is master of none, and converses cleverly on all subjects but lacks genuine knowledge of any. The great contrast between riches and poverty is marked by the ever-present professional beggar, always ragged and often decrepit, insistently urging the cry of his trade: *"Baksheesh, miskeen; baksheesh, miskeen."* Inseparable from the Oriental cities are their odors, not all of which are intriguing. Sanitation is proverbially less than elementary, and the stench of "four thousand years of urine" —to quote a recent dispatch of John Steinbeck—permeates the older sections of the eternal cities of the East.

30. W. F. Albright, "Japheth in The Tents of Shem," *Asia and the Americas*, December, 1942, p. 694.

The main body of the people in the Arab countries—from sixty to ninety percent of the population, outside of Arabia where the Bedouins still prevail—are *fellahin* or tillers of the soil. The *fellah* is hard working, and his use of such tools as he has, not unskillful. But he has a hard struggle against unpropitious nature; he is not generally acquainted with the uses of fertilizer or crop rotation, either following the Bedouin tendency to exhaust the soil or at best letting it lie fallow to recuperate. Tradition, illiteracy and superstition make him slow in adopting new methods; diseases sap his vitality; and he labors in a burden of debt to the rich landowners who live in the cities. He is always poverty-stricken, living on the edge of a subsistence standard at a level not much higher than the starving masses of India and China. Although there are occasional expressions of antagonism against the landlords, there is no rebellious tension between the *effendi* and the peasant; the *fellah* accepts his poverty as "from Allah" along with the evils and disasters of life.

The Bedouin tribesman, the sedentary village cultivator, and the *effendi* landowner and merchant, represent the three major social classes in Arab life. These differentiations are all within the framework of the unitary Arab national self-consciousness. Another line of divergence is along religious and ethnic divisions. Every Arab country, excepting Arabia proper, has its minorities "who are precluded from fully sharing those loyalties and convictions which, by the terms of our definition, constitute the foundations of Arab national consciousness." [31] First, we may note the line of cleavage between the Moslem and Christian speaker of Arabic. There are practically no Christians in Arabia, and the number of native Christians in Libya and French North Africa is insignificant. The Christians constitute small but important minorities: in Egypt (8 percent) and Iraq (3 percent); and in Palestine they represent about 10 per cent of all Arabs. In Syria-Lebanon, however, the Christians constitute almost one-quarter of the population, and in the Lebanon they are in numerical preponderance, being about 55 percent of the population.

The influence of the Christian Arabs on the cultural, economic and political life in the Near East is far greater than the number might imply. They are to a large extent concen-

31. Gibb, *op. cit.*, pp. 7–8.

trated in the cities and this, in part, accounts for their relatively strong position. They are better educated than the Moslems and more receptive to Western ideas. They are regarded as having the support of their European co-religionists and must be taken into account in the political situation. One of the main problems for the Moslems, particularly in Syria and in Palestine, is not to lose the collaboration of the Arab Christians in the nationalist movement, while keeping the effective control in Moslem hands. The position of the Christian Arab is a difficult one despite his undoubted influence. The Christian Arab intelligentsia look upon themselves primarily as Arabs; since they are not sure that their Moslem neighbors so regard them, they are at times impelled to profess a more strident nationalism than their Moslem compatriots. At the same time they are apprehensive of Moslem domination should Arab nationalism succeed.

The Moslems divide into two main groups of *Sunnis* and *Shiis*. The origin of this division was in a political, not in a doctrinal conflict. The *Sunnis* maintain the correctness of the historical order of the succession of caliphs of early Islam, but the *Shiis* claim that Ali, the cousin and son-in-law of the Prophet, was the only legitimate successor and that the others were usurpers. The political quarrel became a religious schism and national differences played their part in producing different outlooks. Broadly speaking, *Sunnism,* although it is the established orthodox view, is more tolerant and less divided by sectarian disagreements. *Shiism,* split into numerous smaller units, has taken on the character of mystic sectarianism, often secretive and intolerant. The schism is an important issue in Iraq where the ruling Hashimite house—descended from the Prophet through the regular succession—are *Sunnites,* while the majority of tribesmen and the population in the Holy Cities of Nejef, Kerbela and Kazimain are *Shiites*. It is also an issue in Arabia as a form of *Shiism* is the dominant creed in Yemen; on the other hand, *Sunnism* is the prevailing religion in the Hejaz, while Ibn Saud and the people of the Nejd are *Wahabis,* a puritanical sect now counted as within the *Sunnite* orthodoxy. The *Kharijites* represent another extreme militant and puritanical sect within *Sunnism,* formerly strong, but now mainly confined to parts of Algeria and to the Emirate of Oman in the southeastern corner of the Arabian Peninsula. In

Syria the religious position is complicated by the presence of several forms of heterodox *Shiism*—the Druses, Nusairi, Ismaili—bizarre sects which include elements of paganism and Christianity as well as of Mohammedanism.

ARAB NATIONALISM AND INDEPENDENCE AFTER THE FIRST WORLD WAR

There is no doubt that a powerful social force which may properly be described as Arab nationalism is at work at transforming the life of the peoples in the Near East, and that this force, besides manifesting antagonism to the alien domination of the British and the French, is also today opposed to the Jewish aspirations in Palestine. At the same time, it is necessary to bear in mind that the term "nationalism" means many things and that the various elements composing it operate with different intensity and with a different effect in the varying contexts of the Near East situation. In some instances, Arab nationalism in the Near East signifies a general attempt at a cultural renascence with Arab culture as the basis, and the achievement of a great Arab state as the goal; in other instances, it appears to be little more than the attempt on the part of persons and groups to replace the French and British administrators and capture the privileges and powers that go along with public office. At times the Arab national movement is clearly associated with a strengthening of Islamic religion and with a general movement for the conservation of tradition; at other times it has imitated the secularism of Western nationalism in its more extreme forms, and has been particularly concerned with breaking away from the past. In one aspect it signifies the unification of all Arab peoples, either in the Pan-Islamic bond with a restoration of the Caliphate, or through a union of States in a Pan-Arabic Confederation; in the actuality, nationalism in the Near East has worked in the direction of the creation of separate nation-states, Egypt, Saudi Arabia, and Iraq. One interpretation of Arab nationalism conceives it to be the product of the rising middle class accompanied by the recognition of the national "we" of all classes; in reality, it appears to be closely connected with an attempt on the part of the land-owning classes to maintain their age-long predominance. Frequently, Arab nationalism speaks in the name of democracy; more often than not—particularly during the last decade—it played the role of the agent of the Axis Powers in the Near East.

Arab Nationalism before the First World War

Arab nationalism, as generally held, arose in the nineteenth century as a reaction, stimulated by Western ideas, against Turkish domination and European imperialism. The rise of Arab nationalism was a revival rather than a new movement: it intensified Arab consciousness and quickened it as a political force, but the feeling of the Arabs that they belonged to a definite group goes back to the pagan tribal days before the advent of Mohammed.[32] No doubt, in spreading Arabism, Islam diluted it; nevertheless, the Arab conquests "were a national movement inspired by a religious faith." [33] Most of the conquered peoples who accepted Islam merged with the Arab nations and lost or submerged their own sense of nationality, and this contributed to the idea that there was no nationality in Islam. However, the Turks who came as conquerors set a different tendency in motion. They refused to dissolve into the Arabic melting pot—at this time saturated with Persian culture. A feeling of disparateness and a certain hostility was early engendered between the Arabs and the Turks, each looking upon itself as superior to the other. The Arabs regarded themselves as representatives of an ancient and brilliant culture with a great literature. The Turks were conscious of their military and political superiority and they identified the Arabs largely with the masses of *fellahin* and the tribes of uncivilized Bedouins. The process of estrangement lasted for centuries; up to the modern era, as long as religion was the recognized communal bond and substratum of cultural life in the Near East, the Turks and Arabs aligned together against the outside world. But as the Turks themselves became Westernized and nationalized, and as Western ideas of national freedom penetrated among the Arabs, the latent national self-consciousness of the Arab peoples began to emerge.

Arab nationalism developed first in those countries which were most open to European influences, i.e., Egypt and Syria. The form that nationalism took in each of these centers was different, but there was reciprocal influence. Egyptian na-

32. G. E. von Grunebaum, *op. cit.*
33. Gibb, *op. cit.*, p. 9.

tionalism was the earlier; it was more closely related to economic and political realities, and it had a longer, more normal development. Napoleon opened up Egypt to European influence in 1799 in his famous Near Eastern campaign. But it was Mehemet Ali, who, as Viceroy of the Sultan, recognized the significance of Westernization for Egypt's development as a modern nation. An Albanian by birth, who never succeeded in mastering Arabic and had no sympathy for the traditional Islamic culture, he sought to make Egypt a strong country, economically and politically. Under his rule, Egypt became the best administered part of the Ottoman Empire. He did away with the Mamelukes and thus detached Egypt from its mediaeval foundations, and built up an efficient army and navy. Utilizing European experts, he overhauled the irrigation system, promoted the cultivation of cotton and laid the basis for sanitation, encouraged technical education and sent promising students to the Western universities. His power grew so great that only the intervention of Great Britain prevented him from entering Constantinople and securing the Caliphate for Egypt and himself. The defeated Sultan had to grant him the hereditary possession of Egypt, including the Sudan, under a suzerainty which became merely nominal.

Mehemet Ali had been able to finance his reforms by extortion and taxation, but his successors had to resort to European loans to continue the modernization of Egypt. The fluctuations in the price of cotton during and after the American Civil War badly affected the finances of the Khedive Ismael (1863–1879), who also involved Egypt in warlike adventures in the Sudan and against Abyssinia. Egypt, in any case, lacking the necessary capital for development of its resources, soon found itself on the verge of bankruptcy. In 1875, the Khedive had to sell Egypt's share in the Suez Canal to Great Britain and to submit to European control of Egypt's exchequer. By 1879, Ismael's financial difficulties had become so involved that the Powers put pressure on the Sultan to depose him, and the latter sent a telegram to "Ismael Pasha, *late* Khedive of Egypt," directing him to abdicate in favor of his son, Tewfik.

The struggle for the independence of Egypt now began to be directed against the Western European Powers as well as against the Turks. Ahmad Arabi, the son of a *fellah,* organized a peasant movement against the Turkish aristocracy, which led to an open rebellion against the government. After a period of unrest, the British, in alliance with the new Khedive and with the acquiescence of the Sultan, defeated Arabi at Tel el-Kebir (September 13, 1882). From that time on, the English occupied and dominated Egypt. The revolt, however, left its mark on Egyptian history; for the first time in the Orient a nationalist slogan had been used in rallying popular support, for Arabi had tried to create a united front of all classes under the slogan of "Egypt for the Egyptians."

The growing anti-European feeling in the Near East was stimulated by the work of the great Islamic scholar and reformer, Jamal Din al-Afghani. He preached freedom from foreign domination as a prelude to moral regeneration, and aimed to unite the Moslem peoples under one universally acknowledged Caliph, as in the golden age of Islam. Afghani made his life an unrelenting crusade for a progressive conception of the Islamic faith as a means of raising the Moslem peoples to the status of free nations. Through revival of religious feeling he strengthened the national loyalty of Moslem intellectuals who did not wish to surrender to the secularism of the West. His influence extended from Persia to Egypt. His chief Egyptian disciple, Muhammed Abduh (1849–1905), became the teacher of the able political leaders of the following generation, among whom was the outstanding Saad Pasha Zaghlul (1860–1927), the organizer of the *Wafd* party. The religious element in Egyptian nationalism acted as a unifying force. However, the hostility toward the worldly-minded nationalist reformers soon became associated with a cultural and social conservatism.

In Egypt, the press played an important part in the diffusion of the nationalist movement. Despite the terror organized by the Ottoman Government, the publications issued in Cairo penetrated to all parts of the Arabic-speaking world. Syrian nationalists were attracted to Egypt where the British offered an open door to Arab political refugees and permitted them freedom of speech. In Syria itself the development of the national movement began in the sphere of cultural aspirations and lacked the economic and political basis that gave Egyptian nationalism a ground in realities. Western ideas came to Syria largely through foreign mission schools. American Protestant missionaries were pioneers in the introduction of Western teaching; their activities, beginning in 1820, culminated in the founding of the Syrian Protestant College at Beirut in 1866 (now the American University of Beirut). French Jesuits following soon after, initiated educational work in 1831, and established the University of St. Joseph in 1875. These schools fired the imagination of the Syrian youth by exalting the beauties of the Arabic language and the glory of the Arabic past. Butrus Bustani (1819–1883), who collaborated with the Americans in translating the Bible into Arabic, and Nasif Yaziji, who strove in his numerous writings to restore the classical purity of Arabic, were leaders in a revival of national enthusiasm on the basis of the Arabic language and literature. In 1847, a society of arts and sciences gathered around these two Lebanese Christians whose efforts were supported and directed by members of the American Mission in Beirut.

During the suppressive rule of Abdul Hamid II (1876–1908), the movement for Arab independence smoldered under cover. He had begun his reign by granting a liberal constitution, promising equality to subject races. But the constitution was soon suspended as he rid himself of the anti-Ottoman coalition of European powers which he had feared. He instituted a highly centralized administration and ruled the country from Constantinople with the aid of a corrupt palace clique and a thorough-going system of espionage and bribery. As Sultan, he maintained a large army in the training of which he had the help of a German mission which had arrived in Constantinople in 1883. As Caliph, he exercised his great religious influence to repress the recalcitrant peoples of the Empire. Among the Arab intellectuals in the Empire the aspiration for the renascence of Arab culture began to be associated with rebellion against political oppression.

As early as 1880 there were the beginnings of a well-defined Arab national revolutionary movement. Reports of the British Consul General in Beirut reveal a progression from rhetorical denunciation of Turkish misrule to the formulation of a basic program of national aspirations. On one of the first placards used is surmounted a device representing a drawn sword below which is the following line: "By the sword may distant aims be attained; seek with it if you mean to succeed." A dispatch posted by the British Consul General on December

31, 1880, gives the outline of a well-defined course of action. The program opened with an indictment of the Turks for attempting to suppress the Arab language; it described the Sultan's tenure of the Caliphate as a usurpation of Arab rights; and stated that after consultation "with our colleagues all over the country" a plan had been drawn up which would be carried out at the point of the sword if necessary. As formulated by George Antonius on the basis of records found in London, the main points of the program were:[34]

(1) the grant of independence to Syria in union with the Lebanon;
(2) recognition of Arabic as an official language in the country;
(3) removal of the censorship and other restrictions on the freedom of expression and the diffusion of knowledge;
(4) employment of locally-recruited units on local military service only.

In contrast to the Egyptian development, which from the beginning had been associated with the immediate achievement of political power and, in a measure, with the improvement of the life of the Arab masses, the Syrian movement in its early phase was largely literary and retrospective and had little contact with the economic-social problems involved in national regeneration. Moreover, because of the prominent part that Christians played in the revival, the unity of all Arabs in Arab history and literature was stressed and the emphasis on the Islamic content of Arabism—which would have been divisive—was avoided. In the late decades of the nineteenth century, as noted, the Syrian nationalist movement began to have more of a political character. Toward the end of the century Moslems began to take the lead out of the hands of the Christians in promoting Arab national feeling, and the Moslem content as well as the political purpose of the movement was emphasized. One of the outstanding leaders was Abdul-Rhaman Kawakebi (1849–1903), nicknamed Abdul-Duafa, the Father of the Weak. He drew a sharp distinction between the Arab and the non-Arab Moslems, emphasizing the intimate connection between the Arab genius and the spirit of Islam. While upholding the doctrine of the unity of Islam,

34. George Antonius, *The Arab Awakening*, Lippincott, 1939, p. 84.

he advocated the abolition of the Sultan's title to the Caliphate and urged instead the setting up as Caliph in Mecca of an Arab directly descended from the clan to which the Prophet belonged. To his appeal for an Arab-inspired religious revival, he joined an impassioned impeachment of the tyranny of the Sultan.

The emerging element of political realism was crystallized by the rise of the Young Turks. At first the Arab nationalists of Syria regarded the Young Turks as brothers in a common cause for the national regeneration of all peoples in the Ottoman Empire. But their enthusiasm was soon dampened when they realized that the apportionment of electoral districts had been designed to secure a Turkish majority in Parliament. The rise of the Committee of Union and Progress (C.U.P.) with their policy of Turkification and their plan for administrative centralization on the French model drove the Arab representatives in Parliament into the ranks of the so-called Liberals who demanded a program of decentralization and local autonomy throughout the Empire. Agitation was organized in secret societies, particularly by Arab officers in the Turkish Army. The appeal was first on the grounds of Islamic brotherhood: the Turks were reproached for neglecting the interests of the Moslem community as a whole in favor of their particularistic national advantage. But this tendency was soon submerged by the increasing secularization of thought along the lines of Western nationalism and by the desire to bring Christian and Moslem Arabs together in the national cause.

In the beginning, the program of the Arab societies was limited to the demand for autonomy within the framework of the Ottoman regime, but the Young Turks were bent on a policy of unification under the banner of Turkish nationalism and suppressed all centrifugal tendencies. The Arabs, on their part, advanced toward a demand for complete independence couched in the embracing phrase: "All Arabic-speaking lands for the Arabs." This significant departure from the pattern of Ahmed Arabi's battle-cry, "Egypt for the Egyptians," may be accounted for by two factors. The Syrian Arabs—who were prominent in the new movement—had become imbued with the nationalist aspiration through the study of Arab history and culture, and tended to regard the new nationalism as a method of resuscitating the glory of the old far-reaching Arab dominion. The other factor was the association of Arab representatives from various parts of the Ottoman Empire in the Turkish Parliament. In their struggle for freedom they faced a common problem which transcended the regional interests of individual countries. The contacts made between Arab leaders in Constantinople helped to cement the bonds of the common political aspiration. This association of the Arab national movement with the struggle against "Turkification" had another consequence: while the Pan-Arab movement spoke vaguely of a union of all Arabs, in practice the effort was devoted to creating a federation of those Arabic-speaking peoples which were subject to the Ottoman Empire before the First World War.

During the War, this broad conception of Arab independence was powerfully strengthened by the Allied slogan of self-determination for all peoples and by the extravagantly worded pronouncements in favor of Arab independence. Such influences played a more important part in giving a basis for the extensive Arab demands than the specific promises in the letters from McMahon to Husain. There may be some doubt as to whether the Syrian nationalists were acquainted with the reservations made by the British which excluded coastal Syria and Palestine, although the Sharif undoubtedly understood the nature of the reservations. But even if the reservations had been precisely worded, the dynamic power of the national idea enforced by the concept of self-determination would have broken them down. It is all the more interesting to note that while the idea of a general Pan-Arab liberation retained a strong driving force, in the actual development Arab independence was obtained piece-meal through the creation of individual states. This has been attributed at times to the fact that the British and the French divided up the Arab countries for their own purposes. The truth is that the realities of the situation did not permit the actualization of Pan-Arabism: the different backgrounds of social-economic conditions in the various regions and the struggle for power of the different dynasties, as well as the lack of a sufficiently strong Pan-Arab feeling among the people at large, were basic causes. While similar tendencies were at work, each country achieved its degree of independence in its own way.

Postwar Development in Arab Lands

The countries and tribes in the Arabian Peninsula—both those who had remained neutral as well as those who aided the Allied cause—became independent with the collapse of the Turkish regime, although a number of them continued to receive subsidies from Great Britain. Husain ben Ali, the Sharif of Mecca, had himself proclaimed King of the Hejaz at the time of his revolt against the Turks in 1916. In 1924, after Kemal Ataturk had abolished the Caliphate, Husain declared himself "prince of the faithful and heir of the Prophet." But this assumption of the Caliphate was strongly resented in the Nejd, in Egypt and in India, and contributed to his downfall. His position had greatly weakened since pre-war times; Ibn Saud, head of the Nejd tribes to the north, was challenging Husain's hegemony in the Arabian Peninsula and the British were getting tired of trying to keep the peace between them. They were also irked by Husain's pretentious demands for the creation of a great Arab Confederation with himself as the head. In 1924, while negotiations between Husain and the British were still going on, Ibn Saud attacked the Hejaz, and Husain was forced to abdicate. He fled the country, leaving the crown to his son Ali who ruled for a short time in Mecca, but soon had to withdraw to Jidda. In 1925, Ibn Saud occupied Medina and Jidda and the rule of the Hashimite family in Arabia came to an end.[35]

Ibn Saud and Arabia

Abdul-Aziz Ibn Saud, who has recently been acclaimed by some American writers as "Prince of the Arabs,"[36] was not widely known during the First World War, although he already had some achievements to his credit. In times past, his family had been a leading dynasty in the Arabian Peninsula. However, in 1880, when Abdul-Aziz was born, the Saudi family had lost control even over their own capital Riyadh, and father and

---

35. While Ali was defending himself at Jidda, the English occupied the Maan-Aqaba district—on the ground that it needed protection from Ibn Saud. The question whether it belonged to Trans-Jordan or to the Hejaz had previously been in dispute. Ibn Saud has never abandoned his claim to this important region.

36. For example, Joel Carmichael, "Prince of the Arabs," *Foreign Affairs*, July, 1942.

son were in exile under the protection of one of the Kuweit chieftains. Ibn Saud achieved his first victory at the age of twenty, when he recaptured Riyadh in a bold attack with the aid of some thirty or forty men.

At the time of the outbreak of the First World War, several British Orientalists—Captain Shakespear, Gertrude Bell and St. John Philby—had recognized the potentialities of the young prince, but Kitchener and Storrs of the Cairo Bureau chose the aged Husain, who, as a descendant of the Prophet, they thought enjoyed great prestige among the Arabs. During the war Ibn Saud remained neutral, receiving a subsidy from Great Britain as did other Arab sheikhs. In 1918, a quarrel developed between King Husain and Ibn Saud, but Britain, through Philby, dissuaded the latter from engaging in hostilities. After the war, Ibn Saud began to round off his territories by conquests of neighboring tribes. Between 1920 and 1922 he captured Hail, the capital of the Shammar tribe, and acquired the fertile oasis Jauf and parts of Assir. Recognizing his growing strength, the Cairo conference in 1921, headed by Churchill, increased his subsidy from £5,000 per month to £100,000 per year, balancing the payment to him against that made to Husain, which was of equal amount.[37] In 1923 the subsidy was discontinued. No longer feeling bound by his promise not to attack Husain, Ibn Saud opened his successful hostilities against the King of the Hejaz and made himself ruler over the major part of Arabia.

Ibn Saud, like his forebears, was inspired by the doctrine of the Wahabis, a puritanical sect founded in the early part of the eighteenth century by Mohammed Abdul Wahab. This reformer aimed to purify Islam and held that everything that the Koran did not order, or did not expressly authorize, was prohibited and sinful. He emphasized three positive virtues: to pray, to read the Koran, and to wage war against infidels— and to him, Moslems who did not live in accordance with his own strict interpretation of the Koran were infidels. His teaching was rejected in his native city Ayaina, but he was welcomed by the rival city Daraya, where the Saud family, the forefathers of Abdul-Aziz, ruled. Abdul Wahab married a daughter of the ruling Prince and the Saudi family, joining

37. Margret Boveri, *op. cit.*, pp. 304–305.

the inspiration of religion with the strength of arms, carried the cleansing sword of Islam across Arabia. They conquered the Hejaz and penetrated Syria, establishing themselves as masters of this entire area until the Turks, rising to the danger, drove them back into the desert.

Ibn Saud is a true follower of the Wahabi doctrine: he has declared that he is in the first place a Mohammedan and only in the second place an Arab.[38] He is supported by the *Ikhwan* —religious communities organized as brotherhoods—which he has developed into a disciplined fighting force. Through these fraternities, which are composed of members of different tribes, a beginning has been made in breaking down the old clan organization with its feuds and jealousies. The *Ikhwan* communities are also playing an important part in turning the Bedouin from nomadic to agricultural pursuits. In peace, the *Ikhwan* cultivate the soil; in war, they are the well-armed core of Ibn Saud's army, ever ready to fight zealously against infidels and against those who are slack in the performance of their Moslem duties.

Ibn Saud's rule over this vast area has been the result of armed conquest and he and his *Ikhwan* have the reputation of ruthlessness in war, but he is moderate in the treatment of his conquered foes. Through drastic measures he has eliminated from his territories robbery—the besetting sin of the Bedouin. Although rated a shrewd politician, he is said to be genuinely interested in the welfare of his country. Like a true Arab chieftain, his ear is open to the voice of the tribesmen, but the decisions rest with him; of democracy, in the modern Western sense, there is, of course, none in this first of the truly independent Arabian states. In one respect he is modern: he has used tanks in warfare against his neighbors; and he is supplied with automobiles and airplanes. He is also ready to consult Western agricultural experts in the development of the country. In another respect he follows thoroughly the good old-fashioned Moslem tradition: he has allowed himself the full flexibility of the Moslem marital law and is reputed to have had over a hundred wives in the course of a quarter of a century of vigorous manhood.

38. Henri Lammens, *Islam: Beliefs and Institutions*, Dutton, 1929, p. 120, quoted by Joel Carmichael in "The Arab National Movement."

National and Social Development in Egypt

Among the Arab countries entertaining European conceptions of government, Egypt was the first to receive formal independence, which was granted in 1922 when the Sultan Fuad was raised to the position of King. The form of government was determined by the Constitution of 1923, under which Egypt was to be governed by a hereditary king, his ministers, and an elected bicameral parliament. Britain reserved her rights in the Sudan and in the defense of the Suez Canal, which necessitated the presence of British troops in Cairo and other cities. These reservations became the target of renewed nationalist agitation by the *Wafdists* led by Saad Zaghlul. The demands of the nationalists were opposed not only by the British, but also by the King, who did not wish to see the development of a strong parliamentary regime. The *Wafdist* Party, which promoted the nationalist cause, had the backing of the middle class, the business people and intelligentsia, aided by some members of the landed aristocracy. There had been peasant elements in the revolt of Ahmad Arabi in 1882, but in this period the effort was narrowly directed toward the purely nationalist goal and the problem of improving the lot of the masses became secondary. In fact, the nationalist movement took on an anti-labor coloring. An Egyptian labor movement began to develop during the twenties but was energetically suppressed in 1927 by the so-called liberal-democratic ministry under Saad Zaghlul.

A certain amount of social legislation has been passed in the fields of child welfare, prenatal and infant care, and there has been some improvement in hospitalization. But these activities have thus far been inadequate, as may be judged by the continued high death rate among the population. A compulsory education law has also been passed and the budget for education increased. However, the education law is not strictly enforced and more is spent relatively on secondary education for the upper middle classes than on elementary education for the masses. According to the figures of 1937, over 70 percent of the Moslem male population and 90 percent of the females still do not know how to read or write. The elementary schools are not articulated with the secondary school system—so that a child who completes the lower school has no opportunity for higher education except in the mainly religious studies offered by the University of al-Azhar. Some legislation for industrial workers has been introduced, particularly to protect juvenile and female labor, and the working day has been fixed at nine hours with a total of fifty-four hours for the six-day week. Farm labor, however, is still exposed to unmitigated exploitation. Egypt's chief problem on the social side is still that of providing a minimum living standard for the *fellahin* who constitute ninety percent of the people.

Although there is interest in the problem of independence for neighboring Arab lands, Egypt's nationalism is mainly centered in Egypt. There is a movement referred to as "Pharaonism" which aims to repudiate Arabism as a basis for Egyptian national development. In accordance with this view, Egypt has never been ethnically Arab; it is claimed that the great masses of the people are descended from the ancient Egyptians and their tradition and culture go back to the Pharaohs. The advocates of Pharaonism generally urge that geographical contiguity, common history and affinity of interests are the determining factors in national development, and that for Egyptians these elements exist only within the Egyptian borders. Professor Gibb, who knows Egypt well, says: "The eyes of Egyptians are focused on Egypt, and while they do not deny Egypt's kinship with the Arab world and interest in its fortunes, they regard Egypt as a separate and independent unit. If we hold to our definition of Arabs, we must exclude from them large sections of Egyptians, for whom the re-emergence of Egypt is a more important fact than the memory of the Arab Empire, and who tend to set the glories of Rameses II alongside the mission of Mohammed as equal elements in their tradition. This attitude may perhaps be modified substantially in the course of the present conflict, but whatever the outcome the relations of Egyptian Nationalism with Arab Nationalism will be one of the decisive factors in the future of the Middle East." [39]

Abolition of the Mandate in Iraq

In Iraq, the struggle for abolition of the Mandate and for complete independence continued throughout the whole decade of the twenties. In his address at the time of his assumption

39. H. A. R. Gibb, *op. cit.*, p. 18.

of the kingship in 1921, Faisal had referred to a treaty to be made between Iraq and Great Britain. There was constant unrest as one draft after another of the proposed treaty was suggested by the British and rejected by the Iraqis. A great gulf divided the British conception of the treaty from that entertained by the Iraqis. The British wished to secure control over the foreign relations of Iraq, to continue a large measure of financial supervision, and to retain the relationship with the League of Nations which gave the British juridical authority to remain in Iraq. The British regarded the treaty not as a substitute for the Mandate—which would remain the document defining the obligations undertaken by His Majesty's Government on behalf of the League of Nations—but as a system of administration which would be less costly to them than the Mandate and which would involve less friction with the native population. "The treaty was, in short, a method of control." [40]

The Iraqis on their part wanted the treaty for the purpose of abrogating the Mandate altogether, for replacing the British officials by their own and avoiding control by a foreign power. At a joint meeting, held in November, 1921, by the two nationalist political parties, an address to the King was presented which culminated in three demands: 1) Immediate termination of British influence; 2) Election of a cabinet made up of "sincere patriots possessing the confidence of the people;" 3) Suspension of treaty negotiations until the meeting of the freely elected Constituent Assembly. Faisal, while recognizing the need of compromising with the British, at heart sided with the nationalists and in the negotiations that followed during the next year, he went as far as he could in defending their demands. On one occasion he informed the High Commissioner that in the event of a rising he disclaimed all responsibility.

In the drafting of the treaty the King and his Prime Minister were consulted, but the work remained throughout in British hands. The draft treaty met a united opposition which included the King, the Prime Minister, the Council of Ministers as well as the nationalists. The main objection was that the treaty did not specifically abrogate the Mandate relation-

---

40. Philip W. Ireland, *Iraq, A Study in Political Development*, Macmillan, 1938, p. 338.

ship. There was much agitation in the press, serious demonstrations against the Government, and seditious disturbances throughout the country. The King happened to fall ill with appendicitis and the High Commissioner took over the reins of Government. Drastic measures were taken, including deportation of notables and crushing of an incipient revolt of tribesmen. After the recovery of King Faisal the High Commissioner told him plainly that the British Government would not tolerate his connection with future nationalist agitation, nor brook any further delay in ratifying the treaty. The Cabinet was brought in line and on October 10, 1922, the Council ratified the treaty; however, in spite of the strenuous objection of the High Commissioner, it reaffirmed a previous resolution that the treaty must be approved by the National Assembly.

The treaty provided that Great Britain would be represented in Iraq by "a High Commissioner and Consul General assisted by the necessary staff." The authority exercised by the High Commissioner as adviser to the King, under the new arrangement, was not essentially different from what it had been under the Mandate. A subsidiary agreement regulated the number and conditions of the employment of British officials. The King of Iraq agreed, according to the treaty, to be guided by the advice of His Britannic Majesty on all important matters affecting international and financial obligations. Moreover, as long as Iraq was under a financial obligation to Great Britain, the King would fully consult the High Commissioner on fiscal policy. The treaty also provided for British military aid to Iraq. Iraq also agreed to accept provisions which Great Britain regarded as necessary in judicial matters to safeguard the interests of foreigners. No territory in Iraq should be ceded or leased to the control of any foreign power. In the event of any difference of opinion as to the interpretation of the treaty, this was to be referred to the Permanent Court of International Justice; and if modification of the treaty were found advisable, this was a matter for the two Governments and the League of Nations.[41]

There was much difficulty in getting the Constituent Assembly organized and inducing it to recommend the ratifica-

41. Henry A. Foster, *The Making of Modern Iraq*, University of Oklahoma Press, 1935, pp. 116–119.

tion of the treaty by the King. But this was finally accomplished on June 10, 1924, after Great Britain threatened to consider the treaty rejected if ratification were postponed any further. Moral suasion and intimidation had been used in order to achieve the ratification, but the most important factor in obtaining consent was the realization on the part of the Iraqis that they needed the help of Great Britain in order to obtain the oil district of Mosul with its great potentialities for revenue. The resolution of the Constituent Assembly had clearly indicated the unsatisfactory character of the treaty, but accepted it because it relied on the "honor of the British Government and the nobility of the British Nation" to assist it in the discharge of its responsibilities. What it meant concretely is indicated in the last sentence: "This treaty and its subsidiary agreements shall become null and void if the British Government fail to safeguard the rights of Iraq in the Mosul Vilayet in its entirety." [42]

The Turks at this time were strenuously disputing the British claim to Mosul and opposing the plan to attach it to Iraq. After an investigation the Council of the League decided in favor of the British. The Turks had at first refused to accept the ruling and applied to the Hague Court, but the latter decided that Turkey had to accept the findings of the League of Nations, and in June, 1926, a treaty was signed between England, Iraq and Turkey in which the Mosul District became part of Iraq. In awarding Mosul to Iraq, the League of Nations laid down two conditions: 1) that the Mandatory regime would be continued for an additional twenty-five years unless Iraq were admitted as a member of the League before the expiration of this period; 2) that guarantees would be given to the Kurdish minority in Iraq for local autonomy. In subsequent negotiations between the British Government and the Iraqis the High Commissioner favored recommending the admission of Iraq to the League of Nations in 1928. His Britannic Majesty's Government regarded this date as premature, but a treaty was finally completed in 1930 which envisaged Great Britain's support of Iraq for its entry into the League of Nations in 1932.

Throughout this period there were internal difficulties in Iraq; struggle between the Shiites and the Sunnites for in-

42. Foster, *op. cit.*, p. 123.

fluence and position in the Government; between the Iraqi majority and religious and national minority groups, e.g., the Kurds and the Assyrian Christians; and between the Administration and the Bedouin tribes who were not accustomed to the payment of taxes and whose economic position, never secure, was deteriorating as a result of modern developments.[43] Observers agree that Faisal's moderation and his success in retaining the confidence of the nationalists was an important element in the achievement of a workable political compromise. There is, no doubt, an element of truth in this; at the same time realistic accounts indicate that the British to whom he was indebted for his kingship had to exert pressure on him to accept their "reasonable" resolutions. After Iraq gained independence, it appears that Faisal had great difficulty in controlling the extremists, and some believe that he was intending to abdicate, when death overtook him in 1933.[44] In 1936, the pseudo-democratic regime gave way to a military dictatorship and the country soon fell prey to Axis intrigue.[45] Faisal's untimely death probably contributed to the deterioration of the situation in Iraq. But the difficulty was more fundamental: the cultural, social and economic conditions of Iraq had not justified so early a granting of political independence —as the Permanent Mandates Commission had feared at the time.

"Divide and Rule" in Syria

Syria was the most complicated problem. Culturally and economically it was more advanced than the other areas of the old Ottoman Empire. France, however, was obstinate in its opposition to the Arab nationalist movement. Syria, which was received as one country in accordance with the Mandate, was divided by the French into five separate units. Lebanon, with a population of 900,000, was made autonomous; this in itself

---

43. The development of motor transportation through the desert made the breeding of camels less profitable, and the improvement of the police force augmented by airplanes made the raiding of caravans too dangerous (Boveri, *op. cit.*, p. 367).

44. Margret Boveri, *op. cit.*, p. 365.

45. The military coup d'état in 1936 was carried out by pro-Turkish elements. In 1941, the former Prime Minister, Rashid Ali Gailani, in conspiracy with the exiled Mufti of Jerusalem, Haj Amin al Husaini, almost succeeded in delivering Iraq with its oil fields to Hitler. See below, Part IV, Chap. XV, p. 963.

was justifiable since the Lebanon with its predominantly Christian population had been an independent *sanjak* under the Turks. However, it received an extension on the coast which enlarged its boundaries beyond those of Turkish times and gave it a large Moslem population. Out of Syria proper (population 1,700,000), two states were carved, one with a capital at Damascus and the other at Aleppo; later, the two parts were again merged into a single "State of Syria." Another separate unit was the territory of Alawiya with the capital at Latakia; this state (population 300,000) also got a strip of territory along the Mediterranean coast. Djebel Druze in the hilly region, with its population of 60,000, was declared a separate entity, and Alexandretta was declared autonomous, in compliance with Turkish wishes.

France was faced with strikes, disturbances and rebellions throughout the decade. In October, 1925, the Government had to resort to shelling Damascus for forty-eight hours in order to restore control. The most serious rebellion was that of the Druses which lasted from 1925 to 1927. Though not a nationalist outbreak in origin, it won the sympathy of the Arab nationalists to whom everything that embarrassed the Mandatory Power was welcome. France attempted to moderate its policy, at least in form. In 1926, Lebanon was declared a republic; in 1928, an election of a constituent assembly for Syria was permitted. However, the extreme nationalists received an overwhelming majority, and the first resolution of the Assembly was a demand for full independence and for the unification of Syria and Lebanon. The High Commissioner thereupon suspended the Assembly. A new republican constitution was promulgated in 1930 and a parliament elected in 1932, but suspended indefinitely in 1933.

From the technical point of view, France gave Syria a good administration: roads were improved, railways developed, airplane fields built and industry encouraged. But France's efforts were regarded by most Syrians as a means of strengthening her military control over the country and securing her economic penetration. Frenchmen controlled the railways, the tramways, the municipal and public works, the telephone installations, and the constructions in the Beirut harbor. The Syrian lire was tied to the franc, giving France a preferential position in trade and subjecting the Syrian middle class to the fluctuations of the French currency. On the cultural side, France enlarged its influence by development of schools and through official use of the French language. A system of public education was founded, but the French-dominated private schools were twice as numerous as the public schools.

The French have been accused of improving on the old "Divide and Rule" principle by a system of "Divide, and Divide Yet Again." [46] On their part, the French have held that the rivalries in the country and the need to protect minorities make a unitary system of government throughout the country impossible. There is no doubt some truth in both contentions, particularly as applied to the decade of the twenties.[47] The minorities wanted autonomy and protection from the Moslem majority, and experience showed that they needed it. While the limitations on democratic government were without doubt motivated by France's desire to continue its domination over the country, there was at the time a basis for the following view offered by Comte de Goutaut-Biron, who in 1928 surveyed the administration of Syria: "One must ask oneself what the so-called democratic constitutional reforms mean in this country. For my part, I see nothing in them but a vast, stupid deception. Only inexperienced newcomers would let themselves be taken in by it, but not men accustomed to the practice of Oriental politics. Far from encouraging the dawn of an era of freedom, this means of applying the parliamentary system by elections is bound to perpetuate the corrupt despotism of the tribal chiefs and of the great landlords and their tyranny over the poor." [48]

ARAB AFFAIRS IN PALESTINE

The General Character of Arab Palestine

From the seventh century to the conquest by the British, Palestine formed a part of the Moslem empires which ruled from Damascus, Bagdad, Cairo and Constantinople. It took

46. Robert L. Baker, *Oil, Blood and Sand*, Appleton-Century, 1942, p. 209.
47. Margret Boveri, *op. cit.*, p. 320.
48. *Ibid.*, p. 321.

no great part in the development of Arab Moslem culture, although for a time it had a local center of Arab learning.[49] The influence of Judaism on Islam, however, has left a trace in giving Palestine a certain religious distinction in the Moslem world. There is a legend that two years before his migration from Mecca, Mohammed was one night miraculously transported from the *Kaaba* in his home city to the *Haram esh-Sharif*, the stone platform on which stands the Dome of the Rock of the Mosque of Aqsa. From there he ascended to the seventh heaven on his magic steed, *al-Buraq*. Originally, Mohammed designated the *Haram esh-Sharif* as the *qibla*, or the point toward which Moslems turn in prayer, and later after Mecca was chosen, Jerusalem remained, along with Mecca and Medina, one of the holy cities of Islam.

On the racial side, Arab Palestine is a mixture of the many stocks that have passed through it in trade, invasion and conquest. The Arabian type of the desert Bedouin is distinguishable throughout the country. The peasants are a highly mixed group in whose veins flows the blood of the ancient Canaanites, Arameans and Hebrews. The *effendi* landowners and city Arabs generally are products of the successive waves of conquerors and of officials who were granted large estates in Palestine by the central government either at Cairo or Constantinople. The predominant type resembles the Southern European, but there are occasional examples of North European types, and these are reputed to be descendants of the Crusaders. In the hot Jordan Valley one may find Negro Sudanese, probably descendants of soldiers who fought under Ibrahim Pasha in the middle of the nineteenth century. In the Gaza district on the southern shore of Palestine, the population is largely of Egyptian origin and contains the racial strains characteristic of the Valley of the Nile. There are also descendants of Moroccan, Tunisian and Algerian emigrants and mercenaries who have brought an admixture of Berber stock.

It is highly improbable that any but a small part of the present Arab population of Palestine is descended from the ancient inhabitants of the land. Apart from the populations brought in by the conquerors, Palestine, like Syria, has from time immemorial been peopled by the drifting populations of

---

49. *Palestine Royal Commission Report*, p. 5.

Arabia, and to some extent by the backwash from its harbors.[50] It is generally agreed that the population of Palestine had been reduced to a low figure in late mediaeval and modern times. In 1882, the population was probably about 300,000, of whom about 35,000 were Jews. A careful estimate made by Cuinet in 1895, placed the figure at 457,592, of whom over 60,000 were Jews.[51] In 1914, at the outbreak of the First World War, the total population had increased to about 600,000, of whom 85,000 were Jews. During the war, the population was reduced through deaths of old people and children, losses in the Turkish Army, deportations by the Turkish authorities, and emigration. In 1920, the population of Palestine was officially estimated at 673,000, of which number 521,000 were Moslems, 78,000 Christians, 67,000 Jews, and 7,000 others, mainly Druses.

The Arab population of Palestine is predominantly agricultural. According to the census of 1922, the total non-Jewish rural population—mostly Arabs—numbered 477,693, which was about 70 percent of the total non-Jewish population. Excluding the Bedouins, who were estimated at the time as 103,000,[52] the number of non-Jewish inhabitants of rural districts was 374,693, who constituted about two-thirds of the non-Jewish settled population. The rural population is mostly agricultural, depending on farming and sheep and goat raising. Those engaged in industry and handicraft—building, stone cutting, carpentry, weaving—are also to some extent dependent on agriculture. Those classed as urban lived in twenty-two towns, only three of which—Jerusalem, Jaffa and Haifa—had populations of 25,000 or more in 1922. The smaller towns, in which more than half of the Arab "urban" population lived, were not cities in the European sense; they were hardly more than enlarged villages as most of the inhabitants engaged in agriculture. The social stratification among the Arabs in Palestine follows the threefold pattern of all Arab countries and comprises: 1) Nomads (bedouin); 2) Peasantry (*fellahin*), agricultural laborers; and 3) Urban

---

50. George Adam Smith, *The Historical Geography of the Holy Land*, Hodder and Stoughten, 21st ed., pp. 7 ff.
51. Vital Cuinet, *Syrie, Liban et Palestine, Géographie administrative, statistique, descriptive et raisonée*, Paris, 1896.
52. This is probably an overestimate. See Chap. VIII.

population. The urban population may be again subdivided into three classes: a) upper (*effendi*)[53] class consisting of large landowners, Moslem religious hierarchy, professional people and some merchants; b) middle class, consisting of merchants and shopkeepers; c) urban masses, consisting of artisans, wage earners, daily laborers, seamen, stevedores, porters and professional beggars.[54]

Poor economic conditions in Palestine and Syria before the First World War led to considerable emigration of the native population. Some migrated to Egypt, but the main stream went to Central and South America and to the United States. Arabs called to military services with the Turkish Army formed a class of involuntary emigrants, since many of them never returned. During the first decade after the establishment of the Civil Administration, emigration slowed down; but the number of recorded Arab emigrants still exceeded the number of recorded immigrants. There was, however, an infiltration from neighboring countries across the frontiers, and it is probable that the increase of the Arab population during the first decade was in some measure due to unauthorized immigration, as well as to natural increase.

The crude birth rate of the Arab population of Palestine is high, due mainly to a very high birth rate among the Moslem Arabs, which during the years 1920–1930 was about 52 per 1,000. The birth rate among Arab Christians is not so high, i.e., about 37 per 1,000 for the corresponding period, not much higher than the Jewish birth rate, which was about 34 per 1,000. However, the Moslem Arabs also have a very high death rate, with the result that the net natural increase, that is, excess of births over deaths, does not show so large a discrepancy. During the first decade, the net natural increase was: for Moslems, 24 per 1,000; Christians, 20 per 1,000; and Jews, 22 per 1,000.

The census of 1922 revealed that there were, outside of the British forces, 668,258 non-Jews in Palestine. Probably 650,000

53. The word "effendi" is a Turkish word derived from the Greek *authentes;* as used in the Levant it means "gentleman" and corresponds somewhat to the English Mr. or Esquire. *Effendis*, generally belonging to the land-owning classes, constituted the governing aristocracy of the Ottoman Empire.

54. For a further analysis of the social composition of the Palestine Arab community, see Chap. VIII, pp. 500.

of these used Arabic as their native tongue and might be designated as Arabs. Close to nine-tenths of the Arabs are Moslems, nearly all of the *Sunnite* denomination. There is no important religious schism among the Moslem Arabs of Palestine as there is in Iraq, and to a certain extent in Syria. The Christian Arabs, however, definitely constitute a self-conscious minority despite recent collaboration in the political field against Zionism. Traditionally, in Palestine as elsewhere, Christians were despised as infidels by the Moslem majority; furthermore, they were envied and resented as they had acquired privileges and economic positions under the protection of foreign Powers.

The difference between the Moslems and Christians is accentuated by the fact that the two groups are markedly divergent in their educational background and their social-economic structure. The Christians are predominantly an urban population; most of the leading merchants are Christians; and, on the whole, the Christians tend to enjoy a higher standard of living than the Moslems. Thanks to the educational opportunities afforded by the missionary organizations, the Christian Arabs are more cultured in the European sense and the better educated among them generally speak one or more foreign languages. Most of the Arab physicians, lawyers, writers and government officials are Christians, and in the early 1920's nearly all Arab periodicals were edited by them. In 1929, the number of Arab Christians in government service still amounted to more than half of the total Arab government employees despite the fact that they were only 10 percent of the population. Notwithstanding the social and religious differences, the Moslem and Christian Arabs have been drawn more closely together as a result of modernization, the development of Arab nationalism, and antagonism toward Zionism.

Personal Factors in Palestine Politics

Before the First World War there was no serious Arab political movement in Palestine. Although Arab nationalism had strong roots in neighboring Syria, it had hardly more than a handful of adherents in Palestine. "Politics" consisted largely of the maneuvers among rival families of the upper *effendi* class, directed toward gaining public offices and maintaining control of local affairs under the Turks. After the war the spread of the nationalist idea and of Western concepts of political organization, and the example and stimulation of Zionism, began to give Arab political life a more impersonal and more patriotic content. In the 1930's, although the different factions still corresponded in the main with family allegiances, parties began to be formed on the Western model where differences of opinion on issues play a part in the formation of groupings. In the first decade of Zionist development, however, family rivalries among the upper classes still lay at the base of political activity and factional differences.

In concrete terms, political activity for the upper class families meant: 1) maintenance of the dominant position which they had held under the Turks; 2) increase of prestige through as great a share as possible of the government positions and municipal jobs; 3) assurance of future control of the country, if and when Britain granted independence. The struggle of the leading families for maintaining their power and prestige became linked with a struggle against Zionism. Jewish penetration of the country would change the whole character of political life and deprive the *effendis* of their privileged position as the ruling elite. The ambitions of the former governing aristocracy inevitably led them to an alignment with those whose opposition to Zionism was on more genuinely national grounds. The coincidence of the interest of the landowning classes with Arab nationalism gave it a reactionary character and contributed toward making Arab nationalism, during the thirties, an easy prey of Axis propaganda. In terms of family rivalry, Arab political life in Palestine was dominated, particularly during the first decade, by two family groupings: the Husainis and their allied families; and the Nashashibis and Dajanis, with their satellites—the group being generally referred to as "the Nashashibis," because Ragheb Bey Nashashibi of Jerusalem was its leader.

The importance of Jerusalem made the offices of mayor and of mufti[55] in that city particularly sought after by the political families. In 1917, on the eve of the British occupation of Palestine, both these offices were in the hands of the Husaini

---

55. Ordinarily, the position of mufti had no political significance; the mufti is a religious official whose duty it is to issue canonical rulings on points of Moslem religious law. There are muftis in all the larger towns.

family.[56] The office of Mayor of Jerusalem was occupied by Musa Kazem Pasha, and that of Mufti by Kemal Effendi Husaini. In 1920, Ronald Storrs, as Governor of Jerusalem, dismissed Musa Kazem for leading a Nationalist demonstration and appointed as Mayor the head of the rival house, Ragheb Bey Nashashibi. In 1921, Kemal Husaini died and the Nashashibi-Dajani faction almost captured the office of Mufti, which had been in the hands of the Husaini family for a number of generations. Due to the intervention of Sir Herbert Samuel, who evidently wanted to keep the honors balanced between the two leading families, Haj Amin al-Husaini, a brother of Kemal, was appointed to the post, for life. Haj Amin had played a leading part in the riots of 1920 and had recently been pardoned.

According to Turkish law which was still in force in Palestine at the time, the Mufti was to be chosen from among the three candidates who received the highest number of votes from a convocation of *ulema* (or Moslem scholars), religious officials and Moslem notables. On this occasion, the three leading candidates for the post were associated with the Nashashibi group of families. The Husainis carried on a widespread propaganda to have Haj Amin elected by the groups entitled to vote, but Haj Amin made only fourth place. Though he had for some time attended the Theological University of Al-Azhar in Cairo, he was not regarded as a competent scholar. Through pressure exerted by the Administration, the candidate who had received the smallest number of votes out of the first three was induced to withdraw so that Haj Amin rose to third place. He then received the approval of Government which was necessary for the appointment and became the Mufti of Jerusalem, the first step in his ascendancy to the leadership of the Moslem community.

Although this now notorious member of the Husaini family is generally referred to as "the Mufti," his real power sprang from the presidency of the Supreme Moslem Council, for which

56. The Husainis are reported to have come to Palestine over two hundred years ago. They married into the family of the greatest landowner in southern Palestine, Sheikh Abou Ghosh. Later they also married into a local family which traced its descent to the Prophet, adopted the name of Husaini which indicated this, and accepted the responsibility for the custody of the shrine of Nebi Musa.

his appointment as Mufti of Jerusalem was the entering wedge. The Supreme Moslem Council was established in December, 1921, as the body authorized by Government to deal with Moslem religious affairs. The Council was granted full authority over all Moslem *Waqfs*—properties under religious custody—and over the *Sharia*—Moslem religious courts. It had the power, with the approval of the Government, to nominate and appoint the judges of the *Sharia* courts and to choose the muftis from among the three top candidates elected by a special electoral college. At the first election, which was held in 1922, Haj Amin was elected President, probably because in the corresponding body in Turkish times the Mufti of Jerusalem was generally recognized as the head. The Supreme Moslem Council had a large income from fees and fines. It also had at its disposal considerable patronage through the appointment of judges of the *Sharia* courts and through recommendations for jobs of a lower order. The presidency of the Supreme Moslem Council enabled the Mufti to build up a supporting organization as efficient as any American political machine. Besides, as head of the highest Moslem authority, the Mufti-President exercised an important psychological influence on the religious-minded peasants of Palestine.

Until the time of the election of the Mufti to the presidency of the Council, there was a fair balance of power between the two leading political families—the Nashashibis and the Husainis. Indeed, there was a rumor in Palestine that the Nashashibis had consented to having one of the candidates withdraw at the time of the elections for the Mufti of Jerusalem in order to make place for Haj Amin among the three leading candidates, the understanding being that the municipal post of mayor would remain in Nashashibi hands and that the religious function would be exercised by the Husainis. But the election of a Husaini to the post of presidency of the Supreme Moslem Council upset this balance and created a lasting cleavage in Palestine politics between the *Mejlissin,* or the pro-Council party, and the *Muaridin,* oppositionists or anti-Council party. These two "parties" corresponded to the two leading family groupings—the Husainis and their allies constituting the *Mejlissin,* and the Nashashibi-Dajani group constituting the *Muaridin.* The conflict was particularly bitter in view of the fact that Haj Amin claimed that his election had been for life, on the basis of the precedent established in the case of the mufti. The Nashashibis challenged this interpretation, and the Government tended to side with them on this issue; but despite this, Haj Amin held onto the post of presidency until 1936, when he was removed by the Government for seditious activity.[57]

The two groupings, the *Mejlissin* and the *Muaridin,* which represented—in large measure, if not altogether—a division between "the ins" and "the outs," have at some time been described as different in their social composition and as divergent in their political attitudes. There is some basis for this, but the differences should not be exaggerated. The *Mejlissin,* "in" or pro-Councilites, were built around the nucleus of the powerful Husaini family, which consisted of great landowners and high Moslem dignitaries, but they also included merchants, professional men and Christians, particularly Roman Catholics. The party included a hard core of employees and beneficiaries of the Supreme Moslem Council of the *Waqf* administration and of the *Sharia* courts. The *Muaridin* opposition, led by the Mayor of Jerusalem, Ragheb Bey Nashashibi, also had a basis of wealthy landowners with a somewhat larger contingent of merchants, professional men and government officials. The party included Moslem functionaries who had been ignored by the Supreme Moslem Council, and the Christian contingent was largely Greek Orthodox. Seen as a whole, both factions were only slightly different divisions of the upper *effendi* classes.

Both factions subscribed to the basic Arab political platform in Palestine, which called for the repudiation of the Jewish national home policy and for the establishment of an Arab National Government. The Nashashibi group was generally represented as being more moderate in its attitude, as more ready to cooperate with the Government and more willing to take into consideration the practical benefits of the Jewish development in Palestine. It is true that Ragheb Bey, of easy conscience, well versed in the practices of Turkish

---

57. Even after he was removed from the presidency of the Supreme Moslem Council, supporters of the Mufti who were trying to arrange for his return to Palestine claimed that he could not be deposed by the British from the position of Mufti of Jerusalem since this was a religious office which he held for life.

officialdom, was more ready to calculate and compromise than the feudal and intransigent Haj Amin al-Husaini. But too great emphasis should not be placed on the moderation of the Nashashibis: they constituted the Opposition Party and their policies must always be judged in the light of the policies of the dominant Husaini leadership. When the Husainis were extreme, as was generally the case, the Opposition might become moderate in order to curry favor with the Government. Yet occasionally, when the Husainis showed signs of moderation—as in 1924, when they appeared to be ready to accept a proposed arrangement between King Husain and the British—the Nashashibi Opposition became extreme in their anti-Government attitude and accused the Husainis of selling out for jobs.[58] In the 1930's, the Nashashibi Opposition found it expedient to compete with the Husaini leadership in extremism, when they bid for the adherence of the Youth Movement.

Ideas and Organization of Early Arab Political Policy

Only a minority of the Arabs of Palestine are politically active and these are mainly of the *effendi* class. Even the so-called "peasant parties" which sprang up for a time during 1924–1925, were organized by city lawyers or religious personages to counteract the dominance of the Husainis or to advance their personal interests. The masses of the people—the Bedouin, the *fellahin* in the villages, and the city day-laborers—are illiterate and easily influenced by propaganda from above. Despite the impression of democratic procedure created by the use of the term "congress," the members of the conventions and meetings which determined Arab policy were appointed or invited by the leaders. An opposition might be disposed of by the simple technique of not inviting delegates from districts or groups when their views were known to diverge from those of the leaders. An alternate method of "election" consisted in the appointment of an organization committee which in turn appointed the delegates. Meetings so organized would vote a program representing a paraphrase of standard Arab demands for independence, including resolutions against the Balfour Declaration, the Mandate, immigration and land sales; sometimes with a broad statement about economic, social and cul-

---

58. *Haaretz,* February 17, 1924.

tural developments thrown in as a decoration. The same group of notables who arranged the elections would constitute the Executive and the main leader would be elected president. The "cooperation" of a whole Bedouin tribe or of a peasant village might be secured through enlisting the support of the sheikhs or the *mukhtars*. This might be done by persuading them of the holiness of the enterprise, by promises of a share in the prospective loot, and, when such means failed, by threats of retaliation.

This portrayal of a personal and class character of Arab political organization in Palestine should not obscure the fact that a certain psychological affinity and some consciousness of a common political purpose existed between the leaders and the people at large. The Arab politicians in a sense reflected as well as controlled the attitudes of the people. Nor can the fact be overlooked that Arab political activity in Palestine was concerned with serious aims and that it exemplified a definite line of policy. The three major ideas underlying Arab politics in other countries—Pan-Islamism, Pan-Arabism and a National Independence—were factors in Palestine as well. As generally in the Arab world, Pan-Islam—the idea of strengthening Moslem unity through the Caliphate—was not a strong motivating idea in and of itself; it was more of a lever for raising the Mufti's prestige and a means of arousing religious feeling for the attainment of national independence. Pan-Arabism was, in general, a stronger force, but again as an activating idea rather than as a concrete program. Just as "democracy" has become a slogan among Western politicians—and some cry it loudest when least believing in it—so every Arab political leader has to make federation of Arab states part of his program, even though he may be opposed to it as not in conformity with his own interest. In Palestine, the idea of federation had even less potency than in other countries of the Levant. It was confined to the group led by Auni Bey Abdul Hadi, who played a minor role in Palestine political affairs during the first decade.

The major and direct motivation of Arab political policy in Palestine was the achievement of national independence under the control of the Arabs; consequently, the major Arab political parties were opposed to the Balfour Declaration and to the Mandate based on it. The major thesis of the Arab political program from the beginning rested on the principle that the Arabs were the "owners" of the country. Their interpretation of the concept ownership was extreme; they refused to accept any proposal which "tends to place them on an equal footing with the alien Jews." [59] They disputed the Zionist claim based on the "historical connection" of the Jews with Palestine and refused to recognize that the Jews had any rights but those of individuals. It was their policy to make a sharp distinction between Jews of the old *Yishuv,* with whom they had lived on good terms—as they alleged—under the Turkish regime, and "Zionist Jews" who were represented as making all the trouble by introducing the political concept of the Jewish national home. While they were ready to cooperate with Jews in business, and their general attitude was not unfriendly to Jews as individuals, they absolutely refused to meet the Zionists as a group or to negotiate with them in political matters.

The ultimate aim of Arab nationalism is to achieve complete independence and do away with the domination of European Powers. However, in the period under discussion, the Arab leaders maintained on the whole a conciliatory attitude toward Great Britain. Their declared policy was to support the British Mandate provided Britain would drop the Jewish national home program. During the first decade, the strategy was not to antagonize the Government unduly and to retain a legal façade in their opposition. When illegal action was resorted to, as in the case of the riots and disturbances, this was alleged to be the natural outbreak of anti-Jewish feeling on the part of the people due to the injustice of the Balfour Declaration policy. The feelings of exasperation of the administrators worried by the difficulties of implementing the Jewish national home policy were played upon. The Arabs represented themselves as the weaker party, lacking the wealth and influence of the Jews, and appealed to the British reputation for fair play in the expectation that the Government would be induced to champion their cause.

Arab political activity in Palestine between 1917 and 1920, which may be regarded as the first phase, was not distinguishable from that of Syria. It emanated from Damascus and demanded a united Syria, rejecting the policy of the Jewish

59. Royal Institute of International Affairs, *Great Britain and Palestine, 1915–1939,* p. 37.

national home in Palestine, along with the claims for a separate regime in the Lebanon. Palestine was always referred to pointedly as Southern Syria by both Palestinian and Syrian leaders. A feature of this period was the organization of the Moslem-Christian societies in the leading towns of Palestine, with the purpose of exercising pressure on the Peace Conference and the British Government to abrogate the Balfour Declaration. The Moslem-Christian societies like the Arab nationalists also demanded the inclusion of Palestine in an independent and united Syria. The organization of these joint societies is significant in that it indicates the beginning of a rapprochement between Arab Christians and Moslems and is indicative of the growing strength of the national as against the purely religious tie. British residents in Palestine and some of the personnel of the Administration encouraged this Moslem-Christian union as a means of counteracting the Jewish national home policy. The Arab leaders were led to believe that London was not absolutely committed to the Balfour Declaration; that with a change of the government in Great Britain, the Balfour Declaration might be rescinded as dangerous and unworkable.

THE COURSE OF ARAB POLITICS IN PALESTINE: 1918–1929

Formulation of the Anti-Zionist Position

As early as 1918, there appears to have been some attempt at an anti-Jewish demonstration, but the Military Administration feared, in the light of experience in Egypt, that this might assume an anti-British character. Consequently, it prohibited the demonstration, strengthened the Jerusalem garrison, and conducted searches for arms in the villages. In January 1919, Arab notables in Palestine met in Jerusalem in what was termed an "All-Arab Palestine Conference." It was presided over by Aref Pasha Dajani, a leading notable of Jerusalem and "a man of long and honorable career in the Ottoman civil service." The resolutions of this Congress were cabled to the Paris Peace Conference and expressed the following demands: 1) repudiation of the promise of a national home to the Jews; 2) rejection of the French claims on Syria; 3) establishment of a united independent Syrian Government "within an Arab nation." [60]

The Nebi Musa celebration in April, 1919, passed off quietly despite Arab warnings that "the Jordan would be filled with blood." This is attributed by Jewish authorities to the strict attitude of the Military Administration. The following year, however, demonstrations were permitted by the new head of the Military Administration, Sir Louis Bols, well known for his opposition to Zionism. The first demonstration took place in February 1920, when there were rumors that matters at the Peace Conference were going unfavorably for the Arabs, and another in March, on the day after the proclamation of Faisal as King in Damascus. It was on this latter occasion that Musa Kazem Pasha, the Mayor of Jerusalem, incurred the disfavor of the Administration by marching at the head of the demonstration. The Nebi Musa riots on April 4, 1920, of which Haj Amin al-Husaini was reputed to have been one of the leading instigators, came as a climax to these more peaceful demonstrations which had been permitted by the Government.

The establishment of the Civil Administration in Palestine in the summer of 1920 and the expulsion of Faisal from Damascus, necessitated a reformulation of the political position of the Arabs of Palestine. There now emerged a definite Palestine policy as separate from the older Syrian policy. To clarify their position, the Arab leaders called a Convention to meet at Haifa in December, 1920. The Husaini and Nashashibi groups and the Moslem-Christian societies united under the chairmanship of Musa Kazem Pasha, the former Mayor of Jerusalem who had recently been dismissed. This meeting became known as the Third Palestine Arab Congress.[61] The resolutions emphasized that the Convention spoke for all the Arabs of Pales-

---

60. M. E. T. Mogannam, *The Arab Woman and the Palestine Problem*, p. 115. It should be noted that once the Mandate was approved, Aref Dajani who headed this first political convention, became an exponent of economic cooperation with the Jews (Kisch, *Palestine Diary*, pp. 64, 67, 82).

61. Palestine delegates attended the General Syrian Congress on July 2, 1919, organized in connection with the King-Crane Commission, and the General Syrian Congress held on March 8, 1920, when Faisal was chosen King. These two Syrian Congresses were regarded as the first two Arab Congresses; hence the designation "Third Palestine Arab Congress," which was in reality the first separate Palestine Arab political convention.

tine; it called for a national government and expressed dissatisfaction with the British Administration for promoting the Zionist policy. It proclaimed that "Palestine, the Holy Land, belongs to the Christian and Moslem worlds and the administration of its affairs should not be entrusted to non-Moslems and non-Christians." The resolutions passed at the Haifa Congress in 1920 formed the basis of Arab policy for the ensuing period. They read as follows:[62]

This Palestine Arab Congress, lawfully representing all classes and groups of the Arab people of Palestine, is now convened at Haifa on this the 13th day of December, 1920.

Basing itself on the treaty entered into between Great Britain and her ally, His Majesty King Hussein, King of Hejaz, in 1915, and on the declarations made by the head of the various Governments of the Allies to the effect that the peoples who were severed from the Turkish Empire should have the right to determine their future and to choose the form of government most suitable to them,

Demands of the British Government in the name of international honour and humanity, and in the name of the Moslem and Christian faiths, to embark on the establishment of a National Government in Palestine responsible to a representative Council, to be elected by the Arab-speaking people who were living in Palestine at the outbreak of the Great War, on the same lines and principles which are being applied in Iraq and Trans-Jordan, in furtherance of the friendly relations which long existed between Great Britain and the Arab Nations.

The Congress, being fully confident that its just demands will receive favourable consideration, desires to confirm that any delay in their execution will mean the continuation of the present undesirable situation, the increase of the disappointment of the Arab people, and the incurrence of exorbitant expenditure on the maintenance of internal and external peace.

Further, the Congress speaking in the name and on behalf of the Arab people, declares its dissatisfaction with the present form of Government in that it does not satisfy their wishes and fails to safeguard their interests for various reasons, the most important of which are the following:

    (a) Government exercises the power of legislation without a representative Council and before the final decision of the League of Nations is given.

    (b) Government recognizes the Zionist organization as an official body.

62. Mogannam, *op. cit.*, pp. 125–127.

(c) Government proceeded with the application of the Zionist policy by allowing the admission of Zionist immigrants, recognizing the Hebrew language as an official language and permitting the use of the Zionist flag.

(d) Government established an Advisory Council in a false attempt to show that there exists in Palestine a Council with legislative powers representing the population.

(e) Many Jews of standing in Zionist circles were appointed to various offices of Government, although Palestine, the Holy Land, belongs to the Christian and Moslem worlds, and the administration of its affairs should not be entrusted to non-Moslems or non-Christians.

Out of the Haifa Congress there developed a new body in Arab political life, namely, the Executive Committee of the Palestine Arab Congress, commonly referred to as The Arab Executive. From its inception it was dominated by the Husainis; Musa Kazem,[63] the former Mayor of Jerusalem, was elected Chairman and Jamal Husaini, Secretary. Thus, in addition to controlling the religious hierarchy, the Husainis now dominated political activity. The first effort of the Arab Executive—their attempt to impress Winston Churchill when he was in the Middle East from December, 1920, to March, 1921—proved a failure, as noted in the last chapter. Whether by design or accident, the May 1921 disturbances followed, resulting in a temporary suspension of immigration and encouraging the Arab Executive to press its demands in London.

Rejection of the 1922 White Paper

The next Arab Congress, designated the Fourth, convened in Jerusalem about six months later, on May 25, 1921. It resolved to send a delegation to London to plead the Arab cause

63. Musa Kazem al-Husaini remained President of the Arab Executive until his death in March, 1934. He was past middle age, and the recognized head of the Husaini family and already had a distinguished career when he assumed political leadership of the Arab Executive in 1920. His father had been Mayor of Jerusalem and he himself a Governor of Yemen and a *Qaimaqam* or Deputy-Governor of the District of Jaffa. To Musa Kazem is attributed the strategy of "demanding everything and conceding nothing." In his manner, however, he was suave and gracious. Later, when his method of sending delegations and submitting petitions proved a failure, it appears that he yielded to the influence of the younger Haj Amin, who was ready to use more drastic means in the promotion of the Arab nationalist policy.

and to demand the rejection of the policy of the Jewish National Home. Sir Herbert Samuel tried to induce them not to go and instead to cooperate with him in the drafting of the proposed Palestine constitution. They absolutely refused to be dissuaded from their purpose. After abortive efforts in London and Geneva, the delegation proceeded to Damascus where they participated in the Syro-Palestine Congress which met in September, 1921. Impressed by the Turkish successes against the Greeks, then the protégés of the British, and encouraged by the lack of unity among the Allies in dealing with resurgent Turkey, this Syrian Congress adopted maximum demands including: a united Arab state, the evacuation of the armies of occupation from Syria, Lebanon and Palestine, and the abrogation of the Balfour Declaration.[64]

Despite the separation of Palestine from Syria at the San Remo Conference, the Syrian political leaders had continued to regard themselves as the older brothers of the Arabs of Palestine. The Executive Committee of the Syro-Palestine Congress with headquarters at Cairo, always included Palestine in the memorials which they repeatedly sent to the Permanent Mandates Commission concerning the grievances of Syria. The Congress established a permanent office in Geneva, known as the Syro-Palestine Delegation, which was headed by the exiled Druse leader, Emir Shakib Arslan. It is not clear whether at this time the Palestine Arab Executive still wished Palestine to be a part of Syria or whether they were aiming for a separate Palestine Arab State. During the same month, September, 1921, the Palestine delegation protested to the League of Nations that no plebiscite had been taken to determine the people's choice of a mandatory, and that the draft mandate did not conform to Article 22 of the Covenant of the League of Nations.

The delegation returned to London early in 1922 with the object of opposing the proposed Palestine constitution of the Legislative Council. In letters dated February 21st and March 16th, the delegation gave a summary of the Arabs' objections to the Balfour Declaration. The essence of their position was that they could not cooperate in the drafting of a constitution for Palestine as long as the Jewish national home policy, in

64. *Oriente Moderno*, Vol. I, October, 1921, pp. 291–292; December 21, pp. 411–412; Medzini, *op. cit.*, p. 192.

any form whatsoever, remained the basis. The introductory paragraphs declared:[65]

Whilst the position in Palestine is, as it stands today, with the British Government holding authority by an occupying force, and using that authority to impose upon the people against their wishes a great immigration of alien Jews, many of them of a Bolshevik revolutionary type, no constitution which would fall short of giving the People of Palestine full control of their own affairs could be acceptable.

If the British Government would revise their present policy in Palestine, end the Zionist *con-dominium*, put a stop to all alien immigration and grant the People of Palestine—who by Right and Experience are the best judges of what is good and bad for their country—Executive and Legislative powers, the terms of a constitution could be discussed in a different atmosphere. If today the People of Palestine assented to any constitution which fell short of giving them full control of their own affairs they would be in the position of agreeing to an instrument of Government which might, and probably would, be used to smother their national life under a flood of alien immigration.

On June 3, the British Government issued the Churchill White Paper of 1922. The Palestine Arab Delegation rejected the British policy, and in a long letter dated June 17 gave a detailed statement of their reasons for doing so. The main points may be summarized as follows:

1. The British Memorandum started by qualifying them as "a Delegation from the Moslem Christian Society of Palestine," and not as "representing the Moslems and Christians of Palestine." The Arabs replied: "Lest it should be imagined that the Moslem Christian Society is like any other society, we would explain that this Society unmistakably represents the whole of the Moslem and Christian inhabitants of Palestine, who form 93 per cent of the entire population."

2. The Memorandum purported to allay the apprehensions which were entertained by sections of the Arab and of the Jewish population. The Palestine Arab Delegation asserted before the war there was never any trouble between the Jews and the Arabs. It was not the Jews of Palestine who had "agitated for the Declaration of

65. Great Britain, *Correspondence with the Palestine Arab Delegation and the Zionist Organisation*, Cmd. 1700, June, 1922, p. 2.

November 1917" but the Zionists outside of Palestine. It was the latter who had "worked for the Balfour Declaration, and who know that the world sees its impracticability, are apprehensive of its abolishment."

3. The Memorandum stated that "The Zionist Commission in Palestine, now termed the Palestine Zionist Executive, has not desired to possess, and does not possess, any share in the general administration of the country." The Palestine Arab Delegation called to witness officers of the Military Administration to prove that the Zionists had interfered with the government of Palestine. They quoted also from a letter by Mr. Charles R. Crane (*The Times,* June 3, 1922) to the effect that during his survey on Palestine together with Mr. King, he had found that "The Zionist Commission which has so much control over the political machinery of Palestine seems to have more power than the authorized government."

4. The Memorandum described the Jewish community in Palestine as possessing national characteristics. The Palestine Arab Delegation remarked that the signs of nationality mentioned in the British statement were possessed also by other communities in Palestine, and these did not constitute a reason why the Jews outside of Palestine should be allowed to enter Palestine as of right and not on sufferance. Incidentally, the Arab Delegation repeated its objection to Hebrew as an official language and reiterated the idea that "the historic rights of the Arabs [to Palestine] are far stronger than those of the Jews."

5. The Memorandum stated that it was necessary for the Jewish community to increase its numbers providing that the volume of immigrants would not exceed the economic capacity of the country. The Palestine Arab Delegation saw no necessity for increasing the numbers of the Jewish community and alleged that the volume of immigrants had already exceeded the capacity of the country to absorb new arrivals.

6. The Memorandum provided for a Legislative Council elected by the people, but the Palestine Delegation pointed out that the proposed Council did not give the people of Palestine control of immigration. Its powers were to be merely consultative in this regard. They said, "Nothing will safeguard the interests of the Arabs against the dangers of immigration except the creation of representative national government, which shall have complete control of immigration."

7. The Memorandum asserted that "the whole of Palestine west of the Jordan was thus excluded from Sir H. MacMahon's pledge." The Arab Delegation did not admit this, maintaining that the exclusion referred to the Lebanon only. Since Great Britain was master of

Palestine and free to act without detriment to the interests of France, a strict interpretation of the pledge to Husain required the inclusion of Palestine as an area of Arab independence.

8. The Memorandum stated that it was the intention of His Majesty's Government to foster a full measure of self-government in Palestine, to be accomplished by gradual stages and not suddenly. The Palestine Arab Delegation replied that they regarded themselves as no less fit for self-government than their neighbors in Iraq and Syria and that they could find no reason for the delay excepting "the eagerness of the Government to allow time to elapse during which the Jews will have increased in numbers and the powers of Zionism become more established in the land."

9. The Memorandum stated that the Departments of Education, of Commerce and of Industry were being advised by representative committees of all sections of the population. The Palestine Arab Delegation maintained that these representative committees had no power to make decisions, and that in general "where their advice clashes with the Zionist policy of the Administration this advice is unheeded."

10. The Memorandum expressed the hope "that a policy upon these lines cannot but commend itself to the various sections of the population." The Arab Delegation, however, regarded the policy as leading to the discontent of 93 per cent of the population. They foresaw continuous division and tension between Arabs and Zionists increasing day by day. It was not to be expected that the Arabs would agree to the entry of Jews into Palestine "by the might of England against the will of the people."

A Fifth Arab Congress was called in Nablus in August, 1922, for the purpose of hearing the report from the Arab Delegation which had now returned from London. After affirming their rejection of the Palestine constitution, the Congress resolved to boycott the elections of the Legislative Council. They also passed a resolution boycotting Jewish business concerns and opposing the sale of land to Jews. Later in the year, in October, the newly elected Executive Committee decided to send delegations to the Hejaz to secure the aid of King Husain, and to Angora (later Ankara) to secure Turkish support on the eve of the Lausanne Conference. When Lloyd George's coalition government was replaced by a conservative cabinet headed by Bonar Law, the Arab Delegation, hoping for a reversal of the Zionist policy, hastened to London. They were, however, disappointed. The new Colonial Secretary, the

Duke of Devonshire, stated that no further changes in policy were contemplated by the British Government beyond those already made by the Churchill White Paper and the offer of the Legislative Council.

The Sixth Arab Congress held in June, 1923, gave consideration to, and finally decided to oppose, the projected Anglo-Arabian treaty between the British Government and King Husain of the Hejaz. Earlier in the year, negotiations had been in progress between Dr. Naji el-Assil, an envoy of King Husain, and the British Government. No official pronouncement on the negotiations was issued, but Dr. Naji, on leaving London, indicated in a public statement that considerable progress had been made in the direction of Arab unity. On May 18th the Moslem Christian Association of Palestine published a telegram purporting to be from King Husain which implied that the proposed treaty was based on the original Arab demands contained in the Husain-McMahon correspondence and that: "His British Majesty promises the active assistance of Britain for general Arab unity in Iraq, Palestine, Trans-Jordania and the States in Arabia, except Aden." [66] The Government of Palestine immediately issued a carefully worded *dementi* to the effect that no change in the political status of Palestine was contemplated.

On June 5th, a summary of the draft treaty was communicated to the press by the Government of Palestine. The provisions relating to Palestine were as follows:[67]

His Britannic Majesty undertakes to recognize and support the independence of the Arabs in Iraq and Trans-Jordan and the Arab States of the Arab Peninsula exclusive of Aden. As regards Palestine, His Britannic Majesty has already undertaken that nothing will be done in that country which may prejudice the civil and religious rights of the Arab community. In the event of the Governments of any or all of these territories expressing the desire to enter into an association for Customs or other purposes with a view to eventual confederation, His Britannic Majesty will, if requested to do so by the parties concerned, use his good offices to further their desire.

His Hashimite Majesty recognizes the special position of His Bri-

66. As quoted in *Report of the Executive to the XIIIth Zionist Congress*, London, 1923, p. 13.
67. *Ibid.*, pp. 13–14.

tannic Majesty in Iraq, Trans-Jordan and Palestine and undertakes that in such matters as come within the influence of His Hashimite Majesty concerning these countries, he will do his best to cooperate with His Britannic Majesty in the fulfillment of his obligations.

Obviously, this treaty contained nothing that would satisfy the Palestine Arab Executive, and their failure to approve it is understandable.[68] Following the Sixth Congress, the Arab Delegation made another trip to London to be on hand at the discussion of Palestine affairs between Sir Herbert Samuel and a committee appointed by the newly formed Baldwin Government. It was at this time that the Arab Agency was proposed by the British and rejected by the Arabs on the ground that "the Arab owners of the country" could not see their way to accepting a proposal which tended "to place them on an equal footing with the alien Jews." [69]

No further congresses were held until 1928. In the interim the Arab delegation continued to express itself in memoranda and petitions addressed to the League of Nations. A petition sent to the Fifth Session[70] of the Permanent Mandates Commission made a double attack: against the Mandate itself and against Herbert Samuel's administration of the country. The petition—the forerunner of similar ones—made a wholesale condemnation of all aspects of the Government policy, its land program, immigration, public security, fiscal administration, concessions for public works, etc. The petition concludes with

68. W. E. Hocking (*The Spirit of World Politics*, Macmillan, 1942, p. 543) quotes Ameen Rihani to the effect that King Husain refused to sign the treaty with Great Britain because of the failure to include Palestine in the area of Arab independence. It is more likely that negotiations were prolonged by the British because of the increasing weakness of the one-time leader of the Arabs, who was now being pressed by the vigorous Ibn Saud. The negotiations were finally abandoned in 1925, when Husain, after having been defeated by Ibn Saud at Mecca, fled and abdicated in favor of his son, the Emir Ali. See above, p. 151.

69. See above, Chap. V, p. 289.

70. This was the first session at which the Palestine Mandate was discussed. Since the Mandate for Palestine did not come into force officially until September 29, 1923, there were no discussions at the earlier meetings. At the Fourth Session of the Permanent Mandates Commission held in the summer of 1924, Mr. Ormsby-Gore as the accredited representative of the British Government came to Geneva prepared to give information on the basis of the report of the Palestine Administration for the previous year, but the Commission was already in session and consideration of the report was postponed until the Fifth Session which was held from October 23 to November 6, 1924.

the "Arab Demands": the establishment of a National Constitutional Government in which the two communities—Arab and Jewish—will be represented in proportion to their numbers as they existed before the application of the Zionist policy —that is to say, as the Arabs viewed the matter, in the proportion of 9 to 1. A threat was also implied: it was alleged that in the past the Arabs opposed the Government's "oppressive policy" with "constitutional methods," but that there must come a time when "the daily slight frictions between Arab and Jew, whose ideas, principles, customs and modes of life take diametrically divergent lines, cultivate and solidify hatred between both communities . . . will accumulate to such a degree as to defy all moral or political restraints. It is a gross error to believe that the Arab and Jew may come to an understanding if only each of them exchanges his coat of extremism for another of moderacy . . ." [71]

Internal Arab Difficulties

In the interim between the Sixth Arab Congress in June, 1923, and the Seventh in June, 1928, a bitter inner struggle developed between the Husaini-led Executive, who were establishing their dominance in the political life, and the Nashashibi Opposition. The Executive had rejected the Legislative Council, had boycotted the Advisory Committee, had refused the offer of an Arab Agency—three institutions in which the Nashashibis could have been strongly represented and which would have competed with the prestige of the Supreme Moslem Council and the Arab Executive. Taking advantage of the fact that the Arab Executive had not accomplished any concrete results, the Nashashibi group organized a new party in November, 1923, under the title of Nationalist Party. At first, Aref Dajani, who had presided over the All-Arab Congress in 1919, hoped to develop the party into an instrument of cooperation with the Government and of common economic endeavor with the Jews. Extremist elements prevailed, however, and Aref, with his nephew, Sidki Dajani, left the party, which then proceeded to elect as its president, Sheikh Suleiman Taji el Farouki, a Moslem theologian who was also a rich orange grower and the owner of the paper *Al Jamia al-Islamia*.

71. Permanent Mandates Commission, *Minutes of the Fifth Session*, Geneva, October 23–November 6, 1924, pp. 172–173.

Factional bitterness reached a high point during King Husain's visit to Trans-Jordan in 1924. The Opposition at this time took an extreme line, accusing the Arab Executive of readiness to sell out to Britain through King Husain and to accept a modified national home policy in a united Palestine and Trans-Jordan. The accusation was that the Husainis expected to get important government posts in the contemplated government. When delegates of the Nationalist Party came to call on Husain in Amman, they were beaten up by a mob at the instigation of Sheikh Muzaffar, a religious fanatic and a Husaini stalwart[72] who had been one of the chief organizers of the boycott against the Legislative Council campaign.

The year 1924 also witnessed the development of Arab peasant parties. As a rule they were formed by urban notables, ambitious lawyers or local sheikhs. The main motivation behind the formation of parties was opposition to the Executive or jealousy of the dominant Nashashibis. Nevertheless, the *fellahin* or local leaders occasionally revealed in their speeches a social and economic emphasis as they remembered that the city politicians represented by the Husainis and Nashashibis, had been office holders and tax farmers under the Turks. The platforms of the peasant parties are noteworthy for their attention to economic needs; the political aspects of their platform are predominantly internal. One of the first groups was the Nablus Peasant Party, which was followed by similar organizations in Hebron, Jenin and Beisan. The resolution of the Nablus Party called on the government to extend the maturity of debts and to grant long-term loans to peasants. Another resolution instructed the executive committee of the party to notify the government in London that the Moslem-Christian Society did not speak in the name of the people.[73] The Hebron Peasant Party led by Musa H'deb[74] directed an attack against the politicians in the Arab Executive for neglecting practical economic questions. The program of the party demanded the building of roads, reduction of taxes, the spread of education and the encouragement of agricultural cooperation. They called for the protection of the Moslem religious properties so that the income should be spent for the benefit

72. *Haaretz*, January 23, 1924.
73. *Ibid.*, January 1, 1924.
74. Later murdered.

of all Moslems—rural and urban. This last demand reflected a general suspicion that the Husaini-controlled *Waqf* administration was using public funds for private and political purposes.[75]

While the peasant and rural parties of 1924 reflected distrust of the Husaini leaders and for that matter of the Nashashibis, they generally also included an expression of opposition to the Mandate. However, the Hebron and Beisan rural parties were an exception and called for Arab-Jewish cooperation. Their main emphasis was on the needs of protecting peasant interests and their opposition was primarily directed against the urban upper class of money lenders rather than against the Jews or the Balfour Declaration. An old peasant speaking at a meeting of the Peasant Party in Nablus is reported to have said:[76]

We have carried our blood suckers on our shoulders long enough. Behold all the villages sinking from year to year in enormous debts which they owe to these leaders. What have they done, or will do, to ease this burden? My village owes to a certain family in Nablus 20,000 Egyptian pounds. We are paying interest of 8,000 pounds a year. We number about 100. Think of our terrible plight. We have become the property of this family, which lives a life of leisure and extravagance at our expense. What has it done for us? The Jews? What can they do for us? Why, they may lend us money to get rid of our terrible oppressors. And who are the leaders of the Moslem-Christian Party if not the publicans who lost their main source of income since the advent of the new [British] Government. Now they are trying to regain their power. They set up the Jews and Zionists as a scarecrow, but this is only a weapon to enslave us, for we need not fear the Jews. They will only better our lot. And the Zionists? But my brethren, that is the whole purpose of these effendis—to oppress us so that they can sell the land to the Zionists. Who sells land to Jews, if not they? They have mocked us and garnered money from all sides, at our expense. Sources of gold they found for themselves. In Angora they received gold to rise against England; from the opposition in London they received money to help them fight Lloyd George, and from King Hussein they received immense sums to oppose Turkey. That is how they are playing politics at our expense.

75. *Haaretz*, June 10, 11, 12, 1924; Kisch, *op. cit.*, p. 125.
76. *Haaretz*, January 1, 1924. Since this quotation is from a Jewish source it may not be wholly impartial. However, as it is not particularly friendly to Zionism, it has been included as probably authentic.

In the early 1920's there were National Moslem Societies in some of the important towns of Palestine, which were openly friendly to Jews. They were accused by the Arab Executive and the Arab press as being financed by Jews. It is not improbable that Chaim Kalvarisky, an old pre-war president of Palestine and official of the PICA, assisted in the organization of these societies; but Kalvarisky, who was an outstanding advocate of Arab-Jewish cooperation, was unquestionably sincere in his purpose and there is no doubt that his desire for rapprochement was reciprocated in a measure by some Arabs. The strongest of these societies—in Haifa—was headed by Hasan Bey Shukri, for many years its Mayor. He had been removed from office by a British military governor after he had wired a message of congratulation to Sir Herbert Samuel on the latter's appointment as High Commissioner,[77] but was reelected in 1925. A high point in the expression of Jewish sympathy was reached in 1922, when the Haifa Society arranged a banquet in honor of Chaim Weizmann at which delegations from various parts of the country were received by him. The National Moslem Societies were also made up of the *effendi* class but of the middle rather than the upper stratum. Unlike the leading *effendi* groups of the Husainis and Nashashibis, they were more concerned with economics than with politics, and were more impressed with the direct advantages that would accrue from Jewish immigration and Jewish development.

Between the years 1924 and 1928 the prestige of the Executive dropped sharply; the great majority of Arab newspapers, with the notable exception of *Falastin*, opposed it, and the 1925–1926 municipal elections were generally won by the Nashashibi candidates. The Executive on its part tried to counteract the tendency to the formation of separate parties, denouncing these as a threat to national unity. Aided by Auni Bey Abdul Hadi, the only genuine nationalist among the Arab notables, who had thus far kept away from the political squabbles, the Executive tried to convene a united Congress in which all factions would be represented. The Nashashibi group held out for guarantees of non-domination by the Husainis.

The Seventh Congress, which had been postponed from year

---

77. Medzini, *op. cit.*, p. 258.

to year, was finally convened in Jerusalem in 1928. The Congress was attended by three hundred delegates, mostly from the urban areas. It elected an enlarged Executive of forty-eight members—double the preceding number—twelve of whom were Christians; the Nashashibi and Husaini factions were represented in approximately equal proportions. Musa Kazem al-Husaini was reelected president, with Taufik Bey Hakki, Mayor of Acre, and Yacoub Faraj (a Greek Catholic of the Nashashibi faction) as vice-president. In addition to Jamal Husaini who had been secretary of the previous Executive, there were two new secretaries—Auni Abdul Hadi and Mogannam E. Mogannam—the latter a Christian. In practice, however, Jamal Husaini continued to be the active secretary. The main resolution of the Congress was as follows:[78]

The Palestine Arab Congress which unites all the Arab parties, both Moslem and Christian, demands as a common right the establishment of a democratic parliamentary government after ten years of absolute colonial regime. Palestine is no more backward than any of the neighboring Arab countries which enjoy on a wide scale parliamentary constitutions of various kinds. The Arabs of Palestine cannot and will not tolerate the present colonial regime, and they demand in accordance with all their rights the creation of a representative body to draft the Palestine constitution which will guarantee the institution of a parliamentary government in Palestine.

Besides its importance in achieving a certain degree of unity among the various factions, the Seventh Arab Congress is significant in that it indicates a somewhat different trend in the method of formulating the Arab objectives. Until now there had been an out-and-out demand for repudiation of the Balfour Declaration. At the Seventh Congress, the emphasis shifted to the establishment of parliamentary institutions on the basis of democratic majorities. The Arab leaders had found the Permanent Mandates Commission deaf to their appeal for a repudiation of the Mandate itself. The Commission could not deal with such appeals because it was empowered only to give consideration to grievances within the framework of the Mandate, whose acceptance was assumed.

78. Royal Institute of International Affairs, *Survey of International Affairs, 1929*, Oxford University Press, 1930, p. 258.

However, in the discussions some of the members of the Commission had emphasized the importance of developing self-governing institutions as early as possible.

The Arab leaders, following this cue, decided on a new tack —to focus their demands on the right of representative government, and to utilize the establishment of a legislature as a means of abrogating the Balfour Declaration, in fact if not in theory, by using the power of the majority to curtail immigration. In this way they made an appeal to those who emphasized democracy and the right of the mandated territories to achieve self-government. They also met internal criticism of the Opposition, who argued that the demands for self-governing status as a Class A mandate would receive more attention than the demand for immediate independence. There is a view to the effect that the Seventh Arab Congress represented a departure from the established policy of maximum demands and that this was due to the influence of the more moderate Nashashibi group. But, essentially, the change was only a change in tactics and not in the basic position of the Arabs.

The demand for the establishment of a representative assembly now became the major theme of Arab politics. In pursuance of the resolution of the Seventh Congress, the new Executive presented to Lord Plumer, the High Commissioner, a demand for the establishment of a Parliament. The subject was discussed at length at the Fourteenth Session of the Permanent Mandates Commission held in the fall of 1928. Dr. Rappard pointed out that the establishment of a democratic and parliamentary government in Palestine while the Arabs were a majority would abrogate the first part of Article 2 of the Mandate, in accordance with which the Mandatory had assumed responsibility for the establishment of a national home for the Jewish people. He said: "The population of Palestine . . . was mostly Arab and was opposed to the establishment of the Jewish National Home. It was, in these circumstances, plain that if a democratic and parliamentary government were established in Palestine, its first action would be to abrogate the disposition foreshadowed in the Balfour Declaration." Other members of the Permanent Mandates Commission indicated a greater inclination to recognize the Arab demand for an early establishment of representative institutions.

The Arabs also succeeded in pressing their point on Sir John Chancellor, the new High Commissioner. As noted in the previous chapter, after their failure with Lord Plumer, they repeated their request for negotiations for a representative assembly in a meeting with Sir John in January, 1929. Chancellor promised to study the question, and before leaving for his vacation in June, 1929, he announced his intention of consulting the Colonial Office regarding the Legislative Council for Palestine. When he appeared before the Permanent Mandates Commission in July, 1929, he made a brief survey of the problem of the development of constitutional government in Palestine. He stated that he had been corresponding with the British Government in regard to the whole question and stated that he intended to discuss the matter with the Secretary of State. It was on this occasion that he remarked: "I think I can say that the relations between the two communities continue to improve." [79]

Arab Intransigence and British Optimism

This optimistic view of continuous improvement in Jewish-Arab relations had been consistently taken by the British representatives speaking before the Mandates Commission. At the fifth session of the Permanent Mandates Commission (1924) Sir Herbert Samuel expressed the view that the Arab opposition was diminishing; that while in the beginning the Arab Executive Committee had represented the view of the majority of the population, the Executive Committee had gradually become less representative and less authoritative.[80] In their observations on the Arab petition submitted to the seventh session of the Permanent Mandates Commission in 1925, the British Government stated that the Arab Executive was not widely representative, that it had been elected by a body of 120 persons which styled itself "The Palestine Arab Congress." [81] Mr. Ormsby-Gore, who was the accredited British representative at the seventh session, said in the course of discussion "that while the political Arab party was intransigent,

79. Permanent Mandates Commission, *Minutes of the Fifteenth Session*, 1929, p. 79.
80. Permanent Mandates Commission, *Minutes of the Fifth Session*, 1924, pp. 54–57.
81. Permanent Mandates Commission, *Minutes of the Seventh Session*, p. 173.

there was evidence that its numbers were not increasing, but were, if anything, on the downgrade." He thought that the mutual knowledge of the two races and the social intercourse between them was increasing, and expressed the view that within ten years' time Palestine would see the development of self-governing institutions in which Jews and Arabs would cooperate. He hoped that the Commission would not press the British Government to move too fast in the direction of ready-made systems of democracy not applicable to the conditions in Palestine. He concluded by saying: "When the Arabs realize that no British Government would abandon the Balfour Declaration, they would change their attitude; and the British Government will be ready to consider any proposals they might make." [82] The same line of thinking was repeatedly expressed by British representatives right up to the month preceding the outbreak of the disturbances of 1929, when Sir John Chancellor made the statement noted above.

In retrospect it appears that this was a superficial judgment. Despite the inner struggle between the Husainis and the Nashashibis, and despite some undercurrent of dissatisfaction on the part of the peasant groups with the leadership of both houses, there is no evidence of any genuine growth of a moderate political policy among the Arabs. The opposition to the Jewish national home policy remained strong and the Husainis were organizing their forces. It has often been suggested that if the British had built up the Nashashibi opposition and had not helped to concentrate power in the hands of the Husaini faction, a more moderate policy would have been developed. Such a view was expressed by the late Colonel Kisch, who was in charge of the Zionist Executive at that time, in the preface to his *Diary*:[83]

The Diary will be found to contain abundant evidence not only of the persistent efforts made by the Zionist Executive to reach an understanding with the Arabs, but also of the fact that there was—and I believe still is—a large body of moderate Arab opinion which would have been ready to follow a lead from the Mandatory Government in coming to an understanding with the Jews on the basis of the policy embodied in the Mandate. Unfortunately that lead was not given, but on the contrary, the Government never

82. *Ibid.*, p. 105.
83. F. H. Kisch, *op. cit.*, pp. 19, 20.

ceased to maintain the authority and power of the Arab extremist group, headed by the Mufti of Jerusalem, Haj Amin al-Husseini.

This judgment is possibly correct; certainly the Government followed a contradictory tactic in strengthening the extremists while professing a policy of moderation. On the other hand, there is no clear evidence that the Nashashibi faction had any sincere desire for cooperation with the Government or with the Jews on the basis of an explicit recognition of the Jewish national home policy. Perhaps it would have been possible to encourage other groups with a greater readiness to recognize the Balfour Declaration from among the urban middle classes and in some of the rural districts. But the question may be raised whether artificial stimulation of parties would be successful when the social and economic conditions and political forces necessary for such a development were lacking. Reasonableness, willingness to compromise, calculation of consequence in terms of general welfare, belief in cooperative relations—these characteristics of modern liberalism are obviously matters of slow development. In the West such qualities, never perfectly embodied, were the product of long schooling in Judaeo-Christian ethics, in the Hellenic balance of reason, in the modern scientific outlook, and not least, were associated with the growth of the middle-class devoted to commerce and industry.

The theory that a policy of reason, moderation and cooperation would succeed in Palestine was the product of wishful thinking rather than of a study of Arab life or of observation of what was happening in Palestine and in the neighboring countries. The optimistic view was largely the projection of Western liberal mentality on to a situation marked by a quite different social and cultural configuration. It failed to give adequate consideration to conditions in the Near East: to the aggressive political character of the Arabic-Islamic tradition; to the growth of Arab nationalism and its manner of expression in neighboring Arab countries; to the general backwardness of economic and educational development among the masses of the Arab population; to the character of Palestine Arab political leadership and its social basis. This is not to say that a policy of extremism would have had better results; the point is that analysis of the problem in terms of moderation versus extremism was an oversimplification. A valid policy for Palestine should, on the one hand—with reference to long-range assumptions—have been based on a more careful study of the social and economic factors, and on the other hand —with reference to immediate application—should have taken into consideration more realistically and more shrewdly the actual nature of Arab politics in Palestine.

CHAPTER VIII

COMMUNITIES, ATTITUDES AND ARAB-JEWISH RELATIONS

THE Zionist Organization as a whole followed Weizmann's policy of compromise and shared his hope of achieving a rapprochement with the Arabs. There was a general belief that as living conditions for the Arab population improved as a result of the Jewish development, the opposition to Zionism would die away. Organized Arab political opinion, however, showed no signs of yielding, and continued its unqualified antagonism to the Jewish national home policy in any form whatever, even as whittled down by the administrative practices of the Palestine Government, and as deflated by the 1922 (Churchill) White Paper formulation.

The Husaini-led Arab Executive had from the beginning of the British administration laid down an extreme policy of resistance to the Zionist purpose. The Nashashibi party was less uncompromising: it did not favor the use of violence as a political weapon and seemed more ready to work together with the Mandatory; had it received encouragement from government circles, it might have been prepared to make such concessions on immigration and land sales as would have offered no serious challenge to Arab predominance. Although the Nashashibis did not differ essentially from the Husainis in their stated political policy, the difference in the attitude between the two groups might possibly have led to a real divergence in policy had the British Government cultivated the more amenable Ragheb Bey instead of strengthening the hand of the more intransigent Haj Amin. The rise of the latter to the position of dominant leader made a reconciliation between the Jews and the Arabs—in any case, surrounded with enormous difficulties—quite impossible.

The difference between the Arab and the Jewish orientation is remarkably well illustrated by the two personalities who guided the respective political policies. On the one hand, was

Dr. Chaim Weizmann, whose background was the non-political milieu of the East European Jewish settlement, permeated with its religious-intellectual tradition of Biblical and Talmudic study. Through his speeches run the themes of Jewish sorrow in exile, of Jewish economic and political insecurity, of the need of a land where Jews would feel "at home." Originally attracted to Ahad Ha'am's spiritual-cultural conception of Zionism, he later became impressed with the force of Herzl's political idea. Weizmann's policy may be conceived as a lifelong attempt to achieve a union of these leading Zionist motifs. His political views, moreover, were developed under the influence of the British pragmatic approach, in which reasonableness and compromise play their parts. His outlook was colored also by the rational approach of the modern scientist who sees in technological progress the key to the creative use of natural resources for social betterment and for ultimate elimination of the struggle between nations.

On the other side stood Haj Amin al-Husaini, scion of the most powerful Palestinian family, in whose hands were gathered the reins of temporal and spiritual power: its members were masters of great landed estates and incumbents of the highest religious offices. As a young man, he was trained in the military college at Constantinople, and seems to have done better there than at the University of Al-Azhar in Cairo, where he pursued religious studies. His mild appearance masked an inordinate ambition for power, and his gracious manner—well befitting his aristocratic and clerical background—concealed an intractable bent of mind. He began his political activities in Palestine with open agitation against the Zionists and the British; and throughout the period of his leadership he carried on shrewd intrigue against both. Finally, guilty of treachery and sedition, he found a place in the entourage of Hitler in Berlin.[1]

To what extent the official views of each political group represented the attitudes of the generality of the Jews and Arabs in Palestine cannot be simply stated. Speaking in the broadest terms and referring to the main points at issue, it may be said

1. After the defeat of Germany he fled to Switzerland by plane, was apprehended by the Swiss authorities and deported to France. He recently made his escape to Egypt, where he is living under the protection of the King.

that the views of the leaders reflected the opinions prevalent in their communities. The Jews of Palestine accepted Weizmann's compromise, but the diversity of opinion was greater than in the World Zionist Organization, and at the two extremes more sharply expressed; on the whole, the Jewish community of Palestine was inclined to be less conciliatory, following the compromise line with a certain diffidence. As to the Arab section of the community, it is even more difficult to speak with definiteness, since the attitudes of the people were not formulated in organized political discussion. Both the upper and the middle classes had their reasons for opposition. Although there is no clear evidence of a general antagonism of the masses of peasants to Jewish settlement, it may be assumed that they did not regard with equanimity the prospect of non-Moslem rule of Palestine.

However, in the light of the great differences within each group and the diversity of conditions in each section of the community, such broad statements as have been ventured in the preceding paragraph are almost without value in attempting to estimate the possibilities of a rapprochement between Arabs and Jews. Ideas do not spring out of the head full grown, but take their rise in definite social contexts. The background of leadership must be known; it is superficial to think that the type of leadership can be changed without changing social conditions. And certainly "good will" cannot be engendered artificially; nor can we jump to the conclusion that if the two communities only "understood each other," political antagonism would disappear; the contrary might well be the case. "Cooperation" is as much the result of united action for specific objectives of common interest as it is an attitude of mind which makes possible common action. It is only in the light of knowledge of the concrete situations, that some estimate may be made of the possibilities of—and of the real problems involved in—bringing the two sections of the population more closely together. It is desirable, therefore, before describing the efforts and proposals made for rapprochement between Arabs and Jews to outline more fully than has been done above, the main characteristics of the several communities of Palestine and to indicate something of their attitudes toward each other and toward the Zionist objectives.

There are many small social units, that may well be called

communities, in Palestine. As throughout the East, groups have tended to retain their ethnic-religious individualities despite changes of ruler and the passing of dominant faith—the Druses, the Samaritans, the Bahais, the Arab-looking descendants of the ancient Hebrews of the Village of Pekiin, are some examples; others within the Christian and Jewish groups will be mentioned in the course of the following presentation. From the point of view of the problems which concern us here, the population of Palestine is generally considered in terms of the two major cultural groupings—Arabs and Jews—and the three major religious groupings—Moslems, Jews and Christians. None of these groups is absolutely pure: the Arabs, predominantly Moslem, include Christians; the latter are mostly native or of Eastern origin, although a considerable—and very influential—number are European. There are, of course, Jews who are culturally almost indistinguishable from Arabs, and some members of the Dönme, Crypto-Jews from Turkey, who are outwardly Mohammedan; the census of 1931 also records 25 persons who signified their nationality as Jewish and their religion as Christian. The Christian group includes native Arabs, Christians coming from other parts of the East, and European Christians.

Dividing the population in accordance with the major cultural distinction, there were, at the time of the 1931 census, 839,457 Arabs (including 66,503 Bedouins), and these constituted 81.2 percent of the total population of 1,035,821. Of these, about 75,000 were Christians, 9,000 Druses, and 350 Bahais. The Jews numbered 174,809, or 16.9 percent of the total. There were 21,555 (1.9 percent) persons who did not indicate their nationality as either Arab or Jewish. There are no later official figures dividing the population into the two major national groupings, but since the figure for the Jews as a religious group approximates their figure as a national group, and since the ratio of Christians to Moslems in the Arab population had not greatly changed, we may accept the figures for the religious divisions as broadly indicative of the relative strength of the two major national groups. The table on the next page shows the official estimates.

Before dealing with each community in detail, some general statement on the social composition of the different sections of the population may be made. It should be noted that the

	Census Figures* 1922		Census Figures** 1931		Government Estimates** December 31, 1942	
	Number	Percent	Number	Percent	Number	Percent
Moslems	589,177	78.4	759,712	73.3	995,292	61.4
Christians	71,464	9.5	91,398	8.8	127,184	7.9
Jews	83,790	11.1	174,610	16.9	484,408	29.9
Others	7,617	1.0	10,101	1.0	13,121	0.8
Total	752,048	100.0	1,035,821	100.0	1,620,005	100.0

* Including unsettled population of 103,000.
** Including unsettled population of 66,553.

religious distinctions are more than differences of creed and practice; the three groups constitute social and cultural communities. In some characteristics, the Christian Arabs are more like the Jews: they are largely urban in character, show a similar occupational distribution, represent on the average an educational and cultural standard closer to the Jewish than to the Moslem. Comparative similarity in standard of living is indicated also by the fact that their birth and death rates are closer to the Jewish than to the Moslem rates.[2] These similarities, however, by no means signify that the interests of the Christian Arabs run parallel to those of the Jews. On the contrary, just because they resemble each other as social groups, Christians and Jews come into competition with each other in many respects. Above all, community of language, as well as political considerations, have aligned the Christian Arabs with the Moslem Arabs against the Zionist program. However, under the cover of unity, there remain tensions between the Moslem and Christian Arabs.

The occupational structure of the population of Palestine, in accordance with the 1931 census, is shown in the table on page 499. This, broadly speaking, represents the situation today, although there was an increase in the second decade in the number and in the proportion of Jews devoted to agriculture. The Moslem population, largely agricultural, is predominantly rural. The rural population, including the Bedouins, was recorded as 648,531. The distribution of urban and rural populations among Moslems, Christians and Jews is indicated in the tables on page 498.

2. See below, Chap. X, p. 667.

URBAN AND RURAL POPULATIONS BY RELIGIOUS GROUPS IN ACCORDANCE WITH THE CENSUS OF 1931

In Relation to the Total General Population

Religious	Urban	Percent	Rural	Percent
Moslems	188,075	18.2	571,637	55.2
Jews	128,467	14.4	46,143	4.5
Christians	69,250	6.7	22,148	2.1
Others	1,499	0.1	8,602	0.8
Total	387,291	37.4	648,530	62.6

In Relation to the Total Urban and Total Rural Population

Religions	Urban	Percent	Rural	Percent
Moslems	188,075	48.5	571,637	88.2
Jews	128,467	33.2	46,143	7.1
Christians	69,250	18.0	22,148	3.4
Others	1,499	0.3	8,602	1.3
Total	387,291	100.0	648,530	100.0

In Relation to Each Religious Group

Religions	Urban	Percent	Rural	Percent
Moslems	188,075	24.8	571,637	75.2
Jews	128,467	73.6	46,143	26.4
Christians	69,250	75.8	22,148	24.2
Others	1,499	14.8	8,602	85.2
Total	387,291	37.4	648,530	62.6

The urban communities were defined as those which were legally recognized as municipalities.[3] These included many small towns which were hardly more than enlarged villages. There were only four cities which would be referred to as urban communities in the European sense: Jerusalem, Haifa, Tel-Aviv and Jaffa. The smaller towns, of which there were sixteen, were nearly wholly Arab, with the exception of Safed

---

3. Tel-Aviv, which was still operating under a local council, however, was also included among the urban communities.

OCCUPATIONAL STRUCTURE OF THE POPULATION IN PALESTINE, 1931
(In Percentage)

	Earners				Earners and Dependents			
	Total	Moslems	Jews	Christians	Total	Moslems	Jews	Christians
Agriculture and Mining	48.8	64.4	19.1	15.7	54.5	68.5	16.0	19.5
Industry and Handicraft	15.8	10.0	28.8	22.8	13.8	8.9	28.4	24.1
Transport	5.7	5.9	4.9	7.1	5.2	5.0	5.5	6.6
Trade	9.4	8.0	13.3	10.3	10.0	8.0	16.5	11.9
Police and Administration	3.4	2.0	2.0	15.7	2.5	2.0	1.9	8.9
Professions and Liberal Arts	4.7	1.6	11.2	9.8	3.7	1.4	10.0	8.4
Unskilled Workers, etc.	6.1	3.8	12.0	7.0	4.7	2.8	11.4	6.6
Persons Living on Their Incomes	1.7	1.0	3.0	3.3	2.4	1.1	4.9	8.3
Domestic Service	3.6	2.4	5.1	8.1	1.8	1.2	3.0	4.1
Others	0.8	0.9	0.6	0.2	1.4	1.1	2.4	1.6
	100.0	100.0	100.0	100.0	100.0	100.0	100.0	100.0

which was mainly Jewish. In reality, then, the rural population was larger and the Moslems formed even a higher proportion of the non-urban communities than indicated above. In the three large urban districts—Jerusalem, Haifa and Jaffa-Tel-Aviv (counting these two adjacent cities as one)—the Jews already constituted a strong element in 1931, as indicated in the table on page 501. By the early forties, the Jewish population in these cities was close to 350,000 and constituted almost half of the total city population, Arab and Jewish. In 1939, Tel-Aviv had a population of 166,000, practically all Jews.[4] In Jaffa, where after the establishment of nearby Tel-Aviv the Jewish population had at first decreased, it rose again, so that out of a total population of approximately 85,000 in 1941, there were probably over 25,000 Jews.[5] By the end of the second decade, in 1939, the Jews constituted 60 percent of the population of Jerusalem and Haifa.[6] Since the political life in Palestine, as in all Arab countries, is centered in the cities, the growth of the Jewish population in the urban districts was replete with political as well as social significance.

SOCIAL CLASS DIFFERENCES AMONG THE ARABS[7]

Different types of categories will be used in describing the life of the several communities. In the case of the Jews, the usual distinctions are between Western and Oriental Jews, and between the "new" and the "old" *Yishuv*. Among the Christians, the guiding distinctions are denominational. The Arab community, mainly Moslem, divides itself into distinct social classes: 1) the Bedouins; 2) the *fellahin;* 3) the *effendis;* 4) the urban middle class; 5) the urban masses.

4. David Gurevich, *The Jewish Population of Jerusalem*, Jewish Agency for Palestine, Jerusalem, 1940, p. 14.
5. The *Luach Haaretz* (a Handbook issued by *Haaretz*) records 27,400 Jews in Jaffa in 1942.
6. David Gurevich, *op. cit.* In Jerusalem (1939) out of a total of 133,850, there were 80,850 Jews, 27,000 Moslems, 26,000 Christians; in Haifa, out of a total of 112,000, there were 68,000 Jews, 27,000 Moslems, and 17,000 Christians.
7. This section, from pages 500 to 516, is largely indebted to the manuscript prepared for the Esco Foundation Palestine Study by Meir Sherman.

POPULATION IN TOWNS
(Official Figures)

	1922 Number	1922 Percent	1931 Number	1931 Percent
Jerusalem				
Moslems	13,413	21.4	19,894	22.0
Jews	33,971	54.3	51,222	56.8
Christians	14,699	23.5	19,335	21.3
Others	695	0.6	52	—
Total	62,578	100.0	90,502	100.0
Haifa				
Moslems	9,377	38.1	20,324	40.3
Jews	6,230	25.3	15,923	31.5
Christians	8,863	36.0	13,824	27.6
Others	164	0.6	332	0.6
Total	24,634	100.0	50,403	100.0
Jaffa				
Moslems	20,699	43.4	35,506	68.5
Jews	20,152	42.2	7,209	13.9
Christians	6,850	14.4	8,132	17.6
Others	8	—	19	—
Total	47,709	100.0	51,866	100.0
Tel-Aviv				
Moslems	—	—	106	0.2
Jews	15,185	100.0	45,564	99.0
Christians	—	—	143	0.3
Others	—	—	288	0.5
Total	15,185	100.0	46,101	100.0
Grand Total	150,106		238,872	

The Bedouins[8] or "Unsettled" Population

The Bedouins are generally referred to as "nomads," but it should be understood that they are not continuously on the move. They are nomads in the sense that they follow the seasons in the search for green grass for their flocks; they may

---

8. The name is derived from *badia* (steppe), referring to the vast stretches in the Arabian deserts over which the nomads wander. Strictly speaking, Bedouin is a plural form, but in English it is most often used as a singular.

also migrate as a result of untoward conditions—expulsion from their habitat by some hostile tribe, or for the purpose of invading some fertile, settled community. In Palestine, some of the Bedouin tribes have lived in the same district for long periods. The distinctive fact about the nomads is that they do not hold title to the lands which they inhabit. They have loose claims over indefinite areas which they have cultivated, or on which they have customarily grazed their flocks. Some of this land is *mewat*,[9] and some private property of little value to the owner.

According to the estimate made in the 1922 census, there were 103,000 Bedouins in Palestine at that time. However, the more careful 1931 census found only 66,553 Bedouins, or 6 percent of the total, and 8 percent of the Moslem, population. Some of the Bedouins may have migrated back to the Hejaz or to southern Trans-Jordan from which they may have come during the war years; others may have migrated into Palestine, becoming agricultural workers or day laborers. The main difference in the two enumerations, however, is probably due to an incorrect estimate in the 1922 census. The Bedouins of Beer Sheba, the largest group, refused to allow themselves to be counted, either because of superstitions or for fear that the enumeration was preliminary to conscription. The estimate was made largely on the report of the tribal heads. As to the main question involved, whether the Bedouin population of Palestine is increasing or decreasing, the census of 1931 offers no definite conclusions. The weight of evidence seems to indicate that it is either stationary or regressive.

The Palestinian Bedouins are *maaza*, that is, breeders of sheep and goats, as are the Arabs of northern Arabia generally, in contrast to the Arabs of southern Arabia, the *jamalin*, or camel breeders. The majority of them are found in the arid, largely desert, area of the sub-district of Beer Sheba. In the census of 1931, they are estimated as consisting of 47,981

---

9. *Mewat* land is waste land which is not held by title deed or which has not been assigned for public purposes of a village; traditionally, it is land lying so far from a town or village that the voice of a person shouting from the nearest inhabited spot cannot be heard there. *Mewat* land in Palestine is governed by the provisions applicable to *miri* land, i.e., property over which the state has right of ownership and assignment, but over which the right of occupation and usufruct is enjoyed by private individuals.

persons. The Beer Sheba tribes are described as "the only true nomads in Palestine today." Even so, they are in a transitory stage tending toward permanent settlement, with agriculture as their main occupation and pasturage secondary. In accordance with the 1931 census figures, 42,868 were supported directly by cultivation and 5,113 by animal husbandry. The relation between the number of earners and dependents seems to indicate that the family as a unit is primarily dependent on agriculture, while the unmarried men are mainly employed in shepherding the flocks. The census figures indicate that the landowners for the most part work their own lands, although a quarter of the agriculturists are tenants. The owners hold their land by "customary" law, as opposed to formal law, since most of the land is *mewat*.

The Bedouin tribes of Beer Sheba derive a bare existence from their scanty agriculture, which is dependent on a small and variable annual rainfall. Each year there is a migration to the central and northern parts of Palestine; when the tribes return they leave behind a great number who find employment as laborers among the settled cultivators or, more recently, in the towns in industrial occupations. The tribal movement from Beer Sheba has intensified the pressure of population on settled Palestine.[10] Beer Sheba is one of the main districts through which Arabs from the Hejaz and from southern parts of Trans-Jordan come into Palestine. The movement from Beer Sheba into the northern part of Palestine could be stopped only if a supply of water were made available and the tribesmen in that area converted into settled cultivators.

The remaining 20,000 Bedouins are scattered throughout other parts of Palestine, particularly in the valleys, those in the Wadi-Havareth area on the coastal plain and in the Beisan area of the Jordan Valley constituting the largest groups. They engage in pasturing flocks—mainly of sheep and goats—cultivating the soil in a primitive fashion, raiding the villages, and in robbing on the highroads. Sir Lewis French describes those dwelling in the Beisan area as follows: "The Bedouin, wild and lawless by nature, were constantly at feud with their neighbours on both sides of the Jordan, and raids and highway robbery formed their industry; while such cultivation as the

10. *Census of Palestine 1931*, Government of Palestine, 1933, Vol. 1, pp. 7–10.

Beduin were capable of filled in the intervals of more exciting occupation." [11] There are also Bedouin encampments near the Jewish villages and on the outskirts of the towns. Sometimes, as in Jerusalem, a family or two may be seen with their tents or petrol-tin houses living in an unoccupied lot in the middle of the city. They may earn their living by supplying milk and vegetables, or as day laborers.

The Bedouins retain the mores and some of the social characteristics of tribal life. They are organized in clans headed by a sheikh and each member of the tribe is regarded as responsible for the others in matters of honor and blood vengeance. As in the case of the *fellahin*, the women go about freely with uncovered faces; polygamy is more frequent than among the settled Moslem population. Although fanatically Moslem, the Bedouins do not know much about the content of Islam and are not always too strictly observant of its ritual and precepts. They are practically all illiterate. Even when ragged and run-down in appearance, they retain a sense of pride of race as the descendants of the true Arabs of the desert. They continue to observe the great virtue of hospitality; they also inherit some of the less praiseworthy traits of the desert Arab. Robbery is considered a worthy occupation rather than a crime, and loot the proper reward for the brave. As Jarvis says of the Bedouin generally: "He is avaricious to a degree and his standard of honesty and truth not high." [12] The police regard the Bedouins as an unruly element in the population, and records indicate that they account for a relatively high proportion of the crimes of violence—murder, robbery, theft of cattle and abduction.[13] Their encampments are also breeding grounds for trachoma, malaria and venereal disease.

Although tourists may regard them as a picturesque and attractive element in the life of the country, the Bedouins are, to quote the Simpson Report, "an anachronism wherever close development is possible and is desired." [14] Quite apart from

11. Lewis French, *Reports on Agricultural Development and Land Settlement in Palestine*, Jerusalem, 1931–1932, p. 36.
12. C. J. Jarvis, *Yesterday and Today in Sinai*, William Blackwood and Sons, Edinburgh, 1938, p. 18.
13. David Tidhar, *Hotim Va'hataim* (Sins and Sinners), Tel-Aviv, 1924, Preface.
14. John Hope Simpson, *Palestine, Report on Immigration, Land Settlement and Development*, London, 1930, p. 73.

the problem of Jewish settlement, their settlements are an obstruction to progress. The extension of the area of improved agriculture, reducing the amount of *mewat* land, would limit the Bedouins in their movements. They also claim traditional grazing rights after the harvest on settled land; the more intensive type of cultivation would not permit this. Their loose property concepts encourage them to enter what are obviously fictitious claims to large undefined areas. They easily become tools of the political intrigue for the promotion of violence. The unsettled tribal population in Palestine proper, outside of the Beer Sheba district, though relatively small, constitutes a very serious problem from the point of view of security, of a more productive agriculture, and the achievement of better health conditions.

The Fellahin or Peasants

The *fellahin*, whose main occupation is farming, constitute the backbone of the Arab population of Palestine. Auxiliary occupations are quarrying, limestone burning, masonry, pottery, weaving of straw mats and baskets, and, to some extent, fishing. They are predominantly Moslems, only about five percent being Christians. The *fellahin* live in small villages of square-shaped houses. In the hills these are generally built of local stone; in the plains, most frequently of mud bricks fortified by straw or dung. Some tourists regard the villages as picturesque, harmonizing with the background out of which they have arisen, but they probably would not care to live in them. The livestock are kept in the front part, where also the seasonal agricultural worker (*harat*) lives. The inner part of the house is on a somewhat higher level; there, the *fellah* and his family sleep on straw mats placed on the earth floor. A clay and stone oven is built in the yard. Sanitary facilities, even the most elementary, are altogether lacking. As a rule there is only one well in the village, and the water, raised by means of a bucket attached to a rope, is used for drinking purposes only. Most of the villages, particularly in the plains, are barren of vegetation, with only a solitary olive or fig tree here and there. Outside the village are stored heaps of dung, sometimes an accumulation of generations. This serves as fuel; until recent times its use as fertilizer was not generally known by the *fellahin*.

The *fellahin* represent a fairly homogeneous group in standard of life and social characteristics. There is of course a range of variation in social conditions: the *fellah* class includes a few well-to-do farmers who own comparatively large tracts of land cultivated by hired help whom they supervise. These comparatively affluent farmers live in stone houses consisting of several rooms equipped with furniture; the livestock is kept in a separate pen; a vegetable garden may be cultivated. At the other extreme is a more numerous group, portrayed by Sir Lewis French as living in mud hovels, suffering severely from malaria, and of "too low intelligence to be receptive to any suggestions for improvement of their housing, water supply and education." [15] Describing the conditions under which these Arabs lived in the Beisan area as it was in 1921, he says: "Large areas of the land were uncultivated and covered with weeds. There were no trees, no vegetables. The *fellaheen*, if not themselves cattle thieves, were always ready to harbor these and other criminals . . . There was little public security and the *fellah's* lot was an alternative of pillage and blackmail by their neighbors, the Bedouin."

The great middle body of the *fellahin* live in what a European would characterize as dire poverty. They are better off than the Egyptian *fellah*, who suffers from continuous malnutrition, and their lot is superior to that of the half-starved Indian peasant. Still the diet of the Palestinian *fellah* is poor and monotonous: his staple is a flat, round, doughy cake of unleavened bread. This, with some onions or radishes, constitutes his morning and noonday meal; in the evening he eats a cooked meal of vegetables flavored with olive oil, onions and pepper. He uses little milk and less meat, the latter most often when an ox, camel or sheep falls ill. The fowl, eggs and cheese are sold by the women in the marketplace, and the proceeds provide a small money income for the *fellah* which is used for what he must purchase. He usually goes barefoot and he may have one or two new garments during his life.

The low standard of the *fellah* is partly due to the primitive system of agriculture; his production would undoubtedly be increased by the use of fertilizer, more carefully selected seed, and the employment of better methods. But he is neither lazy nor unintelligent, as is sometimes thought; nor is the wooden

15. *Op. cit.*, p. 36.

plough pointed with a nail, which is often the subject of ridicule, as inadequate a tool as might at first appear.[16] One major source of backwardness is a system of tenure—*mushaa*—which gives him no incentive to improve his cultivation. Another cause is financial: to begin with, his capital investment —from £20 to £30—is inadequate for the purchase of good working animals and proper tools, and leaves no margin for free working capital. The taxes during the Turkish times and in the first decade of the British administration rested heavily on the cultivator. Worst of all, he has usually been deeply in debt as a result of paying usurious rates of interest to the *effendis* for generations.[17]

Child nurture and education are in a primitive stage. On birth, the infant is bathed in salt water, smeared with oil and swathed in linens for forty days. This treatment is evidently supposed to keep the child healthy for the rest of his life, for the *fellah* rarely bathes. Flies swarm about the child in arms, clustering thickly around the eyes, but the mother never drives them off. Washing, apparently, is not regarded as salutary. Bloodletting is a frequent cure; for eye diseases, fresh dung, mud, or bandages soaked in camel urine are regarded as effective, and talismans are considered helpful. The child is nursed by the mother until the age of three, and then runs about barefoot and half naked. Circumcision of the boys is performed at a great ceremony, usually on the fifth birthday.[18] Traditionally, the training of the boy starts at the sixth or seventh year when he may be given charge of the livestock, and later helps the father in cultivation. At about the same time he may be sent to the *kuttab* where he may learn parts of the Koran orally; reading and writing are sometimes included, but as a general rule few of the *fellahin* become literate.[19]

---

16. See note by Dr. Wilkansky quoted by John Hope Simpson, *op. cit.*, p. 66. For a description of *mushaa*, see *ibid.*, p. 31, quoted below in Chap. X, p. 706.

17. Only during the Second World War was his position in this regard largely improved due to the high prices paid for agricultural products. See below, Chap. XIV, p. 1058.

18. Sometimes, however, at a considerably later age, even during the teens.

19. The census of 1931 showed that of all the Moslems living in rural communities from the age of seven, about 11 percent were literate. However, the literacy is confined practically to the males who are recorded as somewhat over 21 percent literate. The female population is almost

The lot of the woman, the *fellaha*, is unblessed and hard. Her birth is reported without enthusiasm; when the father is asked how many children he has he counts only the boys. As soon as the girl is able to walk she begins to work and continues at it for the rest of her life, aging prematurely through incessant toil and continuous childbirth. On her marriage, which is generally in the late teens—although it may be earlier[20]—she assumes her wifely duties of milling, making dough, baking, carrying water, washing clothes, gathering kindling, cooking, tending the vegetable garden and poultry, sewing, embroidering and mending; and, in addition to this, selling the cheese, eggs and vegetables in the nearby town. When her husband rides to town on his donkey, she walks after him carrying the products she has to sell in a basket on her head. Occasionally, in some parts of the country, a woman may still be seen harnessed to the plough in team with the donkey.

The *fellah* marries as soon as he can afford to pay the purchase price of a bride to the father or next of kin. Poor *fellahin* sometimes have to borrow at usurious rates in order to get married, and thus begin their adult life in debt to the money sharks. With the proceeds of the first wife's earnings, he may purchase a second wife, younger and more desirable. However, although he may take four wives in accordance with the Moslem law, one is the usual number among the *fellahin*. The element of love rarely enters into the marriage and the women generally remain more attached to their families and their brothers, even after marriage. The girl must first be offered to relatives; failure to do so may cause serious trouble, even bloodshed. At the wedding ceremony the groom's kin watch the bride's father closely lest he give the girl in marriage to someone else at the last moment. Failure to deliver the bride may result in violence and start the long chain of blood vengeance.

Religion for the peasant is largely a matter of praying five times a day and observing the holy days. Islam is accepted superficially; as is evidenced in the small white-domed shrines

totally illiterate, only .06 percent being reported as knowing how to read and write.

20. The census of 1931 (p. 185) reports the average age of marriage for women as twenty years, which is higher than the general impression. The *fellahin* are not certain about their ages, and it may be that the statistics are not reliable on this point.

which dot the hills of the countryside, the *fellah's* worship retains elements of ancient Palestinian cults—of early Christian saints cults[21]—or even perhaps of the old Canaanite worship. The saints who dwell in these shrines are considered vengeful; the *fellah* is not likely to break an oath in the name of a "saint," though he may swear with impunity in the name of Allah who is all-merciful. The fear of the evil eye is widespread. He is subject to an extraordinary fatalism; to Allah he attributes everything good or bad which befalls him. A favorite phrase is *Kull shi min Allah*—"It's all from Allah." The peasants have great respect for the members of the Moslem religious hierarchy of the towns: the *mufti* (the authority on law); the *qadi* (the judge); and the *imam* (the leader of prayer). In the villages they meet mostly with the local teacher, or *katib*, who is frequently also a preacher or religious person; the *alim*, who is more learned, more respected than the *katib*; and the dervishes, or holy men.[22]

Like the Bedouin, the *fellah* exalts the virtue of hospitality. Your true *jayd*—as the generous host is called—will stand at the crossroads near the village to invite the stranger to his own home before he reaches the *madafa*—the public guest house—which each village maintains. The *madafa* also serves as the village gathering place in the long winter nights during the rainy season, when the *fellahin* come together to smoke, play games and drink coffee, and discuss local and world affairs. Giving alms is another important virtue, though this is looked upon more as a religious than a social duty. Every celebration —circumcision or wedding—is an occasion for almsgiving, generally in the form of food to the beggars of the village. The *fellah* is fond of celebrations—particularly of elaborate weddings—which are marked by singing, dancing and much eating. The dance consists of body movements repeated indefinitely to the accompaniment of monotonous singing in unison, punctuated by handclapping. The lyrics are simple, singing of love and of incidents in everyday life and everyday work.

---

21. See W. F. Albright in the *Journal of the American Oriental Society*, 1940, pp. 285 ff.

22. The dervishes are in some respects similar to Christian monks, although they may marry. There are innumerable sects, but the *fellah* regards them with a certain awe regardless of sect.

There are other characteristics of the *fellah* which are less likely to evoke the admiration of the Western observer. Lying he considers a great art and he has a proverb which runs: "A lie is the salt in a man." He is excellent at making them up as he goes along, and the bigger the lie the greater are the number of oaths which accompany it. Combined with respect for his superiors, the lie becomes adroit flattery; in litigation, for which the *fellah* has a strong proclivity, it leads to perjury quite usual in Arab peasant lawsuits. As with the Bedouin, stealing is hardly considered a crime and the villagers will think nothing of shielding bandits from the pursuit of the police. Although usually goodnatured and inclined to be peaceful, the peasant inherits the hot blood of the Arabs; he is subject to great outbursts of anger and is easily provoked to violence. The annals of the Palestine police are replete with cases of crimes of violence on the part of *fellahin*—uprooting of one's neighbor's trees and setting fire to his grain stacks; abduction and rape; and murder incidental to robbery or in revenge of a dishonored sister. A dispute in the village may be accompanied by mutual recriminations, an exchange of accusations, lawsuits and perjury; it may also lead to maiming and arson, murder, and a chain of blood revenge which may disturb the peace for generations.

The attitude of the *fellah* toward the city people is a mixture of resentment and respect. In the city live his exploiters: the merchant who cheats him in his purchases; the moneylender who oppresses him with usurious interest; the landlord who bleeds him white with rentals. But these city *effendis* are also the minions of Government—now under British rule, as well as under the Turks formerly. The *effendis* evidently cannot be dislodged from their positions as rulers; it is better to obey them and show them respect. The *fellah's* oldest enemies are the Bedouin nomads, *al-Arab*, as he calls them. An old proverb says: "Four are the ravages of the land: mice, locusts, Kurds and Bedouins." In one night's raid the Bedouins may take the fruit of a season's labor, stealing the harvest and driving off the cattle. The village harbors the memory of ancient tribal strife, of factious disputes between local sheikhs, of vestiges of the never-ending blood feuds. There is struggle between region and region, village and village, and between clans in the same village.

Within the clan or family group there reigns comparative unity sustained by blood relationship and common enemies. In each clan, one elder generally exercises pre-eminent power. Though the peasant society of Palestine is mainly patronal, a certain civil unity is provided by the *mukhtar,* who is the administrative head under the government. The hard life of the tillers of the soil, too, has forged a common bond uniting the *fellahin* in a sense of solidarity which, to some extent, transcends differences and rivalries, and creates to a certain degree a class consciousness among the peasants. At times, this even makes for a sense of kinship with the Jewish tillers of the soil in the neighborhood. But these unities of feeling arising out of a common experience in work and life are not as yet strong enough to counteract traditional forces of disunity kept alive by the patriarchal set-up of the *fellahin* society.

Here and there one sees signs of change. The life of the village, though moving forward very slowly, is not altogether static. Jewish example and government aid have helped the *fellahin* improve his method of cultivation, and the general development of the economic situation has steadily, if slowly, improved his condition. The villages have become cleaner; the houses better built, now frequently having windows; the well with its rope-drawn bucket has been replaced by electric-driven pumps; the water is used for irrigation as well as for drinking purposes. Disease has been reduced and in some villages a higher level of hygiene has been achieved. Increasing numbers of peasants with their wives and children go to the government clinics and missionary hospitals in the nearby towns, and consult Jewish specialists in the cities. The government schools are doing something to reduce illiteracy, and the proportion of girls attending the schools is increasing. Along with these advances, attitudes are changing also: the villager feels himself less dependent on his *effendi* masters and he has begun to be liberated from his sense of worthlessness firmly established in him under generations of tyranny.

The Urban Population

The Upper Effendi[23] *Class.* Although living in the cities, the

---

23. The term *"effendi"* is employed like the English word "sir" in popular usage to indicate an attitude of respect. For origin, see above, Chap. VII.

effendis derive their main income from agricultural land: from rentals, from interest on loans to *fellahin,* and from the profits of plantations. They generally own properties in the cities as well, and in recent years have invested in business and industry. While not comparable to that of the Egyptian aristocracy, the income of the *effendis* is considerable; enough to allow them to live in good style in the cities of Palestine or in neighboring countries, even occasionally in Europe. Their wealth and Oriental charm make them popular in European circles. The class is built around the small aristocracy of landowners who had been admitted by the Turks to the ruling group of the Ottoman Empire. The leading *effendi* families are descendants of the early Arab conquerors of the country or of Moslem soldiers and officials who at various times have been rewarded with grants of land for their services to the ruling dynasty. Some of the Arab notables retain the old Turkish titles of *bey* and *pasha.* To this aristocratic class belong also the more important officials of the Moslem religious hierarchy, who are either members or followers of one or another of the landowning families.

The families most frequently mentioned are the Husainis, the Nashashibis, the Dajanis, the Khalidis and the Abdul Hadis. Unending jealousies exist between them, the inheritance of ancient enmities compounded by rivalries for power in present day Palestine. The Turkish Government had no motive for encouraging unity among them; the British, although favoring the Husainis, have followed a policy of balancing the power between the two leading family groupings—the Husainis and their satellites and the Nashashibis and theirs.[24] In the *effendi* class should be included members in the upper range of the liberal professions—physicans, lawyers, newspapermen. The Moslems in the liberal professions generally belong to the leading families; the Christians, many of whom are of Syrian origin, have more often achieved their positions as a result of the modern education obtained in missionary schools. Even when not of the landowning aristocracy, the members of the liberal professions—Christians and Moslems

---

24. The Khalidis are linked with the Husainis; the Dajanis are closely associated with the Nashashibis. The Abdul Hadis, headed by the nationalist leader, Auni Bey, have played a more independent role in recent decades.

alike—are economically dependent upon it: they emulate this aristocracy socially and follow it politically. No member of the Arab professional class in Palestine has as yet emerged as a leader in any movement for economic and social reform. Their idealism expresses itself mainly in the form of Arab nationalism.

The *effendi* class as a whole is literate and, in a certain sense, even cultured. Most of the leading members of the families have acquired, besides Turkish—in the case of the older generation—some knowledge of Western languages, particularly French, more recently English. Among the professional class a number have attended the American University of Beirut and some are graduates of European institutions of learning. As in the case of the Levant generally, the Arab intellectuals' grasp on Western thought is superficial. The term "democracy" is conceived of as implying national independence, rather than a social and ethical philosophy of life. Particularly noteworthy is the lack of a sense of social obligation on the part of the upper classes; whatever public hospitals and Western educational institutions exist have been established by non-Arab foreign organizations.[25] Moslem charities are limited to almsgiving or to the maintenance of shrines and repair of mosques. Family relations are still largely Oriental; the women of the upper classes are usually veiled; polygamy, though not the general rule, is more frequent among the Moslem aristocracy than among the *fellahin*. There are, however, distinctive signs of emancipation of women in their increasing participation in social and political life.[26]

The Middle Class. Next in economic and social level is the Arab middle class, which includes wholesale merchants, shop-

25. Recently, one of the ladies of the Khalidi family died, leaving a large sum for the establishment of a hospital in Jerusalem. The members of the family, including the late Dr. Husain Khalidi, Mayor of Jerusalem, contested the will.

26. In 1929, a Women's Congress was held in Jerusalem, attended by two hundred women. It was organized by a small group of educated Christian women with a sprinkling of Moslems. Among the participants were wives, sisters and daughters of the well-known Arab leaders —the Husainis, the Nashashibis, the Khalidis and the Abdul-Hadis. A permanent organization was formed for charitable and political activity. However, the political activities were predominant: the women campaigned for use of Arab products, protests were lodged against the Balfour Declaration, and there were pleas for clemency on behalf of three prisoners sentenced to death for murders committed in the 1929 riots.

keepers, owners of bazaars, teachers, minor government officials, and the better artisans. Some of the more prosperous of this class engage in money-lending, orange growing and industry. A relatively large proportion are Christians. As a class, this group was negligible during the Turkish regime; but the economic development since British occupation has made it an increasingly important section of the population. The large ratio of Christians gives this social stratum a literate character, taken as a whole; also, among the Moslems in this class, literacy is gaining ground as the result of the work of the government schools. The large number of government officials and teachers in this group also tends to make it an active political element. Among them are the readers of newspapers and the intellectual nationalists.

The general orientation of this social group is toward the upper class: the more successful use the title *"effendi,"* seek social acceptance by the landed aristocracy, and support the usual political trends. Their attitude toward the *fellahin* does not differ from that of the *effendis,* being also marked by a feeling of superiority. Although here spoken of as a "class," this group is made up of a variety of elements and is essentially individualistic: it lacks the national pride and sense of mutual responsibility of the tribal Bedouins; it is not marked by the uniform social-religious traits of the *fellahin;* nor is it held together by the family loyalties of the upper class. Thrifty and conservative, the business elements in this class are opposed to disorder and violence, an attitude no doubt enforced by the large contingent of Christians. The middle class have been the chief victims of the boycotts, the political strikes, and economic insecurity attending the disturbances.

The Lower Class. The urban masses include artisans, porters, boatmen and unskilled laborers. At the lowest level are a numerous class of professional beggars, men without employment, idlers and urchins—the types who provide the tourist with the characteristic touch of the Orient. These urban masses generally live in the old parts of the cities, in crooked, narrow streets. They are largely illiterate. The Haycraft Commission depicted the working class element which participated in the riots of 1921 as "sociable, credulous, readily collecting in crowds at any moment when any cause of excitement arises." [27] A police officer writes: "Fanaticism and excitability may turn the most quiet among them into a murderer. They tend to respect force and ruthlessness . . . The number of their crimes, consisting of theft, beatings, stabbings and murder is greater than that of other classes." [28] Politicians do not hesitate to use these elements to organize demonstrations, to attack Jews, or to terrorize their Arab political opponents.

The better element of the lower class, consisting of skilled workers, tend to rise to the status of a working middle class. Partly in response to the example of Jewish organized labor, there has been some development of labor unions and cooperatives. In some instances, ambitious lawyers and upper class politicians have organized the labor groups along political lines to prevent their cooperation with Jewish organizations and to obstruct the organization of genuine labor unions which would raise wages and improve terms of service. In recent years the development of Arab national consciousness has also militated against a united labor movement. The greatest difficulty in labor organization, however, lies in the large body of unskilled laborers, uncertain of the next day's wage. This urban proletariat is enlarged in times of agricultural depression by the influx of *fellahin* and *haratin* (hired workers) who come in from the countryside. The problem of raising the standard of the Arab urban masses is thus related to two problems: the improvement and stabilization of agriculture on the one hand, and the development of organized industry on the other.

The Arab urban masses are not imbued with any strong sense of class consciousness; like other city dwellers, they are individualistic. Insofar as they have a sense of cohesion it is, as in the case of the *fellahin,* the religious consciousness of being a Moslem with which the sense of being an Arab is merged. The feeling of being a Bedouin, a *fellah* or an *effendi* is still stronger than the feeling of being a Palestinian, and though nationalism has undoubtedly grown, it has not as yet overridden the class divisions.

The national feeling is strongest in the literate urban middle class and has developed along with the general growth of Arab

27. Great Britain, *Palestine Disturbances in May 1921*, Cmd. 1540, London, 1921, p. 18.
28. David Tidhar, *op. cit.*, Preface, p. xviii.

nationalism in neighboring countries, with Zionism acting as a catalytic agent. The government public schools and the Arab press have been major factors in stimulating its development. Although the British directors of the education department did not intend this, the Arab government schools emphasizing Arab literature and history, and taught by Arab teachers imbued with the national ideal, have contributed to the growth of Arab extremism. The Arab press of Palestine are political propaganda sheets rather than purveyors of news. They are largely the instruments of individuals and support one or the other of the political families. As a whole, the Arab press has helped to promote the agitation of the Arab Executive Committee.[29]

THE MOSLEM AND ARAB ATTITUDES TOWARD THE JEWS

In attempting to understand the Arab attitude toward the Jewish national home, we must bear in mind how the Jewish developments affected each one of the classes described, as well as give consideration to the general reaction of the Arabs to the Jews as an "alien" nationality. As the account of the major Arab social groupings in Palestine indicates, there were many factors which presented difficulties to stable government and offered obstacles to progress. Modern forms of life and thought would have created tensions even if the changes had been introduced by native groups; the introduction of the new forces and ideas by people differing in religion, culture and in social composition necessarily complicated the problem. The attitude of Arabs toward the new Jewish settlements in Palestine was thus not merely a reaction toward a different religious group or nationality or toward an opposing political position. The Zionists represented a European as against an Oriental culture; they constituted a different occupational structure; and they reflected a new social orientation. In the background was the general attitude of Moslem superiority toward the infidel.

The Traditional Moslem Sense of Superiority

It is frequently assumed that, historically, Moslems have been well disposed toward Jews and Judaism; the Arabs of

29. Great Britain, *Palestine Report 1920–1925*, col. 15, p. 43.

Palestine often say that they lived in amity with the Jews until the advent of political Zionism. Like most generalizations, these assertions contain an element of truth; in comparison with their lot under Christian regimes, the position of the Jews under Moslem rule was rather favorable. Nevertheless, the Jews—like Christians and other non-Moslems—were regarded under the law as a politically and socially inferior community. A traditionally minded Moslem would react negatively to the idea of sharing rule with the Jews, let alone admitting the possibility of Jewish political predominance.

A certain antagonism toward the Jews comes down from the days of Mohammed. In the beginning of its career in the Arabian Peninsula, "Islam was by no means friendly to Judaism." [30] Mohammed had hoped to win recognition from the Jewish settlements in Arabia, and at first had tried to identify his new creed with Judaism: he adopted Old Testament narratives, accepted the Fast of Atonement, and designated Jerusalem as the *qibla*—the point to which Moslems should turn in prayer. The Jews, however, looked upon him as an ignorant impostor and derided his pretensions. He then turned against them; replaced the Fast of Atonement by the Fast of Ramadan, and substituted Mecca for Jerusalem as the *qibla*. He attacked the old established Jewish settlements in Medina (which under the name of Yathrib had probably first been settled by Jewish tribes), forced the Jews into exile, and confiscated their lands and properties. The last remaining Jewish tribe in Medina, the *Banu Kuraizah*—who sympathized with the opponents of Mohammed—were brutally murdered.[31] Mohammed declared: "Two religions may not dwell together on the Arabian Peninsula," [32] and his successors, Abu Bekr and Omar I, carried this idea into effect by completely annihilating the Jewish settlements throughout northern Arabia. The Prophet's great animus toward the Jews found expression in discriminatory enactments and the Koran contains a number

---

30. Salo W. Baron, *A Social and Religious History of the Jews*, Columbia University Press, 1937, p. 308.
31. For a brief account of the early relations of Mohammed and the Jews, see Robinson Souttar, *A Short History of Medieval Peoples*, Hodder and Stoughton, London, 1907.
32. Quoted by Baron, *op. cit.*, p. 311.

of derogatory statements which Moslems can turn against the Jews when it suits their purpose.[33]

Outside of the Arabian Peninsula, particularly under the sway of the Caliphs in Bagdad and Cairo, the Jewish position greatly improved after the Moslem conquest, and the Jews became participants in the rising glory of Islamic culture. There were Jewish settlements in both Moslem and Christian countries, and with the unification of the Moslem world and the extension of commerce the Jews began to play an important part in world trade as intermediaries. They had family connections throughout the civilized world and were able to understand one another through the medium of Hebrew, which, as Professor Baron points out, "became the main international language used in the commercial transactions between Paris and Aix-la-Chapelle on the one hand, and Baghdad, Cairo and Fez, on the other." [34] The uniformity of Jewish law and of the Jewish administration of justice throughout the world also contributed to the advance of international trade since the legal systems used by Christians and Moslems differed, and in Europe the codes of different countries varied greatly. During the resplendent period of Islam's ascendancy, the partnership of Jews and Moslems in furthering international commerce was accompanied by collaboration in the cultural realm.

As *dhimmi,* or People of the Book, the Jews enjoyed in common with Christians and Parsees, the status of a minority protected by Islamic law. The Moslems regarded themselves as the ruling class and as such were the military support of the government. To the *dhimmi* was assigned the function of promoting economic life: through a general land and poll tax the non-Moslems provided for the expenses of government—the budgets of the central and provincial administrations, the war expenditures, and the huge outlay for personal expenses of the courts of the Caliphs. This levy was imposed as a substitute for military service, and while it was heavy, it was less onerous

---

33. A summary of the Koran attitude toward the Jews says in part: "They are people highly favored of God, but are said to have perverted the meaning of his Scripture . . . they have intense hatred of all true Moslems and as a punishment for their sins some of them in times past have been changed into apes and swine, and others will have their hands tied to their backs and will be cast into the Fire on the Day of Judgment." (T. P. Wilson, *Dictionary of Islam,* 1885.)

34. Baron, *op. cit.,* p. 322.

than the taxes which had rested on the Jews during the decline of the Byzantine Empire. In many instances, the Caliph entrusted the task of collecting the taxes from the Jews to the Jewish community, which thus became an important governmental agency with large powers of control and extended self-government.

The special status of the tolerated non-Moslem communities entailed a degree of social discrimination and derogatory legislation. Among other things, the *dhimmi* had to wear specially colored robes and other identifying insignia to mark them off from believers. In some places, they were not allowed to ride on horseback and when they rode on their mules they had to use saddles with wooden stirrups. Erection of new places of worship was at times forbidden or limited, and other restrictions were imposed on Jews and Christians. The employment of non-believers in any office of the government which would place them in authority over Moslems was prohibited. There was, however, a wide discrepancy between the law and the practice. The regulations on special dress and insignia were usually disregarded. Jews, Christians and Parsees rose to important positions in public life. The Jews were, in certain periods, particularly close to the courts and had great influence upon them. "Nevertheless," as Professor Baron writes, "there is no doubt that in the period of the caliphate more poignantly than ever before, the Jews felt themselves disparaged as 'infidels,' and that the foundations were then laid for the ghetto, the badge and the oath *more judaico*." [35] Moreover, from time to time the discriminatory laws were invoked with the full force of Moslem fanaticism: synagogues were razed to the ground, the sight of a Jew riding on horseback might provoke a riot, or a Jewish quarter might be attacked in a sudden frenzy against all infidels.

With the gradual weakening of Islamic unity and power, Jewish life also declined in the Moslem countries, although the general social tolerance—broken from time to time by local excesses against infidels—persisted. In the modern period, with the breakdown of central government, instances of local attacks against both Christians and Jews multiplied. In 1625, the local ruler of Jerusalem persecuted the Jews mercilessly in defiance of orders from the authorities in Damascus and

---

35. *Ibid.*, p. 317.

Constantinople. It was not unusual, when the countryside suffered from drought, for the the Moslem mob to attack "Jewish sinners who drank wine and thus caused the rains to stop." [36] To buy off the attackers, Jews had to borrow money from rich Moslems at compound interest, under the threat of further attacks if they failed to repay. Only a little over a century ago, the Moslems of Safed had "to be compelled by force of arms to admit Christians and Jews to any rights at all, and for the gratification of seeing them walk the gutter, forced them to dismount at the sight of the faithful." [37]

During the first half of the nineteenth century, generally when the Ottoman government was weak, the Jews felt the full force of Islamic discriminatory and derogatory legislation.[38] To the Arabs, the Jews as a group were *kuffar* (infidels) and often *frangi* (Europeans).[39] Some hostility to them was always latent, as it was to all foreigners. During the rebellion of 1834 against Ibraham Pasha, Jews were mercilessly dealt with in the general anti-European, anti-Christian and anti-foreign revolt. The ritual murder charge at Damascus in 1840, and the persecution of the Jews in Morocco and in other parts of the Mohammedan world, brought about the intervention of Moses Montefiore and the formation of the Alliance Israélite Universelle to do philanthropic and educational work among the Jews in Arab countries. As a result of the pleadings of Western Powers and the representations of Jewish notables to the Sultan, an edict was obtained which proclaimed "the full equality of Jews before the law and strict justice for them and their property before all courts of justice." [40] But the local pashas did not generally respect this ordinance.

Arab-Jewish Relations in Palestine before and after the First World War

In Palestine the status of the Jews was changed for the better with the strengthening of the Ottoman government in

36. A. Y. Brawer, *Haaretz*, Davar, Tel-Aviv, 1929, p. 169.
37. Great Britain Foreign Office, *Syria and Palestine*, Peace Handbook No. 60, London, 1920, p. 27.
38. Ismar Elbogen, *A Century of Jewish Life*, The Jewish Publication Society, Philadelphia, 1944, p. 76.
39. Because of the prominence of the French in the Crusades, Europeans were generally referred to as "Franks" or *"frangi."*
40. Elbogen, *op. cit.*, p. 76.

the last half of the nineteenth century. The "capitulations," in accordance with which foreigners enjoyed special privileges of protection were extended also to Ottoman Jews. While this change did not affect the social and religious prejudice of the Moslems, the Jews no longer were legal objects of annoyance and were protected from violence by fear of the government. The half century of peace between 1860 and 1914 stabilized Arab-Jewish relations, particularly in the cities where most Jews lived. Business relations developed and a general sense of mutual respect grew up among the upper classes. The attitude of the rural Arab population to the Jews was also marked by increase of good relations in the Jewish colonies; the relatively high wages offered by the Jews to Arab labor was probably an important factor. There remained, however, the underlying disposition to hostility inherited by the masses and in each class of Arabs there were, under the surface, causes for tension between the new and old groups as they came in contact with each other.

In the earlier days of Jewish settlement, the Bedouin applied to the colonists an attitude made up in part of contempt, such as he felt for the peasant, and hostility, such as he bore toward the infidel. This was aggravated in the early years by the practice in some colonies of hiring Bedouin or Circassian guards to watch the fields and vineyards. The formation of the *Hashomer*, a Jewish watchmen's organization, changed the attitude to one of respect. These watchmen often dressed as Bedouins, emulated their skill in horsemanship and adopted Arab customs in dealing with them. Nevertheless, Jewish rural life in Palestine was never secure before the First World War; not a single colony was established without some loss of life resulting from Bedouin attacks. In some instances, the Bedouins claimed grazing rights on lands recently purchased by Jews; at other times, the reasons were relatively trivial, e.g., grudges because Jewish guards had replaced them—as much a slight of honor as an economic loss. The most important single cause was the same as that which led the Bedouins to attack the Arab villages, namely, the traditional raiding and looting habit of the nomad. The attacks were occasional; peaceful relations were generally soon re-established and usually cemented by peace treaties.

On the part of the *fellahin* there does not appear to have

been any overt opposition to Jewish settlement during the first period of Zionist work in Palestine. No scarcity of land was felt, the Jewish colonies employed Arab labor almost exclusively, and the wages paid were higher than those which the *fellahin* received from the *effendi* landowners. In his famous essay "Truth from Palestine," published in 1891 after his first visit, Ahad Ha'am (Asher Ginsberg) notes that the *fellahin* were by no means unaware of the Zionist objectives but they did not regard Jewish colonization as disadvantageous to them. He prophesied, however, that when Jewish development became more extensive, the peasants might not take the matter so complacently.[41] Itshak Epstein, philologist and teacher, writing in 1907, also indicated that the *fellahin* were not altogether unconcerned, but he thought that their suspicions would be allayed as they realized that the Jews were reclaiming the soil from waste and desolation and not taking it from them, and as they came to understand that they were benefiting by the modern agricultural methods which the Jews were introducing.[42]

The attitude of the urban population before the First World War was also largely tolerant, although here the situation is more mixed. With the native Sephardic Jews, who resembled their Arab neighbors in dress and appearance, the relations were friendly. There were even cases of intermarriage among the poorer classes; toward the Sephardic Jewish notables protected by foreign consuls there was a feeling of deference. On the other hand, toward Oriental Jews who came from various parts of Asia—from Persia, Bokhara, Turkestan—and toward the Yemenite Jews who came from the southeastern corner of the Arabian Peninsula, the attitude was less favorable. These recent arrivals lacked the Occidental characteristics and the consular protection which always evoked a certain admiration and respect. The Arabs were inclined to look upon them as infidels and assume toward them the attitude of Moslem superiority. But these Oriental Jews, coming into what they considered their own country, refused to accept the position of inferiority vis-à-vis the Moslem natives.

41. Ahad Ha'am, *Al Parashat Derachim* (At the Parting of the Ways), Berlin, 1921, Vol. 1, p. 25. Also Preface to the 3d ed., p. xxiii.
42. M. Perlmann, "Chapter of Arab-Jewish Diplomacy, 1918–22," *Jewish Social Studies*, Vol. VI, No. 2, 1944, p. 124.

Toward the Jews of the old *Yishuv* who came largely from Eastern Europe for reasons of piety, the attitude was generally neutral. Though markedly different in attire, language and standard of living from other Europeans, they were nevertheless under consular protection. They also offered a profitable market for the Arab peasant and artisan and only rarely competed with the urban Arabs in business. Apart from purchases in the marketplace and other minor business transactions, there was little contact. The attitude of the city Arabs to those who were known as "Zionists" did not differ from their attitude toward other Europeans. (The term "Zionist" before the War was used loosely to describe Jews who came from Europe to settle in Palestine without any obvious religious purpose.) Among the "Zionists" were physicians and well-to-do merchants, who were modern in appearance and enjoyed consular protection.

Nor was there any evidence of opposition to Jewish settlement and development on the part of the *effendis*. The Jews paid high prices for useless lands which were not yielding any income. More often than not they connived with the Jews in evading the Turkish laws which prohibited land sales and the erection of permanent buildings.[43] There was no attempt on the part of Jewish labor to organize Arab labor, and while the Jewish colonists paid the *fellah* a relatively high wage, this did not as yet present any serious problem. Like the peasants, the landowners were not unaware of the danger of Zionist penetration, but they regarded themselves as masters of the situation. The Turkish Government was committed to a policy of discouraging the settlement of non-Moslems and they felt that they could rely upon it to curtail the Jewish development when the time came.

Thus, there was little evidence of opposition to the Zionist immigration and settlement in the early years as far as the majority of the population was concerned. However, signs of antagonism on the part of Arab journalists and political leaders imbued with the nationalist spirit were not wanting; and these multiplied after the Turkish revolution of 1908,

43. In 1891 when immigration and land purchases had reached the proportion of a mild boom—as a result of the growing persecution of the Jews in Russia—the Sultan Abdul Hamid had decreed that Eastern European Jews be prohibited from settling in Palestine permanently and that immigrants could stay in Palestine three months only.

when the franchise granted to Arabs promoted their sense of political importance. The Arab nationalists began to attack Zionism and the Palestine Arab newspapers were guilty of such violent expression that one of them was suspended for a time by the authorities for incitement against the Jews.[44] In the Turkish Parliament, the Arabs more than once denounced Jewish aspirations in Palestine as contrary to the welfare of the Arabs. After the outbreak of the First World War, documents of an Arab secret society seized by the Turks in 1914 outlined a plan for getting rid of Zionism: the colonies to be razed by fire and the Jews driven out. The Zionists were represented as tools of the Turks and as enemies of the Arabs.

On the other hand, some Arab leaders recognized that Jewish capital, labor and intelligence might be valuable for the development of Arab aspirations. Zionist representatives in Constantinople, Nahum Sokolow, Vladimir Jabotinsky and Victor Jacobson, assisted by some Palestinians, kept in touch with Arab leaders. In Palestine, Chaim Margalith Kalvarisky, at this time an officer in the PICA service, promoted contacts in Palestine. Toward the end of 1913, a meeting between several Arab leaders and Nahum Sokolow took place in Damascus, where it was decided to convene an Arab-Jewish Conference in the Lebanon during the following summer with the participation of the Turkish Governor. This project, however, was subsequently abandoned, due perhaps to Turkish suggestion despite the fact that the Turks had originally agreed to negotiations. The Arabs resented the cancellation of the Conference and one of their spokesmen, Nasif Bey al-Khalidi, remarked ominously to a Jewish leader: *"Gardez vous bien, Messieurs les Sionistes, un gouvernement passe mais un peuple reste."* The Zionists were in a difficult position: the Arabs were accusing them of collaborating with the Turks; the Turks on their part accused them of conspiring with the Arabs.

Antagonism to Zionism in the First Decade

It was natural that the first to react to the changed political status implied in the Balfour Declaration were the *effendis*. In a Palestine cut away from Syria, dedicated to the establish-

---

44. M. Perlmann, *op. cit.*, p. 125.

ment of the Jewish national home, they correctly saw an end to their predominance. The Jewish aspiration in Palestine would provide an excuse for prolonging British control and make it necessary to share political power with the Jews, if not ultimately to relinquish it. The *effendi* class had never shared political power with the other Arab classes and certainly had no intention of dividing rule with the Jews. The Jewish development, moreover, offered a serious threat to the hold of the *effendis* over the peasant. The degree of dependence of the peasant upon the landlord was lessened, for now he could find work in Jewish plantations or migrate to the city to find employment in the building trades or in industries established by the influx of capital. The sale of land by individual peasants who had excess holdings enabled them to use the proceeds to repay their debts and to apply some capital to the improvement and intensification of their own cultivation. The Jewish development both in industry and agriculture thus threatened the patronal social-economic structure of Arab Palestine. The socialist ideology enthusiastically proclaimed by the new wave of immigration from Poland and Russia after the First World War certainly did not lessen these apprehensions.

The *effendi* antagonism, as noted in the preceding chapter, expressed itself most clearly in the political field and led to the formation of the Arab Executive which organized the anti-Zionist propaganda under the Husaini leadership. There were also indications of growing opposition to selling land to Jews. As early as 1920, a British Foreign Office booklet stated: "There is . . . a very widespread fear among the Moslem land-owners that the program of Zionism is inimical to their interests; and societies have been formed to organize resistance to the sale of land to Jews." [45] However, this opposition during the first decade was essentially only political propaganda since, in practice, the *effendis* continued to sell land to the Jews. There was much mutual recrimination among the Arab leaders, each side accusing the leaders of the other side of engaging in profitable land sales to Jews. There was evidently a conflict between the private interest of the *effendi* as an individual and his interest as a member of a dominant polit-

45. Great Britain Foreign Office, *Syria and Palestine*, Peace Handbook No. 60.

ical economic class in maintaining the basis of power which he recognized was land ownership.

To the Arab urban middle class, Jewish immigration on a considerable scale signified the introduction of a strong competitive element in the fields of business, government office, municipal services, and the liberal professions. This was true particularly of the Christian part of the population, whose occupational distribution was similar to that of the Jews. The Moslem shopkeeper was usually the owner of a bazaar in the old parts of the cities. The Christian shopkeeper would be more likely to have a modern shop in the new city. The immigration of Jewish physicians was disturbing to the Arab physicians, particularly since Arabs showed no hesitancy in consulting Jewish physicians. Resented particularly was the employment of Jews in government services. This point was stressed by the Melkite Archbishop before the Royal Commission: "The courts as also the administrative and municipal councils had been [in Ottoman days] half Christian and half Moslem. Christian representatives had decreased and were about to disappear owing to Jewish immigration. In former times the vice-president of the Municipal Council of Haifa was a Christian; he had been recently replaced by a Jew." [46]

Among the intellectuals of the middle class were the conscious Arab nationalists. Here too the Arab Christians played a leading part in the activity against Zionism. Common opposition to the Jewish national home policy weakened the traditional hostility between Moslem and Christian Arabs. Moslem acceptance of Christians as political partners strengthened the Arab movement in a number of ways: it was good policy to deprive the government of a minority group which could be played up against the ambitions of the Moslem leaders; and the services of the Christian intelligentsia were needed for propaganda work and as a link with the powerful missionary organizations who were also opposed to the Zionist movement. At times, the Christian Arabs in the middle class opponents of Zionism seemed more zealous than the Moslems themselves in the promotion of Arab nationalism. Despite the profession of Christianity, some of the Arab Christian leaders were evidently ready to join the Moslems in the use of terror and violence. Professor W. F. Albright relates as a witness to the

46. *Palestine Royal Commission Report*, p. 327.

incident that a certain well-known Christian Arab editor, at the time of an anti-Jewish outbreak, "called his little boy of five into the room and told him what he must do to a Jewish boy if he should get a chance. He even put cruel words into the little chap's mouth: 'I will take a knife and stab him; I will take a pistol and shoot him'." [47]

Despite the political antagonisms, Jews and Arabs normally worked together on practical matters of mutual interest. In the mixed municipalities of Haifa, Jerusalem and Jaffa, the Arab mayors and council members generally succeeded in cooperating with the Jews, and questions were, on the whole, determined without regard to national lines. In business, likewise, Arabs worked together with the Jews: Arab and Jewish citrus growers, though maintaining separate organizations, sometimes cooperated in marketing; Jews regularly purchased agricultural products from Arabs, and, despite the separation of Jaffa and Tel-Aviv, Arab women from the latter city, particularly of the upper classes, shopped regularly at Tel-Aviv. The contacts were broken in times of disturbances, but the breaches were eventually healed. It is important to note, however, that the cooperation in practical matters did not appear to affect political attitudes.

As the Royal Commission indicates, despite the by no means negligible record of day-to-day working together, Arab cooperation has never extended to national politics: "Willingness to co-operate with Jews in municipal government is unhappily no evidence at all of willingness to co-operate on a national scale: and Arab councillors, who can agree with Jews about improving an urban water-supply or regulating a market or laying out a park, cannot agree with them about the rate of immigration or land-purchase or the constitution of a Legislative Council. Practically all the Arab mayors, it will be remembered, attended the nationalist meeting at Jaffa which preceded the outbreak of 1933. And of course, the moderates among the Arab politicians have always made common cause with the extremists on major national issues." [48]

It is difficult to estimate whether there was any appreciable change of attitude among the Bedouins and *fellahin* with the

47. "Japheth in the Tents of Shem," *Asia and the Americas*, December, 1942, pp. 692–694.
48. *Palestine Royal Commission Report*, p. 145.

increase of Jewish land purchases. The peasant parties which were active for a while during 1923–1928 were concerned with general agrarian reform rather than with opposition to Zionism.[49] While opposition to the Balfour Declaration was expressed as a matter of course, the main antagonism was reserved for the leaders of the dominant political parties and against the usurious money-lenders. In several cases, as in the peasant parties at Beisan and Hebron, sympathy was expressed for the Jewish national home policy. It is true that *fellahin* participated in the Nebi Musa riots in 1920, but they seem to have been impelled by Moslem religious frenzy and not by any political or economic motivations. The riots in Jaffa in 1921 were initiated by an urban mob; the attacks on the nearby settlements were carried out by Bedouins. There were some incidents where former Arab tenants or Bedouins forcibly resisted Jewish settlement of the land after purchase, but these incidents were not unlike similar ones which had occurred before the First World War. It may be that there was a growth in apprehension, particularly in light of the fact that there was much propaganda among the *fellahin,* but in the first decade expressions of opposition to the Jews because of fear of displacement were not in evidence. The propaganda sent out to the *fellahin* emphasized the religious danger rather than the economic, e.g., the Jews were accused of planting the Zionist flag on the Mosque of Omar. As indicated in the Wailing Wall disturbances of 1929, it was only when the Moslem religious motif was fully exploited by the political leaders that it was possible to arouse the peasant masses.

Arab propaganda has laid emphasis on the disruptive effect of modern and radical ideas introduced by the Zionist pioneers. Such charges are rehearsed in the following paragraphs:[50]

There is another danger which must be borne in mind: the new arrivals usually bring with them some advanced European habits and ways of thought which are not borne out by local traditions. It must be realized that Palestine, being largely Arab, is a country where great importance is attached to matters of social etiquette, decorum and tradition, which have descended from generation to

---

49. See previous Chapter, p. 485.
50. M. E. T. Mogannam, *op. cit.*, pp. 217–218.

generation and which are completely at variance with foreign ideas which are being radically introduced into the country.

It is natural that the Arab should have been irritated by the self-assertion and aggressiveness of the new arrivals and be influenced by the social and bolshevik principles which they bring with them. A strong bolshevist element has already established itself in the country and has produced an effect on the population, not by the success of its propaganda but by the genuine uneasiness which it inspired among the Arabs, especially the poorer classes.

These accusations are designed to appeal to reactionary elements. Zionism was, of course, prohibited in Russia as counter-revolutionary and, conversely, the Palestine Labor movement bitterly opposed the Third International. There was a small number of Jewish communists in Palestine boring from within who were as strongly anti-Zionist as they were anti-British and worked with Arabs in opposition to Zionism. But those who decried Jewish immigration as "bolshevist" made little distinction between the democratic labor movement and communism, since both were anathema to them and both were in their minds calculated to stir up "uneasiness" among the poorer Arabs. The attack against Zionism on the ground that it was bolshevistic was particularly popular in the early 1920's, when the rise of communism was greatly feared in Western countries. This attitude was strongly in evidence also with the development of the Axis anti-communist front in the middle 1930's.[51]

Among the "matters of social etiquette, decorum and tradition" which are referred to in the above quotation, and which are regarded as objectionable to Arab views, no doubt are implied also the evidences of the emancipation of women, indicated in the behavior of the new immigrants. The traditionalists have taken exception to the bare-arm and bare-legged Jewish pioneer girls, to men and women walking together arm-in-arm on the streets, and to the participation of women in public affairs. Even the *Falastin*, though edited by a Chris-

---

51. Jamal Husaini, Secretary of the Arab Higher Committee, giving testimony before the Royal Commission in 1937, declared: "As to the communistic principles and ideas of Jewish immigrants, most repugnant to the religion, customs and ethical principles of this country, which are imported and disseminated, I need not dwell upon them as these ideas are well known to have been imported by the Jewish community." (*Minutes of the Palestine Royal Commission*, p. 236.)

tian, in listing objectionable Zionist manifestations, included, besides giving government jobs to Zionists and opening the gates of Palestine to Russian bolsheviks, the appointment of women for positions which required contact with the public at large.[52] Such innovations of custom were undoubtedly disliked by conservative Britishers and Catholics as well as by the Moslem religious hierarchy, but deviations from convention were practiced by non-Jews throughout the Near East and it is highly doubtful whether the masses of the population cared anything about such matters.

The charges that the Jews are arrogant, tactless and generally lacking in good manners, is made by a certain type of Britisher as well as by the Arab Christian propagandists. These complaints are not unlike those which are sometimes employed in the United States and England in excusing or explaining anti-Semitism. It is not easy to discern how much of the fault lies in the behavior of the Jews and how much in the prejudiced interpretation of the observer; how much indignation against a just grievance; how much is due to a lack of sense of form, and how much to disdain of what is regarded as superficial politeness; how much is due to the exuberance in the newly found freedom in Palestine, how much to the alleged arrogant feeling of superiority. There is no doubt, also, a genuine difference in value judgments: a British official will think nothing of keeping a Jewish subordinate standing on his feet for an hour delivering a report, since this is part of his code; a Jewish subordinate might regard this as inconsiderate and therefore bad manners. On the other hand, the British official might regard it as offensive if a subordinate addressed him informally as an equal, while the Jew might think this an indication of friendliness. Some British are no doubt irritated to find that the Jews will not practice the obsequious courtesy to which they are accustomed in dealing with natives; the Jew may think that he is simply demanding his rights; to the British official he may seem importunate. No doubt there has been much lack of tact and even absence of good manners, but the cases cited are generally trivial. At any rate, there is no ground for thinking that Jewish disregard either for the English or the Moslem routine of conventions has been a serious

---

52. As quoted in *Haaretz*, February 17, 1924.

factor in disturbing good social relations among the people at large.

The differences of customs and general social outlook obviously present barriers to free social intercourse between Jews and Arabs. In view of this basic difficulty and in the light of the continuous stream of political propaganda against Zionism, it is rather significant that, taken as a whole, there has been so little evidence of strong social-economic antagonism between Jews and Arabs. The day-to-day relations have been normal enough: boycotts announced by the political bodies have not prevented Arabs from purchasing from Jews and selling to Jews; Arabs have continued to consult Jewish physicians and even to utilize Jewish skilled labor when expedient. The Jews, on their part, have used Arab agricultural products and employed Arab labor in private enterprise despite the ban on the part of Jewish labor organizations and the Jewish national bodies.[53] While intercourse between Arabs and Jews has not been intimate, nevertheless friendly relations between individuals have persisted and neighborly attitudes between Arab villages and Jewish settlements have been maintained. During the period of riots Arabs frequently warned Jews beforehand, and in certain cases, tried to shield the Jews even at the risk of their own lives. It is significant that normal relations have generally been immediately renewed after strikes and riots.[54]

There are thus many evidences to support the Arabs' contention that they are not anti-Semitic but anti-Zionist. By this, they probably mean that they are opposed to the Zionist objectives; in point of fact, during the disturbances, no distinction was ever made between the Jews of the old *Yishuv* and modern Jews or Zionists. The riots of 1929—which had all of the character of a frenzied Moslem mob assault—were directed against the old centers of Jewish life, and the quarters inhabited by the religious Jews suffered most. The attacks against Jewish colonies generally had the character of Bedouin raids. No sharp line of distinction can be drawn between

53. See below.
54. For some incidents during the 1929 disturbances, see Maurice Samuel, *What Happened in Palestine*, pp. 122, 162, 172, 201 and *passim*, particularly the story of the four Jewish laborers working with Arabs in the government quarry near Bethlehem, pp. 204 ff.

the Moslem opposition to Jewish preponderance and the Arab nationalist objection to the Zionist purpose. If any distinction is to be made it is rather along the line of the Arab attitude toward the Jew as an individual and the Arab attitude toward the Jews as a group. The Jews as a community appear to the Arab as an alien and infidel community over which he wishes to retain a sense of superiority and predominance.

To say that there was no strong opposition on the part of the masses of *fellahin* to Zionist immigration and settlement does not imply that they welcomed it. It is sometimes claimed that the *fellahin* appreciated the advantages of the Jewish development and this counteracted their antagonism. There is undoubtedly some truth in this. On the other hand, it must be realized that the immediate advantages to the *fellahin* were not as obvious as might appear to the student of the development over a course of years. The beneficial changes worked slowly on the mass of the people and they did not affect all parts of the population, or all sections of the country, equally. The advantages derived by the *fellahin* from the Jewish development, moreover, came indirectly as a result of the general improvement of the environment, such as elimination of disease, malaria control, etc. The improvement was not great enough to make any essential difference in the life of the *fellah*. It would have required a revolutionary change and a drastic agrarian reform in Palestine to have left a marked effect on the life of the *fellah*. Thus, while there was undoubtedly improvement, and certainly a great measure of this was due to the Jewish development, there is no reason to believe that the *fellah* was impressed by the benefits to him of Jewish settlement.[55]

There is another important psychological factor that must be taken into consideration. Every social change always brings loss to some, even though it may benefit the majority. The bazaar-keeper who loses his trade when business is transferred to a new district; the small *effendi* landowner who has no sur-

---

55. Even certain changes which may be regarded as beneficial from a general social point of view may not always appear as beneficial to the individual Arab family. One of the most significant changes in Palestine, usually emphasized, is the reduction of infant and child mortality, leading to a great increase in the Arab population; but the Arab *fellah* now has a larger family to support and his somewhat increased income may be more than offset by his larger expenditure.

plus of land to sell but who feels the pinch of rising costs of labor and higher prices; the few tenants who were displaced in the course of land transactions, even though they may have received fair compensation; the Arab worker who is refused a job in a Jewish settlement, even though many other Arabs had gotten jobs—all these will form nuclei of protest against the changing state of affairs. It is natural also that dissatisfaction should cry out with a loud voice, while those satisfied enjoy their benefits in silence. Furthermore, it was unpatriotic to express satisfaction for benefits derived from Jewish development, and those who secretly favored the development were not apt to express their feelings. There was nothing for them to gain thereby. Thus, there may have been a good deal of psychological antagonism to the Zionist development even though there were not any valid reasons for it on economic grounds. The propaganda, of which there was no doubt plenty, stirred up the latent opposition to Jewish settlement and immigration. It was easier to do this in view of the fact that Government did nothing, and the Jewish bodies did little, to counteract the anti-Zionist propaganda.

THE CHRISTIAN COMMUNITIES OF PALESTINE

Diversity among the Moslem Arabs expressed itself in the social-economic differences implied in the terms *bedouin, fellah* and *effendi*. In religion, the Moslem Arabs of Palestine are quite homogeneous, most of them being of the Sunnite or traditional denomination. The Supreme Moslem Council, with its system of courts and control of religious endowments, has given a structural unity to the underlying religious unity. The Christians, on the other hand—including the non-Arabs as well as the Arabs—are socially more homogeneous, being mainly of the middle class, but as religious communities they are characterized by great divisions in church affiliation. Christianity, it will be remembered, is not an indigenous force in Palestine—although it is based on the life and teachings of Jesus; as an organized religion, it is the creation of Rome and always represented in the East the introduction of a foreign civilization. While the Bishopric of Jerusalem dates from the first century, most of the churches today are of foreign origin and are subject to an authority whose seat is in a foreign country. Even in cases where the majority of adherents are native Arabs, the heads of the church are non-Arabs; a fact which is beginning to cause some dissatisfaction as the nationalistic tendencies develop. In varying degrees the different churches of Palestine are associated with specific nationalities, and, in some cases at least, have engaged in political missions as well as religious and educational tasks. The main divisions are the Greek Orthodox Church, with about 45 percent of the Christian adherents; the Roman Catholic Church, with about 23 percent; and the Uniats, or Eastern Christians, who recognize the supremacy of the Pope, somewhat less than 20 percent. There are, however, a large number of churches which, though numerically small, are important in their influence.

Churches and Missions[56]

The Roman Catholic Church

The most important Christian church in Palestine is the Catholic—known in our own country as the Roman Catholic Church—which in 1931 included some nineteen thousand adherents of the Latin Rite and some sixteen thousand Uniats,[57] comprising in all something over 38 percent of the Christians of Palestine. This membership is only seven-eighths as large as that of the Eastern Orthodox Church, but the Catholic Church exercises a far greater influence, since it controls a tremendous investment in real property, is officially supported by a large number of consular officials, and represents a world community of some 350 million persons. All told, there are nearly two thousand Catholic clergy and religious in Palestine, including all the secular clergy of the

---

56. The following sections, to p. 553, written by Professor William F. Albright especially for the Esco Foundation Palestine Study, are reproduced in their original form with some editorial changes.

The first-hand material is drawn almost entirely from Professor Albright's knowledge and experience, as well as that of his wife, who took an active part in Catholic affairs. Dates, figures, etc., have been checked by reference to the official Census of Palestine, to the directories and other official publications of the Christian churches, as well as to pertinent encyclopedia articles, especially in *Religion in Geschichte und Gegenwart* and in the *New Schaff-Herzog Encyclopedia of Religious Knowledge;* for individual items consult further Peter Thomsen's invaluable *Palästina-Literatur*, Vols. I–V. Other references of special interest are listed in the bibliography of this book.

57. See below, p. 536.

Latin and Uniat Patriarchates. The religious are organized in nearly fifty separate orders and congregations, i.e., societies of men or women bound by vows.

The official head of the Roman Catholic Church in Palestine is the Latin Patriarch of Jerusalem. The present incumbent, Msgr. Louis Barlassina, has held office since 1920 and has distinguished himself by his religious zeal and diplomatic skill. He controls the secular clergy of the Latin Rite as well as the religious personnel engaged in parish work; he also advises the congregations of women—nuns and sisters—and exerts a limited authority over the monastic orders. He exercises no supervision over the individual political opinions of the Catholic clergy, but he controls all public preaching and instruction in matters of religion and morals.

As the direct representative of the Holy See, the Latin Patriarchate enjoys steadily increasing prestige. However, it was established only in 1847, after an interruption of more than five hundred years. For this reason, and because it lacks representation in most other countries, it is much poorer than the Franciscan Order, which has been installed in the Holy Land since the early thirteenth century, and has, since the fourteenth, been officially designated as custodian of the holy sites of Palestine. The Franciscan Order now owns or controls nearly all the Catholic holy sites, including those which are regularly visited by pilgrims and tourists. In addition, it receives the Good Friday collections from the entire Catholic world and maintains houses for the support of its Palestinian work in almost every country. Since the First World War, it has devoted more than ten million dollars to the construction of new churches on historic Christian sites, such as Gethsemane, Tabor and Nazareth. The Order also appoints the pastors of the three largest Catholic parishes in Jerusalem, Bethlehem and Nazareth. Owing to the fact that the Patriarchate carries on nearly all the Catholic mission work in Palestine and is forced to do so with very meager funds, there has developed a certain amount of friction between it and the Franciscan Custody of the Holy Land—friction to which other historically determined causes have contributed.

Though the Franciscans are by far the largest and most powerful order in Palestine, more than forty-five other orders and congregations are represented in the country. Some, like the Jesuits and Dominicans, are interested only in maintaining single institutes for Biblical study and research; others do not engage in large-scale institutional work but are rather contemplative in character, e.g., the Trappists and, to some extent, the Carmelites (on Mount Carmel since the early seventeenth century), the Poor Clares and the Reparatrice Sisters. Other groups, such as the Christian Brothers, the Salesians, the Sisters of St. Joseph and the Rosary Sisters, have extensive undertakings, including orphanages and an agricultural school. Historically, the Sisters of Zion, founded by a converted Jew, are most closely associated with missionary work among the Jews, but they have long since ceased to carry on any direct proselyting activity.

The Uniats are Oriental Christian churches, most of them originally tinged with heresy, but which subsequently accepted the primacy of the Vatican and adopted official Roman Catholic doctrine. The Uniat Churches preserve their ancient rites and the secular clergy are allowed to marry before ordination. Celibacy, however, is rapidly increasing among them owing to the fact that most of the Uniat priests are educated in seminaries conducted by Europeans—the Benedictines being in charge of the Syrian Catholic seminary, and the White Fathers of the education of the Melchites. The oldest Uniat group in Palestine is composed of Maronites—thirty-five hundred in 1931—originally from the Lebanon, who accepted the primacy of Rome as early as the fifteenth century. The second oldest group, and now the largest, is the Melchite church—thirteen thousand in 1931—which was formed from the Eastern Orthodox Church by a proselyting activity reaching its climax in the eighteenth century. Much smaller Uniat churches are the Syrian Catholics, the Chaldaeans (Assyrian Catholics) and the Abyssinian Catholics.

The Greek Catholic Church

By far the oldest organized Christian community with a continuous history in Palestine is the Eastern Orthodox Church, which, according to the census of 1931, counted forty thousand adherents—or 44 percent of the Christians. It is popularly known as the "Greek Catholic Church;" its official designation is the "Orthodox Catholic and Apostolic Church of the East," and it is headed by the Patriarch of Jerusalem. From the first century on, the Bishop of Jerusalem was the head of the Christian community in Palestine, his title being successively changed to "Archbishop" and, later in the fifth century, to "Patriarch." In the Byzantine age, the Patriarch of Jerusalem was one of five supreme ecclesiastical authorities: two of them, the Patriarchs of Rome and Constantinople, claimed superior power, though their claim was rejected by the three others, the Patriarchs of Antioch, Alexandria and Jerusalem. The break with Rome came in successive stages, from the political rupture of the early eighth century to the final excommunication of the Eastern Church by the Pope in 1054. In the centuries thereafter, the Patriarch of Constantinople acquired a certain authority which, while nebulous, provided sufficient prestige to make him the head of the Eastern Church. Aside from the parish churches, the Greek Catholic Church has large properties concentrated chiefly in and around Jerusalem; it also owns shrines, churches and monasteries in other sacred spots in Palestine.

There are now some fifteen branches—nearly all national—within the Eastern Church, each of which has its own head. All these autocephalous bodies agree, however, in canonical theology, and none of them, excepting the Russian Church, which became autonomous in 1589, has an independent religious establishment in Palestine. The Russian Church also owns large properties especially in Jerusalem. Before 1914, Russia was recognized as the protector of the Eastern Christians of Palestine. After the rise of the Communist regime in Russia, which broke all ties with the Church, the Mandatory Power kept the property in trust, feeling itself obligated to protect the Russian Church against possible claims by the Soviet Government. The State Church of Russia was again officially recognized by the Soviet Government in 1944, and the Russian property has recently been restored to the custody of the Metropolitan of Jerusalem. It may be expected that the Metropolitan will assume some of the prerogatives which belonged to the Patriarch of Constantinople in the nineteenth century, and he may thus become a leading ecclesiastical figure in the Eastern Orthodox Church as far as Palestine is concerned.

There has been steadily increasing friction between the native Arabic-speaking Orthodox Christians of Palestine and the hierarchy of the Eastern Orthodox Church, practically all of whose members are Greek by origin, coming from Greece, Anatolia, Egypt and Cyprus. Nepotism has been rife and the natives have been deprived of the opportunity of selecting the members of the hierarchy, although the local parish priesthood is almost entirely composed of Arabic-speaking Christians born in Palestine. Under these circumstances, the native Christians will almost certainly call upon the Russians for aid against the power of the Greek hierarchy. There are several much smaller Oriental Christian churches in Palestine—the Armenian, Jacobite, Coptic and Abyssinian—all independent of both the Eastern Orthodox and the Roman Catholic Churches. The largest of these is the Armenian, or Gregorian Church, which numbers over three thousand members, most of them of comparatively recent refugee origin. Being monophysites in theology, they are stamped as heretics by members of the major communities. Since the First World War, they have been assisted by the Anglican mission in Jerusalem, one of whose canons is assigned to foster the relationship. The other three churches are also monophysite and are in communion or loosely affiliated with one another, though not with the Armenians. The Jacobite, or Old Syrian Church, has over a thousand adherents; there are only a few hundred Copts and Abyssinians all told in Palestine. None of these four groups exercises any political influence.

Protestant Churches and Missionary Activities

Protestant missionary activity in Palestine goes back only about a century. The first missionary enterprise in Palestine was launched in 1821 at Jerusalem under the auspices of the American Board of Commissioners for Foreign Missions, a Congregational organization. This effort proved abortive and the mission was transferred a few years later to Beirut in Syria, where it has flourished. The Syrian Protestant College was founded by the American Board in 1865, and now bears the name "American University of Beirut." With two thousand students, this university now leads all other institutions of higher learning in the Near East in significance. Next in the field was the British Church Missionary Society, to which the American Board transferred its interests in Jerusalem in 1943. Immediately prior to this, the Church of England and the State Church of Prussia had collaborated in establishing a joint

Anglican-Evangelical bishopric in Jerusalem, which continued until 1886. Bishop Gobat, a Swiss Protestant, was bishop for a third of a century, and was largely responsible for the expansion of the activity of the Church of England in Palestine. In the forties of the nineteenth century was also founded the Palestine mission of the British Society for the Propagation of the Gospel among the Jews (London Jews' Society), which flourished during the latter part of the nineteenth century, when it made a considerable number of Jewish converts. In subsequent years its success has been so meager as to discourage any extension, and it must now be termed moribund. In 1931, there were about five thousand adherents of the Church of England, which remains much the strongest Protestant body in the country, exerting influence quite out of proportion to its numerical strength. The work of the Church of England in Palestine has been increasingly supported by the affiliated Episcopal Church of America, and there has been an American canon at St. George's Cathedral for over a decade.

Next in importance to the Church of England comes the German Evangelical Church (State Church of Prussia), consisting of the great majority of Lutherans and Reformed Protestants in Germany, with active collaboration on the part of the state churches of Scandinavia and of Lutherans and Calvinists in Switzerland and elsewhere. After the cooperative bishopric in Jerusalem had been given up, the *Jerusalemstiftung* was founded in 1889, which remained in the closest association with the German monarchy until its abolition. This institution became the focus of previously established missionary enterprises, including the hospital of the German Deaconesses (*Kaiserswerther Schwester*), founded at Jerusalem in 1851, the direct missionary work of the *Jerusalemsverein* (since 1853), the Syrian Protestant Orphanage (founded in 1860) and the Leper Hospital, *"Jesushilfe"* (founded in 1867). The German mission remained small in numbers, but through its admirably organized schools and hospitals it exercised very great influence on both Christians and Moslems.[58]

58. The German Temple Society—sometimes confused with the Templars of the era of the Crusades—has no connection with the Lutheran and Reformed missions. It originated as a dissenting Protestant group with a strange combination of apocalyptic and unitarian tenets. After

A number of minor Protestant missionary enterprises may be mentioned. The American Society of Friends (Quakers) has operated an important group of schools at Ramallah for more than half a century. In 1894, the Christian and Missionary Alliance began mission work in Jerusalem and elsewhere, along fundamentalist lines; its Arab missions have been moderately successful, but its Jewish missionary activity has been almost completely futile. To this group, inter-denominational in character, belongs the so-called American Church in Jerusalem. The Church of Scotland Mission to the Jews has long carried on work in Galilee (Tiberias and, formerly, Safed), emphasizing schools and hospital service particularly. Besides these, there have been many smaller undertakings, nearly all quite abortive, such as enterprises of the American Southern Baptists, Mormons, Christian Scientists, Pentecostalists, etc. The Y.M.C.A. in Jerusalem, though scarcely a missionary enterprise, has become known to all foreigners through its palatial building opposite the King David Hotel in Jerusalem.

Protestant missions have become the spearhead of westernization in Palestine. Nearly all the groups have shown a greater interest in education than in other missionary activities. As a result, the Protestants have exerted a far more powerful effect on the people of Palestine than the Roman Catholics, in spite of the fact that the latter were first in the country, have a much larger body of adherents both abroad and in Palestine, and have spent a great deal more money on the country. It is, however, not altogether clear that this influence has been in all respects beneficial. The freedom of conscience and of action encouraged by the Protestants has contributed in no small measure to the breaking up of the smaller Eastern

1868, it was transferred to Palestine by its founder, Christophe Hoffmann. Six successful colonies were founded in Palestine which became the model agricultural settlements before the First World War. No serious missionary work has ever been undertaken by the colonists who have lost their religious fervor. At one time the Temple Society included over fourteen hundred souls, but their number was reduced by emigration. The German Government supported their activity and the colonists remained strongly pro-German. With the development of Zionism, they became increasingly anti-Jewish and during World War II were strongly pro-Nazi in their sympathies. Because they were suspected of treason their property was taken into custody by the British Government and the colonists were interned in concentration camps.

Christian groups, and has not infrequently had a destructive effect on the morale and character of individuals. The origin and growth of Arab nationalism in Syria and Palestine—as well as the development of democratic sentiment—can be traced back directly to Protestant missionary work in Beirut begun a century ago, as explicitly affirmed by such competent witnesses as the late Martin Hartmann and George Antonius.

The Protestant churches in Palestine have not won many converts, a failure which is probably due to the fragmentary character of the groups and the constant friction between them. During the second half of the nineteenth century a certain success—the causes of which will be explained more fully later—was achieved in converting Jews, but this was followed by almost total failure after the growth of the Zionist movement. On a superficial view, it appears that Protestantism has not been very effective in its impact on Islam despite the fact that the Moslem world has found itself in a spiritual stagnation during the past few centuries. However, it is possible that the influence of the Protestant missions acting as a ferment on the Islamic world has, under the surface, been greater than apparent, and a serious religious upheaval among Moslems may take place in the near future. It is to be hoped, however, that such a revival will not assume the violent forms which characterized the messianic and revolutionary *Mahdi* movements of the past century.

Attitudes Toward the Restoration of Israel and Toward Zionism

Pre-millennial Protestantism, which had a powerful revival during the nineteenth century, hopes that the return of the Jews to Palestine, in fulfillment of prophecy, will be followed by the Battle of Armageddon and the Second Coming of Christ. The Adventists, who are the best organized of the pre-millennialist bodies, expect the restoration of many Old Testament institutions along with the return of the Jews to Palestine. In order to pave the way for this reunion of Jews and Christians, they have introduced a number of Jewish practices, such as the seventh day Sabbath, the prohibition of the eating of pork, etc. The Adventists, though a small group, are independently organized; fundamentalist bodies, whose membership is far larger, retain connection with their original churches—Presbyterian, Baptist, etc.—but these pre-millennialist groups have established a common front. In Palestine, the groups are represented by the Seventh Day Adventists mission, the Christian and Missionary Alliances (fundamentalist), as well as by many individuals belonging to the Church of England and the Scotch Presbyterian Church.

With regard to the attitude to the Jewish restoration to Palestine, Christian opinion in Palestine has varied. During the heyday of Protestant missions to the Jews between 1840 and 1890, evangelical Protestants were mostly convinced that the Jews would be converted to Christianity before returning to Palestine or in close connection with their return. This attitude is now reflected especially by Jewish converts to Christianity—mostly calling themselves Hebrew Christians—who number some thousands and maintain a few representatives in Palestine. Since the beginnings of the Zionist movement, as noted above, there has been a rapid decrease in the success of all Christian missionary activity among the Jews. This has naturally brought with it a tendency to regard the Jews as hopeless, accompanied by an increase in anti-Jewish sentiment. Accordingly, several Christian missions in Palestine, originally established for work among the Jews, have shifted their emphasis more and more to work among the Arabs, with consequent hostility toward Zionism. This reaction is evident almost everywhere, in the Christian and Missionary Alliance, in the London Jews' Society, as well as in the much less active Catholic mission of the Dames de Sion.

Nearly a century ago there was a curious offshoot from the messianic movement just described, in the form of an identification of "Israel" of the prophecies with the Anglo-Saxons. The logic of this development was irrefutable, granted its premises: the world was promised by the Prophets to Israel; the English-speaking nations control the world—ergo, the Anglo-Saxons are Israel. According to this view, the Anglo-Saxons are descendants of the lost Ten Tribes, supposed to have been exiled to Armenia and Transcaucasia by the Assyrians and to have migrated from the Caucasus to Scandinavia and Great Britain together with the ancestors of the Teutons. It is believed that there are today at least two million adherents of "British Israel" in the British Empire, of whom most are members of the Church of England. Since this doctrine appeals with peculiar force to British military men and administrators, there can be no doubt that it has had a significant effect on British policy at certain periods. Without "British Israel" it is probable that British sympathy for Zionism would be much less pronounced than it actually is.

Periodically, "British Israel" has invaded America. In one of its first transoceanic movements it won the adherence of Mrs. Eddy, founder of the Christian Science movement. Formerly, many Christian Scientists were, in consequence, favorable to the return of the Jews to Palestine, though the majority of present-day members of this church show little or no interest in this phase of Mrs. Eddy's teaching. Indeed, during recent years the *Christian Science Monitor* has shown a definitely anti-Zionist tendency. About a decade ago there was a remarkable resurgence of "British Israel" in America, followed by a sinister anti-Semitic development during the past few years, centering in Chicago, Dearborn and New England. The adherents of this movement, called the "Anglo-Saxon Federation," hold that Great Britain and America are the true heirs of ancient Israel and the beneficiaries of prophetic promises; the Jews, they hold, are not true Israelites at all, and, having turned away from Christ, should share no part in the coming Restoration to Palestine. Unfortunately, some of the leaders of this movement are in responsible positions in church and industry. It must be emphasized, however, that no Protestant church—except, in part, the Church of Christ Scientist—accepts the vagaries of "British Israel" and that recognized Protestant scholars and theologians are without exception hostile to its claims, which are, of course, both historically and philologically absurd.

On the question of the formal attitude of the different Christian bodies toward Zionism, any statement is necessarily general and approximate, since so far no church has issued any official pronouncement. All major religious groups consider the Zionist issue as strictly political and hence not within the legitimate scope of their official activity. There are, however, in several instances, indications of a general position. In 1917, Pope Benedict XV expressed himself in an interview with Nahum Sokolow[59] as friendly to the proposed Zionist program of Great Britain and France. This attitude later changed

59. See above, Chap. II, p. 97.

under the impact of pressure brought by the Franciscans, who were apprehensive for the future of the holy sites, and by the native Palestinian Catholics and their friends among the European clergy. In 1922, official cognizance was taken of this situation in a letter addressed by the Papal Secretary of State to the Secretary-General of the League of Nations.[60] However, no further official action was ever taken, the Vatican remaining faithful to its tradition of moving slowly and then only when the interests of the Church were directly involved. The present Pontiff has repeatedly expressed his friendship for the Jewish people, but he seems never to have made any public reference to Zionism. In general, the same cautious neutrality has been characteristic of the foreign Catholic clergy of Palestine.

The native Catholic clergy is strongly nationalistic and opposed to any form of Zionism, and their attitude is reflected by some individuals among the foreign clergy. Catholic visitors from abroad generally return from Palestine with more or less hostility toward Zionism, in part the result of propaganda by tourist guides, in part of their own dislike for the intrusion of industrialism and modernism into the Holy Land. In their opposition to Zionist influences in Palestine, Catholics have particularly emphasized the change from traditional mores. Actually, of course, Zionist Jews have merely brought present-day European and American manners to Palestine. However, mixed public dancing was unknown in Jerusalem before the First World War, so it is scarcely surprising that its importation by British officials and Jewish immigrants caused a considerable amount of scandal. The Catholic clergy, led by the Patriarch himself, have repeatedly denounced the immodesty of customs in women's dress, particularly in the early twenties, when skirts and sleeves were unusually short. Despite their strong criticism, however, Catholics have generally been more friendly to Palestine Jewry than Protestants of the same national background. The German Catholics, for instance—Lazarists, Benedictines and others—have been less opposed to Zionism than the German Protestants, who have been strongly influenced by the intransigent attitude of the German colonists in the country and, since 1933, by the official policy of the Protestant State Church of the Reich.

60. Great Britain, *Parliamentary Papers 1922*, Cmd. 1708, 1922.

As an organization, the Greek Church has not taken any stand on the subject of Zionism, but the overwhelming majority of its membership is violently opposed to it on strictly nationalistic grounds. The Armenians are mainly neutral, since they are hopelessly in the minority and know that they are as much disliked by other groups as the Jews are, but they are not trying to use the hostility of the Arabs toward Zionism for their own advantage.

It is more complex and more difficult to analyze the attitudes of the English-speaking Protestant churches toward Zionism. As noted above, it is the messianic and pre-millennial tendencies which have generally led to support of Zionism. However, it must be emphasized that support on this ground is likely to be offset by correspondingly stronger opposition on the part of more conservative or, on the other hand, of the theologically liberal Protestant groups. The latter sometimes resent the literal fulfillment of prophecy by the Zionist movement, because of the comfort which it gives to pre-millennialists and messianists. It must be stated as a general principle that the overwhelming majority of the foreign Protestants in Palestine are more or less strongly opposed to Zionism. The missionaries and resident clergy are naturally devoted to the Arabs among whom they work and with whom they constantly associate. Their friendship for the Arabs and their lack of direct personal contact with Zionists can have only the effect of developing increasing opposition to Zionism on their part.

While this natural partisanship has not in most cases gone beyond incidental expressions of unfrendliness, there have, however, been several notorious incidents of active campaigning against Zionism on the part of Protestant missionaries. In the twenties, the late Miss Frances Newton of Haifa and Carmel, a retired Anglican missionary, became widely known as a bitter protagonist of the Arabs. Her hostility to Zionism went so far that she gladly believed every charge made against the Zionists, however lacking in basis of fact.[61] She deplored activities which benefited Arabs and Jews impartially, such as the health work of Hadassah and certain credit institutions of the Palestine Economic Corporation (directed by Mr. E. N.

---

61. She is responsible for spreading the accusations that Jewish land purchases had led to a widespread displacement of the Arab *fellahin*.

Mohl), which made small loans for business and home building. Her objection was that these Jewish agencies moderated Arab antagonism to Zionism and were thus ultimately the greatest enemies of the Arab cause in Palestine. The late Elihu Grant, widely known as a Palestinian archaeologist, was a missionary in Palestine for three years at the outset of his career, and came to admire the Arabs and to speak Arabic fluently. After his return to the country later as an excavator, he undertook more and more active anti-Zionist propaganda. At the time of his death in 1942, he was president of the American Friends of the Arabs. Though he was a man of great kindliness, and in no sense an anti-Semite, his emotional attachment to the Arabs often got the better of his judgment.

Among the Protestant scholars of Palestine there have been both sympathizers and opponents of Zionism. A notable example of the former is Canon Herbert Danby, now Regius Professor of Hebrew at Oxford, who spent more than fifteen years in Jerusalem, where he warmly befriended the Zionist movement. He is well known to a wider public as the translator of Klausner's *Yeshu ha-Notsri* (Jesus of Nazareth) into English, and more recently as the author of the best modern translation of the *Mishnah*. On the other hand, Gustav Dalman, famous as the leading Christian rabbinic scholar of the past half-century, was strongly opposed to Zionism, principally because of his innate conservatism and dislike for the changes which the Jews brought into the country. His attitude was, however, very different from that of the German colonists in Palestine, described above, and he did not share their Nazi point of view.

There is one Protestant organization in Palestine—the so-called American Colony in Jerusalem—which has been consistently anti-Zionist and which has lost no opportunity to create a spirit of antagonism toward Jewish activity. This group, established in Jerusalem by a Chicago merchant named Spafford, over sixty years ago, began as an antinomian messianic sect, but has gradually lost its religious character and now subsists mainly as a tourist enterprise, maintaining a large shop and a hostel. It has retained enough of its initial character to carry on a small amount of useful philanthropic work and is still regarded in many quarters as a charitable endeavor. Owing to the vast number of tourists with whom it has come into contact, the anti-Zionist point of view of the American Colony in Jerusalem has been diffused far and wide through the English-speaking and Scandinavian countries. In some cases, especially selected guides have been chosen in order to influence important visitors. The violent anti-Zionism of some prominent Americans can be traced to a few days spent at the American Colony years ago.[62]

The anti-Zionist stand recently adopted by the *Christian Century* is in part ultimately traceable to the influence of the American Colony in Jerusalem and to the persons whom it has prejudiced. Its view, moreover, is largely conditioned by its international and anti-nationalistic liberalism, which paradoxically leads it to accept the points of view of the most illiberal advisers. This merely is another illustration of the principle which has led prominent Christian pacifists to share the same platform with fascist and anti-Semitic America First propagandists. Still more recently a rapidly increasing number of Protestants have reacted against these unfair policies and have formed the pro-Zionist Christian Council on Palestine, headed by Henry A. Atkinson, Reinhold Niebuhr, and others of equal standing.

In summarizing, it may be said that just after the First World War the vast majority of Protestant Christians throughout the world favored Zionism, although very few had any clear idea of its significance or of the grave problems involved in its realization. As time went on, this initially favorable attitude became transformed to indifference or open hostility on the part of a great majority. This is not to be accounted for by formal anti-Zionist propaganda which, because of its disregard for Western standards of journalistic accuracy, has been on the whole ineffective. As indicated above, the influence has been directed largely through personal contacts: through tourist agencies and individual guides and chauffeurs, practically all of whom are Christian Syrians; by resident or returned missionaries and teachers in schools and colleges; by Syrians in this country, many of whom emigrated from the Lebanon many years ago. With all this, not all of the non-Arab Christians are anti-Zionists; some are pro-Zionist, and many indifferent.

62. It is probable that the anti-Zionism of Dr. Harry Emerson Fosdick is due to this influence.

The anti-Zionist propaganda may have influenced some of the Christians also in a generally anti-Jewish direction, but it should be clearly understood that the foreign Christians in Palestine are not, generally speaking, anti-Semitic. Their objections to Zionism are for the most part political and not racial or national; many of them feel also that it is not ethical to impose a large Jewish immigration on the unwilling Arab majority. Many illustrations of Christian friendliness to Jews could be given: since 1933 a large number of German-Jewish doctors have been added to the hospital staffs of all the important missionary hospitals, especially the Catholic hospitals and the German Deaconess hospitals. Individually, the relation between Christians and Jews who are brought together by national, social, cultural, professional or other ties has remained satisfactory, and even excellent. Both groups feel themselves drawn together by common interests and common backgrounds, especially when projected against the exotic life of an alien culture. Some Christians believe that the growing breach between them and the Jews in Palestine could be healed partly by the creation of better relations in the home countries, partly by promotion of cooperation between Jewish and Arab groups.

The Attitude of Eastern Christians to Moslems

From the Moslem conquest in the seventh century until the overthrow of the Turkish Empire by the British and French in 1918, the Eastern Christian sects remained uneasy and insecure. For nearly thirteen hundred years their position continued to be precarious, with constant oscillation between extreme danger and relative stability. Under well-established governments, as during the Omayyad and Abbasid caliphates, they were comparatively secure, though heavy taxation and lack of opportunities for political advancement weighed heavily on them and contributed to a swelling tide of apostasy. During periods of anarchy or recurrent religious reformations they were likely to suffer severely. This pattern was interrupted by the Crusades which for the first time in several centuries stirred latent political ambitions and hopes of rescue from the burdensome Moslem yoke. The Eastern Christians flocked eagerly to the standard of the Crusaders, only to be rudely awakened by the discovery that the Latin conquests brought with them imposition of the authority of the Roman church and suppression or even persecution of the Eastern Orthodox and heterdox groups. Moreover, languages and customs were alike foreign and barbarous. Hence the apathy and discontent of the Eastern Christians contributed materially to the ultimate Moslem triumph.

If the Moslems had shown more tolerance at that time, they could have conciliated the Christian population of the liberated countries. Unfortunately, all Christians suffered severely, little distinction being made between Eastern and Western groups. From this time on the Christians were suspected by their Moslem rulers of being potential adherents of the European Powers. Until the final disappearance of the Crusading idea during the sixteenth century, the status of the Eastern Christians was thus exceedingly insecure. The Turkish Empire of the seventeenth century became so vast and so powerful, with its territory extending from Nubia to north of the Crimea, and from the frontier of Morocco to Persia, that the Turks ceased to fear their Christian subjects, and many Christians attained high positions in the Turkish bureaucracy.

The status of the Christians was improved locally by the fact that both Christian and Moslem Arabs became divided into two great political parties, Qais and Yemen, between whom raged a series of local civil wars through most of the seventeenth and eighteenth centuries.[63] The Christians attached themselves as clients to one or the other of the two great Moslem Arab factions and were often drawn into civil war themselves, especially in Lebanon. Under such conditions the country remained undeveloped and declined in wealth and even in population, reaching its lowest point in the late eighteenth century, so far as we can judge from the material at our disposal. At that time it is doubtful whether Palestine had more than one-tenth of its present population. However, the Christians continued to be the favorite target both of factional strife and of tribal raids. Even in Lebanon, where the Christians became semi-autonomous in the eighteenth century, under their own emirs, they became embroiled in the internecine conflicts between Moslem factions. In Trans-Jordan,

---

63. The divisions went back to a long-standing jealousy between North-Arabic (Qais) and South-Arabic tribes (Yemen), which settled in Palestine and Syria after the Crusades and largely transformed the ethnic composition of these countries.

they largely confined themselves to strong hill fastnesses like Kerak and es-Salt, to stand numerous sieges and to endure constant tribute to neighboring Moslem tribes.

A new phase began in the eighteenth century when the French became self-styled protectors of the Latin Christians of the East, followed in the nineteenth by similar protection to native Christians of various orientations from Great Britain and Russia. After a series of civil wars in Mount Lebanon and adjacent districts, in which Moslems, Christians and Druses participated, there was a great massacre of Christians in 1860, followed by the intervention of the European Christian Powers. Thenceforward until 1914, all the Christians of the Ottoman Empire were protected more or less successfully by the Powers. Fear of their armed intervention led repeatedly to the rapid suppression of Arab and Kurdish attacks on the Christians, and the Turkish Empire showed a capacity for extremely prompt action in several cases.[64] It is not accidental that the worst massacres of Christians, especially of Armenians and Nestorians, in the history of the Turkish Empire took place during the First World War, when all three of the traditional protectors of the Christian minorities were at war with Turkey. The Germans were then interested mainly in gaining world-wide Moslem support and they took no official interest in the plight of the slaughtered Christians.

From 1918 until now, native Christian minorities have maintained their existence only with foreign support and protection. The liquidation of the Christians of Turkey continued with accelerated tempo after 1918, and practically all the remaining Armenians of Anatolia were killed or forced into exile, while the Greeks were saved from the same fate only by a gigantic "exchange" of populations, as a result of which great stretches of Anatolia were left uninhabited.[65] One of the first acts of the Iraqians, after obtaining independence from direct

---

64. For instance, in 1911, when the Parker treasure hunt in the area of the *Haram esh-Sharif* in Jerusalem aroused the Moslem population to fever heat.

65. The elimination of the Armenians of Istanbul, who had escaped liquidation because of the watchfulness of the British and Americans, was resumed after 1939, and seems to have disposed of most remaining Armenians in European Turkey. During the past few months it would appear that there has been considerable relaxation in the severity of the process, owing to the representations of the Allied Powers.

British control in 1932, was to massacre a considerable part of the Assyrian or Nestorian Christian refugees in the north, and to begin the systematic elimination of Christians and Jews from public offices. The Copts of Egypt and the Christian communities in Syria outside of Lebanon are in constant danger, illustrated by increasing apostasies on the part of the Copts, who had grown greatly in number during the British occupation of Egypt. It is feared by many that after the Syrians have obtained complete independence, one of their first acts will be to wipe out the colonies of Armenian, Jacobite and Nestorian refugees, which have been established in northeastern Syria by the French mandatory government.

The native Christians of Palestine recognize the acute peril that would confront them if Arab independence were obtained. They are subject to two contradictory impulsions: belonging by language and, in part, by culture, to the Arabs, the leaders have felt obliged to side with the Moslem majority against both the Jews and the Mandatory Power; but they are far from feeling secure in the anticipation of Moslem domination. In 1920, the Christians of Palestine were thrown into panic by the news that Faisal had been crowned king of Syria at Damascus, accompanied by the rumor that the British were about to turn Palestine over to him. In 1928, there was a general Moslem boycott of Christians throughout Palestine, which proved effective and was accompanied by bloodshed. This was touched off by nothing more formidable than an international Protestant missionary conference in Jerusalem, in which the problems of missionary activity among the Moslems were included in the agenda.

The Christian community of Palestine is poor and weak, as well as divided by sectarian differences, and as a consequence, possesses little autonomy. Practically all the Arab Christian leadership comes, accordingly, from Lebanon and centers in the American University of Beirut. Most Christian college graduates in Palestine are alumni of the American University. The Christians of Lebanese origin have seen over eighty years pass by without any serious anti-Christian movement in their own land. Young Christians are conscious of the Moslem peril only as something of historical and therefore of academic interest. Since the movement of Arab nationalism arose under American missionary auspices in Lebanon, they have a strong tradition of Arab patriotism. Moreover, they are saturated with Western liberalism, and a high proportion of them really believe that religious differences are no longer to be feared.

Both of the leading Arab propagandists of the past twenty years, Amin Rihani and George Antonius, were Lebanese Christians who had ceased to practice their ancestral faith and had become typical non-religious intellectuals. Arab nationalism had become a kind of religion with them. On one occasion, Antonius became very angry when asked whether he did not think that the Moslems would turn against the Christian minority if they obtained Arab independence. Evidently he was secretly fearful of just such a contingency. Many of the younger Lebanese Christians show no realization whatever of the existence of this peril. The attitude to the Zionist question of Lebanese who have settled in the Americas is conditioned entirely by prejudice and nostalgic devotion to the land of their fathers. Practically none of them has any clear idea about Jewish problems and many of them are firmly convinced that the Jews would move to Palestine in a body if the way were opened. Most of them have heard fabulous tales about Jewish oppression of the Palestinian Arabs.

The Palestinian Christians, on the other hand, though guided in their outlook and their propaganda largely by the Lebanese, naturally have a much more realistic point of view. While there may have been a few instances where Christians joined the Moslems in active warfare against the Jews, the majority have abstained from violence. In fact, the native Christians actually suffered as much or more than the Jews during the disturbances of 1936–39. Well-to-do Christians were taxed, blackmailed and otherwise forced into making heavy payments to the insurgents. They suffered most from the complete destruction of the tourist industry and from the general disruption of trade relations. In spite of the bitter anti-British and anti-Jewish feeling cultivated in the Arab population during those years, the leading native Christians now feel much less favorable to Arab independence than they did before 1936. It may be expected that the Christians of Palestine will continue to pursue an opportunistic role, sympathizing with the Moslems, at least outwardly, but taking care not to involve themselves in the conflict.

Much will depend upon events after the Second World War.

If the Christian minorities in the Near East will be persecuted in the countries where the Arabs have achieved independence —and this is not unlikely—the Christians of Palestine of course will become increasingly neutral, at least in their overt activity, however strongly they may at heart continue to oppose Zionism. The Lebanese Christians are certain to become disillusioned if Syria is allowed by the Allies to exercise dominion over them. A spiritual revival in Islam and a renascence of the Arab people should be welcomed by the Christian nations, but it is to be hoped that this will not be accompanied by the spirit of the *jehad* and fanatical intransigence which unfortunately has characterized so much of Moslem history in the past. There can be no real progress or inner development of the world of the Near East without assuring the Christian and Jewish communities a secure place, and for the present at least these will need the protection of the European Powers. Particularly, Jewish Palestine and Lebanese Syria must be granted a degree of autonomy which will assure their proper development in an Arab world which greatly needs the stimulus of the energies of these peoples.

THE JEWISH COMMUNITY AND PLANS FOR ARAB-JEWISH RAPPROCHEMENT

The Jewish community, as already indicated, is highly diversified: partly native, largely immigrant, gathered from all corners of the earth, representing various cultural backgrounds and reflecting a great many outlooks. At the Wailing Wall in Jerusalem one may meet the mediaeval mystic *kabbalist,* absorbed in the knowledge of the Messiah and in the meaning of the Redemption; the Socialist pioneer, devoted to the ideal of building a cooperative commonwealth in Palestine in our own day; and every other type between these two extremes.

The emphasis placed on the Zionist political activities and on the practical endeavors of the Labor movement, has at times left the impression that modern Jewish life in Palestine is largely secularistic. In point of fact, though wide diversities of belief and practice exist, the general character of life is rather more religious than in Western countries. The Sabbath and holidays are publicly observed in the traditional manner and, on occasion, even with orthodox severity. Anyone smoking on the streets or riding about in the Jewish sections of the cities on the Sabbath is likely to be reprimanded. Among a considerable number of families the religious ritual is no longer practiced; however, the main body of Jews follows the traditional observances with varying degrees of punctiliousness, ranging from meticulous orthodoxy to respect for accepted conventions. In the atmosphere of freedom and social approval, the Sabbath and holidays are assuming a new vitality. On Saturday afternoon the streets are bright with people promenading leisurely in Sabbath attire; there is much visiting and exchange of talk over the ubiquitous tall glasses of tea. In some places, a Sabbath afternoon gathering at the synagogue or community center, under the name of *Oneg Shabbat* (Sabbath Pleasure), has been instituted, at which noted writers or scholars discourse on some aspect of Jewish literature or on the events of the day.

There are public synagogues and many small congregations in the cities and in the larger colonies. The Cooperative Labor settlements, however—except those established by the orthodox wing (*Poale Mizrahi*)—do not maintain synagogues, and in the past were unsympathetic to institutionalized religion. In recent years some writers in the Labor settlements have indicated an interest in religious forms, in refashioning them and reinterpreting their meaning. Although there is a wide range of religious views, the Jews in Palestine do not divide themselves into organized denominations. The main religious tendency might be called traditional, or, to use the nearest American term, conservative. On the extreme right, there is the ultra-orthodox *Agudath Israel*. There is nothing that corresponds to the Reform movement of Western Europe and the United States. The traditional liturgy and ritual—differing slightly as between the Sephardic and Ashkenazic groups—are always followed. The Rabbinical Courts under Government authority follow the orthodox Jewish law in matters of marriage and divorce, and other forms are not legal for Jews.[66] It may be said that now, after the destruction of the old centers of Jewish life in Eastern Europe, there is no country in the

---

66. This, however, is not due to the wish of the majority of Jews, but to the fact, rather, that Government supports the orthodox view as the only legal one.

world in which Judaism in its traditional religious form is so intensively cultivated as in Palestine.

The Social Composition of the Jewish Community

Besides the differentiation along the lines of countries of origin, there are two distinctions dating from pre-war times that are generally employed in describing the life of the Jewish community in Palestine, which have already been referred to and which may now be more fully explained. One of these is the distinction between the "old" and the "new" *Yishuv;* the other is on the basis of *"edoth,"* or communities. In accordance with the latter division, Jews are divided as "Ashkenazim" and "Sephardim," [67] with minor groupings of Oriental and Yemenite Jews who are sometimes classified with the Sephardim. The term "Ashkenazim" is used to denote Jews coming from Central or Eastern Europe, that is, where some form of German and Yiddish has been adopted as the vernacular. The term also applies to European Jews who are derived from the Germanic-speaking Jews of Europe, and thus is used to describe American and British Jews as well as those coming from the European continent. The "Sephardim" include descendants of refugees from Spain who came to Palestine following their expulsion in 1492, and also the Jews from other countries—Turkey, the Balkans and North Africa—who originated in Spain or in other countries of the Mediterranean area. Some of the Sephardim have adopted Arabic as their vernacular, but more often and more characteristically they use a Judeo-Spanish, called Ladino or Español, derived from a Castilian dialect with a mixture of Hebrew. The Sephardim were the predominant group among the Jews of Palestine in the first part of the nineteenth century and their leaders still claim parity of representation with the now more numerous Ashkenazic group in certain aspects of community life. This tradition has been continued by the Palestine Government in the designation of a Sephardic as well as an Ashkenazic Chief Rabbi in the Rabbinical Council.

The Oriental Jews include some from Morocco and other

---

67. These terms are derived from place names referred to in the Old Testament and traditionally interpreted to mean Germany and Spain, respectively.

556 *Palestine. Jewish, Arab, and British Policies*

parts of North Africa, but consist mainly of immigrants from Iraq, Bokhara, Turkestan and Persia. The Yemenites, who come from the southwestern part of the Arabian Peninsula, form a distinct group. Their origin is obscure; they are the remnants of many Jewish settlements in Arabia dating from ancient times. They are generally small, almost diminutive in size, and dark brown in color. Except for their long curled earlocks and something in the expression of their faces, they might not ordinarily be recognized as Jews. In Yemen they are mostly metal workers, craftsmen and carpenters; in Palestine, they engage in all types of manual work and are regarded as a valuable labor element. In their religious observance, they are orthodox, strictly following the Code of Maimonides and the *Shulhan Aruch*.[68] They retain a pronunciation of Hebrew which is by some regarded as nearest to the ancient Palestinian. Their vernacular is Arabic, but because of their knowledge of the Bible the men learn to speak Hebrew very quickly. In Yemen, they have in recent generations been subjected to indignities and to economic discrimination, and have been coming to Palestine in steadily increasing numbers.

The Sephardic and the Oriental communities have increased about four times in the post-war period; the Yemenites, almost five times. However, in view of the very large immigration in recent years, the Ashkenazic-European element has increased its relative predominance. The following table shows the change in composition of the population between the years 1918 and 1928.[69]

	1918		1928		1943	
	Number	Percent	Number	Percent	Number	Percent
Ashkenazic	33,029	59.0	114,000	71.0	423,000	79.4
Sephardic	12,575	22.0	21,000	13.0	47,000	8.8
Yemenite	4,356	8.0	9,000	6.0	25,000	4.7
Oriental Jews	6,040	11.0	16,000	10.0	38,000	7.1
Totals	56,000	100.0	160,000	100.0	533,000	100.0

68. A code compiled by Joseph Caro of Safed in the middle of the sixteenth century, accepted as authoritative by orthodox Jews.
69. David Gurevich, *Statistical Abstract of Palestine 1929*, Jerusalem, 1930, p. 36.

The distinction between the "old" and the "new" *Yishuv* dates from the eighteen-eighties, when the first groups of settlers, stimulated by the *Lovers of Zion* movement, came to Palestine. These pioneers aspired to earn their living by working the soil of Palestine with their own hands, and hoped to achieve a cultural renascence of the Jewish people on the basis of the revivification of Hebrew, making the language of the Bible the language of life. To them, the Jews already in Palestine were the old *Yishuv*. The latter were concentrated in the four Holy Cities—Jerusalem, Hebron, Tiberias and Safed. They comprised persons—or descendants of persons—who had come to Palestine for reasons of piety to spend their lives in prayer and in the study of the Talmud. They regarded Hebrew as a holy tongue, and used Yiddish in their ordinary discourse.

The Jews of the old *Yishuv* were assisted by their families and countrymen who considered it a sacred obligation to support those who went to Palestine to pursue a life of religious study. This system of support which developed was called *halukah* (distribution or dole). As time went on, this became the only source of support for the greater part of Palestine Jewry. The distribution of the *halukah* was organized through community associations called *kolelim*, which included families from a certain country, city or village. At the end of the nineteenth century, with the increase of the numbers in the old *Yishuv*, and the decline of the *halukah* income some of those hitherto subsisting on these donations, turned to trade or handicrafts as a mode of making a living.

Of the 85,000 Jews living in Palestine before the First World War, 73,000, or 86 percent, lived in the cities, and of these 58,000 lived in Jerusalem, Hebron, Tiberias and Safed. In the postwar period, some of the orthodox immigrants became part of the old *Yishuv;* on the other hand, a greater number turned to the more secular occupations of the new *Yishuv*, being affected in part by modern ideas and, in part, by the economic crisis in various parts of Europe which cut off their means of support from *halukah*. It is noteworthy that the first attempt at colonization—that of Petach Tikvah, purchased and first settled in 1878—was made by Jews from Jerusalem who had abandoned the old *Yishuv* and its *halukah* system.

With the *halutz* immigration during the first decade under

the British Mandate, a great change took place in the social composition of the Jewish population: in distribution between city and rural communities, in occupational classification, and in social alignments. Before the First World War, there were only about 12,000 Jews in the agricultural settlements, comprising about 15 percent of the total Jewish population; in 1922, the number had risen to 17,000, or 20 percent; in 1929, there were over 36,000 Jews in the rural districts, comprising 23 percent of the population. The Jews living in the rural communities were mostly, but not entirely, engaged in agriculture; some were in industrial and professional pursuits. The trend, however, was definitely in the direction of manual work promoted by large-scale road construction, building of dwellings, and the development of transportation. The census of 1931 shows the following occupational structure of the Jewish population.[70]

Occupation	Earners	Percent	Earners and Dependents	Percent
Agriculture	12,720	19.0	27,835	15.8
Industry	19,235	29.0	49,623	29.0
Transport	3,278	4.9	9,629	5.5
Trade	8,881	13.3	28,665	16.4
Public Force and Administration	1,303	2.0	3,410	2.0
Profession and Liberal Arts	7,442	11.1	17,490	9.5
Persons Living on Their Incomes	1,996	3.0	8,545	5.0
Unskilled Workers, Domestic Service, and others	11,828	17.7	29,413	16.8
Totals	66,683	100.0	174,610	100.0

With the development of the Socialist-Labor movement and the organization of workers through the *Histadrut*, a sense of class difference developed: owners of industry and labor-employing private farmers on the one hand, and the labor cooperatives and workers' settlements associated with the *Histadrut*, on the other. It must be understood, however, that these differences resembled the class distinctions in the United

70. Adapted from *Palestine Census*, Part II, 1931, pp. 281–297.

States and other countries where social stratification is fluid and are not comparable to the fixed class divisions among the Arabs. Speaking in social-economic terms, the Jews in Palestine represent a middle-class grouping. Although the great majority are poor as judged by Western standards, the differences between the poorest and the richest are not as great as in Europe and America; their character as a middle-class grouping derives from the fact that there is no aristocratic class descended from a landowning nobility, and no peasant class in the strict sense of the term.

The *Yishuv* became more self-contained in the postwar period as a result of a number of factors, some arising out of the inherent character of the Jewish development, some resulting from special policies adopted. Before the First World War, most Jews lived in cities of mixed population where Arabs constituted a majority. They frequently dwelt in houses owned by Arabs and in the proximity of Arabs. After the war the increase in Jewish population led to the development of more thickly populated Jewish neighborhoods. There was also a movement to build modern quarters in the suburbs, a tendency which was greatly stimulated by the disturbances. In the course of the years, the Jews gradually moved out of the Arab sections of the old cities, partly to find better housing, partly for security, and partly in resentment. The all-Jewish city of Tel-Aviv, founded in 1912, received its great stimulus for growth after the 1921 riots in Jaffa. The increase of the rural population meant an increase in the number and proportion of Jews who lived in self-contained communities. As a result, by far the great majority of the Jews came to live in Jewish neighborhoods, Jewish villages, Jewish suburbs and in the large Jewish city of Tel-Aviv.

A second factor in the development of the *Yishuv's* self-dependence was economic and derived from the principle of *tozeret haaretz* (products of the land) and *avodah Ivrit* (Jewish labor). *Tozeret haaretz* at first connoted locally manufactured or processed products—which were generally Jewish—contrasted with foreign products, e.g., flour milled in Palestine. The principle of *tozeret haaretz* was not at first applied to the native agricultural products—such as vegetables and eggs —which the Arabs brought to market, since the Jews did not produce these products. Later, when the Jews began to produce farm products for sale, the *tozeret haaretz* idea became in essence the principle of buying Jewish products only—not Arab. As in the case of housing, the tendency was accentuated after the riots of 1921, and after the proclamation by the Arab Executive of a boycott of Jewish business and land sales to Jews.[71]

In practice, the *tozeret haaretz* principle was not observed by the generality of the Jewish population, at least in the first decade; the average income was low and the purchase of the more expensive Jewish products was a distinct hardship which only "idealists" would undergo. On the economic side, from the point of view of the general development of the country, the effect of the *tozeret haaretz* was largely beneficial, as a competent neutral observer has indicated.[72] The Arab products were absorbed in the country in any case; the stimulation of local Jewish production reduced the import of foreign products. From the social point of view, however, *tozeret haaretz* had the effect, no doubt, of further accentuating the tendency to develop two parallel economies, one Arab, the other Jewish, and to reduce the amount of economic interchange between the two communities.

Another factor tending to create a dual economy is the principle of Jewish labor only in Jewish-owned economic enterprise. This principle, vigorously advocated by the *Histadrut*, has been attacked by Jews as well as Arabs, and even more vehemently. The attack is on both economic and moral grounds. Jewish citrus growers complain that they cannot compete with the Arab producers if they must pay the higher wages demanded by organized Jewish labor, and thus will ultimately be forced out of the export market on which the success of the orange industry depends. Employers of labor in general hold that it is unwise from the long-range point of view to maintain a wage rate higher than in neighboring countries, at least in such industries as aim to produce for foreign

---

71. See above, Chap. VII, p. 480.
72. A. P. S. Clark, "Commerce, Industry and Banking," in *Palestine, A Decade of Development, Annals of the American Academy of Political and Social Science*, November, 1932, pp. 96–97. Mr. Clark writes: "Thanks to the support of the new population, accentuated by a spirit of loyalty and of devotion to the country's future, the use of home products, which at first was largely uneconomical, was popularized. Without this support, it is doubtful if many of the new ventures would have survived."

consumption. Those who oppose the policy of one hundred percent Jewish labor on moral grounds argue that it undermines the possibility of achieving any social or political rapprochement, that the dual economy which it promotes must keep the two communities forever in isolation from each other.

The *Histadrut* defends its advocacy of the policy of Jewish labor in Jewish enterprise on the ground that the Jewish home land can be built up only on the cornerstone of a large working class immigration. If the principle of one hundred percent Jewish labor is relaxed, the tendency will be to drive the Jewish worker out of the Jewish market altogether. Arabs do not employ Jewish labor—if for no other reason than because it is more expensive. Government public works, made possible in major part by revenue derived from Jewish immigration, and mixed corporations—which have been stimulated by Jewish endeavor—already offer increased employment opportunities for Arabs. To permit Arabs to penetrate the Jewish labor market would mean that the influx of Jewish capital would be used mostly for Arab development and would defeat the Zionist purpose of providing for the Jewish immigrants.

Moreover, employment of Arabs in Jewish industry would lead to a class stratification in Palestine along racial lines, with the Jews acting as capitalist employers and the Arabs as workers—thus repeating in Palestine all the abnormalities that have led to anti-Semitism in the Diaspora. By creating a higher wage standard through organization, the Jewish worker also prepares the ground for adaptation of higher standards among the Arabs. If the Jewish laborer should disappear from the market, the Arab laborers would continue at their old wage as an exploited and oppressed class. Meeting the moral argument, the *Histadrut* proposes collaboration with the Arab worker through the creation of an all-embracing Federation of Labor in Palestine, consisting of two cooperating labor organizations—Jewish and Arab.[73]

In practice, Jewish industrial as well as agricultural enterprise employs a considerable amount of Arab labor. Such industries as the Palestine Electric Corporation and the Palestine Potash Company, based on Government concessions, do so as part of their agreement. Other large private industries, such as the Nir Match Company and Portland Cement, employ

73. See below, p. 1126.

mixed labor, as do some smaller establishments. In the old colonies, Arab agricultural labor predominated, at least until the time of the 1936 disturbances. In some cases, as in Petach Tikvah, Arab labor is used almost exclusively. Arab labor is still employed by Jews in many places despite the political disturbances and its use will probably increase as normal relations are re-established. The Farmers' Federation, composed of private owners, has organized to combat the *Histadrut* principle of unionization and one hundred percent Jewish labor. Arab labor is not employed on lands belonging to the Jewish National Fund. The agricultural settlements founded on such land are based on the principle of "self-labor," and no outside labor—either Arab or Jewish—is employed. In addition,[74] there is a clause in the Jewish National Fund lease which prohibits the lessee from engaging any but Jewish labor. This was intended as an additional precaution for the use of labor in the erection of buildings or for any purpose incidental to cultivating the soil.

Attempts at Political Rapprochement

The hope for a political agreement with the Arabs was kept alive by the memory of the one-time successful negotiations between Weizmann and Faisal. In the formal resolutions of the Zionist congresses there were repeated declarations of a desire for cooperation with the Arab section of the population in the upbuilding of Palestine as the common country of both peoples. Several attempts were made for renewing direct negotiations with leaders of the Arab movement; these proved abortive, but a brief account may be given to indicate the nature of the problems involved.

Dr. Chaim Margalith Kalvarisky,[75] a consistent advocate of

---

74. See Chap. VI.
75. Haim Margalith Kalvarisky was born in Suwalk, Poland, on March 25, 1868, and educated in a Russian *Gymnasium* and University. He was attracted to the *Lovers of Zion* movement and was one of a group of young men who went to France to study agriculture in preparation for rebuilding the land of Israel. He came to Palestine in 1895, acted for a time as instructor in the Mikveh Israel Agricultural School, and then served as an official of ICA as an administrator of the colonization work until 1923. From 1923 to 1931 he was the director of the Arab Bureau of the Zionist Executive and later of a combined Bureau for Arabic Affairs of the Executive of the Jewish Agency and the *Vaad Leumi*. He was a delegate to the Seventeenth World Zionist Congress and to the Round Table Palestine Conference in 1939.

Arab-Jewish rapprochement from the period before the First World War, has recorded an effort made by him in the summer of 1919 to arrive at a political understanding with the Faisal group in Damascus. Faisal, it will be remembered, was at that time King of Syria, having been elected by an all-Syrian Congress in March of that year. According to Kalvarisky,[76] the plan included an outline of a basic constitution for Palestine under the name *Eretz Israel,* and was presented as a basis for negotiations at the request of a number of Faisal's advisers. The document was intended "for the King, for the Minister of Foreign and Internal Affairs, for the head of the All-Syrian Congress, and for the Palestine delegates who participated in this Congress." The main principles of the proposal were as follows:

1. Palestine belongs to all its inhabitants—Jews, Moslems and Christians—all being citizens with equal rights.
2. The Jewish people of Eastern Semitic origin needs a territory for the development of its national culture, and Eretz Yisrael, the land of its origin—a small island in the great sea of lands and peoples of Eastern Semitic origin—should constitute the Jewish National Home.
3. Every official should know the two languages of the country—Hebrew and Arabic—as well as English. In Government schools, particularly in the higher grades, both languages—Hebrew and Arabic—should be required.
4. No differentiation—as between Jews, Moslems and Christians—should be made by public educational or philanthropic institutions in giving social and financial assistance. Similarly, agricultural and industrial banks should serve all sections of the population, and particular attention is to be given to helping the *fellahin.*
5. Since the stream of Jewish wealth and labor to a poor and under-populated country such as Palestine would help all its inhabitants, there must be absolute free Jewish immigration.

The proposal was made by Kalvarisky on his own initiative. He has complained that the Zionist Executive refused to accept the plan as a basis for negotiation and attributes this refusal to the Zionists' "scorn and indifference to the Arab movement and the Arab nation, and exaggerated confidence in our own strength and in the help which we were to get

[76]. C. M. Kalvarisky, *Al Parashat Derakhenu* (At the Parting of Our Ways), Jerusalem, 1939, p. 25.

from Europe and America." [77] However, on the face of it there were more tangible reasons for failing to make this plan a basis for negotiations. Faisal's position in Syria was precarious; the Mandate had as yet not been assigned, British and French interests were involved, and Faisal was not in a position to dispose of the Palestine situation on his own authority. He was moreover bound by the resolution of the Syrian Congress which had definitely rejected the Zionist program in the most vehement terms. Even if Faisal had the power to make a settlement of the Palestine question, the weight of the evidence indicates that at this time he could not have agreed to Kalvarisky's suggestion for an unlimited Jewish immigration into Palestine. The proposal was altogether vague and politically unrealistic; it is difficult to see how the Zionist Executive could possibly have supported it.

A more serious attempt at rapprochement was made in the spring of 1922. At this time both the Jews and the Arabs were experiencing difficulties. The French had driven Faisal from Damascus, and although he had been provided by the British with the kingship of Iraq, the position of the Arab nationalists who had supported him was at a low point. The Palestine Mandate had as yet not been approved by the League of Nations, and its Jewish national home provisions were under attack in Great Britain by opponents of Lloyd George. The Palestine Arab Delegation was active in London and in various capitals on the continent in the effort to have the Zionist provisions of the draft Mandate abrogated.

It was under these circumstances that a series of meetings took place in Cairo between Arabs who represented the "Congress of Parties of the Confederation of the Arab Countries" and representatives appointed by the Zionist Organization. Among the Arabs were leading Syrian nationalists;[78] the Palestinian representatives, however, were conspicuous by their absence. The Jewish delegates were Dr. Montagu David Eder of the Political Department of the Palestine Zionist Executive, Baron Felix de Menache, a leading Egyptian Jewish notable, and the late Ascher Saphir, then a young Palestinian journal-

---

77. *Ibid.*, p. 33.
78. A prominent part in the negotiations was played by Riad Bey Solh, now—since March, 1943—Premier of the newly formed independent Lebanon.

ist with a strong interest in the Arab question.[79] Saphir, who acted as secretary, published a detailed account of the discussions on the basis of minutes he kept at the time.[80]

The first meeting took place on March 18, 1922. Both sides expressed the desire to put an end to the dissensions which retarded "the realization of the legitimate aspirations of both parties," and to inaugurate an era of understanding and collaboration between the Arab and Jewish peoples. The Arab delegation declared that their countries, after the centuries of corrupt Turkish administration, found it impossible to take their place in the world again without collaboration of agents of the more advanced Western civilization, but they realized that the European Powers, who were then the agents of westernization, represented a grave peril to the independence of their countries and to Arab political unity. The Jewish nation, originating in the East and historically related to the Arabs, but now dispersed all over the world, represented "ideal forces on which modern civilization and progress draw." The Arabs did not fear Jewish colonization since it did not represent the entering wedge of a foreign political power. They were truly happy, therefore, to collaborate with the Jews in rebuilding the life of the Arab countries.

The Jewish delegates expressed their appreciation of the recognition of the old relationship between the two peoples and of the confidence expressed in the Jews as collaborators in a Semitic renascence. At the same time they drew attention of the Arab delegates to the "specific legal interest and aspirations which the Jews possess in Palestine, as their historical and national cradle (homeland)." The Arab delegates, however, made it clear that in their view the discussion should not

---

79. Ascher Saphir, the grandson of the famous Jewish traveler, Jacob Sapir, was born in Jerusalem in 1892 and died in London in 1942. From 1912 to the outbreak of the First World War, he was a journalist in Constantinople and Paris. In 1914 he headed ten thousand Jewish volunteers for the French Army who marched with French and Jewish banners; he received a citation for bravery in action and was made a colonel in the French Army. During 1917–1918 he was on the staff of the French forces in Palestine. After the war he continued to live in Palestine as a journalist. In 1939, at the outbreak of the Second World War, he enlisted with the French Army and served as a commandant. In 1940 he escaped to de Gaulle and became head of the Near East Department of the Free French staff, preparing plans for the liberation of Syria and Lebanon. (*Forward* (Yiddish), May 7, 1944.)

80. Ascher Saphir, *Unity or Partition*, Jerusalem, July, 1937, pp. 21–24.

proceed on the basis of any previous political agreements or documents, either the Balfour Declaration or the accord between Britain and King Husain. They said: "Arabs and Jews must discuss today as nation to nation; they must make mutual concessions and must recognize one another's rights." Countering the possible implication of hostility to the Allied Powers, the Arab representatives stated that it was not their intention to ask the Jews to "declare themselves against any foreign powers." They indicated that the labor which should unite the Jews and the Arabs would necessarily be a long process. The work was to commence forthwith and through systematic preparation and by every legal means would have at its end the shortening of the term of the Mandate.

The meeting was held during the month before the Nebi Musa festival and the Jewish delegates laid particular stress on the need of preventing a repetition of Arab attacks against the Jews in the previous years. Their demands were: cessation of hostilities against the settlement of Jews in Palestine within the scope of the economic capacity of the country, and the elimination of anti-Jewish propaganda by the Arab press and Arab Committees in Palestine and abroad. The Arab representatives agreed that it was necessary to prevent the outbreak of disturbances in Palestine and promised to send a delegate, "to proceed to Palestine to carry a message of peace in the name of the Congress." The question of immigration they proposed to refer to other members of the Congress; they would also present their own detailed demands at a subsequent meeting.

Two other meetings took place, on the 2nd and 4th of April. On the former day the Zionist representatives read an official communication from Dr. Weizmann, then in Rome, in which he expressed entire agreement in principle with the course of the negotiations. He nominated representatives to the proposed Mixed Committee which was to draft an accord. However, he asked for greater precision, particularly on the Palestine question. The Jewish representatives, following this up, indicated that they wished to have the following points clarified: 1) whether the Arab delegates could produce documents as to their authority; 2) whether their organization was favorable to Faisal and Husain; 3) whether it would not be of advantage to include Palestinian members in the discussions, since the negotiations would be mainly concerned with Palestine; 4) whether the Arab organizations had among their members representatives of the Christian Arab community; 5) whether the Arab delegates were in full accord with the Jews as to a policy of friendship toward the great Powers, it being understood that such friendship was not to hinder the final object to which both parties looked forward.

The Arab representatives gave what might be considered satisfactory answers, but their formulation was not without an element of reservation on each of the points. The authority of their organization, they said, "could not be proved better than by effective and tangible proofs." They were ready to produce credentials when the Jewish delegates produced theirs and moreover, they proposed "to annex to the treaty of accord a clause providing that in the event of our not being able to prove our authority for the execution of decisions which will be taken by the mixed committee, such accords shall be deemed to be null and void." As to the second point—their relation to the Hashimite dynasty—they said: "Their Majesties, Feisal and Husain, are two soldiers in the Arab cause. Like all the sons of Arabia, they work in harmony with the Arab organization." They declared that they could obtain an indication from these rulers to show that they were in accord with the policy of the Arab Congress. Thus, instead of answering straightforwardly that their organization supported Faisal and Husain, they seemed to say that the latter supported them. To the third point—the inclusion of Palestine members in the discussions—they replied that the constitution and membership of their Executive was a matter to be determined only by themselves, but they could, if necessary, put the Jews in touch with the Palestinian leaders. As to the fourth point, they did not wish to differentiate between Christian and Moslem Arabs in their organizations, but assured the Jews that the Christian element was fully represented. Answering the last point, they called attention to their previous statement that they desired "under no circumstances to manifest any hostility to any of the Allies," adding pointedly, however—"insofar as the Allies themselves desired the realization of the Arab national aspirations." Since the French were opposed to the Arab national aspirations, and the British looked upon them with some reservation, this pronouncement of friendship toward the Allies seems to have been made with tongue in cheek.

At the meeting on April 4th, it was decided that the Mixed Committee should meet at the end of the week; the Jewish and Arab delegates were to prepare their own drafts of the agreements on the basis of the discussions. The negotiations, however, seemed to have been discontinued pending the ratification of the Mandate. In August, 1922, after the Mandate had already been ratified, Saphir, in Europe at the time, was requested by Dr. Weizmann to meet the Emir Habib Lutfallah[81] and the Syrian Palestine delegation at Geneva. Saphir met with the Arab representation on September 7 and 8, 1922, and an agreement entitled "Preliminary Propositions of an Understanding between Arabs and Jews" was drawn up. These "Propositions" followed the lines of the discussions held during the meeting in the earlier part of the year. Besides reiterating the general idea of a union of the Arabs and Jews, with the object of restoring Semitic civilization to its ancient splendor and thus bringing about a renascence of the Near East, the agreement included the following specific points:

The Jews should not use either the Balfour Declaration or the Mandate as approved by the Council of the League of Nations as a basis of argument in the course of the negotiations, and the Arabs, on their part, would refrain from bringing up "the treaty" between Great Britain and the Hejaz of 1915.

Any accord reached should be based on collaboration for the welfare of all the Arab countries, that is, Syria and Mesopotamia as well as Palestine. The Jews were to help the Arabs in these countries to achieve their aspirations for independence by giving economic and political assistance of a legal and constitutional character.

Recognition was to be given to the special attachment of the Jews to Palestine. At the same time, the rights of the Arab inhabitants of the country should be established on the basis of complete equality of all the inhabitants without any distinction of race and religion.

The two parties should exercise their best endeavors "to find a way

81. Emir Lutfallah is a wealthy Syrian Arab who has had ambitions to play a political role in the Arab national movement. He was exiled from Syria with the expulsion of Faisal and established a bureau first in Cairo and then in Geneva. In 1922 he styled himself "Ambassador-at-large of King Husain in Europe."

to regulate and limit the question of immigration into Palestine, or into any other Arab neighboring country, in a manner that will satisfy the two parties concerned."

Cessation of anti-Jewish agitation in Palestine should be immediately proclaimed and an end put to political antagonism between Arabs and Jews in the neighboring countries. A Mixed Committee should be constituted immediately consisting, on the one hand, of representatives of the Syro-Palestine delegation and the Palestine Arabs (Moslems and Christians) and, on the other hand, of representatives of the Zionist Organization which, if it deemed necessary, might coopt influential personalities in the Jewish world. The Mixed Committee should work out the details of a Draft Agreement to form the basis of further action.

For some reason, negotiations were not taken up again. Saphir has supplied the following comment on the cause of the failure of the conversations which had been started in Cairo and which had lasted now for over half a year:[82]

It is difficult to obtain proofs as to the cause of that failure. It was, however, the consensus of opinion in Arab as in Jewish quarters that there were forces that brought pressure to bear with a view to the abortive termination of those negotiations. There is little doubt that members of a certain political school took the view that it was not in the interests of the peaceful administration of the Near and Middle Eastern territories that the two Semitic races who have once played a glorious part in history by close cooperation, should collaborate again on the platform of the recognition of Jewish rights in Palestine. Indeed, some of these, administrators as well as political journalists, made no secret of their anxiety to maintain that part of the Near East free from decisive Jewish influence which, they held, contributed to an unwelcome industrialization and Westernization in a part of the world that had best be left alone in its former Oriental character.

Saphir here evidently means to imply that imperialistic and anti-Semitic elements in the British Government were behind the failure of the negotiations. It may well be that the British disliked the implication of a Jewish-Arab alliance calculated to eliminate them from the East, even though this was to be

82. Ascher Saphir, *op. cit.*, pp. 21–24. Medzini, *op. cit.*, pp. 231–233, also gives an account of the negotiations.

by "constitutional and legal means." But, in all fairness, it is necessary to point out that there must have been objections to the plan on the part of the Zionists and of the Palestine Arabs as well. The Zionists could not have agreed to excluding the Balfour Declaration and the Mandate from the basis of agreement and to relying solely on an understanding with an Arab group which had as yet had neither authority nor power. But the weakest element in the whole matter was the fact that the Palestine Arabs were never party to the agreement; at the very time when these negotiations were being carried on, they were engaged in combating the Legislative Council proposal, boycotting commerce with the Jews, and refusing to consider any plan which denied their right to rule Palestine on the basis that they were the majority.

One more attempt was made by the Jews to come to a political understanding with the Arabs. This happened later, in the fall of the same year, 1922, in conversations carried on under the auspices of the British Government. The British were at the time attempting to straighten out matters with their erstwhile ally, Husain, King of the Hejaz, and the Arab Nationalists. The Arabs were still nursing their grievance at the loss of control over Syria, resulting from the expulsion of Faisal from Damascus. Moreover, although Husain had been recognized King of the Hejaz, and Faisal enthroned as King of Iraq, Abdullah was not satisfied either with his subsidy or with his poverty-stricken domain of Trans-Jordan; it was sparsely populated, with only 250,000 inhabitants, a considerable part of whom were Bedouin. Still working along Winston Churchill's idea of a "Sharifian" solution of the problem of Arab unity —that is, of establishing the basis of an Arab Federation through the dynasty of the Sharif of Mecca, as Husain's family was known—there was some plan of making Abdullah King of Syria and also including in his domain, Lebanon, Palestine and Trans-Jordan, under some autonomous arrangement without interfering with the British or French Mandates. The negotiations with the British were the primary object of Emir Abdullah's visit to London; the conversations with the Zionists were incidental and were designed to find a satisfactory arrangement for Palestine.

The discussions were carried on between Abdullah and H. St. John Philby, on the one hand, and Dr. Weizmann and other Jewish leaders, on the other. There were five conferences; the exact nature of the conclusions has never been determined.[83] Shortly after the Emir's return from England, he gave an interview to the Arab newspaper, *Falastin*, to the effect that when he was in London he had told Dr. Weizmann that "a mutual understanding between the Arabs and the Jews was possible only if an Arab Government were established in Palestine. If this were done," said Abdullah, "we would recognize the Balfour Declaration without prejudicing the rights of the Arabs. Dr. Weizmann agreed, but made the observation that he wished to take counsel first with the American Zionists."

Weizmann, however, denied Abdullah's version as reported in the *Falastin* and asserted that nothing had been said about an Arab Government in Palestine, that the talk was about the creation of a national government in Palestine along democratic lines. Dr. Weizmann said that he personally regarded the idea with favor, but emphasized four preliminary conditions: 1) the Mandate would remain in its complete form; 2) the agreement of Great Britain would be obtained as a preliminary condition; 3) the free development of the National Home for the Jews in Palestine would be assured; 4) he would have to take counsel with Zionists in various countries on the whole matter. Whatever the proposed arrangements were, they fell through. The Sixth Arab Congress, meeting in June 1923, rejected the proposed Anglo-Arabian Treaty between the British Government and King Husain,[84] and soon the British dropped Husain and left him to the mercies of his ancestral enemy, Ibn Saud.

The Histadrut and Arab-Jewish Relations

The Labor Movement in Palestine found itself in a dilemma with reference to the Arab-Jewish problem. Its socialist philosophy forbade too great emphasis on the national differences between Arab and Jew, and required considering the Arabs as partners in a class struggle against feudalism and capitalism. Ben-Gurion, who expresses the dominant view in the *Histadrut*, wrote in a series of essays on Arab-Jewish relations entitled "We and Our Neighbors": "As socialists we have a

83. A summary is given by Medzini, *op. cit.*, p. 233, based largely on an account which appeared in *Haaretz*, Adar 11 (Feb. 27), 1923.
84. See above, Chap. VII, p. 481.

very deep faith in the justice of our Zionist undertaking. For our Zionist movement is a movement for liberation and redemption, a movement which is clean of even a particle of enslavement, oppression, or deprivation. With the strength of this moral conviction we are doing our work in the land—and this same conviction tells us that the Arab laborer is our brother of fate, and our partner in the fatherland. His future is our future and his is our responsibility." [85]

On the other hand, the Labor Movement was dedicated to the idea of the upbuilding of Palestine as the Jewish national home and in its conception this required a large mass Jewish immigration, the creation of a Jewish majority and, thereafter, the establishment of a Labor Commonwealth. Ben-Gurion recognized that the Zionist purpose of concentrating the Jewish people in Palestine and making it a free people on its own land, made the Arab question a grave problem: "Without such a Zionist basis there is no Arab question here, but a Jewish question, as there is a Jewish question in all lands of the diaspora."

There were two fundamental postulates which had to be taken into consideration for an Arab-Jewish understanding: 1) the Arabs must recognize the historical necessity which drove the Jewish people to the stubborn determination to rebuild themselves as a nation in Palestine; 2) the Jews must recognize the rise of the Arab masses who have lived for hundreds of years in Palestine and who regard Palestine as their birthplace where they will continue to live. Fate had decreed that Jews and Arabs must live together: on the one hand, the Arabs of Palestine and the millions of Arabs living in neighboring countries; on the other hand, the Jews of Palestine and the millions of Jews in the Diaspora who stood behind them. Thus, he held that "in order to attain a successful Arab-Jewish cooperation we must come to a political understanding with the Arabs." [86] But he did not believe that such a political understanding could ever be attained as a result of negotiation with the present political leaders who were representative of the landowning *effendi* class. It was only through cooperation in labor organization on the basis of equality and mutual

---

85. David Ben-Gurion, *Anahnu Ushkhenenu* (We and Our Neighbors), Davar, Tel-Aviv, 1931, p. 131.
86. *Ibid.*, p. 230.

respect for each other's national autonomy, that the two peoples could be brought together.

It was the task of the Labor Movement to achieve such a rapprochement with the Arab workers. In the light of these principles the *Histadrut* at its Convention in 1927, formulated the plan for a Palestine Labor Alliance which would encompass the Jewish economy, the Arab economy, and mixed economy. The main points of the plan were as follows:

All Palestinian laborers, without distinction of religion, nationality and race, would be united in the Alliance based on autonomous national sections. The *Histadrut* would constitute the Jewish section of the Alliance; other national sections would be organized in similar autonomous units.

The trade unions would unite all workers in a particular trade for the purposes of protecting working conditions, establishing wage scales, advancing cultural interests, and developing among the members a sense of labor solidarity without distinction of trade, religion, nationality or race.

Until such institutions should be created by the Alliance itself, the self-help institutions of the *Histadrut,* such as the Loan Funds and the *Kupat Holim* (Sick Fund), would extend their services, when necessary, to the non-Jewish members of the Alliance.

The union would conduct negotiations with employers and in case of controversy between them and the workers, the union would act as arbiter. The union would also conduct cultural, educational and sport activities for its members.

Each union should be governed by administration based on parity between the two national groups, Jews and Arabs. Each union should have two national divisions and each division should elect from among its members half of the administrative officers. Hebrew and Arabic would be the official languages of the Alliance.

Socialist Views on Arab-Jewish Relations

The view presented above was that of the majority of the members of the *Histadrut*. There were, however, other conceptions more strongly colored. A frequent view was that a major task of the Zionist Labor movement was to rescue the Arab semi-serfs, that is, the tenant farmers and the debt-ridden *fellahin,* from the clutches of their *effendi* masters. In this view, a fundamental prerequisite for rapprochement between Jews and Arabs was the achievement of a more equal standard of living—not by depressing the Jewish worker's standard to that of the *fellah* or Arab urban worker, but by breaking up the patronal structure of Arab society and raising the level of the Arab worker more nearly to that of the Jewish. Through this transformation of Arab society the social outlook of the Arab worker would be transformed and it would be possible to deal with him on the basis of a democratic conception of equality.

One of the outstanding exponents of such a conception was Moses Beilinson, for many years editor of the Labor daily, *Davar*. He had even less faith than other leaders in the Labor movement of a political rapprochement with the *effendi* landowners, particularly because the latter were not interested in raising the standard of living of the *fellah*, which he regarded as necessary for any social improvement. Moreover, he thought that the general policy of the government and the colonization activities of the Zionist Organization had in the past indirectly worked to strengthen the power of the landed aristocracy and to enrich them, while doing very little that resulted in a radical improvement of the position of the *fellah*. The effort had to be more directly along the line of changing the system of life and the standard of living for the Arab population.

It was Beilinson's basic thesis that Palestine belonged to two communities: "to the Jewish people and to the Arab inhabitants who live in Palestine." [87] The Jewish section of the population had the advantage of large capital accumulated over many years through the *Lovers of Zion* movement, the Baron de Rothschild funds, the *Keren Kayemeth* and the *Keren Hayesod*. In order to make any real dent in the problem of Arab economic improvement, it was necessary to have similar sources of capital for the improvement of Arab life. He recognized that the Jewish funds could not contribute the large amounts needed, for these were insufficient even for the Jewish endeavor. Neither could the government accomplish the necessary improvement with its present means and under the existing economic system. Only the revolutionary step of breaking up the large Arab estates and establishing the Arab peasants on the land as free farmers, with modernized methods of production, could accomplish the drastic agrarian reforms re-

---

87. Moses Beilinson, "Problems of a Jewish-Arab Rapprochement" in Enzo Sereni and R. E. Ashery, *Jews and Arabs in Palestine*, Hehalutz Press, New York, 1936, p. 172.

quired for raising the standard of life of the *fellah* to a level approaching that enjoyed by the Jews.

It was Beilinson's idea that this radical solution of the problem was the task of government aided by the Zionist movement. The spirit of his conception is conveyed in the following paragraph:[88]

The mandatory government must understand that it cannot, by its present administrative policies, be they ever so exemplary, fulfill the special task that it undertook in this country, which has unusual problems. The mandatory government must understand that without a definite line of policy, without truthfully and boldly facing its civilizational objectives, without any pussyfooting, it cannot seriously fulfill the mandate with its two fundamental objectives: the National Home for the Jewish people and the development of the Arab Yishub. The Zionist movement must understand that it cannot accomplish this task in an environment of slavery amidst constant contradictions; that the two provisions of the Balfour Declaration are bound together not only officially, politically, but also are bound together internally, socially, economically. Any desire for peace, whether it come from the mandatory government, from the Zionist movement, or from the Arab Yishub, in part or in whole, will always remain something intangible, based on shaky foundations, as long as such deep social, economic and cultural chasms divide the two communities. The two forces that should be interested in raising the standards of living are the Arab Yishub, the one which is attempting the realization of the Mandate, and the other which is realizing Zionism, must unite in order to fulfill this task of developing the Arab community.

A more doctrinaire socialist analysis was presented by the *Hashomer Hatzair* at its Constitutional Convention held in 1927. The underlying conception was that the dispersed Jewish nation, now deprived of territory, and thus lacking a basis for economic and social development, could solve its problem only through the establishment of a socialist society in Palestine. The Zionist Organization had an historic function to perform in developing an economically, culturally and politically self-supporting Jewish community in Palestine. But the complete solution of the Jewish problem was dependent upon a socialist revolution which would bring with it the abolition of all classes. The Palestinian Labor Movement was an integral part

88. *Ibid.*, pp. 185–186.

of the world proletariat, fighting for the destruction of the existing social economic forms and for the establishment of a new social order. In Palestine the social revolution would be accomplished by the united action of the Jews and the Arab working classes, and a major function of the Jewish Labor Movement in Palestine was the promotion of the class-conscious International Labor Organization.

In the light of this conception, the *Hashomer* regarded the development of relations with the Arabs not merely as auxiliary to political negotiations with Great Britain or any other political body, but as an independent objective and as an integral part of Zionist policy. Since collaboration with the Arabs in building up a socialist commonwealth in Palestine was an indispensable purpose, the *Hashomer* rejected the ultimate aim of a Jewish State. It agreed with the *Histadrut* that mass immigration of the Jews with the object of establishing a majority was an essential of Zionism, but taking into consideration the fact that Palestine already had a large Arab population, which would remain and grow, the ultimate form of government in Palestine could be conceived only in terms of bi-national structure. In line with its general approach to the problem was its repudiation of the principle of one hundred percent Jewish labor in Jewish enterprises.

In its practical program it laid great emphasis on the plan of *irgun meshutaf* (common organization), that is the establishment of a common labor organization of Arabs and Jews as the ultimate goal. As a general principle the *Hashomer Hatzair* accepted the plan for a Palestine Labor Council as outlined by the *Histadrut*, but laid greater emphasis on the importance of the mixed unions and on the necessity of an active program on the part of the *Histadrut* in the organization of the Arab worker. The internal discussions among the labor group revealed continuous criticism on the part of the *Hashomer Hatzair* to the effect that the *Histadrut* had not pursued the program of the promotion of common labor organization with sufficient energy, and that, in effect, the plan for a common alliance had remained to a large extent only on paper.

The Socialist Labor Party (*Left Poale Zion*),[89] a small

---

89. They represented in theory at least, the approach of the urban proletariat rather than the emphasis on agricultural settlement. There were also inner divisions on the question of language; some regarding Yiddish and not Hebrew as the basis for the Jewish national revival.

grouping, followed even a straighter Marxist line. It placed little emphasis on the Zionist and nationalistic elements of the Labor program and stressed more the unmodified socialist ideology. This group had attacked the *Histadrut* as being more nationalist than socialist and because, in pursuit of the Zionist aim, it was ready to make deals not only with the Jewish capitalists but even with the Arab *effendis*. Their leader and spokesman, Moses Erem, maintained that the only way to an Arab-Jewish understanding was by unification of the Jewish and the Arab masses in a class struggle against both the Arab and Jewish capitalists. The eventual rule of the proletariat of both peoples should be the aim and objective of the Jewish Labor Movement. The means for the achievement of this aim was the creation of a single labor organization for both peoples without the bi-national feature of the *Histadrut* and *Hashomer Hatzair* plans. He unequivocally opposed the "conquest through work" policy of the *Histadrut* and its principle of one hundred percent Jewish labor in the Jewish economy. In essence, *Left Poale Zion* demanded that the *Histadrut* divest itself of its Jewish national functions and that it become a socialist labor organization with the primary purpose of organizing the Palestine working class.

In May, 1930, a conference of Jews and Arabs was called on the initiative of some of the *Left Poale Zion* members. Professor Hugo Bergmann, associated with the *Brith Shalom* movement, and a few Arab labor leaders were invited to attend a preliminary conference. The call for the conference was issued in the name of a group which styled itself *Ahvat Hapoalim* (Fraternity of Workers) under the slogan, "From national separation to international cooperation, from national intransigence to a fraternity of workers." [90] In the preliminary discussions, serious differences of opinion developed. Erem, following the line of the *Left Poale Zion*, stressed the necessity of a common union of both peoples and the need to combat the one hundred percent Jewish labor policy. Professor Bergmann emphasized cultural, social and political measures. Some of the Arab labor leaders threatened to organize the Arab masses outside of the Jewish labor organization if the *Histadrut* persisted in its all-Jewish labor policy. The Government stepped

---

90. Unpublished manuscript of the late Elsie Glueck, "Labor and Nationalism in Palestine," Chap. X, pp. 28–39.

in, forbidding the conference on the ground that some of the participating groups were illegal organizations (the *Left Poale Zion* was then under ban). The real reason for its interference —it was alleged—was Government's hostility to a union of Arabs and Jews on a labor basis; implied also was a charge that communists were bent on using the new group for boring from within.

The Brith Shalom Point of View

However far the parties within the Zionist Organization were ready to go in the direction of Arab-Jewish rapprochement, they all based themselves on the Balfour Declaration and maintained that the Jews were in Palestine as of right, not by the grace of the Arab section of the population. While anxious to come to an understanding with the Arabs and to obtain their cooperation in the upbuilding of the country, they repudiated the idea that the Jewish development required the "consent" of the Arabs. Underlying the views of all the Zionist parties, moreover, was the idea that the national home policy was the *primary* purpose of the Mandate, and that Palestine would become predominantly Jewish—if not as "English as England," at least as English as Canada.

Under the slogan *"Brith Shalom"* (Covenant of Peace) there developed a movement in Palestine which, though devoted to the Zionist idea of a Jewish national home, was distinctly different in its general orientation from the official Zionist view, in that it made Jewish-Arab understanding a *sine qua non* of the whole endeavor of upbuilding Palestine. The adherents of *Brith Shalom* were ready to go far in making concessions to achieve Arab consent to the upbuilding of the Jewish national home; so far, indeed, that they were accused of being willing to sacrifice the essence of the Balfour Declaration. The movement was never strong enough to constitute a party within the Zionist Organization, although a number of individuals from among the General Zionist and Labor parties were prominently associated with it.

Though for a short time organized as a society, the *Brith Shalom* was rather a school of thought. Its adherents were mostly intellectual liberals; though small in number, the group included several outstanding personalities of the *Yishuv*, who came from different countries—Russia, Germany and Central

Europe, and America—and reflected a liberal internationalist orientation.[91] Their views varied to some extent, the common theme being an emphasis on the need for mutual understanding and cooperation between the Arabs and Jews in the up-building of Palestine. Stress was placed on each people knowing the other's language, studying each other's history, respecting each other's customs and folk ways, promoting neighborly relations. A frequent theme was that the Arabs and Jews had a common origin as members of the Semitic stock and culture and a common destiny in the revival of Near East civilization.

The *Brith Shalom* movement implied a criticism of the Zionist Organization as having neglected the question of Arab-Jewish rapprochement and as having underestimated the force and the significance of the Arab national movement. Its principles were defined in a series of pamphlets issued between 1927–1931, entitled *"Sheifotenu"* (Our Aspirations). The following quotations indicate the basic ideas:

Brith Shalom aspires to create in Palestine for the Jews a solid and healthy Jewish community which will contain as great a number of Jews as possible, without taking into consideration whether a Jewish majority over the other inhabitants of the country will be attained or not, for the question of a majority in the country does not have any bearing in any way with special rights.[92]

The object of the association is to arrive at an understanding between Jews and Arabs as to the form of their mutual social relations in Palestine on the basis of absolute political equality of two culturally autonomous peoples, and to determine the lines of their cooperation for the development of the country.[93]

91. Among the prominent members were: Dr. H. M. Kalvarisky; Dr. Itzhak Epstein; and Dr. Isaac Louria, for a number of years head of the educational system of the *Vaad Leumi*. These men were all born in Russia but were trained in continental universities. A Central European group was represented by Dr. Arthur Ruppin, for many years the head of the colonization work of the Zionist movement; and Professor Hugo Bergmann, originally from Prague, first librarian and then teacher of philosophy at the Hebrew University. Dr. Judah L. Magnes, for many years the Chancellor of the Hebrew University, and now its president, born and brought up in the United States, represented a mixture of American and German academic influences. He received his rabbinical degree from the Hebrew Union College which was much under the influence of German thought, and did graduate work at the Universities of Berlin and Heidelberg.

92. *Sheifotenu*, Vol. I, 1927, p. 1.
93. *Ibid.*, p. 53.

The organization recognizes that Palestine must not be either a Jewish state or an Arab state, but a binational state wherein will live both the Jews and Arabs with equal civil, political and social rights without distinction whether they are of the majority or of the minority.[94]

The following measures for facilitating common activities were formulated.

I. *Economic:* Mixed chambers of commerce; mixed associations of manufacturers; combined organization for increasing the consumption of Palestine manufactured goods; mixed trade unions in all occupations; a central bank for Jewish and Arab farmers to lend money at low interest rates; assistance to the Arabs in the organization of cooperative societies, including mixed cooperatives; mixed committees to deal with special economic problems; extension of services of the Jewish Agricultural Experiment Stations to Arab zones with the help of the local government.

II. *Education and Medical:* To change the Jewish schools so that they might be attractive to the Arabs; to establish scholarships for Arab students in the Jewish high schools and technical institutes; to establish mixed sport clubs; to organize libraries in both languages; and generally promote social contacts between Jews and Arabs; to increase the scope of Jewish medical activities among the Arabs; combined activities in welfare service, in the scouting movement and in professional organizations.

III. *Political:* To stimulate Arabs to establish an independent group similar to the Brith Shalom; to stop polemic articles in the press, both Arabic and Hebrew; to publish a newspaper in Arabic with Arabs on the editorial staff; to disseminate information for Jewish activities through publishing a bulletin in Arabic for the Arab press.

A central feature of the *Brith Shalom* program was its demand that the Zionist Organization should proclaim "an open and clear surrender of the idea of erecting a Jewish state."[95] Apart from enunciating the general doctrine of a bi-national state, *Brith Shalom* did not outline its political conception in any detail. It hoped for the establishment of the bi-national constitution by mutual agreement with the Arabs, and the point of view implied the elimination of Great Britain as the

---

94. *Ibid.*, Vol. IV, 1930, pp. 31–32.
95. *Ibid.*, Vol. II, No. 5, 1931, p. 153.

trustee for Palestine. For the transitional period, it strongly supported the idea of a legislative council or parliament. However, its functions were to be limited. As formulated by Professor Hugo Bergmann, the *Brith Shalom* agreed to "a parliament based on democratic principles but that the fundamental interests of the Jews—buying land, immigration, and the status of the Hebrew language—shall be taken away from this parliament and be reserved for the Mandatory." [96]

One of the early exponents of the *Brith Shalom* conception was Dr. Judah L. Magnes, President of the Hebrew University in Jerusalem. In his point of view were mingled elements drawn from Reform Judaism's conception of the mission of Israel and Ahad Ha'am's idea of Palestine as a spiritual center. Subscribing to a national interpretation of Jewish history and life, he believed that the people of Israel was not "like all the nations;" it was distinguished by its ethical, spiritual and universal message. The following quotations give an idea of his viewpoint:[97]

I do not at all believe . . . that without Palestine the Jewish people is dying out or is doomed to destruction . . . This eternal and far-flung people does not need a Jewish State for the purpose of maintaining its very existence . . . Palestine cannot 'solve the Jewish problem' of the Jewish people . . . The dispersion of this people, the Diaspora, is a marvelous instrumentality for the fulfillment of its function as a teacher. The dispersion is an irrevocable historical fact, and Palestine can be a means of making this fact into an ever greater blessing.

But as for myself, if I could know that, in the course of a long, long period, a Jewish community of one million souls, one-third of the population, was possible here, I should be well content.

A central thought in Dr. Magnes' view has always been that both the Jews and the Arabs are parts of the common Semitic civilization. This idea looms large also in the views of H. M. Kalvarisky, who has been perhaps the most persevering in the *Brith Shalom* movement. His general conception has already been outlined in connection with his memorandum to King Faisal in 1919. Another plan, in some ways similar, was pre-

96. *Ibid.*, pp. 99–100.
97. J. L. Magnes, *Like All the Nations*, Jerusalem, 1930, p. 7; pp. 22–24.

pared by him for an influential Arab circle, and later published—without Kalvarisky's consent—in an Arab newspaper in September 1931.[98] The theme of this plan was, "Jews and Arabs are brothers and they can live together within the confines of one country and one federation." The plan was even less definite than his previous proposal; it was particularly vague on the question of Jewish immigration into Palestine. Some of the main paragraphs of the plan were:

1. The two Semitic peoples, the Jews and the Arabs, obligate themselves to help each other in all branches of human endeavor; economic, social and spiritual.

2. The Arabs are to welcome their Jewish brothers returning to the Eastern lands, opening the gates of their wide lands to Jewish immigration. The Jews in turn will help in the development of the Semitic East with their wealth, energy and knowledge.

3. In all the lands of the Semitic East, wherever the Jews will dwell, they should have the same rights as are possessed by national minorities in the enlightened countries of Europe.

4. Palestine should become an autonomous country with a special constitution. It belongs not to the Arab or to the Jewish branch of the Semitic nation exclusively, but to both of them on an equal basis without regard to which of them will be the majority or the minority at any time.

5. Hebrew and Arabic, the two cultures, shall develop harmoniously.

6. The Jews declare that they do not wish to rule Palestine; but that they do not want others to rule over them.

7. The country as a whole, including the Arabs, have heretofore gained from Jewish immigration and the Jews obligate themselves in the future not to displace the *fellahin* nor to discriminate against the Arab worker. It will be necessary to form common organizations to increase the direct benefits of the Arabs in the Jewish effort.

8. The Jews obligate themselves not to oppose the Arab national aspirations, and Palestine should enter an Arab federation if such is formed in the future.

Similar in some respects to the view of *Brith Shalom* is the attitude of Moshe Smilansky,[99] for many years the head of the

98. *Sheifotenu*, Vol. III, Nos. 8–9, 1933, p. 245.
99. Moshe Smilansky is one of the old settlers of the colony of Rehovoth. He is well known as a practical expert in agriculture and has achieved note besides for his ability as a writer of short stories. Under the name of Khawaja Musa (Mr. Moses) he has written a number of

Jewish Farmers Organization. Like the *Brith Shalom*, he has emphasized the importance of Arab-Jewish rapprochement through cultural, social and economic cooperation. He has emphasized the following concrete points: the need of an Arab newspaper for Jews, and a Hebrew newspaper for Arabs; the attendance of Jews in Arab schools and of Arabs in Jewish schools; the inclusion of Arabs as partners in Jewish economic undertakings. Most of all, he has been opposed to the idea of the one hundred percent Jewish labor policy and he has proposed that every Jewish enterprise should employ a certain percentage of Arab labor. He regards the Arab labor policy of the *Histadrut* as the greatest obstacle to Jewish-Arab understanding.

His political conception implies that Palestine must remain an indivisible part of the British Commonwealth of nations; both the Arab and the Jewish people must have autonomy in their economic and cultural spheres; the gates of the country must be open to Jewish immigration to the full extent of its economic capacity; acquisition of land must be made free in all parts of the country, but at the same time the rights of the *fellahin* and tenant must be scrupulously protected. In support of his opposition to a Jewish State, he has quoted the warning of Ahad Ha'am:[100]

In the days of the House of Herod, Palestine was a Jewish State. Such a Jewish State would be poison for our nation and drag it down into the dust. Our small State would never attain a political power worthy of the name, for it would be but a football between its neighbours, and but exist by diplomatic chicanery and constant submission to whoever was dominant at the time. Thus we should become a small and low people in spiritual servitude, looking with envy towards the mighty fist.

Brith Shalom was quiescent during the middle 1930's, but reorganized under the name of *Kedmah Mizraha* after the 1936

beautiful stories portraying Arab village life to Jews, in somewhat idealistic terms. He was not a member of the *Brith Shalom* during the first decade, but joined the League for Arab-Jewish Rapprochement which was formed in 1939. He has not been influenced by German ethical neo-idealism, which seems to have been an important strain in the thinking of many members of the *Brith Shalom*, but rather by ideas underlying Ahad Ha'am's Jewishly based ethical conceptions.

100. See M. Smilansky, "Biltmore and After," *Palestine Review*, April, 1944.

disturbances. Former members of *Brith Shalom* were instrumental in forming the League for Arab-Jewish Rapprochement in cooperation with the *Hashomer-Hatzair* and new forces drawn from intellectual circles of recent German immigrants.[101]

Practical Efforts Aiding Arab-Jewish Relations

It is generally agreed that Jewish activities in Palestine benefited Arab life indirectly, e.g., through investment of large sums of capital, increase in government revenue, improvement of sanitary conditions, and raising the general standard of life. From the point of view of rapprochement, it is of interest also to consider such Jewish activities as were calculated to benefit the Arab section of the population more directly.

Most apparent were the services offered to the Arabs by the Hadassah Medical Organization. From the first, the hospitals, clinics and health centers of Hadassah were available to all applicants regardless of race or creed. Between the years 1918 and 1938, some 2,360 Moslems and 1,030 Christians were admitted as patients in Hadassah hospitals. The out patients in Hadassah clinics numbered 123,000 Moslems, who made some 475,000 visits, and 17,000 Christians, who made 105,000 visits.[102] In the early period, during the Military Administration between 1918 and 1920, and before Government established health services, the proportion of non-Jewish patients using Hadassah services was quite large, estimated roughly at 20 percent of the total. After 1920, however, the figures show a very large drop: in hospital services, from almost 7 percent in 1920 to about 1 percent in 1929; and in clinical service, from about 12 percent in 1920 to about 8 percent in 1929. In addition to the increased services rendered by Government, this drop in percentage was due to the growth of the Jewish population; that is, the absolute number of non-Jewish patients visiting Hadassah hospitals did not decline as much as these figures would indicate. The Hadassah clinics in rural districts and in Tiberias, Safed and Haifa, had the highest percentage of non-Jewish patients.

101. See below, Chap. XV, p. 1161.
102. Hadassah Medical Organization, *Twenty Years of Medical Service to Palestine 1918–1938*, p. 50.

Hadassah's anti-malarial work also affected the Arab section of the population directly. In the early postwar period, a system of minor prophylaxis, involving the distribution of quinine at the clinics, aided Arabs as well as Jews. The program of malaria control initiated by the late Dr. I. J. Kligler in 1921, with funds contributed by Justice Brandeis, included three experimental centers in lower Galilee where there were both Jewish and Arab villages. One of the earliest contributions of Hadassah in the field of preventive medicine in Palestine was the establishment of a network of health centers for pre-natal care, infant care, and the supervision of pre-school children. Two such centers were opened in the Old City of Jerusalem between 1921 and 1922, which served Arabs and Jews equally. In 1923, a gift of £6,000 from Mr. Nathan Straus of New York enabled Hadassah to extend such services to other cities and into the rural areas. A center was opened in the Arab district near the Damascus Gate in the Old City of Jerusalem. The unit was later closed in order not to compete with centers opened up nearby by the Health Department of the Palestine Government and the American Colony Aid Association.[103] An infant welfare center on the Hadassah model was also opened in Amman, Trans-Jordan. Nurses were sent from Iraq to observe the work of Hadassah, and on their return organized infant welfare centers along similar lines in their own country. Reference has been made above to the *Nathan and Lina Straus Health Center for All Races and Creeds,* which was formally dedicated in April, 1929.

In the economic field, the Palestine Economic Corporation, organized largely with American funds, made some effort to include Arabs. Many Arabs found employment in the Palestine Potash Company, in which the Palestine Economic Corporation had the controlling interest, and a leading Arab businessman was elected to the Board of Directors. A considerable number of Arabs have found employment in the hotels, including the King David in Jerusalem, operated by the Palestine Hotels Ltd., in which the Palestine Economic Corporation

---

103. Col. G. W. Heron, head of the Health Department of the Government, was one of the Government officials regarded as unfriendly to Zionist effort and unsympathetic to Arab-Jewish rapprochement. The anti-Zionist orientation of the American Colony at Jerusalem has been noted by Professor Albright in the section on "Christian Attitudes toward Zionism," above, p. 534.

has invested a large part of the share capital. The Loan Bank of the Palestine Economic Corporation, originally organized in part with funds from the Joint Distribution Committee to carry on war relief in Palestine, has made small loans from which Arab workers in Jerusalem, Tiberias and Safed benefited. A department for small savings was also organized by the Loan Bank and some of the depositors were Arab workers. The Central Bank of Cooperatives presented a plan to the Government in 1929 for the development of a cooperative movement in which both Jews and Arabs would participate. The Government did not encourage the plan on the ground that it was impractical, and the disturbances of 1929 brought about its abandonment. The Agricultural Mortgage Company which the Palestine Economic Corporation helped to establish, and which began to operate in 1935, grants loans on equal terms to Arab and Jewish farmers. A proposal for a low cost housing project in 1935 was designed to provide for the needs of the Arabs as well as Jews, but the riots of that year prevented carrying it into effect. While the total number of Arabs taking advantage of the credit facilities supported by the Palestine Economic Corporation is not large, nevertheless the opportunity exists.

The Hebrew University in Jerusalem is open to all who qualify, without regard to nationality or race, and in the first decade there were a few Arab undergraduates, despite the fact that the language of instruction at the University is Hebrew. After the development of extreme nationalist tendencies among the intellectual class, the Arab students withdrew, but recently several have returned. Very early in the history of the Hebrew University, emphasis was laid on the promotion of Arabic and Islamic studies for their own sake and as a factor in Arab-Jewish understanding. A school of Oriental studies was established with a broad course of study and research work in Arab literature, philology and the social structure of Moslem countries. The University Library has one of the largest collections of Islamica and Arabica in the world. One of the teachers of the Institute, Dr. J. Rivlin, has recently published a Hebrew translation of the Koran and also of a standard history of Arabic literature. A number of research projects in the social and literary history of the Arabic countries have been completed. Besides the more academic work in research and instruction, the Institute conducts popular courses designed to spread a knowledge of Arabic culture among Jews.

All the Hebrew secondary schools affiliated with the Hebrew Department of Education—formerly under the auspices of the Zionist Organization and now under the *Vaad Leumi*—include the teaching of classic Arabic as a required subject in most of the courses. The late Avinoam Yellin, head of the Jewish Inspectorate for the Palestine Department of Education, was author of an Arabic reader, particularly designed for the Jewish schools of Palestine.[104] The elementary schools of the *Alliance Israélite Universelle* give instruction in Arabic and a number of the Zionist schools in rural districts did so during the first decade. In recent years, Arabic has been eliminated from the elementary schools but still retains its place in the secondary schools. In the cities of mixed population some of the Jews, particularly among the Sephardic families, acquire a knowledge of vernacular Arabic through use.

Of particular interest are the efforts made by the *Histadrut* to promote cooperation between Arab and Jewish workers in the field of labor organization. The plan outlined by the *Histadrut* in 1927 for a Palestine Labor League which would include Arab and Jewish autonomous sections cooperating under one organization has been mentioned above. Some practical activity in the direction of cooperative union activities had been initiated before this. The Jewish workers on the Government railways had established a union as early as 1919 and soon devoted themselves to the effort of inducing their Arab fellow workers to organize with them. At the fifth conference of the Railway Workers' Union, a number of Arab delegates participated for the first time and several were elected to the Joint Central Committee. Contact between the Jewish and the Arab workers on the railways has continued ever since. In the larger railway centers—Haifa, Ludd and Jaffa-Tel-Aviv—hundreds of members, including Arabs and Jews, joined the union. In

---

104. Avinoam Yellin was the son of the late David Yellin, noted student of the Hebrew poetry of the Arabic period and head of the Jewish Teachers' Training School of Jerusalem. Avinoam Yellin was shot and killed during the riots of 1938. About the same time, Dr. Levi Billig of the School of Oriental Studies at the University, met a similar fate. Both were interested in advancing Arab-Jewish relations through the promotion of an understanding of Arabic culture among the Jews.

some of the smaller branches such as Kantara and Samakh, the membership was wholly Arab.

In 1925 the Haifa Labor Council of the *Histadrut* opened a club for Arab workers, under the name of General Workers' Club. The following year the Arab carpenters and tailors in Haifa went out on a general strike in protest against the long working day which frequently amounted to fourteen hours. This was the first Arab strike in Haifa and all the local Arab employers joined forces, enlisting the aid of the religious elements. Speakers in the mosques and churches denounced the attempt to break the time-honored Arab custom of working "from sunrise to sunset." The strikers were also told that if the Arab working day was reduced to that of the Jewish laborers, the latter would benefit, for there would then be no inducement to employ the Arab worker. With the aid of the moral and material assistance of the Haifa Labor Council, the Arab workers succeeded in holding out for a fortnight and won a nine-hour working day and extra pay for overtime. Again in 1927, assistance was given by the Jewish organizations to the strike of Arab and Jewish workers in the Jewish-owned match factory Nir in Acre, and in 1928, in the cigarette factory Mebruk in Haifa.

In April, 1926, the *Histadrut* began to publish, in Jerusalem, a labor newspaper in Arabic called *Ittihad el-Amal* (Unity of Labor). This was the first Arabic labor newspaper in the Middle East. The economic crisis between 1927–1929 prevented the *Histadrut* from doing much in the way of realizing the Palestine Labor League plans. The riots of August, 1929, were a further hindrance. However, a few weeks after the disturbances, the Haifa Labor Council resumed activities among the Arab workers and reopened the General Workers' Club. The situation is described as follows in the 1929 report of the Haifa Labor Council:[105]

At first we used to meet in private dwellings and out-of-the-way cafes, talking to the Arab workers about the possibilities of renewing contact. It was still dangerous to engage in this work in the open, and no little courage was required by the Arab comrades in those days which were rife with incitement and terrorism, to begin

105. As quoted by Abba Khushi in "The Palestine Labor League," *Jewish Chronicle*, March, 1944, p. 24.

organizational work and renew ties of friendship and common activity with the Jewish workers and Federation. But little by little the number of members increased. Life in the town gradually returned to normal. With the help of the Executive Committee of the Histadrut we rented premises for a club in a public place at the suggestion of the Arab members.

The Arab membership of the General Workers' Club included mostly skilled workers. Evening classes were organized in Arabic, Hebrew and English. An athletic club developed, with the assistance of the *Hapoel,* the *Histadrut's* sports club. The Arab workers were assisted in the setting up of a Loan Fund, and the *Kupat Holim* (the Workers' Sick Benefit Fund), extended medical and other services at a nominal rate. During the decade of the thirties, the Palestine Labor League helped in the organization of Arab workers and in the conduct of a number of strikes. Arab employers raised the racial and nationalist issues and in competition to the Palestine Labor League, a Palestine Arab Workers' Society was organized to counteract the influence of the *Histadrut*.

Some of the difficulties accompanying the organization of Arab workers were brought out in a large Arab strike which occurred at Haifa among the workers employed by Arab contractors at the quarries of the Jewish-owned Nesher Cement factory. The strikers (about 130 men), mostly from the rural districts, received a wage of 100 mils (fifty cents) for a working day of from twelve to fourteen hours, and moreover were compelled to buy their provisions at a canteen owned by the contractors. The Haifa Labor Council supplied food for the strikers and raised a relief fund through voluntary contributions all over Palestine. The strike was settled in favor of the workers; their wages were raised by 25 mils per day and their hours of work reduced to nine. The strikers immediately joined the Palestine Labor League en bloc, forming a separate trade union of quarry workers.

This, however, did not end the matter. The contractors brought in 150 new men affiliated with the Palestine Arab Workers' Society and finally locked out all the Arab workers who were members of the Palestine Labor League. Seventy Jewish workers employed in a department of the Nesher Cement factory which was directly dependent on the quarries went out on a sympathy strike and the remaining 250 Jewish workers in the factory were ready to join. Thereupon, the contractor suggested that the matter be brought for arbitration before the District Commissioner who appointed one of the district officers as arbiter. The Government arbiter made an award which justified the workers' demands, but he did not make the award binding and refused to compel the contractor to recognize the representative of the Haifa Labor Council whom the workers deputed to deal with the contractor on their behalf. The Arab workers, inexperienced and illiterate, were not able of themselves to defend their interests. The provisions of the award were never carried out by the contractor and the Government took no action in the matter.

Another example is furnished by a strike organized in 1935 against the Iraqi Petroleum Company. In this, 600 to 800 workers were involved, comprising a heterogeneous group of different nationalities and different trades, with varied interests and demands. The strike was complicated by the fact that it was conducted by two hostile organizations—the Palestine Labor League, associated with the *Histadrut*, and the Palestine Arab Workers' Society, the Arab nationalist group. The purpose of the strike was to prevent a threatened reduction of wages and to obtain an improvement in working conditions, including sick leave with part pay and an interim of notice before dismissal.

The Palestine Labor League provided a fund of over £1,000 ($5,000) from Jewish workers. The Palestine Arab Workers' Society contributed nothing and from the beginning exploited nationalist factors to introduce dissension among the strikers. Moreover, the skilled workers were urged to dissociate themselves from the unskilled peasants, on the ground that it would then be easier for them to gain their objectives. Finally, Fakhri Nashashibi (a member of the political family of that name) conducted negotiations with the company's managers and induced a number of the strike leaders to sign an agreement. Fakhri told the strikers that most of their demands would be met, provided that no outside organization appeared on their behalf, and that, furthermore, Iraqi Petroleum was ready to set up a company union. This induced a number of the workers to go back to work, and the remainder, disheartened, also returned. The company adopted a policy of encouraging dissension and soon the workers' organization which had been set up under the Arab Palestine Workers' Society was dissolved. The strike ended in failure both from the point of view of organization and Arab-Jewish relations.

Contacts were maintained between the Jewish workers and the Arab workers through the Palestine Labor League throughout the disturbances between 1936 and 1939. Even during 1936 and after, hundreds of Arabs participated in the *Histadrut's* May Day celebrations, came to meetings and marched in procession despite threats against them. After the May Day celebration of 1937, two active members of the Palestine Labor League were murdered, and after the 1938 celebration a number of Arab workers were kidnapped, taken to the hills and tried before the terrorist tribunals. Some were sentenced to death, while some were released on payment of large ransoms.

The port workers of Haifa were particular targets for the attacks of the terrorist leaders in their effort to paralyze the work of the Haifa harbor. Delegations of Arab leaders, including the Mufti himself, came to Haifa to persuade the dock workers to strike. The efforts of the Arab leaders were unavailing and work at the port was not suspended for a single day throughout the disturbances. The failure of the efforts of the Arab leaders is ascribed to the presence of a large number of Jewish workers engaged in port activities and to the contacts that had been built up through the Palestine Labor League between them and the Arab workers. During the disturbances the League issued a number of circulars and pamphlets to counteract the propaganda of the nationalist extremists, and in March, 1937, during the worst part of the riots, the *Histadrut* commenced publication of the Arab newspaper, *Hakikat el-Amr*, which aimed at rapprochement between the workers of the two communities. The distribution of the paper among the Arab workers in the towns and villages called for considerable courage and a number of the Arab members risked their lives in order to carry the paper to remote places. In 1937, also, the Jaffa customs porters requested the *Histadrut* to aid them in a strike against their employer, who had been appointed by the Government customs authorities.

At the end of 1942, there were 1,000 or more active members

of the Arab section of the Palestine Labor League. About two-thirds of these were unskilled workers and the remainder, skilled workers and clerks. A slight beginning in the organization of women workers was made, there being 16 women workers enrolled. The skilled workers were usually townsfolk; the unskilled workers were villagers who came to the city for seasonal work. The trade union activities during World War II affected also some 2,500 to 3,000 Arab workers for the Government in the Arab camps at Haifa. The total number of Arab workers organized through the League, therefore, was not very large. However, a wider influence was undoubtedly exerted by the League indirectly.

The above brief summary indicates that the practical work carried on by the Jewish bodies with the direct purpose of benefiting Arabs or with the object of advancing Arab-Jewish rapprochement, although not negligible, was relatively small. The inadequacy of the activity, however, was due not to a lack of a favorable attitude but to several causes: insufficient funds, unreadiness of the Arabs to take advantage of opportunities offered, and, not least, to difficulties inherent in the two types of culture and levels of civilization. The American bodies—Hadassah and the Palestine Economic Corporation—were most clearly conscious of the necessity of extending benefits to the Arab section of the population. The Zionist Organization itself did relatively little except insofar as it supported the activities of the *Histadrut*. The endeavor of the *Histadrut* to raise the wages and standard of life of the Arab worker, it might be claimed, was motivated as much by the desire for self-protection as it was by altruistic interest in the Arab worker. Its policy of excluding Arab labor from the Jewish market, whatever its justification may have been, was not calculated to make the Arab worker feel that the Jewish labor organization was directly concerned with his welfare.

Despite these limitations, the Jewish activity in the direction of Arab-Jewish rapprochement looms large in relation to what the Arabs, or even the Government, did in this direction. The effort of the Arab leaders was purely negative, designed in every instance to increase the antagonism between the two groups. While undoubtedly some of the Government officials favored increasing contacts between the Arabs and Jews, there were others who were not anxious to see any rapprochement, and the general impression is that the latter predominated. Although it is not possible to substantiate the idea frequently advanced that the Administration wished to keep the two communities apart on the principle of "divide and rule," there was certainly no active policy on the part of Government designed to promote cooperation between the Jews and the Arabs during the first decade. The Government confined itself largely to lecturing both sides on the virtues of political moderation. Whether a greater amount of cooperation in the economic and social fields would have led to a political rapprochement is quite another question. It is possible that it would have had a moderating effect; on the other hand, it may also be argued that a stable political situation was prerequisite for the improvement of social and economic relations. One thing seems clear, that both the British and the Jews underestimated the complexity of the problem.